AF333667

Biblical Hermeneutics in Context
and the Struggle for Meaning

Biblical Hermeneutics in Context
and the Struggle for Meaning

A Festschrift in Honor of Gerald O. West

EDITED BY

Aliou Cissé Niang

Andrew M. Mbuvi

Alice Yafeh-Deigh

Tinyiko Maluleke

AND

Kenneth N. Ngwa

PICKWICK *Publications* · Eugene, Oregon

BIBLICAL HERMENEUTICS IN CONTEXT AND THE STRUGGLE FOR MEANING
A Festschrift in Honor of Gerald O. West

Pickwick Publications
An Imprint of Wipf and Stock Publishers
199 W. 8th Ave., Suite 3
Eugene, OR 97401

www.wipfandstock.com

PAPERBACK ISBN: 979-8-3852-1990-2
HARDCOVER ISBN: 979-8-3852-1991-9
EBOOK ISBN: 979-8-3852-1992-6

Cataloguing-in-Publication data:

Names: Niang, Aliou Cissé, editor. | Mbuvi, Andrew M., editor. | Yafeh-Deigh, Alice, editor. | Maluleke, Tinyiko, editor. | Ngwa, Kenneth N., editor.

Title: Biblical hermeneutics in context and the struggle for meaning : a festschrift in honor of Gerald O. West / Edited by Aliou Cissé Niang, Andrew M. Mbuvi, Alice Yafeh-Deigh, Tinyiko Maluleke, and Kenneth N. Ngwa.

Description: Eugene, OR: Pickwick Publications, 2024. | Includes bibliographical references and index.

Identifiers: ISBN 979-8-3852-1990-2 (paperback). | ISBN 979-8-3852-1991-9 (hardcover). | ISBN 979-8-3852-1992-6 (ebook).

Subjects: LCSH: West, Gerald O. | Bible—Hermeneutics. | Bible—Criticism, interpretation, etc.

Classification: BS1192.6 B2024 (print). | BS1192.6 (ebook).

VERSION NUMBER 10/03/24

Contents

Abbreviations

AA	*African Affairs*
ABH	African Biblical Hermeneutics Unit of SBL
ACSA	Anglican Church of Southern Africa
AE	*Applied Economics*
AOG	Assemblies of God Church of South Africa
ASR	*African Studies Review*
AT	*Acta Theologica*
ATJ	*African Theological Journal*
ATR	*Anglican Theological Review*
BCT	*Bulletin for Contextual Theology*
BI	*Biblical Interpretation*
BIFAN	*Bulletin de l'Institut Fondamental d'Afrique noire*
BIS	Biblical Interpretation Series
Bridges	*Bridges: A Jewish Feminist Journal*
BT	*The Bible Today*
CBQ	*The Catholic Biblical Quarterly*
CBS	Contextual Bible Study
CCAHSCZ in SA	The Christian Catholic Apostolic Holy Spirit Church of Zion in South Africa

CI	*Critical Inquiry*
Contagion	*Contagion: Journal of Violence, Mimesis, and Culture*
CS	*Chicago Studies*
CSR	*Christian Scholar Review*
CT	*Christianity Today*
FA	*Foreign Affairs*
FP	*Foreign Policy*
GC	*Geography Compass*
HO	*Human Organization*
HTR	*Harvard Theological Review*
HTS	*HTS Teologiese Studies/Theological Studies*
HUCA	*Hebrew Union College Annual*
IdK	*In die Skriflig*
IJS	*International Journal of Sociology*
JAAS	*Journal of Asian and African Studies*
JBL	*Journal of Biblical Literature*
JBT	*Journal of Black Theology*
JBTSA	*Journal of Black Theology in South Africa*
JCAS	*Journal of Contemporary African Studies*
JCT	*Journal of Constructive Theology*
JEPER	*Journal of Educational Policy and Entrepreneurial Research*
JETS	*Journal of Evangelical Theological Society*
JIBS	*Journal for Interdisciplinary Biblical Studies*
JIT	*Journal of Inculturation Theology*
JITC	*Journal of the Interdenominational Theological Center*
JRT	*Journal of Religious Thought*
JSHJ	*Journal for the Study of Historical Jesus*
JSNT	*Journal for the Study of New Testament*
JSNTSup	*Journal for Study of the New Testament Supplements*
JSOTSup	*Journal for Study of the Old Testament Supplements*
JSR	*Journal for the Study of Religion*

JTSA	*Journal of Theology for Southern Africa*
LAI	Library of Ancient Israel
LHBOTS	Library of Hebrew Bible/Old Testament
MC	*Modern Churchman*
McQ	*McCormick Quarterly*
MF	*Ministerial Formation*
NCR	*National Catholic Reporter*
Neot	*Neotestamentica*
NLH	*New Literary History*
NNK	*Nytt Norsk Kirkeblad*
NTM	*Norsk Tidsskrift for Misjon*
NYT	*New York Times*
OTE	*Old Testament Essays*
OTL	Old Testament Library
QR	*Quarterly Review*
RBS	Resources for Biblical Studies
RS	*Religion and Spirituality*
RT	*Religion & Theology*
SAHJ	*South African Historical Journal*
SJOT	*Scandinavian Journal of the Old Testament*
ST	*Social Text*
STJ	*Stellenbosch Theological Journal*
TEC	*The Ecumenical Review*
TJ	*Trinity Journal*
TMW	*The Muslim World*
UKZN	University of KwaZulu-Natal
VE	*Verbum et Ecclesia*
VT	*Vetus Testamentum*
WCC	World Council of Churches
ZAW	*Zeitschrift für die alttestamentliche Wissenschaft*
ZMR	*Zeitschrift für Missionswissenschaft und Religionswissenschaft*

Contributors

Editors

Aliou Cissé Niang, PhD, Associate Professor of Biblical Interpretation—New Testament—at Union Theological Seminary, New York. His scholarship, research, and teaching combine New Testament Exegesis, Greco-Roman and African Identity Constructions, Postcolonial Biblical Criticism, Negritude, and spirituality. Niang is the author of *Faith and Freedom in Galatia and Senegal* (2009) and *A Poetics of Postcolonial Biblical Criticism: God, Human-Nature Relationship, and Negritude* (2019).

Andrew M. Mbuvi, PhD, Visiting NEH Chair and Associate Professor in the Religion Department, Albright College, PA. Mbuvi's research and teaching interests combine postcolonial biblical interpretation, African and African American biblical hermeneutics, African American religious traditions, race and religion, literature and religion, and social science and the Bible. His latest book is *African Biblical Studies: Unmasking Embedded Racism and Colonialism in Biblical Studies*.

Alice Yafeh-Deigh, PhD, Professor of Biblical Studies, Azusa Pacific University, Azusa, CA. Her areas of expertise, research, and teaching interests include New Testament exegesis, Greco-Roman sexual ethics, cultural hermeneutics, feminist hermeneutics, postcolonial hermeneutics, and literary and rhetorical methods of biblical interpretation. She is the author of *Paul's Sexual and Marital Ethics in 1 Corinthians 7: An African Cameroonian Perspective*.

Tinyiko Sam Maluleke, PhD, Vice-Chancellor and Principal at Tshwane University of Technology in Pretoria, South Africa. Maluleke's extensive leadership includes previous administrative positions at, University of South Africa (Unisa), University of Johannesburg, and the University of Pretoria. His areas of research and teaching are in the fields of religion and theology. He is the co-editor of *Ecumenical Encounters with Desmond Mpilo Tutu: Visions for Justice, Dignity, and Peace.*

Kenneth N. Ngwa, PhD, Donald J. Casper Professor of Hebrew Bible and African Biblical Hermeneutics at Garrett-Evangelical Theological Seminary in Evanston, Illinois, USA and directs the Religion and Global Health Forum. He is the author of *Let My People Live: An Africana Reading of Exodus.*

Authors

Dorothy BEA Akoto, PhD (Hebrew Bible) Vice President and Associate Professor of Hebrew Language, Old Testament and Gender Studies, Trinity Theological Seminary, Legon (TTS), Accra, Ghana. Author of numerous articles on the biblical book of Proverbs, including *Proverbs and the African Tree of Life: Grafting Biblical Proverbs on to Ghanaian Ewe Folk Proverbs*(2014).

L. Juliana Claassens, PhD, Professor in Old Testament and Head of the Gender Unit at the Faculty of Theology, Stellenbosch University, South Africa. Publisher of numerous articles and essays, with Carolyn Sharp she edited *Feminist Frameworks and the Bible: Celebrating Intersectionality, Interrogating Power, Embracing Ambiguity.*

Belinda Crawford, MTh, Founder/Director, Ebenezer Stone Women's Empowerment Center, University of KwaZulu-Natal

Philippe Denis, PhD, is a Professor of History of Christianity, at the School of Religion, Philosophy & Classics University of KwaZulu-Natal, South Africa. An established scholar, he has authored on topics of the Church in South Africa.

Jonathan Draper, PhD, Professor of New Testament (Emeritus) at the University of KwaZulu-Natal, South Africa. A prolific author of over 80 books, articles, and essays, covering topics on the New Testament, the second-century Christian document Didache, and African Christianity. With Clayton N. Jefford, he edited the two-volume *Orality, Literacy and Colonialism in Antiquity*, and *The Didache: A Missing Piece of the Puzzle in Early Christianity*).

Musa W. Dube, PhD, (Botswana) is the first African woman president of the Society of Biblical Literature (2023) and currently serves as William Ragsdale Cannon Distinguished Professor of New Testament Literature in the Candler School of Theology at Emory University, USA. A prolific author with over 160 publications (books—as author and editor, articles and essay/book chapters, including the groundbreaking *Postcolonial Feminist Interpretations of the Bible*) she is also a Humboldtian awardee (2011) and recipient of the Gutenberg Teaching Award (2017) from Gutenberg University, Germany.

Bob Ekblad, ThD, is an Associate Professor of Old Testament Studies at The Seattle School, and Executive Director of Tierra Nueva and the People's Seminary in Burlington, Washington. His research focuses on the book of Isaiah.

Nathan A. Esala, PhD, is an Adjunct Professor of Religion at Capital University, Columbus, Ohio and is the part time Translation Coordinator for Lutheran Bible Translators, USA. He lived in Ghana for 10 years involved in Bible translation. He holds a PhD in Religion with a focus in Biblical Studies from the University of KwaZulu-Natal (2020). Esala is the author of Translation as Invasion in Post-colonial Northern Ghana, forthcoming SBL. He is the author of several articles.

Kjetil Hafstad, Full Professor in Systematic Theology at the University of Oslo, Norway. He has published in the area of eschatology including "Looking for a Miracle: On the Point of Eschatology" in *Eschatology as Imagining the End*.

Knut Holter, PhD, Professor, Centre of Mission and Global Studies Faculty of Theology and Social Sciences, VID Specialized University, Stavanger, Norway, and Extra-ordinary Professor at Stellenbosch University, South Africa. He has published extensively on African biblical studies while compiling the most exhaustive data on African biblical publications, and his publication: Yahweh in Africa and Old Testament Research for Africa.

Richard A. Horsley, PhD, Distinguished Professor of Liberal Arts and the Study of Religion (Emeritus), University of Massachusetts, Boston. A prolific author his seminal publications on the Greco-Roman world and the New Testament, including *Jesus and Empire: The Kingdom of God and the New World Disorder* and *Paul and the Roman Imperial Order*, have been influential in New Testament studies.

Robert W. Kuloba, PhD, Associate Professor in the Department of Religious Studies and Philosophy, Kyambogo University, Uganda. A 2022 Fellow at Leeds University, UK, he is working on a project titled "Afro-Biblical Reading of Genesis 2–3 in Response to Climate Change."

R. Simangaliso Kumalo, PhD, Dean and Head of School of Theology, and Associate Professor of Public Theology and History, University of KwaZulu-Natal, South Africa. Author of numerous publications on theology in Africa. He is the editor of *Religion and Politics in Swaziland: The Contributions of JB Mzizi to Religion, Culture and Politics.*

Madipoane Masenya (Ngwan'a Mphahlele), PhD, Professor of Old Testament Studies, University of South Africa (UNISA) in Pretoria. Has authored multiple articles and essays and author of *How Worthy Is the Woman of Worth?: Rereading Proverbs 31:10–31 in African-South Africa*, which introduced *Bosadi* (African womanist) readings to biblical studies.

Dora R. Mbuwayesango, PhD, George E. and Iris Battle Professor of Hebrew Bible/Old Testament and Dean of Students, Hood Theological Seminary, Salisbury, North Carolina. She co-edited, with Musa Dube and Andrew Mbuvi, *Postcolonial Perspectives in African Biblical Hermeneutics.*

Gilbert O. Ojwang, PhD, Professor of Old Testament and Semitic Languages, Oakwood University, Huntsville, Alabama. Including many published articles and essays, he has authored the book *The House of Omri: A Sociohistorical Study of Israelite Political and Economic Systems (885–841 BCE).*

Jeremy Punt, PhD, Professor of New Testament, Theology Faculty at Stellenbosch University, South Africa. With over twenty publications on biblical interpretation and hermeneutics, including the volume *Postcolonial Biblical Interpretation: Reframing Paul*, Leide.

Robert Vosloo, PhD, Professor of Systematic Theology, Faculty of Theology, Stellenbosch University, South Africa, and serves in the editorial team of *Stellenbosch Theological Journal*. A prolific author, his most recent publication is *Reforming Memory: Essays on South African Church and Theological History*.

Robert Wafawanaka, PhD, from Zimbabwe, is an Associate Professor of Biblical studies and the Old Testament/Hebrew Bible, at the Samuel DeWitt Proctor School of Theology, Virginia Union University. Author of author of *Am I Still My Brother's Keeper? Biblical Perspectives on Poverty*.

Trygve Wyller, PhD, Dean and Professor of Theology (Emeritus), University of Oslo, Norway, and former President- International Academy of Practical Theology (2017-2019). He is co-editor of *Borderland Religion. Ambiguous Practices of Difference, Hope and Beyond*.

Sithembiso S. Zwane, MA., Director of the Ujamaa Centre for Biblical and Theological Community Development and Research, and lecturer in the Bible and Social Change within Biblical Studies, University of KwaZulu-Natal, South Africa. His publications include "Transition, Reflection, Rethinking and Reimagining: The Relevance of Black Liberation Theology in South Africa post-1994—A Tribute to Vuyani Vellem," *HTS Theological Studies* 76/3 (2020) a6078.

Editors' Note: Our greatest debt of gratitude goes to Elizabeth Renee Niang for her invaluable assistance in proofing, providing editorial suggestions, and singlehandedly creating indices for the volume. Her devotion and commitment to the work greatly enhanced the completion of this Festschrift.

Introduction

No "Ordinary" Person!

Andrew M. Mbuvi

Celebrating an Amazing Activist-Scholar

THERE IS NOTHING "ORDINARY" (to borrow his terminology) about the person and work of Gerald Oakley West, as this introduction will attest. Rather, this well-deserved Festschrift celebrates the *extra*-ordinary life of a South African biblical scholar, anti-apartheid activist, ordained priest, community organizer, social justice advocate, role model, husband, colleague, and friend, a citizen of the world.

I met West through his publications before I met West the man. Like any two people whose academic lives are separated by 6,000 miles and an ocean, he in South Africa and I in the USA, our personal meetings and encounters were confined to the annual AAR/SBL meetings. Nonetheless, over time, email communications and eventually Zoom sessions, provided opportunities for contact between the annual meetings. My continued participation during the annual Society of Biblical Literature meetings in the African Biblical Hermeneutics (ABH) Unit sessions, allowed us to continue meeting and getting to know each other better. Our serving together in the ABH unit's Organizing Committee, and especially after I later assumed the leadership of the unit in 2010, a unit which, along with

Justin Ukpong, Musa Dube, and Dora Mbuwayesango, West had been instrumental in its inception, helped cement our friendship.

West was born on April 10, 1956, in Zimbabwe (then Rhodesia), to South African parents working in the country (his cartographer father was working for the Rhodesian federal government in the waning years of British colonial rule there). The family returned to South Africa when West was a young boy and during his High School years, he became acutely aware of the injustices of the Apartheid system that racially segregated people on the basis of skin color, and his activism and commitment against the Apartheid system took root. Ordained (1980) in the Assemblies of God Church of South Africa (AOG), Gerald's increased involvement and active participation in anti-apartheid events, eventually led to his forced resignation from the AOG Church.[1] Ultimately, he would join the Anglican Church of Southern Africa (ACSA), whose active political stance against apartheid as manifest in leaders like Bishop Desmond Tutu, was welcomed and encouraged.

A declaration of a State of Emergency was announced in 1985 by the South African apartheid government which was facing growing national and international resistance. West had already become a conscientious objector by this stage and actively campaigned to end military conscription which had been in operation since 1967. By leading resistance to the conscriptions, West put himself in a vulnerable position that eventually resulted in his having to flee the country. Ending up in England, West embarked on academic studies, completing a PhD at the University of Sheffield. On returning to South Africa, West joined the School of Theology at the then University of Natal and served a term as Head of School (now the School of Religion, Philosophy, and Classics, University of KwaZulu-Natal), where he would remain for the next three decades. At UKZN, West would become instrumental in serving as the Director of the Ujamaa Centre for Development and Research and pioneering the Contextual Bible Study method which is now used in community groups, academic classrooms, and churches worldwide. In addition, while at UKZN he assisted in establishing a publishing house (Cluster Press, Pietermaritzburg) and continues to serve as editor of an academic journal (*Journal of Theology for Southern Africa*).

It is perhaps in the Ujamaa Center's work, described on its website as a context for reading the Bible as an "interface between socially

---

1. West, "The Vocation of an African Biblical Scholar."

engaged biblical and theological scholars, organic intellectuals, and local communities of the poor, working-class, and marginalised . . . [for] individual and social transformation," that West's contribution to biblical studies would find its most profound articulation and impact. (http://ujamaa.ukzn.ac.za/Homepage.aspx—Accessed: 08/09/2023) That his scholarship is undergirded by the notions of justice, empowerment, and liberation of the oppressed, marginalized, and materially deprived, aligns well with the Spirit's transformation of the Early Church in Acts 2.[2] The Ujamaa center had to reflect an idealized image of what Bishop Tutu would come to call the "rainbow nation," a multiethnic community of people of different heritages and backgrounds working together toward liberation and transformation.

Rather than disconnect the Ujamaa Center from his academic pursuits, he chose to situate in one of the South African "ivory towers." This seemed to serve two main purposes: to bring to the academic center the value of the community's knowledge and experience in the struggles for liberation, health, livelihood, etc.; second, to make it clear that the Eurocentric "ivory tower" model had to be undone. Embedded in his earliest publications would be the foundational elements of what would become his life's pursuit—liberation, empowerment, and justice for the poor and marginalized.[3] From liberationist readings of West's first book/dissertation (*Biblical Hermeneutics of Liberation: Modes of Reading the Bible in the South African Context*, Orbis, 1995) to his prolific publications on a vast range of topics (see below), there remains the balance between theory and praxis. To West, *theory* ("collaborative dialogue") and *praxis* ("liberative action") are inextricably linked, because one can only arrive at a good theory through praxis and, in turn, good theories find full expression only through praxis. To model praxis, West has mentored and supervised (and continues to do so even in retirement) more than fifty master's and PhD theses, students from all over Africa and beyond, at UKZN and other universities, several of whom have made chapter contributions in this volume.

---

2. In my personal estimation, while West's greatest influence has been "partially constituted" by the poor and marginalized, he seems to have retained the democratizing notion of the AGC's teaching emphasis concerning the Divine in-filling, in Acts 2, which liberates, empowers, and vivifies, in his academic life.

3. West, "Can a Literary Reading Be a Liberative Reading?"; *Idem*, "Two Modes of Reading the Bible," 34–47.

Those who may be materially poor, oppressed, and marginalized communities nevertheless have banks of knowledge and experience that are vital in the transformation of society for the better. At the height of the HIV-AIDS pandemic in the 1990s, Ujamaa Center became a location of solace and spiritual healing for many who sought guidance with crises of faith resulting from stigmatization associated with the disease. Ujamaa Center then became a conduit for the readings guided by the everyday needs and concerns of the community, which resulted in a rethinking of such, oft-neglected biblical stories, as the rape of Tamar (2 Samuel 13). The center also helped West remain grounded in an academic environment where individuals easily get lost in quests of the esoteric and banal that have little value for the "real" world.

West also never lost sight of his pastoral calling, even as he entered academia, turning upside down the isolationist inscrutability of the "ivory tower" of academia by giving voice in the institution to those typically marginalized and downtrodden (those materially less fortunate, those devoid of formal (western) education, those with tenuous connection with political and religious leadership, etc.). To these, he gave the term "ordinary"—not in the generic sense of lacking something that sets them apart but—in the sense of academically non-initiated readers. West was fully aware of how the academy had perceived a virtually unbridgeable chasm between academic readings (considered more accurate and reliable) and the "un-trained" Bible readers, whose reading was regarded as spurious and uncritical, or "precritical." It is in bridging this chasm that West has patiently and committedly labored for over three decades of professional academic and community-based life to build a firm bridge.

In what was, otherwise, deemed as simply the difference between academic readings and "ordinary" readings (if ever the "ordinary" reading was considered at all), West had rightly understood a deeper imbalance of power and control reflected in the colonialist structure of "center-periphery" entrenched in biblical studies, through which voices of the uninitiated who also tend to be the powerless, marginalized, and colonized were ostracized from academic discourse and its platforms (e.g., publication houses). Over time, the relevance of the academic discipline of biblical studies beyond its academic corridors has meant increasing irrelevance to everyday concerns of those outside of the academy, even as its pursuits become ever more abstruse. Denigration of the untrained and un-initiated reader of the Bible not only privileges the few but also effectively silences the majority of African Bible readers. "Ordinary" readers and their readings, in West's scholarship, are thus transformed from sub-jects of academic scrutiny and inquiry (even derision) to generators of independent and viable readings and ideas, which, more often than not, challenge long-held academic interpretations.

It was inevitable then, that West's interpretive approaches would be grounded in liberationist and postcolonialist ideologies that strive for freedom, justice, equality, and inclusion. By harnessing the African social spirit of "community," the nature of communal readings prioritized in the "ordinary reader" models developed at the Ujamaa Center, West has been able to also counter the extreme individualism that has been idol-ized within the Western "ivory tower" academic model. In giving voice to those typically silenced, usually, those from the lower socio-economic strata of society, whom he christened the "Academy of the Poor" (also, a title of one of his important books), West *anchors* the voice of the voice-less, *centers* the marginalized, oppressed, and colonized, and *challenges* the esoteric proclivity of scholarly biblical studies.

As a white middle-class South African of British heritage, taking the path of least resistance may have meant simply remaining quiet and uninvolved, as many did. However, for West, this was not an option; or, this was an option he refused to take. Publicly airing his opinions via the pulpit and academic publications became the means by which to play an active role in calling for justice and freedom for the oppressed Black South Africans. This was a choice he made, driven by his un-derstanding of the biblical teachings on human active agency in the divine call for justice and salvation. He chose, as his life's central work, to establish a center in a South African "ivory tower," but instead use it to work with, and in the midst of, South African materially poor and marginalized communities.

West has managed to do all this while maintaining a robust schol-arly life with an astounding publication record. Over the years he has given twenty-three visiting lectureships in Europe, India, Australia, and America; given over forty public lectures worldwide; presented over one hundred and fifty conference papers, and presided in over 90 workshops; and written, co-authored, or edited a dozen books and 99 book chap-ters; and, published over one hundred and ten peer-reviewed academic journal articles (see C.V.—https://ukzn.academia.edu/GeraldWest). As a longtime member of the Society of Biblical Literature (SBL), the flagship academic organization of biblical scholars worldwide, West has also been very active, over the years serving in multiple committees and leadership positions, including as general editor of the SBL experimental journal *Semeia* (2010–2016). During his tenure at *Semeia*, significant volumes addressing important topics often overlooked in western academic journals were published.[4] Together with Musa W. Dube, West edited a massive groundbreaking tome titled *The Bible in Africa: Transactions, Trajectories, and Trends* (Leiden: Brill, 1998). In 2014, he had conversations with Adele Reinhartz, the then-editor of the Society's flagship *Journal of Biblical Literature* (*JBL*), about opening the journal to scholarship that exceeds historical-grammatical questions; specifically, West wanted a space where African biblical scholarship could be published in the journal. The result was a "Special Occasional Exchange" *JBL Forum,* 2015, featuring articles by African biblical scholars that showcased the distinctive contributions of African Biblical Hermeneutics.[5]

With Beverley Haddad (his spouse and an academic theologian in her own right, and professor at UKZN) he jointly published articles embracing a "feminist" stance very early on. This was a conscious undertaking on West's part as reflected in his approach of emersion when it comes to his academic endeavors. And even perhaps an embodied stance against African and biblical patriarchies which dominate both the biblical and African worldviews.

In this celebratory Festschrift, the breadth of West's impact on the Academy, Community, and Church, is evident in the chapter contributions done by former students, professional colleagues, community leaders, and friends from Africa, Europe, and America. The diversity of interests and topics reflected in the chapters in this volume—poverty, HIV/AIDS pandemic, liberation, social justice, gender and sexuality, creative literature, hermeneutics and interpretation, postcolonialism, Bible translation, etc.—run the gamut of subject matters that have constituted West's impressive vocation. The five-section subdivisions are an attempt to map out or "track" West's manifold interests into organized groupings, to reflect this same breadth of his impact as a scholar, a church leader, organizer, anti-apartheid activist, and community leader whose calling brought him to those often marginalized and ostracized members of society.[6] From the beginning, West understood Liberation to be more

---

4. Cf. West and Dube, eds., *Reading With.*

5. *JBL* 134.4 (2015). Included are articles by Kenneth Ngwa, Aliou C. Niang, Musa W. Dube, L. Juliana Claassens, with a framing introduction by Gerald O. West.

6. West prefers the term "tracking" for its evocation of African imagery. Interesting, coming from a cartographer's son! Cf. West, "African Biblical Scholarship as Tripolar,"

than just a fanciful academic interest, but to be at the core of the biblical teachings about salvation and justice, embodied by prophets and Jesus. He has always embodied this as an activist-scholar.

West can be said to embody the saying from my Akamba community about the refreshing that happens to the goat's kid after visiting the rivers—"Undu ka-endaa usini ka-ambite tiwo ka-syokaa ka-ambite" (*She does not come back from the river hollering [from thirst] the same way she left.*) Like the visit to the river, an encounter with West provides quenching knowledge, and inspirational commitment as the essays in this volume attest.

Ujamaa: Academy of the Poor[7]

West's former student and, subsequently colleague at UKZN Ujamaa Center, kicks things off by paying homage to his mentor and providing a personal reflection on West's impact on the discipline of biblical studies in South Africa and beyond. In South African R. Simangaliso Kumalo's chapter, we glean some of the significant influences of Black theologians and biblical scholars on West's academic interests over the years. An overview examines the impact of certain literature (e.g., *Kairos Document*), terminology (the Bible as a "site of struggle," "socially engaged biblical scholarship," etc.), and societal events (HIV/AIDS Pandemic), in shaping West's diverse academic and social interests. In turn, Kumalo allows us to see West's impact on the academy (modes of reading), on the community (poor, marginalized, LGBTQ+, HIV-AIDS, etc.), and on the Church (rethinking social justice and Christian calling).

Because Bible translation is key in how local communities interact with the biblical text, Nathan Esala, an American Bible translator who worked in Ghana, analyzes how the postcolonial African Bible translators in Ghana have engaged in the decolonization of the Bible by performing activist translations that resist western translators' "social invasion." According to Esala, African translators do this by "strategically subordinat[ing] the text to their ideological concerns for liberation from oppression." To have a better chance at countering the colonial "social invasion," whose intent was control, exploitation, and subordination, Esala proposes that the more marginalized communities in Ghana have avoided the colonial gaze

---

240–73, 240.

7. Cf. West, *Academy of the Poor.*

as much as possible. The marginalized, he argues, would provide a less infiltrated source by the colonial entanglements that have already shaped the political, social, and economic structure of contemporary Ghana. And none more than the disabled members of the community. Only in this way can "activist translations" be both liberatory and life-giving. It was in this regard that utilizing West's contextual bible study (CBS) developed in Ujamaa Center in South Africa proved vital for Esala's work in Ghana when applied to the book of Job.

Senegalese New Testament scholar, Aliou C. Niang, invites us to consider the notion of hospitality embedded in the story of the Lukan Jesus about a disgruntled host whose invitations were spurned by his preferred guests, and who went against the grain of social practice by opening his doors to the poor and disabled or differently able people to his snubbed feast in Luke 14:16–24. Drawing on some African cultural elements of hospitality, Niang proposes that an understanding of the story as a basis for an "enough to go around" approach toward shared resources is what is being called upon. Unlike Greco-Roman meals, particularly symposia meals (which may have formed the conceptual backdrop to Luke's critique), which deliberately excluded the poor and differently-abled members of society, Niang perceives a more commensurate alignment of the Lukan teaching with African hospitality codes embedded in teachings of Negritude, of a Senegalese prophetess Aline Sitoé Diatta and the Qur'an.

Reading with the "ordinary reader" in the African context essentially implies siding with the plight of those who have been victims of society's social structures and laws. In this spirit, Ugandan Hebrew Bible scholar, Robert Wafawanaka reads Deuteronomy 15 and the notion of the *Shemmitta* year (when material restitution and redistribution in Israel would have been enacted) in the context of African social values of hospitality, sharing, and concern for the poor. In highlighting certain parallels between the biblical text's context and some African cultural elements, Wafawanaka helps us see how such connections, when applied appropriately, can help address and alleviate poverty by rethinking the redistribution of resources. Colonialism's introduction of a capitalist economy eroded these conscientious African socio-economic structures that Wafawanaka would like to see recovered and reinstituted.

Jonathan Draper, West's colleague and fellow South African at UKZN, interrogates the concept of "reading *with*" which was developed and championed by West through his scholarship and praxis via the

Ujamaa Center at UKZN. While acknowledging an eventual methodological parting of ways with West, Draper concedes to the inevitable influence of West's work in engaging with the materially and economically underprivileged churches and their members. He utilizes Bourdieu's theory of *habitus* to revisit a session carried out at UKZN in 2009, with members of The Christian Catholic Apostolic Holy Spirit Church of Zion in South Africa (CCAHSCZ in SA), one of the oldest African Indigenous Churches in Southern Africa. To do so, Draper examines the reading of the Lukan "Parable of the Rich Man and Lazarus" (Luke 16:19–31), with a focus on CCAHSCZ's special interest and focus on the role of angels in death rituals. Draper concedes, however reluctantly, that academia would need to integrate and pursue a different set of questions if a "reading *with*" approach were to be more widely adopted by the academy because the true transformative engagement with the Bible, in the African context, has been occurring outside of academia.

Methodology and African Biblical Hermeneutics

West has maintained that a distinct African biblical interpretation has to be an outgrowth of the symbiotic engagement of the Bible and the African context that results in mutual enlightenment and transformation.[8] In this regard, the Botswana New Testament scholar, Musa W. Dube, gives a fascinating methodological proposition drawn from the African folk tale genre, as a possible means of engaging some biblical stories. Dube explores the world of African storytelling by analyzing how the trickster narratives, often associated with the hare in African stories, provide a mode of reading that opens up possibilities for authentic and distinct African liberative interpretations. Employing a decolonial framework, Dube demonstrates how reading from the trickster position means recognition of one's "vulnerability but not incapacity." The subversiveness of the trickster as a means of resistance, escape, survival, and liberation, is utilized to defy oppressive forces that attempt to limit, control, or subjugate. The trickster is not a deceiver, but a resister of oppression in its different forms, and so a template for emancipatory and liberative readings. The gender neutrality of the trickster, for Dube, also offers avenues of upstaging the dominant male voice in both the biblical text and patriarchal African communities. The trickster, by

8. West, "On the Eve of an African Biblical Studies," 99–115.

questioning and challenging the oppressive societal structures (racism, patriarchy, sexuality, etc.), opens up the possibilities of reimagining a more equitable, just, and fair social existence.

West's former student, American Bob Ekblad, takes a bold approach in comparing West's approach of reading with "ordinary readers" to the Isaianic "Servant" text. Juxtaposing the Isaianic text with some of the foundational aspects of West's Ujamaa project, Ekblad explores what he perceives as the prophetic nature of reading the Bible with and among the poor and oppressed. The Isaianic prophetic message, which oscillated between judgment and hope, provides a viable background to analyze the different ways that the prophet and his "disciples" were called to engage the floundering people of Judah and Israel. For Ekblad, West exemplifies a faithful Isaianic "disciple" who has chosen to commit his life's work to the suffering and oppressed members of the Black South African communities, despite his otherwise racially, socially, academically, economically, and politically privileged background as a white South African of British heritage, in Apartheid and post-Apartheid South Africa. Over the years of utilizing the Contextual Bible Study approach at Ujamaa, West has mastered and trained many in the art of listening, distilling of ideas, and empowering communication that has transformed reading with "ordinary readers" into a means of providing a voice to those often silenced, ignored, oppressed, and marginalized.

The distinguished Greco-Roman world and New Testament scholar, the American, Richard Horsley, highlights how works like those of West, by resisting the "Imperial Bible" with its propensity to oppression and domination of the weak by the powerful, help to bring about the kind of desired transformation and inclusivity lacking in the larger biblical studies forum. Learning from the undercurrents of the biblical texts that sought to undo the imperialistic tendencies replete in the ancient world, and which find parallels in modern world history, Horsley posits the significance and impact of postcolonial readings articulated by African scholars like West. Horsley finds these continued challenges of western approaches' persistent colonialist tendencies quite warranted and necessary.

Issues of methodology, as they relate to African biblical interpretations, have been a mainstay of West's academic publication from the onset.[9] In choosing to make his contribution to the ongoing vibrant discussions

9. See, for example, West, "Reading the Bible in Africa," 1–5; and West, "On the Eve," 99–115. Other publications include West, "Re-Reading the Bible with African Resources," 3–32; West, "African Biblical Scholarship as Tri-Polar," 240–73.

on the nature of African Biblical Hermeneutics (ABH), South African Pauline scholar, Jeremy Punt, cautions about the unwitting over-emphasis on the contextual readings which may result in readings that lack broader relevance. While not downplaying their significance, Punt would also like African biblical scholars to exercise awareness of the pitfalls of such an interpretive enterprise and has provided several warning signs to pay attention to. ABH, Punt argues, should not lose focus of constant self-awareness that the "meaning-making" process needs to be self-examing and renewing, so as not to end up in the same unfortunate fate of calcification that has plagued the western biblical enterprise.

On Race, Gender, and Sexuality

Examining her liminal existence as a bi-racial person in apartheid South Africa, Belinda Crawford revisits her earlier Honors research on the subject, where she analyzed Gen 2–3 using Social Identity Theory (SIT). This time she incorporates the Contextual Bible Study (CBS) approach, to re-read the Genesis 2–3 story. Paying close attention to CBS's "See–Judge–Act" model to biblical reading, Crawford does an autobiographical re-reading of the Genesis story. She examines the expulsion of the humans from the Garden which, though traumatic and bearing semblance to her own exile-like existence (without a home or a community to belong to), nevertheless opens up the possibility that even in the divine judgment there remained divine compassion and mercy, assuring continued divine presence even in exile. This creative and resilient aspect of the biblical narrative supplies a sense of comfort for Crawford that, despite her struggles to belong, in a world defined strictly in black-and-white terms that excluded her, as a biracial person, she still looks back and sees the presence of a divine hand guiding her along. Not fitting in the socially constructed categories did not stop her from connecting with such a God.

Hebrew Bible professor, Madipoane (Ngwan'a Mphahlele) Masenya, employs (South) African proverbs to interrogate and problematize the assumptions that lie behind some of the passages concerning warnings to young males about sexual deviance (Prov 7). In reading Proverbs 7 with select Sotho/African proverbs, Masenya finds both parallels and divergencies between the biblical instructions and the African proverbs. However, in both, the presumption of the public space as a male domain is challenged by non-conformist females whose presence, while vilified by the male voice, nonetheless calls the presumed normative social structure into question. In celebrating West's scholarship, Masenya points out how he never shied away from addressing gender and sexual oppression within racialized South African and patriarchal communities in the South African context, and the biblical text.

Both the biblical world and the majority of African communities are predominantly patriarchal. These shared social aspects often allow for parallels between some biblical worldviews and African traditions, but they also, unfortunately, perpetuate gender inequality and continued subordination of women. These gender-based exploitative relationships undermine the freedoms and agency of females in society, making it challenging for those who may seek to cultivate liberative feminist movements. One such relationship in Cameroon that exploits the socio-economic vulnerabilities of young girls and women, is the "sugar daddy" phenomenon, where older economically affluent men prey on young, economically desperate university girls and young women. The "sugar daddies" offer ongoing financial support to these girls and young women, who usually need the money to pay for university education, in exchange for sexual favors. Utilizing Gerald West's liberationist reading, and building on an article published by West and Beverley Haddad on the "Sugar Daddy" phenomenon and HIV, in South Africa, Alice Yafeh-Deigh explores the Pauline language of 1 Cor 6:12–20, as encoded with liberating aspects about the female body, to confront and challenge the Cameroonian "sugar daddy" situation.[10] Employing an "Afro-womanist-intersectional" interpretive approach, Yafeh-Deigh argues for the Pauline constructs of the human body, including the female body, as subject to the freedom and liberation afforded in being part of the Christian community. Putting the Cameroonian Christian community in the spotlight, Yafeh-Deigh challenges it to offer significant alternative means of support to the vulnerable members of the community, to enable them to avoid the trap of the "sugar daddy" exploitation.

Continuing the theme of patriarchy, Zimbabwean Hebrew Bible scholar, Dora Mbuwyesango explores how West's positive appraisal of the teachings of one of the African pioneers of independent indigenous Christian churches in Southern Africa, Isaiah Shembe, overlooks how the role of women in marriage and divorce, falls short of granting agency and

10. West and Haddad, "Boaz as 'Sugar Daddy,'" 137–56.

full equality to the community's women. While Mbuwayesango agrees with West's appraisal of Shembe's progressive stance on women, in contrast to that of the European missionary teachings, she takes issue with the ways in which the interpretations remain trapped in patriarchal strictures. While granting women a voice in certain decisions on marriage and divorce, in a manner beyond those proscribed in the biblical text and African tradition, Shembe's religio-cultural revolution failed to extricate itself from the constraints of patriarchal dominance.

Choosing to focus on the aspect of "see," in the CBS interpretive model of "See–Judge–Act," Cameroonian Hebrew Bible scholar, Kenneth Ngwa does a fascinating re-examination of the story of Lot's wife who "looked back" and turned into a "pillar of salt" (Gen 19). Challenging the traditional reading of the narrative being about Lot's wife's divine judgment, for disobeying the command of the men/angels (Gen 19:17) rescuing her family, Ngwa instead postulates how her "looking back" (תבט) was an act of defiance and resistance to oppressive, colonial and patriarchal, powers. Told from a patriarchal perspective, Lot's wife's role in the story has been *hidden from sight*—mutilated and dismembered by the narrator's focus on her husband even when it is clear that, for example, she would be in charge of the hospitality offered to the strangers.[11] She is also not seen, even as her husband insanely offers her daughters to the men of Sodom to be raped (the silencing of the daughters, who likely resisted their father's vulgar proposal, indicates the likelihood of the narrative's muting of any of their mother's resistance, too). Salt, as both a preserver and a corrosive, occasions an ambiguity of meaning that allows the questioning of what becoming a "pillar of salt" represents. Ngwa constructs a compelling re-reading that "re-members" Lot's wife where laughter and seeing become means of resistance to violence and marginalization.

On Politics and Theology

Norwegian theologian Kjetil Hafstad finds in Pope Francis a kindred spirit to West's long work among the poor and the vulnerable. Surmising the possible influence of South American Liberation Theological thinking

---

11. Rabbinic tradition's attempt at filling in the biblical text's gaps, include naming of Lot's wife (either Idit in *Midrash Tanhuma*, *Vayera* 8, or Ado in *Book of Jasher* 19:52), and connections to salt (*Genesis Rabbah* 50–51), retained a decidedly patriarchal alignment with Lot.

on the then Cardinal Bergoglio of Buenos Aires, Argentina, Hafstad believes it prompted the cardinal to exemplify affiliation with the poor by choosing a simple life and work among the *favelas*. It is the spirit of St. Francis to care for all life, especially of those most vulnerable, that as, Pope Francis, Bergoglio has continued to evidence his continued guidance by the same principles. He has prioritized the concerns and voices of those traditionally marginalized by the Catholic Church—the gay community, ordination of women, marriage of priests, etc.—and ventured into issues like Climate Change and the environmental crisis. At the heart of Pope Francis's vision is a life of simplicity whose impact is profound. A willingness to listen to and learn from those otherwise not considered by society to be knowledgeable, influential, powerful, experts, etc., and whose voices are suppressed or ignored aligns West's work among the "ordinary readers" with Pope Francis' focus on the marginalized.

Comparing Miriam's bold challenge to Moses' leadership in Numb 12:1–16, Ugandan Hebrew Bible scholar, Robert Kuloba, examines her bravery and the resultant fallout and punishment, casting it against the experiences of today's Ugandan and Rwandan female politicians. While both Uganda and Rwanda have set quotas for women representatives in political leadership, women's roles remain largely limited in political influence and authority. Resultantly, those women politicians challenge the imposed limits to power and authority set by the dominant patriarchal political structure, be it discrepancies, injustices, abuse of power, etc. Like Miriam, who for Kuloba, simply sought (with Aaron) equality of power with Moses (yet was the only one punished of the two, and thereafter written out of the story, as she dies soon after) such African women politicians find themselves punished, ostracized, and even criminalized for doing so. Kuloba faults both the biblical narrative and the Ugandan and Rwandan political structures for their blind adherence to and perpetuation of, patriarchal structures and ideologies that harm, rather than build, a more equitable society.

Hebrew Bible scholar, Gilbert Ojwang of Kenya, turns our focus to the tumultuous post-colonial African political scene to make the case for the relevance of the Deuteronomic construct of a sovereign's role (Deut 16:18—18:22) as a model for African political leadership. Using his native Kenya as a focal point, Ojwang appeals to the Deuteronomic prescription and circumscription of the Israelite kingship in order to draw lessons for contemporary African leadership that would ultimately forestall the leadership challenges that have plagued the pursuit of democracy for many post-independent African countries. For Ojwang, the ideals of leadership laid out in the Deuteronomic text, if adhered to, could help address the challenges of corruption, injustice, poverty, empowerment of the populace, and the checks-and-balances that make a modern democracy function to the benefit of all.

In analyzing how space impacts participants' responses to questions of social identity and cross-cultural communications between those living in animosity, Norwegian scholar Trygve Wyler put to test West's CBS approach in a non-religious setting. The aim was to see how, in trying to seek a more "neutral space" participants, both university students and local leaders of diverse political, religious, and civic group affiliations in the city of Oslo could learn to listen to one another. For comparison and analysis, Trygve uses the doctoral research of a Tanzanian student at the University of Oslo, who also organized similar groupings in Tanzania. The nature of what parameters are set in constructing a space for the purpose of addressing controversial and portent community concerns such as social justice, racism, etc., is determined to be critical for a successful outcome.

On Decolonization and Liberation

Ghanian Hebrew Bible scholar Dorothy Akoto hails West as a living "memorial stone," drawing inspiration from the stones set up in Joshua 4 to prompt the Israelites to always remember God's actions on their behalf. West's role now, as an "elder statesman" among African biblical scholars, and the trailblazing that he has done (and continues to do, even in retirement) for African biblical scholarship, marks him out for such meaningful recognition. Juxtaposing a critical historical reading of the text with African reality, Akoto draws connections between the ancient Israelite history and African reality, as the premise for her reading of the biblical text. West is postulated as an example to be emulated in his proficiency, efficiency, service, and productivity, whose contributions should be celebrated among other "memorial stones," as an ongoing witness to future generations of African scholars.

L. Juliana Claassens (Hebrew Bible) and R. R. Vosloo (Theology) of South Africa, engage with South African author Damon Galgut's novel, *The Promise,* the winner of one of literature's most prestigious awards, the Booker Prize, in 2021. The novel, which echoes the failures of post-apartheid South Africa to live up to the promise of restoring the lost heritage, especially land, of Black South Africans, is compared to the plight of Hagar in Genesis 16, providing an intriguing interplay between the failure of justice for both. The impact of the prevailing trauma on the Black South African community, is evident in the struggle to justly address the delayed promise of restitution and reparation. This is reminiscent of the Black Lives Matter (BLM) movement's struggle for justice for African Americans, which the authors reference but, also, South Africa's own continued struggle to address the still festering historical atrocities of wealth and land displacement during apartheid rule. It is among the members of the latter group that West's work on "reading with the poor" continues to take place.

While the history of Dutch and British missionary activities in South Africa is dominant, not much of the Norwegian mission in Southern Africa gets scholarly examined. So, Norwegian Hebrew Bible scholar, Knut Holter, inspired by West's research on the mission history of the BaTlhaping, a Tswana community in South Africa in his groundbreaking *The Stolen Bible*, takes the opportunity to explore this not-so-well-publicized presence of Norwegian missionaries in South Africa in the 18th and 19th centuries.[12] He focuses on the encounter between a Norwegian Mission Society called Jan Kielland, and his encounters with the Zulu prince, Cetshwayo, during which Kielland offered the prince an American ax, both as a gift and as a symbol; of the technological progress awaiting the Zulu people should they convert to Christianity. Relying on Kielland's original writings, Holter translates his fellow Norwegians' notes in analyzing the account, showing that Kielland's progressive views about race and religion reflected a rare positive perspective in the context of Western missionaries of the period.

Philippe Denis, West's colleague and history professor at UKZN, examines three events in recent history that reflect ways in which the Bible has been misused, in defense of a systemic racist structure of apartheid in South Africa by the Dutch Reformed Church (DRC), in justification of genocidal killings in Rwanda, and the atrocious cases of priestly sexual abuses in the Catholic Church. Denis sees an underlying interpretive pattern in the three situations where the oppressors have turned to the Bible to mind-bogglingly make the case for their violent actions. In all three cases, the Bible's authority was appealed upon because the oppressors themselves believed in its content, but also because they

---

12. West, *Stolen Bible*.

believed they could impose their interpretations on those they sought to control or subdue, thereby silencing them. While disagreeing with these biblical interpretations, Denis does point out the culpability of the Bible in its portrayal of divinely sanctioned violence, the mistreatment of strangers, and the deceptive character of some religious individuals. Like the Ujamaa Center's "Tamar Campaign," which gives voice to the victims of rape in confronting their trauma, Denis contends that only in giving voice to the victims of apartheid, genocide, and sexual abuse, is any form of healing for the victims possible.

Having opened this Festschrift with West's former student and colleague, the volume appropriately closes with another of West's former students, and a subsequent colleague at the Ujamaa center. South African, Sithembiso Zwane, offers us an invaluable historical overview of the Ujamaa Center at UKZN, and West's long period of service as director of the center. Zwane provides an especially helpful analysis of West's vital contribution and ministry during South Africa's devastating HIV/AIDS pandemic period, which threatened to upend the South African social and religious fabric. Advocating for the rights of LGBTQ+ community members, who were especially hard hit by the HIV/AIDS pandemic and ostracized by the Church, Zwane shows how West made it the Center's priority to seek out and serve such marginalized members by providing a safe space to grapple with issues of faith, HIV/AIDS stigma, and Christian compassion. This foundation of the Center continues to play a critical role in conversations that many religious institutions in South Africa and beyond, are still grappling with or have struggled to appropriately address. Driven by the need to empower "ordinary readers," and Church leadership, to engage meaningfully with the biblical text, it meant taking their everyday experiences and situations seriously as a starting point in the interpretive process. It also meant embracing the whole person as an *agent* of interpretation, not just a *recipient* of often authoritarian ecclesial interpretations. This, for Zwane, remains the enduring distinction of the Center and of West's unwavering commitment and contribution.

Nkosi Sikelel' iAfrika!

For the editorial team:
Andrew M. Mbuvi, PhD
Albright College, Reading PA, USA.

Bibliography

West, Gerald O. *The Academy of the Poor: Towards A Dialogical Reading of the Bible.* Interventions 2. Sheffield: Sheffield Academic, 1999.

———."African Biblical Scholarship as Tri-Polar, Post-Colonial, and a Site-of-Struggle." In *Present and Future of Biblical Studies: Celebrating 25 Years of Brill's Biblical Interpretation,* edited by Tat-Siong Benny Liew, 240–73. BIS 161. Leiden: Brill, 2018.

———. "Can a Literary Reading Be a Liberative Reading?" *Scriptura* 35 (1990) 10–25.

———. "On the Eve of an African Biblical Studies. Trajectories and Trends." *JTSA* 99 (1997) 99–115.

———. "Reading the Bible in Africa: Constructing Our Own Discourse," *BCT* 2.2 (1995) 1–5.

———. "Re-Reading the Bible with African Resources: Interpretative Strategies for Reconstruction in a Post-Colonial, Post-Apartheid Context on the Eve of Globalization." *JCT* 4.1 (1998) 3–32.

———. *The Stolen Bible: From Tool of Imperialism to African Icon.* BIS 144. Leiden Brill, 2016.

———. "Two Modes of Reading the Bible in the South African Context of Liberation." *JTSA* 73 (1990) 34–47.

———. "The Vocation of an African Biblical Scholar on the Margins of Biblical Scholarship." *OTE* 19.2 (2006) 307–36.

West, Gerald O., and Musa W. Dube, eds. *Reading* With: *An Exploration of the Interface Between Critical and Ordinary Readings of the Bible. Semeia* 73. Atlanta: Society of Biblical Literature, 1997.

West, Gerald, and Beverley G. Haddad. "Boaz as 'Sugar Daddy': Re-Reading Ruth in the Context of HIV." *JTSA* 155 (2016) 137–56.

PART ONE

"Academy of the Poor"

Reading the Bible with the Materially Underprivileged

1

Turning Swords into Ploughshares

Gerald West's Bible in Communities of the Poor

R. Simangaliso Kumalo

Introduction

GERALD WEST HAS BEEN my teacher, colleague, and friend. So, in a way, I guess I am biased in the content of this paper. On the other hand, I am also an academic who is committed to the integrity of my scholarship and, therefore, I have adhered to the principles of critical analysis when writing this reflection. In this essay, I aim to pay tribute to West's scholarship legacy as I have observed and experienced it.

A Life Spent in the Re-reading of the Bible

Growing up in apartheid South Africa as a white person, West witnessed the denial of God-given humanity on the people of colour by a vicious system that, ironically, used the Bible to justify racial hierarchy and treatment of Black people as second-class citizens. That experience was to have an immense impact on his life and scholarship. As a young biblical scholar-activist, influenced by South African Black and Contextual Theologies the dominant strands of liberation theology at the time, West sought to use his scholarship to effect social transformation. And what better place to do it, than at the Ujamaa Center for Community

Research and Development Center (previously, the Institute for the Study of the Bible & Worker Ministry Project)?

For the next thirty years, West would dedicate his career to making the Bible contextually relevant in Southern Africa and beyond, by reading it with organized, marginalized groups of the poor, working-class, ordinary people. Throughout his decades-long career, he did not tire from talking and writing about the agency of the marginalized, insisting that "ordinary readers" of the Bible have resources that are valuable and useful for trained readers. He, therefore, argued that it is important for trained readers to "read with" ordinary readers. The story of West is the story of a white male English-speaking South African, a socially engaged biblical scholar, who deliberately situated himself on the margins of South African society, to read the Bible with the marginalized people.

Yet, he would prove his academic prowess by producing over two hundred academic works and delivering innumerable guest lectures, throughout the world. Through his scholarship, West has become one of the foremost authorities in biblical hermeneutics, not just on the continent, but globally. This chapter highlights West's contributions to biblical scholarship over the years and the impact that it has had on communities with which he has worked.

The Making of a Radical Biblical Scholar

Although West grew up in a Christian home and attended a church-related boarding school, he had not actually read much of the Bible as a young person. Rejecting Christianity in his experimental teen years did not help his limited knowledge of the Bible. It was not until he was "born again," and attending a Pentecostal church as a young adult, that he began to be immersed in the Bible. Accepted as a pastor in a Pentecostal church, it was only a matter of time before tensions emerged between his "strange" reading of the Bible and his conservative church. The dangerous mistake that he made was to reconcile the importance of the Bible and his faith, with the struggle against apartheid, and consciously choosing to side with the oppressed Black South Africans, resulting in his expulsion from the church. Fearing of detention, and the consequences that came with it, he went into exile in England for graduate studies. He returned home to a country boiling from the heat of Apartheid's racial injustice and oppression. Amid the ruins of the violence, he founded a vibrant Black Theology frame, that would shape his scholarship and activism.

A cursory reading of West's works shows the debt that he owes to South African Black Theology and Contextual Theology of the 1980s. The apartheid regime was getting more draconian. South Africa was literally on fire. Various anti-apartheid activist groups and individuals coalesced to reflect on what God could be saying to South Africa in "a time such as this." These included the Institute for Contextual Theology (ICT), the South African Council of Churches (SACC), and various theologians scattered throughout the country's universities, seminaries, and parishes, as well as ordinary Christians. Out of their efforts emerged the iconic *Kairos Document* and numerous other theological works. *The Kairos Document*, in particular, looms large in West's work. The notion of 'Prophetic Theology' as identified and defined by *The Kairos Document* was primarily useful to West. *The Kairos Document* argues that there can be no prophetic theology without a "people's theology."

West picked up on that notion of "people's theology" and made it the starting point of the institution he founded, the Ujamaa Centre's work. The Contextual Bible Study methodology that Ujamaa Centre pioneered is, in his view, a process that enables the people's theology to become "prophetic theology."[1] Furthermore, West was impressed by the method that was used to produce the antiracist and antiapartheid *Kairos Document*. It convinced him that theology is not reserved for professional theologians and priests, but ordinary Christians can participate in theological reflection and should be encouraged to do so.[2]

Some South African theologians who inspired him, and whom he frequently mentions in his works, are Itumeleng Mosala, Takatso Mofokeng, James Cochrane, Albert Nolan, Allan Boesak, Musa Dube, and Frank Chikane. He was also influenced by the African-American theologian, Cornel West. From the pioneers of South African Black Theology, West borrowed the term "site of struggle" which permeates his work. His later work with communities of the marginalized would confirm that the Bible is, indeed, a site of struggle with a multiplicity of often contending voices.

West was impressed by Mofokeng's nuanced view of the Bible, which saw it as being both a solution and a problem, at a time when many liberation theologians and activists in the ecumenical movement regarded it as

1. West, "Contextual Bible Study," 144.
2. Kairos, *The Kairos Document*, 34–35.

essentially a "book of liberation" that represented hope for Black South Africans.[3] In his own scholarship, West shows, now and again, that the Bible is a "site of struggle," representing both liberating and dominating discourses engaged in covert and/or overt contestations.[4] In his reading of the Bible with the organized marginalized, West would endeavor to show that, indeed, the Bible is frequently (and successfully) used as an instrument of death, rather than as a book of life. For example, as we shall see later with regard to his work with HIV-AIDS and the LGBTIQI+ people in faith communities, West shows how the Bible has been used to condemn and marginalise these sections of society in South Africa.

Thus, it is clear to him that the Bible has a multiplicity of often contending voices. Aware of the reality of the importance of the Bible among the oppressed Black communities, West notes that Mofokeng had suggested that it would not be prudent to rid Black communities of this book, as suggested by many young activists, at the time, who regarded it as an oppressive document. Rather Mofokeng suggested that "[B]lack theologians who are committed to the struggle for liberation and are organically connected to the struggling Christian people have to engage this reality and do their best to shape the bible into a formidable weapon in the hands of the oppressed instead of leaving it to confuse, frustrate, or even destroy our people."[5] While accepting Mofokeng's argument, West noted that Mofokeng did not say *how* Black theologians can take up this task. Instead, the *how* part, in West's view, was Mosala's key contribution to South African Black Theology.

West's debt to Mosala is quite huge and is evident in the numerous citations of the latter's work in his own scholarship. In his own words, "Mosala's work, and the work of the generation of black theologians who have followed him, especially Tinyiko Maluleke, has remained the sounding point for all of my work."[6] West accepts Mosala's critique of earlier scholar-activists, such as Desmond Tutu and Boesak, who had as their starting point the notion that the Bible is the revealed word of God, and that "the bible is rent apart by the antagonistic struggles of the warring classes of Israelite society in much the same way that our world is torn asunder by society's class, cultural, racial and gender divisions."[7]

3. West, *The Stolen Bible*, 328.

4. West, "Locating Contextual Bible," 120.

5. West, *Stolen Bible*, 329.

6. West, "Vocation of an African Biblical Scholar," 310.

7. West, *Stolen Bible*, 331.

We can imagine West smiling and agreeing with Mosala who argues that "The insistence on the bible as the Word of God must be seen for what it is, an ideological manoeuvre whereby ruling class interests evident in the bible are converted into a faith that transcends social, political, racial, sexual and economic divisions."[8]

If the Bible is a ruling class document that represents the ideological and political interests of the ruling class, West quotes Mosala as arguing that the Bible cannot be the starting point for a theology of liberation. Rather, it requires a de-ideologization before it can be hermeneutically straightforward, in terms of the liberation struggle. What impressed West in Mosala's argument is the methodological framework used for the de-ideologizing hermeneutical project, something that Mofokeng had not done. Black Theology could only derive from the Bible if it could link the struggles of the oppressed in South Africa with those of ancient Israel. It is with this one thing that Mosala won West over to his intellectual and ideological camp.

It is exactly this linking of the struggles of the oppressed in ancient Israel with those of the organized marginalized groups in South Africa that West has worked with in contemporary, post-apartheid South Africa, that has made the Contextual Bible Study methodology of the Ujamaa Centre very impactful. In line with South African Black Theology, West also argues that the Bible cannot be the primary starting point for Black biblical hermeneutics of liberation because it is itself a "site of struggle" with contending ideo-theological voices.

West also found Norman Gottwald's Marxist analysis of ancient Israel's social life quite appealing. Gottwald's *The Tribes of Yahweh* left a mark on West's mind. Having read it "from cover to cover, including every footnote,"[9] West notes, that it was a pivotal experience in his life. It enables him to provide lines of connection not only between the present struggles that socially engaged biblical scholars are in solidarity with and the struggles of early Israel but also between socially engaged biblical scholars located in various contexts of struggle.[10] Economic concerns that are an integral part of Gottwald's work feature prominently in West's scholarship.

---

8. West, *Stolen Bible*, 331.

9. West, "Tribes in Africa," 85.

10. West, "Tribes in Africa," 85.

Having drunk from the "wells" of Mosala, Gottwald, and Mofokeng, among many other socially engaged scholars, the stage was set for West to begin his own scholarship. West admits that the works of Mosala and Mofokeng, together with those of West, made him conscious of the agency of the oppressed.[11] However, he notes that, although neither Mofokeng nor Mosala reflects much further on the agency of the oppressed, they provided the starting point and trajectory for his own work on Black African agency.

Reading the Bible in Community, with the Marginalized

West's praxis uses biblical and theological resources for social transformation. His decades-long work has been committed to systemic or structural analysis, critique, and advocating for change of oppressive structures. His view is that, in African contexts, theological change is a prerequisite for social change. For systemic change to happen in communities of faith, there is a need for theological change. The tool that he and his colleagues at Ujamaa Centre have used consistently is Contextual Bible Study (CBS), which emerged in South Africa in the 1980s. CBS is a form of biblical liberation hermeneutics and prophetic theology, in which socially engaged biblical scholars and ordinary readers of the Bible collaborate in the interpretive process, each bringing different sets of critical resources.[12] The beauty of such collaboration is that it produces forms of local theology that can be articulated and owned by those producing it, to whom it is organic. CBS is dialogical, not only in terms of a dialogue between ordinary and scholarly readers but also a dialogue between the context of the readers and the biblical text.

The emphasis on the context is crucial because, as West rightly points out, all biblical reading is contextual and, therefore, context is not something to be reluctantly acknowledged and then bracketed. It is an integral part of the interpretive process.[13] Working with his colleagues at Ujamaa Centre, West has designed numerous Bible Studies that are potentially appropriate to the contextual realities they work with or within. Some of the contextual issues he has been grappling with over the years

11. West, "Vocation of an African Biblical Scholar," 318.

12. West, "Locating Contextual Bible," 109.

13. West, "Locating Contextual Bible," 109.

include land rights, patriarchy, rape, HIV and AIDS, economic injustice, casual labor, disability, sexual orientation, race and class.

The CBS interpretive process follows the "See–Judge–Act" method that moves from social analysis, to biblical reflection to social action. The "See'" part is done by the organized marginalized community, who share a lived reality and analyze this reality together. In the "Judge" section, the analyzed reality is viewed in the light of what God intends for that community's lived reality, whether or not it conforms to God's will. The last step, "Act," is about transformation and change of that reality, if it does not conform to divine will. It is clear, therefore, that the communities of the marginalized are in charge of the process. The role of the socially engaged theologian is only a facilitating role. CBS begins and ends in the hands of a particular group of the marginalized community. This is what makes people's theology, prophetic theology.

Ujamaa Centre has a clear ideo-theological commitment shaped by liberation theology. Of course, this is because there is no non-ideological interpretation of the Bible. To this end, CBS privileges the experiences of marginalized communities and recognizes, and affirms, the agency and analytical competency of the marginalized sectors with whom it works. It gives theological form to the lived reality of the marginalized and emphasis is placed on the voices of the ordinary poor, working-class, marginalized African Christians. It allows the embodied theologies of the participants to find articulation. CBS provides a sacred and safe space for the subaltern to talk about things that are not usually spoken about in the Church where the Bible is often read "against" the marginalized in a life-denying way. For example, the Bible has done a lot of damage to the LGBTQIA+ and HIV-positive people in South Africa (and the rest of Africa).

Because of the contested nature of the Bible, West's contribution as a socially engaged biblical scholar has been to open up the ideo-theological dimensions of the redactional interpretive process, identifying the different ideo-theological voices contending within, and behind, the biblical text.[14] Rather than provide a biblical "solution" to contextual concerns, CBS is concerned with creating an environment within which religious resources can be used to engage with contextual concerns that are not readily taken up by the Church. To this end, Ujamaa Centre often uses unfamiliar texts not usually read in churches (for example, the rape of Tamar in 2 Sam

---

14. West, "Reconfiguring a Biblical Story," n.p.

13:1–22) and also reads familiar texts in unfamiliar ways. CBS grapples with the biblical text to bring forth life-affirming readings.

Another reason that attracts West to CBS is that it pays close attention to the details of the biblical text. By focusing on the details of a text, CBS disrupts "settled" and "normative" theologies through which the Bible has been typically read, enabling "new," and contextually relevant theologies, to be born.[15] Dominant theologies often marginalize certain sectors of society such as HIV-positive people and the LGBTQIA+ community. Readings that disrupt such theologies have the potential to contribute to the formation of more contextually relevant and more life-giving theologies. Detailed readings also enable the biblical text to connect with the lived realities of the marginalized readers, and to construct prophetic theology, which becomes a tool of resistance, and hope, in contexts where the dominant theologies have marginalized, oppressedand condemned others. West has labored with his team at Ujamaa Centre to resist doctrinaire "'church theologies" of stigmatization, discrimination, and retribution, and to construct "prophetic theologies" of justice, acceptance, inclusion, and redemption.[16]

Impact of Gerald West's Work On Communities of the Poor and Marginalized

HIV-AIDS

West is not known to accept accolades. Even though his work with his team at Ujamaa Centre has had a huge impact on the communities he has worked with, he remains modest in describing their successes. In the 1990s, the HIV and AIDS pandemic was wreaking havoc in South Africa. HIV-positive people were being marginalized because they were seen as sexual perverts, who were now "reaping what they had sowed." (Matt 25:24; Luke 12:22) Many of them had been pushed out of their churches because of stigmatizing theologies of retribution. The Ujamaa Centre sprang into action, conducting CBS sessions in churches and communities, including accompanying support groups for HIV-positive people.

The book of Job became their favorite resource for the CBS in this context of HIV and AIDS. The dominant theologies of stigmatization

15. West, Contextual Bible Study, 146, 148.

16. West, Contextual Bible Study, 151–52.

of HIV-positive people were disrupted with the detailed readings of Job 42:6–11 allowing the "people's theology," of those living with HIV, to draw on this text to construct alternative redemptive prophetic theologies. That God instructs Job's friends to offer a public sacrifice, to ask Job publicly for forgiveness for their false theology (Job 42:8), and to embrace him back, was taken by the CBS groups to mean that holders of the theology of retribution and stigmatization, in the context of HIV, have a wrong theology.

Theologies of "redemption" challenged and contended with theologies of retribution and stigmatization. Many Christians living with HIV, who had been forced out of their churches, found a safe and sacred refuge within CBS. Many of them had discarded their Bibles because they saw in them only condemnation and judgment against them. But, CBS reconnected them with their Bibles.[17] For example, Siyaphila, a support group for people living with HIV that Ujamaa Centre worked with, evidenced the impact of CBS. Before joining the group, the Bible was far off and at a distance from members of this group, and had become a silent book, which could only be made to speak to condemn them, by the preacher or pastor. These negative associations with the Bible were positively transformed by their membership of the Siyaphila support group, about which West writes,

> What was far from them had now been brought close to them; what had no place in their lives now had a place within their lives; what belonged to others now belonged to them; what had nothing relevant to say to them now spoke directly to their condition; what could not be touched or made to speak by them or for them was now in their hands, they could ask their questions of it, and they heard it speaking to them directly; what had brought judgment, stigma, and discrimination now brought healing, hope, and life. The bible was no longer far off. It engaged them personally and as a group; it dealt with the daily concerns that constituted their lives.[18]

It is amazing to see what a simple Bible study can do to the marginalized. To them, the Bible gave hope and renewed interest in their faith. It ceased to be this unequivocal "Word of God" that could not be engaged with or questioned and became a book that they could engage with, interrogate, and relate their struggles to, in line with the marginalized

17. West, "Contextual Bible Study," 150.
18. West, "Contextual Bible Study," 150–151.

in ancient Israel. They felt that they now "owned" the Bible and became acutely aware of how it had been used selectively in their churches, to marginalize them. They began to see themselves anew, as human beings created in the image of God. CBS empowered Siyaphila members to resist their churches' biased use of the Bible.

LGBTQIA+ and the Struggle for Recognition

The struggle of the LGBTQIA+ community for acceptance is also related to that of HIV-positive people. Their struggle has become a public contextual issue. Many have become alienated from their churches and the Bible. Like in other struggles, Ujamaa Centre situated itself within the justice framework of the struggle and adopted a clear ideological stance that took sides with the marginalized.[19] After a CBS session on Genesis 18–19, members of the group reported that the CBS process had given them a different perspective on the Bible. It enabled some of them to return to their faith and churches, equipped to confront their churches' selective reading of the Bible. Some of them appropriated the re-read biblical text as a resource with which to hit back at the Church: "The church is like Sodom, just as the men of Sodom wanted to subject others to their power, so the church wants to subject us to its power."[20]

Rape and Women's Rights

Perhaps the most famous of the CBS done by Ujamaa Centre is the story of the rape of Tamar by her elder brother, Amnon (2 Sam 13). It is a text that does not appear in the lectionary. Yet it is a very important resource in the struggle against rape, in particular, and gender-based violence, in general. It is as a CBS that it became a huge international campaign, the "Tamar Campaign," which was launched in the year 2000. This CBS had a profound impact within faith-based communities by providing resources for resisting abuse, and for articulating and owning local life-giving theologies.[21]

Because it was an unfamiliar text, "Women are amazed that such a text exists, are angry that they have never heard it read or preached,

19. West, "Reconfiguring a Biblical Story," n.p.
20. West, "Contextual Bible Study," 157.
21. West et al., "Rape in the House of David," 36.

are relieved to discover that they are not alone, are empowered because the silence has been broken and their stories have been told."[22] South African women felt that the story of Tamar was empowering because it was a story in the Bible and, therefore, could be used in the Church and community to break the silence around rape and abuse. They argued that rape must be acknowledged as a reality and that society should learn to listen to those who claim to have been raped.[23] Perhaps more importantly, CBS and the "Tamar Campaign" gave a voice to many victims and CBS was a therapeutic praxis. This is because, as West argues, "Human dignity, even in the most damaged and denigrated subaltern, demands some form of 'speaking.'"[24]

The Land Issue

The land issue in South Africa is a very sensitive one and many people would rather not touch it, to avoid "getting their hands dirty." While the government dithers on the ownership issue, white commercial farmers pray that the government does not touch their farms. West, and his Ujamaa Centre team, organized a CBS on land ownership, dispossession, and evictions in their location of Zululand, to assist the villagers in their struggle to regain land. The choice of the location for the CBS was quite significant. It is a rural area in which there have been struggles for land. Being rural, patriarchy reigns supreme. Thus, it is difficult for women to air their views in public or influence public discourse. The party-political dynamics are also very complex, given the area's historical links with the opposition Inkatha Freedom Party (IFP).

A CBS on "Leadership and Land," based on Gen 37–50, enabled the group to mobilize other villagers to participate in their local struggle for land. The CBS also helped local land activists overcome traditional beliefs and stereotypes, especially gender prejudice, that are an obstacle to social progress. It also provided a safe space for the community to discuss the politics of land and political leaders' roles in addressing issues of land reform without fear of political reprisals. This worked because the bible is associated with the Church which is viewed as non-partisan. The CBS

22. West et al., "Rape in the House of David," 38.

23. West and Zondi-Mabizela, "The Bible Story that Became a Campaign," 5.

24. West, "Between Text and Trauma," 218.

served as a non-threatening but effective and empowering tool in drawing participants into a space of critical but sensitive dialogue.[25]

Conclusion

West has made an outstanding contribution to African biblical hermeneutics, the center of gravity for much of this work being the articulation of an Africa-centric theology in which the poor and marginalized become agents of theological reflection. Spending three decades re-reading the Bible with the marginalized was not just out of intellectual curiosity or the fulfillment of academic demands. As he has put it himself, "I do believe that there is a sense of calling to what I do."[26] For that, the Church in South Africa and beyond owes West's tones of gratitude. To him, we can only *Siyabonga!* (thank you), Comrade.

Bibliography

Kairos. *The Kairos Document: Challenge to the Church: A Theological Comment on the Political Crisis in South Africa*. Rev. 2nd ed. Braamfontein: Skotaville, 1986.

West, Gerald O. "Between Text and Trauma: Reading Job with People Living with HIV." In *Bible through the Lens of Trauma*, edited by Elizabeth Boase and Christopher G. Frechette, 209–30. Semeia Studies 86. Atlanta: SBL Press, 2016.

———. "Contextual Bible Study and/or as Interpretive Resilience." In *That All May Live! Essays in Honour of Nyambura J. Njoroge*, edited by Ezra Chitando et al., 143–59. Bamberg: University of Bamberg Press, 2021.

———. "Locating Contextual Bible Study and Intercultural Biblical Hermeneutics within Biblical Liberation Hermeneutics." In *New Perspectives on Intercultural Reading of the Bible*, edited by Daniel S. Schipani *et al.* 107–35. Elkhart, IN: Institute of Mennonite Studies, 2015.

———. "Reconfiguring a Biblical Story (Genesis 19) in the Context of South African Discussions about Homosexuality." In *Christianity and Controversies over Homosexuality in Contemporary Africa*, edited by Ezra Chitando and Adriaan van Klinken 184–98. Religion in Modern Africa. London: Routledge, 2016.

———. *The Stolen Bible: From Instrument of Imperialism to African Icon*. BIS 144. Leiden: Brill, 2016.

———. "Tribes in Africa: The Impact of Norman Gottwald's *The Tribes of Yahweh* on African Biblical Hermeneutics (With an Emphasis on Liberation and Inculturation Paradigms)." In *Tracking the Tribes of Yahweh: On the Trail of a Classic*, edited by Roland Boer, 85–97. JSOTSup 351. London: Sheffield Academic, 2002.

———. "The Vocation of an African Biblical Scholar on the Margins of Biblical Scholarship." *OTE* 19.1 (2006) 307–36.

25. West and Ndlazi, "Leadership and Land," 187.

26. West, "Vocation of an African Biblical Scholar," 330.

West, Gerald O., and Thulani Ndlazi. "Leadership and Land: A Very Contextual Interpretation of Genesis 37–50 in KwaZulu-Natal, South Africa." In *Genesis*, edited by Athalya Brenner-Idan, et al., 175–90. Texts@Contexts. Minneapolis: Fortress, 2010.

West, Gerald O., and Phumzile Zondi-Mabizela. "The Bible Story That Became a Campaign: The Tamar Campaign in South Africa and Beyond." *Ministerial Formation* 103 (July 2004) 4–12.

West, Gerald O, et al. "Rape in the House of David: The Biblical Story of Tamar as a Resource for Transformation." *Agenda* 61 (2004) 36–41.

2

Re-Translating the Logics of Social Invasion

Lamenting with People with Disabilities and Job for Life

Nathan A. Esala

Introduction: Activist Translators Entangled with Social Invasion

Translation Studies scholars have described translation activities that emphasize agency as activist translation[1] or as committed approaches to translation.[2] Activists who have a particular skill set in cultural mediation and communication engage in translating to inspire and enact social change.[3] African scholars with activist dispositions are challenging the assumptions of coloniality in Bible translation.[4] In an important article written at the end of the 20th century, Tinyiko Maluleke surveys several possibilities for an activist African theology. Maluleke coined the term "translation theology" to characterize the innovative and far-reaching proposals of Lamin Sanneh and Kwame Bediako.[5] "Translation theology" emphasizes African agency in the reception, interpretation, and appropriation of African language Bibles

1. Tymoczko, *Enlarging Translation,* 209–16.
2. Brownlie, "Descriptive vs Committed Approaches," 79–80.
3. Tymoczko, *Enlarging Translation,* 213.
4. Dube and Wafula, *Postcoloniality.*
5. Maluleke, "Half a Century," 19–20.

for active theologizing.[6] Activist African translators have the option of leaning into the potential of African translation theology in their contemporary translation practices. African translation theology argues that African languages and African language Bibles carry with them the presuppositions of African life worlds. Activist translators may choose to translate biblical texts in ways that intentionally revitalize African religio-cultural life worlds, recognizing that African religions (including African Christianities and practices of Islam) have contributions to make in social discourse in Africa and the world.

Translation Studies scholars Maria Tymoczko and Mona Baker have noted that activist translators often work in groups, making explicit a set of ideological commitments that inform how they engage the translation industry.[7] Sometimes translators strategically choose to translate, other times they refrain from translating, based on their analysis of the dynamics of oppression in a particular situation. Translation scholars note that activist translators do not translate in a consistent style. They make different strategic decisions, depending on their emancipatory priorities, and the power dynamics of the situation.[8] Activist translators strategically subordinate the text to their ideological concerns for liberation from oppression. The way activist translators foreground ideology over texts makes scholars who privilege texts uncomfortable— such as many Bible scholars and translators. Tymoczko points out that colonizers also subordinate texts in favor of their ideological agendas.[9] Colonizers engaged in translation projects to enact change in favor of their social, political, and economic goals to assert their will for social invasion, political domination, and economic extraction.

My analysis of translation practices in northern Ghana shows that colonial actors camouflaged assertions of power in translation, developing an influential form of translating I call "translation as invasion."[10] One of the key characteristics of the "translation-as-invasion" paradigm is "social invasion," which, in translation, involves establishing and asserting the perspective of social elites (usually foreigners) in the translation process and presenting those elite sectoral perspectives in translated

6. West, *The Stolen Bible*, 238–43.

7. Tymoczko, *Enlarging Translation*, 215; Baker, "Translation and Activism," 30.

8. Tymoczko, *Enlarging Translation*, 215; Baker, "Translation and Activism," 34–35; Simon, *Gender in Translation*, 121–25.

9. Tymoczko, *Enlarging Translation*, 216.

10. Esala, "Translation as Invasion," 146–59.

texts as the definitive and legal starting points for the whole population.[11] All other social perspectives were normed by elite perspectives in what the colonizers called 'customary law.'[12] The articulation of customary law involved a process of translation that flattened the diversity of social perspectives expressed in pre-colonial translation.[13]

This act of "norming" diverse social perspectives was the basis of establishing a legal hierarchy inside a defined and contained colonial territory.[14] Social invasion in translation was particularly useful in locales governed by the colonial policy of "territorial indirect rule," a policy that was applied to Africans living outside of colonial centers.[15] For example, colonial-era translation used the logic of social invasion to translate the concept of "tribe" into a legal colonial category with clear boundaries and hierarchies.[16] Social invasion in the colonial era involved identifying, strengthening, and projecting a paramount chief's viewpoint as the starting point that established the rights of conquest and the present right to rule inside a limited territory. Social invasion further established the paramount chief's viewpoint as the standard for making legal judgments about the past.[17]

The practice of social invasion, established by colonization embedded in colonial translation practice, ensures that elite foreign perspectives shape a translated text so that when other social agents and social groups with different points of view hear the translated discourse, they are likely to assume that the elite social perspective embedded in the discourse is the ideal perspective from which to view the world. Social invasion is often implicit in translation activities that are entangled with the world economic system, such as the Bible translation industry. The focus of social invasion is to normalize elite social domination and to strengthen material relations between elite sectors across societies. The logic of social and territorial invasion implicit in colonial translation, and

11. Esala, "Translation as Invasion," 157.

12. Esala, "Translation as Invasion," 140–44.

13. Esala, "Translation as Invasion," 95-101.

14. Mamdani, *Citizen and Subject*, 51.

15. Mamdani, *Neither Settler nor Native*, 13; Esala, "Translation as Invasion," 120–25.

16. Mamdani, *Neither Settler nor Native*, 11.

17. Mamdani, *Citizen and Subject*, 43, 48; MacGaffey, *Chiefs, Priests, and Praise-Singers*, 50.

in Western humanist education itself,[18] presents a challenge to activist translators or activist interpreters of the Bible who may want to use a translated Bible to attempt to change unjust relations in a particular post-colonial context. Social invasion implicit in translation carries along the logics of hierarchy. Activists may use translation to address one oppression, but as they do so, they assert another oppression in the process, an oppression that may be difficult for them to perceive.

The example of the Konkomba of northern Ghana is illustrative. After the British colonial invasion, ethno-linguistic communities were ranked hierarchically.[19] Ethnic groups who were marginalized through the colonial manipulation of chieftaincy and "tribe" resisted their marginalization in various ways.[20] After political colonization ended in 1957, tribal-based social activism continued. Missionary-initiated Bible translation resumed in different forms. Some rural Konkomba social activists perceived that Bible translation and especially literacy in the Konkomba language were useful tools in "tribal" activism,[21] that helped elevate groups who had been marginalized by the colonial making of tribal hierarchies.[22] In the context of northern Ghana, some activists understood Bible translation in their language to support the notion that marginalized kinship groups deserved to be a 'tribe' just like other colonially privileged tribes.[23] The activists were using the same centralizing logic of tribe that was asserted by colonial-era translation.[24] Bible translation was reinforcing those same centralizing logics of social invasion. As Mahmood Mamdani argues, tribalism involves intra-ethnic and interethnic dimensions.[25] A set of ethnic groups may assert their interethnic/intertribal equality in part through translation, but in the process the ethnic groups start internalizing the logic of intra-ethnic/intratribal hierarchy, thus becoming a hierarchically organized tribe. In

18. Wynter, "Unparalleled Catastrophe?," 9, 23; Yusoff, *A Billion Black Anthropocenes*, 34–35.

19. Horowitz, *Ethnic Groups in Conflict*, 29.

20. Talton, *Politics of Social Change in Ghana*, 1–108.

21. Hasselbring, "Cross-Dialectal Acceptance," 148.

22. "My point is that modern tribalism has to be understood not only as a historical phenomenon, but also as one that is contradictory. It signifies both the form of rule, and the reform of revolt against it. Whereas the former is oppressive, the latter *may be* emancipatory." Mamdani, *Citizen and Subject*, 183. (Emphasis original.)

23. Esala, "Translation as Invasion," 387-391.

24. Talton, *Politics of Social Change in Ghana*, 182-184.

25. Mamdani, *Citizen and Subject*, 1996, 184.

the process, the logics of social invasion are internalized, perhaps making them more difficult to recognize and resist.

In other words, earlier assumptions about the nature of translation are embedded in later practices. Achille Mbembe's description of African time as a *"time of entanglement"* helps illustrate this dynamic of embedded practices in translation. Mbembe writes,

> This time of African existence is neither a linear time nor a simple sequence in which each moment effaces, annuls, and replaces those that preceded it, to the point where a single age exists within society. This time is not a series, but an *interlocking* of presents, pasts, and futures, each age bearing, altering, and maintaining the previous ones.[26]

Present acts of translation/interpretation remain entangled with past acts of translation, but not necessarily in strictly linear ways. One era's practice of translation does not necessarily lead to the next. People engage in translating at the site of a translation's production to change things in a particular way, within a particular context, by translating this text in this language, in this way, and projecting this viewpoint into the world, by disseminating a discourse to an audience through certain media. The community who receives a translation, at various sites of reception, also use the translation they receive in particular ways, sometimes in ways unanticipated by the translation's producers.

African translation studies have shown how Africans received their translated Bibles in ways that most missionaries never anticipated.[27] What complicates things even further is that (biblical) texts pass on remnants of earlier sites of textual production and earlier sites of textual reception. Those who pass on texts, such as activist translators, and those who receive texts, such as ordinary Africans, may or may not be consciously aware of the internalized perspectives the text embodies.[28] Thus, translated texts are entangled with earlier sites of production and reception, and contemporary translation practices are entangled with earlier practices of translation. Entanglement helps show that contemporary translation, in post-colonial/neo-colonial times, carries with it some of the logics of colonization. The question becomes, how can activist translators contribute

---

26. Mbembe, *On the Postcolony*, 16. (Emphasis original.)

27. Sanneh, *Translating the Message*, 53.

28. Mosala, *Biblical Hermeneutics*, 32, 101; Briggs, "Contested Mobilities," 287.

to reworking or recalibrating entangled translation practices in ways that counter the logics of social invasion?

To counter the logics of social invasion, I suggest that activist translators should collaborate with marginalized groups in African contexts, engage native speakers, and facilitate processes that reassert the legitimacy of diverse social perspectives in translation processes. Marginalized groups are differently entangled with African pre-colonial life worlds. Their perspectives are necessary for African translation theology to express its holistic life-giving social vision!

Being Translators, Becoming Translation Facilitators for Others

I now turn to describing the journey my colleagues and I took toward learning an alternative mode of re-translating biblical texts for liberation and life. I am focusing on professional Bible translators because that is my experience; however, I understand translators to include anyone who translates discourses in African language communities. After being involved on a team translating the New Testament into a language of Northern Ghana for ten years, I was unsatisfied with standard Bible translation processes. I had already been exploring African Biblical Hermeneutics and orality studies as potential pathways for destabilizing some of the missionary-colonial ideo-theologies entangled with Bible translation.[29] Having already read about his work,[30] I met West at an African Biblical Hermeneutics section of the Society of Biblical Literature's annual meeting at which point I started reading his work directly. West gave a lecture at the 2014 Nida School of Translation Studies that connected "African Translation Theology" and "South African Black Theology" with the method of Contextual Bible Study, an emancipatory approach to reading biblical texts developed in South Africa over the past 30 years.[31] At that point, I introduced my translation colleagues in northern Ghana to Contextual Bible Study (CBS), and I began thinking critically about how CBS can be utilized as a method of translating biblical texts from other sectoral perspectives. I was coming to a greater awareness about how sectoral perspectives were suppressed by the logics of social invasion implicit in colonial translation.

29. Esala, "Skopostheorie."
30. Maxey, *From Orality to Orality*, 62–65.
31. West, "Translation for Liberation"; West, "Contextual Bible Study."

As translators learning the CBS method, the first difficulty we faced was how do traditional translators like my colleagues and I who have been socialized and educated to promote our social point of view learn another way of translating which prioritizes other social viewpoints? It was difficult to wrap our minds around alternative options. Acknowledging that difficulty is part of the reason I now describe CBS as an alternative method of re-translating biblical texts for life. The way I have come to describe the change is that those who are educated and socialized to be translators in society can use the CBS method to help them learn how to facilitate processes of (re-)translating biblical texts with others, so that other sectors of society can practice translating from their own perspectives aided by some of the critical resources of biblical studies and the supportive presence of translation facilitators. In circumstances where marginalized groups have established their own sequestered spaces outside the view of dominant social groups, they are already practiced in asserting their own points of view in discourse. The difference in CBS is that marginalized groups are encouraged to speak from their own points of view in spaces, such as in churches or schools, where they are not normally encouraged to speak openly from their own bodily perspectives. Secondly, in CBS marginalized groups are offered resources from the discipline of critical biblical studies, resources they do not normally have access to. These additional critical resources, offered in the form of carefully constructed critical questions, walk participants through a hermeneutical process of slowly and carefully (re-) reading, (re-)translating, and (re-)interpreting a biblical text from their point(s) of view. For our newly formed group of aspiring translation facilitators, the process of identifying a social issue and an organized group was a collaborative effort.[32] One of the CBS facilitators, Samson Bilafanim, was a Bible translator, a pastor, a prince in his kinship group, and a person with a significant limp—a physical disability. Bilafanim volunteered with a local group that offered surgeries, prosthetics, wheelchairs, and job training for people with disabilities in the area. He was also the secretary for the organized group of people living with disabilities in the local area.

The Bible translation office, with the help of Bilafanim, invited participants to a workshop. The people living with disabilities understood they were invited to come to "our" workshop in the same way they might be invited to come to development workshops sponsored by different

---

32. Esala, "Towards Contextualizing 'Contextual Bible Study,'" 113–16.

national and international development agencies. Sithembiso Zwane has provided analytical language that aptly describes the power dynamics that characterize development workshops. This CBS engagement took place in what Zwane calls "invited spaces": "Invited spaces, characterized by exclusion or at best-supervised participation, deprive the community of the ability to participate in development processes."[33] As facilitators we had to use our best facilitation skills, drawing upon the values of CBS,[34] to signal to the participants that we wanted to do something different in this CBS engagement compared to what they are used to doing in typical "invited spaces." We wanted to read the Bible with them,[35] not to beat them over the head with it, or to teach them how to act from it. Rather, we wanted to affirm that God was on their side, and that God affirmed their perspectives on the world, and wanted to help them in their social struggle. As facilitators, we had to make sure we signaled to the participants that, we too, affirmed their social experiences, perspectives, and desires for a better life. We were, intentionally, trying to construct what Zwane calls an "invigorated space," where people living with disabilities were, at least, partially in control of the discourse. Ideally, invigorated spaces will lead to "invented spaces" where marginalized groups are substantially in control of the space where the discourse is taking place.[36]

At the beginning of our time together, before we referenced the Bible directly, one of the facilitators, James Adongo, communicated using a storytelling genre that was familiar to the participants. Storytelling is a useful tool to express what James Scott calls a discourse of "infrapolitics," that critiques power relations in a way that has a "double meaning."[37] Adongo told a story about a farmer who hated his horse and who even tried to bury his horse alive. Adongo openly revealed the double meaning of the story when after his telling he said, "I am telling you today, my people, shake yourselves, before they bury you."[38] This story offered a trans-textual hermeneutic for participants to use as they interpreted the

33. West and Zwane, "Re-Reading 1 Kings 21:1-16," 187.

34. West, "The Value/s of Contextual Bible Reading."

35. West and Dube, "Read With."

36. West and Zwane, "Re-Reading 1 Kings 21:1-16," 187.

37. James C. Scott defines "infrapolitics" as "a politics of disguise and anonymity that takes place in public view but is designed to have a double meaning or shield the identity [and/or ideology] of the actors." *Domination*, 19.

38. For the full translation of the story, see Esala, "Contextualizing 'Contextual Bible Study,'" 126.

soon to be referenced biblical text. The shouts and cheers at the end of Adongo's story clearly signaled to the participants that this engagement was not going to be a normal Bible study; its purpose was to help people struggling for life in the context of systems that bring death. Adongo helped shift the space from a clearly "invited space" to an "invited/invigorated space." We hope our engagement will lead to "invigorated/invented spaces." I have intentionally skipped over describing the collaborative process of choosing a biblical text in the process of "reading with" people living with disabilities. Prior to choosing a biblical text we attempted to do some social analysis with people living with disabilities. What does the world look like from their point of view? Where are they experiencing pain? And what is causing it? This shift in point of view is a crucial adjustment as translators seek to become facilitators of translation. Traditional translators have been trained to assert their own point of view as they translate. To become translation facilitators, they must learn to engage in what liberation theologians have called "the epistemological privilege" of poor and marginalized social groups.[39]

Learning to see things from the perspective of a marginalized group, in their own community, is especially important for translators, *even* activist translators. My colleagues and I were aware that decentralized kinship groups in northern Ghana had been actively marginalized by the legacy of colonization, intertribally. We perceived our work in Bible translation to counter that colonial legacy. However, we lacked a "critical lens" to help us see how translation processes inherited from the missionary-colonial past also participated in establishing intratribal social hierarchy. Engaging in social analysis from the perspective of people living with disabilities within the language community is an important step in learning to view things from 'other' social sectoral points of view and a crucial part of learning to become a facilitator of translation with others. The next step was to apply what we were learning in social analysis to biblical interpretation. Our method, social analysis, was teaching us to see things from other points of view, and now we needed to consider alternative points of view in biblical texts as we formed our CBS questions. CBS questions are intended to prompt CBS participants to read and re-translate a biblical text from their own points of view in pursuit of imagining, expressing, and enacting social healing.

39. Hall, *Reading the Bible with the Poor*, 29–30.

CBS questions walk participants through a process of carefully reading and re-reading a biblical text in whatever language is accessible to them. (Sometimes, participants explore alternative media to the written text such as how art or drama semiotically translates the story.) As they re-read a text, the questions prompt them to explore re-translating and re-interpreting the story from their own social location and bodily point of view. CBS questions are designed to take participants on a hermeneutical journey. They begin by identifying an aspect of the participants' contemporary experience that is thematically related to a biblical discourse. Then they move from the participants' contemporary experience into the biblical narrative world. In the process of exploring the narrative world, sometimes participants will question aspects of the social world that produced the biblical narrative world. Finally, participants return to their contemporary realities, with resources from their journey with the biblical text, which may help them engage in their contemporary struggle in more life-giving and emancipatory ways.

When I asked my colleagues which biblical texts have the potential to offer life-giving resources to people living with disabilities, our colleague Samson Bilafanim identified the question of Job's wife in chapter two—"Why don't you curse God and die?"—as a question that many people living with disabilities have heard. Drawing on my own prior knowledge of CBS as practiced by the Ujamaa Centre in South Africa, I thought of the ways that the Ujamaa Center worked with HIV positive people to read Job's lament.[40] Together, my colleagues and I developed a set of questions that we hoped would prompt participants to perceive redemptive details in the biblical text and re-translate that detail in a way that would bring life to their bodies. Before I describe some of the ways participants journeyed into the narrative of Job and started re-translating it from their own perspective, I would like to back up and explore how people living with disabilities are treated as passive objects by contemporary theologies. This next section is part of our ongoing social and theological analysis of the world from the point of view of people living with disabilities in northern Ghana.

---

40. West and Zengele, "Reading Job 'Positively.'"

Social Analysis: What is the Good News for People Living with Disabilities?

In northern Ghana, Africa's "new Christianity" proclaims an African version of the prosperity gospel.[41] The new Christianity has become the most salient version of Christianity for most Africans. The new Christianity understands the Bible to be a book that illustrates God's desire for all followers to prosper by intervening in people's lives.[42] The new Christianity like missionary-colonial Christianity before it, interprets the Bible doctrinally. Drawing on the African tri-polar approach to hermeneutics, the prosperity doctrine is the ideo-theological third pole of interpretation that interpreters use to engage the two poles of text and context in dialogue.[43] The new Christianity teaches that every Christian can share in Christ's victory of sin, sickness, and poverty by making a confession of faith. When individuals experience blockages, believers give gifts to men of God who are called upon to remove spiritual blockages located in and around the individual supplicant.[44]

Theologically, the presence of people living with disabilities presents a problem for new Christianity's prosperity gospel, because if God wants all followers to be healed and successful, how does one explain those whose bodies are not being healed? This must be part of the reason people living with disabilities are kept from public view in their homes, or sometimes even in cages at prayer and healing camps in remote locations.[45] The bodily entanglements of people living with disabilities require a different ideo-theological orientation to connect text to context in a way that is life-giving for them. The mainline Christian churches and Non-Governmental Organizations (NGOs), often affiliated with mainline Christianity, offer an alternative to the health and wealth gospel, which Anthony Balcomb has described as a developmentalist approach.[46] A developmentalist perspective assumes African countries should imitate Western countries on their pathway to development. Paul Gifford exhibits a developmental approach when he

---

41. Gifford, *African Christianity*; Gifford, *Ghana's New Christianity*.

42. Gifford, *Ghana's New Christianity*, 72.

43. Draper, "African Contextual Hermeneutics."

44. Gifford, *Ghana's New Christianity*, 89.

45. Lambert et al., *Mental Health Treatment*, 12.

46. Balcomb, "Counter-Modernism," 44–45.

promotes the notion of "getting to Denmark."[47] Denmark is perceived as the ideal state other states should emulate. This developmental approach to nation building operates within a similar life world of translation as missionary-colonial Christianity.

The life-worlds of people living with disabilities in African contexts have quite different presuppositions from the life-worlds operating within the developmentalist paradigm. African religions (including Christianity and Islam as African religions) have understood disabilities in relation to spiritual forces. If people living with disabilities in African contexts are to be the agents of their own liberation, their religio-cultural lived reality cannot be ignored. These two "gospels," the prosperity and developmental gospels, have different ideo-theological orientations. They connect text to context in different ways, yet they both split apart what indigenous/pre-colonial African life worlds hold in tension. This is most obvious in the missionary-colonial assumptions of the developmentalist approach.[48] In the developmentalist paradigm, the material world is largely split from the spiritual world. The material world is governed by science. The political world should be governed by rational-bureaucratic structures. In this ideal Western life world individuals must trust science and push past the "ignorant" assumptions of their pre-scientific worldviews. People living with disabilities, like all Africans, must emulate this Western bifurcation of the spiritual and material worlds to develop. Theology primarily applies to the spiritual realm, dealing with matters of life after death. Increasingly, the Western world is realizing that theology affects the material world. The devastation of the environment on a global scale is one example of why this bifurcation of the spiritual and material does not result in the flourishing of life. Unlike missionary-colonial Christianity, Africa's new Christianity does not disregard the religio-cultural assumptions of African Christian supplicants.

Africans experience problems in the world, and they discern that their material problems are influenced by underlying spiritual relations.

47. Gifford, *Christianity, Development,* 154.

48. Missionary-colonial Christianity is a predecessor in different ways to the developmentalist approach and to the new Christianity. The missionary "ancestors" of mainline Christianity in Africa translated the Bible to communicate the church's doctrine to African communities. From the perspective of missionary-colonial Christianity, the biblical narratives illustrate the doctrine of the church, which everyone needs to understand to belong to the church and to be saved. The confession of the church proclaims a gospel content that is fixed. The Bible's message is understood to reflect that fixed confession.

New Christianity takes this understanding as its starting point.[49] However, when supplicants present their problems to African practitioners of health and wealth theologies, these theologies limit the diagnosis of spiritual-material problems to individual and localized causes. Put differently, the systems of power in the state and economy are precluded from new Christianity's spiritual-material assessment of a supplicant's social problems.[50] Just as we observed a separation of the spiritual from the material in missionary-colonial Christianity's relation with secularism, we observe that the new Christianity separates the causes of an individual's spiritual-material problems, from an individual's spiritual-material interdependency with other human and more-than-human agents in the shared environment.[51] A more holistic analysis recognizes that economic and state relations are spiritually-materially interconnected to the manifestation of individual problems.

Indigenous/pre-colonial African life worlds hold spiritual-material relationships together in a holistic tension. Individual problems are dependent on collective relations to human, and more-than-human, agents in a shared environment. People living with disabilities, by virtue of their marginalization through the missionary-colonial legacy of privileging elite social perspectives, are differently entangled with indigenous/pre-colonial African life worlds than most Bible translators. Thus, people living with disabilities, and other marginalized social sectors, approach entanglements in biblical texts differently. Their bodily entanglements hold the potential for re-translating dynamics in texts in relation to spiritual-material social problems in ways that enact holistic social healing from colonial translation's legacy of social invasion.

CBS and the Alternative Logics of Re-Translation

I need to remind the reader that it was hard for me at first, to conceive of CBS as a form of translating. The legacy of colonial translation and its practice of social invasion has become embedded in dominant social consciousness. That is why I have turned to describing CBS as a practice of, post-colonial, re-translation. I use the hyphen in both "re-translation" and

49. Dube, *Postcolonial Feminist Interpretation*, 40–41; Gifford, *Ghana's New Christianity*, 89.

50. Mbamalu, "The Use of 'Abundant Life,'" 132; Gifford, *African Christianity*, 380; West, *The Stolen Bible*, 535.

51. Balcomb, "The War of the Trees," 36.

"post-colonial" to indicate the entangled and contested nature of African time and space, held in tension. Re-translation is a topic taken up by translation studies scholar Sharon Deane-Cox. Deane-Cox has studied the motivating logics for retranslating texts in Euro-American thought and practice. Deane-Cox observes, "To say the same thing twice (or multiple times) would appear to be a redundant enterprise, unless it is motivated by an *alternative* logic."[52] In a 2015 paper presented at the annual meeting of the Society of Biblical Literature, Deborah Shadd discussed the motivating logics for retranslating texts as discussed in Translation Studies and applied it to the practice of Bible Translation.

Translation Studies scholars have identified two primary motivating logics for retranslation in Euro-American contexts: retranslation for social progress, and retranslation as challenge.[53] Both of these logics reflect the logics of modernity and by extension, they encompass the logics of coloniality.[54] To these two motivating logics, Shadd added a third, the logic of dialogue. Shadd's alternative logic can be characterized as reflecting a logic of postmodernity/postcoloniality in that it views all retranslations as options.[55] West responded to Shadd's analysis a few months later by suggesting that the logic of liberation could be a fourth post-colonial motivating logic for re-translating a biblical text.[56] For people struggling under the weight of the death-doling effects of modernity and colonization, re-translating for life is more than one option among many possibilities, it is a precondition for social dialogue. I now turn to the ways people living with disabilities re-translated the lament of Job.

52. Deane-Cox, *Retranslation*, 2–3.

53. Shadd, "Response to Carolyn J. Sharp."

54. Mignolo and Walsh, *On Decoloniality*, 109.

55. "Without losing sight of the source text which gave rise to the subsequent versions, the logic of dialogue trains its gaze on the interaction of the various translated iterations of the text, much as the logic of challenge did, with the key difference being that these retranslations are now welcomed as partners in a dialogic endeavour to enrich the understanding of all, rather than denigrated as inferiors, as competitors or, worse, as threats. Instead of casting individual translations or translation choices in negative light, criticizing them for the particular manner in which they constrained a given alternative or excluded a given potentiality, the logic of dialogue would by contrast invite us to consider all retranslations in the textual sphere collectively, stepping back to see how together they draw an outline of these spaces in which different voices, different languages and different cultural perspectives can be heard." Shadd, "Response to Carolyn J. Sharp."

56. West, "Necessity of Re-Translation," 12–14.

Re-Translating Job's Lament for Life

CBS purposes and processes are intentionally emancipatory in character. CBS questions are designed to foreground participants experiencing redemptive detail in a biblical text in light of their lived experiences of marginalization. But, the logic of liberation does not presume to know what liberation looks like for people living with disabilities in their context. As participants dialogue about CBS questions, individuals express their points of view in small groups with whom they share sectoral affiliations based on gender, age, and any other relevant social marker. Then small groups are offered the opportunity to report back in large group settings some of the things that were said in their small groups. Those group statements are written down on paper by a scribe, so the whole group can see and read each sectoral group's contribution. Once the CBS questions are asked, facilitators are supposed to listen and facilitate processes that encourage participants to speak with one another, as they dialogically re-translate moving from their contemporary experience to the life world of the text, sometimes including the worlds that produced the text, and then back again to the present.

The critical study questions of CBS offer an array of critical tools from the discipline of biblical studies to a community that is already engaged in its own struggle for liberation. The questions respect the prior experience of the host[57] community with the biblical text, offering additional critical detail about that text from biblical studies. The study we developed has taken the following form:

Retelling the basic outline of the introduction of Job.

Read Job 2:7-9.

1. How does Job/Ayoub's wife's statement sound to persons living with disabilities?

2. If you were to respond to Job/Ayoub's wife, what would you say?

Read Job 2:10-13.

Read Job chapter 3 fully.

3. What is Job trying to say in this text? (What did you hear?)

4. What does Job 3 say to people <u>living</u> with disabilities?

57. Maxey, "Hostile Hosts and Unruly Guests."

5. What would be your own version of Job 3?

Read Job 42:7-8.

6. What is God's view of how Job has spoken in chapter 3?

7. How can you share your version of Job 3 with your local church or community?

Space will not permit a fulsome description or analysis of all the ways people living with disabilities re-translated Job's narrative and lament.[58] I will focus on the alternative logics that sectors of people living with disabilities utilized as they re-translated Job's lament in Chapter 3.

Prior to question three, the facilitators invited the participants to read Job 3 in two local languages. While Job 3 was being read, one could hear a pin drop. People were listening intently to Job's dark rhetoric. After it was read, there was silence. We observed a pause before inviting people to respond to question three, which asked, "What is Job/Ayoub trying to say in this text? What did you hear?" Some of the group answers were:

Because of suffering.

- Job was right to have said so because God had failed to help Job.

- Because of the pain, but Job was still having his faith.

- Maybe the devil came to Job.

In these answers, we can see the re-translational logic of dialogue at work within an emancipatory frame. Using CBS as an alternative mode of re-translating means that no singular sectoral translational perspective is privileged above all others. Groups were willing to disagree with one another and, even disagree, with Job. Participants felt free to jump back and forth between the story of Job and their own experience rather freely. For people living with disabilities in African contexts, a post-colonial mode of re-translating biblical texts that responds to dominant theologies necessarily involves reworking translation practices to include multi-sectoral dialogue. I am quick to add, multi-sectoral dialogue begins with excluded and marginalized sectors re-reading, re-translating, and re-interpreting among themselves. Question five asked, "What is your version of Job 3?" Here are some of their re-translations of Job's rhetoric for their own situations:

58. Esala, "Translation as Invasion," 290–305.

- "The suffering we are undergoing should not get to any other one, but we alone, so that when we die, other healthy people can bury us well. We don't attribute our cases to anyone, but God, and He knows why." (Older women's group)

- We pray and hope that God will turn things around, so we look unto him. We do not have another power to look unto." (Mature women's group)

- "We leave our suffering unto God who created us and the sickness." (Mature women's group)

- "We will not do anything that will deny us God's kingdom because there no one will experience suffering." (Mature women's group)

- "God knows the plan he has for us. We do not know why we face these problems. We hope we shall overcome these problems." (Youngest women's group)

- "We will encourage our friends to give all to God because God know all things. It is God who gives and takes, also no condition is always the same, time changes as well as conditions. It is God who created us, and he knows what is good for us. If it is good, we thank him. If it is bad, we still thank him because he knows what is the best for us." (Youngest men's group)

- "I will ask my friends to keep me in prayers because it is God who has made me. I am not the first person that this has ever happened to because it has happened to people before me. It is Satan's desire that sickness should come to me, but I know that God is more powerful. I will tell my friends that God has made me." (Elder men's group)

- "We should fear God in every situation we find ourselves. It was a test and God still tests people today. Trust in God. We should pray always and hope that God will answer our prayers." (Mature men's group)

- "What we have comes from God. Pray always. Look up to God. Wait to be called by God, do not try to kill yourself." (Mature men's group)

- "God you are the power, you are driving your things without asking anybody. So, this problem has already done to a lot of people, but we do not forget about God so try and help me with this problem. We thank God that you know the reason why you are giving me this problem. If anything is happening to your life you have to give back to God." (Young men's group)

- "God created us this way. Let's live and see what happens." (Older men's group)

A key theme in many of the versions of Job 3 as articulated by sectoral groups of people living with disabilities was that they did not attribute their suffering to another human being. This redirected the focus from other people who may have contributed to disabilities through "witchcraft" or cursing—to God.[59]

Dominant ideo-theologies at work in the secular developmentalist model dismiss witchcraft concerns as unreal, the result of an "enchanted worldview" that must be changed for Africa to develop.[60] In contemporary Africanist religious practice, disabilities are often seen as a sign a family has fallen short of societal standards, a result of being cursed by the Gods.[61] The dominant theologies, in the new African Christianity, often assume that disabilities are caused by other able-bodied people in the family with better fortune, who exhibit ambition, or who have uncommon creativity or skill.[62] To respond to the invasive logic of challenge implicit in these theologies, it is important that people living with disabilities consider the causes of disability from inside their own bodies and religio-cultural life worlds. They do not need to accept the terms of translation that colonial translation has set for them.

In other words, for instance, "witchcraft" is an English term that has been infused with Eurocentric baggage by missionary-colonial Christianity and the Enlightenment. The new Christian churches do not bypass this baggage, because they largely accept the understanding of witchcraft offered to them by missionary-colonial translation. Re-translating "witchcraft" from an alternative ideo-theological entanglement requires engaging the terms for witchcraft in the local languages. As such, I have been told the term kusɔɔg[63] in the Likɔɔnl (or Komba) language, often translated "witchcraft," is something every person has. It can be used positively and negatively. However, only some people

59. Kirby, *Gods, Shrines, and Problem-Solving*, 91; Kirby, "Christian Response to Witchcraft," 20–21.

60. Gifford, *Christianity, Development and Modernity*, 154.

61. Kuloba, "'Homosexuality Is UnAfrican and Unbiblical,'" 27.

62. Asamoah-Gyadu, "Witchcraft Accusations and Christianity," 24.

63. I make a conscious choice not to mark words as foreign with italics.

are usɔɔn "a witch." Grillo's, more in depth, research in Côte d'Ivoire confirms that not everyone is agn "a witch" in the Adioukrou language. Furthermore, the power behind "witchcraft" is ambiguous. It is a singular power that can be used positively and negatively.[64] Grillo claims "the problem is that the Western construct itself is so heavily weighted by the moral judgment that witchcraft is singularly negative."[65]

Experienced practitioners of CBS have often found that it is more effective to address a fraught, and potentially dangerous discussion, indirectly. The narrative of Job offers just such an indirect approach to discussing the causes of disability. Re-translating, governed by an emancipatory logic, begins when marginalized groups dialogically rework the logic of challenge for themselves. Their bodies understand the kind of damage that dominant theologies do. Not only do they deal with disability, but they also deal with theologies that marginalize them, operating through their kinship groups and their religious communities—Africanist, Muslim, and Christian. As "pain-bearers"[66] in their communities, people living with disabilities may be well-positioned to navigate through pain and trauma in their context, toward addressing the sources of that pain, and healing that pain, from the inside out, in a manner that other social locations cannot. This is largely born out in the re-translations of Job's lament, translated into English above. Remarkably, groups of people living with disabilities did not express retaliation or a desire to reenact harm upon others. They began reworking the individualist, and sometimes retaliatory logics of the health and wealth gospel, to focus on collective aspects of sectoral healing. Their entanglements with African indigenous/pre-colonial life worlds facilitate a holistic integration of the spiritual and material, the individual and the collective.

I return now to responses to question four, which asks, "What does Job 3 say to people *living* with disabilities?"

- Suffering is not only one person.

- I was somebody, but now I am not.

---

64. Grillo, *An Intimate Rebuke*, 36–38; Asamoah-Gyadu, "Witchcraft Accusations and Christianity," 23.

65. Grillo, *An Intimate Rebuke*, 39.

66. Drawing on Walter Brueggemann's notion of the embrace of pain, June Dickie writes, "'Pain-bearers' is a general term including those who bear physical or emotional pain, and those caught in situations of political, social, and economic distress." Dickie, "African Youth Lament," 7.

- If you lose hope, still take your time, and do not lose hope.

- Give your house people patience.

The response of one of the young men's groups was to "Give your house people patience." I believe this response was directed at able-bodied young men who, in their eagerness and ambition to achieve higher levels of social status and in their frustration at the lack of opportunities the northern Ghanaian context offers them, find it easy to pin any lack of success or any misfortune on vulnerable people, especially vulnerable older women in their homes. This perspective is especially important for those young men who may be practicing a version of the health and wealth gospel. At the same time, this response offers the same grace to young men who have their own set of struggles and frustrations. If we all give our house people patience, then perhaps we will not resort to scapegoating them[67] and begin to find ways to help them address the spiritual-systemic causes of their frustrations. The response of the young men's group could also have been partly directed at older men present in the group, who had only recently become disabled. These older men may have been tempted to blame vulnerable others as the cause of their disability, rather than recognizing that all bodies are in the inevitable process of becoming disabled.

I have spent significant time discussing how these re-translations responded to the logic of challenge in an emancipatory manner. How did the re-translations of CBS participants articulate an emancipatory vision of social progress that was not constrained by the paternalism of the developmentalist gospel?

Consider again the older women's group response to question 5, what is your version of Job 3?

> The suffering we are undergoing should not get to any other one, but we alone, so that when we die, other healthy people can bury us well. We don't attribute our cases to anyone, but God, and He knows why. (Older women's group)

The older women's group version of Job 3 recalls the story told at the beginning of the study about the farmer who hated his horse, but their version changes the narrative of that story. The narrative, as told at the beginning of the CBS by an able-bodied facilitator, suggested that some able-bodied people wanted to bury people living with disabilities

---

67. Girard, *Sacrifice*.

prematurely out of hatred. The older women's version of the story refuses to address other people's motives. Their narrative does not eschew being buried. As Job said, burial would be an end to suffering. What they desire from other people is a good burial. They express a vision of social progress that people living with disabilities would be buried with dignity by kin members and friends as part of God's "*kin*-dom." If religious communities and extended families would bury these women well, it would be transformational.

Conclusion: Re-Translating Social Invasion for Life

My colleagues, and I, were moved by these encounters with people in the community, some of whom were my colleagues' relatives and friends. The participants invited us to begin to see life from their point of view—with Job. Afterward, one colleague remarked in a serious tone, "I didn't know our people felt that way." This colleague from his own social position was not content just to listen to his people; he was lamenting with his people from inside his own body, experience, and position in society. CBS offers an opportunity for activist translators to learn to hear what re-translating for liberation looks like from the perspective of those who have been made invisible several times over by the hierarchical logic of social invasion. CBS offers an opportunity for those who are "pain-bearers" in the underlayers of contemporary contexts to rework the colonial logics of oppression from the inside out. CBS as a form of re-translation is not simply about marginalized groups translating back the oppressive logic of social invasion. Instead, this case study shows that marginalized groups have the power to rework and re-translate the very logics of social invasion, holding spiritual-material relations in tension in ways that are life-giving, resurrecting processes of social healing for all sectors of society to experience and enact.

Bibliography

Asamoah-Gyadu, J. Kwabena. "Witchcraft Accusations and Christianity in Africa." *IBMR* 39/1 (2015) 23–27.

Baker, Mona. "Translation and Activism: Emerging Patterns of Narrative Community." In *Translation, Resistance, Activism*, edited by Maria Tymoczko, 23–41. Amherst: University of Massachusetts Press, 2010.

Balcomb, Anthony. "Counter-Modernism, the Primal Imagination and Development Theory: Shifting the Paradigm." *JTSA* 157 (2017) 44–58.

Balcomb, Tony O. "The War of the Trees: Analysing the Rise and Fall of an Indigenous Mass Greening Movement amongst the Shona in Southern Zimbabwe Using Actor Network Theory (ANT)." *JTSA* 154 (2016) 28–42.

Briggs, Charles L. "Contested Mobilities: On the Politics and Ethnopoetics of Circulation." *Journal of Folklore Research* 50/1 (2013) 285–99.

Brownlie, Siobhan. "Descriptive vs Committed Approaches." In *Routledge Encyclopedia of Translation Studies*, edited by Mona Baker and Gabriela Saldanha, 77–81. 2nd ed. London: Routledge, 2009.

Deane-Cox, Sharon. *Retranslation: Translation, Literature and Reinterpretation.* Bloomsbury Advances in Translation Series. London; New York: Bloomsbury Academic, 2014.

Dickie, June. "African Youth Engage With Psalms of Lament to Find Their Own Voice of Lament." *JTSA* 160 (2018) 4–20.

Draper, Jonathan A. "African Contextual Hermeneutics: Readers, Readings, and Their Options between Text and Context." *RT* 22/1–2 (2015) 3–22.

Dube, Musa W. *Postcolonial Feminist Interpretation of the Bible.* St. Louis, MO: Chalice, 2000.

Dube, Musa W., and R. S. Wafula, eds. *Postcoloniality, Translation, and the Bible in Africa.* Eugene, Oregon: Pickwick Publications, 2017.

Esala, Nathan. "Skopostheorie: A Functional Approach for the Future of Bible Translation in Africa?" *JACT* 15/2 (2012) 26–32.

———. "Towards Contextualizing 'Contextual Bible Study' among the Bikɔɔm Peoples and Their Neighbors in Ghana." *JTSA* 154 (2016) 106–26.

———. "Translation as Invasion in Post-Colonial Northern Ghana." Ph.D. diss., University of KwaZulu-Natal, 2020. https://researchspace.ukzn.ac.za/handle/10413/19690.

Gifford, Paul. *African Christianity: Its Public Role.* Bloomington: Indiana University Press, 1998.

———. *Christianity, Development and Modernity in Africa.* London: Hurst, 2015.

———. *Ghana's New Christianity: Pentecostalism in a Globalizing African Economy.* Bloomington: Indiana University Press, 2004.

Girard, René. *Sacrifice.* Translated by Matthew Pattillo and David Dawson. Breakthroughs in Mimetic Theory. East Lansing: Michigan State University Press, 2011.

Grillo, Laura S. *An Intimate Rebuke: Female Genital Power in Ritual and Politics in West Africa.* Durham: Duke University Press, 2018.

Hall, Crystal L. *Insights from Reading the Bible with the Poor.* Minneapolis: Fortress, 2019.

Hasselbring, Sue Ann. "Cross-Dialectal Acceptance of Written Standards: Two Ghanaian Case Studies." Ph.D. diss., University of South Africa, 2006. http://uir.unisa.ac.za/bitstream/handle/10500/715/thesis.pdf?sequence=1&isAllowed=y.

Horowitz, Donald L. *Ethnic Groups in Conflict.* Berkeley: University of California Press, 1985.

Kirby, Jon P. *Gods, Shrines, and Problem-Solving among the Anufɔ of Northern Ghana.* Collectanea Instituti Anthropos, vol. 34. Berlin: Reimer, 1986.

———. "Toward a Christian Response to Witchcraft in Northern Ghana." *IBMR* 39/1 (2015) 19–22.

Kuloba, Robert W. "'Homosexuality Is Unafrican and Unbiblical': Examining the Ideological Motivations to Homophobia in Sub-Saharan Africa - the Case Study of Uganda." *JTSA* 154 (2016) 6–27.

Lambert, Jessica E., Jeannette Kørner, Nikolaj Mølgaard Thomsen, and Fred Nantogmah. *Mental Health Treatment in Traditional and Faith-Based Healing Centers in Ghana: Field Study.* DIGNITY Publication Series on Torture and Organised Violence No. 29, 2019 https://www.dignity.dk/wp-content/uploads/publication_series_no29.pdf.

MacGaffey, Wyatt. *Chiefs, Priests, and Praise-Singers: History, Politics, and Land Ownership in Northern Ghana.* Charlottesville and London: University of Virginia Press, 2013. http://www.jstor.org/stable/j.ctt6wrkqq.

Maluleke, Tinyiko S. "Half a Century of African Christian Theologies: Elements of the Emerging Agenda for the Twenty-First Century." *JTSA* 99 (1999) 4–23.

Mamdani, Mahmood. *Citizen and Subject: Contemporary Africa and the Legacy of Late Colonialism.* Princeton Studies in Culture/Power/History. Princeton: Princeton University Press, 1996.

———. *Neither Settler nor Native.* Cambridge: Harvard University Press, 2020.

Maxey, James A. *From Orality to Orality: A New Paradigm for Contextual Translation of the Bible.* Biblical Performance Criticism 2. Eugene, OR: Cascade Books, 2009.

———. "Hostile Hosts and Unruly Guests: Bible Translation as Hospitality and Counterinsurgency," 1–13. Presentation at the Bible Translation Conference, Dallas, TX, October 11-15, 2013. https://map.bloomfire.com/posts/692586-hostile-hosts-and-unruly-guests-bible-translation-as-hospitality-and-counterins.

Mbamalu, Abiola Ibilola. "The Use of 'Abundant Life' in John 10:10 and Its Interpretation among Some Yoruba Prosperity Gospel Preachers." Ph.D diss., University of KwaZulu-Natal, 2010 http://hdl.handle.net/10413/3497.

Mbembe, Achille. *On the Postcolony.* Berkeley: University of California, 2001.

Mignolo, Walter, and Catherine E. Walsh. *On Decoloniality: Concepts, Analytics, Praxis.* On Decoloniality. Durham: Duke University Press, 2018.

Mosala, Itumeleng J. *Biblical Hermeneutics and Black Theology in South Africa.* Grand Rapids: Eerdmans, 1989.

Sanneh, Lamin O. *Translating the Message: The Missionary Impact on Culture.* American Society of Missiology Series, no. 13. Maryknoll, NY: Orbis, 1989.

Scott, James C. *Domination and the Arts of Resistance: Hidden Transcripts.* New Haven: Yale University Press, 1990.

Shadd, Deborah. "Response to Carolyn J. Sharp – Translating Alterity: Conflict, Undecidability, and Complicity." Presentation at the Annual Meeting of the Society of Biblical Literature Atlanta, GA, Nov 21-24, 2015.

Simon, Sherry. *Gender in Translation: Cultural Identity and the Politics of Transmission.* London: Routledge, 1996.

Talton, Benjamin. *Politics of Social Change in Ghana: The Konkomba Struggle for Political Equality.* 1st ed. New York: Palgrave MacMillan, 2010.

Tymoczko, Maria. *Enlarging Translation, Empowering Translators.* Manchester, UK; Kinderhook, NY: St. Jerome Publishing, 2007.

West, Gerald O. "Contextual Bible Study and/or as Interpretive Resilience." In *That All May Live! Essays in Honor of Nyambura J. Njoroge,* edited by Ezra Chitando, Esther Mombo, and Masiiwa Ragies Gunda, 143–59. Bamberg: University of Bamburg Press, 2021.

———. "On the Necessity of Re-Translation." Presentation at the Nida School of Translation Studies Misano Adriatico, Italy, May 30–June 10, 2016.

———. "Reading the Bible between Alterity and Appropriation: Translation for Liberation." Presentation at the Nida School of Translation Studies Misano Adriatico, Italy, May 26–June 6, 2014.

———. "Reading the Bible with the Marginalised: The Value/s of Contextual Bible Reading." *STJ* 1/2 (2015) 235–61.

———. *The Stolen Bible: From Tool of Imperialism to African Icon.* BIS 144. Leiden: Brill, 2016.

West, Gerald O., and Musa W. Dube. "An Introduction: How We Have Come to 'Read With.'" *Semeia* 73 (1996) 1–16.

West, Gerald O., and Bongi Zengele. "Reading Job 'Positively' in the Context of HIV/AIDS in South Africa." *Concilium* 4 (2004) 112–24.

West, Gerald O., and Sithembiso Zwane. "Re-Reading 1 Kings 21:1-16 between Community-Based Activism and University-Based Pedagogy." *JIBS* 2/1 (2020) 179–207.

Wynter, Sylvia. "Unparalleled Catastrophe for Our Species? Or, to Give Humanness a Different Future: Conversations." In *Sylvia Wynter: On Being Human as Praxis,* edited by Katherine McKittrick, 9–89. Durham: Duke University Press, 2015.

Yusoff, Kathryn. *A Billion Black Anthropocenes or None.* Forerunners: Ideas First from the University of Minnesota Press 53. Minneapolis: University of Minnesota Press, 2018.

3

"Enough to Go Around" at God's Table

Sharing Meals with the Poor in Luke 14:16–24

Aliou Cissé Niang
Union Theological Seminary

Introduction

> There will, however, be no one in need among you, because the LORD is sure to bless you in the land that the LORD your God is giving you as a possession to occupy . . . "For there will never cease to be poor (*endeēs*) in the land. Therefore, I command you, you shall open wide your hand to your brother, to the needy and to the poor, in your land." (Deut 15:4, 11)

> For you always have the poor (*ptōchos*) with you, and whenever you want, you can do good for them. But you will not always have me. (Mark 14:7)

> Go out at once into the streets and lanes of the town and bring in the poor (*ptōchos*), the crippled, the blind, and the lame. . . Go out into the roads and lanes, and compel people to come in, so that my house may be filled. (Luke 14:21c, 23b)

Social action, and its admirable accomplishments, is the modern form of charity and one of the faces of social justice. They

> constitute a categorical imperative for all . . . It is easy to choose
> between loud, empty statements and the critical feats of those
> who have humbly put themselves to the task. Because poverty
> does not wait.
>
> Paulette Nardal, *Poverty Does Not Wait*, 41.

ONE OF THE MOST challenging universal human dilemmas in the biblical and modern worlds is understanding the nature and causes of poverty and its antidote. The above epigraphs bear witness to the fact that poverty was in the mind of God and is especially a divine summons for human participatory agency. On the human side, many socially engaged clergy, laypersons, and scholars such as Gerald O. West, have risen up to the challenge with innovative ways to renew communal life by tackling poverty. These epigraphs echo my reading of West's crucial contribution to biblical studies and African Biblical Hermeneutics (ABH).

During the first International PhD Seminar organized by the Universities of KwaZulu Natal, University of Oslo, and Union Theological Seminary and held on 1–3 October 2013, in Oslo, Norway, I read and heard papers presented by Gerald O. West and other participants. After my presentation on "Identity Construction in Postcolonial Contexts," Gerald asked me a crucial question paraphrased from my notes as follows, "Your argument has analogical echoes to my work on Isaiah Shembe. Was Aline Sitoé Diatta influenced by Christianity?"[1] I recall saying "yes and no" to his question. As a follow-up to that knee-jerk response, this essay offers some broader insights on how Aline Sitoé Diatta fed all who joined her faith community.

Other crucial collaborations in which West's and my work intersect are in the 2015 *SBL Forum* special publication on African hermeneutics that includes an insightful introduction by West,[2] with responses to Kenneth Ngwa's intriguing article[3] by other scholars and myself,[4] and a panel discussion on postcolonialism that Brigitte Kahl and I organized at Union Theological Seminary in 2016. These collaborations shaped my thoughts on how I might engage and innovate on West's African

---

1. West, *Stolen Bible*, 232–317. His work on Isaiah Chembe is invaluable—a figure whose life and thought he engaged for many years.

2. West, *"Twice Called, Thrice Rebuked,"* 850–54.

3. Ngwa, "Making of Gershom's Story," 855–76.

4. Niang, "Space and Human Agency," 887–89; Claassens, *"Memories of Midwives,"* 877–81; Dube, *"A Luta Continua,"* 890–902.

indigenous hermeneutics construed as "Reading Other-Wise"[5]—a locution that includes reading with the poor, but to which I would also add people afflicted with all forms of oppression. Herein lie elements constitutive of my reading lens that I will apply to the parable Jesus told in Luke 14:16–24.

A handful of western social scientists[6] and socially engaged biblical exegetes and hermeneuts,[7] mostly living at the margins of societies (within or outside empires) around the globe, fully reckon with the need to make scripture, especially Jesus' ministry in Roman Palestine, relevant to their own lived experiences as imperially shaped contexts by promoting freedom, social, religious, and ethnic/racial economic justice. In agreement, I argue with Hans-Georg Gadamer that "If we [interpreters] fail to transpose ourselves into the historical horizon from which the traditionary text speaks, we will misunderstand the significance of what it has to say to us: we must place ourselves in the other's situation in order to understand."[8] Therefore, I place myself "into the historical horizon from which the traditionary text speaks" by placing "texts into a relationship with other texts to create meaning" convinced "that texts from quite different communities and traditions participate in various ways in common cultural contexts and interact with various other texts."[9] Conflict theorists place themselves into this horizon when they apply a social-scientific optic[10] to offer actionable insights from biblical texts that expose the interactions between the "haves" (elites, retainers. . .) and "have-nots" (e.g., Galileans peasants, and the poor) in Roman Palestine, which a Bible interpreter might use to read texts. Interpreters must cross their cultural pattern of thought and linguistic meaning-making, and learn from that of the host culture, in order to apply its content and message. In spite of the various nomenclatures one may encounter while navigating variegated exegetical works, "cross-cultural encounters," "cultural

5. West, ed., *Reading Other-Wise*.

6. Rohrbaugh, *The New Testament in Cross-Cultural Perspective*, 1–76; Smith-Christopher, "Cross-Cultural Exegesis," 138.

7. West, ed., *Reading Other-Wise*.

8. Gadamer, *Truth and Method*, 303.

9. Carter, *Jesus and the Empire*, 3.

10. Herzog, *Parables as Subversive*; Oakman, *Jesus and the Peasants*; Oakman, *The Radical Jesus*; Eck, *The Parables of Jesus the Galilean*; Rohrbaugh, *The New Testament in Cross-Cultural Perspective*; Rohrbaugh, *The Biblical Interpreter*; Hanson and Oakman, *Palestine in the Time of Jesus*.

intertextuality," "cross-cultural perspective," or "cross-cultural exegesis" all seek to articulate such a reading lens.

Taking my cues from West's reading with the poor, as articulated in his *The Academy of the Oppressed*, "Reading Other-Wise," and his magnum opus *The Stolen Bible*,[11] I transpose myself "into the historical horizon from which the traditionary text speaks," which in this case is Luke 14:16–24,[12] to argue that the unnamed elite of Luke 14:16–24 underwent a gradual transformation. Luke's Jesus shows the "good news" inspires a revaluation of Greco-Roman *patron-client* relationship so as to incubate liberation within it for the poor, the captive, the blind, and the oppressed (Luke 4:18–19)—that is, people confined to certain liminal spaces. In so doing, Jesus subverts Greco-Roman clientelism and creates a community that exercises, what I argue, is the art of practicing the daring, divine, timeless model of sustaining life—*the organic art of Looking Around and Practicing "Enough to Go Around"* mentality. *"Enough to Go Around"* as Webster's Dictionary has it, it is "enough of something for all of the people who want or need it."[13]

To my surprise, a Google search turned up a children's book entitled *Enough to Go Around: A Story of Generosity*.[14] The primary title comes from Kristin Johnson's character, a child named Kevin, who related to his grandmother a conversation he had with his peers during lunch. He recounts the fact that while Olivia, Jayden, and he talked about the kind of dinner they had the night before, their friend Michael said nothing. Wondering why he said nothing about what he had, his grandmother extrapolated that "Maybe Michael didn't know what to say . . . Not everyone has enough to eat . . . there just isn't enough to go around."[15] This inspired generosity in the heart of Kevin who invited Michael and his friends to have a food drive that led to the creation of a food pantry. This is a children's story with a message for both children and adults.

We have heard stories of children immersed in the Civil Rights Movement, and see children holding adults responsible for climate change, and leading food drives. Some thinkers, and even children, believe climate

---

11. West, *Academy of the Poor*; West, *Reading Other-Wise*, West, *The Stolen Bible*; *Contextual Bible Study*.

12. This parable is often read with Matt and Q.

13. https://www.merriam-webster.com/dictionary/enough%2Fplenty%20to%20go%20around.

14. Johnson, *Enough to Go Around*.

15. Johnson, *Enough to Go Around*, 10

change is responsible for mass human movements around the globe due to drought, diseases, wars, and famine. Given the literary context of Luke 14, could it have been the reason for Jesus' punning of this parable in the context of a meal? To explore my claim, I will frame my contextual analysis of Luke 14:16–24 by building on Hebrew Bible antecedents (Exod 3:7–8; Lev 25; and Deut 15:4, 11) and their relevance to my Diola reading of Luke 14:16–24 and Senegalese solidarity with the poor and the people who are differently able. And then, I will offer closing remarks which I hope would contribute to the ongoing quest of *Reading With* and *Eating With the Poor* and people who are differently able.

Divine "Enough to Go Around" in Human Hands: Hebrew Bible Antecedents

Though the historical, cultural, linguistic, and theological distance between the worlds of the Two Testaments and ours cannot be underestimated, human need for sustenance, especially food (a central concern for this chapter) remains a perennial human experience irrespective of the span of cultures or time. Many causes of human movement in the world include colonial occupations, wars, drought-related famines, diseases, and other forms of human suffering which we often blame on natural disasters, but can now also be linked to human action—the human destructive hand. In the context of the Lukan Jesus and ours, imperial systems of control of land and subsistence-level economies also reduce many to poverty. A modern interpretation of scripture that ignores these realities fails to take seriously Jesus' call to discipleship— a summon, I argue, that inspires an organic, other-centered praxis, namely, *"Enough to Go Around"* praxis. In his explorations of various forms of assistance, Garret Keizer observes:

> Help is a part of our humanity; it is what human beings do. If it is complicated, inconclusive, that is because we are. Its paradoxes define us. Alone in the universe, I am as helpless as a stone. But with my disappearance, or the turning of one stone into bread, the universe is bereft . . . I distinguished help from altruism by saying that altruism is what it is but that help, being action, must always submit to a verdict.[16]

16. Keizer, *Help*, 237–38.

To say that "Help is a part of our humanity" but it is "its paradoxes" that "define us,"[17] is a daring vocation. However, my question is, if "help" is human, how do "its paradoxes define us"? To answer this question in conversation with West's work, I build on some select Hebrew Bible texts to foreground my reading of Luke 14:16–24. I find Exod 3:7–10 illuminating for its centrality to Ngwa's riveting *Let My People Live*. God consults Moses, son of a Hebrew slave who is adopted by Pharaoh's daughter, a murderer, and refugee, a shepherd to his father-in-law, Jethro's sheep, by using strong verbs to communicate the divine intimate experience of oppressed Hebrews to whom the deity would like to send Moses to deliver and transform into a community of free persons.

> I have surely *seen* (εἶδον) the affliction of my people who are in Egypt and have *heard* (ἀκήκοα) their cry because of their taskmasters. I *know* (οἶδα) their sufferings, and I *have come* (κατέβην ἐξελέσθαι) down to deliver them out of the hand of the Egyptians and to bring them up out of that land to a good and broad land, a land flowing with milk and honey. . . (Exod 3:7–10, LXX)

After a failed attempt to reject the divine call to free Israel, Moses returns to Pharaoh and delivers the prophetic command of God: "Let my people go, so that they may celebrate a festival to me in the wilderness" (Exod 5:1). God, through Moses, creates a ritual calendar layered with meticulous instructions, and imperatives for the perpetual observance of the Passover, and preempts future generational queries about such a ritualized life (Exod 12:1–26). The redeemed people's answer must be to "say"/"speak of"/"proclaim" אָמַר—as in the retelling of a ritualized story—divine acts of liberation (Exod 12:29–51). The significance of this ritualized liberative journey from Egypt to other spaces is multidimensional and, as Ngwa rightly argues, "lives beyond the story's original setting and timing (Exod 13:14–15)."[18] As the journey unfolds, the deity provides water and food (Exod 15:22–25) for the freed (Exod 16:4–5) thirsty and hungry community. Raining "bread from heaven" (Deut 16:4; Pss 78:24–27) does not preclude divine provision of meat from quails.[19] Observance of Sabbath ritual, feeding, and quenching thirst are existential lessons to resurrect, shape, reposition, and rehabilitate Israel's nearly erased ontologies and epistemologies by servitude,

---

17. Keizer, *Help*, 237.

18. Ngwa, *Let My People Live*, 2.

19. Propp, *Exodus*, 593.

to exercise and practice abundant life in all spaces—in the wilderness, Canaan, and exilic communities.[20]

Lessons learned through this journey should be transmitted to future generations to ensure they remember and emulate divine liberative acts in their midst. They must be forever etched in Israel's memory as rehabilitating ontologies and epistemologies inspired by mighty divine acts of liberation. This is why the *manna* [מָן (MT)/μάννα (LXX) Deut 8:2–3] feeding, and provisions of water, are inextricably linked to Israel's obedience to divine commandments *miṣwôt* (מִצְוֺתָו). The work of liberation is an organically multidimensional praxis-oriented ontology and epistemology—for the divine-human presence and provisions of water and food. The work of liberation continues as the deity guides, feeds, and quenches the thirst of the liberated (Exod 12–16). Freedom and space are heavenized as the deity instructs the liberated community members to practice mutualism in the land they will inhabit (Deut 11:10–12; 15:1–15). As heavenized estate/space, the land—a non-human entity with a perennial agency (Lev 25:23b)—"shall observe a sabbath for the LORD" (Lev 25:2) and "must not be sold in perpetuity" (Lev 25:23a). The identity of freed community members is divinely transformed from God's "people" or "Israel" (Exod 3:7, 9–11) to "aliens and tenants" (Lev 25:23c). Unfortunately, as society's structure transformed over time, some elites failed to heed these existential lessons.

As Fernando Belo observes, there are two main Torah codes: the "debt codes" anchored in divine liberation from Egypt, and the "Levitical purity codes." Whereas the former advocates inclusive life sustenance for all people, regardless of the stipulations of the latter, the "purity codes" construct a non-negotiable binary in life of "clean versus unclean"[21]—a conclusion that William Herzog rightly welcomes, and I concur with. He writes:

> The debt codes begin with the liberation from slavery in Egypt and the gift of the land. The land belongs to Yahweh and is Yahweh's to distribute as he sees fit. Leviticus picks up this theme in a very pointed manner: 'The land shall not be sold in perpetuity, for the land is mine; with me you are but aliens and tenants. Throughout the land that you hold, you shall provide for the redemption of the land' (25:23–24). According to the debt codes,

20. Ngwa, *Let My People Live*, 1–53.

21. Belo, *A Materialist Reading*, 37–59 [trans. Matthew J. O' Connell from the French, *Lecture Materialist*, 63–92].

> everyone is a debtor to Yahweh. The land was given to be a bless-
> ing to the people of the land, and that blessing was to be realized
> through the principle of extension, which means that the yield
> of the land was to be shared with all so that none would be in
> need. The more one gets, the more one gives.[22]

The work of sustenance and liberation is one of the most daring divine calls for the community (Exod 16; Lev 25; Deut 15:1–15). However, the human voice translating divine intention is often mired in the human construction of reality. Most Jews would subsequently become familiar with miraculous stories[23] of God sustaining life inside (Gen 2:15) and outside the Garden (Gen 3:22–24), liberating the oppressed (Exod 1–3), feeding them with a divine menu—quails and manna (Exod 16:13, 31), land to farm that will be lavished with abundant rain, and *enough to go around* if they remain faithful (Deut 15:1–15). Thus, Herzog writes, "The purpose of the debt codes was to create a contrast society in which '*jus-tice* would roll down like waters and righteousness like an ever-flowing stream'" (Amos 5:24)." Citing Belo, Herzog writes:

> the debt codes were intended to avoid the violence that arises
> when a ruling class begins to exploit and oppress a peasant base.
> 'This is . . . the locus of violence that must be exorcized: the desire
> that is brought to bear on the other's source of subsistence, the
> desire that is the origin of aggressive violence . . . This violence
> . . . is the source of the class system, the enrichment of some at
> the expense of others, and the formation of large-scale owner-
> ship. Unfortunately, the debt codes harbored an inner contra-
> diction. As the land yielded abundantly, providing the means
> to fulfill the principle of extension, it also triggered the desire
> to accumulate rather than redistribute the wealth of the land . . .
> "Blessing and abundance engender the covetous desire to have
> more; this means that the blessing may well develop under its
> aegis the violence that is the curse." This was certainly the case
> by the first century in Galilee and Judea.[24]

Clearly, lessons from the debt codes etched in Israel's memory ended up creating a vision of scarcity under Empire that undermined the practice of *Enough to Go Around*, as Herzog rightly observes.

---

22. Herzog, *Prophet and Teacher*, 127.

23. Lexically, the two Testaments do not use the word "miracle."

24. Herzog, *Prophet and Teacher*, 128.

> Take the issue of poverty as an example. Seen through the lens of the purity codes, poverty is the result of impurity or uncleanness. If people lived by the purity codes of the Torah, they would be blessed and prosperous, so poverty *is* a sign of God's judgment on the unclean. The problem is with the poor, not the rich who are reaping the rewards of their faithfulness to Torah. Seen through the eyes of the debt codes, however, poverty is the result of covetous greed. It is the consequence of a ruling elite alienating peasants from their land and reducing them to forms of dependency such as tenants or day laborers. The problem is not with the poor but with the rich.[25]

Reading with the poor is not just a process of conscientizing them, it is also an invitation to exorcise scarcity with the wisdom of *Enough to Go Around* as the deity of liberation in Exodus did (Exod 12—Num 16), and would be later demonstrated in Jesus' teachings and feedings of the poor and outcasts. Could this historical concern reflected in Exodus have precipitated Jesus' parable? To this question, I now turn.

"Enough to Go Around": A New Testament Imperative

According to Exod 12:25, children's inquiry about the Passover ritual is situated in the context of Israel entering (בּוֹא) into Canaan, namely settling in the land: "When you come to the land that the LORD will give you, as he has promised, you shall keep this observance. And when your children ask you, 'What do you mean by this observance?'" (Exod 12:25–26). The answer should include liberation from bondage and impartial divine sustaining acts in the wilderness that liberated Israel should not fail to emulate to ensure the poor have enough to live on. A failure to exercise debt codes would reduce some to poverty—a situation Herzog, citing Belo, blames on some religious elites, and I would add rich landowners, especially under Imperial-Herodian Rome. It is in this social and religious milieu that Jesus Christ encouraged his disciples to "strive for" the reign of God (Luke 12:31; Mark 1:15; Matt 12:28). He was not begging, imploring, or beseeching, but commanding Jewish peasants, who perhaps were nudging each other while being tightly squeezed by the sharp claws of Imperial Rome. As I argued above, some of the wealthier Jews engaged in the insatiable accumulation of wealth and power, thereby

---

25. Herzog, *Prophet and Teacher*, 128.

betraying the vision of the Mosaic debt codes[26]—*Enough to Go Around*. Jesus, thus, revives such a revolutionary vision.

Many Africans, shaped by the European transatlantic slave trade and colonization, would have sympathized with many first- century poor Galilean Jewish peasants. Jesus lived in agrarian Galilee affected by a host of intersectional needs that mired the relationships among urban elites, peasants, and the poor. Jesus describes his ministry this way: "The Spirit of the Lord is upon me, because he has anointed me to bring good news to the poor. He has sent me to proclaim release to the captives and recovery of sight to the blind, to let the oppressed go free, to proclaim the year of the Lord's favor" (Luke 4:18–19).

Responding to the emissaries of John the Baptist, Jesus said: "Go and tell John what you have seen and heard: the blind receive their sight, the lame walk, the lepers are cleansed, the deaf hear, the dead are raised, the poor have good news brought to them" (Luke 7:22). Who are being represented here? πένης and πτωχός belong to a wide semantic field and convey ideas ranging from hardworking to destitute persons,[27] as opposed to πλούσιος—a wealthy or propertied individual.[28] Only in Exod 22:24 and Prov 28:15; 29:7 is πενιχρός[29] used to specifically describe visible poverty.[30] While the LXX uses πενιχρός to refer to intrinsic poverty (Exod 22:24, and Prov 28:15; 29:7), the MT prefers עָנִי (Exod 22:24)[31] and דַּל "poor people"[32] (Prov 28:15; 29:7). These lexical meanings evince different levels of destituteness in antiquity, with some more severe than others. The same can be said of the present-day Global South in contrast to the opulent Global North, especially the United States of America and Europe, a reality that led to the making of such movements as Martin Luther King Jr.'s "The Poor People's Campaign" and "The Poverty Initiative" led by Liz Theoharis, and others. On

26. Myers, *Biblical Vision*, 3–35.

27. *LSJM*, "πενιχρός 1359; Hauck, "πένης, πενιχρός" *TDNT*, 37–40; Coenen, "πένης," *NIDNTT*, 2:820–1. Although πένης and πενιχρός are synonyms, only πένης conveys a wide range of meanings from the idea of being economically destitute to oppressed. In contrast to πένης, πενιχρός speaks of those who need assistance, namely the economically poor.

28. *LSJM*, "πλούσιος" 1422–3.

29. Hatch and Redpath, *A Concordance to the Septuagint*, 1118, 1239–40.

30. Coenen, "πενιχρός," 821.

31. Kohlenberger and Swanson, *HECOT*, 6714.

32. Kohlenberger and Swanson, *HECOT*, 1924.

this note, I now turn to *Enough to Go Around* in the mind of the God of liberation, according to the Lukan Jesus.

When the Rich Eat with the Poor and Persons of Different Ability: A Senegalese Diola Reading Luke 14:16–24[33]

Luke contextualizes the parable in an unnamed city and as Rohrbaugh opines,

> [T]he patterns of pre-industrial cities were very much the consequence of the role played by the city in the larger urban system. As the center of control, the city gathered to itself those non-elite necessary to serve its needs as it carried out the specialized functions it had collected. It was a system characterized by the dominance of a small center, by sharp social stratification, and by a physical and social distancing of component populations that were linked by carefully controlled hierarchical relations. The city was a ready example of human territoriality in which the elite occupied a fortified center, ethnic, socioeconomic and occupational groups the periphery, and outcasts the area immediately outside the city walls.[34]

Gospel scholars unanimously agree that Luke is the only synoptic author to describe economically poor or destitute persons such as the "poor widow" as πενιχρός (Luke 21:2, 3; cf. Mark 12:42 who has μία χήρα πτωχὴ—"one poor widow").[35] Luke places Jesus' teaching (Luke 14:16–24) in a parable modeling Greco-Roman literary symposia. Scholars have long argued whether conflicts between Jesus and some of the Pharisees over who should recline with whom at meals are structurally parallel to, but subvert, those in Plato's symposia.[36] Evidence from Greco-Roman symposia may be traced to Plutarch who shows that rank or social status was a benchmark for ordering and sharing meals

---

33. For versions of Luke 14:16–24, see Matt 22:2–14 and Thomas 64:1–12.

34. Rohrbaugh "The Pre-Industrial City in Luke–Acts," 136–7.

35. Kohlenberger, Goodrick, and Swanson, *ECGNT*, 4293. While Luke uses πλούσιος eleven times, πενιχρός once, and πτωχός nine times, he never uses πένης in his redaction.

36. Braun, *Feasting and Social Rhetoric*, 43–61; Smith, *From Symposium to Eucharist*, 219–76. See also Sterling, *Historiography and Self-Definition*, 370–71; Schmidt, *Hostility to Wealth*, 45–58; 145–50.

among many associations of elites, sophists, and other social groups.[37] Such banquets were contexts for philosophical debates, as Dennis Smith notes, citing Plato and Atheneus.[38] In spite of much disdain for such ordering of banquets based on "rank" (Plutarch, *Moralia* 616), and on making or "keeping up friendship," (Plutarch, *Moralia* 149a–b) the practice among elites persisted especially in walled cities. And, in even one example, a nuanced reading offers striking exceptions.

> Phylarchus says that Ariamnes, who was a very rich Celt [πλουσιωτάτων], publicly promised to give a feast [ἑστιᾶσαί] for all Celts for a year, and he fulfilled this promise by the following method . . . Many victims were slaughtered daily—bulls, hogs, sheep, and other cattle—casks of wine were made ready, and a large quantity of barley-meal ready mixed. . . "Not merely the Celts who came from the villages [κωμῶν] and towns [πόλεων] profited by this, but even passing strangers [οἱ περιόντε ξένος] were not allowed to depart by the slaves who served, until they had had a share of the food which had been prepared" (Atheneaus, *Desp.* 4d–c; trans. C. B. Gulick).

Although Athenaeus' Phylarchus might have exaggerated the length of this feast, his account begs for a nuanced interpretation of Greco-Roman exclusive elitist conviviality maintained by many scholars[39] which has been challenged by evidence of mixed social strata—the poor, slaves, and women as shown by Ascough, Harland, Evans, and others.[40] Conceivably, before the Christian era, and perhaps during the Hellenistic period, Ariamnes entertained urban and rural Celts as well as strangers passing by, irrespective of their social status/rank, ethnicity, gender, political standing, or religious adherence. My point is that it would be an unnuanced argument to say all Greco-Roman elites gave dinners, banquets, or feasts[41] that were exclusively attended by their

---

37. Braun, *Feasting and Social Rhetoric*, 43–61.

38. Smith, *From Symposium to Eucharist*, 256.

39. Klinghardt, "Topology of the Communal Meal," 9–22; Smith, "Greco-Roman Banquet," 23–33.

40. Ascough, "Social and Political Characteristics," 59–72; Harland, "Banqueting in the Associations," 73–85. Evans, "Evidence for Slaves at the Table," 149–64.

41. Athenaeus uses ἑστιᾶσαί (from ἑστιάω—"give a feast") which shares the same root with the word ἑστιατορία meaning "allowance of food" or "feast" (LEH) and ἑστιατήριον "banqueting hall" (LSJM, "ἑστιάω," 698) instead of Luke's δεῖπνον μέγα "great dinner" as modified by the adjective μέγα "great" from a simple dinner to a "great" meal, supper, banquet, dinner or feast (Behm, "δεῖπνον," *TDNT*, 2:34–35).

wealthy peers. Athenaeus, I argue, offers a crucial exception to such broad conclusions held by many scholars.

As I noted above, Luke's Jesus subverts exclusive Greco-Roman elitist social arrangements over meals that may have affected his ministry. To recontextualize Jesus' teaching, Luke redacts Luke 14:16–24 and structures it the same way he does in Luke 5:29–39; 7:36–50; 11:37–54; and 14:1–24,[42] to have Jesus wisely subvert such segregated banquets with the inclusive practice of *Enough to Go Around*. Luke's Jesus reclines with the marginalized—*erased, alienated, and singularized*[43]—as a decisive act of liberation, sabbatical, and jubilee legislations delivered by the divine Liberator of the Exodus. Luke's Jesus sizes the banquet as a context for teaching and re-evaluating banqueting (Luke 14:1, 7–14; 19:1–9). Convivial Greco-Roman clientelism, as *status quo*, erases the needy and persons with different abilities from being seen at table fellowships, but Jesus reimagines it, especially as the divine table. Rohrbaugh is thus correct when he notes:

> The point is that the parable of the Great Supper is placed in the context of a larger discussion of eating and associating with the unexpected people whom the kingdom includes. The question to which we must return then is one about the reason meals, rich hosts and unexpected guests are of such obvious concern to Luke.[44]

What Difference Does It Make?

Luke's Jesus begins by sharing about an inclusive invitation to a banquet given by a certain person (Luke 14:16b–17) to which three unnamed elitist guests unanimously declined invitations to attend (Luke 14:18–20). The host's subversive invitation of the marginalized (Luke 14:21–3) is then followed by his radical subversion of convivial clientelism (Luke 14:24). Jesus offers insightful clues prior to his telling of the parable by instructing his hearers not to sit "at the place of honor" so as to avoid being disgraced by being assigned to "the lowest place" (Luke 14:8–9). Instead, sitting at "the lowest place" might result in being moved or assigned by the host to a place of honor (Luke 14:8–10). It is from this perspective

42. Sterling, *Historiography and Self-Definition*, 370–1.

43. Ngwa, *Let My People Live*.

44. Rohrbaugh "The Pre-Industrial City in Luke–Acts," 138.

that he instructs his host—"a leader of the Pharisees"—"When you give a luncheon or a dinner, do not invite your friends or your brothers or your relatives or rich neighbors (γείτονας πλουσίους), in case they may invite you in return, and you would be repaid. But when you give a banquet, invite the poor, the crippled, the lame, and the blind" (Luke 14:12–13). To me, this is what Luke's Jesus illustrates in Luke 14:16–24.

He tells his hearers that someone gave δεῖπνον μέγα ("a great dinner") and invited πολλούς ("many") but to which three invitees declined, justifying their excuses as follows. The first cited expediency to see ἀγρὸν ("a field") he bought (ἀγοράζω), the second the obligation to try "five pair of oxen" (ζεύγη βοῶν . . . πέντε) he had just bought (Luke 14:19), and the third could not come because γυναῖκα ἔγημα (γαμέω) "he married a wife" (Luke 14:20). Whether these excuses are final or not, the point that Luke's Jesus is communicating has to do with convivial clientelism practices. The adjective πολλούς "many," to me, implies people of lower status may have been numbered among initial invitees whose presence the three elites implicitly objected.

Whereas the adverbial expression ἀπὸ μιᾶς "from one" complicates the syntax by implying a feminine noun missing in Luke 14:18, Nolland agrees with Fitzmyer that it is "probably an Aramaism, related to an idiom known in later Christian Palestinian Aramaic or Syriac [so: 'once'] or it could involve an ellipse with φωνῆς, 'voice,' γνώμης, 'opinion.'. . . since the shared opinion is most striking in the storyline development, the latter is preferable."[45] If Luke means to convey the idea that ἤρξαντο ἀπὸ μιᾶς πάντες παραιτεῖσθαι "all began to excuse themselves," then my question is why would a unanimous defection by many (πολλούς) be reduced to just the three invitees' clearly stated but lame excuses? Only the slave/servant knows the excuses the rest might have voiced out to him. However, as Rohrbaugh explains,

> Their excuses, seemingly irrelevant to the Western, industrialized mind, are standard fare in the dynamics of honor-shame societies. The point is not the excuses at hand, but social disapproval of the arrangement being made, a point to which their seeming irrelevance contributes. Something is wrong with the supper being offered or the guests would not only appear, social opinion would demand that they do so.[46]

45. Nolland, "Luke 9:21—18:34," 755; Fitzmyer, *Gospel According to Luke (X-XXIV)*, 1055.

46. Rohrbaugh "The Pre-Industrial City in Luke–Acts," 141–42.

Welcoming the poor and persons with different abilities (Luke 14:17–18) is consonant with the visible manifestation of the reign of God.[47] To me, whether they had errands and would later attend the main dinner, as Eta Linnemann maintains,[48] is unlikely.

The excuses of the most valued guests that angered the host imply they must have known the day and time of the banquet and could have avoided a conflict of schedule. Some scholars, for example, have already pointed to the fact that the first invaluable guest would have inspected the field prior to closing the deal, not after.[49] The same argument applies to the second guest. As for the newly married person, it is unthinkable that, if the host were his close friend, he would not have been invited to the wedding. In other words, the host would have known about his friend's wedding since both weddings and banquets involved some degree of planning. Conceivably, all the three invitees would not have been oblivious to each other's planned events—great banquet, errands involving economic transactions, and wedding. This might be the reason why their declining angered (ὀργίζω) the host/banqueter, who is also later referred to as "master/lord" (κύριος) and "householder" (οἰκοδεσπότης) in Luke 14:21.

The gist of Jesus' parable rests on verses 21–24 to which I now turn. The householder makes a strategic and subversive move to welcome others. He re-sent his servant to invite the poor and differently able—"the poor (πτωχός), the crippled (ἀνάπειρος), the blind (τυφλός), and the lame (χωλός)" on the streets (πλατύς) and lanes (ῥύμη) of the unnamed city. Initial invitees, as I argued earlier, may have included people of lower status (Luke 14:23–24) in line with the programmatic mission of Luke's Jesus to bring the "good news to the poor," marginalized people, restore "sight to the blind," and proclaim cancelation of debt (Luke 4:18–19). I concur with Rohrbaugh that "Luke is using the parable to confront the rich of his own community who are avoiding association with poor Christians, the question about why guests stay away is exactly the question that the parable intends to force upon the reader."[50]

---

47. I encourage readers to consult Braun, *Feasting and Social Rhetoric*; Scott, *Hear Then the Parable*; Snodgrass, *Stories with Intent*; Rohrbaugh; "The Pre-Industrial City in Luke–Acts;" and Bailey, *Poet and Peasant*.

48. Linnemann, *The Parables of Jesus*; Eck, *The Parables of Jesus the Galilean*.

49. Bailey, *Poet and Peasant*; Linnemann, *The Parables of Jesus*.

50. Rohrbaugh "The Pre-Industrial City in Luke-Acts," 141.

In a conversation with Kenneth Ngwa, he asked if there might be a function of the slave/servant in Luke 14:16–24 worth exploring. Curious about his insightful question, I thought there was something revolutionary about the slave/servant relationship in this story. After he returned from inviting persons with different abilities and noticing that the host could have done better in filling up his table, the slave/servant said: "Sir, what you ordered has been done, but there is still room" (Luke 14:22 adapted). Conceivably, his words inspired the householder's command. "Go out into the roads and lanes, and compel people to come in, so that my house may be filled" (Luke 14:22–23). I argue that the role of the slave/servant in advocating for more invitees corrects the householder's perception to further expand his vision.

It was not enough to just invite persons of different abilities within the city limits. The imperially created urban and rural binary must be subverted as no geographical space is immune to human basic needs for sustenance, and is often exacerbated by the elites' geographical control of the economy. Clearly, slave/servant in Luke's imaginaire sympathizes with the "have-nots" of both spaces—urban and rural (those outside the "walled city"). As if to say, snubbing divine debt codes gave rise to exclusive elitist conviviality and patronage—bad and terrifying news to non-elites, poor, peasants, and the differently able.

The most valued invitees in Luke 14:16–24 may have been adhering to "performances of belonging" which, according to John Kloppenborg, are "segregative commensality" which "serve to reinforce the 'We' by rejecting the 'not We'—strangers, rivals, enemies."[51] In comparison, Paul performed belonging by excluding church members (1 Cor 5:11) but was silent about the ordering of meal-sharing space in 1 Cor 11:23–26. But, by Luke's time, sitting during meals became a contested issue as Kloppenborg argues citing Luke 14:7–14 and Jas 2:1–13.[52] To Kloppenborg's "not We," I would add the poor and persons with different abilities. Luke denounced his community members for engaging in greedy and egotistic pursuits of wealth (Luke 12:13–15; 16:14–15), promoting clientelism (Luke 6:32–34), and contemptuously gazing at the poor/destitute (Luke 18:9), instead of generously practicing *Enough to Go Around* (Luke 6:20–49). True discipleship means relinquishing the pursuit of wealth (Luke 14:33).

---

51. Kloppenborg, *Christ's Associations*, 147.

52. Kloppenborg, *Christ's Associations*, 151, 239.

Seen from this perspective, Luke's inclusive banquet (Luke 14:21, 23) echoes Deutero-Isaiah's prophetic justice and *Mother Wisdom's* (Prov 9)[53] persistent creative sustenance,[54] which is consistent with Jesus' life restoring and sustaining ministry to the oppressed and marginalized in the context of Imperial Rome. The poor have enough to eat and drink (John 2:9; 4:14; 6:9, 12, Pss 22:26) in the creation God sustains. And, just as the exilic community members were invited to the divine banquet, irrespective of social rank or status, so was Luke's audience. Other than being hungry and thirsty, attendants do not need silver (*kesef*)[55] to buy water or food or reciprocate, that is "everyone who thirsts, come to the waters; and you that have no silver [*kesef*], come, buy and eat! Come, buy wine and milk without silver and without price" (Isa 55:1–2; cf. 25:6). Jesus' reassuring of John the Baptist that "the blind receive their sight, the lame walk, the lepers are cleansed, the deaf hear, the dead are raised, the poor have good news brought to them" (Luke 7:22) was quintessential.

Conceivably, that "the poor have good news brought to them" includes Jesus' feeding stories—four thousand and five thousand.[56] Luke's Jesus also revaluates the commensality of some priests at Qumran that would have excluded invitees whom the householder of Luke 14:21–23 ended up inviting.

> . . . of fifties and of tens, and the levites, (each one) in the mid[st of his divi]sion of service. These are the famous men, those summoned to the assembly, those gathered for the community council in Israel under the authority of the sons of Zadok, the priests. No man, defiled by any of the impurities of a man, shall enter the assembly of these; and everyone who is defiled by them should not be established in his office amongst

53. Perdue, *Wisdom and Creation*, 94–100.

54. . . . "the LORD of hosts will make for all peoples a feast of rich food, a feast of well-aged wines, of rich food filled with marrow, of well-aged wines strained clear (Isa 25:6 NRSV) . . . everyone who thirsts, come to the waters; and you that have no money [silver], come, buy and eat! Come, buy wine and milk without money [silver] and without price. . ." (Isa 55:1–2 NRSV with minor correction from money to silver).
". . . Wisdom has built her house. . . hewn her seven pillars. . . slaughtered her animals. . . mixed her wine. . . set her table. . . sent out her servant-girls, she calls from the highest places in the town, 'You that are simple, turn in here!' To those without sense she says, 'Come, eat of my bread and drink of the wine I have mixed" (Prov 9:1–5 NRSV).

55. Alter, *The Hebrew Bible Volume 2*, 806–7.

56. Five thousand mixed group of people fed in Mark 6:32–44; Matt 14:13–21; Luke; 9:1–17; John 6:1–15 and four thousand people fed in Mark 8:11–13; Matt 15:32–39.

> the congregation. And everyone who is defiled in his flesh, paralysed in his feet or in his hands, lame, blind, deaf, dumb or defiled in his flesh with a blemish visible to the eyes, or the tottering old man who cannot keep upright in the midst of the assembly, these shall not enter to take their place among the congregation of famous men, for the angels of holiness are among their congre[gation.] (1QSa 2.4–7)[57]

Greco-Roman physiognomics also would have excluded the householder's group of "differently able" invitees on the basis of their reading of the human physical appearance, since bodies would have been read (as one reads texts), taxonomized (Ps-Aristotle, *Physiognomics*, I.805–VI.814), objectified, and ridiculed. For example, Ps-Aristotle states that persons with "fleshy and ill-jointed ankles are weak (μαλακός)[58] in character" (Ps-Aristotle, *Phys.* 810a); in contrast, he writes "the lion manifestly exhibits the male type in its most perfect form. . ." (Ps-Aristotle, *Phy.* 809b.14b-35). The appearance of the lion translates into its fearless and powerful character and thereby became the ideal body portraiture emperors craved to have their images modeled after. On persons with back curvatures and stooping, Adamantius the Sophist opines, "a broad, solid back makes a man noble and spirited, while the opposite means the opposite" (B 11) and "A stooping man is not good, unless he also has suppleness of limb and the other signs are elegant" (B 12).[59] Robert Garland observes that, "By their own imperious reckoning, the Greeks and the Romans stood head and shoulders, culturally speaking, above all other races on earth in part because they alone exemplified the ideal human type . . . In short, ethnic deformity exemplified the critical difference between the Graeco-Roman Self and the other."[60]

Luke's Greco-Roman audience was not impervious to these negative judgments. Mikeal Parsons has convincingly argued that,

> Luke at times employs physiognomic categories in his literary presentation of certain characters, usually for the purpose of subverting them . . . For Luke this is a radically inclusive community, comprised not only of sinners and social outcasts but also of the physically disabled and the disfigured who, on the

57. Martínez, *The Dead Sea Scrolls Translated*, 127; Vermes, *The Complete Dead Sea Scrolls in English*, 161; Fitzmyer, *Luke X–XXIV*, 1057.

58. For the semantic field of the word "weak," see *LSJM*, "μαλακός," 1076.

59. B 11 and B 12 are cited in Swain, *Seeing the Face*, 523.

60. Garland, *The Eye of the Beholder*, viii.

basis of the appearance of their physical body, have been ostracized as misfits from the body politic (or religious).[61]

Building on Parsons' thesis, I argue that Luke subverts physiognomics to include the marginalized and "differently able." They are "God's able-bodies" who embody God's vision for humanity. To Jesus, the reign of God calls for radical inclusion. My focus is on the model Jesus offers for people of faith to emulate—meeting the needs of the destitute and persons with all kinds of ability by including and sharing meals and other provisions.

I began by arguing that *Enough to Go Around* was central to God's work of liberative justice. God hears and identifies with the suffering or oppressed—those inflicted with the brutalism of what Ngwa calls the ideology of "erasure, alienation, and singularity."[62] Feeding stories of the liberated (Exod 15:22–25; 16:4–5; 17:1–6) and the divine command for Israel to ensure there is enough for everyone (Deut 15:4, 11), especially the poor, are meant for Israel and the followers of Jesus to emulate.

As Leslie J. Hoppe observes, some rabbis believed in the permanence of poverty based on Deut 15:11, but that the messianic age would upend servitude to foreign powers. That perennial poverty should engender practical generosity to the poor and the divine injunction "there will be no poor in the land" (Deut 15:4) meant that "it was in people's power to eliminate poverty from the land."[63] Strack's and Billerbeck's comments on rabbinic midrashim on Luke 14:13 insightfully compares the hospitality of Abraham and Job to the people in need. Job is said to have had a four-door household intentionally open to the poor people who after they had eaten and drank to their fill share their experience with whomever they would encounter on their way out. In contrast, Abraham surpasses Job[64] for he does not sit and wait for the needy to come. He seeks them out, invites travelers he might encounter, leads them to his house, feeds, and gives them a drink. He built palaces and

61. Parsons, *Body and Character in Luke and Acts*, 14. See also Hartsock, *Sight and Blindness in Luke-Acts*.

62. Ngwa, *Let My People Live*, 7. For more insights see 2–34.

63. Hoppe, *There Shall Be No Poor*, 166.

64. Strack and Billerbeck, *A Commentary*, 241. See 241–43 for a detailed midrash on Job 31:17, 20. For translations of 1QSa 2:4–7, see Martinez, *The Dead Sea Scrolls*, 127; and Vermes, *The Complete Dead Sea Scrolls*, 127. See the critical study editions of 1QSa 2:4–7 in Martinez, *The Dead Sea Scrolls: Study*, 125–26.

highways leading to each where he stored food and drinks, for people to help themselves and "thank God."[65]

Eating with All People

Many religious leaders exhort their community members to meet the needs of the poor and persons with different abilities. Having transposed myself into the Lukan *Sitz im Leben*, I found his vision for communal meal-sharing to be analogous to many people of faith in African Traditional beliefs, Christianity, and Islam in Senegal. For example, Aline Sitoé Diatta was a Diola prophetess born around 1920s in the Her/Haer Diola subgroup in Kabrousse, a southern district of the Casamance region of Senegal, West Africa bordering the country of Guinee Bissau, who confronted French colonial exploitation of her people. She contracted an illness that left her limping—a condition thought to have resulted from her many attempts to avoid *Émitai's* (Diola supreme deity—*Émitai* or *Émit*) calls. She finally responded to the commission from *Emitai* to liberate her people, in 1941. In this study, I focus only on her liberative ministry centered on the exercise of charity and hospitality.

Sent by *Emitai*, Aline Sitoé Diatta refuted French colonel Sajous' accusation of being a political insurrectionist against French imperial interests saying: "God, who appeared to me many times, sent me. I am just transmitting the orders he dictated to me."[66] There were many reported dimensions of her crucial ministry, such as rainmaking and healing rituals which she performed with convincing results. However, I emphasize here her communitarian ethic built on mutualism, egalitarian lived experience communing with people of all ages and from all walks of life—wealthy, poor, rich, male and female, and I would add, persons with different abilities, like herself. Aline Sitoé Diatta decries proselytism and performs rituals that engender *une organisation socio-*économique *nouvelle* ("a new socio-economic organization")[67]—an alternative religious and socioeconomic organization she deployed against French colonial exploitation. The practice of universal human equality, hospitality,

65. Strack and Billerbeck, *A Commentary*, 241. Though pp. 241–43 cite Gen 21:33, I argue that Gen 18:1–8 embeds some actionable ideas on Abraham's radical hospitality to strangers.

66. Girard, *Genèse*, 240. His use of the male pronoun "he" is foreign to Diola ungendered references to their supreme deity, Emitai.

67. Thomas, "Les rois," 163.

"fraternity, love, and peace"[68] is fundamental to the ministry of Aline Sitoé Diatta. As Thomas observes:

> The cult gathers into a fellowship, almost a church, the totality of adherents to the truth of Alinsitüé, whatever their ethnic origins and their other religious practices, a kind of initiation on a human scale that takes on the appearance of a mystery open to all people of goodwill, regrouping them into a unitary movement focused on the Good. The latter responding to the economic aspirations of the era: meeting food needs through agriculture; the key to it remains the rain, dispensed by Alinsitüé, on behalf of Ata Émit (God), to help suffering humanity.[69]

Clearly, her ministry sided with the poor and people with all kinds of needs. She instructs her community members with songs/poems to withstand French imperial oppression and practice of meal sharing. They are to cook meals for the strangers God is sending to the inclusive community of persons she is creating.[70] Divine agency empowers her prophetic songs (poems).[71] Similar to Jesus' teaching, Aline Sitoé Diatta teaches her followers with aphorisms. The sound of her songs is moved by the force/wind/spirit of *Emitay/Emit*[72] to inspire strangers. They are performative songs that create reality and inspire people to join the hospitality lavished on the would-be-new members of her community. The meals prepared for strangers echo Abraham's radical hospitality (Gen 18:1–8).

For Aline Sitoé Diatta, sharing meals with strangers was a model for new adherents to emulate clearly expressed in the following imperative: "take a cooking pot and prepare a meal for the strangers . . . cook the food for strangers." Loving the neighbor, mutual help, solidarity, and the exercise of charity translates into mutualism in meal sharing and welcoming strangers.[73] To me, her meal-sharing praxis with people, especially

68. Thomas, "Les rois," 165.

69. Thomas, "Les rois," 165.

70. Girard, *Genèse*, 348–49, 347–56, who first recorded many of the known poems/songs of of Aline Sitoé Diatta.

71. Girard, *Genèse*, 348–49.

72. The word "wind" implicitly bespeaks of Diola belief that it comes from *Emitai/Emit* and has power to create reality, shape creation, and inspire humans. There is life in God's wind. This belief is analogous to the Genesis myth of creation where רוּחַ אֱלֹהַּ [MT]/πνεῦμα θεοῦ [LXX] (Gen 1:2) was hovering or better (רָחַף/ἐπιφέρω) brooding/incubating life.

73. Darbon, "La Voix de la Casamanace," 131–2; Diédhiou, *L'identité Jóola en Question*, 280.

marginalized persons, is analogous to the conviviality Jesus proclaimed in Luke 14:1–24, which Paul (1 Cor 11:23–26) and the earliest followers of Jesus practiced (cf. Acts 2:42–47; 4:32–37; Pliny the Younger's Letter to Trajan—*Epistulae* X. 96). To me, Jesus, Paul, the earliest followers of Jesus, and Aline Sitoé Diatta were subverting *scarcity* with the intentional praxis of *Enough to Go Around* at God's Table.

Most Senegalese Muslims and Christians also encourage solidarity with the poor. Sufi Muslims practice *zakat*, the third pillar of Islam, that prescribes a fixed portion of one's income to palliate poverty caused by unequal distribution of wealth—a pillar hermeneutically innovated to address not just poverty but the needs of qur'anic students, the sick, and persons with all forms of disability.[74] Similarly, Senghorian *Négritude* sees scriptural and spiritual relevance in the praxis of Senegalese socialism.[75] Quoting Luke's rendition of Isaiah in Luke 4:18–19, Senegal's first president Léopold Sédar Senghor, writes of Christian ethics: "Jesus was a revolutionary. In his sermons, he protested against Roman ethics—that of the colonizers—and against the ancient law of Israel. Born poor, he took a sympathetic interest in the fate of the poor and oppressed of all races and religions."[76] Building on the multivalence of his *Négritude*, he sees what I call the same *divine–human ethic* in Islam, and referencing the Qur'an (4:36), Senghor observes further that:

> Mohammed, who appears on the scene to confirm the teaching of the Bible and Jesus . . . writes: "serve Allah. Ascribe no thing as partner unto Him. Show kindness unto parents, and unto near kindred, and orphans, and the needy, and unto the neighbour who is of kin unto you and the neighbor who is not of kin, and the fellow-traveller and the wayfarer and the slaves whom your right hands possess. . .."[77]

74. Tamba, *Histoire et sociologie*, 326–27. Abuses of noble acts of solidarity with the poor, according to Tamba, led some "marabout-teachers" to encourage mendicancy upholding it as the only venue for their students to learn the Qur'an cultivates humility, spiritual knowledge, self-control, lucidity, and resilience toward hunger and thirst. Citing Sheikh Hamidou Kane, he adds "as long as the student (disciple) seeks God, he can only live by begging."

75. Senghor, "What Is Negritude?" 54–55, defines Negritude as an encompassing "whole complex of civilized values—cultural, economic, social and political which characterize the black peoples, or, more precisely, the negro-African World."

76. Senghor, *On African Socialism*, 162.

77. Senghor, *On African Socialism*, 162

To Senghor, Jesus (Jews) and Mohammad (Arabs) worked to transform the human nature of their respective followers into new persons[78] (an echo of Paul's καινὴ κτίσις "new creations" in 2 Cor 5:17; Gal 6:15 who practice the art of *Looking Around* (implied in Luke 14:7) and exercising *Enough to Go Around.*

Practices of solidarity as demonstrated in African conviviality reflected among Senegalese people, is a pre-transatlantic slave trade and pre- and post-colonial temperament rooted in traditional African beliefs—a lived experience that does not succumb to individualism. African socialism is the function of African ontology, fostering not only solidarity but also hospitality, beyond family relationships, to all persons in obedience to ancestors. Seen from this perspective, African traditional beliefs such as hospitality, to Senghor, shun egotism and greed and instead foster the idea that *humanity is its own antidote* to suffering and destruction. *Solidarity* and *hospitality*, as African virtuous temperaments, are fundamental virtues that shaped Senghor's vision civilization of the universal.[79] My point is that Senegalese Christians, Muslims, and those who practice African indigenous spiritual beliefs all strive to alleviate poverty and destitution of all forms, thus adhering to Jesus' exhortation to exercise an "other-centered" praxis. Théodore NDok Ndiaye cites the words of Pope John Paul II delivered at the diocese of Thiés, Senegal, in 1992 on being a Christian witness:

> Ce règne qui doit affranchir la création de l'esclavage, de la pauvreté et de la misère fait de nous des comptables: nous aurons à rendre compte de notre être dans la société, de notre comportement quotidien face à nos concitoyens et nos frères ou sœurs que nous côtoyons tous les jours. Le chapitre 25 de Mathieu devrait convaincre tout chrétien de son rôle et sa vocation clans la nation, la ville, le quartier et son milieu de vie. Il est dramatiquement et quotidiennement interpelle face à ceux qui ont faim, soif, qui sont nus, malades, prisonniers étrangers, dans leur corps, leur esprit et leur cœur.[80]

> [This reign that must free creation from slavery, poverty and misery makes us accountable: we will have to account for our being in society, for our daily behavior in front of our fellow

---

78. Due to the language of the time, Senghor's rendition is captured by Cook's translation as "birth of a new man" in *On African Socialism*, 163.

79. Senghor, *On African Socialism*, 62–165.

80. Ndiaye, *Qu'el Sénégal pour demain?*, 138.

> citizens and our brothers or sisters we encounter every day.
> Chapter 25 of Matthew should convince every Christian of his
> role and his vocation in the nation, the city, the neighborhood
> and his living environment. He is dramatically and daily chal-
> lenged in the face of those who are hungry, thirsty, naked, sick,
> foreign prisoners, in body, mind, and heart].

Aline Sitoé Diatta's ministry, as I discussed earlier, was built on extant Diola communalism that predated the French colonization of West Africa. My point is that Diola traditional beliefs have long inspired and shaped divine-human-nature relationships since time immemorial, but were later disrupted by the transatlantic slave trade and colonization.[81]

Luke 14:16–24 embeds more than a "wait-and-see" eschatology or messianic banquet as many commentators maintain, at the expense of the present needs of persons impoverished by Roman exploitation, as I discussed above. Jesus' revaluation of sharing meals with the poor and differently able persons is quintessential for Luke. Seen from this angle, West's *Reading with the Poor*, does not preclude *eating with* given the fact that Jesus tells the parable to teach lessons about the nature of com-mensality that his disciples, and other followers, ought to practice. An eschatological or a Messianic meal, indifferent to human needs in this age, is useless to Jesus' hearers.

As an African transposing myself into the Lukan *Sitz im Leben*, I am struck by his vision for community and identity construction. The house-holder is one of those wealthy individuals who can afford banquets and would likely host his peers, a predilection to the kind of "reciprocity" Luke challenges.[82] To his surprise, each of the first three invited guests refused to honor his invitation, using their respective pursuit of wealth as legitimate excuses.[83] For Luke, friendship should not be limited to wealthy insiders. It must be extended to the poor—insiders and outsiders alike.[84]

Luke is concerned with the indifferent behavior of his wealthy community members. Since the social outcasts cannot maintain the rec-iprocity expected in the Greco-Roman world, as Willi Braun observes, Luke has them dine with the householder "to overcome the affective dis-tance between urban outsiders . . . and élite insiders, to which group the

81. Niang, *A Poetics of Postcolonial Biblical Criticism.*

82. Moxnes, *The Economy of the Kingdom*, 131, 129–33.

83. Braun, *Feasting and Social Rhetoric*, 80.

84. Moxnes, *The Economy of the Kingdom*, 133.

inviting host belongs."[85] That being the case, the Gospel of Luke not only has a predilection for the needy, it also addresses the appropriate use of wealth with regard to the needy. The οἰκοδεσπότης, ("householder") after being shamed by his peers for not honoring him, decides to re-define his previously held social values--a decision Braun rightly calls "conversion."[86] While the woes addressed to the wealthy suggest that reciprocity is being practiced in the community, the story of the great dinner shows that some rich Lukans have given up such a practice and become examples of the Good News.

Conclusion

Retelling the story of Jesus to community members who are heavily influenced by Greco-Roman thought, and Jewish debt and purity codes, Luke has Jesus revaluate conviviality that would have excluded most of his followers—the poor, peasants, tax collectors, differently able persons, and the so-called sinners. A performative subversion in words tempered by concrete deeds that manifest the impartial "Good News" of God's kinship empowers the ridiculed and those marginalized in society to become participatory community members—God's "abled bodies," and Abraham's children, according to God's promise (Gen 12:1–3; Luke 19:9; Gal 3:26–29). The poor, Luke argues, must not only have the "Good News" preached to them, they should also be treated appropriately, as invaluable children of God at the deity's table fellowships[87]—a concern Paul also addresses, much earlier, on the significance of Eucharistic meals at Corinth (1 Cor 11:18–21). The affluent should not only give the poor a share of their possessions, but also eat together with them, and extend non-reciprocal hospitality. Women who supported the teething ministry of Jesus (Luke 8:3), the householder (Luke 14:21), the Samaritan who offered to pay for the care of the traveler beaten on the road to Jericho (Luke 10:25–37), the shepherd who lost a sheep, the woman who lost her coin, the father with two sons (Luke 15), and Zacchaeus the tax collector (Luke 19:1–8) all (eventually) practiced *Enough to Go Around*.

Aline Sitoé Diatta, Senghorian *Négritude*, and most Senegalese Muslims and Christians believe God's vision for *Enough to Go Around* is

---

85. Braun, *Feasting and Social Rhetoric*, 96.

86. Braun, *Feasting and Social Rhetoric*, 97.

87. Osiek and Balch, *Families in the New Testament World*, 194–206.

a way of subverting the disproportionate distribution of wealth by alleviating poverty, in their respective communities. Eating with the poor, and persons with different abilities, should also include reading and reflecting on sacred texts and songs (e.g., the Bible, Senghorian poems/speeches, and Aline Sitoé Diatta's poems/songs). I suspect that West's *Reading with the Poor* does not preclude such inclusive commensalities—itself, a form of carrying the cross of Jesus Christ (Luke 14:21). Thus, in line with the Ujamaa Centers' CBS Bible Study model of "See–Judge–Act," seeing ["see" (ὁράω) Exod 3:4 LXX; Luke 10:33)], and observing ["observe" (ἐπέχω) (Luke 14:7)] should inspire liberative actions such as freeing, healing, teaching, feeding, and "eating with" the poor and marginalized. We should look around and practice *"Enough to Go Around"* hospitality in times like these and minister to all peoples.

Bibliography

Alter, Robert. *The Hebrew Bible,* Vol. 2: *Prophets Nevi' im: A Translation with Commentary.* New York: Norton, 2019.

Ascough, Richard S. "Social and Political Characteristics of Greco-Roman Association Meals." In *Meals in the Early Christian World: Social Formation, Experimentation, and Conflict at the Table,* edited by Dennis E. Smith and Hal Taussig, 59–72. New York: Palgrave, 2012.

Autero, Esa. *Reading the Bible across Contexts: Luke's Gospel, Socio-Economic Marginality and Latin American Biblical Hermeneutics.* BIS 145. Leiden: Brill 2016.

Bailey, Kenneth E. *Poet and Peasant, and Through Peasant Eyes: A Literary-Cultural Approach to the Parables in Luke.* Grand Rapids: Eerdmans, 1983.

Balch, David L. *Jesus, Paul, Luke-Acts, & 1 Clement: Studies in Class, Ethnicity, Gender, and Orientation.* Eugene, OR: Cascade Books, 2023.

Becker, Matthias. "Plutrach's Septem sapientium convivium: An Example of Greco-Roman Synoptic Literature." In *T. & T. Clark Handbook to Early Christian Meals in the Greco-Roman World,* edited by Soham Al-Suadi and Peter-Ben Smit, 31–43. New York: T. & T. Clark, 2019.

Behm, J. "δεῖπνον." In *Theological Dictionary of the New Testament.* Abridged Edition. Edited by Gerhard Kittel and Gerhard Friedrich. Translated by Geoffrey W. Bromiley. Grand Rapids: Eerdmans, 1985.

Belo, Fernando. *A Materialist Reading of the Gospel of Mark.* Translated by Matthew J. O'Connell. Maryknoll, NY: Orbis, 1981.

Braun, Willi. *Feasting and Social Rhetoric in Luke 14.* Society for New Testament Studies Monograph Series 85. Cambridge: Cambridge University Press, 1995.

Cadbury, Henry J. *The Making of Luke–Acts.* New York: Macmillan, 1927.

Carter, Warren. *Household and Discipleship: A Study of Matthew 19–20.* JSNTSup 103. Sheffield: Sheffield Academic, 1994.

———. *Jesus and the Empire of God: Reading the Gospels in the Roman Empire.* Cascade Companions. Eugene, OR: Cascade Books, 2022.

Claassens, L. Juliana. "Memories of Midwives." *JBL* 134 (2015) 877–81.

Coenen, L. "πένης." In *The New International Dictionary of the New Testament Theology.* Vol. 2. Edited by Colin Brown. Grand Rapids: Zondervan, 1967.

Darbon, Dominique. "'La Voix de la Casamance' une parole diola." *Documents* 14 Janvier 1985.

Degenhardt, Jans-Joachim. *Evangelist-der Armen: Besitz und Besitzverzicht in den Luanischen Schriften.* Stuttgart: Katholisches Bibelwerk, 1965.

Diédhiou, Paul. *L'Identité Jóola en question (Casamance).* Paris: Karthala, 2011.

Dube, Musa W. "*A Luta Continua:* Toward Trickster Intellectuals and Communities." *JBL* 134 (2015) 890–902.

Eck, Ernest van. *The Parables of Jesus the Galilean: Stories of a Social Prophet.* Matrix: The Bible in Mediterranean Context 9. Eugene, OR: Cascade Books, 2016.

Evans, Nancy A. "Evidence for Slaves at the Table in the Ancient Mediterranean: From Traditional Rural Festivals to Urban Associations." In *Meals in the Early Christian World: Social Formation, Experimentation, and Conflict at the Table,* edited by Dennis E. Smith and Hal Taussig, 149–64. New York: Palgrave, 2012.

Fitzmyer, Joseph A. *The Gospel according to Luke (X–XXIV): Introduction, Translation, and Notes.* Anchor Bible. New York: Doubleday, 1992.

Gadamer, Hans-Georg. *Truth and Method.* Translated by Joel Weinsheimer and Donald G. Marshall. 2nd ed. New York: Continuum, 1994.

Garland, Robert. *The Eye of the Beholder: Deformity & Disability in the Graeco-Roman World.* Ithaca: Cornell University Press, 1995.

Girard, Jean. *Genèse du pouvoir charismatique en basse Casamance (Sénégal).* Dakar, Senegal: IFAN, 1969.

Green, Joel B. *The Theology of the Gospel of Luke.* New Testament Theology. Cambridge: Cambridge University Press, 1995.

Hanson, K. C., and Douglas E. Oakman. *Palestine in the Time of Jesus: Social Structures and Social Conflicts.* 2nd ed. Minneapolis: Fortress, 2008.

Harland, Philip A. "Banqueting Values in the Associations: Rhetoric and Reality." In *Meals in the Early Christian World: Social Formation, Experimentation, and Conflict at the Table,* edited by Dennis E. Smith and Hal Taussig, 73–85. New York: Palgrave, 2012.

Hartsock, Chad. *Sight and Blindness in Luke–Acts: The Use of Physical Features in Characterization.* BIS 94. Leiden: Brill, 2008.

Hatch, Edwin, and Henry A. Redpath. *A Concordance to the Septuagint: And Other Greek Versions of the Old Testament (Including the Apocrypha).* Grand Rapids: Baker, 1897.

Hauck, Friedrich. "πένης, πενιχρός." In *Theological Dictionary of the New Testament.* Edited by Gerhard Kittel and Gerhard Friedrich. Translated by Geoffrey W. Bromiley. Grand Rapids: Eerdmans, 1968.

Herzog, William R., II. *Prophet and Teacher: An Introduction to the Historical Jesus.* Louisville: Westminster John Knox, 2005.

———. *Parables as Subversive Speech: Jesus as Pedagogue of the Oppressed.* Louisville: Westminster John Knox, 1994.

hooks, bell. *Yearning: Race, Gender and Cultural Politics.* Boston: South End, 1990.

https://www.merriam-webster.com/dictionary/enough%2Fplenty%20to%20go%20around.

Hoppe, Leslie J. *There Shall Be No Poor among You: Poverty in the Bible*. Nashville: Abingdon, 2004.

Jeremias, Joachim. *New Testament Theology: The Proclamation of Jesus*. Translated by John Bowden. New York: Scribner, 1971.

Johnson, Kristin. *Enough to Go Around: A Story of Generosity*. Minneapolis: Millbrook, 2018.

Johnson, Luke T. *The Literary Function of Possessions in Luke-Acts*. SBL Dissertation Series 39. Missoula, MT: Scholars, 1977.

———. *Sharing Possessions: Mandate and Symbol of Faith*. Overtures to Biblical Theology. Philadelphia: Fortress, 1981.

Karris, Robert J. "Missionary Communities: A New Paradigm for the Study of Luke-Acts." *CBQ* 41 (1979) 80–97.

———. "Poor and Rich: The Lukan Sitz im Leben." In *Perspective on Luke–Acts*. Edited by Charles H. Talbert. Edinburgh: T. & T. Clark, 1978.

Keizer, Garret. *Help: The Original Human Dilemma*. New York: HarperCollins, 2004.

Klinghardt, Matthias. "A Topology of the Communal Meal." In *Meals in the Early Christian World: Social Formation, Experimentation, and Conflict at the Table*. Edited by Dennis E. Smith and Hal Taussig, 9–22. New York: Palgrave, 2012.

Kloppenborg, John S. *Christ's Associations: Connecting and Belonging in the Ancient City*. New Haven: Yale University Press, 2019.

———. *Q Parallels: Synopsis, Critical Notes & Concordance*. Sonoma, CA: Polebridge, 1988.

Kohlenberger, John R. III, and James A. Swanson. *The Hebrew-English Concordance to the Old Testament: With the New International Version*. Grand Rapids: Zondervan, 1998.

Kohlenberger, John R. III, Edward W. Goodrick, and James A. Swanson. *The Exhaustive Concordance to the Greek New Testament*. Grand Rapids: Zondervan, 1995.

Liddell, H. G., and Robert Scott. "πένης." In *Greek–English Lexicon*. Oxford: Clarendon, 1996.

Lim, Chin Ming Stephen. *Contextual Biblical Hermeneutics as Multicentric Dialogue: Toward A Singaporean Reading of Daniel*. BIS 175. Leiden: Brill, 2019.

Linnemann, Eta. *Parables of Jesus: Introduction and Exposition*. Translated by John Sturdy. London: SPCK, 1966.

Marshall, I. Howard. *Commentary on Luke*. New International Greek Testament Commentary. Grand Rapids: Eerdmans, 1978.

Martinez, Florentino Garcia. *The Dead Sea Scrolls: Study Edition*. Edited by Eibert J. C. Tigchelaar. Leiden: Brill, 1999.

———. *The Dead Sea Scrolls Translated: The Qumran Texts in English*. 2nd ed. Translated by Wilfred G. E. Watson. Leiden: Brill, 1996.

Miller, Robert J., ed. *The Complete Gospels*. Sonoma, CA: Polebridge, 1992.

Moxnes, Halvor. *The Economy of the Kingdom: Social Conflict and Economic Relations in Luke's Gospel*. Overtures to Biblical Theology. 1988. Reprint, Eugene, OR: Wipf & Stock, 2005.

Myers, Ched. *The Biblical Vision of Sabbath Economics*. Washington, DC: Church of the Saviour, 2002.

Ndiaye, Théodore NDok. *Quel Sénégal pour demain? Une vision Chrétienne et Citoyenne*. Paris: L'Harmattan, 2012.

Ngwa, Kenneth. *Let My People Live: An Africana Reading of Exodus*. Louisville: Westminster John Knox, 2022.

———. "The Making of Gershom's Story: A Cameroonian Postwar Hermeneutics Reading of Exodus 2." *JBL* 134 (2015) 855–76.

Niang, Aliou Cissé. *A Poetics of Postcolonial Biblical Criticism: God, Human–Nature Relationship, and Negritude*. Eugene, OR: Cascade Books, 2019.

———. "Space and Human Agency in the Making of the Story of Gershom through a Senegalese Christian Lens." *JBL* 134 (2015) 882–89.

Nolland, John. *Luke 9:21—18:34*. Word Biblical Commentary 35B. Dallas: Word, 1993.

Oakman, Douglas E. *Jesus and the Peasants*. Matrix: The Bible in Mediterranean Context 4. Eugene, OR: Cascade Books, 2008.

———. *The Radical Jesus, the Bible, and the Great Transformation*. Matrix: The Bible in Mediterranean Context 12. Eugene, OR: Cascade Books, 2022.

Osiek, Carolyn, and David L. Balch. *Families in the New Testament World: Households and House Churches*. Louisville: Westminster John Knox, 1997.

O'Toole, Robert F. "Poverty and Wealth in Luke–Acts." *CS* 30 (1991) 30–31.

Parsons, Mikeal C. *Body and Character in Luke and Acts: The Subversion of Physiognomy in Early Christianity*. Grand Rapids: Baker Academic, 2006.

Perdue, Leo G. *Wisdom and Creation: The Theology of Wisdom Literature*. Nashville: Abingdon, 1994.

Poirier, Jean-Louis. *L'antiquté en détresse: Catastrophes et épidemies dans le monde Gréco-romain*. Paris: Les Belles Lettres, 2021.

Propp, William H. *Exodus 1–18: A New Translation. With Introduction and Commentary*. Anchor Bible 2. New York: Doubleday, 1999.

Rohrbaugh, Richard L. *The New Testament in Cross-Cultural Perspective*. Matrix: The Bible in Mediterranean Context 1. Eugene, OR: Cascade Books, 2006.

———. "The Pre-Industrial City in Luke-Acts: Urban Social Relations." In *The Social World of Luke-Acts: Models for Interpretation*, edited by Jerome H. Neyrey, 125–49. Peabody, MA: Hendrickson, 1991.

———. *The Biblical Interpreter: An Agrarian Bible in an Industrial Age*. 1978. Reprint, Eugene, OR: Wipf & Stock, 2018.

Schmidt, Thomas E. *Hospitality to Wealth in the Synoptic Gospels*. JSNTSup 15. Sheffield: Sheffield Academic, 1987.

Scott, Bernard Brandon. *Hear Then the Parable: A Commentary on the Parables of Jesus*. Minneapolis: Fortress, 1989.

Senghor, Léopold Sédar. *On African Socialism*. Translated by Mercer Cook. London: Pall Mall, 1964.

———. "What Is Negritude?" *Atlas* (1962) 54–55.

Smith-Christopher, Daniel. "Cross-Cultural Exegesis." *The Oxford Encyclopedia of Biblical Interpretation*, edited by Steven L. McKenzie, vol. 1, 138–50. New York: Oxford University Press, 2013.

Smith, Dennis E. *From Symposium to Eucharist: The Banquet in the Early Christian World*. Minneapolis: Fortress, 2003.

———. "The Greco-Roman Banquet as a Social Institution." In *Meals in The Early Christian World: Social Formation, Experimentation, and Conflict at the Table*, edited by Dennis E. Smith and Hal Taussig, 23–33. New York: Palgrave, 2012.

Snodgrass, Klyne R. *Stories with Intent: A Comprehensive Guide to the Parables of Jesus*. Grand Rapids: Eerdmans, 2008.

Sterling, Gregory E. *Historiography and Self-Definition: Josephus, Luke–Acts and Apologetic Historiography*. Novum Testamentum Supplements 64. Leiden: Brill, 1992.

Strack, Hermann L. and Paul Billerbeck. *A Commentary on the New Testament from the Talmud and Midrash*. Volume 2. Edited and Translated by Jacob N. Cerone. Bellingham, WA: Lexham, 2022.

Swain, Simon, ed. *Seeing the Face, Seeing the Soul: Polemon's Physiognomy from Classical Antiquity to Medieval Islam*. New York: Oxford University Press, 2007.

Tamba, Moustapha. *Histoire et sociologie des religions au Sénégal*. Paris: L' Harmattan, 2016.

Thomas, Louis-Vincent. "Les 'rois' Diola, hier, aujourd'hui, demain." *BIFAN* 34.1 (1972) 151–74.

Vermes, Geza. *The Complete Dead Sea Scrolls in English*. Rev. ed. New York: Penguin, 2004.

West, Gerald O., *The Academy of the Poor: Towards A Dialogical Reading of the Bible*. Interventions 2. Sheffield: Sheffield Academic, 1999.

———. *Contextual Bible Study*. KwaZulu Natal, SA: Cluster, 1993.

———, ed. *Reading Other-Wise: Socially Engaged Biblical Scholars Reading with Their Local Communities*. Semeia Studies 62. Atlanta: Society of Biblical Literature, 2007.

———. *The Stolen Bible: From Tool of Imperialism to African Icon*. BIS 144. Leiden: Brill, 2016.

———. "Twice Called, Thrice Rebuked: Doing African Biblical Scholarship." *JBL* 134 (2015) 850–54.

4

The Joy of Release in Deuteronomy 15:1–11

Reading the Bible with the Poor

Robert Wafawanaka

Introduction

THIS ESSAY SEEKS TO provide a contextual reading of the release (*shemittah*) law in Deut 15:1–11 from an African perspective of community values and the common good. It argues that while release laws may imply loss and ill-will for creditors, the goal was to foster community building, sharing of resources, and experiencing the joy of release when this law ultimately engendered goodwill and gratitude. Reading this text from the perspective of the poor and interpreting it from an African communal context facilitates our understanding of the intention of the *shemittah*. The benefit of reading this text with the poor is that it highlights their world-view and response to biblical texts on poverty and wealth. This contextual reading is also applicable to other similar biblical texts.

Wealth and Poverty in African Context

In traditional African culture, wealth and poverty are not only defined in individual material terms but in terms of communal values and principles. More than economic status, wealth relates to human flourishing, social cohesion, relationships, satisfaction in life, communal and spiritual values, or that which promotes the common good. Consequently, poverty is anything devoid of such values, or that which promotes individual rather than collective good. Someone with all material success is considered impoverished if they have no family, relationships, or community support. For the African poor, families are still "the main sources of support," as John Iliffe argued in the late 1980s.[1] Visitors to the poorest African villages are often surprised by the joy that permeates families everywhere because wealth is not defined only in material success but by communal values and relationships. In the same context, hospitality is one of the prized values, especially for strangers, because the intent is to make visitors feel welcome and part of the community. The poorest African will go out of their way to provide hospitality to a visitor or passing stranger. Some African theologians like the late John Mbiti highlight the strong kinship ties that bind Africans, in such a way that it would seem "everybody is related to everybody else."[2] Such strong relationships ensures that people regard one another as relatives who must be cared for by members of their community. Even the poor have the assurance that they can expect care and solidarity from their families and communities, due to the hospitable nature of African communities.

Hospitality in the African context means sharing with anyone within one's proximity. Even if resources were limited, people would always want to share what they have. This sharing can take place in families, villages, or tribes. Indeed, sharing with strangers is considered a great virtue. For example, the Shona people of Zimbabwe have a proverb *nzara ishuramweni* which translates as "hunger forecasts (the coming of) a stranger." According to Hamutyinei and Plangger, "It often happens that visitors turn up just at a time when the host is least prepared with provisions. But even so, the host will try his level best to satisfy his guest and the whole family."[3] People instinctively know that visitors are always afforded the best, even if the family might be poor.

---

1. See Iliffe, *African Poor*, 7.

2. Mbiti, *African Religions and Philosophy*, 102.

3. See Hamutyinei and Plangger, *Tsumo-Shumo*, 73. Growing up poor in Zimbabwe, we did not eat meat or delicacies everyday but only on special occasions such as holidays or whenever a visitor showed up. Even then, the family would eat after the guest has been served first.

Africans also have a very communal cultural heritage. A spirit of community is evident in their day-to-day relations where people often come together in good and bad times. Celebrations like weddings bring the whole village together, invited or uninvited. So also in times of sadness, people gather to comfort one another, to mourn the loss of a loved one, or simply, to lend a supportive hand. Before the pandemic of the twenty-first century that has required social distancing, the traditional African funeral was a communal event. Once it was known that someone had died, especially an important person, everything stopped and the whole village came together to mourn the deceased and comfort the bereaved family.

In short, African societies have strong cultural values which are deeply humanistic. These values enable people to confront any problem with confidence and the support of the community. People know they can support one another and confront any situation, be it disease, hunger, death, or poverty. Joy is experienced when the whole village shares together whatever life brings. Just as poverty is addressed at the communal level, so also is wealth. In the African context, the rich are expected to share their wealth with their extended families and the entire community. These values approximate the biblical vision of community in Deuteronomy 15. They also stem from the larger African religious worldview.

African Religious, Cultural, and Moral Value Systems

Mbiti, famously stated that "Africans are notoriously religious, and each people has its own religious system with a set of beliefs and practices. Religion permeates into all the departments of life so fully that it is not easy or possible always to isolate it."[4] Therefore, religion plays a central role in people's lives, their practices, and interpersonal relationships. Since religion is so pervasive, there is no distinction between the sacred and the secular, the spiritual and the mundane. Any distinctions people might make are artificial. Therefore, one cannot claim to be non-religious in the African context. For Mbiti, "Religion is the strongest element in traditional background, and exerts probably the greatest influence upon the thinking and living of the people concerned."[5]

---

4. Mbiti, *African Religions and Philosophy*, 1. For Dopamu, Africans are "incurably religious," and "from the womb to the grave, religion governs everything." See *Readings in African Traditional Religion*, 23.

5. Mbiti, *African Religions and Philosophy*, 1.

Traditional African culture is also "communitarian" or "corporate" and socially constructed. There is generally a sense of the well-being of the group rather than the individual. As Mbiti attests, people exist communally, not individually.[6] Africans tend to seek the common good rather than that of the individual. Families are closely knit, and one does not exist as an individual, but as part of a group. Mbiti aptly states, "In traditional life, the individual does not and cannot exist alone except corporately. He owes his existence to other people, including those of past generations and his contemporaries. He is simply part of the whole."[7] Therefore, it makes sense that one suffers or rejoices corporately, for "whatever happens to the individual happens to the whole group, and whatever happens to the whole group happens to the individual."[8] Like the ancient Israelites, Africans also believed in corporate responsibility.

Branching from the family unit, Africans always have kinship ties of some sort among themselves. Whole villages are related, in one way or another, such that society as a whole is built on strong kinship ties. According to Mbiti, "The deep sense of kinship, with all it implies, has been one of the strongest forces in African traditional life. Kinship is reckoned through blood and betrothal."[9] Kinship controls social relationships, binds people together, and even extends to cover animals, plants, and non-living objects through the totemic system. As stated before, kinship embraces everybody such that there is really no stranger among African communities.[10] When strangers meet, they first determine how they are related, and then behave toward each other accordingly. Because of this, one has literally hundreds of fathers, mothers, wives, and children.[11] The

---

6. Mbiti, *African Religions and Philosophy*, 204, 209–10; see also Mbiti, *Introduction to African Religion*, 174–79.

7. Mbiti, *African Religions and Philosophy*, 106.

8. Mbiti, *African Religions and Philosophy*, 106. Hence, one can only say, "I am because we are; and since we are, therefore I am," 106.

9. Mbiti, *African Religions and Philosophy*, 102.

10. Mbiti, *African Religions and Philosophy*, 102.

11. Mbiti, *African Religions and Philosophy*, 102. In Shona culture, family relationships are very close and may sound too complicated for Westerners. For example, all my brothers' children call me "father" (not uncle) and I call them my "children" (*vana*). My nephews and nieces are only the children of my sisters. My father's father did not permit my siblings and I to call him grandfather (*sekuru*). Instead, he demanded that we call him "*baba/bambo*" ("father/big father"). Our grandfather (*sekuru*) was only our mother's father. These relationships also extend to strangers or other people such that I would call any man or woman my parents' age father or mother, any man my age brother, any woman my sisters' ages sister, any man or woman my grandparents' age

totem is the visible symbol of unity, kinship, belonging, togetherness, and common affinity. A totem therefore acquires sacred status such that it may neither be harmed, killed, nor eaten.[12]

Hospitality is expressed in the value put on the other. Africans usually put the other first, and in many situations, the well-being of the other usually takes precedence over one's own. A person would go out of their own way to ensure that the other person has been taken care of first. African tradition dictated that strangers and the poor should be well cared for, even if one was poor himself or herself.[13] In Nigeria, Bolaji Idowu describes hospitality among the Yoruba in this way: "The Yoruba are by nature a hospitable race and are particularly hospitable to strangers . . . The Yoruba teach that one should be hospitable because it is right to be so, as also because one can never tell when one might be in need of hospitality oneself."[14]

From this brief survey, we can conclude that African societies have very strong social and cultural values. These are deeply oriented toward the well-being of the other, rather than the self. Such value systems enable people to confront many problems facing them with the confidence of communal support. People intuitively know that they can depend on each other and confront situations, be it disease, hunger, death, or poverty. These values will enable us to interpret biblical texts like the *shemittah* with a new vision, and from the perspective of the poor who reside within this African religio-cultural milieu.

Mbiti's research on African morality also increases our appreciation of communal values. African moral values have to do with the other person's welfare or livelihood. It is an ethic of the other, and Mbiti puts it succinctly:

> The essence of African morality is that it is more "societary"
> than "spiritual"; it is a morality of "conduct" rather than a

---

grandfather or grandmother, and any young person, *mwana* (child).

12. Mbiti, *African Religions and Philosophy*, 103. See also Radcliffe-Brown and Forde, *African Systems of Kinship*.

13. Mafico writes, "There were no inns or hotels in traditional Africa, but there were dangerous wild animals such as lions, hyenas and leopards. In search of food, or in search of work, strangers needed to find shelter at night. African traditional ethics required that one offered strangers some shelter and food." See Mafico, "The African Context," 75; Mafico, "Tradition, Faith," 41.

14. Idowu, *Olodumare*, 157. The argument that "one should be hospitable because it is right to be so" is what ethicists call a deontological argument. Such arguments are "absolutist" and "one cannot argue beyond them." For further discussion of this concept, see Gill, *Textbook of Christian Ethics*, 5–6, 157–60.

> morality of "being." This is what one might call "dynamic eth-
> ics" rather than "static ethics," for it defines what a person *does*
> rather than what he *is*. Conversely, a person is what he is be-
> cause of what he does, rather than that he does what he does
> because of what he is. Kindness is not a virtue unless someone
> is kind; murder is not evil until someone kills another person
> in his community. Man is not by nature either "good" or "bad"
> ("evil") except in terms of what he does or does not do.[15]

These ethical values have many dimensions all of which promote the existence of a more just, humane, and equitable social order. For example,
inherent in these cultural models are the values of generosity, selflessness,
community, equality, justice, and many others. A society built on these
principles is likely to be better, more just, and more equitable than one
devoid of these norms. In such a context, the poor are guaranteed to fare
much better than they would if they were left to struggle by themselves.

These perspectives of African religion, culture, and morality gives
us a viable lens to interpret biblical texts such as the *shemittah* year, because what this text calls for is exactly reflected in African value systems.
Reading this text with the poor easily resonates with their experiences
and cultural values. As West has demonstrated in his numerous writings, reading with the poor has its potential benefits for both the trained
professional and ordinary readers. Both groups of readers draw from
their "life contexts" to enrich biblical interpretation.[16] Both the African
context and the biblical context of the *shemittah* call for an ethic of car-
ing for the other and not the self. We will briefly examine one more
context, the larger ancient Near Eastern context of the Bible, where the
same altruistic values are also expressed.

15. Mbiti, *African Religions and Philosophy*, 209 [author's emphasis]. See also Mbiti, *Introduction to African Religion*, 174–79, and Uka, "Ethics of African Traditional Religion," 180–94.

16. See among many of Gerald West's writings: "1 and 2 Samuel," 92–104. Here, West shows many of the ways Samuel resonates with Southern African readers and interpreters, p. 94. See also West, "Reading the Bible Differently," 21–41. This entire issue is devoted to "Reading With" African Overtures; West, "Contextual Bible Study," 595–610; West, "Indigenous Biblical Hermeneutics," 85–96.

The Context of the *Shemittah:*
Ancient Near Eastern Antecedents

Ancient Near Eastern societies wrestled with the problem of poverty, debt, and social inequity about 5000 years ago.[17] Material evidence from ancient Mesopotamia suggests that debt obligation was an established tradition. Due to an agrarian economy, most debt involved agricultural products. Debt involved soft loans, typically given by royalty or wealthy citizens, to subjects for survival. Commercial loans were granted to merchants for travel and acquisition of goods. Graeber's research shows that monetary debts evolved later.[18]

Since many fell into debt, they had an obligation to pay it. The general evidence suggests that when debts were repaid, high-interest rates were charged. Michael Hudson argues that the origins of interest lie in the palaces and temples of ancient Mesopotamia.[19] Because of high interest rates, debtors were often unable to repay a loan, and as a result, they often sold themselves or a family member, into indentured servitude. For an economy based on extraction, debtors often lost their land and property or found themselves at the mercy of the creditor. The earliest evidence of a loan has been found in royal inscriptions from the city of Lagash in Southern Mesopotamia.[20]

To ameliorate the problem of debt and insolvency, ancient Near Eastern rulers often announced freedom proclamations or debt cancellation decrees, usually at accession to the throne or to curry favor with the subjects. These measures were intended to provide what scholars refer to as a "clean slate," whereby rulers restored equity and economic viability in the land. According to Paul Hanson, these measures were also "a means of winning the popular support necessary for a peaceful reign, and of maintaining social and economic stability in the land."[21] Mesopotamian Bronze Age clean slates seem to have influenced the biblical concept of Jubilee because these edicts "canceled debts, freed debt-servants and restored land to cultivators who had lost it under

17. See the comprehensive and definitive work of Graeber, *Debt.* See also Hudson, *Lost Tradition;* and Husdon and Van De Mieroop, *Debt and Economic Renewal.*

18. Graeber, *Debt,* 387.

19. See Hudson and Van De Mieroop, *Debt and Economic Renewal,* 10.

20. See Van De Mieroop, "History of Ancient Near Eastern Debt?," 62. In Mesopotamia, barley interest was about 33⅓% but it could be 50% for a defaulting debtor; silver interest was 20%, Van De Mieroop, *Debt and Economic Renewal,* 64, 79, 82, 84–85.

21. Hanson, "Ancient Near Eastern Roots," 13.

economic duress."[22] Such freedom proclamations were made by rulers as part of their attempt to maintain economic justice. Scholars however debate the benefits of these measures.

Material evidence from Sumerian texts (Enmetena, a ruler of Lagash—2404–2375 BCE) shows debt cancellation in the city of Lagash.[23] The prologue and epilogue of Hammurabi's Law Code also express concerns for justice and equity.[24] Ur-Nammu (2112–2004 BCE), the ruler of the Third Dynasty of Ur, proclaimed *misharum* as part of a long-established tradition. Hudson believes "the Israelites likewise seem to have picked up the Clean Slate idea from Babylonia."[25] He argues, "If rulers had not proclaimed clean slates, creditors would have reduced debtors to bondage and taken their lands irreversibly. In canceling . . . crop debts, rulers acknowledged that the palace had taken all that it could."[26]

Evidently, justice was at the core of Mesopotamian legal documents, though these measures seem to have vanished over time. As Hudson explains, they waned when wealth-seeking individuals replaced kings who normally restored order.[27] Moreover, the parts of the Hebrew Bible that deal with debt cancelation and release issues are the most documented in ancient Near Eastern literature.[28] The African and ancient Near Eastern perspectives concerning the social order provide us with viable contexts to interpret the *shemittah* law in Deut 15:1–11 from the perspective of the poor and marginalized for whom these measures were intended. These contexts demonstrate the provision of social safety measures designed to care for the poor and other underprivileged members of society. While some scholars doubt the effectiveness or intention of these measures in the ancient Near East; however, the ethos behind them is laudable.[29] Reading Deuteronomy 15 with the poor can

22. Hudson, *Lost Tradition*, 6.

23. Hudson, *Lost Tradition*, 15.

24. Pritchard, *Ancient Near Eastern Texts*, 164, 178. (Henceforth *ANET*).

25. Hudson, *Lost Tradition*, 29. He notes that the Hebrew word *deror* is cognate to Assyrian *andurarum* rather than to Babylonian *misharum*.

26. Hudson, "Reconstructing the Origins," 37.

27. Hudson, *Lost Tradition*, 11.

28. Hudson, *Lost Tradition*, 13.

29. Harold V. Bennett argues that such measures were legalized injustice that worsened the condition of the poor because they primarily benefitted the rich and powerful kings who proclaimed them. See Bennett, *Injustice Made Legal*.

assure them that they will not be abandoned or neglected because there is a safety net designed to care for their needs.

The Year of Release: Deuteronomy 15 and Release Laws

Deuteronomy 15 is part of the Deuteronomic Code (Deut 12–26) and, unlike the Covenant Code in Exodus (Exod 20:22—23:33) and the Holiness Code in Leviticus (Lev 17–26), it has a humanitarian attitude toward the poor and needy. According to Jeffries, though Deut 15 "holds out the ideal of a land without poverty (Deut 15:4), [it] recognizes that it is the ongoing existence of the poor which causes the law to be given."[30]

Deuteronomy 15:4 states that there shall be no poor people among the Israelites. If Israel obeys the Torah, then the poor would not exist because community members would care for the needy. The perspective of African culture and ancient Near Eastern values can relate to the idea of a land without poverty given the close cultural and community bonds and the centrality of hospitality that uplift the welfare of the other.

Deuteronomy 15 also discusses the poor in the context of the year of release.[31] This release is viewed as a remission of debts every seventh year.[32] It seems a release or cancellation is intended because of the parallel release from slavery in Deut 15:12–18. It is significant that both texts call for a release—either from debt obligation or slavery.

The *shemittah* law attaches blessings for obeying the command to care for the poor (Deut 15:1–6). In other words, the release of the debtor leads to the joy of divine blessings. Should there be any poor people among them, Israel is to give ungrudgingly and liberally in order to continue receiving God's blessings (Deut 15:7–10). This concept appeals to the African idea of hospitality. People often experience joy when they know that they have satisfied the needs of others. Reading this text with the poor ushers them into a very familiar environment. They know that they can depend on the care and generosity of the community. The

---

30. Hamilton, *Social Justice*, 3.

31. The Deuteronomic Code refers to the poor as either the *'ebyon* or *'ani* and most of the occurrences are in chapter 15. The word *dal* is not used at all in this Code. See also Wafawanaka, *Am I Still My Brother's Keeper?*, 50–58.

32. Some scholars have argued that the *shemiṭṭah* presupposes the Fallow or Sabbatical Year of Exodus 23:10–11 and the Sabbatical Year of Lev 25:1–7. See Wright, *God's People in God's Land,* 143–51; Hoppe, "Deuteronomy and the Poor," 371–75, esp. 372; and Miller, *Deuteronomy,* 134–35.

poor are also encouraged to give because they know that they will receive something in return. The Shona have a proverb that says *"kandiro kanopfumba kunobva kamwe"* (one good turn deserves another). This proverb expresses the reciprocal relationship that exists among people, whether rich or poor. In the *shemittah* law, we can imagine the joy of release on the part of the poor debtor. In fact, the poor continue to receive interest-free loans even as the *shemittah* year approaches (e.g.). Such loans are virtual gifts since they will soon be canceled. The text commands the hearer not to be tight-fisted but to extend one's hand to the needy. According to Deanna Thompson, this is "a radical vision" that challenges our economic practices.[33] She further states that, "If the need exists now, the time to give is now." That is, "give to anyone in need, for any reason."[34]

When the African poor read or hear this text, there is nothing radical about its vision. Just as religion is a way of life among Africans, giving to the needy is already a way of life. Such readers do not need to be commanded to give to the needy because they already do so on a daily basis. The recipients also expect to receive even if they might not be able to reciprocate in kind. The culture determines that the other's physical and material needs be satisfied first before economic benefit accrues to the individual.

Deuteronomy 15:11, often misunderstood because it is not read in context, states that since the poor will never cease from the land, Israel is to give generously to the poor in its midst. The poor exist in the land *because* Israel has disobeyed its divine mandate.[35] Cited in the New Testament (Matt 26:11; Mark 14:7; John 12:8), v. 11 is often understood to mean that "the poor will always be there." Instead, however, this verse explains *why* the poor are always there contrary to the law. As Patrick D. Miller argues, this is "exactly the opposite of what this text says."[36] Read in its proper context, Deut 15:11 urges community members to care for those in need. In addition to calling for benevolence toward the poor, Deuteronomy also calls for a regular cancellation of debt to ensure

33. Thompson, *Deuteronomy*, 125.

34. Thompson, *Deuteronomy*, 127.

35. See Wafawanaka, *Am I Still My Brother's Keeper?*, 3–21. See also Work, *Deuteronomy*, 159.

36. Miller, *Deuteronomy*, 137. He translates v. 11a thus: "For the poor will never cease *off the earth*" (137; Miller's emphasis). This verse makes sense when read fully, in context, and in conjunction with v. 4. See also Sugirtharajah, "'For You Always Have the Poor,'" 102–7; and Davies, "Poor You Have with You Always," 37–48.

equity.[37] These ideas are in line with ancient Near Eastern concepts and African values. Reading this text with the poor confirms that people should do as the Africans do—take care of your poor relatives because it is expected. There is no need to mandate it because it is a way of life.

Scholars have interpreted the "release" as either suspension or cancellation of the debts of the poor.[38] In light of the slave release law of Deut 15:12–18, whose structure is similar to that of Deut 15:1–11, and the language of the text, I agree with most scholars that a full release or cancellation is meant here.[39] The poor exist when the law is broken and a release is denied.[40] This text "commands generosity, regardless of the borrower's motives."[41] Read from the perspective of the poor, the primary motive for giving is to address immediate needs. Since "everybody is related to everybody else" in African culture, the poor can identify with this text because anyone they meet is a "relative" who is culturally bound to address their needs.

The book of Deuteronomy also deals with the subject of loans, pledges, and the wages of the poor (Deut 24:10–13; Exod 22:25–27; c.f., Lev 25:35–36). Loans are to be interest-free (Exod 22:26–27; Deut 23:19; Lev 25:35–38) and wages must be paid daily. This injunction resonates with African readers because in traditional culture, if a loan was given, it was to be returned without interest, whenever the borrower could afford to return it, if at all. There was no interest or late fees that further exacerbated the condition of the poor in the modern world. In the biblical context, a pledge garment taken as collateral for a loan must be returned before nightfall (Exod 22:26–27; Amos 2:8; Prov 20:16; 27:13; Job 22:6) since it is that person's only source of warmth. Creditors are forbidden

37. Hoppe, "Deuteronomy and the Poor," 372; Hoppe, *Being Poor*, 17.

38. The scholars who favor a suspension include Wright, *God's People in God's Land*, 148; Driver, *Critical and Exegetical Commentary*, 179; and North, *Sociology of the Biblical Jubilee*, 186. Those who favor a full release or cancellation are: Miller, *Deuteronomy*, 135; Gnuse, *You Shall Not Steal*, 34; Patrick, *Old Testament Law*, 112; and Hoppe, *Being Poor*, 17.

39. See also Hamilton, "*Ha'arets* in the Shemiṭṭâ Law," 214–22; Hamilton, *Social Justice and Deuteronomy*.

40. According to vv. 4–6, there should ideally be no poor and therefore no need for a release as long as Israel fully obeys the law. After this qualification or hortatory reminder, the law of vv. 1–3 continues in vv. 7–11. Miller notes that because of the human reality that there might be some poor people, a series of prohibitive actions and commands are given, prescribing the proper way to act. Miller, *Deuteronomy*, 136. He focuses on prominent "body language" used here (vv. 1–2, 7–11, 18).

41. Work, *Deuteronomy*, 159.

from entering a poor person's house to take a pledge item. They must wait outside. According to Leslie J., "Deuteronomy's concern is to maintain the dignity of the poor in what was already a humiliating situation."[42] Traditional Africans did not take pledge items. They simply gave, whether something was to be returned or not. The law also prohibits taking interest on loans to fellow Israelites (see Exod 22:25; Deut 23:19–20; Lev 25:35–38; Neh 5:1–13; Ps 15:5; Prov 28:8; Ezek 18:5–8, 10–13; 22:12; 2 Kgs 4:1; Isa 50:1).[43] These measures were intended to level the playing field and create social cohesion in the Israelite family.

The thrust of the *shemittah* is that Yahweh mandates releasing the poor from debt obligations, and slaves from exploitation by powerful landowners. African concepts of kinship view such less fortunate people, not as economic pawns for the rich, but as family members in need of assistance from the group. Ancient Near Eastern laws also encourage release from any obligation as a means to ensure social cohesion and equity.

The Meaning of Release Laws

The problem of the persistence of poverty, according to Deuteronomy 15, stems from disobedience to the Torah. Read in its proper context, Deuteronomy 15 argues that the poor ought not to exist in Israelite society. This is the biblical mandate, to care for the poor, and the book of Deuteronomy demonstrates specifically how Israel was to do this.[44]

This mandate is evident throughout the biblical period as it was in the surrounding cultures. Gerhard von Rad correctly argues, with regard to Deuteronomy, that "this sermon is a summons to meet the poor *at all times* with an open hand and an open heart. It is just the appeal to the heart which is characteristic."[45] This text "calls for a radical restructuring of how the people of God are to live in community . . .

42. Hoppe, "Deuteronomy and the Poor," 373. He adds that "to allow creditors inside the homes of their debtors in order to rummage about for a suitable item to take as collateral was demeaning to the families that found themselves in severe economic need. Keeping creditors outside the home of their debtors preserves at least a modicum of dignity and self-respect for the poor" (373).

43. Malchow, *Social Justice*, 23. For further studies on interest law, see the following works: Gamoran, "Biblical Law," 127–34; Sutherland, "Usury: God's Forgotten Doctrine," 9–14; and Ballard, "On the Sin of Usury," 210–28.

44. Wafawanaka, *Am I Still My Brother's Keeper?*

45. von Rad, *Deuteronomy*, 106. See also Deut 10:16; 11:18.

[and] love of God and service of neighbors in need go hand in hand."[46] Reading this text with the poor will confirm what they already know and practice. The communal nature of African culture determines their response to any member who is poor and in need.

In the modern context, the duty to care for the poor falls on human governments, creditors, and community members who can ameliorate the situation of the poor by sharing resources equitably, canceling debt obligations, and giving the poor a hand-up rather than a handout. These ancient concerns are still relevant in our modern societies, if not more so. Reading the *shemittah* text with the poor has enormous implications on the question of global debt forgiveness for the Two-Thirds World.[47]

Contextual Implications of Reading with the Poor

Reading the *shemittah* law with the poor and from an African and ancient Near Eastern context broadens our perspectives and views. Such contextual interpretation makes the text more accessible because in both contexts, release from economic obligations, the welfare of the other, and the treatment of the other as a family member in need of a helping hand, are paramount values. Reading such a text with the African poor, not from an individualistic perspective but a communal one, affirms their cultural connections and sheds greater meaning on this ancient text.

The release commanded by the *shemittah* engenders joy in the creditor who is asked to view the victim as a family member rather than as a source of credit extraction. The joy of the creditor is doubled when the creditor receives divine blessings and the dependent persons become independent. The joy of the recipient of such largess is realized when he or she is now a family member, debt-free, independent, and not a victim.

There is joy when the blessed master who releases his slave is blessed even more (Deut 15:14, 18). There is joy when the slave is released, not empty-handed, but with liberal supplies from the master's flock and agricultural products. In this context, the joy of release is double-edged as it affects both groups—rich and poor, creditor and borrower, slave and master—who each now has a new reason to rejoice. The poor who read this text will find it affirmative of their culture and traditional way of life.

46. Thompson, *Deuteronomy*, 128.

47. I have already addressed the global debt crisis elsewhere, see Wafawanaka, "Global Crisis of Debt," 163–90.

Conclusion

This essay has attempted to argue that reading Deuteronomy 15 with the African poor introduces them to a familiar context and affirms their communal way of life. There is a joy for both lender and receiver, rich and poor, when a lender gives unselfishly and the receiver's needs are met. By interpreting the release text of Deut 15 in the context of African traditional values and ancient Near Eastern economic concepts, we gain a better appreciation of this text. In these contexts, poor readers no longer see exploiters and victims, but family members ensuring that the well-being of the other comes before individual need, and personal gain and comfort.

I close with the words of Pope Francis on his "Third World Day of the Poor" on Nov 17, 2019. Pope Francis essentially claimed that economic inequality is largely unchanged since biblical times and may haunt us when the condition of the poor explodes before us. The Pope stated: "Certainly, the poor come to us also because we give them food, but what they really need is more than our offer of a warm meal or a sandwich. The poor need our hands, to be lifted up; our hearts, to feel anew the warmth of affection; our presence, to overcome loneliness. In a word, they need love."[48] These papal remarks also resonate with the African context where reading biblical texts with the poor confirms African cultural values and practices.

Bibliography

Ballard, Bruce. "On the Sin of Usury: A Biblical Economic Ethic." *CSR* 24 (1994) 210–28.

Bennett, Harold V. *Injustice Made Legal: Deuteronomic Law and the Plight of Widows, Strangers, and Orphans in Ancient Israel*. Grand Rapids: Eerdmans, 2002.

Davies, Paul Ewing. "Poor You Have with You Always: The Biblical View of Poverty." *McQ* 18 (January 1965) 37–48.

Dopamu, P. Adelumo. "Towards Understanding African Traditional Religion." In *Readings in African Traditional Religion: Structure, Meaning, Relevance, Future*, edited by E. M. Uka, 19–38. New York: Lang, 1991.

Driver, Samuel R. *A Critical and Exegetical Commentary on Deuteronomy*. International Critical Commentary. New York: Scribner, 1895.

Francis, Pope. "Message of His Holiness Pope Francis: Third World Day of the Poor, 33rd Sunday in Ordinary Time, 17 November 2019." Available at: https://ethicsdaily.com/pope-economic-inequality-largely-unchanged-since-biblical-times/. Accessed November 11, 2021.

48. Pope Francis, "Message of His Holiness."

Gamoran, Hillel. "The Biblical Law against Loans on Interest." *Journal of Near Eastern Studies* 30 (1971) 127–34.

Gill, Robin. *A Textbook of Christian Ethics.* Edinburgh: T. & T. Clark, 1985.

Gnuse, Robert K. *You Shall Not Steal: Community and Property in the Biblical Tradition.* 1985. Reprint, Eugene, OR: Wipf & Stock, 2011.

Graeber, David. *Debt: The First 5000 Years.* Brooklyn, NY: Melville House, 2011.

Hamilton, Jeffries M. "Ha'areṣ in the Shemiṭṭ Law." *VT* 42 (1992) 214–22.

———. *Social Justice and Deuteronomy: The Case of Deuteronomy 15.* SBL Dissertation Series 136. Atlanta: Scholars, 1992.

Hamutyinei, Mordikai A. and Albert B. Plangger. *Tsumo-Shumo: Shona Proverbial Lore and Wisdom.* Shona Heritage Series 2. Gwelo: Mambo, 1974.

Hanson, Paul D. "The Ancient Near Eastern Roots of Social Welfare." In *Through the Eye of a Needle: Judeo-Christian Roots of Social Welfare,* edited by Emily Albu Hanawalt and Carter Lindberg, 7–28. Kirksville, MO: Thomas Jefferson University Press at Northeast Missouri State University, 1994.

Hoppe, Leslie J. *Being Poor: A Biblical Study.* Wilmington, DE: Glazier, 1987.

———. "Deuteronomy and the Poor." *BT* 24 (1986) 371–75.

Hudson, Michael. *The Lost Tradition of Biblical Debt Cancellations.* New York: Henry George School of Social Science, 1993.

———. "Reconstructing the Origins of Interest-Bearing Debt and the Logic of Clean Slates." In *Debt and Economic Renewal in the Ancient Near East,* edited by Michael Hudson and Marc Van De Mieroop, 7–58. International Scholars Conference on Near Eastern Societies, vol. 3. Bethesda, MD: CDL, 2002.

Hudson, Michael, and Marc Van De Mieroop, eds. *Debt and Economic Renewal in the Ancient Near East.* International Scholars Conference on Near Eastern Societies, vol. 3. Bethesda, MD: CDL, 2002.

Idowu, Bolaji. *Olodumare: God in Yoruba Belief.* London: Longmans, 1962.

Iliffe, John. *The African Poor: A History.* African Studies Series 58. Cambridge: Cambridge University Press, 1987.

Mafico, Themba L. J. "The African Context for Theology." *JITC* 16/1–2 (1988/1989) 69–83.

———. "Tradition, Faith, and The Africa University." *QR* 9/2 (1989) 37–51.

Malchow, Bruce V. *Social Justice in the Hebrew Bible: What Is New and What Is Old.* Collegeville, MN: Liturgical, 1996.

Mbiti, John S. *African Religions and Philosophy.* 2nd ed. London: Heinemann, 1990.

———. *Introduction to African Religion.* 2nd ed. London: Heinemann Educational, 1989.

Miller, Patrick D. *Deuteronomy.* Interpretation. Louisville: John Knox Press, 1990.

North, Robert. *Sociology of the Biblical Jubilee.* Rome: Pontifical Biblical Institute, 1954.

Patrick, Dale. *Old Testament Law.* Atlanta: John Knox Press, 1985.

Pritchard, James B., ed. *Ancient Near Eastern Texts Relating to the Old Testament.* 3rd ed. Princeton: Princeton University Press, 1969.

Radcliffe-Brown, A. R., and Daryll Forde, eds. *African Systems of Kinship and Marriage.* 9th impression. London: Oxford University Press, 1967.

Sugirtharajah, R. S. "'For You Always Have the Poor with You': An Example of Hermeneutics of Suspicion." *AJT* 4.1 (1990) 102–7.

Sutherland, John. "Usury: God's Forgotten Doctrine." *Crux* 18/1 (1982) 9–14.

Thompson, Deanna A. *Deuteronomy*. Belief: A Theological Commentary on the Bible. Louisville: Westminster John Knox, 2014.

Uka, E. M. "The Ethics of African Traditional Religion." In *Readings in African Traditional Religion: Structure, Meaning, Relevance, Future*, edited by E. M. Uka, 153–56. New York: Peter Lang, 1991.

———, ed. *Readings in African Traditional Religion: Structure, Meaning, Relevance, Future*. New York: Lang, 1991.

Van de Mieroop, Marc. "A History of Near Eastern Debt?" In *Debt and Economic Renewal in the Ancient Near East*, edited by Michael Hudson and Marc Van de Mieroop, 59–94. International Scholars Conference on Near Eastern Societies 3. Bethesda, MD: CDL, 2002.

von Rad, Gerhard. *Deuteronomy: A Commentary*. Translated Dorothea Barton. OTL. Philadelphia: Westminster, 1966.

Wafawanaka, Robert. *Am I Still My Brother's Keeper? Biblical Perspectives on Poverty*. Lanham, MD: University Press of America, 2012.

———. "The Global Crisis of Debt in Context: Biblical and Postcolonial Reflections on the Ideology of Empire." In *Reading the Bible in an Age of Crisis: Political Exegesis for a New Day*, edited by Bruce Worthington, 163–90. Minneapolis: Fortress, 2015.

West, Gerald O. "1 and 2 Samuel." In *Global Bible Commentary*, edited by Daniel Patte, 92–104. Nashville: Abingdon, 2004.

———. "Contextual Bible Study in South Africa: A Resource for Reclaiming and Regaining Land, Dignity and Identity." In *The Bible in Africa: Transactions, Trajectories, and Trends*, edited by Gerald O. West and Musa W. Dube, 595–610. Leiden: Brill, 2000.

———. "Indigenous Biblical Hermeneutics: Voicing Continuity and Distinctiveness." In *Postcolonial Perspectives in African Biblical Interpretations*, edited by Musa W. Dube, Andrew M. Mbuvi, and Dora R. Mbuwayesango, 85–96. Global Perspectives on Biblical Scholarship 13. Atlanta: Society of Biblical Literature, 2012.

———. "Reading the Bible Differently: Giving Shape to the Discourse of the Dominated." *Semeia* 73 (1996) 21–41.

Work, Telford. *Deuteronomy*. Brazos Theological Commentary on the Bible. Grand Rapids: Brazos, 2009.

Wright, Christopher J. H. *God's People in God's Land: Family, Land, and Property in the Old Testament*. Grand Rapids: Eerdmans, 1990.

PART TWO

Methodology and African Biblical Hermeneutics

5

Lazarus and the Angels

(Reluctant) Confessions of an (Unwitting) Colonial Agent?

Jonathan A. Draper
University of KwaZulu-Natal

Introduction

I LEFT THE ANGLICAN parish ministry in the Diocese of Zululand in 1986 to join Professor Gunther Wittenberg in his ambitious project to set up a Bachelor of Theology at the then University of Natal (UN) in Pietermaritzburg.[1] His vision was to provide an ecumenical program based on cooperation between the university and the existing programs in Pietermaritzburg, which would be focused on the South African context of the struggle for justice, democracy, gender equity, and non-racialism. My appointment was to a newly created post in New Testament studies and my arrival followed closely the declaration of a state of emergency by the racist regime in South Africa as the apartheid era became more violent and resistance to it more vocal and determined. A formidable group of theologians and activists gravitated towards Pietermaritzburg and the UN—later merged with the University of Durban-Westville and

1. The four posts in theology required to set up the programme by supplementing the existing Religious Studies department were initially funded by the Lutheran World Federation and various other Lutheran sources local and international. To their credit—this initiative was from the start ecumenical in scope and practice and has remained so in its various permutations.

was renamed the University of KwaZulu-Natal (UKZN)—and its growing partnerships with the Federal Theological Seminary (FedSem), St. Joseph's Theological Seminary, and the Evangelical Theological House of Studies (ETHOS). Among those who saw the potential of this emerging vision of a *Cluster of Pietermaritzburg Houses of Study* was Gerald West, who had found his role as an Assemblies of God pastor untenable and had moved to Sheffield University to undertake a PhD in liberation hermeneutics. He joined FedSem, and subsequently, the UN to develop an Institute for the Study of the Bible (ISB), which has had an important impact on contextual Bible Study in Africa and beyond.

"Reading *With*": A Retrospect

As it happened, in 1988 I was asked to contribute an article on South African Anglicans and Scripture to a volume on the Anglican Church. In seeking an appropriate angle to take this, I soon noticed that, apart from the controversy around Bishop John William Colenso, there was little or nothing to indicate how Anglicans understood or read the Bible. Impressed by West's passion, enthusiasm, and incisive grasp of transformative hermeneutics, and commitment to working with the grassroots, I invited him to work with me to find out. The project was to ask Anglicans across the diverse spectrum of parishes in Pietermaritzburg to participate in an empirical study, undertaking a carefully non-directive common Bible Study on Mark 10:17–22, facilitated by trained students as fieldworkers and then to tabulate the results on a range of criteria. While the study was a joint project, my contribution initially was interested in a historical perspective, the theoretical expertise and fieldwork model was largely provided by West. The study produced fascinating results and cried out for further analysis of how communities actually read the Bible and its role in resistance to apartheid.[2] His influential book, *Biblical Hermeneutics of Liberation: Modes of Reading the Bible in the South African Context* (1991, 19952) drew not only on this pilot project as a case study, but also on three other South African case studies of grassroots Bible readings: The Institute for Contextual Theology's "Church and

---

2. Draper and West, "Anglicans and Scripture," 30–52.

Labour Research Project;"[3] "Readings in the Young Christian Workers (YCW);"[4] and "Readings in the African Independent Churches."[5]

In the conclusion to *Biblical Hermeneutics of Liberation*, West argued that the key question[6] facing biblical studies in universities was the gap between "trained readers" and "ordinary readers," in which the very relevance of the discipline is at stake:

> In this study we have come to a recognition of an interpretive crisis both in the wider interpretive debate and within biblical interpretation . . . This scrutiny . . . exposed the limitations of objectivity and uncovered the powerful negative hermeneutic potential of moving beyond objectivism.[7]

He is not alone in this analysis of the problem posed by objectivism, but what makes his study particularly relevant in South Africa under apartheid is his rejection of "skepticism and nihilism" and his insistence on "a positive hermeneutic [that] would require a prophetic vision of resistance and hope that was rooted in an active and transformative solidarity with the community of the poor and oppressed."[8] In other words, trained academics needed to read *with* ordinary readers taking an "option *for* the poor," as so often advocated by South American liberation scholars and activists.

His study made him the obvious choice to lead Wittenberg's new establishment of an Institute for the Study of the Bible in 1989. This was a watershed in the South African study of the Bible in universities and academic societies, which was well established in the academy but often, though not always, served as an instrument to support and

---

3. Cochrane, "Already . . . But Not Yet," 176–89.

4. Young Christian Workers, "National Team Meeting," YCW National Secretariat, Durban." See also Stevens, "Role of the Church."

5. West's discussion is based on research by Mosala, "Race, Class and Gender," 43–57.

6. In the initial process of developing a contextual biblical model, we shared the enjoyment and stimulation of our first international conferences of the Society of Biblical Literature, often sleeping rough and surviving on food and coffee from conference displays and receptions so as to be able to buy books and computer resources with our limited grant resources. Gerald was, with other engaged scholars, instrumental in pushing successfully to make the resources of the SBL available to under-resourced scholars from Third World countries and foregrounding their work through the International Cooperative Initiative.

7. West, *Biblical Hermeneutics of Liberation*," 163. I am using the 1st ed. as my much-thumbed treasure.

8. West, *Biblical Hermeneutics of Liberation*, 163.

legitimate apartheid.[9] West provided the vision, patience, and commitment required for anyone working with base communities in the mode of Paulo Frere.[10] My contribution to this Festschrift both celebrates his achievement and explores some of the theoretical and practical challenges West posed for me and others in his considerable experience and analysis of reading the Bible *with* local communities, together with his research and publications.[11]

As so often happens, academics working together start out sharing a common agenda, but the exigencies of research and its reception raise issues that challenge their initial work and solidarity.[12] This is not necessarily a bad thing where collegiality can be preserved, since it clarifies the issues involved and can be mutually enriching.[13] Looking back to the paper West wrote in a *Semeia* issue titled "Reading With: African Overtures," he edited with Musa W. Dube, "Reading the Bible Differently: Giving Shape to the Discourses of the Dominated,"[14] I presented a final report on sharing our joint empirical Reader Response study of "ordinary" Zulu Anglican readers in Pietermaritzburg.[15]

However, West's new direction of understanding and praxis defined as "reading *with*" reflected strongly Gramsci's theory of the "organic intellectuals."[16] West views such biblical scholars as having been "converted" and "called."[17] Here West's re-use of missionary language rather

9. There were notable points of resistance to apartheid within the various Reformed Churches in South Africa and attempts to challenge the use of the Bible to support it, sometimes at great personal cost. That, however, would be another story.

10. Freire, *Pedagogy of the Oppressed*.

11. West's publications have been prolific and probing throughout his career, capped appropriately by his major work, West, *The Stolen Bible*.

12. A classic example of this is disclosed by the turbulent relationship and correspondence between Karl Barth and Rudolf Bultmann over what they both called "dialectical theology" as exegetical key to reading the Bible in the turbulent times of the rise of Hitler, Nazism, and the Second World War. I do not see myself in such illustrious company nor did our relationship when our understandings differed as exhibiting such bitterness.

13. To his credit, where academic paths sometimes parted, he continued to engage dialectically with colleagues in a positive and affirmative way. See, for instance, his response to the sharp challenge of Tinyiko Maluleke and Sarojini Nader.

14. West, "Reading the Bible Differently," 21–41.

15. Draper, "Confessional Western," 59–78. My interest remained strongly determined by "reading for" in its theoretical framework and socio-historical in its use of orality theory in methodology.

16. Gramsci, *Selections*.

17. Admittedly he does not use the words "sent" or "commissioned."

startled me when I re-read it for this paper, but it was an authentic reflection of the direction and dedication of his personal and academic life to the poor and the oppressed in the South African context. Such "organic intellectuals" he differentiates from "engaged biblical scholars":

> Remarkably in contexts like Brasil and South Africa, biblical scholars are continually being 'called' by ordinary readers of the Bible. Trust of intellectuals is reserved, however, only for those with whom the people choose to speak. The biblical scholars who are part of this 'contextual Bible study process' are committed to doing biblical studies with and from the perspective of the poor and oppressed. So there has always been a clear recognition of their role as servants. Their contribution may be distinctive and different, but it is not in any way better or more significant. While not all of these biblical scholars are organic intellectuals, they all work closely with organic intellectuals.[18]

I certainly honor and celebrate West as a scholar who really attempted and in many ways succeeded in following this calling throughout his whole academic career.

My own engagement was more like a political commitment than a hermeneutical choice—less a claim to be an "engaged intellectual" working with "ordinary readers."[19] Besides, I found that I was singularly clumsy at this, even as a parish priest in my former parish in Matubatuba. What I had been committed to doing was engaging in the critical interpretation of the Bible in the South African context of apartheid and its aftermath, in the belief that at its heart and its axis, the Bible was potentially liberative. Not that there are no oppressive texts and narratives. Of course, there are. Here the biblical scholars should unmask unjust domination and read in that light. Where I fully agreed with West was on the need to construct a model of contextual biblical study that might enable me and other readers, especially post-graduate students, to read critically but constructively, in a way that could speak to the social and political questions of the moment in their context.[20]

---

18. West, "Reading the Bible Differently," 28.

19. See also Bernard Lategan's rejoinder to West ("Scholar and Ordinary Reader," 244–46). He argues that the hegemonic potential of the relationship remains a key factor in West's model.

20. I concede that this is potentially not that far from preaching, though without its directive assertiveness.

Oppressive texts need to be acknowledged and contested in dialogue with the liberative axis of the Bible as we find it.[21] Nevertheless, I clung then, and to some extent still cling (often to my embarrassment), to a conviction that the liberative potential of the Bible is actually there, historically and materially, as a living legacy from the struggles of historical Israel and the historical Jesus, despite my awareness of the problems, and even perhaps the impossibility, of such a notion. West, on the other hand, brought a conviction inspired in the first instance by Postmodernism and Reader Response theories that academic Bible readers could partner with poor and oppressed communities, non-prescriptively.[22] Despite these differences, our common goal was to engage the resources of the academy in a liberative way to the needs of ordinary Bible readers, especially in a time of crisis in South Africa.

In the various responses to the papers in "Reading With: African Overtures," West's "manifesto" of how "engaged readers" could be "reading with" ordinary readers has found widespread interest, mostly positive. However, the most strident attack on "reading with" as a hermeneutics of liberation came from two former colleagues at the University of Natal, in 2003–4 after a decade of the election for a new South Africa in 1994, namely Tinyiko Sam Maluleke and Sarojini Nadar, "Alien Fraudsters in the White Academy: Agency in Gendered Colour," *JTSA* 120 (2004), 5–17. Far from such "reading with" enabling the agency of the poor and marginalized through contextual Bible studies, they argued that it represents a hijacking of the debate on the agency of the oppressed to the benefit only of white male academics:

> Above all we shall not let the matter rest at the distant level of an imaginary agent interlocutor in some imaginary South African township—we shall venture to problematize our own space as agents of change and transformation in the academy to our own detriment.[23]

---

21. There are, of course, those who view the whole Bible as oppressive in their experience, but if that oppression is to be combated, critical academic voices against such texts are needed to contest the terrain. Mosala's use of reading "against the grain" of texts (from Terry Eagleton, "The Revolt of the Reader," in *Against the Grain*), provides one way to contest such texts, even if few "grass roots" Christians may not be willing to buy into it. If academic scholars do not engage in such a hermeneutical study, they abandon the field to the oppressors.

22. Cf. West, *Academy of the Poor.*

23. Maluleke and Nadar, "Alien Fraudsters," 7. They echo the words of Gayatri Spivak ("Can the Sub-Altern Speak?") "Does an Alien Fraudster Speak and If So, How, to

They also challenged the whole discussion of the concept of agency among anthropologists,[24] historians, and sociologists, as well as biblical scholars, since the data these academics depended on was tainted by their Western hegemony. Moreover, Maluleke and Nadar saw in "reading with" a kind of false consciousness in which rather than them enabling the voices of the poor to be heard, organic intellectuals were entrenching the continuation of their domination of the discourse.

Maluleke and Nadar demand that White and male academics who engage in the agency discourse ". . .must come clear and 'elaborate on the precise and particular implications of their identity to the discourse including the reparative actions invoked thereby.'"[25] In effect, Maluleke and Nadar reject the theory of agency as "fraudulent," but in doing so simply replace White male academics with Black male and female academics. And, in such a scenario, the poor and oppressed are no more agents than they were before the debate of "fake "or "authentic" agency.[26]

Of course, it is reasonable to ask such questions in particular cases, but if White males were to do this in everything they wrote, it would forever be talking about themselves rather than dialoguing with others. The question *cui bono* should be asked of ourselves, even if others don't ask. Such a "lifestyle audit" should then be made by all those participating in the interpretive discourse. Therefore, for me, such cynical rejection of any possible agency of communities reading the Bible (or any other religious text) belittles the spirituality and Bible readings of the majority of South Africans—largely "ordinary" untrained Black men and women—and creates a new (and potentially "fake") dichotomy.[27]

Whom and with What Authority?"

24. Especially Scott, *Domination* and Comaroff and Comaroff, *Revolution*.

25. Maluleke and Nadar, "Alien Fraudsters," 16. I acknowledge with gratitude the welcome I received from members of St. Christopher's Parish in Sobantu, and its rural "outstations" for their inviting and accepting of my presence in the parish as a non-stipendiary priest and congregant. For around 30 years, following our initial empirical research in the Parish, until Covid-19 and retirement brought an end to my presence.

26. Maluleke and Nadar, "Alien Fraudsters," 16.

27. Lategan, "Scholar and Ordinary Reader," 244, already notes the problems with the dichotomy of "critical/ordinary readers" which West sets up, since it disguises a range of other dichotomies which are not explored. The same challenge could be posed to Maluleke and Nadar. In his own inimical way, the late Archbishop of Cape Town Desmond Tutu in his "Foreword" to *Bounty in Bondage*, opposed "the dualism that spouts the dichotomies so much loved by those who usually are the beneficiaries of a socio-political and economic dispensation that others condemn as unjust." In terms of the hermeneutical retrospect above, we can perhaps benefit from his warning that

West has trained up and enabled a cohort of Black and women leaders who now run *Ujamaa* and continue to build an institute that can engage in transformative "reading with" poor and oppressed communities in South Africa and indeed with many international partners.[28] And, in his work in the "Institute for the Study of the Bible," tested and modified over thirty-three years, including his manual on reading with the Bible translated into *isiZulu*, has proved a valuable tool for "ordinary readers" and also "engaged Black scholars" concerned with the failure of Church and/or Society, in general, to assist them in undertaking their contextual Bible studies.

"Reluctant Confessions"

While West continued to focus on *reading with* "ordinary readers," after those initial projects my own focus turned back to producing, *inter alia*, contextual studies of the concrete issues of the day, with research and writing academic papers in a responsive and transformative way. Often these would arise from discussion with students in the classroom. My rather simplistic starting point was from the premise that the Bible presents a set of historical texts in foreign languages with very different cultures and experiences, yet which with all its problems of interpretation "has something *good* of value to 'listen to,' but which could be dangerous if simply taken literally and therefore cease to be *good* at all.[29]

"My second point was that many modern South African Christian readers of the Bible interpret it as the "Word of God," so that Bible

could cut both ways.

28. Ironically, considering that "reading with" had links with a request to write a paper on "Anglicans and Scripture in South Africa," West was asked to organize a *read with* style daily Bible Studies before his retirement at the last Lambeth Conference, a gathering of Anglican primates from around the world, providing a model of *reading with* the Bible. It enabled many of the participants to read with those who disagreed with them, and found each other at a time of considerable turbulence and threats of schism in the worldwide Anglican Communion.

29. My biblical exegesis was deeply influenced by the *Kairos Document*. Mofokeng, "Black Christians," 34–42, has poignantly outlined the problem of using the Bible in this way, by stating that the problem lies in the "bourgeois biblical-hermeneutical assumptions and methodologies of the academies." His critique has been a "pebble in my shoes" in my own work, discomforting me and challenging me, as I have tried to present liberatory readings of recalcitrant texts. I must admit that he was right in much of his critique of historical criticism as "the hermeneutical yoke of slavery," and that I have in many ways continued to use it and teach it, even as I have tried to change what I do.

reading does matter, not just for Christians, but for us all. People continue to find meaning from it for their own context, whatever it is. They continue to act on it but often do so uncritically in a way that simply repeats it in worn clichés which impede it from being good *news*. Hence "trained readers" have an important role to play in providing background reading and other information.

Thirdly, their readings often did not move on to bring the Bible into dialogue with the real issues of contemporary importance which could provide liberatory or healing *praxis*.[30] Greatly influenced by Hans-Georg Gadamer's hermeneutic of "conversation,"[31] together with "orality theory" of John Miles Foley and social linguistics of M. A. K. Halliday,[32] I proposed a dynamic, dialogical "Tripolar" model of hermeneutics, which I hoped recognized the presence of *readers* in their own contexts, the *texts* in their own literary and socio-historical context and the appropriation of the results of the "conversation" in a transformative *praxis*.

The three poles proposed were: *Contextualization*, *Distanciation*, and *Appropriation*. In my first draft, I suggested that it did not matter in which order one began the dialectical process which culminated in praxis, as long as all three poles were given equal space. In my understanding, the model required that the text be engaged as "other," as not written for us, and as addressing different situations to ours, as alien from us. The model allows for any explicit use of methodologies that provoke and address the otherness of the text. It also requires that we do an equally in-depth analysis of our own context recognizing its otherness to the biblical context. The two contexts could then be engaged in a process of conversation which could be questioning, even hostile and rejecting, especially in the interrogation of "texts of terror"[33] for women and slaves and the poor and the colonized underclasses of empire. I then suggested that the outcome of the dialogue might enable a new "praxeological interpretation," oriented towards change and transformation.

---

30. I used the opportunity offered by an invitation of St. Paul's College, Limuru, Kenya, to give a series of three papers on biblical hermeneutics for their centenary celebrations, 21–24 May 2002. Past and present Kenyan graduate students at the time were wonderful hosts and introduced me to East Africa and its vibrant congregations, as well as the past achievements and ambitious developments at St. Paul's College. See Draper, "Reading the Bible," 12–24.

31. Gadamer, *Truth and Method*.

32. Halliday, *Language as Social Semiotic*.

33. A designation coined by Phyllis Trible, *Texts of Terror*.

The model seemed to "make sense" to me, and to many of our graduate students, but it was flawed at many points and was rightly and strongly challenged by Gerald West among others.[34] His sympathetic but stimulating discussions have always proved helpful and fruitful, for which I am grateful. The first problem it confronts is that, while deep conversations are possible between *living people* who can question and challenge each other, gain clarification, and effect change through dialogue, even agree to differ with each other's points of view completely and walk out the door, texts do not dialogue: obviously, they cannot. Texts do not choose themselves: obviously, they cannot. Texts cannot decide what qualifies as evidence for their meaning: obviously, they cannot. Only people can dialogue with texts and bring them into dialogue with other texts.

The language of conversation is thus always in danger of providing a species of false consciousness in which the author of the exegesis of the Bible appears to disappear.[35] The voice of the interpreter sounds like the voice of the text and obtains an English, Zulu, or other accent! In the context of South Africa's ugly colonial and apartheid legacy, claims to represent an "African context" will inevitably mean entering a contested space.[36] A more complex model of dialogue between texts is needed, one that recognizes the reader as an "interested party" as well as the initiator and controller of the "interested reading," an idea well-articulated in West's writings.

In addition, while I initially argued that one could begin the process from any of the poles, my Black students insisted rightly that for it to be an *African* Contextual Biblical Hermeneutic, the discussion *must* begin with their African context. I believe they are right. And, I have tried to modify my model accordingly. I have usually begun any study of any text with a socio-historical analysis, followed by a modified structural/ narrative analysis where necessary, whereas for this model to be viable it requires that African readers foreground their context, anchor themselves in an African context, and work within that context as their theoretical framework. In addition, the Bible as a "dialogue partner" in this kind of "conversation," can, obviously, still only be encountered from an author's

34. For the history and progress of my model and its modification over the years, see Draper, "African Contextual Hermeneutics," 3–22.

35. For a vigorous criticism of this model from a neo-Marxist position, see Wright, "Re-Appropriating Appropriation," 25–45.

36. White South Africans, including myself, need to acknowledge and "fess up" to this.

reconstruction of a culture and experience different from ours, whichever methodology we adopt to initiate the dialogue.

Moreover, for me, however similar any particular text of the Old or New Testament may be to a modern context, it needs to be critically, narratively, socially, or historically interrogated in some way to open up its potential and unmask uncritical hegemony. Yet, "reading *with* ordinary readers" runs the risk of being drowned out by the task of historical reconstruction by trained readers. However, one must try to distance oneself and foreground "the reader," without further ado. Furthermore, most of the textbooks used by the academy for training undergraduates are replete with Western assumptions of reality and Western culture. One way forward is to understand the role of "reading communities"[37] in determining what constitutes the issues, what tools are acceptable, and what constitutes an answer to the questions posed to the Bible, et cetera. Taken seriously, this makes me a "trained reader," answerable to a Western- "First World "-community of scholars.

However, how then does this make me accountable to "untrained" South African readers as those to whom I am also answerable? How then are we to have a critical and transformative dialogue with the Bible which honors the agency of "ordinary readers" as well? We have to find a way to take account of human potential to act and to change, but also the limitations of that agency. Is "reading *with*" entirely ruled out as a possibility for a mutually enriching bridge between the trained and the ordinary readers?

Rethinking the "Reading *With*"[38]

I would like to suggest we revisit the concept of transformative "reading *with*" in a way suggested by Pierre Bourdieu's concept of *habitus, doxa, and field*.[39] As we have seen, many Black intellectuals have challenged the

37. Draper, "African Contextual Hermeneutics," 3–22. Here I take up the suggestion of Stanley Fish asking the question of "what constitutes a text," namely that specific communities of readers perform that role. See Fish, "Interpreting the *Variorum*, 465–85. Fish, *Is There a Text?*, 147–74.

38. The research project on the *Enyonini Church* was undertaken jointly with Rev. Dr. Kenneth Mtata as my postdoctoral student. It included fieldwork, observing worship and joining the annual pilgrimage to Newcastle, discussions with the Church's leadership and secondary sources and the CBS which follows. I would like to acknowledge and thank him for the friendship, help and insightful cooperation over many years.

39. Draper, "Pierre Bourdieu," 35–69.

concept of agency, while at the same time remaining skeptical about the biblical interpretations of the African Initiated Churches or Zionists as representing genuine agency.[40] My mind has been influenced by a project I participated in with Professor Ulrich Berner of Bayreuth University and our students, partly funded by NRF and FRD, to examine the relevance of Bourdieu's social theory in the African context.[41] It seemed to me that it might provide the theory that can overcome the great divide between a model of agency and a skeptical determinism.

Central to the theory is his model of *habitus,* in which a person's socialization is a lifelong accumulation of social/cultural capital, and it is inscribed on the body as well as the mind, in the world as a species of "memory pad."[42] This constitutes within the *habitus* of the individual, a structuring of the structures of life that replicate themselves, and which partly determine a person's response to context, though never completely.[43] The *habitus* constitutes what is taken for granted within a given community, regarded as the way things are and always were: the "rules of the game" in which people exercise their mastery of the *habitus* so as to maximize their participation in the *field* of contestation in and between communities.[44] A person's mastery of this cultural capital in any given *field* is exercised within the *habitus.* The ability of persons to succeed in a situation is a factor of their ability to maximize their control of the cultural capital in their *habitus.*

As we have noted, the nature of the cultural capital and *habitus* of the social universe of meaning, by which a person acts, is unknown to them—rather taken for granted as the way things always are—whereas these are changing imperceptibly all the time. This is what Bourdieu calls *doxa* ("opinion").[45] In this respect, the agency of a given individual in a community to understand and act in a new way is limited and repetitive and lasts only as long as the *habitat* and its relevant cultural capital remain hidden as taken-for-granted *doxa.*

However, when a crisis is presented by a new situation, or a failure of an outcome taken for granted as a consequence of action, or when forced

40. Draper, "Pierre Bourdieu," 35–69.

41. See Draper, "Pierre Bourdieu," 35–69. In the earlier paper, I set out the theory more fully than can be done here.

42. Bourdieu, *Logic of the Practice,* 141.

43. Bourdieu, *Logic of the Practice,* 141.

44. Bourdieu, *Outline of a Theory.*

45. Bourdieu, *Outline of a Theory.*

obedience by colonizers, for example, to their different *habitus* presents a moment of contest and agency, it can no longer be determined by the previous exercise of social and cultural capital in the *habitus*.[46] The hiddenness of the *habitus* is exposed to view. The *doxa* which was taken for granted as a pre-supposition of everything now becomes *ideology*, the realm of debate and re-definition, and hence, above all, a moment of agency—limited as it may be. The *doxa* is reformulated by the competition with the "other."[47] New ways of thinking and doing, which address the crisis in the contest over *ideology*, adjust the *habitus* since they come to be accepted, unawares once more, as has been always the way things were since, now, what are new stands in some continuity with the old.[48]

In the end, aspects of the contested *ideology* which successfully address the challenge become part of a new *doxa* that is only partly new. Winners and losers are not necessarily what they appear. The language and instruments of the conqueror may be adopted *per force* but peopled with the meaning of the existing *habitus*. The proliferation of attempts to avert or address the crisis means that the outcome will be messy and diverse. What interests me is the extent to which, in this process, the Bible continues to be viewed as the unchanging "Word of God" even though its understanding will have shifted in obvious ways. The creation out of the contested religious *field* results in interpretive moves which provide a number of options in constructing a new African *habitus*.

In other words, the imperial conquest and cultural colonization of much of Africa could enforce a semblance of compliance when there are no other choices for survival, but this creates a contested *field* or set of *fields*, especially the religious field since religion is the ultimate guardian of a culture. A variable in the boundaries of the religious field is provided by the account of the gift of the Holy Spirit of God to all believers in the Bible and its confirmation by the experience of the Spirit in the *habitus* in Zionist Churches determines the form of Christianity with which they began to contest the religious *field*. The missionaries, even of the "mainline Pentecostal churches" such as those founded by Peter Le Roux, had no convincing answer.[49] I will briefly look at the example of the first Zionist Church, which I have tried to "read *with*" in different ways. The *Enyonini* Church (1906) has gone through many changes but

46. Bourdieu, *Outline of a Theory*.

47. Bourdieu, *Outline of a Theory*.

48. Bourdieu, *Outline of a Theory*.

49. See the discussion in Draper, "Role of the Spirit," 51–67.

is still very much alive, and it requested from us and the field workers a *Contextual Bible Study* (CBS). I have focused narrowly on the question of the role of angels which play a big role in several accounts of Zionist Churches, and in which some play the role of ancestors, or at least gatekeepers, to the entry of the dead to the afterlife.

Rethinking "Reading *With*": The Bible in Christian Catholic Apostolic Holy Spirit Church of Zion, South Africa

This short paper was occasioned by a challenge to the possible agency of the poor and oppressed resulting from Contextual Bible Study in the shape of Gerald West's formula of "reading *with*." The Christian Catholic Apostolic Holy Spirit Church of Zion in South Africa (CCAHSCZ in SA) was the first Zionist Church.[50] It began as the Dutch Reformed Mission Church in Wakkerstroom in the Transvaal Republic under Pieter Le Roux, which broke away to join the Pentecostal Chicago Zion in the U.S.A. under John Alexander Dowie (1847–1907).[51] Subsequently when Le Roux abandoned the Chicago Zionist Pentecostalism and became the founder, among others, and the first president of a largely white Apostolic Faith Mission, the majority of its Black members refused to leave and insisted on staying in "Zion" and renamed themselves: "The Christian Catholic Apostolic Holy Spirit Church of Zion in South Africa (CCAHSCZ in SA)."[52]

After their expulsion from Wakkerstroom by Le Roux, they moved to Charlestown over the Transvaal boundary to Natal; there, they were expelled a third time, from Charlestown to Madedeni outside Newcastle, by the apartheid government.[53] So they called themselves *Enyonini* "the place of the bird/Spirit."[54] For his part, Le Roux believed that the "breakaway" congregation was apostate.[55] He tried and failed to enforce a ban on staffs, stoles, the prohibition on pork, bare feet in worship, and the

---

50. Draper, "Role of the Spirit," 51–54.

51. Draper, "Role of the Spirit," 51–54.

52. The addition "in South Africa" reflects tensions between the South African and KwaSwathi branches of the Church. See Dlamini, "Christian Catholic Apostolic," II, 314. This tension, especially in the purchase of a car for the President of the Church, was confirmed in field work discussions.

53. Draper, "Role of the Spirit," 52.

54. Draper, "Role of the Spirit," 51.

55. Draper, "Role of the Spirit," 51–54.

prohibition of smoking.[56] All of these factors impacted how this particular Church ended up looking and acting.

Bengt Sundkler was a pioneer in the study of Zionist Churches and the first scholar to give an account of the *Enyonini* Church in its original Wakkerstroom location.[57] However, the most authoritative account of the *Enyonini* is provided by Timothy Dlamini's massive and meticulously indexed two-volume Master's thesis on this Church in Swaziland.[58] Sundkler often misinterprets what he observes.[59] The religious *field* they were contesting was a stern Calvinist Reformed tradition, but the *habitus* was Black African and more specifically Swazi and Zulu. In the CCAHSCZ, the pastor (and vice president of the Church) wore a formal pure white Geneva gown and stole. Other leaders wore simple green/blue gowns, while the congregants wore white robes and plain green/blue. The pastor carried a metal hooked staff (of Moses), while all others carried one or two wooden sticks/staffs, matching the major focus on healing and combat with Satan in the Church, which also reflects Le Roux's emphasis on healing. His account indicates that they used *isiwasho* for healing (a mixture of water and ashes),[60] but they did not seem to do so in Elandskop. However, I was given some to drink after a service. On inquiry, I was informed that it is sometimes, but not routinely, used.

Healing was carried out on supplicants who knelt while the leaders circled ritually around and ended with the staffs stretched out over them. On one occasion, a young woman was beaten by the wife of the pastor to drive out Satan. Otherwise, the service consists of prayer, song and dance, and a reading of Scripture followed by a sermon on the text. Dlamini provides many transcripts of *Enyonini* sermons based directly on Scripture and "orthodox" in their theology.[61]

So, Dlamini's account argued that the sticks carried by Zionists were crude crosses, but this is mistaken. A cursory glance at the photos Berngt Sundkler provides in his *Bantu Prophets in South Africa* and *Zulu Zion*,[62] and our own fieldwork, reveal that they are not crosses.

---

56. Draper, "Role of the Spirit," 51–54.

57. Sundkler, *Bantu Prophets*; Sundkler, *Zulu Zion*.

58. See above Dlamini, *CCAAHSCZ*.

59. Sundkler, *Bantu Prophets*.

60. Dlamini, *CCAHSCZ*, II, 311.

61. Dlamini, *CCAHSCZ*, II, 313. His assertion is borne out by a perusal of the Sermons and Testimonies, provided in the second volume as a whole.

62. Sundkler, *Bantu Prophets*; Sundkler, *Zulu Zion*.

Either they are curling on top (a symbol of the healing snake of Moses which becomes explicit in the staff of some leaders), or else made into two sticks either by affixing a small one crossway, or by holding two sticks (a symbol of a weapon against witchcraft and Satan). They are named *izikhali* following a widespread tradition as weapons of protection in Zulu culture, frequently placed in the thatching of huts in the homestead.[63] Every member in the congregation in Elandskop near Pietermaritzburg carried one or two sticks in worship as the Spirit dictated, and the two sticks for healing and/or protection were chosen from specific trees known to have either healing properties or protective powers *inter alia* against lightning, by a dedicated community member, who has to fast while collecting and preparing the sticks.

Viewed from the perspective of Bourdieu's theory, contestation within a specific religious field of Calvinist Christianity which carried over into the Apostolic Faith Mission led to the re-formation of the boundaries of the *field*, the structures, and externals of the Reformed colonial churches, now came to be populated by a particular Zionist Church with aspects of the cultural capital of the indigenous *habitus*.[64]

So, for instance, their worship was orderly and not ecstatic as in many other Zionist Churches. Participants were barefooted so that the predominant sound was often the swishing of robes and bare feet in dance. We did not notice any particular emphasis on prophecy. While there were overlaps with other Zionist Churches, there were clear differences resulting in the symbolic structure and rootedness in particular pre-Christian cultural formations and the kind of Christianity they received from the missionaries. He might have added, as other missionaries did, worship on Saturday as the true Sabbath.

Lazarus and the Angels in *Enyonini*

As a small test of Bourdieu's hypothesis of the *habitus* and contestation of *field*, I am drawing on an important CBS Workshop with the *Enyonini*, although it is more than a decade old (5th September 2009).[65] After a sus-

---

63. Sundkler, *Bantu Prophets*; Sundkler, *Zulu Zion*.

64. See the differences reflected in the color coding choices of "white robed" and "red robed" Zionists in Draper, "Pierre Bourdieu," 54–59.

65. The data was not analysed, published or taken further, because of changes in the posts and engagement of staff and students. So, it seems appropriate for my contribution to this Festschrift.

tained period of engagement and worship with the *Enyonini*, the Church requested us[66] to share a Bible Study with them. When we undertook to "read" a Bible Study "with" the Church, I had no idea of the existence of Dlamini's thesis. Nevertheless, his earlier study agreed at most points with our fieldwork in Elandskop, though we could not claim the depth he provides on the eSwathini branch of *Enyonini*.

We agreed to set up a day-long Bible study at the UKZN, in co-operation with Ujamaa Centre, and utilizing West's model of "reading *with*." We met and discussed this with the local and national *Enyonini* Zionist Church and obtained the "informed consent" of the leadership, their agreement to attend the event themselves, and to its being video recorded—widely done at the Church's major events in any case. The agreed text was the "Parable of Lazarus and the Rich Man" in Luke 16:19–31. The theme was "Search for Transformative Leadership Principles in a Context of HIV and AIDS." About 60 participants arrived at the University (UKZN) on 5th September 2009. The President of *Enyonini*, Rev. Madide, was present, having come down from Johannesburg, as was the Deputy President of the Church from Elandskop, Pietermaritzburg, namely Rev. Maphumulo.

This year was a mid-point in the HIV-AIDS crisis in South Africa, and we decided to take the parable of the Rich Man and Lazarus as a somewhat open and complex narrative: rather different from most of Jesus' parables. It provided the potential to open up discussion on ostracism for unclean skin disease, or to open discussion on wealth and poverty in Church and Society, or to explore questions of Christian or social leadership in general. Our questions were designed to allow options as to what aspects interested them. Our School of Theology at UKZN had just hosted a Conference on HIV-AIDS and Healing, conjointly with the Faculty of Theology at Oslo University, at which both staff and doctoral students gave papers. The papers were published.[67] Most papers emphasized the problem of the shame associated with sexual activity, stigma, and social ostracism. We were interested to see whether "reading with" "untrained readers" would yield similar findings to those of the "trained readers" from the conference.

---

66. "Us" here serves to designate the research team led by Kenneth Mtata as my post-doctoral student and myself, as well as a number of fieldworkers from *Ujamaa*, including Bongi Zengele, Maria Makgamathe, and my then graduate student, Xabiso Sebeni. Their assistance in facilitating is acknowledged with appreciation.

67. Richardson, ed., *Broken Bodies*.

I had engaged and wrestled with this difficult text as a "trained reader" testing narrative and socio-historical analysis.[68]

- The study opened in plenary with repeated readings of the text aloud in the group.

- Then, the provision of background information to the text, which might generate closer reading, discussion in smaller groups to discuss open questions provided.

- Finally, a report back from the groups to the plenary session and general discussion.

When the plenary divided into groups, they were asked to discuss *four* questions to structure their reading:

- The first question posed to the text of the parable was, "Why was Lazarus outside the gate?"

- The second question was, "What kind of leadership position was the rich man providing?"

- Thirdly, "Are there people as sick and neglected as Lazarus in our Church?"

- Fourthly, "What kind of leadership will help us to respond to the ministry of such need?"

The model also presents relevant background information to provide a new angle for the study of this text and to feed into the discussion of the small groups.

- First it was pointed out that all kinds of people would turn up when a rich person gave a feast, hanging on the fringes inside the gate, hoping for scraps or just to look at what was going on: even prostitutes and sinners, even dogs. The Syro-Phoenecian woman whose daughter had an unclean spirit pointed out in her pleading with Jesus that even dogs can forage for scraps under the table. Likewise, the immoral woman wiping Jesus' feet in public with her hair.

- Secondly, in Jesus' time, people got into leadership positions and power by making big donations to a city, giving extravagant feasts, dressing in expensive clothes that made them shine and made the rags of the poor even more obvious, also giving expensive gifts and

68. Finally published in Draper, "Disease, Table and Economy," 125–44.

public donations. This practice was part of the nexus of a patron–client, honour–shame cultural system.[69]

- Thirdly, it was noted that Lazarus is not called a righteous man nor is the rich man called a sinner. Why? What might this mean?

A summary of reports in the groups

8. "Why was Lazarus outside the gate?" This elicited considerable discussion and suggestions: because he was dressed in rags, had sores, was smelly, and was not of the same class or status as a rich man. We were asked to give more information and pointed out that in that society feasting was usually done publicly and uninvited people such as beggars, prostitutes, and even dogs might hang around beneath the table to catch scraps. People might turn up from the vicinity hoping for some food and drink, but only those invited would be seated at table. Some suggested Lazarus was not outside because he was poor but because he was sick and might infect others in the same way that those visiting HIV-AIDS patents should use appropriate protective gear.

9. "Why is Lazarus never called righteous nor the rich man called a sinner?" This did not elicit much sympathy. Someone declared to great applause and laughter, "Don't think because you are poor that you would automatically enter God's kingdom because you are poor nor that a rich person will not enter because of their riches"— someone even went as far as arguing that beggars make themselves poor and street children are making deliberate choices. This was clearly not a majority viewpoint. Nevertheless, they agreed that one should look at people, not on outward appearances, but as they deserve and as God sees inside.

10. "Are there people suffering like Lazarus in your community?" The answer was emphatically yes. It was generally agreed that there were many, even members of the Church, and yet they were not being cared for. They should be visited and the fear of infection should be allayed by the use of protective gear.

69. See for instance Malina, *New Testament World*, 47–49.

11. Fourthly, the question of transformative leadership in a time of HIV-AIDS and the financial question of excessive display of wealth by the rich man in the presence of downright poverty in the case of Lazarus caused much discussion. Interestingly, the groups felt able to discuss this question with their Church leadership present—although the groups did not openly differentiate Church leaders from National government leaders. While obsequiousness to leaders was disapproved, it was also insisted that when people are elected leaders they need to be respected since it is us who put them there: "There needs to be a balance." The question of leadership in the community was taken seriously. It was noted that some people wanted offices such as leadership in the Church and/or a big organization like the ANC for personal advantages. The group argued for "leadership as a collective that is elected by virtue of their dedication and suitability to lead" which gains respect. There was a suggestion that some leaders only took a "top-down approach" and only listened to people of high positions and ignored anyone who was just an ordinary person: "The Lazarus and the rich man syndrome is very much alive in us . . . even when we are believers."

Two group observations did raise some interesting points:

12. The first one was the connection made by one respondent that the rich man asking Lazarus to dip his finger and cool his burning tongue is appropriate because he used his tongue to harm Lazarus: "The issue here is concerning the tongue because the man seems to be burning in the tongue as he was using his tongue to chase away Lazarus during his living days. Therefore, he is burning in the tongue . . . and as leaders, we need to be careful of what we say because it has the potential to destroy the church . . . in Isa 6:5 he says, "'Woe to me!' I cried. 'I am ruined! For I am a man of unclean lips' . . ." "The lips say everything but, at the end, Lazarus is asked to touch the tongue . . . because tongues have been used to destroy the Church instead of uniting it."

13. The angels carrying Lazarus away drew a good deal of interest which may point to unresolved questions in the groups concerning the possibility of dead people returning to warn their kin, because

warning their kin is the role of the ancestors in Zulu culture. As one person put it:

> I'm going to speak to the time when Lazarus was dead. . . the rich man cries out and asks for a person to wake up from the dead and go back to warn his five brothers who are still living. . . maybe they will be shocked into obedience, but the response is that they will not listen because there are prophets and Moses are with them. So, I'm thinking that as we are here we might not listen and use this gospel as we have heard it; instead prefer what we hear from someone returning from beyond the grave.

This speaks to the acting out of the parable by one of the groups in a summary final drama in performing the story, with makeshift props, done to great enjoyment and audience participation. The central feature of the play was the angels (male and female symmetrically on each side of the man) picking up the dead Lazarus and carrying him literally and ceremonially for about 15 minutes singing "*Ngcwele, Ngcwele, Ngcwele*" (Holy! Holy! Holy!) moving rhythmically as they moved around the room and deposited him in Abraham's bosom. In the end, everyone joined in the singing and dancing. The rich man, on the other hand, is graphically castigated and rejected by Abraham. There is a great separation between him and the father Abraham, which cannot be crossed. Abraham is often termed 'Father Abraham' in popular piety but, in the Zionist Church, it is more usual to draw a parallel between Moses and their leaders, especially in the dual role of healer and that of defeating Pharaoh.

On the face of it, for the *Enyonini,* readings of the angels in Luke's Gospel play a minor and purely instrumental role in the narrative of Lazarus' entry into heaven of the dead man. Yet appearances may be deceptive. In other Zionist Churches, angels play a major role. So in Isaac Shembe's *Nazarite* Church, Shembe also has angels bringing back to life a little girl (Elizabeth Gunner, 39), taking either the form of birds and stars or of Shembe's mother.[70] Indeed, the boundaries around the holy spaces and the impure world are guarded by angels.[71]

---

70. Gunner, *Man of Heaven,* 39.

71. Muller, *Rituals of Fertility,* 66–67: "Nazarites construct this alterity by setting up boundaries between 'heavenly' spaces and the defilement characteristic of the wider South African state. These boundaries cannot be crossed other than the figurative 'gate' at which the symbolic angel watches those who enter. This angel stands guard, checking that everyone who enters this space is ritually clean." Cf. Draper, "Worshipping with Angels."

In the *Enyonini* group, the angels in their acted, dramatic inter-pretation play the part of connecting the living and the dead, so they transport the suffering Lazarus to Abraham as the father of the "ances-tors." It is not important to determine whether this has reached the level of consciousness which, in Bourdieu's terms, would be *"ideology."* But germane to this is that the (dead) rich man cries out and asks for a person to wake up from the dead and visit the living. In fact, the parable presumes that it is possible for the dead man to come back to the living and warn the five brothers that their conduct may exclude them from the bosom of Father Abraham. This is a key role played by the ancestors in African Traditional Religion: to warn the living when they are cross-ing the lines of Zulu culture.

The threat of a final separation from the living is one's worst fear in the Zulu *habitus.* Abraham refuses to allow the rich man to go because they already have Moses and the prophets. Most Zionist churches claim to have prophets like Moses (promised by Deut 18:15–22) who warn and counsel the members of the Church. Moreover, the role of Moses who heals and defeats Pharaoh in battle is suggested by the bronze staff in the Zionist churches, though not so clearly in *Enyonini,* which barely men-tions Moses and Abraham.[72] In fact, in Dlamini's study of the Church, he finds it so hard to classify that he calls it "independent orthodoxy" because of its lack of socio-political ambitions and lack of distinctive Zionist characteristics, such as no polygamy allowed; no veneration of the ancestors; no "revival of divination or magic;" no reference back to its founding prophet.[73] Indeed, Dlamini observes that "The supposition that the Bible alone can be the rule of faith was implicitly accepted by everyone–church officials and ordinary worshippers alike." Enyonini appears to accept the main traditional Christian Doctrines, though it has no eucharist.[74]

Conclusion

In the Bible reading of the "Parable of the Rich Man and Lazarus," the angels are not significant for *Enyonini,* as we have noted, although the

72. George Khambule, for instance, carried a staff with a snake on top, inspired by Moses' healing power.

73. Dlamini, *CCAHSCZ,* II.313.

74. Dlamini,*CCAHSCZ,* II, 311–12. The ceremonial washing of the feet as at the Last Supper appears for some Zionist Churches to replace the eucharist.

involvement of angels has the potential to take on a different meaning, as does the reference to Moses and the prophets. It hovers in the dance but does not come explicitly to consciousness. This is not surprising when looked at from the perspective of Bourdieu because this Bible reading was not conducted at a time when their *doxa* was challenged. In fact, participation in a Bible Study at the university would tend to affirm the validity of their *doxa*, in their eyes. In specific crises in which their *habitus* is under threat, I would like to suggest that angels as ancestors might allow Bible reading in *Enyonini* to engage with the text in a more agency-like role.

Moreover, an advantage of paying attention as an "engaged scholar" is that it opens up avenues to new questions and possibilities for interpretation of the Bible itself which challenges our received understandings (*doxa*). Jesus when asked about the resurrection of the dead, answers in terms of angels:

> For when they rise from the dead, they neither marry nor are given in marriage, but are like angels in heaven. And as for the dead being raised, have you not read in the book of Moses, in the story about the bush, how God said to him, 'I am the God of Abraham, the God of Isaac, and the God of Jacob'? 27 He is God not of the dead, but of the living; you are quite wrong. (Mark 12:25–27 NRSV)

Following up on the question of whether "reading with the poor and the oppressed" can enable them to exercise agency by "reading *with*," it is difficult to affirm or deny it, since the poor and the oppressed are not as much an immediately obvious group as they might have been under apartheid. Moreover, Zionist or "prophetic" Churches are no longer automatically part of the social underclass, but their members can, like Judge Mgoeng Mgoeng, obtain high social positions, and even become the Chief Justice of South Africa.

The "mainline" colonial churches and missions are by way of contrast, in my opinion in serious decline, whereas prophetic churches mushroom. In the thirteen years since the Bible Study, we helped facilitate and record, the social location of many of the people from Zion Church whom we got to know have been upwardly mobile. This is not at all to deny that there is still great poverty, glaring inequality, and different forms of oppression and domination, especially in the rural areas and the urban fringes of informal settlements. Moreover, problems of leadership, even among "struggle heroes" (those involved in the struggle against apartheid) are only too obvious in some sectors of leadership in South Africa in the churches and among the political elite.

Even in 2009, it was obviously a concern within the group in this study, which they raised in their interpretations. For example, Daniel Nkonyane's church's modest retention of their Reformed African *habitus* enabled them to survive the repeated attempts to drive them out by the colonial authorities and to create a safe space for their agency. The result is a church that is well suited to profit from the new South Africa because of its emphasis on education, ethical lifestyle and moderation, and the compatibility of their appropriation of cultural capital.[75] George Khambule's church, on the other hand, which made a big impact in the beginning because of its virtual deification of its prophet and its wholesale adoption of a literal reading of the Bible in terms of Zulu cultural capital, was short-lived and did not survive long after Khambule's death. It also did not, in my opinion, leave much by way of heritage in the long run.

This leaves the question of the agency in Zionist Church readings of the Bible, and "reading *with* them," as this paper has tried to utilize what is proposed by West. Perhaps taking a long view, we can see that the Zionist movement as a whole did exercise a positive agency in its resistance to colonial attempts to make them conform to an alien agenda in the religious field, but not all of its expressions are positive. Perhaps Zionist Churches might borrow and redefine the concept used by Roman Catholicism of a *sensus fidelium,* in which there is a gradual adoption by a religious community of theological understandings and practices which gives them the status of received doctrine. From that perspective, one might argue that the majority of positive practices of prophetic and Spirit-driven Zionist churches have exercised and continue to exercise positive agency in their challenge to "orthodox readings of the Bible," as difficult as these terms are to define.[76] It would, however, help both religious and secular authorities if they could develop and adopt some form of accountability by agreeing on what is acceptable and what is not acceptable to them as a broad movement.

75. I was struck by the findings of the late Robert Garner in Dawid Venter, *Concepts and Theories.* He found that the so-called "Apostolic" Zionist Churches—of which *Enyonini* is an example—were faring much better financially in the new circumstances and opportunities offered by liberation than those heavily invested in retaining a more conservative version of the African *habitus.* It certainly matched my own experience in engaging with *Enyonini* and a few other churches.

76. Not that I would wish to see any notion of "infallibility" associated with my use of the term.

Tony Balcomb provides a fascinating response to statistics of the *Atlas of Global Christianity* emerging from the 2010 Edinburgh Conference of the World Council of Churches, which noted the phenomenal growth of Christianity to a majority religion in Africa south of the Sahara. Considering whether this success should be viewed as a victory of imperialism and colonization, as Chinua Achebe concluded [in his novel, *Things Fall Apart*][77] and noting that throughout Africa south of the Sahara, it is the "prophetic," "prosperity" and other forms of AICs which present a very "non-Western style of Christianity" and constitute the majority of Christians, Balcomb concludes:

> More credence needs to be given to the agency of ordinary people in the way that the Christian faith has been transacted, assimilated and insinuated into their lives. Such stories need to find another way into our theological curricula and become part of shaping our theological agenda.[78]

This perspective on the phenomenal growth of Zionist/prophetic/prosperity Churches is a given in the modern Christian *field* and needs to be interrogated in terms of its agency and to ensure a positive contribution to African well-being. As Balcomb insists:

> [It should not be] assumed that the species of Christian faith that was brought to the continent by western missionaries is the one that has always been appropriated by Africans. Far from it. The really successful forms of faith are those that have been translated, in the broad sense of the word, by Africans themselves.... [W]hat Africans have done to the gospel is as important as what the gospel has done to Africans.[79]

Balcomb's analysis is convincing and perhaps confirms the agency of the "untrained grassroots intellectuals" in reading the Bible.

But what can be said about the concept of "engaged intellectuals" *reading with* the poor and the oppressed, as a means to liberate their

---

77. Balcomb, "Christianity in Africa," 8–21. He provides a new perspective on Achebe's epic *Things Fall Apart*.

78. Balcomb, "Christianity in Africa," 20. As I noted above, I would have to concede that my own lecturing and research career was characterized by providing very Western analytic and exegetical tools to students—even when my goal was intended to empower African Contextual interpretations of the Bible by my students. To what extent I was, as I grudgingly admitted I might have been, an agent of colonialism, I leave to others to determine.

79. Balcomb, "Christianity in Africa," 11.

agency? "Engaged intellectuals" may have moved closer to *reading* the Bible *with* the various forms of Christianity and in listening to the large section of it which claims to be "Spirit led" in Zionist or prosperity churches. This paper records an attempt to do just that. However, we ["trained biblical intellectuals"] are a long way from empowering the poor and the oppressed through the agency of Bible Study, if only because the "poor and oppressed" are a fluid and unstable group who do not want to stay poor and oppressed.[80] However, the dignity and sense of self-worth provided by a general process of mutual *reading* and above all listening to the Bible *with* those who have been our others could make a small contribution to their journey, and ours.

Bibliography

Achebe, Chinua. *Things Fall Apart*. Exp. ed. with notes. Portsmouth, NH: Heinemann Educational, 1996.

Balcomb, Anthony O. "Christianity in Africa: Watchdog of Imperialism or 'Drops of Frozen Rain Melting on the Dry Palate of the Panting Earth.'" *Alternation* Special Edition 14 (2015) 8–21.

Bourdieu, Pierre. *The Logic of Practice*. Translated by Richard Nice. Stanford: Stanford University Press, 1990.

———. *Outline of a Theory of Practice*. Translated by Richard Nice. Cambridge Studies in Social Anthropology 16. Cambridge: Cambridge University Press, 1977.

Cochrane, James R. "Already . . . but Not Yet: Programmatic Notes For a Theology of Work." In James R. Cochrane and Gerald O. West. *The Threefold Cord: Theology, Work, and Labor*, 177–89. Pietermaritzburg, SA: Cluster, 1991.

Comaroff, Jean, and John L. Comaroff. *Of Revelation and Revolution, Volume 1: Christianity, Colonialism, and Consciousness in South Africa*. Chicago: University of Chicago Press, 1991.

Dlamini, T. L. L. "The Christian Catholic Apostolic Holy Spirit Church in Zion" as it exists in Swaziland: Its Development, Life and Worship." PhD diss., University of Botswana and Swaziland, 1976.

Draper, Jonathan A. "African Contextual Hermeneutics: Readers, Reading Communities, and Their Options between Text and Context." *RT* 22 (2015) 3–22.

———. "Confessional Western Text-Centered Biblical Interpretation and an Oral or Residual-Oral Context." *Semeia* 73 (1996) 59–78.

———. "Disease, Table and Economy in Luke 16:19–31." In *To Set at Liberty: Essays on Early Christianity and Its Social World in Honor of John H. Elliott*, edited by Stephen K. Black, 125–44. Social World of Biblical Antiquity Series 2/11. Sheffield: Sheffield Phoenix, 2014.

———. "George Khambule and the book of Revelation: Prophet of the Open Heaven." *Neot* 38.2 (2004) 101–24.

---

80. This is, after all, the reason for the popularity of prosperity churches.

———. "Pierre Bourdieu and the Role of the Spirit in Some Zulu/Swathi African Initiated Churches." In *Bourdieu in Africa: Exploring the Dynamics of Religious Fields*, edited by Magnus Echtler and Asonzeh Ukah, 35–69. Studies on Religion in Africa 44. Leiden: Brill, 2014.

———."Reading the Bible as Conversation: A Theory and Methodology for Contextual Interpretation of the Bible in Africa." *Grace and Truth* 19.2 (2002) 12–24.

Draper, Jonathan A., and Gerald O. West. "Anglicans and Scripture in South Africa." In *Bounty in Bondage: The Anglican Church in South Africa: Essays in Honour of Edward King, Dean of Cape Town*, edited by Frank England and Torquil J. M. Paterson, 30–52. Johannesburg: Ravan, 1989.

Eagleton, Terry. *Against the Grain: Essays 1975–1985*. London: Verso,1986.

England, Frank, Torquil Paterson, and Desmond Tutu. *England Bounty in Bondage: The Anglican Church in Southern Africa, Essays in Honour of Edward King, Dean of Cape Town*. Randburg, SA: Ravan, 1989.

Fish, Stanley. "Interpreting the *Variorum*." In *Is There a Text in This Class?*, 147–74. Cambridge: Harvard University Press, 1980.

Freire, Paulo. *Pedagogy of the Oppressed*. Translated by Myra Bergman Ramos. New York: Seabury, 1970.

Gadamer, Hans Georg. *Truth and Method*. Translated by William Glen-Doepel. New York: Seabury, 1975.

Gramsci, Antonio. *Selections from The Prison Notebooks of Antonio Gramsci*. Edited and translated by Quintin Hoare and Geoffrey Nowell Smith. New York: International,1971.

Gunner, Elizabeth. *The Man of Heaven and the Beautiful Ones of God: Umuntu Wasezulwini Nabantu Abahle Bakankulunkulu: Writings from Ibandla IamaNazaretha, A South African Church*. Studies on Religion in Africa 24. Leiden, Brill, 2002.

Halliday, M. A. K. *Language as Social Semiotic: The Social Interpretation of Language and Meaning*. London: Arnold, 1978.

The Kairos Theologians. *The Kairos Document: Challenge to the Church: A Theological Comment on the Political Crisis in South Africa*. Braamfontein, SA: Skotaville, 1986.

Lategan, Bernard C. "Scholar and Ordinary Reader: More Than A Simple Interface." *Semeia* 73 (1997) 244–46.

Malina, Bruce J. *The New Testament World: Insights from Cultural Anthropology*. 3rd ed. Louisville: Westminster John Knox, 2001.

Maluleke, Tinyiko, and Sarojini Nadar. "Alien Fraudsters in the White Academy: Agency in Gendered Colour." *JTSA* 120 (2004) 5–17.

Mofokeng, Takatso. "Black Christians, the Bible and Liberation." *JBTSA* 2.1 (1988) 34–42.

Muller, Carol A. *Rituals of Fertility and the Sacrifice of Desire: Nazarite Women's Performance in South Africa*. Chicago Studies in Ethnomusicology. Chicago: University of Chicago Press,1999.

Richardson, Neville, ed. *Broken Bodies and Healing Communities: The Challenge of HIV and AIDS in the South African Context*. Pietermaritzburg, SA: Cluster, 2009.

Scott, James C. *Domination and the Arts of Resistance: Hidden Transcripts*. New Haven: Yale University Press, 1990.

Spivak, Gayatri. "Can the Subaltern Speak?" In *Marxism and the Interpretation of Culture*, edited by Cary Nelson and Lawrence Grossberg, 24–28. London: Macmillan, 1988.

Sundkler, Bengt. *Bantu Prophets in South Africa: 1909–1995*. Cambridge: James Clarke, 1961.

———. *Zulu Zion and Some Swazi Zionists*. Oxford Studies in African Affairs. London: Oxford University Press, 1976.

Trible, Phyllis. *Texts of Terror: Literary-Feminist Readings of Biblical Narratives*. Overtures to Biblical Theology. Philadelphia: Fortress, 1984.

Venter, Dawid. "Concepts and Theories in the Study of African Independent Churches." In *Engaging Modernity: Methods and Cases for Studying African Independent Churches in South Africa*, 13–44. Westport, CT: Praeger, 2004.

West, Gerald O. *The Academy of the Poor: Towards a Dialogical Reading of the Bible*. Interventions 2. Sheffield: Sheffield Academic, 1999.

———. *Biblical Hermeneutics of Liberation: Modes of Reading the Bible in the South African Context*. Maryknoll, NY: Orbis, 1991.

———."Reading the Bible Differently: Giving Shape to the Discourses of the Dominated." *Semeia* 73 (2001) 21–41.

———. *The Stolen Bible: From Tool of Imperialism to African Icon*. BIS 144. Leiden: Brill, 2016.

Wright, Matthew. "Re-Appropriating Appropriation On the Road to an Adequate Theory of Text Production—A Dialogue with the Tri-Polar Exegetical Framework." *RT* 22.1–2 (2015) 25–45.

6

When the Subaltern Speaks[1]

Reading the Mmutle[2] (Hare) Way[*]

Musa W. Dube

Introduction

AFRICAN ORATURES[3] CONSIST OF a significant corpus of trickster stories. This article investigates indigenous frameworks of reading texts by exploring the philosophical stance of Mmutle, the trickster of Southern Africa, by analyzing eight stories. The analysis of the Mmutle trickster discourse

1. This title is drawn from the famed essay of Gaytri Spivak, "Can the Subaltern Speak?" 271–313, who concludes that the subaltern cannot speak, for the subaltern defines one who is politically silenced, hence she proposes strategic essentialism. My argument in this essay is that Mmutle, who recognises her/himself as a perpetual subaltern, provides a language and philosophy of resistance, survival, speaking and thriving amongst the powerful and oppressive.

2. The Hare has different names according to various ethnic groups. Mmutle is a Setswana name. Among the Ndebele the Hare is known as Uvundla, and Tsuro among the Shona.

* This chapter was previously published in the *Journal of Africana Religions* 4.1 (2016) 54–75. Published here with permission in honor of Professor Gerald Oakley West's indelible contribution to African Biblical Studies and Hermeneutics—researching, teaching, and reading scripture/the Bible with humans.

3. Oratures is a term I adopted from Ngugi' wa Thiongo, the Kenyan novelist and writer; he uses it to refer to oral literature. It is, however, attributed to the Ugandan scholar, Pio Zirumu, who first coined it.

highlights four postures of reading for liberation.[4] First, the vulnerable and oppressed should keep a permanent vigil towards the powerful and always watch out for their interests without fail. Second, the vulnerable and oppressed should be willing to be in solidarity with other vulnerable and oppressed members of the society and to use teamwork. Third, sharp and transgressive thinking skills are vital weapons of resistance, survival and liberation. Fourth, the Mmutle trickster philosophical framework demands skills of rewriting and redirecting a story towards new and unexpected ends in the service of resistance, survival and liberation—a skill most needed by women and other groups, who, more often than not, occupy the position of subalterns due to their gender.

Methodologies

The quest for theories, methods, and frameworks of reading and writing normative texts in the African context includes exploring African ways of knowing and analyzing social reality and relationships.[5] The frameworks of analysis may be drawn from classic African philosophies found in their proverbs, stories, sayings, songs, rituals, art, riddles, language, divination, belief systems, and cosmology.[6] African frameworks of reading texts can also be drawn from modern and contemporary historical experiences such as colonialism, post-independence, globalization, economic challenges, HIV & AIDS, among others. These two streams of interpretation are not parallel, for they intersect in different ways and levels in the history and work of African scholars.[7] Indeed, to speak of

4. Mmutle, as a border-crosser, will always be read in multiple ways depending on the contexts and agendas of readers. For example, some critics have seen the ruling elites of the postcolonial state as tricksters who have tricked all members of the nation, for their own ends. Colonizers who came as minorities and tricked the majority by disposing them of the lands have also been read as tricksters. Maluleke, "Of Lions and Rabbits," 41–55, represents one such an example.

5. The specification of biblical texts here reflects the writer's area of literary specialization. The proposed trickster frameworks of reading can be applied to any other literature.

6. Masenya, "Esther and Northen Sotho Stories," 27–49, where she explores reading the book of Esther through proverbs and folktales of the Sotho people of Southern Africa.

7. Various volumes represent the work of African biblical interpretations and various frameworks of reading. These include West and Dube, eds. *The Bible in Africa*; Dube, ed., *Other Ways of Reading*; Dube, Mbuvi, and Mbuwayesango, eds., *Postcolonial Perspectives*.

African biblical interpretation is at once an acknowledgement of a hybrid practice of standing between cultures, worlds, time and texts as well as to acknowledge a practice of crossing multiple boundaries and bridge building. In this article, I seek to contribute to the quest of constructing African-centred frameworks of reading biblical texts by exploring the character of Mmutle, hare, the main trickster of Southern Africa, who also appears in other regions, such as East, West and Central Africa. In African oratures, stories and their philosophical stance are meant to provide lenses for reading and analyzing life as it exists in relationships and to provide indicators of how one may have to position her or himself in particular situations.

While most African scholars of normative texts (e.g., Bible, Quran) have been trained in Western ways of reading and analysis of social relations in scriptures, most African indigenous Churches have always used African perspectives such as divination and storytelling in their interpretation.[8] In fact, the earliest indigenous response to the encounter with the Bible in Southern Africa named biblical interpretation/reading as divination.[9] Consequently, the first generation of African biblical scholars developed inculturation hermeneutics, which often meant reading the Bible with and through African cultures, or searching for aspects of African concepts that resonated with the act of reading and interpretation. The earliest forms of inculturation, unfortunately, often subjugated African indigenous religions to the Bible and Christianity.[10] Indeed in many cases inculturation was developed as a tool for evangelization.[11] However, several other inculturation approaches such as Canaan Banana's call for rewriting the Bible, Mercy Oduyoye's work in general and Seratwa Ntloedibe-Kuswani's reading of Jesus as *Ngaka* (indigenous

---

8. For a detailed development of divination and storytelling as interpretive frameworks drawn from African Independent Churches, see Dube, "Divining Texts for International Relations (Matt. 15:21–28)," 315–28; Dube, "Divining Ruth For International Relations," 67–80; Dube, "Fifty Years of Bleeding," 26–49; and Dube, "Readings of *Semoya*," 111–29.

9. See Moffat, *Missionary Labours and Scenes in Southern Africa*, 258; and Comaroff and Comaroff, *Of Revelation and Revolution*, 299.

10. See Antonio, "The Hermeneutics of Inculturation," 29–61, who summarizes different forms of African inculturation hermeneutics.

11. Ntloedibe-Kuswani, "The Religious Life of An African," 121–39, who problematizes how early inculturation hermeneutics tended to see African cultures as preparatory ground for planting the Christian gospel rather than traditions in their own right.

African doctor) shift the approach towards valuing African indigenous beliefs than overt subjugation to colonizer's religions.[12]

This article seeks to explore the figure of the trickster in African oratures and how its philosophical perspectives can provide ways of reading normative/texts as well as ways of reading the world and the relationships that African people inhabit.[13] The article focuses on the Southern African main trickster, Mmutle, the hare.[14] The latter might also be a trickster in West, Central and East African oratures. Different African regions and people feature different tricksters. In Ghana, for example, Ananse the spider is the most celebrated trickster. Ananse is credited with divine status as s/he is also held to own all the stories and taught people. Among the Yoruba of Nigeria and other West African ethnic groups, Eshu, the Trickster, also has divine qualities, for he functions as the messenger between all other gods and human beings, thus multi-talented with various languages and interpretations.[15] According to Audre Lorde, Eshu is "The mischievous messenger between all the other Orisha-Vudo [gods] and humans, he knows their different languages and is an accomplished linguist who both transmits and interprets. Eshu is a prankster, also, a personification of all the unpredictable elements in life."[16] Richard Patterson states that "in the folklore of the Central African Republic one encounters the tales of the Tere. Of Divine descent, Tere is the implementer of all that contributes to mankind's wellbeing. He is also a trickster."[17] Other tricksters of African oratures include the Tortoise, the Monkey and the Jackal.

African trickster figures have been intensely studied and theorized in the African Diaspora. There have been different African diaspora movements, including current political and economic ones, yet human enslavement marked the biggest and most historical African diaspora. Exiled from their lands, cultures and communities through enslavement to the Americas and Europe, black people occupied the most vulnerable

12. Banana, "The Case for a New Bible"; Oduyoye, *Beads and Strands*, 12–17; Ntloedibe-Kuswani, "Ngaka and Jesus as Liberators," 498–510.

13. The application of the Mmutle trickster perspectives will be explored in another paper.

14. Studying Southern African oratures indicates that there are other animals which also trick such as the Jackal and the Tortoise, but the Hare almost always tricks in every story, where s/he appears.

15. Eshu's role closely resembles that of Hermes, who was also a trickster.

16. Provost and Lorde, "Becoming Afrekete," 45–59.

17. Patterson, "The Old Testament Use of an Archetype," 385–94.

social positions as they had no human rights. They had, however, in their memories African indigenous traditions,[18] including African oral tales, which they continued to tell and retell among themselves as traditions of self-identity and self-empowerment as compared to the imposed status of enslavement. African trickster stories functioned, among the enslaved Africans, as a sign of hope in hopelessness.

Despite their seeming powerlessness, as enslaved people, the trickster stories continually said, "you can resist, you can survive, you can get out, you can in fact beat the master." Consequently, African trickster stories were and are still very popular among people of African descent in the diaspora (North America, Haiti, Brazil and the Caribbean Islands). The trickster stories were not only preserved, but they also informed modern and contemporary African American writers in the formation of their characters.[19] In some cases, they have been reconstructed[20] while in others they have been constructed as a theory of reading literature.[21]

Within the African contemporary writers, the trickster, together with other genres of African oratures, such as proverbs, myth, legends, riddles, and rituals has been central to creative writers.[22] Reminiscing about the stories he heard around the fireplace in his family, and how they informed their political thinking during colonial and post-independence times, Ngugi Wa Thiongo says:

> Hare, being small, weak but full of innovative wit and cunning, was our hero. We identified with him as he struggled against the brutes of prey like lion, leopard, hyena. His victories were our victories and we learnt that the apparently weak can outwit the strong. We followed the animals in their struggle against hostile nature—drought, rain, sun, wind—a confrontation

18. See Olupona and Rey, eds. *Orisa Devotion as World Religion*, which documents the spread and survival of African Indigenous Religions in the African Diaspora.

19. See Hurston, *Their Eyes Were Watching God*, who is credited with the earliest and most intensive use of African oral literature in novels. See also Provost and Lorde, "Becoming Afrekete," 45–59.

20. Provost and Lorde, "Becoming Afrekete," 45–59, who discuss not only Audre Lorde's use of the African Trickster Eshu, but how she also makes many attempts to reconstruct the gender of Eshu by highlighting his feminine side.

21. See Gates, *The Signifying Monkey*, which perhaps represents the most extensive work to develop the African Trickster, Eshu, as a theory of reading literature.

22. See Okpewho, *African Oral Literature*, considered a landmark in the exploration of the relationship between oral and written African literature. The book reviews indigenous African writers, underlining their rootedness in African cultures and languages, including performance.

often forcing them to search for forms of co-operation. But we were also interested in their struggles among themselves, and particularly between beasts and the victims of prey. These twin struggles, against nature and other animals, reflected real-life struggles in the human world.[23]

Analysis of African written literature indicates that the trickster figure has provided narrative plot, theme, style, characterization, social commentary among African writers. Achebe, one of the earliest African writers, for example, used the trickster story of the Tortoise, who flew to a feast in the sky through the assistance of birds. The Tortoise, however, ate all the food alone without sharing with his transporters, who then abandoned him and flew back to Earth. The Tortoise had to throw himself down and he broke into several pieces upon landing. His wife picked the pieces and reconstructed him. According to Nadia Naar Gada, Achebe uses the rise and fall of the Tortoise to develop the character Okonkwo in *Things Fall Apart* and to discuss the theme of exile, return and dislocation.[24] The trickster framework has been used to describe both the authors and contemporary literature of postcolonial Africa. Writers as political critics of both the colonial and post-independence structures of oppression are regarded as tricksters, since the stories they tell are told from the perspectives of the powerless, seeking to expose the powerful and to outwit them. Underlining the subversiveness of African postcolonial literature Gada thus speaks of African creative writers as "intellectual tricksters,"[25] while Roger Kurtz notes that among some writers "entire texts function as tricksters, making subversive reading available."[26]

My reasons for entering this ongoing conversation on the African trickster discourse are multiple. First, decolonizing the production and analysis of knowledge remains an unfinished project.[27] This includes decolonizing what we read and how we read, for theories and methods that we employ are culturally situated. Most scripture books, such as the

23. See Thiong'o, *Decolonizing the Mind*, 10. Unfortunately, Thiong'o does not seem to be gender sensitive, since he describes the stories using male gender, which is contrary to the indigenous narration.

24. See Gada, "Modern African Literature Revisited," 156–60.

25. It seems the phrase "Trickster Intellectuals" was first used by Sean Kicummah Teuton, *Red Land, Red Power*, 82.

26. See Kurtz, "Peter Nazareth," 317.

27. Thiong'o, *Decolonizing the Mind*, problematizes both the content and structure of presenting our literary works in the academic halls as privileging colonial knowledge.

Bible and Koran, which are now African books, but they are more often that not tied to the history of modern colonization and marginalization of women.[28] While in the past seventy years most African countries have acquired their liberation, it is increasingly clear that colonization was not only political and geographical, but also economic, cultural, spiritual, psychological, and ideological. African economic systems remain tied to the western structures of trade (and other new powers) in a relationship that does not equally empower both parties. The academic institutions in the African continent and elsewhere remain largely organized according to Western ways of knowing and producing knowledge.[29] In exploring Mmutle trickster perspectives and applying them to biblical interpretation, I seek both decolonization and expansion of knowledge to include, *Other Ways of Reading*, so to speak.[30] Not only have we, African scholars, opened ourselves to learning Western ways of knowing and applied them to our scholarly work, we also seek to present the world with African ways of knowing and production of knowledge.[31] As said above, the theorization of African trickster perspectives has already been championed by people of African descent in the historic diaspora of enslavement,[32] that preceded modern colonialism. Second, the trickster philosophical perspectives are pertinent to the African scholar, women and other oppressed people of the world, because increasingly, the continent continues to be marginalized among the rising world superpowers of different ages. To read from the trickster perspective is to first and foremost recognize one's situation of vulnerability but not incapacity.[33] It is to take a position for one's own empowerment and to be in solidarity with many others who find themselves living with and among the powerful, who are potential oppressors, and in many cases, indeed oppressors. A trickster reading perspective is the insistence that regardless of one's vulnerability, one still has the power

28. Dube, *Postcolonial Feminist Interpretation of the* Bible.

29. See Thiong'o, *Decolonising the Mind.*

30. Dube, *Other Ways of Reading*, 1–221.

31. See Diakite and Hucks, "Africana Religious Studies," 61, who argue "for a vision of ARS as a transdisciplinary field with capacity to support new models of research." It is this paper's agenda to highlight Mmutle philosophical perspective as offering some frameworks of reading texts.

32. See Gates, *The Signifying Monkey*; and Provost and Lorde, "Becoming Afrekete," 45–59.

33. Niditch, "Genesis," 24, points out that most trickster stories have the following pattern: "a problem in status, deception to improve status, and success of the plan."

to resist, survive and liberate themselves, but one must always take his/her own side and the side of others who are oppressed.

While there are many tricksters in African oratures, in this article I focus on the Southern African trickster, Mmutle. This is the tradition I grew up with, as a citizen of Botswana in Southern Africa. I therefore focus on the Setswana Mmutle trickster discourse, since even among Southern African ethnic groups oral cultures allow for individuality, creativity and contextualization of storytelling. This applies also to different storytellers within the same community.[34] This focus allows me to give this specific tradition its particular attention, even though it shares many similarities with other trickster traditions of Southern Africa and the world. Further, African trickster traditions that have received more attention are the West African ones, (Eshu and Ananse) since more people of African descent in the historic diaspora of enslavement identify with this region. This is not to suggest, however, that the rabbit trickster has not traveled into the historic African Diaspora. Indeed, the rabbit is also well known and celebrated as Brer Rabbit in the African Diaspora.

Third, the gender neutrality of Mmutle is also a motivating factor. African oratures feature animals as personified characters, which appear gender-neutral. Whereas it is largely documented that most trickster figures are male,[35] this is hardly the defining feature of Mmutle the trickster of Southern Africa. In almost all the Mmutle trickster stories, Mmutle is gender-neutral. Hardly ever is Mmutle named as male or female.[36] This gender-neutrality enables the listeners who hear the stories to identify with Mmutle, without emasculation or stereotyping of one gender. All listeners (boys and girls, men and women) can learn/adopt the Mmutle strategies of resisting oppression, surviving and working in solidarity with other oppressed members of the world. In an attempt to respect gender neutrality of the Mmutle trickster discourse (and African oratures in general), this article makes effort to maintain its

34. Consequently, a grandmother telling a story to a child may slightly change the characters to address issues that the particular child needs to learn. Thus, a story told among men's evening gathering space and at the women's traditional space may be changed accordingly.

35. Hansen, *The Trickster and Paranormal*.

36. I found one story where a married couple of Mmutle was supposed to work on their farm. The female Mmutle expected the male partner to clear the field so that she may cultivate the crops. The male Mmutle was, however, too lazy to clear the field and decided to trick the rhino and the elephant into fighting. Since they are both big animals, their fighting automatically cleared the ground for Mmutle's field.

gender neutrality. Mmutle as a gender-neutral trickster should also land an interesting reading of the biblical tradition's tendency to characterize women as tricksters in a patriarchal world.[37]

Mmutle: The Southern African Trickster

Mention Mmutle to most citizens or children of Southern Africa, you will see people smile or laugh. By mentioning Mmutle, you have automatically produced and lifted a trick card, loaded with humor and transgression of socially accepted norms. Mmutle is quintessentially a trickster in Southern African oratures.[38] In the Mmutle tales, nothing seems to be what it is. With Mmutle, the trickster, what is said and what is done, at various points of the story, are two different things. With Mmutle the trickster, what should be and what becomes are two different things. Mmutle changes his/her views and stance several times. Mmutle is an unpredictable performer, who inhabits multiple perspectives and realities all at once. Consequently, Mmutle twists the plot, and changes the story and its outcomes several times. The only predictable aspect about Mmutle is her or his unpredictability. Mmutle is thus a character who challenges listeners and readers to deeper listening and interpretation. Since the trickster discourse in general tends to feature a small animal, surviving and defeating the powerful through wit, Mmutle like most trickster traditions, features a great deal of irony.[39] There is always a space that one must read that is beyond what is verbally expressed and what is actually meant. Mmutle, who relies much on her/his own wit, thus challenges listeners to a great deal of careful listening and thinking beyond the obvious words and actions. Noting this particular use of words in trickster traditions, Audre Lorde and Kara Provost hold that, "through multi-voiced, outspoken and disruptive discourse, the trickster models ways of speaking, writing, enacting those contradictions of who we are."[40] The trickster discourse, thus

37. That being said, quite a number of biblical patriarchs played the trickster several times. Examples include Abraham claiming that Sarah is his sister; Isaac claiming that Rebekah is his sister; Jacob tricking his father to get Esau's blessing; Laban giving Jacob a wrong daughter for a wife; Simon and Levi tricking the Hivites into circumcision in order to attack them while weak; Joseph placing an expensive cup in the purchase of his unknowing brothers.

38. The Mmutle character has inspired many songs in Southern Africa. It would be interesting to investigate how the character has informed contemporary novelists.

39. See Booth, *A Rhetoric of Irony.*

40. Provost and Lorde, *Becoming Afrekete,* 57.

tease and challenge the listener to multiple levels of interpretation and keeps the reader constantly unsettled.

The Mmutle trickster philosophy of Southern Africa is stringent and relentless, as the stories below will highlight. Mmutle need not be provoked to trick. The powerful need not have obvious bad intentions or plans. The powerful need not overtly oppress or exploit Mmutle. They need not be unkind, uncompassionate, unfair, unhelpful, inhospitable, or exclusive. The trickster must, always, without any compromise and regardless of the circumstances, trick the powerful in all his/her dealings with them—and at all times. Further, Mmutle tricks are not just good games, where it is all fun and no one gets hurt. Indeed Mmutle is not hesitant to lie, cheat, steal, and kill for his/her own way. It seems fair to say in the Mmutle trickster discourse, the powerful or potential oppressors have already been tried and judged and found deserving of perpetual trickery. But to call the powerful potential oppressors in the Mmutle discourse is an understatement. They have been tried and found to be irredeemable oppressors. Consequently, in the Mmutle trickster discourse of Southern Africa, Mmutle is incapable of ever avoiding tricking, seemingly good members of the society and bad ones, the well-intending and the evil planning, the kind and the unkind, the seemingly fair and unfair. No powerful person is exempt. Mmutle must trick, always, and everyone—as long as they are powerful.

In so doing, the Mmutle trickster discourse underlines that the powerless must never lose guard, never compromise, never trust, or ever relax in their dealings with the powerful, hence potential oppressors. The stakes are high. The vulnerable must remain perpetually suspicious and on guard to a point where it is almost an ongoing war. In adopting this stance, the Mmutle trickster discourse underlines, fairly or unfairly, that the powerless must realize there are no fair dealings with the powerful, at any time. Indeed the tradition underlines that to assume such a position is to subject oneself to further exploitation and oppression. The analysis of Mmutle tradition thus encourages the vulnerable to be consistently on guard and to use the most powerful tool they have; namely, thinking for themselves and to center their own interests, always. This position is consistently demonstrated by Mmutle's dealings with all the powerful/potential oppressors, to the point where one might be embarrassed by what seems to be Mmutle's singular selfishness. This characterization of Mmutle, however, serves to underline the point to the powerless: "never cease to be suspicious, for the playing ground is already biased against you."

Mmutle's characterization embodies this commitment and caution. The stories of Mmutle acting in solidarity with the other vulnerable members are central to interpreting the rest of the trickster stories. They caution against equating Mmutle's approach with selfishness by highlighting that Mmutle does take a position for other vulnerable animals, when they are oppressed by the powerful through using his/her skills to save them (two cases shall be discussed below). In so doing, the Mmutle philosophical perspective does not only underline that the vulnerable should always take an option for their own liberation and interests, it also encourages them to be in solidarity with one another.

With this background, I want to highlight some of the above discussed aspects of the Mmutle trickster discourse by providing hard data (stories) under three categories. The first category shall examine Mmutle with the Big Five. These will include the Elephant, Lion, Whale, a White man and everybody else. The second category examines a story where Mmutle was tricked by Tortoise. The third category examines stories where Mmutle acted in solidarity with other vulnerable members to resist their oppression and give them means of surviving as liberated members among the powerful and potentially oppressive members. The Mmutle storyteller is her/himself a performer, to present the complex character of the trickster. The written translations that follow are, therefore, limited since they do not adequately carry the performance that comes with oral storytelling. The nuances of gesture, song, tonality, audience participation, among others, are lost in translation. Be that as it may, I invite you to the narrative world of Mmutle the trickster to witness that the subaltern can, and must, speak.

Tricking the Big Five: Lion, Elephant, Rhino, a White Man, and Everyone Else[41]

Mmutle and the Elephant

Once upon a time, Mmutle met the Elephant in the forest. Mmutle looked at the elephant and said, "You are so big and so fat, but you are not strong. I can pull you and throw you into the ocean." The Elephant was stunned to be challenged by such a small animal. The two agreed on a day when they could pull each other. When the concerned day arrived,

---

41. All the translations and retelling used in this article are mine.

Mmutle went to give the Elephant one end of the robe saying, "Hold this until I give you a signal to pull, that is, when I start pulling you." Then Mmutle went to the Whale and said. "You are so big, but I am stronger than you. I can pull you out of that water of yours into the forest if you doubt." The whale said, "No way." Then Mmutle said, "Okay. Hold this robe. When I pull it, then start pulling for your life. Give me some time to find my place in the forest." Mmutle ran to the middle point, where s/he began to give a signal to both animals. The Elephant and the whale began to pull each other. None of the animals moved from its place, since their strength was almost equal. After a while the rope broke into two and the elephant fell down on its back. With a big splash, the Whale also plunged into the water. Mmutle first ran towards the Elephant, who was struggling to stand up, and said, "You see! You could not pull me. If the string did not break, you would be in the ocean right now." The Elephant[42] said, "Mmutle, from now onwards I will truly respect you for your strength." Mmutle left and headed to the seashore to see the Whale who also gave Mmutle the same acknowledgement.

Mmutle and the Lion

Once upon a time, Mmutle met an Old Lion, who was unable to hunt other animals. The Old Lion grabbed Mmutle and said, "I am going to eat you." Mmutle said, "Grandfather, instead of eating me, why don't we plan to get a larger amount of meat so that we can eat together? Here is my idea. Let us build a kraal and then you can go inside and pretend that you have fainted or are dead. I will call other animals to come and see a dead Lion. Once they are inside, I will close the kraal and give a shout and you can wake up and kill as much as you want." The Lion said, "But who will build the kraal? I do not want to build a kraal." Mmutle said, "Aagh, that is not difficult at all. Apparently, if I say, "Kraal be made, the kraal will make itself." So Mmutle said Kraal make yourself, and a new kraal appeared. The Old Lion went inside and slept as if he was dead, while Mmutle went out to call animals to come and see a dead Lion. As soon as the animals were inside, Mmutle closed the kraal and called, "Lion get them!" The Lion woke up and killed several animals while others ran away. Thereafter Mmutle and Lion began to cook the meat in big pots. But then great

42. There are four other stories where Mmutle tricked Elephant in the Setswana tales.

clouds began to gather and then Mmutle said, "We need a house. I can command a new house to appear, but you must help me to roof it." Then Mmutle said, "May a house appear." And the house appeared so while they were knocking the nails into the rafters, Mmutle nailed the tail of the Old Lion into the rafters and jumped down and began to open the pots of meat. Mmutle picked the biggest and most succulent piece and showed it to the Lion and said, "Should I eat this piece grandfather?" The Lion said, "No. That one is mine." Mmutle sat down and started to eat the whole piece. Then again Mmutle went to the pot and picked out another richest piece and asked the Lion, "Grandfather, can I eat this one?" The Lion said it was suitable for himself, but Mmutle ate it. The Lion in great anger tried to jump down but ended up suspended in the air. Mmutle ate all the meat in the same style and when s/he was really full s/he left the Lion to die, hanging down the roof.

Mmutle and All Other Animals

Once upon a time, there was a great drought. Water and food were very scarce. The king of all animals decided to call a compulsory meeting to discuss the situation and strategize. The animals agreed to dig a well for their water supply. Mmutle refused to participate, stating that s/he will not need to drink from their well. All other animals spent days digging until they had a big and reliable well. The following day when the animals had gone searching for food, Mmutle descended upon the well, drank as much as s/he wanted, washed her/himself and even pooped in the water. When the animals returned, and discovered that Mmutle drunk their water, they decided to leave one animal guarding the water each morning when they go searching for food. The Hyena was the first to remain as the guard. While watching, there came Mmutle carrying succulent honeycombs, dripping of sweet honey. S/he said to Hyena, "If you let me drink water from your well, I will give you one of these honeycombs." The Hyena, feeling hungry, agreed. While s/he was busy eating honey, Mmutle, drunk the water, washed and peed in the water. When the animals realized the guard's failure, they were disappointed. The Hyena was dismissed from the job. They decided to elect a different animal on a daily basis to guard the well. All the animals took their turns, but each time Mmutle managed to drink, wash, and contaminate the water.[43]

43. There are two other Mmutle trick stories featuring Mmutle against all animals

The animals decided to come up with a new plan to arrest Mmutle. They build a man with a sticky wax next to the well. When Mmutle arrived, Mmutle said, "Hello!" The man did not answer. Mmutle greeted again, but there was no answer. Mmutle said, "If you do not reply to me, then I am going to hit and knock you down with my fist." And still, there was no response. Da! Mmutle hit the silent man with a fist. Mmutle 's right hand got stuck. Mmutle screaming said, "You, let me go! Let me go, or I will kick you." There was no response. Da! Mmutle kicked the man and his whole foot stuck in. "Let me go! Let me go!" Mmutle screamed and kicked with another foot and hit with another hand and they all stuck." Let me go! Let me go," cried Mmutle desperately. "Let me go, if you don't I will knock you down with my head." The man did not reply. Da! Mmutle headed the man, and now the whole of Mmutle was stuck. No amount of wriggling could set Mmutle free until the animals returned from searching for food. The animals decided that Mmutle deserved to die for the numerous crimes s/he committed against the whole animal community. Elephant was given the task to kill the culprit. Mmutle said, "Please, Elephant, just one thing I request from you as you kill me. First, throw me high up, after that, you can crash me with your feet as you wish." The Elephant threw Mmutle high in the air and when s/he landed on the ground, Mmutle sprung away!

Mmutle and the White Man

Once upon a time, Mmutle was cooking porridge on the fire. The pot was very hot and the porridge was "boiling." Just then Mmutle saw a white man coming towards the direction of her/his house. Mmutle rushed and took the pot off the fire and destroyed the fire until there was no trace of fire. But because the pot had been very hot, the porridge continued to "boil." When the white man arrived he was surprised to see a pot boiling without any fire or source of heat. The white man asked the Mmutle about the pot. Mmutle said this is the only pot that can cook without fire every morning. All you need to do is to command the pot to cook in the morning and it will cook." The white man said, "I would love to have a pot of this kind." Mmutle said, "I can sell it to you, but it will cost you a lot of money." The white man said, "I am willing to pay what you ask for this pot." "Good, then the pot is yours," said Mmutle. "Let me empty the pot

---

and winning.

of the porridge, wash it and give it to you." Mmutle soon came back with a clean and empty pot and received a lot of money from the white man, who happily went away with his pot. The following morning the white man was eager to use his pot. So he said, "Pot make porridge." The pot did not respond regardless of his repetitions. Realizing that he has been cheated the white man went to report Mmutle at the court. Meanwhile, Mmutle, gathered all other Mmutle species. When the white man was asked to identify the Mmutle who cheated him, he could not identify him/her. The white man was thus charged for falsely accusing the Mmutle clan.

Brief Analysis

Consistent with the above description in the introductory sections, these four stories highlight that the Mmutle trickster discourse is largely about challenging the powerful and demonstrating that the vulnerable are not powerless. It underlines that the vulnerable need not subject themselves to domination. In the first story, quite unprovoked, Mmutle challenges Elephant's power and sets it against the Whale, while claiming credit for himself. In the second story, featuring the Lion, Mmutle is indeed confronted with death. The Lion wants to eat Mmutle. Mmutle escapes by seemingly collaborating with the Lion. In the end, Mmutle does not only save him/herself but also uses Lion to gather food for her/his own ends and leaves the Lion to die of hunger. The moral of the story is, even when the powerful seek to oppress and kill the vulnerable, there is a way of beating them at their game and getting away. To evoke Lorde's famous question ("Can the master's tool bring down his own house?"),[44] perhaps the Mmutle trickster discourse demonstrates that one can use the master's tool for one's end. The third story, featuring all animals, seals the effectiveness of Mmutle trickster resistance and survival skills. Mmutle refuses to participate in a community project but wants to benefit from its fruits. By tricking all the animals who had guarded the well, including the Elephant who was supposed to kill him, the Mmutle's trickster discourse underlines its own effectiveness: the vulnerable can live among the big and powerful and even in communities, but they should know how to apply skills of resistance, survival and liberation. Indeed, by tricking all animals as they took their turns, Mmutle is elevated to the status of a

---

44. See Lorde, *Sister Outsider*, 110–13.

hero.[45] The last story, featuring a white man, underlines that the Mmutle trickster discourse is not a frozen tradition, rather it is also applicable to contemporary giants and circumstances. Historically credited with having used cheap goods (beads, bibles, mirrors and bottles of whisky) to take African lands, economic and human resources from African people, in this story the tables are turned. Mmutle is the one who sells a white man a useless pot while s/he gets away with his money.

When the Trickster Got Tricked: Mmutle and the Tortoise

While Mmutle, being one of the small and vulnerable animals, learned to resist and survive among the big, the strong and potential oppressors, by using her/his own wit and always taking his/her own side, the expert trickster once got tricked by the Tortoise.[46] The Tortoise is held as a trickster in some West African traditions; however it does not, carry the same features in Southern Africa. In this particular tale, the Tortoise is featured as a trickster and successfully beats Mmutle, the expert Trickster, at the game. The question to ask is: why does the trickster discourse allow Mmutle, the expert, to get beaten at her/his own game? And what does the story add to the philosophy of being in the world as a trickster? First, let us consider this tale.

It is said Mmutle once said to Tortoise, "I can run much faster than you." Tortoise said, "You are not serious. I can beat you flat in a race." After a long argument, they agreed to solve the issue by running a specified race on a specified date and time. Tortoise being aware of his/her slow pace organized a whole team of tortoises and placed them at different points of the specified route. Mmutle and Tortoise started to run at the agreed time and point. Mmutle effortlessly sprung ahead and Tortoise was slowly crawling behind. After running for a while Mmutle stopped, looked behind and said, "Where are you Tortoise?" And Mmutle heard Tortoise answering, "I am here, ahead of you!" Stunned, Mmutle decided

45. See Scheub, *Trickster and Hero,* for an elaborate exploration of the trickster and hero. He holds that "the trickster embodies the essential traits of the hero: everything except vision. And the trickster often moves on the grand scale of the hero," 12.

46. In fact, in another story, Mmutle and Tortoise are shown to be in a very close trickery competition: Mmutle first tricked Tortoise of his bag of food, by jumping on it and claiming he found it for himself. The court granted Mmutle the bag. Tortoise got back by jumping on Mmutle's tail and claiming that s/he found it for him/herself. The court was forced to grant the Tortoise Mmutle's tale, which explains why the Hare has no tail up to today.

to spring faster and passed Tortoise. After a while, Mmutle stopped and asked, "Where are you Tortoise?" Again, Mmutle heard the Tortoise answering ahead of him and saying, "I am here, ahead of you." Mmutle lifted his/her head and indeed saw the Tortoise ahead. Mmutle sprung ahead and passed the Tortoise and after a while, s/he stopped and asked, "Where are you Tortoise?" Mmutle received the same answer. The Tortoise was crawling ahead of her/him. Mmutle's response was the same. S/he sprang and ran faster toward the finishing line. As Mmutle gazed towards the finishing point, Mmutle saw Tortoise already there. The Tortoise said, "I won the race! Now you have to agree that I run faster than you, Mmutle." Although puzzled, Mmutle had to consent that the Tortoise runs faster than him/her.

In this story, which is often used to highlight that teamwork is effective, Mmutle the expert trickster is successfully tricked by the Tortoise. Why? Mmutle has virtually tricked all animals but fails in the case of Tortoise. Unlike in other cases, where Mmutle was overtly aware of his/her physical powerlessness, Mmutle trusted in his/her physical capacity. In other cases, Mmutle knew that the best tool available to him/her was the brain and wit. Mmutle always knew that while there were big-sized and powerful animals in his/her world, s/he was equally gifted with brains. So Mmutle always thought for him/herself and used wit to resist and survive as a liberated person. In the case of Tortoise, Mmutle was convinced that s/he can actually run much faster than a Tortoise and did not have to use her/his head to survive. Consequently, Mmutle was beaten by Tortoise, who, being terribly aware of his/her slow pace, immediately resorted to her/his mind to design a way of winning the race. Consistent with the rest of the stories featuring Mmutle, the story underlines that the vulnerable need not ever relinquish their major tool of resistance and liberation; namely, thinking and acting for their own interests and own survival. They can only do so at their own peril. On the flip side, the story also underlines that the powerless actually need teamwork and solidarity, as demonstrated by Tortoise's strategy.

Mmutle in Solidarity with the Vulnerable and Oppressed

While the portrait of Mmutle as a trickster may seem too self-centered and border on selfishness, two stories do save face and offer a framework for interpreting the Mmutle trickster discourse. The two stories highlight that the character of Mmutle serves as a model for other smaller and vulnerable animals in the world of the big, the powerful and the potential oppressors. The first story is the tale of the Baboon and the Python, the snake that kills by constricting its victims. It is said one day the Baboon was hunting for fruits in the mountains when s/he came upon a groaning Python. A big boulder had rolled on top of Python. Upon seeing the Baboon, Python begged, "Please help me. Roll this rock off my back." Please. The Baboon rolled the rock away. But as soon as Python was free, s/he jumped on to the Baboon and rolled him/herself all around the Baboon in preparation for eating the Baboon. Desperate, the Baboon begged for his/her life: "Please Python, this is not fair. I just saved you, but you want to eat me. Is this the way to thank a compassionate friend? Please, let me go." But Python tightened his/her grip and said, "I am hungry. I was caught by this rock while searching for food and I have been under this rock for a long time. I am going to eat you."

Just then Mmutle appeared and heard the Baboon's cry for help. "What is going on here?" asked Mmutle. The Baboon explained the story. Mmutle said s/he does not understand. The Python explained the story. Again, Mmutle said s/he does not understand. Finally, Mmutle said, "I really cannot understand what happened here. I think the best way to assist me to understand is that everybody must go back to the place where they were. Let us reenact the whole story." So the Python loosed her/his hold on the Baboon. The Baboon rolled back the boulder on the Python again. Then the Baboon started narrating the story, "I came walking around this rock, searching for fruits, when I found Python trapped and groaning under a rock. He was calling for help. I began to roll the rock away, like this . . ." "Stop!" interrupted Mmutle. "It's alright, Baboon. It's alright! I understand your story now. Here is my advice: You Baboon, just walk away from Python and continue searching for your own food." So the Baboon was saved by Mmutle, as s/he walked away from the trapped Python and continued with his /her own search for food.

This story highlights the ethical commitment of the Mmutle trickster discourse. In other words, the Mmutle trickster philosophy of being in the world of the big and powerful as a small and vulnerable member, involves recognizing other vulnerable members in the community who may be subjected to oppression. This recognition means that the Mmutle trickster discourse includes being in solidarity with other oppressed members. Consequently, in this story, Mmutle tricks are not only used for her/his own interest, but also to save other vulnerable animals subjugated by a powerful member. The story highlights the Mmutle trickster discourse as salvific and embracing solidarity with other smaller animals in danger of being eaten up by powerful ones.

The second story is about the horses' experience of oppression. It is said horses were oppressed and overworked by human beings. After enduring much, the horses decided to consult Mmutle about their situation and how they can overcome their oppression. After listening to their plight, Mmutle informed the horses to return to him on a specified date. All horses were expected to turn up. Mmutle promised to administer medicine on all horses that would deter human beings from oppressing and exploiting them. On the specified date all the horses arrived, Mmutle was sitting down with two containers, one with white paint and another with black paint. Mmutle began to paint each horse black and white stripes. Since there were so many horses and it was taking so long to get the job done, some horses became impatient, awaiting their chance. They began fidgeting and kicking around. In the process, they spilt Mmutle's paint. Mmutle said, "Sorry, only those who have been painted will be protected from human oppression." This is how we came to have zebras that are free from human control and the tame horses, which remain under human control.

In this story, Mmutle's trickster skills are elevated to sage skills. Whereas in the constrictor story, Mmutle happened to find the baboon in trouble and voluntarily used her/his skills, in the second story the oppressed approach him/her. Since s/he is known for the capacity to escape all forms of oppression from all the most powerful and potentially oppressive members of his/her community, Mmutle is consulted by those who find themselves subject to oppressive powers. In fact, the story encourages the vulnerable and oppressed to seek the wisdom of Mmutle. In so doing, the story indicates that Mmutle's resistance and survival techniques can be used for the benefit of other vulnerable members of the community if they adopt them. Mmutle, in other words, does not only act for her/his own interest but can also use her/his wisdom for other oppressed members. The story also indicates that the oppressed members who fail to adopt Mmutle's wisdom for liberation (horses) do so at their own peril—they are likely to remain under the yoke of their oppressors. The two stories, featuring the Baboon and Horses, elevate Mmutle trickster skills, beyond seemingly individual interests to a level where they are useable to all who may, in different times and circumstances, find themselves subjugated by the powerful. Seen against the background of these two stories, the rest of Mmutle's stories are clearly not about irredeemable selfishness of the trickster. Rather the whole Mmutle trickster corpus models for the vulnerable ways of being in the world and the importance of being committed to resistance and liberation from all oppressors and potential oppressors, as well as being in solidarity with the Other, who is oppressed.

It is this particular perspective that makes Mmutle (trickster) framework relevant for liberation-oriented African biblical reading. The African continent and its people are, in more ways than one, the powerless and vulnerable among many world giants. Yet there shall never be a time when the African continent and its people will live apart from the giants and potential oppressors of their world. The Mmutle trickster framework of thinking and being, while ancient, remains relevant as a strategy of reading relationships and texts for resistance, survival and liberation. In particular, the diaspora trickster discourse and the contemporary African compositions highlight the usability of the Mmutle trickster philosophy in today's relationships and reading situations and texts.

Reading with and through the Mmutle Framework

In sum, the above, analysis of the Mmutle trickster discourse indicates that trickster frameworks of interpretation involve the art of

1. Recognizing one's low social status in the community and world they inhabit and the potential of being exploited and oppressed, a stance that challenges the listener/reader to identify their own social location in relation to other members.

2. Not giving up, not becoming helpless, not becoming dependent on the powerful/potential oppressors nor excluding oneself from the relationship with the powerful, but never ever trusting them. Trickster reading is, to use feminist language, to be a suspicious reader of relationships and to treat almost all relationships with the powerful/ potential oppressors as a crime scene, which must always be subject to resistance and survival techniques of trickery.[47]

3. Developing unshakeable confidence in one's capacity to resist, survive and beat the powerful through thinking—wit. In the Mmutle

47. Schüssler Fiorenza, *Bread Not Stone*, 1–223.

discourse, the weak and vulnerable are not helpless or powerless. They must develop great skills of thinking.

4. Developing an uncompromising stance of a self-centered approach in all the dealings with the powerful and potentially oppressive members of one's world. Consequently, foregrounding thinking skills for resistance, survival and staying free through wit, which should be consistently applied at all times and all circumstances.

5. Using language in a complex manner for one's own self-protection, a fact that challenges the trickster reader/listener to complex analysis of relationships and meaning, purpose and manner of communication.

6. Redirecting the plot of the story towards one's own ends for resistance, survival and liberation—basically rewriting the story.

7. Giving solidarity to other vulnerable members, to defeat the powerful and oppressive members (Baboon and Horses' stories, even the gathering of hares to trick a white man). A Mmutle reading framework takes the side of the marginalized and oppressed.

8. Realizing that teamwork and solidarity is needed to overcome the powerful (Tortoise and Python story).

9. Being a multiple border crosser: crossing social class, gender, animal and cultural norms, among many other social categories.

10. Self-transformation—consistently changing from one state to another, one position to another, one perspective to another, from oppression to liberation.

11. Radical non-conformist to social standards at home and with strangers.

12. Performing different characters all at once, thus eluding predictability.

13. Assuming positions of trickster intellectuals in reading and writing texts.

These Mmutle philosophical principles can also be articulated in question form and applied to analyzing texts and relationships for resistance, survival and liberation as follows:

1. What is my social status in relation to those in power in my world?

2. How should I approach any issue and read any text for resistance, survival, and liberation?

3. In the text/story that I am reading, who are the powerful, the vulnerable and the powerless?

4. Who are the powerful and potential oppressors and how can I apply the trickster strategies of reading a situation to evade their potential or given oppression towards the vulnerable?

5. How can I read from the perspective of the vulnerable and in solidarity with them?

6. How can I use my language and my wit to put a twist to the story for my resistance, survival and liberation and for other vulnerable members of my world and community?

7. How can I retell any text from the perspective of the powerless and the vulnerable and change its outcome completely?

8. How should I remain committed to inclusive and gender-neutral language?

9. How can my reading demonstrate commitment to multiple border-crossing of all social categories and structures?

10. How can my reading and writing of social texts remain faithful to unpredictability?

11. How can I become a trickster intellectual in my writing and interpretation of social texts and relations, by assuming a position of perpetual challenge and resistance to structures of oppression and potential oppression?

While I have used the Southern African trickster figure, Mmutle, other African regions can add to this effort by theorizing trickster frameworks according to their regional figures. For West Africa, this would be Ananse and Eshu philosophical frameworks, who more often than not, are also characterized as culture heroes with divine status. Yet even within regions, the particular trickster traditions have developed in various directions, given the flexibility of oratures. Tracing the various genealogies of the trickster discourse is also important, as it might tell us about both the storytellers and their social contexts. Understanding and defining the philosophical frameworks offered by various tricksters and tracing their genealogies are important steps towards application of such perspectives on the interpretation and writing of texts and social relations for resistance, survival and liberation.

Bibliography

Antonio, Edward P. ed. *Inculturation and Postcolonial Discourse in African Theology.* Society and Politics in Africa 14. New York: Lang, 2006.

Banana, Canaan S. "The Case for a New Bible." In *"Rewriting" the Bible: The Real Issues,* edited by I. Mukonyora, et al., 17–32. Gweru: Mambo, 1993.

Booth, Wayne. *A Rhetoric of Irony.* Chicago: University of Chicago Press, 1974.

Comaroff, Jean, and John Comaroff. *Of Revelation and Revolution: Christianity, Colonialism and Consciousness in South Africa.* Vol. 1. Chicago: University of Chicago Press, 1991.

Diakite, Dianne M. S., and Tracy E. Hucks, "Africana Religious Studies: Towards a Transdisciplinary Agenda in an Emerging Field." *JAR* 1.1 (2013) 28–77.

Dube, Musa W. "Divining Ruth For International Relations," In *Postmodern Interpretations of the Bible,* ed. A. K. Adam, 67–80. St. Louis: Chalice, 2001.

———. "Divining Texts for International Relations (Matt. 15:21–28)." In *Transformative Encounters,* edited by Ingrid Kirtzberger, 315–28. Leiden: Brill, 1999.

———. "Fifty Years of Bleeding: A Storytelling Feminist Reading of Mark 5:24–35." In *Other Ways of Reading: African Women and the Bible,* edited by Musa W. Dube, 26–49. Atlanta: SBL, 2001.

———, ed. *Other Ways of Reading: African Women and the Bible.* Global Perspectives on Biblical Scholarship 2. Atlanta: SBL and Geneva: WCC, 2001.

———. *Postcolonial Feminist Interpretation of the Bible.* St Louis: Chalice, 2000.

———. "Readings of *Semoya*: Batswana Women Interpretations of Matt. 15:21–28." *Semeia* 73 (1996) 111–29.

Dube, Musa W., Andrew M. Mbuvi and Dora Mbuwayesango, eds. *Postcolonial Perspectives in African Biblical Interpretations.* Global Perspectives on Biblical Scholarship 13. Atlanta: SBL, 2012.

Gada, Nadia Naar. "Modern African Literature Revisited a Study of Literary Affinities in Selected Early Novels." PhD diss., Mouloud Mammeri University of Tizi-Ouzou, Algeria, 2014.

Gates, Henry Louis, Jr. *The Signifying Monkey: A Theory of African-American Literary Criticism.* New York: Oxford University Press, 1988.

Hansen, George P. *The Trickster and Paranormal.* Bloomington: Xlibris, 2001.

Hurston, Zora Neale. *Their Eyes Were Watching God: A Novel.* New York: Harper & Row, 1937.

Kurtz, Roger. "Peter Nazareth." In *Postcolonial African Writers: A Bio-Bibliographical Critical Sourcebook,* edited by Pushpa N. Parekh and Siga Fatima Jagne, 312–17. Westport, CT: Greenwood, 1998.

Lorde, Audre. *Sister Outsider: Essays and Speeches.* Crossing Press Feminist Series. Berkeley: Crossing, 1984.

Masenya, Madipoane. "Esther and Northern Sotho Stories: An African-South African Women's Commentary." In *Other Ways of Reading: African Women and The Bible,* edited by Musa W. Dube, 27–49. Global Perspectives on Biblical Scholarship 2. Atlanta: SBL, 2001.

Moffat, R. *Missionary Labours and Scenes in Southern Africa.* London: Snow, 1842.

Niditch, Susan. "Genesis." In *The Women's Bible Commentary,* eds. Carol Newsom and Sharon H. Ringe. Louisville: Westminster John Knox, 1992.

Ntloedibe-Kuswani, Seratwa. "Ngaka and Jesus as Liberators: A Comparative Reading," In *The Bible in Africa: Transactions, Trajectories and Trends,* edited by Gerald O. West and Musa W. Dube, 498–510. Leiden: Brill, 2000.

———. "The Religious Life of An African: A God-given Preparation Evangelica." In *Talitha Cum! Theologies of African Women,* edited by Nyambura Njoroge and Musa W. Dube, 121–39. Pietmaritzburg, SA: Cluster, 2001.

Oduyoye, Mercy Amba. *Beads and Strands: Reflections of An African Woman on Christianity in Africa.* Maryknoll, NY: Orbis, 2004.

Olupona, Jacob, and Terry Rey, eds. *Òrìṣà Devotion as World Religion: The Globalization of Yorùbá Religious Culture.* Madison: University of Wisconsin Press, 2008.

Okpewho, Isidore. *African Oral Literature: Backgrounds, Character and Continuity.* Indianapolis: Indiana University Press, 1992.

Patterson, Richard D. "The Old Testament Use of an Archetype: The Trickster." *JETS* 42 (1999) 385–94.

Provost, Kara, and Audre Lorde. "Becoming Afrekete: The Trickster in the Work of Audre Lorde." *Melus* 20.4 (1995) 45–59.

Scheub, Harold. *Trickster and Hero: Two Characters in the Oral and Written Traditions of the World.* Madison: Wisconsin Press, 2012.

Schüssler Fiorenza, Elisabeth. *Bread Not Stone: The Challenge of Feminist Biblical Interpretation.* Boston: Beacon, 1995.

Teuton, Sean Kicummah. *Red Land, Red Power: Grounding Knowledge in the American Indian Novels.* Durham: Duke University Press, 2008.

Thiong'o, Ngugi wa. *Decolonizing the Mind: The Politics of Language in African Literature.* London: Curry, 1986.

West, Gerald O., and Musa W. Dube, eds. *The Bible in Africa: Transactions, Trajectories and Trends.* Leiden: Brill, 2000.

7

Training for Prophetic Social Engagement Informed by Isaiah and Gerald West

Bob Ekblad

Introduction

GERALD WEST'S PIONEERING WORK developing his Contextual Bible Studies (CBS) provides training in prophetic liberatory seeing, discernment, and action that lines up with the prophetic traditions of Scripture. The prophet Isaiah provides a vast corpus of material valuable for equipping and empowering a prophetic movement today which interfaces well with West's vision and pedagogy. The prophet Isaiah launched a prophetic movement in his day that lasted approximately 225 years—from pre-exilic times in Judah (740 BC to 686 BC), through the deportations to Babylon (598/7 and 587/6 BCE), the Babylonian exile (586 to 516), return to the land of Israel and rebuilding of the second temple (520 BC to 515 BC).[1]

Within the anthology of prophetic oracles that make up Isaiah's 66 chapters, we can find diverse prophetic stances and emphases that are context-specific. Isaiah 1–39 prophecies expose injustices of Judah's ruling elite and their demise, presenting what is likely a description of Isaiah's call, the role of his disciples, and prophecies regarding

1. Freedman, ed., *The Anchor Bible Dictionary*, 3:478–79.

surrounding nations. In Isaiah 40–55, the movement adjusts to a new context, announcing comfort to the oppressed exiles, and identifying them as "the servant of the Lord" through whom God will bring salvation to the nations. Finally, Isaiah 56–66 contains diverse oracles addressing people returning and rebuilding their lives after devastating exile. West's life as a socially engaged Bible scholar fits well within Isaiah's prophetic movement.

Growing up in South Africa during Apartheid, he made the difficult, and continual, choice to engage in active solidarity with poor Black South Africans in their liberation struggle. West's privileged status as an educated white man, stamped irrevocably by British colonial ancestry, could have intimidated him into indifference, denial, or flight. However, he chose the narrow path of offering his life and gifts to the Black South African poor, despite the near impossibility of this vocation in the brutal Apartheid and post-Apartheid contexts. West pursued academic excellence through graduate studies in Scripture at the University of Sheffield in the UK and then returned to South Africa to translate that knowledge to serve his community.

As Professor of Old Testament at the University of KwaZulu-Natal, West engaged in "prophetic research" addressing the oppressive colonial use of Scripture on the African continent, while simultaneously embodying a liberating approach to reading the Bible for the freedom struggle. West has taught generations of pastors and theologians from across the African continent. He leveraged his theology and pedagogical expertise to found Ujamaa Center, a training centre committed to empowering the poor to read the Bible in ways that challenged systemic oppression in South Africa. At the same time, he took what he learned amongst the South African poor and marginalized into the international academic world of the Society of Bible Literature and American Academy of Religion (SBL/AAR), where he influenced scholars and activists the world over.

West has mastered listening skills born out of a lifelong commitment to humbly and conscientiously serve those oppressed by people of the same race and class. He models grace-filled refusal of power, choosing instead to forge a gentle, simple, yet comprehensive approach to empowerment through dialogical education. His giftedness as a listener and facilitator has made him the most effective trainer of prophetic pastoral theologians I have ever witnessed.

I will look now at some ways that the book of Isaiah provides insight and training for empowering a prophetic movement, showing how West's pedagogy effectively aligns with, and enhances, capacity-building for social change today.

Seeing and Embeddedness

Isaiah's message is described from the beginning as a vision that he "saw," concerning Judah and Jerusalem "during the reigns of Uzziah, Jotham, Ahaz and Hezekiah, kings of Judah" (Isa 1:1). Isaiah's prophetic "seeing" is described as rooted in particular contexts, the reigns of different kings. There's much we can learn from Isaiah's "vision" and "seeing" that can inform prophetic seeing today. For example, this interfaces well with the "see" category in Gerald's articulation of the "see, judge, act" methodology, reflected in the Ujamaa CBS manual.

> "'See' involves careful social analysis of a particular context 'from below', by organized groups of the marginalised. This 're-ality' is then 'judged' by the biblical and theological tradition of 'God's project'. ("Ujamaa CBS Manual," part 1, 27)

The Hebrew term for vision, *ḥāzôn* (חָזוֹן), in Isa 1:1, occurs only here in the whole book, and is preceded only by 1 Sam 3:2 which references the boy Samuel, who lived during a time when "visions were infrequent." Jeremiah and Ezekiel critique prophets for false visions (Jer 14:14; 23:16; Ezek 13:16).[2] Yet visions are one of the primary ways God spoke to the minor prophets (Obad 1; Nah 1:1; Hab 2:2), which is stated most positively as a mode of God's revelation in Hosea 12:10: "I have also spoken to the prophets, and I gave numerous visions, and through the prophets I gave parables" (*NASB*).

Isaiah's (Isa 1:1) seeing is presented using the Hebrew verb *ḥāzaʿ* חָזָה, meaning "to gaze at; mentally perceive, contemplate (with pleasure); specifically, to have a vision of: behold, look, prophesy, provide, see."[3] Isaiah sees a "word" (Isa 2:1), and an "oracle" (Isa 13:1). Isaiah then speaks in the first-person for the Lord, establishing that the subsequent descriptions of injustices are rooted in people's rebellion against God, and the resulting lack of understanding and relational disconnect.

2. In the LXX, ὅρασις (vision) and *horaō* (ὁράω) are used to match the Hebrew terms.

3. *Key Dictionary of Hebrew Bible.*

> Sons I have reared and brought up, but they have revolted against me. An ox knows its owner, and a donkey its master's manger, but Israel does not know, my people do not understand. Alas, sinful nation, people weighed down with iniquity, offspring of evildoers, sons who act corruptly! They have abandoned the Lord, they have despised the Holy One of Israel, they have turned away from him. (Isa 1:2–4 NASB)

Isaiah speaks out what God "sees" first, and then God shows him from out of his own relational connectedness with YHWH, which assumes Isaiah himself knows YHWH, having returned, after he perhaps also abandoned God. At the same time, Isaiah's graphic descriptions of rebellion and injustice show that he was himself deeply rooted in his community, embodying "embeddedness."

From his embedded stance, Isaiah launched a liberation movement that included the recruitment of converted disciples. There are signs throughout Isaiah's writings that he was engaged in a process of facilitation, that animated and formed disciples, who responded to God's call to his people through the prophet. Might there have been a kind of CBS-like process underway that was embedded in diverse communities over these 225 years? West's description of the value of embeddedness may suggest so:

> The starting point for facilitation is to be embedded in particular communities of struggle, particularly communities of the poor, the marginalized, the working classes. To experience with them the things they are struggling with, to work with them and then to be invited by them to work with contextual Bible study. It is the immersion; it is the embeddedness in those communities that makes one attentive to the kinds of things you need for facilitation. Facilitation begins with the feet. Unless your feet are in these communities of the marginalized, I don't think you can be a facilitator of contextual Bible studies. It sensitizes you to the other, it sensitizes you to yourself. You become aware of who you are and of your own limitations, but also of your contributions.[4]

Isaiah speaks as one embedded in his community, recounting with great detail the injustices and empty religion that he "sees," using God's first-person voice in ways that align with the second phase "judge": "When you come to appear before me, who requires of you this trampling of my courts? Bring your worthless offerings no longer . . . I will hide my eyes

4. West, "On Facilitation," unpublished talk in Bogota, Columbia, January 29, 2015.

from you; Yes, even though you multiply prayers, I will not listen. Your hands are covered with blood." (1:12–13; 15 NASB)

The prophet appeals to the people on behalf of God to "act":

> Wash yourselves, make yourselves clean; Remove the evil of your deeds from my sight. Cease to do evil, learn to do good; Seek justice, reprove the ruthless, defend the orphan, plead for the widow. (Isa 1:16–17 NASB)

Between these appeals to change their ways, the prophet also exposes the injustices of the powerful: "Your rulers are rebels and companions of thieves; everyone loves a bribe and chases after rewards. They do not defend the orphan, nor does the widow's plea come before them" (Isa 1:23 NASB). In Isa 2:1, the prophet "sees" a word (*dabar* in Hebrew, *logos* in the LXX), before going on to describe both positive visions of an ideal future with God (Isa 2:2–4) and injustices that continue to be committed by God's people (Isa 2:5–9). Seeing a "word" might well include a form of front-line reporting, and even social analysis, which when publicly stated "for God," makes clear that the status quo now exposed and denounced, is not God's sovereign will.

Isaiah's words of judgment on behalf of God reveal to the humble poor that the status quo is not God's sovereign will: "The proud look of man will be abased and the loftiness of man will be humbled, and the Lord alone will be exalted in that day. For the Lord of hosts will have a day of reckoning against everyone who is proud and lofty and against everyone who is lifted up, that he may be abased" (Isa 2:11–12 NASB).

"Born from Below"

We see from the quality of Isaiah's Hebrew poetry that he was likely an educated man, and probably from the priestly class. In West's language, Isaiah is a "trained reader" about to become a socially engaged Bible scholar of sorts. In Isaiah 6, we see what is likely the "call" narrative that turned Isaiah from an establishment voice to a subversive prophet.[5] Isaiah's call likely took place in the temple, where he "saw the Lord sitting on a throne, lofty and exalted, with the train of his robe filling the temple" (Isa 6:1 NASB). "Seeing God" becomes catalytic for Isaiah,

---

5. Seitz, *Isaiah 1–39*, 54. Watts identifies Isa 6:1–13 as an "authenticating vision." Watts, *Isaiah 1–33*, 71.

suggesting that divine encounter is the necessary initiation into prophetic social engagement.

Isaiah "saw" the Lord sitting on a throne at the moment when there was a power vacuum left by King Uzziah's death. In the Masoretic Text, the verb *rā' â* ("to see") is used here, which doesn't link exegetically with *ḥāzâ* ("to see") in Isa 1:1. In the LXX, however, ὅραω is used, linking this text contextually with Isaiah's seeing of the vision, ὅρασις, in Isa 1:1. The LXX thus presents prophetic seeing as linked directly to the originating vision, highlighting the Lord's appearing/revealing.

Strange heavenly beings call out to one another: "Holy, Holy, Holy, is the Lord of hosts, the whole earth is full of his glory." Only someone "clean," is ritually qualified to enter the temple, in contrast to the unclean masses. Isaiah's vision of God's glory filling the entire earth—unclean and clean together, subverts the soon-to-be prophet's self-understanding. He responds: "Woe is me, for I am ruined! Because I am a man of unclean lips, and I live among a people of unclean lips; for my eyes have seen the King, the Lord of Hosts" (Isa 6:5 NASB). Isaiah's recognition of his equality with unclean, disqualified sinners initiates a kind of birth from below (initiated from above). Sudden awareness of his true condition before God causes him to perceive that his life is in immediate danger and leads him to confess in a pre-"baptism of repentance for the forgiveness of sins" way.

This activates God's heavenly beings, who bring him a lump of coal with tongs from the altar, that touches his lips followed by a declaration of forgiveness: "Behold, this has touched your lips; and your iniquity is taken away and your sin is forgiven" (Isa 6:7 NASB). Isaiah is now available to the Lord, and readily receives his commissioning. "Then I heard the voice of the Lord, saying, "Whom shall I send, and who will go for Us?" Then I said, "Here am I. Send me!" (Isa 6:8 NASB). Isaiah's conversion and calling could be interpreted as comparable to the shift required for a Bible scholar to become socially engaged in the service of the poor. Isaiah is presented as a religious insider, and the Hebrew used in the Book of Isaiah is that of an educated writer. Yet when the Lord encounters him, he is undone and becomes available to serve the unclean as their equal. West describes this "conversion from below,"[6] or

---

6. West, *Academy of the Poor*, 37.

being "born from below,"[7] as an Isaiah-like journey of seeing himself as equal to marginalized people this way:

> I am still learning what it means 'to be made use of', and I am discovering in the process that I am becoming partially constituted by my work with them . . ." "Work with poor and marginalized communities enables white, middle-class, male biblical scholars like me to be constituted partially by the experiences, needs, questions and resources of such communities. This does not mean that my 'whiteness', 'middle-classness' and 'maleness' cease to be the major factors that constitute me, but they are no longer the whole story. I will need to be reminded again and again that I am indeed substantially shaped and indelibly inscribed by my whiteness, middle-classness and maleness, but I know that I need not remain content to always be so.[8]

Elsewhere, West writes that "It is only the 'called' and 'converted' biblical scholar who may be of service to poor and marginalized communities—those who have betrayed the hidden discourse of the dominant and who have chosen to be partially constituted by the hidden discourse of the dominated."[9]

Isaiah is given a difficult message to the powerful, which sets him apart. He is to declare their inability to see and hear: "Go, and tell this people: 'Keep on listening, but do not perceive; Keep on looking, but do not understand.' Render the hearts of this people insensitive, their ears dull, and their eyes dim" (Isa 6:9–10). This vocation most certainly interferes with a "see, judge, act" pedagogy. Yet, a way out of blindness is offered. Isaiah asks the Lord how long this spiritual blindness and deafness will last, which is followed by a declaration of leveling judgment: "Until cities are devastated and without inhabitant, houses are without people and the land is utterly desolate, until the Lord has removed men far away, and the forsaken places are many in the midst of the land" (Isa 6:11–12 NASB). Isaiah's oracles are, in turn, entrusted to his disciples, who are mentioned for the first time in Isa 8:16: "Bind up the testimony, seal the law [Torah/teaching] among my disciples."

In the chapters that precede Isaiah 40, the prophet continues to challenge the powers, warning them of an impending exile. Jerusalem is

---

7. West, *Academy of the Poor,* 55.

8. West, *Academy of the Poor,* 36–37.

9. West, *Academy of the Poor,* 111.

subsequently destroyed by Babylonian invaders and its elite are carried off into exile—the anticipated blindness-ending judgment.

Prophetic Embeddedness amongst Exiles

A new phase in Isaiah's prophetic ministry starts with a second-person-plural appeal, to come alongside the suffering exiles in Isa 40:1: "Comfort, O comfort my people," says your God. "Speak kindly to Jerusalem; and call out to her" (NASB). I suggest that these imperatives are addressed to disciples active in Isaiah's prophetic community, embedded amidst the ex-iled people.[10] These same second-person plural imperatives persist in Isa 40:3, preceded by "A voice is calling," which some scholars think indicates a second-call text.[11] "Clear the way for the Lord in the wilderness; make smooth in the desert a highway for our God." The comforters and those who clear the way are likely an already-initiated group of "disciples" from Isaiah's prophetic community. I see them as constituting a "socially engaged Bible scholar-" or "trained reader"-type group, amongst the downtrodden exiles. Whether they were or were not, they most certainly were part of the "Servant of the Lord" community.

Early in Deutero-Isaiah, the Servant of the YHWH is introduced. Many of the over forty occurrences of *ʿābad* in Isaiah 40–55 clearly refer to Israel in her exiled state.[12] Servant Israel was dislocated from her home-land, and oppressed by an imperial power who enslaved her. Simultane-ously, the Servant is called to a high vocation, identified in more cryptic texts contained within what scholars refer to as the "Servant Poems."[13] So, the Servant's highest vocation must not be disassociated from servant Israel's lowly state, articulated in these sample texts below. "But you, Is-rael, my servant, Jacob whom I have chosen, the descendant of Abraham my friend, you whom I have taken from the ends of the earth, and called from its remotest parts and said to you, 'you are my servant, I have cho-sen you and not rejected you.'" (Isa 41:8–9)

10. The LXX inserts "priests" as the subject of "comfort" in this verse, possibly showing that the Jewish community of Alexandria understood that this prophetic move-ment was contained within the priesthood.

11. Ekblad, *Isaiah's Servant*, 69–70.

12. Isaiah 41:8, 9; 42:19; 43:10; 44:1, 2, 21, 26; 45:4; 48:20; 49:3. Other occurrences of *ʿābad* are more cryptic, occurring within the four poems often referred to as the "Servant Poems" (Isa 42:1; 49:5, 6, 7; 50:10; 52:13; 53:11).

13. Isaiah 42:1; 49:5, 6, 7; 50:10; 52:13; 53:11.

The next reference to the Servant is found in what's often referred to as the first "Servant Poem," Isa 42:1–9. In this poem, the Servant is not overtly associated with Israel but appears more cryptic. Yet, since the Servant is elsewhere associated with the dispossessed, exiled people of God (Israel), this text alludes to their highest vocation; which, since Israel is not named here, may also include those not associated with Israel, with YHWH, and with Israel's anticipated Messiah. "Behold, my Servant, whom I uphold; my chosen one in whom my soul delights. I have put my Spirit upon him; he will bring forth justice to the nations" (Isa 42:1 NASB).

YHWH calls the slaves of Babylonian colonizers "my Servant," much as Moses, speaking for YHWH before Pharaoh, identified the Israelite slaves as "my people." God declares preferential choice, and, in delight, places his Spirit upon the Servant, whom YHWH empowers to engage in a prophetic movement among the enslaved, to bring justice to the nations. This vocation is further expanded in the following verse, announcing: "And I will appoint you as a covenant to the people, as a light to the nations, to open blind eyes, to bring out prisoners from the dungeon and those who dwell in darkness from the prison. I am the Lord, that is my name; I will not give my glory to another, nor my praise to graven images" (Isa 42:6–7 NASB). To further clarify that YHWH's glory will not be given to just anyone, other than the "untrained" and oppressed Servant, the very next mention of ʿāḇaḏ highlights the Servant's not-yet-enlightened nor liberated state. The Servant is associated with the failed addressees of Isaiah's original message who "keep on listening, but do not perceive; keep on looking, but do not understand" (Isa 6:9 NASB).

YHWH then offers guidance to the blind: "I will lead the blind by a way they do not know, in paths they do not know I will guide them. I will make darkness into light before them" (Isa 42:16 NASB), as an alternative to trusting in idols (Isa 42:17). The Lord appeals to people mediated by the prophetic spokesperson(s), who address them:

> Hear, you deaf! And look, you blind, that you may see. Who is blind but my servant, or so deaf as my messenger whom I send? Who is so blind as he that is at peace with me, or so blind as the servant of the Lord? You have seen many things, but you do not observe them; your ears are open, but none hears. (Isa 42:18–20 NASB)

The servant is not enlightened or educated but remains in an enslaved state, which becomes clearer in the verses that follow: "The Lord was pleased for his righteousness' sake to make the law great and glorious. But this is a people plundered and despoiled; all of them are trapped in caves, or are hidden away in prisons; they have become prey with no one to deliver them, and spoils, with no one to say, "give them back!" (Isa 42:21–22 NASB). This Servant will use humble, even subversive, means reflecting an empowering pedagogy. The Servant "will not cry out or raise his voice. His voice will not be heard in the street."

The Servant "will faithfully bring forth justice," not becoming discouraged "until he has established justice in the earth; and the coastlands will wait expectantly for his law" (Isa 42:4 NASB). In Isa 42:4 the islands wait for the Servant's law. Here the term "law," *Torah*/teaching has the meaning of Israel's most sacred Scripture. In the book of Isaiah, the *Torah* is always associated directly with YHWH,[14] identifying the Servant here with YHWH. Later, in Isa 42:21, YHWH is described as making "the law great and glorious." Yet Isaiah also clearly states that it was the Lord, "against whom we have sinned, and in whose ways they were not willing to walk, and whose law they did not obey," who gave Israel over to plunderers (Isa 42:24 NASB). The law [*Torah*/teaching] of the Servant, for which the isles wait expectedly (Isa 42:4), is the sacred revelation that the exiled Servant-people had themselves rejected. Yet this does not disqualify them from their prophetic vocation. Rather their disobedience now qualifies them for a ministry of the Word to the non-Jewish world.

The gentle means of the Servant's faithful justice-bringing described in Isa 42:2–4 bring to mind West's empowering pedagogy, which is not about fore-fronting his own voice, "making it heard in the streets." On numerous occasions, I have witnessed his special ability to make room for people who are not accustomed to being respectfully listened to and learned from, by the powerful. This makes them feel safe and free to express their authentic, uncensored voices. West recognizes the value of Biblical scholarship and seeks to sensitively bring these resources to the service of people who have not had access to formal or academic education. One of the ways he does this is to help these "not-yet-trained" readers learn to read the biblical text seriously, taking

14. Isaiah 1:10; 2:3; 5:24; 8:16, 20; 30:9; 42:21,24; 51:4, 7. In the LXX version of Isa 42:4 "name" (*onoma*) matches the Hebrew *Torah*, which allowed early Christians to associate this with the name of Jesus, which still identifies the Servant with God. See Eugene R. Ekblad, Jr, *Isaiah's Servant*, 69–70.

into account "the text," that which is "behind the text," and that which is "in front of the text."[15]

> So one of the commitments of the contextual Bible study process is to facilitate the development of critical consciousness by beginning with critical Bible reading. This is a small beginning, but through critical Bible reading we participate in the important process of building a critical church and community that can play a role in analyzing the past and present and in shaping the future (*sic*). Readers of the Bible are not the only ones who are contributing towards constructing a more critical society, but we can make a small (and significant) contribution, particularly in the church.[16]

As a White South African Bible scholar, West is keenly aware of his privilege, educational training, and power, based on the country's social-political setting. The authority he wields due to his race, social class, and education might typically block the true empowerment of "ordinary" African readers he engages. And, without a sensitive and prolonged effort to build trust through authentically honoring reading partners, the result could easily be that the true voice of the poor remains hidden, as people often unconsciously comply with (or consciously) the perceived "right" or "official" interpretation.[17] As West notes,

> Participants are testing the waters to see if it is really safe to venture any deeper. As trust and a sense of security grows, a more nuanced listening usually discloses a more ambiguous and polysomic expression that is capable of two readings, one which is innocuous, so providing an avenue of retreat if challenged, and one which is subversive, 'smuggling . . . portions of the hidden transcript, suitable veiled, onto the public stage.'[18]

West builds trust through a very deliberate process of designing questions that engage people in careful analysis of the biblical text (text questions) along with "community consciousness" and "critical consciousness"

---

15. For a detailed description of these categories, see West, *Contextual Bible Study*, especially Chapter 2, "Three Modes of Reading the Bible," 26–50.

16. West, *Contextual Bible Study*, 19.

17. In his chapter "Reading With: A Call to Conversion," West goes into great detail describing the "official transcript" that marginalized communities feel beholden to, while holding their "hidden transcripts" closely at a distance from trained readers, who cannot simply "listen to" untrained readers without themselves going through a profound conversion. West, *The Academy of the Poor*, 34–62.

18. West, *The Academy of the Poor*, 110.

reflection questions.[19] These questions are not imposed on people, but are developed in collaboration with the communities,[20] who then work through them together, *seeing* their lives in the light of the text, and, often, leading to social transformation. The very process of Ujamaa CBS sets into motion a consciousness-raising experience that simultaneously empowers people to find and strengthen their voices.

West listens to people in such a way that makes them feel respected and empowered. Given that sensitive facilitation of dialogical Bible studies is essential, he has become, over time, a master of this practice like no other person I know. Regarding the overall process, he writes:

> Contextual Bible study is a process, and this process will not just happen; it needs to be facilitated . . . In a recent workshop on contextual Bible study, participants agreed that the five most important characteristics of a facilitator were the following: the facilitator should use a method that encourages the whole group to participate; the facilitator should manage conflict and make the group a safe place for member contributions; the facilitator should train others to become facilitators; the facilitator should clarify what is not clear and should summarize the discussion; and the facilitator should enable the group to become aware of and involved in the needs of the community. A facilitator, then, is one who helps the progress and empowerment of others, who makes it easier for others to act, to contribute, and to acquire skills. Anyone can be a facilitator, provided they are willing to learn to be enablers and not dominators. Community consciousness and critical consciousness cannot develop in authoritarian forms of Bible study. Democratic processes can only develop where there is mutual respect and trust and where there is a deep sense of community. Only in such a context do self-confidence, responsibility, and accountability grow.[21]

19. "Community consciousness questions are "designed to encourage participants to engage with the text from their own experience." Critical consciousness questions "ask for a more critical response to the text, and create a measure of distance between 'reader' and the text. By facilitating a close and careful reading of the text and by exploring the relationship between the text and its socio-historical context, the text as literary and socio-cultural artifact is taken seriously. In a variety of ways such questions draw out the critical resources of both ordinary 'readers' and socially engaged biblical scholars, and enable a critical appropriation." West, *Contextual Bibles Study*, 129–30.

20. West emphasizes repeatedly his commitment to only work with the "organized poor and marginalized," which makes sense in the South African context, but is impossible in many settings, such as jails and prisons. See West, *Contextual Bible Study*, 25.

21. West, *Contextual Bible Study*, 24.

The Ujamaa CBS process involves dividing a larger group into smaller groups, in which participants read the biblical text and work together through carefully crafted questions. After a set amount of time, the groups return to the plenary where a spokesperson from each group presents their responses to the set questions, whose responses are carefully recorded for all to see on newsprint paper.

West's particular way of facilitating involves making use of what he calls "analytic listening" and "analytic summarizing." This involves summarizing, gathering, and organizing people's responses to questions around themes.[22] Observing West actively listening and summarizing is where I have witnessed his most effective training of prophetic activism. He models an artful facilitation involving helping the scribe to record respondents' comments through modeling an active condensing and summarizing, of responses. In this regard, he has stated that "It's very hard for a scribe to summarize, especially if they're not educated. They may be conscious of their spelling. Analytic summarizing is a way to help the scribe summarize. That's a way to help them document."[23] Repeating back his re-stating of their condensed responses models a kind of "prophetic listening" in that, respondents hear their words so clearly summarized that they feel truly heard and, simultaneously, inspired to seek still greater clarity. The process involves a certain reciprocity, as West notes,

> When you summarize you encourage condensation. How do you do that?. . . By asking permission, feeding it back to people, some will talk for a few minutes. So what you're saying is . . . Hopefully, you've established a sense of safety, where people will tell you if you didn't summarize it rightly.[24]

West's analytic listening and summarizing are practical facilitation tools that, when implemented conscientiously, artfully, and consistently, can empower speakers, in this case, the poor and often voiceless people, to step into greater agency. Learning this art of conscientious facilitation also involves mastering some of its mechanics. As West explains in his *Academy of the Poor*:

> The primary role of the facilitator is to enable 'group process' to take place—to manage group dynamics, to promote turn-taking, to keep time, to summarize and systematize the

22. West, Unpublished Talk, Bogota, Columbia.
23. West, Unpublished Talk, Bogota, Columbia.
24. West, Unpublished Talk, Bogota, Columbia.

reading results, to find creative and empowering ways of reporting back to plenary the findings of the group, and to move the group from reflection into action. Besides the more general group process concerns, the facilitator's task in the contextual Bible study process is to stimulate the use of local reading resources and to introduce critical reading resources—in the specific sense that this term is used within biblical studies—into the reading process as they are requested and required. This is no easy task, and so much of the work of the ISB involves training facilitators in local communities. Contextual Bible study, then, is committed to corporate and communal reading of the Bible in which the trained reader is just another reader with different resources and skills, not better resources and skills. As I have argued, really believing that our modes of reading are 'different, but not better' requires some form of conversion. Remaining within the categories and concepts of ordinary 'readers', resisting the temptation to 'translate' local articulations in the terms of the dominant discourse, takes considerable conversion, and careful facilitation.[25]

As I have witnessed West practice his analytic listening, summarizing, and condensing on many occasions, I have witnessed people's surprise and delight. He models a prophetic posture and gifting that manifests when he articulates back to people what they are saying with such precision that they feel truly heard, seen, understood, and empowered.

"From Blindness to Sight" in Isaiah 42–48 and in Ujamaa Contextual Bible Study

The poor and oppressed Servant-people of God in the Babylonian exile continued to be referred to as blind and deaf, despite their highest calling to bring justice to the nations. There's no romanticization or idealization of the oppressed,[26] nor naïve over-empowerment here. Rather they are presented as especially dependent upon YHWH as their essential guide and liberator. "I will lead the blind by a way they do not know, in paths they do not know I will guide them. I will make darkness into light before them" (Isa 42:16 NASB). YHWH's shepherding appears

---

25. West, *Academy of the Poor*, 133–34.

26. West, *The Academy of the Poor*, 37, writes that "biblical scholars either romanticize and idealize the contribution of the poor and marginalized or they minimize and rationalize that community's contribution."

unmediated, as God speaks in the first person. And yet YHWH calls on a second plural group to free the prisoners: "Bring out the people who are blind, even though they have eyes, and the deaf, even though they have ears" (Isa 43:8 NASB).

This certainly makes room for disciples in Isaiah's prophetic movement, those very "comforters" commissioned in Isa 40:1, so that, despite the Servant-people's blind and deaf status, YHWH still calls them "my witnesses," and "my Servant who I have chosen," (Isa 43:10). For what they are witnesses to is YHWH's saving action, as we see in Isa 43:10–11. "So that you may know and believe me and understand that I am he. Before me there was no God formed, and there will be none after me. "I, even I, am the Lord, and there is no savior besides me." (Isa 43:10–11 NASB).

In the verses that follow, imagery from the Exodus is brought into the Isaianic age. YHWH makes "a way through the sea," quenching and extinguishing the chariots, horses and mighty men like a wick (Isa 43:17). But, despite God's saving actions, YHWH challenges the people: "Yet you have not called on me" (Isa 43:22). In spite of the people's resistance and refusals, the prophet never minimizes their role, instead, repeatedly proclaiming God's commitment to save them: "I, even I, am the one who wipes out your transgressions for my own sake, and I will not remember your sins" (Isa 43:25 NASB). And because the worship of idols is the greatest obstacle to God's exiled people stepping into active awareness that YHWH is their Savior, which the prophet describes in graphic detail in Isa 44:9–12, YHWH's critique through the prophet is followed by yet another declaration of the people's blindness: "They do not know, nor do they understand, for He has smeared over their eyes so that they cannot see and their hearts so that they cannot comprehend. No one recalls, nor is there knowledge or understanding" (Isa 44:18–19 NASB). The prophet speaks for God in calling the people to "remember these things," followed by yet another affirmation of the people's irrevocable calling and a declaration of forgiveness: "I have formed you, you are My servant, O Israel, you will not be forgotten by me. I have wiped out your transgressions like a thick cloud and your sins like a heavy mist. Return to me, for I have redeemed you" (Isa 44:21–22 NASB). YHWH "confirms the word" of his Servant (Isa 44:26). Yet the Servant-people are in need of being addressed internally by ministers, within their ranks, who are stepping into the high calling that Isaiah has pioneered.

Isaiah's prophetic tradition also includes the public exposure and denunciation of Babylon as an oppressive power, which happens in Isaiah 46–47. At the same time, the prophet doesn't hold back criticism on the Israelite exiles, who are called out for invoking God but "not in truth and righteousness," and for being "obstinate." YHWH's words are hard-hitting: "Your neck is an iron sinew and your forehead bronze" (Isa 48:4 NASB); "You have been called a rebel from birth" (Isa 48:8). Through the prophet, YHWH calls Servant-Israel to "come near and listen" (Isa 48:16), and to "go forth from Babylon! Flee from the Chaldeans!" (Isa 48:20). Let's, now, look at how this ministry of the Word is further developed in Isaiah's second and third Servant Poems.

Prophetic Proclamation: The Servant's Ministry of the Word in Isaiah 49–50

In the second Servant-poem, the Servant's prophetic role is further defined. The Servant will be listened to by the "islands" and "peoples from afar" (Isa 49:1). YHWH has made the servant's "mouth like a sharp sword," and "like a select arrow" hidden in YHWH's quiver, to both "bring Jacob back to him, so that Israel might be gathered to him" (Isa 49:5), and to be a "light of the nations so that my salvation may reach to the end of the earth" (Isa 49:6). The Servant's prophetic calling is further clarified in the third "Servant poem," (Isa 50:4–11), which begins with an emphasis on receiving revelation. "The Lord God has given me the tongue of disciples, that I may know how to sustain the weary one with a word. He awakens me morning by morning, he awakens my ear to listen as a disciple" (Isa 50:4 NASB).

Stepping into Isaiah's prophetic movement, clarified by the Servant's mission, involves receiving one's voice—literally the "tongue of a disciple." This tongue is "given" by the Lord God. The underlying Hebrew word for "disciple" here, is the plural participle of *limmud*, *limmûdim* (לִמּוּדִים), which means literally "ones who are taught." The Lord's disciples, each have a highly defined purpose for their education: "That I may know how to sustain the weary one with a word." YHWH takes the initiative to "awaken" the disciples, "morning by morning," which is followed by a separate divine action of awakening the ear to hear. YHWH is the recruiter of the "taught" community.

The Servant's obedience to God's word, despite increasing persecution, culminates in the famous final Servant poem of Isa 52:13—53:12. There the Servant's solidarity with God's sinful people reaches an extreme. The suffering of the Servant figure identified with Israel, yet also clearly differentiated for it, is presented as redemptive, even as it ends in his death (Isa 53:8). A spokesperson for Isaiah's prophetic movement asks listeners or readers the probing question: "Who has believed our message?[27] And to whom has the arm of the Lord been revealed?" The response given elevates the image of an oppressed figure who is not attractive but rather despised, forsaken, a man of sorrows (Isa 53:2–3). Yet, this "Suffering Servant" bears the people's sin:

> Surely our griefs he himself bore, and our sorrows he carried;
> Yet we ourselves esteemed him stricken, smitten of God, and
> afflicted. But he was pierced through for our transgressions, he
> was crushed for our iniquities. (Isa 53:4–5)

The Servant's outrageous suffering and death appear to have functioned like the seed that falls into the ground and dies, in order to then multiply. After Isaiah 53 the term "Servant" only occurs in the plural,[28] (though the singular figure still appears in Isaiah 61) embodying the entire tradition.

> The Spirit of the Lord God is upon me, because the Lord has
> anointed me to bring good news to the afflicted; he has sent me
> to bind up the brokenhearted, to proclaim liberty to captives
> and freedom to prisoners; to proclaim the favorable year of the
> Lord. (Isa 61:1–2 NASB)

In Luke 4:17–20, Jesus cites this very text in his inaugural sermon, fulfilling in his earthly life the Servant's liberating mission. West's lifelong commitment as a socially engaged Bible scholar, teacher, and activist, has certainly advanced the Isaianic concept of the Servant's universal mission as articulated by the prophet and embodied by Jesus. West has effectively trained and inspired many socially engaged Bible scholars and now, more-fully-trained and empowered "ordinary readers," setting the course for many more to carry on the Jesus Movement in Africa, and around the world.

27. The term translated "message" here comes from the feminine Hebrew noun *šᵉmûʿâ* (שְׁמוּעָה), which comes from (שְׁמוּע) "to hear."

28. Isaiah 54:17; 56:6; 63:17; 65:8, 9, 13, 14, 15; 66:14.

Bibliography

Accordance electronic ed. *Key Dictionary of Hebrew Bible*. Oaktree Software, 2010.

Ekblad, Eugene R., Jr. *Isaiah's Servant Poems according to the Septuagint: An Exegetical and Theological Study*. Contributions to Biblical Exegesis and Theology 23. Leuven: Peeters, 1999.

Freedman, David Noel, ed. *The Anchor Bible Dictionary*. 6 vols. New York: Doubleday, 1992.

Seitz, Christopher R. *Isaiah 1–39*. Interpretation. Louisville: John Knox, 1993.

Watts, John D. W. *Isaiah 1–33*. Word Biblical Commentary. Waco, TX: Word, 1985.

West, Gerald O. *The Academy of the Poor: Towards a Dialogical Reading of the Bible*. Interven-tions 2. Sheffield: Sheffield Academic, 1999.

———. *Contextual Bible Study*. Pietermaritzburg: Cluster, 1993.

———. "On Facilitation." Unpublished talk in Bogota, Columbia, January 29, 2015.

8

(Under)Mining the Imperial Bible in the Face of the New Form of Empire to Recover a Tradition of Peoples' Resistance

Richard A. Horsley

Introduction

Gerald West has probably done more than anyone to deepen, expand and change the course of biblical studies in general, and especially in Africa, so that it serves the interest of people rather than aid and abet debilitating transnational forces. He nurtured and catalyzed the development of biblical studies among African peoples well beyond his South African home base. And he has been the most widely influential voice in pushing the wider field to take into account the concerns and views of peoples still under the hegemony of imperial metropolises. I offer these ruminations in tribute and gratitude to a distinguished colleague and good friend, Gerald West.

One of the most important connections in which he has been a critical, indeed prophetic, voice has been the burgeoning development of postcolonial studies in general, and of postcolonial biblical interpretation in particular. He warned prophetically that "post-colonial [with the hyphen, then] discourse within Biblical studies will make the shift from

East to West and from South to North, as it has done in literary studies, altering its forms as it moves from projects which struggle to change the world to programmes which re-describe the world."[1] At the time, I was still busy pursuing a more extensive analysis of how the Roman Empire was not just the context of Judean and Galilean resistance movements, including that catalyzed by Jesus of Nazareth, that led to the mission of Paul and coworkers. I was still unaware that postcolonialism was developing into an "industrial enterprise" (West's term). When asked to contribute to a volume on *The Postcolonial Bible,* it did not take me long to discover the criticism that postcolonial theory had developed and changed form and orientation in just the way West had predicted.[2]

Originating primarily in literary studies, postcolonial criticism emerged from attention finally being given to literature produced by Caribbean writers such as M. L. R. James, and others located mainly in former British colonies. As exemplified by James and others, however, it initially also owed a great deal to Marxist political-economic ideas, as well as cultural analysis. Its burgeoning development was mainly in literary criticism. In response to the confusing label "postcolonial" (imitating "postmodernist," another of its roots) by those who pointed out that political-economic and cultural power relations were rather neo-colonial or neo-imperial, apologists claimed that "postcolonial" still included colonial relations. Arif Dirlik and others, however, criticized postcolonialism for diverting attention from contemporary problems of social, political, and cultural domination by obfuscating its relationship to the conditions of its own emergence. That is, the growth of global capitalism had come increasingly to dominate local, as well as, global economic, political, and cultural relation.[3] Ten years later, West produced a much wider-ranging and more profound critique of postcolonial theory which had forgotten its deeper roots in Marxist criticism (including non-western forms of Marxism) of colonialism and imperialism.[4]

1. West, "Finding a Place."

2. Horsley, "Submerged Biblical Histories."

3. Horsley, "Submerged Biblical Histories," drawing on Dirlik, "The Postcolonial Aura"; also, Ahmad, *In Theory*; Prakash, "Postcolonial Criticism"; Shohat, "Notes on the Post-Colonial."

4. West, "Doing Postcolonial Biblical Interpretation."

The Imperial Bible

Perhaps it should not be surprising that a relatively new version of literary criticism would divert attention from issues of political, economic, and cultural domination. Literary criticism, a new academic field at the beginning of the twentieth century, had long operated on the assumption that literature and other modes of culture were separate from, and often claimed as a humanizing antidote to, the travails caused by industrialization. It is even less surprising that a new criticism in biblical studies would also ignore and obfuscate the conditions of its emergence, insofar as biblical studies, as a division of (Christian) theology, operated on the assumption that religion, increasingly narrowed to personal piety, was separate from political and economic life. This was doubly ironic in the case of postcolonial biblical interpretation because it was partly as a result of this new criticism that biblical scholars were beginning to recognize that the Bible was, and is, *the imperial Bible*. Other recent initiatives and new lines of research have reinforced recognition that this is not simply a matter of the Bible's rhetorical use in interpretation, but of the text of the Bible as we know it and as it has functioned historically.

A particularly important aspect of the imperial Bible is simply that the collection of books that comprise it had become "Sacred Scripture," "Holy Writ," the "Word of God." Recent research into the severely limited literacy, and the forms and functions of writing in antiquity, has shown that *writing* in its various forms has historically been an *instrument of power*. Before the invention of the printing press, the vast majority of people had no use for writing. Oral communication was dominant. Especially in societies where writing was rare and not often consulted, even by the literate elite, writing had a numinous sacred aura of special authority. The Code of Hammurabi was inscribed on steles erected in prominent public places. The emperor Augustus had his *Res Gestae* inscribed on massive monuments in the cities of the Empire. Earlier in ancient Athens, laws were inscribed on large blocks of stone as monumental, constitutional writing, even though few could read them.

Somewhat similarly, in ancient Judea, texts of *torah* in the archaic language of Hebrew were inscribed by scribes on huge, heavy parchment scrolls and laid up in the temple. An illustration of the numinous authority of such scrolls is the narrative (in Nehemiah 8) of the legendary learned scribe Ezra, an envoy of the Persian imperial regime. Standing on a raised platform, he held aloft a great scroll of Mosaic torah as the people raised their hands and acclaimed "Amen! Amen!," and then bowed their heads and worshiped YHWH with their faces to the ground.[5] The numinous scroll, inscribed with "the words" of God, was a sacred object of worship. The core of the "books" that were included in the Hebrew Bible, centuries later, were "monumental" constitutional writings which authorized God's establishment of the Jerusalem temple-state. This became the representative, in Judea, of the rule of a succession of imperial regimes. Still today, "The Bible" is hedged about with special awesome sacred authority, and not just in somber sacred ceremonial moments in churches.

The New Testament (NT) was the creation of the Roman Empire in late antiquity, centuries after the "books" were composed. After Constantine established Christianity as the "glue" that might hold his disintegrating Empire together, later Roman emperors convened "ecumenical" councils of the monarchic bishops of the Church to establish which "books" were authoritative. When the books included in the Septuagint (and later the Hebrew Bible) as the "Old Testament" were joined with the canonized "books" of the New Testament, however, they together became *the imperial Bible* in support of, and approved by, the Roman Empire. Thereafter, throughout the European Middle Ages, the texts of the Bible were in a "sacred language" unintelligible to ordinary people.

Certain texts in this imperial Bible give powerful expression to the awesome authority of Empire. The combination of what are called the Enthronement Psalms and the Royal Psalms proclaims the eternal cosmic order over which the imperial God rules and, at the center of that order, the unchallengeable authority and power of God's earthly regent, the imperial king. The royal psalms were ceremonial investments of the king/emperor but, because they were also inscribed on a scroll, they externalized and eternalized that empowerment. Western culture made texts prominent in certain eras and places, then extended and intensified the authority of Empire. I think of G. F. Handel's *Messiah* being performed in elite circles of eighteenth-century London. *Messiah* was ostensibly about the enthronement of Christ as "King of kings and Lord of Lords," but also authorized the enthronement of the British monarch in the Empire on which "the sun never sets." The *Messiah* was revived in the USA, in the 1960s and 1970s, in thousands of performances in symphony halls and (audience-participation) concerts and churches at Christmas-New Year time, which had become the climax of the annual economic cycle in

5. Horsley, *Scribes, Visionaries*, 93–99; Niditch, *Oral World*.

lavish gift-giving. This was not so much about the advent of Christ as the ceremonial sanctification of the civil order, that gave cover to the climax of the annual economic cycle in sync with the cosmic order.[6]

The irony, and the genius, of the imperial Bible was/is that it also included an individualist piety for the faithful. God has established the political-economic order within the cosmic order, and because it is established by God, it is not to be challenged, much less changed. But God has also graciously provided the forgiveness for, and salvation of, individual sinners. Believers need only accept their salvation ensured by, and focused on, the sacrifice of Christ in expiation for sin. (This concept is not prominent in the Gospels but, as the Church became established, it elevated key passages from Paul's letters, and elsewhere, as authorization for forgiveness and expiatory salvation.) Luther only made explicit what was implicit in other churches and theologies, that there are two kingdoms—the temporal kingdom of this world, and the spiritual kingdom of Christ which is effective only through individual salvation and devotion. The imperial Bible thus operates by authorizing imperial domination in the worldly kingdom, and offering individual salvation in the spiritual kingdom of Christ: a separation of religion from political-economic life and a reduction of salvation to individual believers.

The canon of authoritative NT "books"[7] was not formulated until the Roman emperor convened "ecumenical" councils of bishops in the 5th and 6th centuries. This canonization meant that New Testament "books" were transformed from subversive stories and letters, into sacred scriptures in support of the Roman Empire and Emperor. In his ad hoc letters, Paul had insisted that the new *assemblies* (communities or subjected people in pointed opposition to the assemblies of the cities of the Empire) be *loyal* (the meaning of *pistis/fides* in the Roman imperial context) to Christ, whom the Romans had crucified, as their *Lord* and *Savior*. This was in pointed resistance to loyalty to Caesar who was honored as the *Lord* and *Savior* throughout the Empire. But the establishment of Christianity and the creation of the NT canon transformed

---

6. Horsley, "Christmas."

7. It has become standard to refer to the texts included in the Bible as "books." Books, however, is at best a metaphor derived from modern Western print-culture and projected onto ancient texts that had been inscribed on scrolls or codices. The great variety of texts included in the Bible, however, were *not* books that had been written by authors and available for private reading by literate readers.

Christ into the Imperial Lord, who further mystified and legitimated the Roman Emperor.

Coinciding with the Reformation and Counter-Reformation, the new technology of the printing press made possible mass production of identical texts. Relatively inexpensive, printed Bibles played a role in limited democratization in some European countries. The printing press, however, also led to the generation of "national" languages and literatures, beginning with translations of the Bible "authorized" by the ruling authorities, such as the KJV and the Luther Bibel. This, in turn, enabled the rise of Western nation-states and nationalisms that, thanks partly to the grand-narrative of the Bible as well as nascent capitalism, had a sense of destiny to expand.[8]

The biblical underwriting of Western imperialism was sometimes blatant. Some of this happened in the translation of the Hebrew or Greek, into authorized versions. In a prime example, the Hebrew construct יֹשְׁבֵי כְנַעַן—(*yosheve* [*of fortified cities in*] *Canaan* (lit: "those who sit in [the fortified cities of] Canaan") was a synonym, in parallel lines of Hebrew poetry, of "kings" and other rulers (e.g., in the Song of the Sea in Exodus 15). Had that meaning of the construct phrase been taken as an indication of its historical meaning, then its occurrence in prose passages of "books" such as Joshua would have been discerned as references to peasant guerrilla attacks against local "kings" and their chariot forces who dominated peasant villagers from fortified cities such as Ai or Hazor.[9] In their service of early modern European rulers and/or established churches, however, Christian scholars read the construct as "the inhabitants of [the cities in] Canaan." Those passages in biblical books were thus transformed from stories of peasant uprisings against their exploitative rulers into a charter for conquest and extermination of indigenous peoples by the European Christians, successors of the ostensibly chosen people. The result was a grand narrative of the conquest of "the inhabitants" of Canaan ("the Canaanites") that became the biblical charter for the English, French, and Spanish conquest and extermination of "the Indians" in the Americas, the conquest of African peoples in what is now South Africa by the Dutch and later the English, and more recently the conquest and displacement of the Palestinians in the "Holy Land"—and many other instances of imperial/colonial conquest and domination.

8. Eisenstein, *Printing Press as Agent*; Anderson, *Imagined Communities*.

9. Gottwald, *Tribes of Yahweh*.

A central aspect of European colonization of Africa, India, and East Asia were the Christian missions that brought the Bible (in various national translations) to colonized peoples, the sacred word of God that displaced or overlaid indigenous cultures and native traditions and customs.[10] The Bible imposed on colonized peoples and their descendants was the imperial Bible. The grand-narrative and particular stories it told were, and are, the European and European-American grand-narrative and stories. This was brought home to me thirty-some years ago when I was teaching, as "migrant labor," across the river at Harvard Divinity School. Purity Malinga and Michael Mkize, two Zulu students who became good friends, already having completed traditional European-style theological school degrees in South Africa, understood the Gospel of Mark as a European story. In discussions with other students from the two-thirds world, however, they made it their own story. The Bible, including Mark, had come to them as the God-given charter for taking over the land (and later of confining the Zulu and other indigenous people to "homelands"). But they discovered Mark as the story of a resistance movement among conquered people to their imperial subjugation. As Musa Dube pointed out in no uncertain terms, the Bible, which is now also a sub-Saharan book, will always be connected to the European expropriation of African peoples' lands.[11] Thus what many of us in biblical studies, including feminist, liberationist, and postcolonial critics were, and are, struggling against is basically the Western imperial Bible.

Biblical Studies: Offspring and Facilitator of Western Empire

Centuries before there were fields of study in the social sciences or literature, biblical studies was developing as a division of theology in Western European universities. It was a product of the cultural elite and its print-culture, and its assumptions and controlling concepts and agenda, were derived from Christian theology. It was tied in with Western history in which Christendom was central. It assumed, and built on, the dominant Western European-Christian meta-narrative (derived from the imperial Bible) of creation, the dispersal of the different races and peoples, the chosenness of the people Israel and their promised land, which gave way to *Spaetjudentum;* then early Christianity, and finally the European Christian

10. See further Kwok Pui-lan, "Discovering the Bible."

11. Dube, *Postcolonial Feminist Interpretation,* 3.

nations that had superseded the Jews as the chosen people. The field's response to the Enlightenment did not change the meta-narrative. But it sharpened the sense of historical distance between the supposed height of civilization in modern Western Europe and the more "primitive" or "mythical" worldview of some biblical texts, and of non-Western peoples. The still dominant constructs and discourses of biblical studies emerged more fully in the heyday of European empires, as Germany and Belgium joined the Netherlands, Spain, France, and Britain in taking over distant territories and subjugating dark-skinned peoples.

Biblical studies functioned very much as the handmaiden of Western imperialism. A few examples should suffice to indicate the close relationship between biblical studies and Western empires. The grammar, understanding, and translation of "biblical" languages were developed in the field of biblical studies. This was a key part of the development of Western Orientalism, as Said explained.[12] The Hebrew and Greek texts of biblical books were the products of biblical studies. By closely and painstakingly poring over the Hebrew and Greek (and Latin) manuscripts and fragments, teams of text-critics "established" the "early" or the best texts, from which modern translations were made. These texts established by text-critics, of course, never existed anywhere or anytime in antiquity.[13] They are modern Western scholarly constructions. The very texts being interpreted in the diverse, recently evolved new criticisms (e.g., narrative criticism, postmodern criticism, postcolonial criticism) are the products of modern Western biblical studies.

The imperial Bible and its official interpreters, however, could not always completely dominate subordinated peoples. Even though most of them could not read, subjugated peoples heard other voices and stories underneath the grand narrative when priests and preachers read from the imperial Bible. For example, in late medieval times, European peasants inspired by stories of the exodus and the Gospel stories, rebelled against their overlords. Most widespread, sustained, and now well-known was the S.W. German peasants' assertion of their own independence, after realizing that God-given covenantal commandments and mechanisms contained in the Bible supported their own sense of economic rights, as articulated in the "Twelve Articles," among other sets of demands they formulated.[14]

12. Said, *Orientalism*.

13. Kelber, *Imprints, Voiceprints*, 327–30, 448–54 (here 449).

14. That great biblical scholar Martin Luther, on the other hand, wrote a pamphlet

As Renita Weems has explained, Africans enslaved in the USA and their descendants "heard other voices" in the Bible, different from what their owners wanted them to hear from the plantation preachers.[15] African Americans put together their own "Jubilee Bible."[16] The Civil Rights movement took inspiration from voices, stories, commandments, and prophecies completely assimilated into the imperial Bible, often as "translated," and transformed them into "spirituals" and then "freedom songs." Among various African peoples, several leaders of anti-colonial movements had been influenced by stories, and laws, and prophecies they learned in the missionaries' schools. When *campesinos* in Central America were finally able to hear stories from the Bible, they tended toward resistance to their plight, for example, organizing to retake control of their ancestral lands that had been expropriated by powerful landlords living in the cities.

It seems clear, and not just in retrospect, that liberation theology in Latin America, Black liberation theology in the USA (and elsewhere), and Feminist and Womanist liberation theology derived from, and were rooted in, such popular movements that had found precedents and authorization in the voices and stories they heard and read in the Bible. And, some of these liberation interpretations found a constituency in North American biblical studies in the 1980s and 1990s. While liberation theology had become strong in Latin America, it did not resonate widely or deeply in conservative North American biblical studies.

The lines of innovation in establishment biblical studies, however, led elsewhere. Following the dominant currents in Western culture and academy, biblical studies also took the "literary turn" into narrative, structuralist, and deconstruction criticisms. By the time I completed the revised edition of *The Bible and Liberation*, replacing the apolitical social science selections with various liberationist essays, however, postmodernism had become the dominant stream in non-traditional biblical studies.[17] These new criticisms began to lead biblical studies away from interest in concrete historical political-economic relations in historical contexts, then and now. And, what became postcolonial criticism in biblical studies was rooted mainly in that "literary turn"

Against the Murderous, Thieving Horde of Peasants encouraging the knights and other overlords to subdue peasants.

15. Weems, "Reading Her Way."

16. *KJV African-American Jubilee Bible, 400th Anniversary Edition.*

17. Horsley, *Bible and Liberation.*

and postmodern criticism. These exciting innovative new "criticisms" simply ignored and, in effect, obfuscated the rapidly changing conditions of their own operation.

The New Form of Empire: Global Capitalism

It should not be surprising that postcolonial biblical studies, a new "criticism" in biblical studies more generally, like literary studies and other fields in the humanities, paid little or no attention to the new form of Empire that was emerging in the late twentieth century: global capitalism. After all, from its beginnings, biblical studies had proceeded on the assumption that religion was separate from concrete political-economic life. And, academics in general seemed oblivious to what was happening in their own lives—although the fact that Harvard University Press published the book *Empire* by Michael Hardt and Antonio Negri means that at least some leading economists and historians were aware of the world-historical transformation that was happening.[18]

The attacks of 9/11 dramatically illustrated how the new form of Empire worked: the World Trade Center towers were the symbols of global capital and the Pentagon the symbol of the US military that served as its enforcer, when needed. The transnational power of finance capital became only too obvious in the financial crash of 2008 resulting from mega-banks foisting sub-prime mortgages on marginal home-owners (disproportionately people of color) and then slicing and dicing the value of the collateral into inflated securities. The mega-banks had become too powerful to be disciplined, even by the US government: labeled "too big to fail," lest the global capitalist economy be weakened. Of course, some biblical scholars outside of the imperial metropolises might have been aware of what was happening: the World Bank and the IMF had been disintegrating and ruining the local economies in many countries by forcing them to take loans at high interest rates and then imposing structural adjustments on them.

Globalized consumer capitalism had become skillful in generating and channeling people's desire, manipulating consumers by marketing that wormed its way into people through all the senses, through every orifice of peoples' heads. Advertising through mass media, and then electronic media, effectively atomized people, dissolving

18. Hardt and Negri, *Empire*.

neighborhoods, local communities, church parishes, and civil society. Capitalism also began to cannibalize cultures, fragmenting and then exoticizing them, transforming pieces of people's culture into commodities.[19] For several decades now, capitalism *produces* much of the culture that is consumed. Especially through the mass media and, particularly, the production of images it commodifies and capitalizes racial, ethnic, and gender diversity. Global capitalism has long figured out how to monetize and thrive on multicultural diversity. Its reach is extensive and expanding. It even appropriates images from local movements (of resistance), then exoticizes them into commodities for consumption in innocuous depoliticized form.

The power of globalized capitalism to fragment and exoticize, and then offer for consumption, reached right into biblical studies and even postcolonial biblical criticism. While there may have been a separation between Church and State in some countries, there is none between religion and the reach of global capitalism. Eager to sell its product, the neo-liberal "Jesus Seminar," aided and abetted the burgeoning global capitalism in this process by its fragmentation and commodification of exoticized sayings of Jesus in books heavily marketed by a Rupert Murdock publishing house.[20] As West[21] pointed out with regard to postcolonial biblical criticism, "anything particular and local is prone to commodification and consumption by postcolonial theory in general," citing how Mosala's liberation hermeneutics was co-opted.[22]

Considering the pervasive power of global capitalism, it is almost impossible to be *in* the new Empire but not *of* it. It would be possible to minimally lessen our individual and collective contribution to how it "grows wealth" for the corporations that wield the power of capital by, for example, not using credit cards, shifting our mortgages and bank accounts from mega-banks to credit unions, and not shopping on Amazon (a division of Empire that has, for example, gobbled up Whole Foods, an expansive chain of grocery stores that sources appetizing-looking produce from expanding industrial farms in Mexico, Brazil, and East

19. Boer, "Remembering Babylon"; West, "Doing Postcolonial Biblical Criticism," 152–53.

20. E.g., Crossan, *Historical Jesus*; Funk et al.,

21. West, "Doing Postcolonial Biblical Criticism," 151–52.

22. Sugirtharajah, *The Bible and the Third World*, 241–52; compare Sugirtharajah, *Voices from the Margin*, and Sugirtharajah, "Afterword," in *Voices from the Margin*, 3rd ed., 494–97.

Africa). But our livelihood is inextricably tied up in the machinations of global capitalism. To focus on only one example, the pensions of state employees, including most academics, are embedded in, complicit in, and dependent on the growth of new global capital.

While biblical scholars did participate in the consumption modes of global capitalism, they mainly allowed its free reign by withdrawing further into individualism by separation of political-economic life and critical historical inquiry. The "literary turn" became, in effect, mainstream interpretation, and literary interpreters obligingly confined their attention to the world of the text. Even less attention was given to the context and conditions of the production and appropriation of texts that became "biblical." After all, biblical texts had taken on a life of their own as sacred scripture for pious individual readers.

While it may not be possible for biblical studies not to be *in* the Empire of global capitalism, might it be possible for it not to be *of* the Empire? The question for biblical studies now is whether it would be possible: (1) to no longer submit to the authority of the imperial Bible and subservient biblical studies, and instead, (2) find resources in the sources that were coopted by the imperial Bible that could aid in imagining an alternative to global capitalism, and perhaps even find resources for resistance.

What did Not Happen as a Result of the Innovative Criticisms in Biblical Studies

Surely, a factor in what postcolonial biblical interpretation did not become is *what did not happen* as a result of the many innovative new "criticisms" in biblical scholarship in the 1980s and 90s. The challenges to, and departures from, the objectivist depoliticized scientific (historical-critical) scholarship—the new literary criticisms, applications of social scientific schemes, the different liberationist criticisms, and the critical deconstruction of modernist assumptions and conceptualizations—did not result in any explicit criticism, much less serious deconstruction of the basic established theological schemes and controlling synthetic constructs at the center of biblical studies, as established interpretation of the imperial Bible.

Most fundamental was the assumption, a projection of modern Western culture and society, that the texts were religious and that the historical context consisted (vaguely and abstractly) of two religions, (early) Judaism and (early) Christianity, as the latter originated in and then broke away from Judaism. According to the Christian theological view that became standard in 20th-century NT studies, moreover, the driving theology or worldview of the followers of Jesus and the apostle Paul was apocalypticism, with its expectation of the imminent end of the world. Apocalypticism had supposedly become dominant in late second-temple Judaism, in contrast with the more "this-worldly" orientation of the earlier prophets. Further, texts such as the "books" of the Pentateuch or Torah and the "books" of the Prophets were understood as already biblical or Scripture, and the Gospels and Pauline letters were understood as the New Testament "books" of (early) Christianity. The historical context in which these "biblical" books originated and were operative, moreover, continued to be understood as the biblical world. All of these synthetic concepts that continue to control discourse in the field of biblical studies are anachronistic modern scholarly constructs that biblical scholars have imposed on texts and history.

What many scholars realize, but do not admit publicly, is that what are usually understood as Judaism and Christianity did not develop until late antiquity. Something that could intelligibly be referred to as Christianity did not develop until well after "the New Testament period," and what became dominant and "orthodox" was the branch of "Christianity" that was "established" by the Roman Empire in late antiquity. The New Testament did not come into being until those church councils were convened by Roman emperors in the fifth century. What could be intelligibly referred to as Judaism emerged, perhaps, in very late antiquity, while the process by which the Hebrew Bible emerged remains unclear. Apocalypticism is a synthetic (Christian) scholarly construction that attempted to comprehend, somewhat literally, misunderstood "cosmic" images and fragments from a range of Judean texts, many of which were newly discovered in the 19th century.[23] To begin to understand texts in their historical contexts (long before they became biblical) it would be necessary to wriggle out from under these anachronistic scholarly constructs and guard critically against reverting to them.

The combination of more comprehensive and precise investigations of the historical contexts of texts and several (largely separate) lines of recent research into ancient communications media are undermining

---

23. Horsley, *Scribes, Visionaries*, chaps 8–9; *Prophet Jesus*, chaps. 1–5.

and challenging these standard constructs together with the assumptions on which they were based. The implications of these more recent lines of research can be reinforced and deepened by reviving earlier research that was left behind in the excitement over innovative new "criticisms." This may enable us to, at least, imagine alternatives to the Empire of global capitalism and even discern a sustained history of resistance movements in search of a more just social-economic order.

Ancient Communications Media and the Historical Contexts of Texts

A brief summary of the largely independent lines of research into ancient communications media can expose the unwarranted assumptions of standard biblical studies that are deeply rooted in modern print-culture. Most basic is research demonstrating that literacy was limited to a tiny percentage of people, around 10% in the Roman Empire and only around 3% in ancient Palestine.[24] Oral communication dominated. The vast majority of the populace had little or no use for writing and were even hostile to it; they knew it mainly from the way it was used to document their debts and to estimate levels of tribute and taxation that could be extracted from them. Even the literate scribes serving the Judean temple-state learned and cultivated their texts and other traditions by repeated recitation so that the texts were "inscribed on their hearts" (Prov 3:3), i.e., in their memory—collective as well as individual memory. Thus, scribal texts were oral as well as written, and should not be imagined as having been "written" by "authors" and widely available for individual "readers." Insofar as inscribed scrolls were confined to the temple and scribal-priestly circles (such as the Qumran community), villagers would have had little contact with written texts. They knew very well their often-localized Israelite popular traditions of stories, legends, covenantal commandments and laws, and ceremonies such as Passover in which they celebrated their liberation in the exodus.[25]

The recent research on communications media drives us to seriously rethink how we understand the historical contexts of the texts we

24. Harris, *Ancient Literacy*; Hezser, *Jewish Literacy*.

25. Fuller (provisional) discussion in Horsley, "Oral Communication, Oral Performance"; and most recently, "Can Study of the Historical Jesus Escape?" The pioneer in studies of ancient communications was Werner Kelber; see his now collected essays, *Imprints, Voiceprints*.

interpret, which have recently been investigated more comprehensively and precisely than previously. This rethinking is resulting in more critical awareness of "the power/knowledge relations" evident in texts-in-contexts. That is, the broader historical contexts of the texts later included in the Bible were a succession of empires that conquered and then ruled the subjected people(s) in Judea through the temple-state in Jerusalem.

The composition and development of the texts that became the "books" of the Torah/ Pentateuch, and the "books" of the Deuteronomic history, may have begun in support of the Davidic monarchy. But it seems clear that scribal circles, serving in the temple-state, also shaped and further developed the "books" of the Torah/ Pentateuch as authorization of the temple-state that represented a succession of imperial regimes. The "book" of Deuteronomy adapts earlier traditions and covenantal laws in a centralization of political-economic-religious power in "the (sacred) place that YHWH will choose" for the temple (i.e., Jerusalem). Parts of Exodus and Numbers provide the grounding of the Jerusalem temple-state in the formative history led by Moses, who mediates revelation. But the law(s), for an almost powerless king, suggest deference to the dominant imperial regime. The "book" of Leviticus consists of the establishment of, and instructions for, the priests who staffed the temple. It was previously assumed that these texts of *torah* had become "the Scripture" during second-temple times.

Close analysis of the manuscripts of these "books," and other texts of *torah* found among the Dead Sea Scrolls (DSS) by highly regarded text-critics, however, has undermined this assumption. These DSS manuscripts are more than a thousand years older than those previously known. Text critics such as Eugene Ulrich and Emanuel Tov have found that these new-found manuscripts attest to multiple versions of "books"—such as Exodus, Leviticus, and Deuteronomy—and that all of these different versions were still undergoing development.[26] There thus was no standard "text" of the Torah/Pentateuch that was supposedly "the Scripture." These "books" did not constitute a sacred set of solely authoritative written texts that groups of scribes then "interpreted." Scribes serving the temple-state, or perhaps dissident scribes, were rather adapting the texts, or even composing new texts, of *torah*.[27] These books, evidently, had only relative authority, mainly for the temple-state

---

26. Ulrich, *Dead Sea Scrolls*.

27. Horsley, *Scribes, Visionaries*, chaps. 5–6.

rulers, and its priests and scribes. It is quite unclear what sort of author-ity these "books" would have held for the vast majority of the Judean people who had little or no contact with them.

As Hellenistic conquest and imperial rule replaced Persian and Ro-man conquest and domination replaced Hellenistic, the historical context became increasingly complex and conflictual, as indicated in the increas-ing information from available sources. The Hellenistic and Roman im-perial rule became increasingly invasive and violent, evoking increasing resistance, not only by the people but even by some scribal circles. The dream-visions included in Daniel 7–12 and 1 Enoch 85–90, standardly labeled as "apocalyptic" texts, were rather attempts by scribal circles who remained loyal to the Judean tradition of a covenant with "the Most High," to understand and voice opposition to the increasingly invasive Hellenis-tic imperial rulers and the attempt by the priestly aristocracy to transform the Jerusalem temple-state into a Hellenistic *polis* that abandoned the covenant with God for Hellenistic political cultural forms.[28] Resistance begun by these scribal circles expanded into the Maccabean Revolt by Judean villagers and 1 Maccabees was composed as propaganda by other scribal circles in support of the Hasmonean dynasty that took power, as high priests, in the outcome of the revolt. The scribal-priestly group that formed the community of the DSS withdrew in protest.

Hiring mercenary troops in an increasingly military state, the Hasmonean high priests proceeded to conquer the people of Samaria and take over Galilee, expanding Jerusalem's rule over most people of Israelite heritage in Palestine. Galileans thus came under Jerusalem's rule for the first time (in, at least, hundreds of years) only in 104 BCE. According to Josephus' accounts both the people and, evidently, the Pharisees who had become the leading scribal retainers of the Has-monean temple-state with expert knowledge of "the laws," offered per-sistent resistance that escalated into virtual civil war under the brutal Alexander Jannai.[29] The temple-state had become increasingly remote from, and repressive of, the people.

Roman conquest of the expanded area ruled by the temple-state was prolonged, brutal, and destructive, complicated by war between rival warlords and Hasmonean factions. Their client "King of the Judeans," the

---

28. See my *Scribes, Visionaries*, chap. 9; and the parallel analysis of Daniel in Port-ier-Young, *Apocalypse against Empire*, both "deconstructions" of the older synthetic construct of apocalypticism.

29. Josephus, *War* 1.88–98; *Antiquities* 13.372–383.

military strongman Herod, finally conquered his subjects with the help of Roman troops after three years' resistance by Galileans and Judeans. He then subordinated the temple and high priesthood as instruments of his own rule. He massively rebuilt the temple, in grand Hellenistic style, and expanded the high priestly aristocracy with his own favorites as high priests, while transforming the areas of Palestine into a model Roman client kingdom adorned with the principal institutions of Roman imperial rule. Following the death of Herod and the end of his tyrannical rule, widespread revolts erupted in the principal districts of Galilee, Judea, and the trans-Jordan. After the Romans reconquered the people, they placed Herod's son Antipas in charge of Galilee, who built two new cities in the area, continuing the exploitative rule of his father. In Judea they restored the temple-state to power; under a Roman governor, the high priestly aristocracy became predatory on the people. The resulting turmoil of continuing resistance by the people, and the declining ability of the high priests to maintain control, eventually led to the outbreak of widespread popular revolt against both Roman and high priestly/Herodian rule. This was the context of the mission of Jesus and the emergence of the Jesus movements that produced the Gospel stories.

Salvaging Some Resources for Resistance from the Imperial Bible

By combining the implications of recent research on ancient communications media and continuing historical investigations of the historical contexts with earlier literary analysis of the complex "layered" "books" included in the Bible, it is possible to uncover memories and stories of historical movements of resistance to domination, in creating or renewing alternative social-economic forms. Such memories and stories may offer both visions of an alternative to domination by Empire and, perhaps, even resources and precedents for current resistance.

The literary turn in biblical studies often left behind earlier critical scholarly analysis of the processes in which those "books" that were later included in the Bible were probably produced. The scribal composers of the "books" of the Torah/Pentateuch had drawn on legends of the ancestors in hoary antiquity and of the people's supposed formative origin in the exodus, from bondage under the Egyptian Pharaoh. In multiple stages of composition, these scribes also drew on collections of laws and customs we know as the "Covenant Code" in Exodus 21–23, the "Holiness Code" in Leviticus, and Deuteronomy, that drew extensively on and adapted (or perhaps coopted) what had been (and continued as) popular customs cultivated in village communities.[30] These were, evidently, the Mosaic covenantal commandments, laws, and customs that guided social-economic relations in the village communities before the rise of a monarchic state.

The scribal composers of the "books" of the Deuteronomic history had, evidently drawn on memories of peasant revolts against the kings of fortified cities in Canaan (in Joshua); popular stories of "liberators" such as Gideon and the archaic "victory song" of the movement led by the prophetess Deborah (in Judges);[31] memories of the young David who had been "messiah-ed" as the leader of the struggles against the Philistines (in 2 Samuel); the sustained narratives of the revolts of the tribes of Israel against David who had become an exploitative king (in 2 Samuel); and, continuing revolts of the people against exploitative kings led by popular prophets such as Ahijah and Elijah/Elisha (in 1–2 Kings).[32] In prophetic "books," where the framing prophecies are exhortations (evidently to rulers) to suddenly do justice, and promises of future restoration of Jerusalem/Zion to glorious imperial status and glory, scholars discerned earlier prophetic pronouncements of YHWH's judgment against kings and their officers for having manipulated peasants into debt and expropriated their land (Coote; Mosala; Chaney). [On this basis, Mosala formulated a hermeneutics of liberation applied to apartheid South Africa.]

The (perhaps unintended) consequence of earlier critical studies of these "books" has been to provide access to popular traditions central to the collective identity and social-economic life of the people who were ruled by earlier monarchies and later by the temple-state. These memories and stories, lying "underneath" and adapted in the imperial Bible, offer both visions of an alternative to domination by global capitalism and, perhaps, even resources and precedent for current resistance.

---

30. See the extensive more recent survey in Knight, *Law, Power, and Justice*; Cf. also Chaney, *Peasants*; and Horsley, *Covenant Economics*.

31. What we know from Exodus 15 and Judges 5 are renderings of the two oldest examples of poetry in (archaic) Hebrew; "The Song of the Sea" celebrating YHWH's victory over the military forces of Pharaoh in a storm at the Red Sea, and "The Song of Deborah," celebrating the victory by YHWH and the people of Israel over the chariot forces of kings in the Great Plains.

32. Coote, ed., *Elijah and Elisha*.

Continuation of Israelite Popular Movements of Resistance as Alternative to Empire

Israelite alternate traditions adapted in scribal texts, moreover, evidently continued to be cultivated orally by peasant villagers, "underneath" the scribal texts that were later included in the Bible.[33] Villagers hardly needed to have been trained to read in order to celebrate Passover, to recite the song of Deborah or the song of Hannah, or to tell and retell stories of the exodus or of prophets such as Elijah. Village elders hardly needed to consult a scroll in order to deal with local conflicts or hunger from crop failure, according to time-honored popular customs. The central importance of Israelite popular tradition for village community life is parallel to the central importance of indigenous peoples' traditions and practices that continue to function "underneath" the imposition of colonial rule and practice and, more recently, the pressures of capitalist "development." This is central to presentations of African scholars such as that of Aliou Niang.[34] The Israelite tradition of popular resistance to imperial rule, and renewal of an independent community life, reemerged in popular movements against the intensified imperial rule of Rome and its client rulers in Palestine. The resilient power of this tradition, moreover, emerged dramatically in the mission of Jesus, and the movements that formed, in response as evident in Gospel stories they produced.

The resilience of Israelite popular tradition (or social memory) is evident in the distinctively Israelite forms taken by several instances of two kinds of popular movements in the same historical context as the mission of Jesus, according to the accounts of Josephus. The revolts of the people at the death of Herod in 4 BCE, and again in 66–70 CE, took the form of popular movements led by "kings" acclaimed by their followers. These were evidently patterned after the young David's example, having been "messiah-ed" by the Israelites struggling against Philistine invasions. These movements successfully maintained the independence of Galileans and Judeans from Jerusalem and Roman rule, for periods of up to three years. In the mid-first century, popular prophets called out Judean (or

33. I have been explaining the existence and importance of Israelite popular tradition (or social memory) in many books and articles since the late 1970s; see most recently Horsley, *Text and Tradition,* chap. 5; and Horsley, "Can Study of the Historical Jesus Escape."

34. See the recurrent discussion in every chapter of Niang, *Poetics of Postcolonial Biblical Criticism.*

Samaritan) villagers into the wilderness to experience new acts of deliverance patterned after those led by Moses or Joshua.[35]

Jesus and the Gospels: Continuing the Tradition

The literary turn in biblical studies surely helped professional interpreters recognize that the Gospels are stories (sustained narratives) and not mere collections of Jesus' sayings and "miracle stories." But it also domesticated the Gospel stories as if they were modern *novellas*, and not ancient stories, decontextualizing them from any historical (political-economic-religious) significance. Recognizing, rather, that the Gospels were ancient historically oriented stories responding to and addressing a particular historical context of crisis for the Galilean and Judean people, makes a significant difference in how they are understood.[36] They were/ are sustained narratives and speeches of a popular prophet generating a movement of the renewal of Israel among villagers in Galilee and beyond, who was opposed to, and by, the Roman-client high priestly rulers in the Jerusalem temple-state and other Roman-client rulers. The Gospel stories then, evidently, developed in movements of Jesus-loyalists and were orally performed in communities of those movements of the renewal of Israel that were deeply rooted in Israelite popular tradition.[37]

The Gospel stories stand in direct continuity with the Israelite popular tradition (and movements) that can be discerned "underneath" or "adapted" in the scribal texts later included in the Hebrew Bible. Jesus, like other popular prophets active in the mid-first century, would have interacted with villagers in the terms and forms of Israelite popular tradition in which they were mutually embedded. The overall Gospel stories,

---

35. See my first forays into critical historical investigations of these popular movements in the series of articles behind *Bandits, Prophets, and Messiahs*, chaps. 3–4; those articles are now published in Horsley, *Politics, Conflict, and Movements*.

36. Extensive analysis and discussion of the Markan Gospel story in Horsley, *Hearing the Whole Story*.

37. See more recently the explanation in "Can the Historical Jesus Escape," which draws partly on the recent "revisionist" text-critical analysis of David Parker and Eldon Epp. They conclude that extant ancient manuscripts (and fragments) of the Gospels were so "multiform" in their particulars (although fairly consistent in the overall stories). They were thus what have been called "oral-derived" texts. As noted above, the written Gospel texts as we have them (and interpret them) are the products of modern scholars, experts in text-criticism, who work on the assumptions of print-culture. See especially Parker, *Living Text*; and Epp, "It's All About Variants."

and many of their episodes, present Jesus' mission among the people as a new exodus and Jesus as a new "Moses" and "Elijah." The Gospels portray Jesus and his disciples as working in village communities, the basic social-economic form of Israelite society.

Contrary to the fragmenting practices of established biblical studies, Israelite tradition took the format, not of individual verses in print, but of broader cultural patterns such as stories of the exodus and the Mosaic covenant (that can be seen in Joshua 24, Deuteronomy 5, and the overall structure of Deuteronomy, and the Community Rule from Qumran).[38] In a repeated theme and form in the Gospels, Jesus is portrayed as renewing the Mosaic covenant in performative speech. The first long parallel speech in the Matthean and Lukan Gospels, for example, is a renewal of the Mosaic covenant both in overall covenantal structure (declaration of deliverance, covenantal demands, and sanctions) and in the demands for the people's social-economic interaction (explicitly, a sharpening of the covenant commandments in Matthew).

Many of Jesus' prophetic statements continue Israelite prophetic forms familiar from the earlier prophets. Like the ancient prophets, Jesus in the Gospel stories pronounced condemnation of the (high priestly) rulers' exploitation of their people.[39] He even declares that the people do not owe tribute to (the divine) Caesar, as it is not lawful according to the first two covenantal commandments. The Gospel stories thus present the prophet Jesus carrying out a renewal of the solidarity and cooperation of village communities as well as pronouncement of God's judgment against the rulers' exploitation of the people. The Gospels provide paradigmatic stories of strengthening local communities in resistance to the ruling institutions that extract resources from people to expand the wealth and power of the wealthy and powerful.

Some Interrelated Conclusions

Post-colonial criticism has helped undermine the authority of the imperial Bible. It is difficult to discern reasons to continue allowing the imperial Bible to exercise authority as "the Scripture." Established Western biblical studies served as the handmaid of Western imperialism

38. Extensive discussion in Horsley, *Covenant Economics*, and most recently in Horsley, *You Shall Not Bow Down*, chaps. 1–4.

39. See most recently Horsley, *Jesus and the Politics of Roman Palestine*, chaps. 2 and 6; and Horsley, *You Shall not Bow Down*, chap. 5.

and colonialism. More recently it has ignored the conditions of its own operation, failing to discern the consolidation of imperial power by the new form of empire, global capitalism. In its literary turn, excitement over new criticisms has turned attention further away from the concrete circumstances of ancient and recent contexts of texts toward individualistic interpretation. Recent research into ancient communications media that are undermining the print-cultural assumptions in which biblical studies are embedded and the theological constructs that control investigation and interpretation, are also further undermining the authority of the imperial Bible. Combined with these researches, more comprehensive and precise historical investigations illuminate the political contexts and functions of biblical texts.

Rather than throw the imperial Bible onto the scrap heap, however, a combination of neglected earlier critical research into the formation of the "books" later included in the imperial Bible, and the recent research into communications media and the investigations of historical contexts, enable us to mine those same "books" as sources to recover the long history of peoples' resistance to domination and insistence on just social-economic practices in supportive communities.[40] This tradition of peoples' resistance to domination offers images of possible alternative political-economic forms to the imperial domination of global capitalism and examples of collective resistance.

40. Moreover, the popular tradition of stories and customs "underneath" and/or included in "books" of the imperial Bible, and the further development and adaptation of Israelite popular tradition in the Gospel stories continued in the collective social memory of other peoples, as alternative to, and often in opposition to, the imperial Bible and its dominant reception. In the European Middle Ages, village priests' translation of the Gospel lessons into the vernacular that serfs could understand tended to touch off local peasant revolts against local lords in their castles. Translations of Bible stories told to the people became part of the motivation of wider popular movements of resistance or revolt among late medieval European peasants (Lollards, Hussites). In 1524–25, prior to their widespread revolt, several groups of peasants in S.W. Germany formulated sets of principles, such as the "Twelve Articles," that summarized their traditional rights to the resources of the land, forests, and streams that their lords had been expropriating for their own use. These Articles were clearly influenced by Israelite popular customs recognizable to us from adaptations in Exodus 21–23 and Deuteronomy. Africans enslaved in America heard subversive voices in the Bible lessons read to them by their enslavers' clergy, voices that helped them develop their own "hidden transcript of resistance" and engage in hidden forms of resistance (see Scott, *Domination and the Arts of Resistance*). When *campesinos* in late twentieth century Central America heard certain Bible stories told by "delegates of the Word," some of them organized resistance to their landlords who had taken over their ancestral land. Many more examples of resistance to domination from peoples in Africa and India could be added.

Bibliography

Ahmad, Aijaz. *In Theory: Classes, Nations, Literatures.* London: Verso, 1992.

Anderson, Benedict R. O'G. *Imagined Communities: Reflections on the Origin and Spread of Nationalism.* New York: Verso, 1983.

Boer, Roland. "Remembering Babylon: Postcolonialism and Australian Biblical Studies." In *The Postcolonial Bible,* edited by R. S. Sugirtharajah, 24–48. Bible and Postcolonialism 1. Sheffield: Sheffield Academic, 1998.

Chaney, Marvin L. *Peasants, Prophets, and Political Economy: The Hebrew Bible and Social Analysis.* Eugene, OR: Cascade Books, 2017.

Coote, Robert B. *Amos among the Prophets: Composition and Theology.* 1981. Reprint, Eugene, OR: Wipf & Stock, 2005.

———, ed. *Elijah and Elisha in Socioliterary Perspective.* Semeia Studies. Atlanta: Scholars, 1992.

Crossan, John Dominic. *The Historical Jesus: The Life of a Mediterranean Jewish Peasant.* San Francisco: HarperSanFrancisco, 1991.

Dirlik, Arif. "The Postcolonial Aura: Third World Criticism and the Age of Global Capitalism." *CI* 20 (1994) 328–56.

Dube, Musa. *Postcolonial Feminist Interpretation of the Bible.* St. Louis: Chalice, 2000.

Eisenstein, Elizabeth L. *The Printing Press as an Agent of Change: Communications and Culture Transformations in Early Modern Europe.* Cambridge: Cambridge University Press, 1979.

Epp, Eldon J. "It's All About Variants: A Variant-Conscious Approach to New Testament Text Criticism." *HTR* 100 (2007) 275–308.

Gottwald, Norman K. *The Tribes of Yahweh: The Sociology of the Religion of Liberated Israel, 1250–1050 B.C.E.* Maryknoll, NY: Orbis, 1979.

Gottwald, Norman K., and Richard A. Horsley, eds. *The Bible and Liberation: Political and Social Hermeneutics.* Rev. ed. Maryknoll, NY: Orbis, 1993.

Hardt, Michael, and Antonio Negri. *Empire.* Cambridge: Harvard University Press, 2000.

Harris, William V. *Ancient Literacy.* Cambridge: Harvard University Press, 1989.

Hezser, Catherine. *Jewish Literacy in Roman Palestine.* Texts and Studies in Ancient Judaism 81. Tübingen: Mohr Siebeck, 2001.

Horsley, Richard A. "Can Study of the Historical Jesus Escape its Typographical Captivity?" *JSHJ* 19 (2021) 1–65.

———. "Christmas: The Religion of Consumer Capitalism." In *Christmas Unwrapped: Consumerism, Christ, Culture,* edited by Richard A. Horsley and James Tracy, 165–87. Harrisburg, PA: Trinity, 2001.

———. *Covenant Economics: A Biblical Vision of Justice for All.* Louisville: Westminster John Knox, 2009.

———. *Hearing the Whole Story: The Politics of Plot in Mark's Story.* Louisville: Westminster John Knox, 2001.

———. *Jesus and the Politics of Roman Palestine.* Revised with a new Preface. Eugene, OR: Cascade Books, 2021.

———. "Oral Communication, Oral Performance, and New Testament Interpretation." In *Method and Meaning: Essays on New Testament Interpretation in Honor of Harold W. Attridge,* edited by Andrew McGovern and Kent Harold Richards. Resources for Biblical Study 67. Atlanta: Society of Biblical Literature, 2011. Reprinted as chap. 1 in *Text and Tradition in Performance and Writing*. Biblical Performance Series 9. Eugene, OR: Cascade Books, 2013.

————. *Politics, Conflict, and Movements in First-Century Palestine*. Edited by K. C. Hanson. Eugene, OR: Cascade Books, 2023.

————. *The Prophet Jesus and the Renewal of Israel*. Grand Rapids: Eerdmans, 2012.

————. *Scribes, Visionaries, and the Politics of Second Temple Judea*. Louisville: Westminster John Knox, 2007.

————. "Submerged Biblical Histories and Imperial Biblical Studies." In *The Postcolonial Bible I*, edited by R. S. Sugirtharajah, 52–173. The Bible and Postcolonialism 1. Sheffield: Sheffield Academic, 1998.

————. *You Shall not Bow Down and Serve Them: The Political-Economic Projects of Jesus and Paul*. Eugene, OR: Cascade Books, 2021.

Horsley, Richard A., with John S. Hanson. *Bandits, Prophets, and Messiahs: Popular Movements at the Time of Jesus*. Minneapolis: Winston, 1985.

Kelber, Werner. *Imprints, Voiceprints, and Footprints of Memory: Collected Essays*. RBS 74. Atlanta: Society of Biblical Literature, 2013.

Knight, Douglas A. *Law, Power, and Justice in Ancient Israel*. LAI. Louisville: Westminster John Knox, 2011.

Kwok, Pui-lan. "Discovering the Bible in the Nonbiblical World." *Semeia* 47 (1989) 25–42. Reprinted in *The Bible and Liberation: Political and Social Hermeneutics*, rev. ed., edited by Norman K. Gottwald and Richard Horsley. Maryknoll, NY: Orbis, 1993.

Mosala, Itumeleng J. *Biblical Hermeneutics and Black Theology in South Africa*. Grand Rapids: Eerdmans, 1989.

Niang, Aliou Cisse. *A Poetics of Postcolonial Biblical Criticism: God, Human-Nature Relationship, and Negritude*. Eugene, OR: Cascade Books, 2019.

Niditch, Susan. *Oral World and Written Word: Ancient Israelite Literature*. LAI. Louisville: Westminster John Knox, 1996.

Parker, D. C. *The Living Text of the Gospels*. Cambridge: Cambridge University Press, 1997.

Portier-Young, Anathea. *Apocalypse against Empire: Theologies of Resistance in Early Judaism*. Grand Rapids: Eerdmans, 2011.

Prakash, Gyan. "Postcolonial Criticism and Indian Historiography." *ST* 31/32 (1992) 8–19.

Said, Edward. *Orientalism*. London: Penguin, 1985.

Scott, James C. *Domination and the Arts of Resistance*. New Haven: Yale University Press, 1990.

Shohat, Ella. "Notes on the Post-Colonial." *ST* 31/32 (1992) 99–113.

Sugirtharajah, R. S. *The Bible and the Third World: Precolonial, Colonial and Postcolonial Encounters*. Cambridge: Cambridge University Press, 2001.

————, ed. *The Postcolonial Bible*. Bible and Postcolonialism 1. Sheffield: Sheffield Academic, 1998.

————, ed. *Voices from the Margin*. Maryknoll, NY: Orbis, 1991, 1995, 2006.

The KJV African American Jubilee Bible, 400th Anniversary Edition. Philadelphia: American Bible Society, 2012.

Ulrich, Eugene. *The Dead Sea Scrolls and the Origins of the Bible*. Grand Rapids: Eerdmans, 1999.

Weems, Renita J. "Reading *Her Way* through the Struggle: African American Women and the Bible." In *Stony the Road We Trod*, edited by Cain Hope Felder. Minneapolis: Fortress, 1991. Reprinted in *The Bible and Liberation* rev. ed., edited by Norman K. Gottwald and Richard A. Horsley. Maryknoll, NY: Orbis, 1993.

West, Gerald. "Doing Postcolonial Biblical Interpretation @home: Ten Years of (South) African Ambivalence." *Neot* 42.1 (2008) 147–64.

———. "Finding a Place among the Posts for Post-colonial Criticism in Biblical Studies in South Africa." *OTE* 10 (1997) 322–42.

9

African Biblical Hermeneutics

Contexts amidst "Meaning Making"

Jeremy Punt

Strivings, Contexts, and "Meaning Making"

Gerald West has contributed, in many important ways, to biblical studies in Africa and beyond. His poignant and tireless work on biblical hermeneutics in South Africa, the broader African continent, and the global context would be impossible to pin down in a brief essay. In fact, his very own assessment of African Biblical Studies, including hermeneutics, was an attempt to assess such works conducted over almost a century of scholarship, in which he identified three significant features, and contemplated how "African futures might reconfigure them."[1] Scholars will inevitably review and emphasize different qualities in his work, driven by a spectrum of scholarly interests, institutional prerogatives, guild-related considerations and strictures, and social concerns. However, his concern with and for hermeneutics as social engagement, for *interested* rather than *interesting* readings, and with resilient inclusion of "ordinary readers," stands out to a fellow South African biblical scholar.

To the extent of his own proclivities, at least, such work aligns well with the somewhat broader area of African biblical hermeneutics, which he, in all fairness, spent more time practicing than theorizing

---

1. West, "African Biblical Scholarship as Post-Colonial, Tri-Polar," 240.

in, as a concept.[2] Tasked to reflect on African Biblical Hermeneutics (ABH) as a discipline, I will engage the topic by attempting to emulate West's non-partisan, scholarly-engaging inquisitiveness, in some small way. Over two decades ago, West already identified an "interpretive crisis" in the academic reading of the Bible. While emphasizing the Bible's importance in the South African society, and its significance for poor and marginalized societies, in particular, he identified the problem with the Bible in Africa as hermeneutical.[3] Rather than allowing the Bible to become divorced from the lives of regular people and to be relegated to the so-called religious or spiritual realms of their lives, West proposed that cooperation between professional exegetes and theologians with poor and marginalised societies be established in a form he labeled "reading *with*" or "speaking *with*" approach.[4] This, he argued, would let the Bible speak, once again, to regular people and their lives in South Africa by stimulating interdependency between the professional biblical scholars and those he called "ordinary readers," in hermeneutical processes and practices which produced readings in support of the "struggle for full liberation and life."[5]

Throughout his career, West's work has been both an example of illocutionary value for engaging with African biblical hermeneutics, which is irrevocably tied to (and at times perhaps also tied up, in the sense of strangulation) both its colonial past, and a resilient postcolonial present. The danger of a "North Atlantic captivity and inheritance" of theology in Africa, in tandem with the dualisms of Western liberalism that include a church-state separation, the tensions between faith-life and individual community, and the denominationalism of faith communities living off historical events in Europe and America pose many challenges for African biblical hermeneutics.[6] So does an idealist (or Platonist-Kantian) approach to biblical studies, which promotes unarticulated epistemological presuppositions of western content-oriented

2. See, e.g., West, "Reading the Bible in Africa"; West, "On the Eve"; and West, "Re-Reading the Bible,"

3. West, "Reading the Bible in Africa," 1–5. Other scholars agree: "the problem does not arise out of the Bible but out of the context of the interpreter and the interpretation" (Maimela, "Religion and Culture," 169), and even with specific concerns such as the debate between the inculturationists and liberationists, hermeneutics seems to be at the core (Martey, *African Theology*, 37–38).

4. Bediako, *Theology and Identity*, 7; cf. Segovia, "Reading Across."

5. West, "Reading the Bible in Africa," 4.

6. Pobee, "Comments on the Future," 2, 4.

curricula, with their hermeneutical assumptions, that can be nestled into fundamentalist positions on the Bible as a source of timeless and universalist, normative messages.[7]

Can the promotion of African biblical hermeneutics assist in shifting the focus from "meaning" to "meaning-making," which involves greater attention also to the endeavour of interpretive ventures and various stakeholders' roles and contributions, and requires accountability for approaches and methods, as much as for results and meanings?[8] This question touches on the theological setting of ABH. While a hermeneutical approach is so theologically laden that texts, overtly or otherwise, become substantiation of positions, is best avoided. Rethinking theological tradition does not imply the denunciation of past efforts nor unbridled optimism for current or future interpretive work.[9] It does, however, mean a break with biblical studies' overemphasis on "meaning," to the detriment of "meaning-making." "Meaning" is all too often still the driving force, even if subtly or covertly so, in search of the hidden semantic value of words, which are only recoverable through intensive decoding.[10]

Amidst the work of West, and many others, ABH is a contested area, not only for each of the three terms ("Africa(n)" in particular) but especially for the interplay between the terms. In a world filled with an ever-widening spectrum of hermeneutical approaches (although questions ranging from depth to purpose to orientation may need more attention),

7. Deist maintained the untenability of the Kantian epistemology and hermeneutic in South Africa based on a perceived total contrast between so-called Western and African styles of thinking: "idealist, theoretical" as opposed to "pragmatic, practical" (Deist, "South-Africanizing Biblical Studies," 33–39). See also Segovia, "And They Began to Speak," for a more comprehensive overview and comparison.

8. "[M]eaning—to the extent that there is such a thing—does not inhere in a text any more than it might inhere in a dream . . . Meaning is what we make of texts, not an ingredient in texts" (Adam, *What Is Postmodern?*, 33).

9. For a more comprehensive consideration of the role of the Bible in African Christianity, see e.g., West, "Role of the Bible."

10. "[T]he etymological conviction, still regnant, that there is something of surpassing value hidden 'beneath' the words, a something that is essential, as opposed to the verbally accidental, and that may be uncovered only by decipherment" (e. g., Smith, "Twice-Told Tale," 134). Some scholars, in fact, have also pointed out that, unlike meaning often implying finality (*a la* Foucault), the problem of "meaning-making" may be a more interesting focus than "meaning" itself (McCutcheon, *Discipline of Religion*, 28). Biblical scholarship increasingly experiences the tension between questioning and deconstructing the source-compendium approach to biblical interpretation to secure meaning versus relishing intertextual interplay of ideas and materiality together with ongoing interpretive meaning-making.

and concerns about the Bible's position and role in various significations, "Africa" as a notion, as much as a reality in all its complexity and comprehensiveness, offers as many possibilities as it poses challenges. In what follows, a prescriptive, regulatory approach is avoided. I also deliberately steer away from evaluating specific proposals for ABH, striving instead to engage with the more significant concerns of meaning(-making), contexts, and their connections in African biblical hermeneutics.

Meaning Abounds: African Meaning Making

Over the years, various attempts have been made to formulate an African hermeneutic, or at least to identify vital aspects which are to be included in such a hermeneutic.[11] At times, the search for an appropriate hermeneutic has been called the "dilemma" of the African theologian (Onwu 1985) and the appropriate use of exegesis and hermeneutics, for making sense of the Bible, identified as "a primary concern."[12] The development of a hermeneutic deemed particularly suitable for African readings of the Bible therefore largely depends on the perceived relationship between the notion of "Africa," its cultures, its (pre-mainstream religions) religiosities, and the relation to Christianity.[13] Many tools generated and applied by scholars from the Global North can, and continue to, be used in Africa. Still, the quest for exegesis and hermeneutics of the Bible, relevant to the African context remains. And, as Benezet Bujo argued, rereading the Bible from an African perspective is the appropriate starting point for an "African Christian Theology."[14]

11. Cf. Adamo, "Task and Distinctiveness;" Adamo, "What Is African Biblical Hermeneutics?;" Mburu, *African Hermeneutics*; Ntreh, "Toward an African;" Ukpong, "Rereading the Bible;" Wambudta, "Theologia Africana." Criticism has not stayed out, with Wambudta taken to task for being too much aligned with the New Hermeneutic (Parratt, "African Theology," 92) and other scholars stressing the importance of an indigenous African hermeneutic without defining it (e.g., Muzorewa, "A Definition," 175–76).

12. For example Mukonyora, Cox, and Verstraelen, *"Rewriting" The Bible.*

13. Bediako, "Understanding African Theology," 5–6, typology of "indigenisers," "biblicists," and "translators," for respectively those stressing radical continuity between Africa and Christianity, those insisting on radical discontinuity between the two, and those who occupy the middle ground can be further refined, but already identified points on the spectrum.

14. See Bujo, "Afrikanische Theologie," 125; Farisani, "Current Trends;" Punt, "Reading the Bible." In the words of West, "The details of scripture disrupt 'settled' theologies, enabling 'new' and contextually relevant theologies to be born" ("Contextual

Rather than stressing difference(s), biblical hermeneutics in Africa often focuses on looking for parallels and connections between the biblical and contemporary contexts (e.g., LeMarquand 1995).[15] In the past, the idea was even mooted that the role of the reader in locating similarities between the African context and the biblical (Old Testament) world could become the basis for a "genuine" African biblical hermeneutic.[16] However, African biblical scholars have since questioned the perceived close relationship between the Bible and African traditions, on at least three levels: i) Methodological deficiencies in comparative approaches include attempts to provide biblical justification for certain African traditions, in order to incorporate them into Christianity; ii) Biblical and African viewpoints, sometimes, tend to contradict one another, rather than exist symbiotically; iii) Many of the socio-religious aspects that are identified as parallels are not core to the biblical texts (Parratt 1983, 90, 93 n.7).

The emphasis on exploring parallels may be related to a dispensation biased towards relevance in contrast to a focus on textual content and the stronger involvement of "ordinary" readers in the "meaning-making" processes. Since ABH also tends to focus on the meaning and relevance of biblical texts for contemporary readers and listeners (LeMarquand 1995, 6), it is inclined to produce predominantly readings set "in front" of the text:[17] "This mode of reading concentrates on discerning the predominant themes, metaphors, and symbols . . . which

---

Bible Study," 146). As much as African Theology and African Biblical Hermeneutics are bedfellows, along the lines of African and Black Theology (Tutu, "Black Theology/African Theology"), their distinctive foci remain important (Mosala, *Biblical Hermeneutics*).

15. Identifying differences between African and Western hermeneutics remains slippery since not only is the Bible extensively infiltrated in the life and thought of the West, but this Bible also suffused context at times constitutes the framework in which the Bible is read and in intertextual sense, even produced. The continuity between Africa and the Bible is at least implicitly and in part questioned by African scholars who suggested the "rewriting" of the Bible (Banana, "The Case;" Punt, "From Rewriting").

16. Dickson, "African Traditional Religions," 157, 164, cautioned many decades ago already against any superficial equation of the African and biblical worlds, but the over-simplification of similarities leads even in his work to Africa becoming virtually homogeneous; insufficient distinctions are made between religious and cultural ideas; and apparent similarities may indeed be only that, apparent.

17. Ntreh, "Toward an African." But not exclusively. For example, Mosala specifically identified Desmond Tutu's and Allan Boesak's hermeneutical practices as inhibiting Black Theology from providing a liberatory paradigm because the text itself was not challenged. In contrast, he advocated a "behind the text" reading aimed at a materialist identification of the class struggle underlying the biblical documents (Mosala, *Biblical Hermeneutics*; see also Farisani, "Current Trends," 9–12).

then form the focus of the reading process."[18] However, the tendency to read texts with hardly any, if at all, attention to matters historical (at least as far as it concerns the text's production or context of production) has become more widespread and prevalent. Some would even argue, it is characteristic of the postmodern time.[19]

In the past, scholars have argued that a visible gap exists between academic and popular biblical interpretation, even if this division is by no means limited to the African continent, and that the divide in the case of ABH, is caused by African scholars using "an interpretive grid developed in the western culture."[20] However, is the realization that readers play a more significant role in the "meaning-making" processes than is often acknowledged by academic interpreters not, perhaps, greater on the African continent than elsewhere?[21] And, that "ordinary" readers doing everyday readings are allowed more theoretical and methodological assumptions, choices, and processes in ABH?[22] Had not ABH already started to engage in what are now areas of development in biblical hermeneutics elsewhere, such as exploring engagements between the Bible and popular culture or even cultural criticism?[23] ABH underscores how meaning is made, not found, and points also to the role of readers, including "ordinary" readers, and their contribution to the "meaning-making" processes.

18. West, *Contextual Bible Study*, 36.

19. Aichele et al., *The Postmodern Bible*, 1–19.

20. Ukpong, "Rereading the Bible," 4. As long as Western scholarship remains the dominant tradition, it will be characterized by its "ex-nomination" (i.e., the power not to be named) and likely to remain the normative, regulating discourse, and therefore remain both the yardstick (to measure others) and goal (to which others [are required to] aspire).

21. Ntreh, "Toward an African," 249, argues that "the Bible becomes meaningful only through a dialogue between the reader and the text," and insists that the reader as, an African scholar, should be "firmly grounded" in both the church and the community for his/her interpretation of the Bible to have an effect.

22. Others also suggest that by engaging hermeneutically with the Bible as well as with other sources and interlocutors, African theologians can avoid its entrapment that renders a professed allegiance to the Bible, which in reality, boils down to creatively pragmatic and selective use of the Bible (Maluleke, "Black and African Theologies," 12–14; see Isichei, *A History of Christianity*, 4–5).

23. As Blount, "Souls of Biblical Folks," 14, has noted; "A cultural-studies approach to biblical interpretation invests passionately in this contextual engagement with text meaning potential."

Contexts and Meanings: "Meaning Making" in Africa

Biblical interpreters generally agree that meanings only exist, (i.e., make sense, function, or are credible) in contexts. Still, the complex and complicated nature of the diversity of contexts that are all around, yet (or perhaps) nowhere, constrain "meaning making." To put it another way, while the meaning potential of texts is appropriated culturally—in and through cultural contexts—contextuality contributes to hermeneutical challenges.[24] Context is essential in ABH in different ways, but this emphasis does not always sit well with the regnant master paradigm of interpretive neutrality and hermeneutic objectivity.[25] Biblical hermeneuts increasingly acknowledge that historical experience and cultural reality are always and inevitably particular and contextual, which follows that no particular hermeneutical iteration can be universalized as normative for the entire human experience and reality. Therefore, such normalization of a singular approach into the norm for all is possible only through power imbalances where the reality, and experience, of the power-center are established as a yardstick for those inside, and outside, the center. In turn, those on the outside are excluded and marginalized, unable to transcend their social locations on the margins.[26] It is worthwhile asking, therefore, if the struggle for meaning is not, perhaps, a struggle between contexts. That is, how contexts, old and new, figure in(to) reading and interpretation.

The contexts of engagement of the Bible in Africa cannot be divorced from a whole range of ideological issues concerning power which naturally impacts the interpretation of the biblical texts in different ways, in different communities. As a renowned scholar of religion pointed out some years ago, "Controlling, owning, and operating the Bible . . . have become strategic appropriations of power to be deployed against a white man's faith that has systematically disempowered blacks in South Africa."[27] It is no surprise, then, that ABH is characterised by both *resistance* and *retrieval*. The importance of resistance is visible in readings that challenge dominant and conventionalist biblical interpretations

24. Blount, "Souls of Biblical Folks," 14.

25. The alternative postmodernist construct of a narrator and observer who is always situated and engaged (Segovia, *Decolonizing Biblical Studies*, 175) has started to replace the singular, universalized Western reader.

26. See, e.g., Segovia, *Decolonizing Biblical Studies*, 173.

27. Chidester, "Worldview Analysis," 25.

(western) and those that expose sinister impositions on, and negative allegations about, African readings.[28] Resistance, thus, often challenges the biblical texts through constructive (re)readings of both the texts and their interpretations, exposing their complicity in historical atrocities ranging from raced-based oppression and enslavement of Africans to misogynist and homo-transphobic attitudes and practices of the present.[29] The retrieval dimension of ABH seeks to unearth, and, at times, reappraise traditional African customs, traditions, and practices without exoticizing Africa and carefully avoiding the danger of repeating eccentric colonialist and modernist presentations of, and engagements with, African peoples, material, and intellectual culture.[30]

This privileging of contemporary contexts, however, does not mean denying or denigrating the importance of biblical texts' historical settings.[31] The historical dimension of texts which relates to the underlying assumptions derived from the ancient social spheres, link text and reality.[32] Nevertheless, focus on contemporary contexts in "meaning making," thus, implies a shift from the historical reconstructionist focus of reading texts, as exemplified in historical-critical readings and practices. That is hermeneutical perspectives attuned to the present-day context such as ABH, attempt to take seriously the consideration that texts are perceptions of reality much in the same way that "meaning

28. The smug comfort deriving from conventionalist interpretation feeds into its self-perpetuation and contributes to its analytical debilitation—a risk that is run not only by traditional hermeneutics. Resisting readings go beyond resistance against externally imposed propositions such as from the Global North to include also more local hermeneutical impositions; if postcolonial work has taught us nothing else, it has pointed out the ever-present danger of repeating colonizing tendencies today (Rukundwa and Van Aarde, "The Formation").

29. See also Punt, "Countering Bible-Based."

30. Liberation remains a key concept, and one which West also explores (see his early and important work in West's *Biblical Hermeneutics of Liberation*) but in postcolonial and at times a very neo-colonial that is not-yet-decolonial world, the content or shape but not the intensity has changed—and also goes beyond political power, or economic wherewithal.

31. For example, recent work on ancestors and cross-cultural hermeneutics, where the consideration of both ancient and contemporary, both the Greek and Roman worlds and Africa today, inform interpretation (Z. Dube, "The Statue Debate;" Kamudzandu, *Abraham as a Spiritual Ancestor*, and *Abraham our Father*). African American biblical scholars are also concerned with the importance of historical understanding of texts to facilitate a new, liberatory interpretation, referring, primarily, to the socio-political-cultural liberation of Black people (Wimbush, "Biblical Historical Study;" see especially Hoyt, "Interpreting Biblical Scholarship").

32. Schüssler Fiorenza, "Text and Reality."

making" is guided by perceptions of, and about, the reality of texts and contexts's that all perception of reality is exactly that, *perceived* reality. However, this perception and its communication are culturally determined, which necessitates taking the cultural context into consideration when interpreting texts.[33]

The claim that "all meaning is contextual," whose accuracy is beyond dispute, given that it is self-evidential that all interpretation is socially situated, remains, nevertheless, complicated and compromised in at least two ways: the tendency to prioritize meaning above context and the interpretive imperative regarding context. First, then, context can be all but drowned out by a vigorous focus on textual meaning rather than "meaning making." Meaning, then, becomes a distillate rather than an active ingredient in the ever-continuing combustion process of hermeneutics. Second, context itself is not autochthonous, and is always, also, in need of interpretation and analysis. Perhaps, then, is the very aspect that is ABH's *raison d'être*, the African context(s), also the reason for its contestation? "Meaning making" that inevitably takes place contextually, like all interpretation, requiring navigating between the Scylla of generalization and the Charybdis of eccentricity, has seen ABH develop amidst concerns with lived experiences, a range of readers, and socially engaged hermeneutics.[34]

African Biblical Hermeneutics as Contextual African "Meaning-Making"

The continuing search for, or development of, an adequate ABH cannot be constrained by the ongoing validation of some (generalizing) claims concerning biblical interpretation in Africa focused on the two aspects of

33. Deist, "South Africanising Biblical-Studies," 328–29 and 337–38. The culture-critical call that "textual studies must be pushed beyond the discrete boundaries of the page and the book into institutional practices and social structures" (Leitch, "Cultural Studies, 2," 281), does not trip up African biblical hermeneutics; nor the nudging to take up, besides the roles of biblical critics and even constructive theologians, also that of cultural critics, a task which includes a focus on issues of construction, representation, and power, and the investigation of various other dimensions of the biblical interpreter's social context besides the socio-religious (cf. Segovia, "Biblical Criticism," 51 n.2, and *Decolonizing Biblical Studies*, 59).

34. West, "Contextuality," 212: "By locating the biblical text in its literary and socio-historical contexts, we not only allow the text to speak to us out of its ancient past, we also provide today's readers of the Bible with additional lines of connection between their contexts and the Bible."

the biblical and African worlds' continuity and the connection between the biblical text's historical and readers' contemporary settings. The search for a truly authentic ABH has come a long way, understandably so, because methods are scholarly homes that create and define where and how scholars work and that inform their identity.[35] Recently Nyiawung (2013) has pleaded for an African hermeneutic that shifts from the primary focus on texts or on their authors or contexts, to the context of interpretation and to the exegetical agent's context, in particular. Apart from emphasizing the hermeneutical benefits of the African context for biblical hermeneutics, without any suggestion of assigning superiority to African culture, Nyiawung concludes that an ABH will contribute to the development of an authentic African Christian theology.[36]

The quest for an authentic ABH is akin to African theologies of identity, which are related to the search for identity and meaning in Africa. The devastation wrought by missionary enterprises, colonialism, and Apartheid, and more recent economic structural adjustment programs (SAPs), impact of urbanization, conflicts, migration, and globalization, and natural disasters, have all impacted indigenous African cultures, languages, and traditions, requiring a redefinition of how "self," "others," and "the world" are understood.[37] West's work, if I am not misrepresenting it, has pushed beyond the search for pristine hermeneutics in Africa, instead of seeking to promote the African context as the primary point of reference for ABH while avoiding the temptation to lump different African contexts together (that, typically, sees the promotion of some general traits as though representative of the full spectrum with its variety).[38] His work has succeeded in emphasizing

35. Cf. Punt, "From Rewriting." However, some African biblical scholars appear to have given up on African biblical hermeneutics. For example, Speckman, "African Biblical Hermeneutics," 221, notes that, "Africans have for long been going through a liminal phase as a result of historical cultural ties and that they were consequently unable to cross the threshold. Hence, recent proposals for a Biblical Hermeneutics model appear to reflect a cul-de-sac. While the celebration-of-life approach can be shared by various cultures, it has a uniquely African dimension in that it is not a compliance with any religious prescript, but an appropriation of an African worldview."

36. Tarus and Lowery, "African Theologies," 307. As found on other continents, Africa has a rich diversity of faith formations and expressions of Christianity, with different hermeneutical approaches; for the growing Pentecostal or Charismatic positions, see Abosede and Paul, "African Biblical Hermeneutics."

37. See Kwame Bediako's *Theology and Identity* for analysis in this regard.

38. West did this by making, in the words of Ukpong, "African peoples, identified social-culturally as groups and defined in terms of their common identities and

particular, focusedly-significant elements in different Southern African cultures without laying claim to any distinctiveness that may serve to deepen or entrench existing scholarly and social biases. It has promoted appreciation for the valuable and significant contributions originating from, and because of, the "African soil."

The constructive use of such Afrocentric reading practices, where African peoples and perspectives are the subjects, entails more than opposition to dominant Global North readings.[39] Afrocentric hermeneutics, which often avails itself of the "hermeneutics of suspicion" or "ideological criticism," is hardly naively accepted as authentic to Africa (or African Diaspora) and certainly not considered neutral or objective. "[B]orrowed theological concepts and tools such as Western Philosophy," can, and do, distort the efforts of African theologians. In similar ways, traditional theological thought forms of the African worldview have to be scrutinized for their accompanying baggage, including the presuppositions and assumptions carried within these thought forms including African worldviews' ideological strictures.[40] Some scholars hold ABH as "vital to the wellbeing of African society," feeding into a social imaginary where African social cultural contexts are the subjects of interpretation both constructively reappraising ancient biblical tradition and African world-views, cultures, and life experiences, as well as countering cultural, ideological conditioning imposed on African interpretation.[41]

The inevitable contextual nature of biblical interpretation means that worldview and culture are part of making sense of biblical texts. African biblical scholars often express concern both concerning the wilful neglect of including African contexts in western interpretations of the

---

concrete historical social life situations, the subject of interpretation of the Bible" (Ukpong "Rereading the Bible," 22; Cf. West, "African Biblical Scholarship as Tripolar," 240.

39. Cf. Wimbush, "Afrocentric Interpretation."

40. Muzorewa, "A Definition," 169, 173. Ideology in the (Mannheim) sense of one's particular perception of and alignment in life, and to life itself; see also Kawale, "Divergent Interpretations," 24, who claims that the Bible has been used to sanction both Western and African cultures.

41. Adamo, "What Is African Biblical Hermeneutics?," 59. Other dangers accompany African biblical hermeneutics, especially when it is universalised and abstracted for other(s') goals and ideologies, e.g., "one can recognize the ready grasp of IBS methodology by the African mind. As such, it is imperative that the discipline of inductive study be vigorously promoted in Africa to combat the ideo-theological tendencies of the African academy, but also the uncritical embrace of the populist western preacher-propagandist all too easily accessed through the medium of television and internet." (Meenan "Biblical Hermeneutics," 272)

Bible, and the often-unacknowledged Western worldview's permeating of most hermeneutical approaches. Some suggest that biblical parallels to African contexts, the theological context, the literary contexts, and the historical and cultural contexts are vital components for an ABH that is intent on both interpretive integrity and cultural-contextually appropriate readings.[42] David Tuesday Adamo has developed a seven-fold task for ABH, including as a liberational and transformational hermeneutics; dismantling of Eurocentric hermeneutical hegemonies and ideological strangleholds; using African culture and tradition to make sense of biblical texts; highlighting existential interpretation; "blackening" the Bible; reappraising the Bible to correct its cultural, ideological conditioning; and to promote African cultures, traditions, and identities.[43] ABH, according to Adamo, deliberately opts for an "Africentric" perspective, interpreting biblical texts from the perspective of an African worldview, and culture.[44]

Can the hermeneutical flow also be reversed? Can mainstream biblical studies, rethink its "ghetto"-like existence in a narrow religious sphere to create space for considering the Bible's legacy within cultural heritages—informative as such heritages have been and still are for all interpretive ventures? Not unlike in other parts of the world, in Africa, the Bible continues to be a "book for life," in the sense of an identity cultural marker that reaches beyond mere interesting notions, but which are considered informative for people's sense of self and community.[45] Even

42. Mburu, *African Hermeneutics*.

43. Adamo, "The Task," 31.

44. Adamo, "The Task," 59, also the discussion of the Circle of women biblical scholars' hermeneutical methods and their achievements, and possible further areas of investigation. Togarasei's conclusion is that not unlike other African biblical works, Circle biblical scholars put a premium on engagement for the sake of intellectual growth and to address their communities' urgent concerns (Togarasei, "The Legacy of Circle," 1). For a demonstration of the "diverse, heterogenous, dynamic, contingent, evolving, and constantly under negotiation" (Page, ed., *Africana Bible*, 1) nature of Afrocentric readings, see the volume edited by Hugh Page which reflects a broader range of Afrocentric engagements with the Bible, and Dube, Mbuvi, and Mbuwayesango, *Perspectives*, a volume dedicated to Ukpong. In Yorke's, "The Bible and the Black Diaspora," 149–57, typology is applied to two different appropriations of the Bible in the Black Diaspora context which fails to convince; some liberationist socio-political readings are equally literalist if not magical, and vice versa; is it simply a matter of inadequate terminology amid valid distinctions, or are the latter flawed as well? For a brief historical overview of readings of the Bible in the Black Diaspora, see however, Wimbush, "The Bible and African Americans."

45. Brenner, "Forward."

when it has been used both in life-threatening and life-affirming ways over many centuries in Africa. In addition, ABH has the African context as a point of departure, as a reference point, and also as a goal. However, this does not mean that it is self-serving, to the exclusion of hermeneutical work more broadly, or that it is peripheral to the biblical hermeneutical enterprise. In fact, ABH has also been explored in the global village and beyond ("transcending") the boundaries of inculturation and liberation.[46] Shifting the focus from *meaning* to *meaning making* involves greater attention, also to the role and contribution to interpretive ventures, and requires accountability for approaches and methods as much as for results and meanings.[47] Not only are hermeneutics and methods scholarly homes but as much as hermeneutics allows for meaning(-making), meaning(-making) also defines hermeneutics.

Conclusion

West's work nudges biblical scholars to think broadly and inclusively about hermeneutics, and, certainly also, on the African continent. More than it being merely postulated, ABH is distinctively multi-dimensional in its contextuality, its (inter)culturality, its social engagement, and its geographical focus.[48] As is generally befitting of hermeneutical projects, and in particular those which set stock in "meaning-making," contextuality, and social engagement, ABH is an ongoing enterprise—not in the sense of an un(der)developed venture, but rather in the sense of a dynamic undertaking. African biblical hermeneutics cannot be held ransom to the specific theory or model of any particular exponent of such work. Since all interpretation is contextual, and interpreters make meaning within their contexts, the question that accompanies biblical hermeneutics is how (and sometimes, if) contextuality is theorized and set to use by biblical

---

46. Cf. Ukpong, "Reading the Bible;" and Ukpong, "Biblical Interpretation of the Bible."

47. The tradition of eschewing the notion of any overt political agenda in biblical studies and attempts to disentangle such work (along with religious studies) from theological studies is often equated with pursuing biblical studies as a separate academic discipline in its own right. Such vaunted neutrality is characteristic of the work of more recent decades, unlike the work of the beginning of the twentieth century with its overt questions about relevance (see e.g., Penner and Lopez, *Re-Introducing The New Testament*).

48. See Mbuvi, "African Biblical Studies."

interpreters.[49] West's lasting legacy will remain the challenge to do authentic African biblical interpretation or meaning-making, a hermeneutics consciously deriving from the interaction of the Bible and the context of the African continent and its peoples.

Bibliography

Abosede, Oderinde Olatundun, and Kolawole Oladotun Paul. "African Biblical Hermeneutics: An Excursus on Covenant in Yoruba Context." *Cyber Journal for Pentecostal-Charismatic Research* 27 (July 2020). http://pctii.org/cyberj/cyberj27/AbosedePaul.html.

Adam, A. K. M. *What Is Postmodern Biblical Criticism?* Guides to Biblical Scholarship: New Testament. Minneapolis: Fortress, 1995.

Adamo, David Tuesday. "The Task and Distinctiveness of African Biblical Hermeneutic(s)." *OTE* 28.1 (2015a) 31–52. https://doi.org/10.17159/2312-3621/ 2015/ v28n1a4.

———. "What Is African Biblical Hermeneutics?" *Black Theology* 13.1 (2015b) 59–72. https://doi.org/10.1179/1476994815Z.00000000047.

Aichele, George, Fred W. Burnett, Elizabeth A. Castelli, Robert M. Fowler, David Jobling, Stephen D. Moore, Gary A. Phillips, Tina Pippin, Regina M. Schwartz, and Wilhelm Wuellner. *The Postmodern Bible: The Bible and Culture Collective.* New Haven: Yale University Press, 1995.

Banana, Canaan S. "The Case for a New Bible." In *'Rewriting' the Bible: The Real Issues. Biblical and Religious Studies in Zimbabwe*, edited by Isabel Mukonyora, James L. Cox, and Frans J. Verstraelen, 1:17–32. Religious and Theological Series. Gweru: Mambo, 1993.

Bediako, Kwame. *Theology and Identity. The Impact of Culture upon Christian Thought in the Second Century and in Modern Africa.* Oxford: Regnum, 1992.

———. "Understanding African Theology in the 20th Century." *BCT* 3.2 (1996) 1–11.

Blount, Brian K. "The Souls of Biblical Folks and the Potential for Meaning." *JBL* 138 (2019) 6–21. https://doi.org/10.15699/jbl.1381.2019.1382.

Brenner, Athalya. "Foreword." In *Culture, Entertainment and the Bible*, edited by George Aichele, 7–12. JSOTSup 309. Sheffield: Sheffield Academic, 2000.

Bujo, Bénézet. "Afrikanische Theologie. Rückblick Auf Eine Kontroverse." *ZMR* 2 (1977) 118–27.

Chidester, David. "Worldview Analysis of African Indigenous Churches." *JSR* 2 (1991) 15–29.

Deist, Ferdinand E. "South-Africanising Biblical Studies. An Epistemological and Hermeneutical Enquiry." *Scriptura* 37 (1991) 32–50.

———. "The Bible as Literature: Whose Literature?" *OTE* 7.3 (1994) 327–42.

---

49. The realization dawning increasingly but hardly fully is that all hermeneutics and exegesis are contextual (e.g., West, "Contextuality," 399) but contextuality can be a double-edged sword, wielded to expose/cut through layers of authorial intention invoked to protect against interpretive intention but at the same time running the risk of rendering balkanised positions, islands of interests drifting unconnected and listlessly on their own in the ocean of hermeneutical enterprise.

Dickson, Kwesi A. "African Traditional Religions and the Bible." In *The Jerusalem Congress on Black Africa and the Bible, April 24-30, 1972: Proceedings*, edited by E. Mveng and R. J. Z. Werblowsky, 155–66. Jerusalem: Israel Interfaith Committee, 1972.

Dube, Musa W., Andrew M. Mbuvi, and Dora R. Mbuwayesango. *Postcolonial Perspectives in African Biblical Interpretations*. Global Perspectives on Biblical Scholarship 13. Atlanta: SBL, 2012.

Dube, Zorodzai. "The Statue Debate: Ancestors and 'Mnemonic Energy' in Paul and Now." *HTS* 71.3 (2015) 1–5. https://doi.org/10.4102/hts.v71i3.3035.

Farisani, Elelwani B. "Current Trends and Patterns in African Biblical Hermeneutics in Post-Apartheid South Africa: Myth or Fact?" *Scriptura* 116.1 (2017) 1–20.

Felder, Cain Hope, ed. *Stony the Road We Trod. African American Biblical Interpretation*. Minneapolis: Fortress, 1991.

Hoyt, Thomas, Jr. "Interpreting Biblical Scholarship for the Black Church Tradition." In *Stony the Road We Trod. African American Biblical Interpretation*, edited by Cain Hope Felder, 17–39. Minneapolis: Fortress, 1991.

Isichei, Elizabeth. *A History of Christianity in Africa: From Antiquity to the Present*. Grand Rapids: Eerdmans, 1995.

Kamudzandu, Israel. *Abraham as a Spiritual Ancestor: A Postcolonial Zimbabwean Reading of Romans 4*. BIS 100. Leiden: Brill, 2010.

————. *Abraham Our Father. Paul and the Ancestors in Postcolonial Africa*. Paul in Critical Contexts. Philadelphia: Fortress, 2013.

Kawale, W. R. "Divergent Interpretations of the Relationship between Some Concepts of God in the Old Testament and in African Traditional Religions—a Theological Critique." *OTE* 8.1 (1995) 7–30.

Leitch, Vincent B. "Cultural Studies, 2: United States." In *The Johns Hopkins Guide to Literary Theory & Criticism*, edited by Michael Groden and Martin Kreiswirth, 179–82. Baltimore: Johns Hopkins University Press, 1994.

LeMarquand, Grant. "A Bibliography of the Bible in Africa: A Preliminary Publication." *BCT* 2.2 (1995) 6–40.

Maimela, Simon S. "Religion and Culture: Blessing or Curses?" In *Culture, Religion and Liberation. Proceedings of the EATWOT Pan African Theological Conference, Harare, Zimbabwe, January 6-11, 1991*, edited by Simon S. Maimela, 1–17. Pretoria: Penrose, 1994.

Maluleke, Tinyiko Sam. "Black and African Theologies in the New World Order: A Time to Drink from Our Own Wells." *JTSA* 96 (1996) 3–19.

Martey, Emmanuel. *African Theology: Inculturation and Liberation*. Maryknoll, NY: Orbis, 1993.

Mburu, Elizabeth W. *African Hermeneutics*. Carlisle, UK: HippoBooks, 2019.

Mbuvi, Andrew Mūtūa. "African Biblical Studies: An Introduction to an Emerging Discipline." *Currents in Biblical Research* 15.2 (2017) 149–78.

McCutcheon, Russell T. *The Discipline of Religion: Structure, Meaning, Rhetoric*. London: Routledge, 2003.

Meenan, Alan John. "Biblical Hermeneutics in an African Context." *Journal of Inductive Biblical Studies* 1.2 (2014) 268–73.

Mosala, Itumeleng J. *Biblical Hermeneutics and Black Theology in South Africa*. Grand Rapids: Eerdmans, 1989.

Mukonyora, Isabel, James L. Cox, and Frans J. Verstraelen. *"Rewriting" the Bible: The Real Issues. Perspectives from within Biblical and Religious Studies in Zimbabwe.* Gweru, Zimbabwe: Mambo, 1993.

Muzorewa, Gwinyai. "A Definition of a Future African Theology." *ATJ* 19.2 (1990) 168–79.

Ntreh, Benjamin A. "Toward an African Biblical Hermeneutic." *ATJ* 19.3 (1990) 246–54.

Onwu, N. "The Hermeneutical Model: The Dilemma of the African Theologian." *ATJ* 14.3 (1985) 145–60.

Page, Hugh R., ed. *The Africana Bible: Reading Israel's Scriptures from Africa and the African Diaspora.* Minneapolis: Fortress, 2010.

Parratt, John. "African Theology and Biblical Hermeneutics." *ATJ* 12.2 (1983) 88–94.

Penner, Todd, and Davina C. Lopez. *De-Introducing the New Testament: Texts, Worlds, Methods, Stories.* Chichester, UK: Wiley Blackwell, 2015.

Pobee, John S. "Comments on the Future of Theological Education in Africa." *Scriptura* 28 (1989) 1–23.

Punt, Jeremy. "Countering Bible-Based, Culturally-Ensconced Homophobia: Un-African Meets Unambiguous!" *JTSA* 149 (2014) 5–24.

———. "From Rewriting to Rereading the Bible in Postcolonial Africa: Considering the Options and Implications." *Missionalia* 30 (2002) 410–42.

———. "Reading the Bible in Africa: On Strategies and Ownership." *RT* 4.2 (1997) 124–54.

Rukundwa, Lazare S., and Andries G. Van Aarde. "The Formation of Postcolonial Theory." *HTS* 63.3 (2007) 1171–94.

Schüssler Fiorenza, Elisabeth. "Text and Reality—Reality as Text: The Problem of a Feminist Historical and Social Reconstruction Based on Texts." *Studia Theologica* 43 (1989) 19–34.

Segovia, Fernando F. "'And They Began to Speak in Other Tongues': Competing Modes of Discourse in Contemporary Biblical Criticism." In *Reading from This Place. Vol. 1: Social Location and Biblical Interpretation in the United States*, edited by Fernando F. Segovia and Mary Ann Tolbert, 1–32. Minneapolis: Fortress, 1995.

———. "Biblical Criticism and Postcolonial Studies: Towards a Postcolonial Optic." In *The Postcolonial Bible*, edited by R. S. Sugirtharajah, 1:49–65. The Bible and Postcolonialism 1. Sheffield: Sheffield Academic, 1998.

———. *Decolonizing Biblical Studies: A View from the Margins.* Maryknoll: Orbis, 2000a.

———. "Reading Across: Intercultural Criticism and Textual Posture." In *Interpreting Beyond Borders*, edited by Fernando F. Segovia, 59–83. The Bible and Post-colonialism 3. Sheffield: Sheffield Academic, 2000b.

Smith, Jonathan Z. "A Twice-Told Tale: The History of the History of Religions' History." *Numen* 48 (2001) 131–46.

Speckman, McGlory T. "African Biblical Hermeneutics on the Threshold? Appraisal and Way Forward." *AT* Supplement 24 (2016) 204–24.

Tarus, David Kirwa, and Stephanie Lowery. "African Theologies of Identity and Community: The Contributions of John Mbiti, Jesse Mugambi, Vincent Mulago, and Kwame Bediako." *Open Theology* 3.1 (2017) 305–20. https://doi.org/10.1515/opth-2017-0024.

Togarasei, Lovemore. "The Legacy of Circle Women's Engagement with the Bible: Reflections from an African Male Biblical Scholar." *VE* 37.2 (2016) a1582. http://dx.doi.org/10.4102/ve.v37i2.1582

Tolbert, Mary Ann. "Afterwords: The Politics and Poetics of Location." In *Reading from This Place*. Vol. 1: *Social Location and Biblical Interpretation in the United States*, edited by Fernando F. Segovia and Mary A. Tolbert, 305–17. Minneapolis: Fortress, 1995.

Tracy, David. *Analogical Imagination: Christian Theology and the Culture of Pluralism*. New York: Crossroad, 1981.

Tutu, Desmond. "Black Theology/African Theology—Soul Mates or Antagonists?" In *Black Theology: A Documentary History, 1966–1979*, edited by Gayraud S. Wilmore and James H. Cone, 483–91. Maryknoll, NY: Orbis, 1979.

Ukpong, Justin S. "Biblical Interpretation in Africa: Transcending the Boundaries of Inculturation and Liberation." *JIT* 5.2 (2003) 105–22.

———. "Reading the Bible in a Global Village: Issues and Challenges from African Readings." In *Reading the Bible in the Global Village: Cape Town*, edited by Justin S. Ukpong, 9–39. Global Perspectives on Biblical Scholarship 3. Atlanta: Society of Biblical Literature, 2002.

———. "Rereading the Bible with African Eyes: Inculturation and Hermeneutics." *JTSA* 91 (1995) 3–14.

Wambudta, Daniel N. "Hermeneutics and the Search for Theologia Africana." *ATJ* 9.2 (1980) 29–39.

West, Gerald O. "African Biblical Scholarship as Post-Colonial, Tri-Polar, and a Site-of-Struggle." In *Present and Future of Biblical Studies*, edited by Tat-siong Benny Liew, 240–73. BIS 161. Leiden: Brill, 2018.

———. *Biblical Hermeneutics of Liberation: Modes of Reading the Bible in the South African Context*. Pietermaritzburg: Cluster, 1991.

———. *Contextual Bible Study*. Pietermaritzburg: Cluster, 1993.

———. "Contextual Bible Study and/or as Interpretive Resilience." In *That All May Live! Essays in Honour of Nyambura J. Njoroge*, edited by Ezra Chitando, Esther Mombo, and Masiiwa Ragies Gunda, 143–59. Bible in Africa Studies 30. Bamberg: University of Bamberg Press, 2021.

———. "Contextuality." In *Blackwell Companion to the Bible and Culture*, edited by John F. A. Sawyer, 399–413. Blackwell Companions to Religion. Oxford: Blackwell, 2006.

———. "On the Eve of an African Biblical Studies: Trajectories and Trends." *JTSA* 99 (1997) 99–115.

———. "Reading the Bible in Africa: Constructing Our Own Discourse." *BCT* 2.2 (1995) 1–5.

———. "Re-Reading the Bible with African Resources: Interpretative Strategies for Reconstruction in a Post-Colonial, Post-Apartheid Context on the Eve of Globalization." *JCT* 4.1 (1998) 3–32.

———. "The Role of the Bible in African Christianity." In *Anthology of African Christianity*, edited by Isabel Apawo Phiri, Dietrich Werner, Chammah Kaunda, and Kennedy Owino, 76–78. Oxford: Regnum, 2016. https://doi.org/10.2307/j.ctv1ddcqdc/.

Wimbush, Vincent L. "Afrocentric Interpretation." In *New Interpreter's Dictionary of the Bible*, edited by Katharine Doob Sakenfeld. Nashville: Abingdon, 2006.

———. "The Bible and African Americans: An Outline of an Interpretive History." In *Stony the Road We Trod: African American Biblical Interpretation*, edited by Cain Hope Felder, 81–97. Minneapolis: Fortress, 1991.

———. "Biblical Historical Study as Liberation: Toward an Afro-Christian Hermeneutic." *JRT* 42/2 (1985) 9–21.

———. "Reading Texts through Worlds, Worlds through Texts." *Semeia* 62 (1993) 129–39.

Yorke, Gosnell L. O. R. "The Bible and the Black Diaspora." In *The Bible in African Christianity: Essays in Biblical Theology*, edited by Hannah W. Kinoti and John Mary Waliggo, 145–64. African Christianity Series. Nairobi: Acton, 1997.

PART THREE

Bible, Race, Gender, and Sexuality

10

An Autobiographical Reading of Genesis 2–3 as an Examination of My Biracial Identity and Belonging

Belinda Crawford

Introduction

How might an autobiographical interpretation of Gen 2–3, help me, a biracial South African woman in perpetual liminal existence, analyze the concept of belonging in the South African culture, through aspects of the Contextual Bible Study (CBS) approach?[1] This was my Honours research project where I utilized the Social Identity Theory (SIT) as a lens to interrogate my liminal state as a biracial South African woman in relation to reading Gen 2–3.[2] In my segregated social context of South Africa, where, as a biracial woman I did not fit neatly into the dominant

1. I have answered these questions in the paper under the See–Judge–Act methodology.

2. Social identity theory was developed by Henri Tajfel and John Turner ("An Integrative Theory of Intergroup Conflict") and presented in various influential psychological research articles. Social identity is not limited to individual-level identification but extends to more significant social categories. For example, people may identify strongly with their nationality or view themselves as part of a broader collective. Various factors influence social identity, including culture, upbringing, social interactions, and personal experiences. It plays a significant role in shaping attitudes, beliefs, behaviours, and social interactions. However, it may be essential to note that social identity is not static and can change over and constructing self-narratives.

"Black" or "White" categories, I examined identity and belonging as one occupying the liminal space. In South Africa, there are diverse cultures and traditions, but there is also racial diversity. And, during the Apartheid period, interracial marriage was considered illegal. While it was not morally wrong to have interracial marriages, the legal restriction applied specifically to marriages between European settlers and Black Africans. Therefore, when the "Coloured" children (the term for biracial people in South Africa) emerged illicitly, it became a challenge, since the "Whites" who parented such children, typically rejected them. On the other hand, the "Coloured" children often avoided identification with the "Black" South Africans.

What makes the Contextual Bible Study (CBS) method useful for my analysis is that, while similar to other forms of Bible Study, it focuses on the interface between trained biblical scholars and "ordinary" readers. The trained scholars are individuals who have acquired advanced biblical scholarship from either seminaries or tertiary institutions while "ordinary" readers of the Bible (whether literate or not) lack formal training. CBS, as developed at the Ujamaa Centre by Gerald West, utilizes an interpretive approach framed as the "See–Judge–Act" method, where the Bible Study process begins with an analysis of the local context ("See") and then re-reading of the Bible to allow the biblical text to speak to the local context ("Judge"), and then, finally, moving to action, as the "reader" responds to what God is saying to them ("Act"). Because social analysis enables us to understand our reality, re-reading the Bible encourages us to judge whether our reality is as God intends it to be. Our action plan helps us work with God to change our reality.[3]

Contextualization: My Story

My Zulu mother, who worked in Kwa Zulu Natal, specifically in Durban, for R12.00 per month, was misled by my European father (non-Black) to think that when they had a relationship, my mom would receive an identity book (called "dompass"), and have access to other services such as housing accommodation and social security. However, my father abandoned us, and my mother could not raise me under these difficult circumstances. As such, she resolved to give me up to the State, also known as social welfare or government. She gave me an English name,

---

3. "Ujamaa Manual."

Belinda, hoping I would be sent to an English school, and be in a safe house with such an English name.

From the age of two years, I moved from foster home to foster home within the Coloured community in Durban, KwaZulu Natal. At the age of nine, my foster mother abruptly told me that I was not her child, and introduced me to my biological mother, for the first time. This new knowledge inflicted psychological trauma on my young self and initiated what would become the trajectory of my identity crisis. However, I would remain a State child, and I was sent to a place of safety in Kimberly, in the Northern Provincial State, and later to a reformatory in the Western Province of South Africa. These institutions were made up, predominately, of Coloured children, like myself. Having come to understand that my stays in the different places were temporary, I had no emotional or sentimental attachments to them. There were no traditional cultures, faiths, or customs and no denominational values for those of us growing up as State children to maintain. We were free to have whatever faith we wanted, but prayers, said while having meals, were a regular part of these homes. Also, Christian ministers from different denominations would visit periodically for devotions.

When I was released from the reformatory, I had only one motive, self-sustainance, since I did not have a family to count on. My liminal and transitory existence did not allow me to fit into any of the larger South African communities. I remained socially classified as "Coloured" but I did not have any "Coloured" traditions, culture, or religious beliefs to identify with, because adolescents from the reformatory were stigmatized and marginalized leaving them unable to fit into the Black, White, or even the few Coloured communities. By the time I turned 18 years old and, therefore, considered an adult who could make my own decisions, I was already self-sufficient and living independently. I worked in a predominantly Black community as a manager in a retail store. But, because I could not speak *isi*Zulu, I was continually marginalized in this community, also, and lived an isolated life. The predominant Zulus made it clear I was not Zulu enough. But, according to the law, I was not White. But when I interacted or engaged with the other Coloured people in my community, I was held at arm's length as a "form girl" (from the reformatory, where many children had ended up) and not a full member of the community. So, all my life, I have lived in a liminal state, always between places, but not meaningfully belonging to any.

Liminality and Social Identity Theory (SIT)

I agree with a similar study by Angella Enders on biracial identity and belonging, where she explores different meanings of "liminality."[4] However, it's important to note that "liminality" is not found in standard dictionaries like Merriam-Webster or Oxford Dictionary. Instead, they list the adjective "liminal," meaning "related to a sensory threshold." In her study, she used "liminal" in this sensory context. Despite the historical work of ethnologist Arnold van Gennep and anthropologist Victor Turner in defining liminality as a stage in rites of passage, Enders shows that it's also relevant to biracial individuals living between racial groups and trying to find their sense of belonging.[5]

Tajfel and Turner identified three phases through which community members establish their group identity. Namely, "social categorization," "social identification," and "social comparison."[6] At the social categorization phase, we organize people to make sense of the social environment by using social categories such as male, female, Coloured, Black, white, Zulu, South African, foreigner, etc. The second social identification phase is about adopting the identity of the group we have categorized ourselves as belonging to. If the members have categorized themselves as Zulu, for example, they begin to act how they believe Zulus are meant to act. They become emotionally attached to their group.

Membership in a group is not something foreign or artificially attached to the person. It is a real, authentic, and vital part of the group members.[7] As such, we often prefer to classify individuals based on their social categories rather than their individual characteristics. Once we have categorized ourselves as part of a group and have identified with that group, we move to the third phase: social comparison. This is where we tend to compare our group with other groups. At this stage, groups

4. Enders, "Finding Wholeness," 8.

5. Turner, *Ritual Process*; van Ginnen, *Rites of Passage*.

6. Tajfel and Turner, "An Integrative Theory," 38–40. 1. "Social Identification" refers to the part of an individual's self-concept derived from group memberships. It highlights the importance of identifying with and feeling belonging to specific social groups. 2. "Social Categorization" is the process of mentally classifying people into different social groups based on shared characteristics. It involves perceiving individuals as members of distinct categories, such as gender, race, age, or occupation categorization. 3. "Social Comparison" involves evaluating one's group and oneself in relative to other groups or individuals.

7. McLeod, "Social Identity Theory," 2.

boost and enhance their own self-esteem by favorably comparing themselves with other groups.

An "in-group" (the community in which one is a member), thus, will seek to find negative aspects of an "out-group" (all other groups) to improve its self-image. For an in-group's self-esteem to be maintained, members must consider their group more socially significant than the out-groups. Placed in this context, such things as stereotyping of one group by another, discrimination, competition, and hostility between social groups should not always be viewed simply as competing for resources but also as the result of competing identities.[8]

In comparison to West's CBS, who argues that its origin is in the interface between socially engaged biblical scholars (organic intellectuals) and ordinary Christian "readers" of the Bible," one can see some "liminality" aspects in the interface.[9] Participants of the CBS apply the "See–Judge–Act" analysis in the following ways: "See": causes one to analyze the social context. "Judge": the scripture reading is a tool to judge or discern the researched context theologically, and "Act": applying action to transform context positively. Liminality, the state of being in-between or undergoing transition, can connect with the "See–Judge–Act" model through a shared focus on the in-between space, and shared interest in transformation and reflection. For example, at the "See" stage, liminality would encourage a heightened awareness of the transition, leading to a deeper understanding of the situation; in the "Judge" stage, the liminal space allows for critically examining values, beliefs, and societal norms, promoting thoughtful evaluation, finally, in the "Act" stage, the liminal experience can inspire innovative and intentional actions that align with the insights gained from the preceding steps. In essence, both concepts emphasize change, introspection, and deliberate decision-making. It is worth noting, however, that the CBS ("See–Judge–Act") model goes further as it begins by assessing the social context of the "reader," thereby creating a justice road map that calls for action and influences any resulting application's logical path.

The SIT approach analyzes belonging to an "in-group" and having positive thoughts and feelings about the group. Belonging to the in-group contributes to our sense of self. This is where individuals gain a sense of belonging, self-esteem, and a framework for understanding their social

---

8. McLeod, "Social Identity Theory," 2.

9. West, "The Bible and the Poor."

place by identifying with the group. It is the aspect of identity based on a person's affiliation with a certain group, such as their nationality, ethnicity, religion, gender, occupation, or any other group that holds significance to them. SIT was developed by Tajfel and Turner and presented in various influential psychological research articles. Social identity is not limited to individual-level identification but extends to other significant social categories. For example, people may identify strongly with their nationality or view themselves as part of a broader collective. Various factors influence social identity, including culture, upbringing, social interactions, and personal experiences. It plays a significant role in shaping attitudes, beliefs, behaviors, and social interactions.

However, it is essential to note that social identity is not static and can change over and construct self-narratives. Social categories may change and one's place in them may change too, e.g., from poor to rich, and vice versa. Social comparisons, which involve evaluating one's group and oneself relative to others may change e.g., from rulers to being ruled. People develop new identities, modify existing ones, or shift their emphasis on different aspects of their identity depending on their contexts and life experiences. I used SIT to investigate my biracial identity and liminal status in the context of Gen 2–3 because, as defined below by McLeod it provides a useful framework:

> Social identity is a person's sense of who they are based on their group membership. Social groups are an important source of pride and self-esteem and give members a sense of social identity and belonging. By belonging to and identifying with a particular group, members divide the world into "us" and "them." By so categorizing people, we tend to exaggerate the differences between groups and the similarities of members of the same group.[10]

McLeod further explains that "the central hypothesis of social identity theory is that group members of an in-group ("us") will seek to find negative aspects of an out-group ("them"), thus enhancing their ("us") self-image." Furthermore, according to Gazi Islam, the SIT method explains prejudice, racism, and social identity tensions between groups by characterizing these phenomena as the result of an in-group's categorization, and self-improvement.[11] Thus, how social categorizations and values attributed to

---

10. McLeod, "Social Identity Theory," 2. Cf. also, Tajfel and Turner. "An Integrative Theory."

11. Islam, "Social Identity Theory," 741–63.

different groups are portrayed in an individual's self-conception, can be either positive or negative, according to S. Trepte and L. S. Loy.[12]

Therefore, Tajfel's claim that social identification is about embracing the group's identity makes my liminal condition more obvious and explains my sense of social isolation. Since I grew up constantly moving from one home to another, and being exposed to various forms of social, religious, and cultural structures where I did not fit well, my liminality deepened. In this chapter, I build on my earlier Honours project by comparing how SIT and CBS share some characteristics that can help me further examine my liminality but also try to find a positive way to construct my identity. I want to show that, while SIT assisted me in analyzing my context as one with no particular South African cultural, traditional or denominational identity, CBS may offer a different way of how I perceive myself in my community.

My Bi-Raciality in Terms of Social Identity Theory (SIT)

L. Bloom cites American James Baldwin approvingly concerning the plight of South African "Coloured" persons.[13] For Baldwin, South African Coloureds are in a similar position to that of African Americans, who have lived in an "entirely hostile" environment set to cut them down and risk "the gates of paranoia" closing in on them, as it "begins to be almost impossible to distinguish a real from a fancied injury." In confirmation of Baldwin's insight, Bloom then quotes A. Kardiner and L. Ovesey as follows:

> It is a consistent feature of human personality that tends to become organized about the main problems of adaptation, which tends to polarise all other aspects of adaptation towards itself. This central problem of Negro adaptation is orientated toward the discrimination he suffers and the consequences of this discrimination for the self-referential aspects of his social orientation . . . In addition to maintaining an internal balance, the individual must hold a social facade and some kind of adaptation to the offending stimuli to preserve some social effectiveness.[14]

Bloom further goes on to say,

12. Trepte and Loy, "Self-Categorization Theory."
13. Bloom, "The Coloured People," 148.
14. Bloom, "The Coloured People," 148.

> The Coloured man or woman in a discriminatory society is operating within a matrix of values that permits only low self-esteem. He is in a society which does not permit the full control of his life that alone can enable the individual to develop an unimpaired self.[15]

Bloom's insights have merit since social categorization is the first step in social identity formation.[16] In this phase, people use recognized social categories to classify themselves and others in an attempt to make sense of their social environment. As can be seen from my story, above, I struggled with that. I did not know how to classify myself at all. Moreover, white society classified Coloured persons as inferior and, on top of that, Coloured people classified one part of me, my African side, as inferior. It was exceedingly difficult for me to form a stable identity.

The second phase of SIT is social identification, which is the process of identifying with a particular community and behaving in an appropriate, valuable, emotionally significant way that would improve their self-esteem in communities. Regarding social identification, I could not identify with any group in particular. Instead, I learned to adapt to the societal norms of each group. For example, when I was around white people, I spoke eloquently and conducted myself with elegance and sophistication. On the other hand, I learned to speak *isi*Zulu and conducted myself in a manner respectful to the cultural norms of Black Zulu people, when I was with them. I behaved similarly within the Coloured community, where I conducted myself in as non-offensive a manner as possible.

To maintain the self-esteem derived from belonging to a group, members tend to regard their group as socially more significant than others. The resultant clash of identities produces acts of discrimination, competition, and hostility, which, in terms of identity, attempt to maintain self-categorization and self-enhancement of the group and its members. And, with continued social comparison, people envision their group more favorably compared to others. For their self-esteem to be maintained, they need to consider their "in-group" as being more socially significant than all "out-groups" according to G. Islam.[17]

In such a context, there is a long history of Coloured people, like myself, being stuck in the middle of a racial political segregation

15. Bloom, "The Coloured People," 149.
16. Tajfel and Turner, "An Integrative Theory," 38.
17. Islam, "Social Identity Theory," 742.

struggle. In South Africa, for example, according to Bloom, O. D. Wollheim assumes that:

> [There] is a basic 'identity of interest and of common loyalty' between Coloureds and Whites and claims that 'coloured people have until recent years been regarded as part and parcel of the white people owing to their traditional proximity and identity of interests and cultural background' . . . . Lastly, Wollheim regrets that the Nationalist governments persist in rejecting the Coloured people, who are allies of the Whites' almost as sophisticated as themselves.[18]

Bloom responds to Wollheim as follows:

> It is naive to think of the Coloured people merely as appendages of the White community. Their three centuries of history have steadily compelled them to realize that they are a group apart from the dominant Whites and that it is an illusion that one day they might become equal to, though separate from, the Whites. The realization by the Coloured people that they must make common cause with Africans can be their psychological as well as their political salvation.[19]

Bloom's argument holds merit. From the perspective of SIT, the Coloured people were an "out-group" to the white minority ruling culture in South Africa, and also an "out-group" to the larger Black dominant culture. This made it particularly difficult for me to fit in either group. In the first place, as a bi-racial woman who is part of a group that is still considered an "out-group" (by the whites and Blacks) and, secondly, as a bi-racial woman who was rejected by the Coloured community, because I had been in a reformatory.

Application of the Biblical Text to My Context

I will now apply my contextual analysis to the reading of Gen 2–3 to determine the possibility of using my liminal self's autobiography to analyze Gen 2–3. I chose the Gen 2–3 narrative because the narrative is about the creation of man and woman, and there is no racial segregation. When I engage the text, I hope to get insights from it about my

---

18. Bloom, "The Coloured People," 149–50.
19. Bloom, "The Coloured People," 150.

own life experience by applying an "autobiographical analysis" of the biblical text. According to P. J. Schutte,

> Autobiographical biblical criticism entails an explicitly autobiographical performance within the Act of criticism. Autobiographical biblical criticism is to implement personal criticism as a form of self-disclosure, wittingly while reading a text as a critical exegete. It thus has to do with a willing, knowledgeable, outspoken involvement on the part of the critic with the subject matter."[20]

Schutte further highlights that,

> . . .an autobiographical critic does not claim to uncover absolute truth and or to practice pure science. Instead, the critical text provides an opportunity to introduce the flesh and blood author as a scholar. It makes the point that no writing or academic research takes place in a vacuum. An autobiographic critical text creates space for contextualization, culture, and experience.[21]

My mother is represented by the earth in Gen 2:7, as she is not only of lower socio-economic status but also one with far fewer privileges and compromised human rights. My father, like God, blew his breath into my mother, and I became a living being. In reading the text, this way, I have a dualistic view of God. The first view is that the human being cannot represent "my father" since, he and the woman, had not yet procreated. My second view is where I lean towards the notion of God representing "my father." In Gen 2:7, God is alone and breathes himself into the earth, suggesting that God was in a better position of power and control; he had more resources, political authority, and social privileges than my mother. My foster mother played the role of the serpent in Gen 3:1–5.

Since I lived in a Coloured community for some time, moving from foster home to foster home, and like the human being and the woman in Genesis 2, I was content with my environment because I lacked nothing (or so I thought). On the day that my foster mother informed me that I was not her biological child, was when I questioned who I was. Like the humans in the biblical story, I had now "eaten of the fruit" of this hidden knowledge. When she introduced me to my biological mother, at the age of nine years, that day, like the human beings in Genesis, my eyes were "opened" and I realized that I was "naked" as in Gen 3:7. I

---

20. Schutte, "When They, We," 104.
21. Schutte, "When They, We," 105.

took the "fig leaves" of identity crisis and sewed them into coverings for myself for, suddenly, I was neither Black as an African nor white like a European. And even though I was classified as a Coloured, I was not personally a member of a Coloured household.

For the remaining nine years, my identity was determined by the politically constructed social system while, internally, I toiled with the psychological and emotional trauma of who I was. To make matters worse, at the age of 18, when I was released from the government system, all the privileges, such as being well-fed, free access to medical benefits, and skills training and education, had come to an end. I no longer had access to any of them. On leaving the reformatory, the clothing given to me when I arrived was taken back and I was given back the clothes I had arrived with. Just like in Gen 3:21, where the humans had to leave their fig leaf coverings in the garden and wear new garments as they left the garden, so had I done. I no longer was a child of the state but had become a member of the larger society. However, I questioned where in society I belonged and, for many years struggled in a South Africa that is so deeply culturally rooted and diverse. I wore a new robe of liminality with the trauma of homelessness, toiling through the community by the sweat of my brow, looking for belonging. Only with the SIT model analysis of my context was I enabled to define my identity as a liminaly situated person which opened up the idea that, maybe, I do not need to belong but rather be a social human being.

While Gen 2–3 not only informs us of human creation, it also introduces us to how these first humans experienced the trauma of homelessness and the toil of navigating their lives in an environment that was harsh. The author of the Genesis story does not explain where God lives after bringing human beings into the garden or even when God removes them from the garden. Because of this, the use of SIT method had a limitation. Since the method has a clear distinction between "in-group" community and "out-group membership" which are not represented in the story, it was problematic. However, I still gained insight through analysis of the human-to-human identity using the SIT model, which was based on the proclamation of Adam to Eve. When he saw Eve for the first time, he gave himself an identity by calling himself "a man" (Gen 2:23). The narrative exposes the issue of self-reflectivity, meaning self-identification. Later, when the humans had eaten the fruit, they did not look at each other, but each one looked down, at themselves. The author leaves the reader to wonder if there was a conflict between them about the consequence of their actions or just internalized shame.

The narrative suggests that the humans reflected on themselves, covered themselves in shame, and hid among the trees from God. I did a similar thing when my eyes were "opened" to this new knowledge. I looked at myself and proceeded to live a life of "covering" myself up while wrestling with the issue of my identity crisis. There were very few spaces where I felt welcomed as I am, a biracial woman. Whenever I was approached by a non-white person, I was typically asked about my last name, assumed to be African. The first question they asked was, "*What are you?*," which meant, "From which racial group do you originate?," wishing to place me in the existing South African social categories. It is only the lens of the SIT method that has allowed me to look at the character of God in a remarkably redemptive way in Gen 2–3, given my life experience, and given me a different idea of my identity.

I always heard the dominant narrative of the creation story, that God is retributive in nature and action, because of how Adam's and Eve's disobedience was handled. However, I have observed that God, in the narrative, could be seen as more merciful and redemptive in the response to Adam and Eve. God's love for humans is steadfast, despite their behavior. The animal skin clothing was God's Act of mercy, love, and compassion. There was no banishment or separation from God, only from the garden and from the "tree of life" (Gen 3:24). Hence, the humans had a daily reminder that, though they no longer lived in the Garden of Eden, they still belonged, and remained connected, to God.

Through this biblical analysis, I have discovered that with the help of the SIT method, my biracial identity could extend beyond social categorization boundaries through these heuristic tools of self-exploration. I was able to find a sense of belonging as a social human being with the ability to appreciate similar human values and beliefs and have the ability to respect and accept differences.

My Lived Reality in the Context of the Liminal Space

Based on my personal experience, and through research, I can say that I have become content with my biracial identity and accepted its versatility. Through my autobiographical reading of Genesis 2–3, I have developed a clearer theological understanding of belonging in my South

African context. The narrative goes beyond the social, and cultural, norms that promote racial inequalities, injustices, and segregation. The text demonstrates that I, a social human being, can gracefully use this versatility to interact with others in society because I understand the world of liminality. I had questioned if this research could translate into autobiographical biblical criticism and I found that Enders' insights hold merit, stating, "When dealing with an individual struggling with his or her biracial identity, for instance, there would need to be some exploration of his or her cultural background and some historical research might be necessary."[22] Many individual contexts vary and, therefore, this research approach may not be used as a universal tool, but it can be helpful for those who struggle with multiple forms of identity searching for theological affirmation of belonging in their society.

The research was a transformative journey, in the sense that, since I began the process, I found my marginal status becoming more affirmed as an authentic identity. I realized that I do not have to fit into extant societal categorizations but rather belong in society as a social human being. During this research journey, this realization of the possibility of a new understanding of my liminal existence has become more meaningful for me. I discovered that, on the one hand, I could appreciate similarities in terms of values and, on the other, respect differences in a deeply rooted cultural society, and still find a way to fit in that space.

I used the CBS ("See–Judge–Act") model and the SIT model as theoretical frameworks to guide my study. I looked at the biblical text in comparison with my surroundings through the lens of SIT. As such, both CBS and SIT served theoretical frameworks and heuristic lenses to interpret both the biblical texts' and my autobiographical contexts. I discovered that the main focus of the Genesis narrative was both the relationship of the creator God with humanity and the relationship between the human couple. Both SIT model phases I applied to the Genesis story, and which represents the individual self-concept, found that God is the root of existence for humans, and chooses to create an extension of himself to be on the earth. God is therefore dominant in the "social categorization" stage, perceiving human beings as extensions of the Godself creating an "in-group" not determined only by other humans.

22. Enders, "Finding Wholeness," 67.

Bibliography

Bloom, Leonard. "The Coloured People of South Africa." *Phylon* 28.2 (1967) 139–50.

Crawford, Belinda. "Activist Profiles." Emerging Voices, 2020. https://www.emergingvoices.co.uk/profiles-of-activists.

Enders, Angella. "Finding Wholeness: Understanding Liminality through My Experience as a Biracial Woman." PhD diss., Pacifica Graduate Institute, 2011.

Gennep, Arnold van. *The Rites of Passage.* Translated by Monika B. Vizedom and Gabrielle L. Caffee. Chicago: University of Chicago Press, 1960.

Islam, Gazi. "Social Identity Theory." *Journal of Personality and Social Psychology* 67 (2014) 741–63.

McLeod, Saul A. "Social Identity Theory." *Simply Psychology.* (2009) np. https://www.simplypsychology.org/social-identity-theory.html (Accessed: 11/3/2020).

"Ujamaa Manual: Doing Contextual Bible Study." May, 2015. https://www.theologyjustice.org/wp-content/uploads/2017/09/Contextual-Bible-Study.pdf/.

Schutte, P. J. "When They, We, and the Passive Become I: Introducing Autobiographical Biblical Criticism," *HTS: Theological Studies* 61/1–2 (2005) 401–16.

Tajfel, Henri, and John C. Turner. "An Integrative Theory of Intergroup Conflict." In *The Social Psychology of Intergroup Relations,* edited by W. G. Austin and S. Worchel, 33–47. East Sussex: Psychology Press, 1979.

Trepte, Sabine, and Laura S. Loy. "Social Identity Theory and Self-Categorization Theory." In *The International Encyclopedia of Media Effects.* Malden, MA: Wiley, 2017.

Turner, Victor. *The Ritual Process: Structure and Anti-structure.* Chicago: Aldine, 1969.

West, Gerald O. "The Bible and the Poor." In *Bible in Mission,* edited by Pauline Hoggarth, Fergus Macdonald, B. Mitchell, and K. Jørgensen, 158–67. Oxford: Regnum, 2007.

Wollheim, O. D. "The Coloured People of South Africa." *Race & Class* 5/2 (July 1963) 25-41.

11

Masculinities Problematized?

*A Wisdom Gaze at the נַעַר Na'ar (Youth) in Proverbs 7
through the Lens of Select African Proverbs*

MADIPOANE MASENYA (NGWAN'A MPHAHLELE)

Introduction

IN THE POST-APARTHEID SOUTH African context of the writing of this essay, and where both the honoree and the present author are located, traditional and/or normative notions of masculinity/manhood appear to be increasingly problematized. Why so? First, there exists a social category labeled as "Ben-Tens" here in South Africa. This is a practice where younger males are sexually used by older females, usually more elite ones, for their own personal gratification and/or pleasure, among other things. Second, and related, there exists the phenomenon of some single South African women (by choice or otherwise), who being socio-economically well-off, are not persuaded that their humanity or womanhood (*bosadi*) should be validated by marrying a man as a marital partner. Third, there is the problematization of the idealization of traditional notions of marriage, where the affirmation of the rights of all, including the rights of the gender non-confirming persons, are respected.

With the preceding frame of reference and, especially informed by notions of masculinity/manhood as they are derived from select African proverbial sayings, I will pose and analyze the following critical questions: Which masculinities are displayed by the sage in Proverbs 7, in his portrayal of the נַעַר—*na'ar* (youth) to his sons, in their interactions with the figure of Woman Stranger? And, even more importantly, what kind of reading may emerge if the text of Prov 7 is read through the African proverbial lore in search of the kind of masculinity revealed by the actions and/or non-actions of the נַעַר חֲסַר-לֵב "youth without heart" (*na'ar hăsar-lēb*) in this text?

Celebrating the Honoree

First, I would like to acknowledge Professor Gerald West and, his related contribution to issues of masculinity, the Bible, and the South African context. In his article titled, "The Contribution of the Tamar Story to the Construction of Alternative African Masculinities," West enables his readers to get a glimpse of the kind of masculinity that Tamar had anticipated from Amnon, her half-brother. Elsewhere, in his argument that Tamar's story can assist us in the construction and exercise of redemptive/liberating masculinities, West contends:

> Reading together trans-textually discerns kindred sectoral struggles across biblical time and space, enabling Tamar to summon Jesus to join her in contesting and trans-forming dominant forms of masculinity, contending for redemptive, anomalous, forms of masculinity.[1]

As he usually does in his interaction with the biblical text, West does not read the text on the Tamar narrative as an end in itself. No! The end result should be the transformation of the contexts of present-day readers of the ancient texts and, thus, argues West:

> While Pierre Bourdieu is right to remind us of the socially habituated body and its limited capacity to recognize and resist socialization, particularly in the case of masculine domination, I want to argue here that the social space produced by the Tamar Contextual Bible Study is significant for enabling what is embodied to come to some kind of articulation, and for this articulation to lead, potentially, to some kind of social transformation.[2]

---

1. West, "Tamar Story," 200.
2. West, "Tamar Story," 194.

Indeed, right from early on in his journey in biblical scholarship, in the heydays of apartheid in South Africa, a context where doing liberationist biblical hermeneutics and/or theology was not only taboo but could have landed one in prison or make one a perpetual recipient of death threats, West, a fellow Old Testament/ Hebrew Bible scholar, a friend/a brother in the context of the Circle of Concerned Women Theologians, and an African biblical hermeneut, engaged in this mission as a socially engaged biblical scholar. It thus gives me a great sense of exhilaration to be able to write this piece to ululate him as a scholar, as well as to appreciate his immense contribution to biblical scholarship in general, and African biblical scholarship, in particular.

For West, the act of Bible interpretation should not be the preserve of trained biblical scholars only. "Ordinary" Bible readers also have a role to play in the process of Bible interpretation in our varying, Bible-conscious and Bible-reading African contexts. West argues that "It is the organized poor and marginalized, working with socially engaged biblical scholars, in their struggles for justice[,] who have the capacity to discern the ideological identity and agenda of particular biblical source texts."[3] The classification of the "organized poor and marginalized" is what West categorized as "ordinary readers." South Africa is a context where the Bible is a text that was used by the powerful (including the missionaries) of South Africa's colonial past, the Afrikaners, to justify South Africa's apartheid system, and by men (both African and non-African) to perpetuate patriarchy amongst other ills.

Through West's scholarly and practical efforts, the Bible can also be used by the powerless for the social transformation of readers' contexts. Thus, getting my cue from this socially engaged biblical scholar who, to my knowledge, is one of the very few (or possibly the only) male South African Hebrew Bible scholar to engage the theme of masculinity in Hebrew Bible biblical scholarship, I would like to venture an engagement with the theme of the notions of masculinity/ties/manhood as glimpsed from an African folklorist reading of the text of Prov 7.

Notions of Masculinity/ies in the South African Context(s)

Our varying African contexts and, dare one say, the global contexts, are largely hetero-patriarchal. However, in the South African contexts,

---

3. West, "Tamar Summons Jesus," 194.

definitions of manhood and/or masculinity will always be tied to certain notions of femininity. Hence, Paul Leshota can rightly argue from Lesotho perspective that,

> [I]n a man's world, nothing could be as ill-omened [as] being and behaving as a woman . . . For a man to be portrayed as a woman is demeaning and contemptuous. This is simply because a man can only become a man by not becoming a woman, who is fainthearted, powerless, emotional and weak."[4]

As can be expected, in such contexts, notions of masculinity or manhood, are still pretty much trapped within the duality of male vis-à-vis female categories at the expense of other forms of sexualities, such as those within the gender non-conforming categories, for example. Similar narrow definitions of manhood, and/or femininity, may also undergird notions of manhood/masculinity in the Prov 7 context, as will be gleaned from the key texts of this investigation.

In varying African heteronormative contexts, the concept of manhood/masculinity is linked to the following norms and values, among others. First, the unquestioned capacity of a youth to go out of the homestead at will, and not be restricted to the private sphere of the home. The tenor underlying the (Northern Sotho) proverb, lesogana le le sa sepelego le tšea kgaetšedi ("A young male adult who does not go out of the homestead, will marry his sister") assumes this male privilege. The lad who is the object of the sage's teachings and/or proverbial exhortations, and/or warnings in Prov 7, is also apparently (as I will argue in the following paragraphs) not barred from leaving the homestead *per se* (Prov 7:7–8)

> 7. . . . and saw among the simple ones,
>
> I discerned among the youths,
>
> A young man void of understanding,
>
> 8. passing through the street corner;
>
> And he went the way to her house . . . .

As a matter of fact, if we were to hold on to the view that there existed schools in Yehud, and that these teachings and commandments by the sage to his "son" (Prov 7:1) or "sons"/"children" (Prov 7:24), happened in that public instructional setting (cf. the genre of "Instruction" (Prov 1–9) that hosts these teachings and commandments), we could

---

4. Leshota, "Under the Spell," 153.

argue that this "son," (a "man-in-the making") was assumed to be in the public domain, a gendered space that could not be inhabited by his female counterpart (i.e., the sage's "daughter"). In that way, while the "son" (presumably, together with his female sibling) would, however, have been exposed to the teachings of his mother and his father in the home space, in his earlier life (Prov 1:8; 4:1–4), at some point, even in the parents' attempt to shape him into "a man of worth," (*ish chayil*) the "son" would eventually be permitted into the public educational sphere for exposure to the wisdom traditions of the community.

Noteworthy, however, is that in Prov 7, the sage still seems to be concerned about the destination and/or motives of the *na'ar's* external ventures. Therefore, in the wisdom teacher's view, the "son"'s manhood/masculinity would be better served by a deliberate designation of wisdom as his "sister." Wisdom is embraced as a "sister," not for a potential (albeit metaphorical) marital partner, but in order to allow wisdom to protect the "son" from the lures of the alternative nemesis, the "loose woman" (Prov 7:4–5; 5:23–35).

Comparatively, in some traditional African societies, like the Northern Sotho, an older biological sister in some circumstances almost takes the place of one's mother in terms of her role to the younger siblings, both male and female. She would nurture and protect them from any possible harm just like the parents would. Even during marriage negotiations, this paternal sister would play a crucial role in the lobola (bride's prize negotiations) of her younger brothers. In that context, it makes sense that the biblical sage would deploy the metaphor of wisdom being embraced by the son, as a "sister" protector and nurturer.

The irony here is that Wisdom, portrayed as a "sister," a female sibling, would be expected to protect male kin from another seducing female if she is not permitted into the public domain. A similar exhortation is reminiscent of the words of the mother of Lemuel in her instruction to her son:

> "Do not give your strength to women,
>   nor your ways to that which destroys kings."
>   (Prov 31:3, MEV)

In the former case, however, it is ironic that it is a female wisdom teacher, albeit with some form of influence (where does she get her authority from in a patriarchal society where, a son-of-age, can do whatever he likes?), while in the latter a mother, transmits parental wisdom in an educational setting, warning her son against fellow females!

The "loose" woman/"strange" woman, whatever her real identity, appears, at least as she is constructed by the sage in Prov 7, to have defied the critical role of women as household managers.[5] On "Woman Stranger"'s ambivalent portrayal, Christine R. Yoder rightfully remarks: "The poetry dances such diverse images of her that they blur" (2012: 235). However, that is not the only reason that the son is warned to avoid her. The sage seems also to be irritated massively by the incapacity of "Woman Stranger" to be confined to the house: "She is loud and stubborn; her feet do not abide in her house" (Prov 7:11, MEV).

Unlike the *na'ar* who could, apparently go out of the house, but is advised to be discerning in terms of the places and/or people he would encounter, "Woman Stranger" must be tied to the household, according to the sage. Regarding her alleged "loudness," "Woman Stranger" may be compared to the proverbial goat in some African proverbs, which is representative of womanhood or femininity. An example is the Sotho proverb *Monna ke nku, mosadi ke pudi* ("A man is a sheep, a woman is a goat"). In this African proverb, the latter part alludes not only to a woman's incapacity to keep secrets but also to her tendency to be "loud and noisy" in contrast to the "quiet" sheep.[6]

In many (traditional) African cultures, the official transition to manhood, for a male child, would be an initiation rite, typically circumcision. Regarding the role of initiation rituals, John S. Mbiti reminds us that one of their great importance is to introduce the candidates to "adult life."[7] Among the Northern Sotho people, for example, the act of "going to the mountain," that is, undergoing initiation into manhood, would happen in two stages; *koma* and *bogwera*. The actual initiation/circumcision (*koma*) happens during the first stage and the initiation into manhood would naturally happen at this stage. The second one, *bogwera*, is a follow-up stage in which the traditions introduced at the initial stage would be further entrenched and endorsed. In some contexts, the latter stage remains optional. The act of going out of the homestead for male initiation (*koma*), also points to the communal mentality of Sotho people. The parental responsibility of jointly raising "the sons," that is, "men-in-the-making" who would transmit the wisdom of the community and

5. Cf. Masenya [Ngwana Mphahlele], *How Worthy.*

6. Rakoma, *Marema-ka-dika.*

7. Mbiti, *African Religions and Philosophy.*

later teach other initiates acceptable notions of manhood, among other things, would not simply be their fathers, nor their male relatives, who lead events during the initiation space. This would fall instead to "other men/elders" (*baditi*) from the community.

As the designated elderly men, who themselves would have been initiated into manhood, steeped the "sons" into the community traditions, norms and values, they would have gotten their cues from such proverbs as the following: *rutang bana ditaola, le se ye natšo badimong* (lit. "teach children divining stones and do not take them [the bones] along to the ancestors"). The proverb's implication is that the parental responsibility the elders/*baditi* had as "the guardians of the initiates"), involved teaching the young (both male and female) the wisdom and traditions of their people, to enable them to grow into responsible men (and women).[8] It is in this secret and sacred initiation male space, that the African male youth would be introduced to the wisdom of their people, about what a man should be, and which features would typify an ideal African man.

A similar commitment seems to have undergirded the commitment of the wisdom teachers (both in the family and school settings) of the "Instruction genre" in Prov 1–9. The book of Proverbs as a whole is characterized by admonitions with regard to character and behavior; on modesty, self-control, honesty, reliability, careful speech, respect for superiors, and concern for truth and justice.[9] Prov 1–9 are typified by the direct address, "my son," a basic feature of the "Instruction genre" which uses imperatives, commands and exhortations within motive clauses.[10]

Prov 7 falls within this part of the "Instruction genre" of Prov 1–9. It opens with the words of the (male) wisdom teacher to his male student. Typical wisdom vocabulary can be identified in this text, including *misw't* (commandment), *bînāh* (understanding), *torah* (teaching/law) and *hôkma* (wisdom), among others. As it is typical in the instructional setting, enabled by the sage's wealth of experience gained over the years, the teachings and commandments that the young man has to guard jealously, would of necessity keep him from the lures of "an adulteress." As he listened/ kept the words of wisdom from his parent in the educational setting, the son would have been enabled to grow into a man of integrity,

8. Masenya, "In the School of Wisdom."

9. Scott, "Study of Wisdom," 26.

10. McKane, *Proverbs*, 3.

a worldview reminiscent of the optimistic wisdom outlook underlying the book of Proverbs. And, as noted above, the traditional African context typified in the Sotho case, the instructional setting featured in Proverbs 7 could be compared to an initiation "school" for males.

In the African setting, one could safely conclude that among other teachings, notions of what it meant to be a man in marriage, would have been unpacked. Manhood would most probably have been linked with male sexual prowess. Thus, the second feature of manhood to be gleaned from several African proverbs, is that of virility or sexual prowess. Mbiti is on target when he explains that, "The initiation rites prepare young people in matters of sexual life, marriage, procreation and family responsibilities."[11] Due to the fact that the initiation space mainly had to do with initiating boys into manhood, it may not be far-fetched to speculate that the following Sotho proverbs about male virility would have featured on the agenda. It is probably not coincidental that all the proverbs start with the phrase: "*monna ke*" literally, "a man is." In a nutshell, the proverbs spell out what manhood/masculinity is in the context of sexual intimacy. The general tenor of these proverbs can be summarized as follows: "A married man's body, unlike its female counterpart, is "a communal space." Such a communal space, by virtue of its designation, can be shared with women who are not the man's legitimate wives.

> *Monna ke tšhwene o ja ka matsogo a mabedi*:
> ("A man is a baboon, he eats with two hands.")

> *Monna ke thaka o a naba*:
> ("A man is a pumpkin plant, he spreads.")

> *Monna ke phoka o wa bošego*:
> ("A man is fog, he falls in the night.")

> *Monna ke selepe o lala a adimilwe*:
> ("A man is an axe, sharpened in the night.")

In this context, "a man" who is a baboon, a pumpkin plant, fog, or an axe, is a married man. Although he has a wife (or wives) to whom his sexual virility should be directed, he is legitimated by these "sacred texts" (read: "wisdom sayings") to share his body with women outside the confines of his marriage(s).

---

11. Mbiti, *African Religions and Philosophy*, 119.

Although it is not explicit from these proverbs, it can be implied from their general tenor that a male person is typified by his going out to seek sexual favors from the public space (*read*: "the private spheres of other men!"). For example, as a pumpkin plant, he cannot be restricted to his field only. He is allowed to spread into other men's fields. His manhood is also compared to a metaphoric fog that defies restrictions and falls in the night. Could the mention of the nocturnal time at which the fog falls, be ascribed to the shame connected to such extra-marital relationships? In the same vein, the man who is a proverbial axe, is loaned in the night. Whatever explanation one may come up with, one thing for sure is that the going-out feature that typifies masculinity in this context remains. An intersection thus exists between masculinity, the public space (symbolized by going out), and male virility.

As previously noted, the concern of the sage in Prov 7 is not about the *na'ăr*'s going out, *per se*, but implies the motives and toxic places that the young man would need to learn to avoid. Among those, are places that could expose him to women like "Woman Stranger." As a matter of fact, the young man in Prov 7 is barred from allowing his body to be "a communal space" for a "loose/stranger woman." However, what would have been the view of the sage if the woman in question was not another man's property or wife, we may ask? What seems to have frustrated the wisdom teacher in the Instruction genre with his "son" falling into sexual traps with women outside the confines of his own marriage included the involvement with the "wife of another" (Prov 7: 24–27).

But is this still "Woman Stranger" of Prov 5:4–5? If so, is "Woman Stranger" married? Is she "an adulteress"? If so, she is the one whose untypical behavior is in this context, especially for married women, who go out to seek sexual favors from a young man. So, "Woman Strangers" would be the one, like the African men portrayed in the preceding proverbs, who views her female body to be "a communal space." (A parallel that has emerged is the female "blessers" and "sugar mammas" in the South African context who would probably also fall under the category of "Woman Stranger" according to the sage of Prov 7). Sexual intimacy with such women, whose sexuality is supposed to be controlled and contained by their husbands, would of necessity, according to the sage, have led to the demise of the sage's "son(s)."

Listen to me now therefore, O children, and attend to the words of my mouth: do not let your heart turn aside to her ways, do not go astray in her paths; for she has cast down many wounded, and many strong men have been slain by her. Her house is the way to Sheol, going down to the chambers of death (Prov 7:24–27, MEV).

The woman who is the object of the sage's irritation is a married man's wife. Was the warning of the sage informed more by his concern in shaping the *na'ar* and/or his "son(s)" into a man/men of worth, one/ones who would drink water from his/their own cistern(s) only? (Prov 5:15–17). Was it a matter of the expression "an injury to one is an injury to all" since in the preceding line of thought, the sage would have been empathizing more with the husband of "Woman Stranger," a man who would have failed to control the sexuality of his wife?

If indeed motivated by the sage's defense of monogamous sexuality, a rare exhortation to men in the Hebrew Bible, the masculinity propagated by the wisdom teacher in Proverbs 7 stands in stark contrast to the masculinity propagated by the preceding four African proverbs. The sage's exhortation to his "son" to drink water from his own cistern (Prov 5:15–17) would thus not make sense to notions of masculinity and virility in the preceding African context. It occasions no surprise though, that even those African men (whether young or old) who claim to adhere to the Christian tradition with its propagation/celebration of monogamy, would still find the instruction from the four African proverbs affirming of their masculinity.

There is, however, the following African/ Northern Sotho proverb, which is one of its own kind. Why? Because it reverses the male-focused proverbs and seems to affirm female sexual prowess. I am of the view that this particular proverb could have appealed to the biblical "Woman Stranger" as she is constructed by the sage in Prov 7. Interestingly, the proverb, like the preceding four proverbs on the features of an "ideal Sotho man" also starts with the phrase, *monna ke*—"a man is." However, there is an ironic twist, especially in comparison to the kind of masculinity constructed in the other four wisdom sayings:

Monna ke kobo re a apolelana: "A man is a blanket, we share."

Those who typically affirm/use this proverb are women. The proverb boldly displays not only female sexual desire for a man, but also reveals the women's affirmation of the male body as a "communal space" (for women) and to "be shared" among women. Yet it does so without undoing the affirmation of women's bodies as part of the communal space sharing with other men.

Although this reversed proverb does not stipulate the age of the man in question, in light of the expectation regarding the link between masculinity and initiation noted previously, a man, whose body is a female's "communal space," would most likely not have been the age of the *na'ar* featured in Prov 7. One is thus hesitant to assume that in the traditional African context, in which the proverb would have been uttered, the present South African trend of the involvement of female "blessers" and "sugar mammas" with the "Ben Tens," would have been embraced. Thus, "Woman Stranger"'s concerted efforts in Proverbs 7:13-21 to lure the *na'ar*, would have been detested by the utterers of the African proverbs, even in a context that celebrated and affirmed female sexual prowess. The South African "Ben Tens" (perhaps like the youth in Prov 7?) may have embraced the luring actions of the rich, mature woman. The following public advertisement example on a social contact app (https://www.hep-ays.com/) can serve as cases in point:

> "I am just a boy seeking rich old women to love me (pmb)."

> "Looking for rich sugar mom (Bronkhorstsruit, SA)."

> "Handsome Boy Looking for Rich Women Mummies in Bloem."

Noteworthy in Prov 7 is the "silence" and "passivity/non-action" or constructed silence of the *na'ar*, who is the object of the teacher's lesson. One is here reminded of the Sotho proverb mentioned above designating a man the proverbial "sheep," typifying him, in contrast to the noisy and loud "goat" (female), as one with few words as a measure of his self-discipline. What is one to make of the (constructed) silence of the *na'ar* in this biblical text? In that ancient patriarchal context, it is the woman who approaches a male for sexual favors. She also talks (acting like a goat?) to him in public. "Woman Stranger" takes the young man and kisses him (Prov 7:13). With smooth words she massages his male ego by letting him know that she has been searching for him and has found him by "invading" his public space. She, like the female-centered Sotho proverb, seems to operate from the assumption that a man's body is a "communal space," a blanket shared among women. For that one night's stand, her body will be available for the *na'ar* in the absence of the legitimate owner of her body, her husband. As I have argued elsewhere:

> A reversal of gender roles happens here. The active-male-seeker-husband is replaced by the active-female-seeker-wife whose prey is not elderly men, but younger men! The latter

> are portrayed as real helpless victims who have fallen prey to a highly sexualized woman. The prostitute attire that she wears makes her potential male victims yield easily to her seductions, for who, in their right minds, would dare tamper with the property of a married man?[12]

The tenor of Prov 7 reveals yet another feature of manhood in the Sotho/African context. A man must be a family's breadwinner. If "Woman Stranger"'s husband was to take the words of the preceding Sotho proverbs seriously, his wife would allow a young man to have a share of his resources (cf. the bed and the expensive linen), even if temporarily. Perhaps "Woman Stranger"'s husband heeded the proverb of the man whose grave is next to the road (*lebitla la monna le thoko ga tsela*). She will commit the following crime: to share the body that is supposed to belong to her husband as its legitimate master, with another man; a younger one to boot!

In the case of the South African "Ben Tens" and the transactions with the "sugar mammas" involved would actually enable the young man (if married) to win bread for his family for that specific night. As "Woman Stranger" speaks and acts, the male youth initially, like a silent sheep, remains passive. However, he eventually acts by succumbing to the trap of "Woman Stranger"! Is it a calculated silence and passivity? Has his ego been massaged by his being sought after by a woman of class or is he simply weak? If he was married, could it be that he, like many an Israelite man, especially in the context of the lives of women who were not attached to men in marriage (e.g., prostitutes among others), and like many an African man, was persuaded that his body was "a communal space"? Who will be affirmed by the kind of masculinity displayed especially in the *na'ar*'s interaction with the wife of another man? May younger African women be affirmed by the encounter between "Woman Stranger" and the *na'ar* of Prov 7.

Conclusion

Multiple shades of masculinities could be identified from our engagement with the text about the *na'ar* in Prov 7. Depending on one's worldview, perspective, ideological orientation, and sexuality among other things, and viewed through the African proverbial lens, the male youth's action and non-action reveal different types of masculinities. This is apparent

12. Masenya, "Reading Proverbs 7."

especially when read side by side with South African proverbs. The South African "Ben Tens" would view their masculinity as redemptive, especially if their activities with "sugar mammas" and "female blessers" are economically and not sexually motivated.

A typical patriarchal African man who believes that, while his body can be shared with other females extra-maritally and that his wife dare not do likewise, would find the *na'ar's* masculinity to be toxic. Many men who benefit from hegemonic masculinities, will find the masculinity of a man who yields to the lures and dictates of a woman, to be soft. If the young man was married and may have reveled in yielding to the lures of "loose women," his masculinity would not be celebrated by those men who link ideal manhood with male virility.

In contrast, if the biblical wisdom teacher is foregrounding monogamous sexuality, he would view the young man's masculinity as toxic by daring to tamper with the body of another man's wife, as well as neglecting the sage's teachings and commandments. In the sage's view, this would be the masculinity displayed by a fool (*ě'wîl*) who dared to ignore and neglect "parental instruction" to make wisdom his "sister" because, so says an African proverb, *popotela ye e sa hwego, e wetše retheng la mohwelere*; "A child who does not listen (to his parents) will have negative consequences to bear."

Bibliography

Leshota, Paul. "Under the Spell of Discrete Islands of Consciousness: My Journey with Masculinities in the Context of HIV and Aids." In *Redemptive Masculinities: Men, HIV and Religion*, edited by Ezra Chitando and Sophie Chirongoma, 147–70. Geneva: World Council of Churches Publications, 2009.

Masenya, Madipoane J. *How Worthy is the Woman of Worth?: A Feminist Reading of Proverbs 31: 10–31*. Bible and Theology in Africa 4. New York: Lang, 2004.

———. "In the School of Wisdom: An Interpretation of Some Old Testament Proverbs in a Northern Sotho Setting." MA thesis, University of South Africa, Pretoria, RSA, 1989.

———. "Reading Proverbs 7 in the Context of Female Blessers and Sugar Mammas in South Africa." *Scriptura* 116.1 (2017) 120–32.

Mbiti, John S. *African Religions and Philosophy*. 2nd ed. New York: Praeger, 1969. Reprint, 1989.

McKane, William. *Proverbs: A New Approach*. OTL London: SCM, 1977.

MEV—Modern English Version Bible

Rakoma, J. R. D. *Marema-ka-dika tša Sesotho sa Leboa*. Cape Town: Van Schaik, 1971.

Ratele, Kopano. *Liberating Masculinities*. Cape Town: Human Sciences Research Council, 2016.

Scott, R. B. Y. "The Study of Wisdom Literature." *Interpretation* 24 (1970) 20–45.

Yoder, Christine Roy. "Proverbs." In *Women's Bible Commentary*, edited by Carol A. Newsom, Sharon H. Ringe, and Jacqueline E. Lapsley, 232–42. 3rd ed. Louisville: Westminster John Knox, 2012.

West, Gerald, O. "The Contribution of the Tamar Story to the Construction of Alternative African Masculinities." In *Bodies, Embodiment, and the Theology of the Hebrew Bible*, edited by S. Tamar Kamionkowski, and Wonil Kim, 184–200. LHBOTS 465. London: T. & T. Clark, 2010.

———. "Tamar Summons Jesus: A Trans-Textual (2 Samuel 13:1–22; Mark 5:22–43; Matthew 20:17–34) Search for Sectoral Solidarity with Respect to Gender and Masculinity." In *Transgression and Transformation: Feminist, Postcolonial and Queer Interpretations as Creative Interventions*, edited by L. J. Claassens, Christl M. Maier, and Funlola O. Olojede, 184–203. LHBOTS 707. London: T. & T. Clark, 2021.

12

The Female Body as a Site of Struggle for Agency

*The Theological Implications of Paul's Theology
of the Body for Cameroonian Christian Women*

ALICE YAFEH-DEIGH

Introduction

FIRST CORINTHIANS 6:12–20 IS incontrovertibly the *locus classicus*, or foundational text, for Christian perspectives on a believer's physical body.[1] Paul focuses on the human body sustainably in 1 Corinthians 6:12–20. The main concern of Paul's arguments in the pericope is three faith claims[2]: (1) that eschatological salvation involves the whole person, including the physical body (1 Cor 6:15); (2) that the believer's physical body is God's body and is the temple of the Holy Spirit (1 Cor 6:19);[3] and (3) that for believers living between the "already" and "not

---

1. As Kenneth Bailey aptly points out, "there is an important double meaning to the word 'body' that was known to all of Paul's readers. The 'body' meant the physical body and also referred to the 'body/church'" (Bailey, *Paul Through Mediterranean Eyes*, 188).

2. It should be noted here that Paul's letters, in general, ". . .are not systematic treatises but real letters, written to address a variety of practical problems within churches for which Paul felt some pastoral responsibility" (Thielman, *Paul, and the Law*, 11). They are contextual responses to concrete problems taking place within the church.

3. This valuation of the body is antithetical to the general perception in the ancient Mediterranean culture that "the physical body with its desires and longings, and indeed

yet," the exclusive function of the physical body is to glorify God (1 Cor 6:20). My basic premise is that, within its own context, Paul's alternate contextual moral reasoning about the physical body provided the early Christians with a different vision of the body. It also provided the most powerful framework for early Christian contestation and subversion of seemingly natural codes of representation of physical bodies, especially a prostitute's body, often the victim of unbridled male lust.

Paul infers that believers have the grace-empowering agency to adhere to his theological and ethical imperatives. Thus, he concludes his arguments with a resounding exhortation, "Do you not know that your body is a temple of the Holy Spirit within you, which you have from God, and that you are not your own? For you were bought with a price; therefore, glorify God in your body" (1 Cor 6:19–20). Paul's fundamental presupposition is that believers can comply with his appeals; that is, they can exercise agency over their bodies, even though he is persuaded that God's grace enables choice and agency (Phil 2:12–13).[4] Accordingly, Paul is confident that his own moral and theological reasoning can transform his readers' behavior, and vision of their bodies, through grace-energized actions that honor God.

---

the whole of the material world, is a distraction and impediment to the soul's highest pursuits" (Hollinger, *The Meaning of Sex,* 44).

4. Indeed, it is beyond the scope of this chapter to address the exact contours of this agency and how human agency and divine grace are related. See Yafeh, *Paul's Sexual and Marital Ethics,* 239 n.60. I argue that

". . .both divine and human agency are simultaneously operative in the believer. Therefore, God's gracious gift does not negate human responsibility or free will. Paul's view of agency is exemplified in passages such as Phil 2:12–13, where he encourages the Philippians believers to be responsible moral agents. Yet, he ascribes the powers and causes of all moral actions to God. The moral injunctions are based on the assumption that the Philippians believers are endowed with the competence to pursue moral values. Paul engaged in a radical reconfiguration of human agency through the eyes of God's apocalyptic in-breaking into human history in the events of Christ. Through these events, human agency has been restructured."

Also, the emphasis on God's energizing and enabling grace is a central thread that runs through 1 Corinthians (Cf. 1 Cor 3:16–17; 4:7; 6:19; 12:4–11). I equally argued, elsewhere, that the same argument for grace and agency is found in 1 Cor. 7. I also show that, "by collocating the verb *enkrateuomai* ('to practice self-mastery') within the same discourse context as charisma (7:7–9), and viewing v. 7 as a transition between vv. 2–5 and vv. 8–9, where the verb form of *enkrateia* (1 Cor 7:9) and its opposite *akrasia* (1 Cor 7:5) appear, it is plausible to identify *enkrateia* as the contextual reference of charisma. Consequently, Paul uses *enkrateia* to denote grace-gift for abstention" (Yafeh, *Paul's Sexual and Marital Ethics,* 12).

Teasing out the implications of Paul's theological and ethical reasoning for contemporary Christian attitudes toward the body, this essay engages in a contextual reflection on Paul's theology of the physical body, particularly the female body, using an Afro-womanist,[5] intersectional recontextualization of Gerald West's hermeneutics of liberation and life within the social location of Cameroon.[6] A socially engaged Afro-womanist-intersectional (AWI) approach is oriented primarily toward a liberationist Christian social justice praxis.[7] Second is its acknowledgment that the intersection of gender, religion, disability status, class, socioeconomic status, and other salient social identity markers shape Cameroonian women's experiences with their bodies.

Therefore, an intersectional analysis of 1 Cor 6:12–20 privileges diversity in reading conclusions that are variously life-giving and transformative for believing communities in diverse social locations over against the quest for a single, consistent, and unified meaning. The emphasis on multivalency in the AWI approach subverts and problematizes universalizing interpretations of Paul's moral reasoning about the body. It highlights that Paul's discourse about the body speaks differently to different women and at different times, based on their entry points into the discourse.

With the female body at the center of my analysis, this essay explicitly explores and unpacks the differential impact of Paul's moral reasoning

5. An "Afro-womanist-intersectional" approach recognizes the complexity, multidimensional, and intersectional nature of identity. It underscores a quest for a transgressive and contested space where women can constructively address holistic concerns. The approach carries the weight of the collective and multilateral experiences of women. It assumes, and recognizes, shared and unique aspects, thereby holding up the tension between fundamental differences and commonalities, which binary definitions do not adequately capture. Indeed, various positions are used within gender-sensitive hermeneutical frameworks (Mujerista, Asian Feminists, Black Feminists, and many others). These different gender-sensitive approaches share several key features central of which is a focus on gender justice as a critical dimension of biblical analysis and interpretation.

6. A hallmark of Gerald West's trailblazing work is his emphasis on recontextualizing the Bible to speak to the holistic reality of readers' experiences. He insists on the importance of "enabling believing readers of the Bible to connect their contexts with biblical narrative contexts, across both time and space, finding and forging lines of connection between their own contexts and the narrative world of the biblical text" (West and Haddad, "Boaz as 'Sugar Daddy,'" 150).

7. West's works emphasize the dialogic interactions between the "socially engaged biblical scholars and ordinary African 'readers' of the Bible" (*Reading Other-wise*, 56). For West, such interaction yields contextually relevant meanings of biblical texts within diverse African communities.

about the body for Christian women within patriarchally structured relationships in Cameroon through two contextual examples taken from the lived experiences of Cameroonian women and girls.[8] In the first example, we consider whether deeply-rooted patriarchal marriages offer women of faith possibilities for agency and choice relative to their bodies. Can Paul's transgressive claims serve a liberationist goal of righting the wrongs perpetrated by centuries of patriarchal control over women's bodies and sexuality? In the second example, we contextualize Paul's theologizing about the body within the concrete socioeconomic, political, and religious reality of impoverished Cameroonian university students who resort to "sugar daddy" relationships for financial sustenance.

Presupposing Paul's moral reasoning aims to transform believers' behavior and vision of their bodies; how can students in "sugar daddy" relationships make independent decisions about their bodies being heavily constrained by socioeconomic systems, gender structures, educational barriers, and norms? In other words, can a socially and economically marginalized person, relegated to the fringes of society with no access to resources and opportunities, have an active voice to make independent decisions about her body? Are those decisions not always constrained? Indeed, how can Paul's theological and ethical perspectives about the body support the struggle for full liberation and life among students in "sugar-daddy" relationships who are discriminated against based on several aspects of their identity? These questions reveal complexities and dilemmas in actualizing Paul's exhortations about the body within the lived realities of women and girls in Cameroon.

As such, a recontextualization of Paul's discourse within the lived experiences of women in Cameroon must take seriously contextual variables and the reality that women are constrained within "interlocking systems of oppression."[9] Before rereading Paul's discourse within the social location of Cameroon, let me briefly discuss the general context of Paul's theology of the body. A fundamental premise here is that socioeconomic and cultural constraints, such as the androcentric

---

8. I want to note that most believing Cameroonian women who read the Bible take it as the authoritative literal Word of God that holds religious significance over their beliefs and moral behavior. A "hermeneutic of trust" characterizes the general posture of the reading community of women toward the Bible, even though their understanding and appropriation of the Bible is influenced by their contextual perceptions and mindsets (cf. West, "Some Parameters of the Hermeneutical Debate in the South African Context," 10–11).

9. hooks, *Yearning*, 59.

determinants of status and worth, hinder women's ability to make independent decisions over their bodies. Such structures do not encourage women and girls to use their agential capacities.

The Context of Paul's "Theology of the Body"

Rather than being peripheral to Paul's ethical and theological reasoning, Paul focuses on the human body sustainably in 1 Corinthians 6:12–20. The pericope about the body, 1 Cor 6:12–20, is situated within the overall context of a broader socio-theological reflection on the topos of *porneia* "sexual morality", in 1 Cor 5-7). Elsewhere I have noted that:

> Although a plurality of specific issues are raised in chapters 5–7, the common theme of the larger argumentative unit is sexual morality, understood more broadly under the umbrella term *porneia* (construed as symptomatic of a larger theological problem in the church.[10]

The term *porneia* has an extensive semantic dynamic range such that ". . .its concrete import for behavior remained ambiguous."[11] Union with the Lord is exclusive of and incompatible with *porneia* in all its forms.[12] Paul's fundamental motivation and core theological conviction are that believers' ". . .bodily actions stand under the eschatological judgment of God and that we should use our bodies in ways that point towards the wholeness for which we hope in the resurrection."[13]

My analysis below will show that Paul addresses believers individually and attends to their concerns. However, individuals are never viewed as discrete individuals pursuing *autarkeia* ("self-satisfaction" or "self-sufficiency"). Rather, individuals are always within the community since Paul's primary objective is to shape communal identity. Such an orientation de-emphasizes the self by ascribing the ability to own

10. Yafeh, *Paul's Sexual and Marital Ethics*, 14. Cf. the noun and its cognates [*porneuō, pornē,* and *pornos*] in 1 Cor 5:1, 9–11; 6:9, 13, 15–16, 18; 7:2).

11. Horsley, *Paul, and Politics*, 116; Furnish, *The Theology of the First Letter to the Corinthians*; Barrett, *Commentary on the First Epistle to the Corinthians*, 155; Lightfoot, *Notes on the Epistles of Paul*, 221.

12. Caragounis' argues a Greek Jewish understanding of *porneia* "does not involve the idea of prostitution, but of the legitimate sexual urges" ("Fornication" and "Concession," 551).

13. Hays, *First Corinthians*, 108.

the body to the Lord and locating the discourse about the body within a communal context.

The pericope begins with a maxim, probably a Corinthian adage (1 Cor 6:12ab). It ends with the theologically charged phrase *doxasate dē ton theon en tō sōmati hymōn* (1 Cor 6:20). Interpreters remain divided over ". . .the meaning and rhetorical function of 1 Cor 6:12–20."[14] It is unclear whether 1 Cor 6:12–20 is responsive to the community's queries in the first part of the epistle or not.[15] Different from 1 Cor 5:1 and 7:1, in which Paul explicitly mentions oral and written reports from the congregation, the introductory maxim in 1 Cor 6:12 leaves no clues as to the nature of the discourse. It is equally unclear whether it is part of an oral report (cf. 1 Cor 5:1), whether Paul has a specific case in mind, or whether it is articulated as part of a general discourse on *porneia*. Different hypotheses have been suggested, but none have received general consensus.[16] The various hypotheses center on whether Paul addresses a general or specific situation of *porneia*. Whatever the particular issue addressed, Paul's argumentative procedure suggests that he understands the various issues as symptomatic of a more significant theological problem in the church of Corinth.[17] The ultimate theological problem Paul confronts and refutes in 1 Cor 6:12–20 is the idea that the physical body is inconsequential in terms of "what you do with it."[18] Against this claim,

14. Fisk, "*Porneuein* as Body Violation," 540. Cf. Fee, *The First Epistle To The Corinthians*, 251; Rosner, "Temple Prostitution," 336.

15. Keener argues that in 6:12–14, "Paul cites the opinion of an imaginary opponent similar to his readers, and then refutes or qualifies it" (*The IVP Bible Background Commentary*, 472).

16. For a detailed analysis of the different hypotheses, see Rosner, "Temple Prostitution," 336–48. Rosner's own suggestion postulates a concrete case of prostitution. He argues that Paul's address in 1 Cor 6:12–20 is directed explicitly to "prostitutes who offer their services after festive occasions in pagan temples." His contention that Paul moves from the specific discussion of sexual intercourse with a *pornē* in 1 Cor 6:12–20 to a general discussion of the topic in 7:2 is clear from using the plural *porneias* in 7:2 ("Temple Prostitution," 337). This proposal is attractive and plausible. However, we contend that the discourse is shaped by a complex blend of language drawn from the Jewish and Greco-Roman contexts of which the discourse was a part. Thus any attempt to ascribe the influences to one tradition rather than the other is necessarily too restrictive and consequently fails to convince.

17. As Grindheim cogently phrases it, "for Paul, sociology is indicative of theology" ("Wisdom for the Perfect," 689–709).

18. The fact that the physical body is transitory made the Corinthians assume it was spiritually inconsequential. However, this does not mean the body has no value or consequence—the ranking of the body or body type results from such valuation. The point here is that, in the Greco-Roman society, the body was "perceived as a location

"Paul insists both here and in 1 Cor. 15, that the body is created by God as a good part of creation and that God will redeem the body through resurrection."[19]

The rhetorical function that this discourse is meant to accomplish is the redefinition of the *topos soma* ("idea of body") within the parameters of the cross and the resurrection—the body will be resurrected, it is the temple of the Holy Spirit, and it is bought for a massive price through Christ's sacrificial death on the cross. This framework serves as a theological warrant to the emphatic claim that the body is not a site of moral indifference since *ho theos kai ton kyrion* ēgeiren *kai hēmas exegerei dia tēs dynameōs autou* ("And God raised the Lord, and will also raise us, by his power," 1 Cor 6:14). Hence it is emphasized that both the individual and collective body (1 Cor 6:13c, d, 15, 16, 18a, b, 19, 20) are not peripheral to Christian identity, but are central in understanding believers' newfound identity in Christ.[20] Rather than being an instrument for immorality, the body is God's property (*to de sōma ou tē porneia alla tō kyriō, kai ho kyrios tō sōmati*, 1 Cor 6:13),[21] and comprises the "members of Christ" (1 Cor 6:15), with its function redefined as an instrument for glorifying God (*doxasate dē ton theon en tō sōmati hymōn*, 1 Cor 6:20).

---

in a continuum of cosmic movement. The body—or the "self"—is an unstable point of transition, not a discrete, permanent, solid entity" (Martin, *The Corinthian Body*, 1995, 25). Martin additionally notes that the gendered body was a mark of hierarchy: "A firm social hierarchy existed within the body of the ancient person, favoring male over female, strength over weakness, superior over inferior. Each individual body, moreover, could be placed confidently at some location in the physiological hierarchy of nature" (34).

19. Hays, *First Corinthians*, 103. As Martin correctly points out, Paul insists "on the future resurrection of the body, thereby denying the lowly status attributed to the body by Greco-Roman elite culture" (Martin, *The Corinthian Body*, 135).

20. According to Martin, *The Corinthian Body*, 176, Paul "rejects a hierarchical notion of the body according to which relative importance is attached to the actions of the different levels of the human self as if the body and food are lower on a hierarchical scale of meaningfulness than the human mind or will and therefore simply do not matter very much."

21. The phrase "God's property" is potentially problematic and can legitimately hurt or offend the ethical sensibilities of black persons who still experience the psychological trauma of slavery and institutionalized racism, including women with a long history of being viewed and treated as property. However, Paul coopted the language to subvert and redefine God's liberative or redemptive purchase in terms of freedom. Believers can belong to God's household as freed people with complete agency to glory or not to glorify God with their bodies. Agency here is not constrained or coercive. A crucial theological statement that underlies Paul's moral reasoning is that God will resurrect the body. Believers are not done with the body at death, as was the cultural commonplace (see Keener, *The IVP Bible Background Commentary*, 472).

Believers, therefore, no longer have the freedom to devalue the bodies in favor of the spirit or to do with God's body as they please (1 Cor 6:15–19) because the individual body is a gift from God—they come from God, they belong to God. God, through the Holy Spirit, resides in each Christian's body. Again, it is essential to note that when Paul talks of the individual, he is not talking about a discrete/isolated individual but an individual within the collective body of Christ. Thus, Paul's theological reflection here does not authorize a dichotomy between the individual and corporate bodies. I think that Hans Conzelmann states it cogently when he avers: "What was said in 3:16 of the community, that it is the temple of God, that the Spirit of God dwells in it, is here transferred to the individual."[22]

This theological understanding of the human body, especially when it included the female body as God's body and the temple of the Holy Spirit, is radical and countercultural.[23] It challenges culturally accepted perceptions about bodies that contradict this theological claim.[24] As Richard Hays accurately maintains, ". . .the resurrection of the body is an integral element of the Christian story. Those who live within that story, then, should understand that what they do with their bodies in the present time is a matter of urgent concern."[25] This theological imperative that believers glorify God with their bodies coheres with Paul's general attitude of theologically presenting Christ crucified as a pattern for re-evaluation of all things (cf. 1 Cor 1:18–25; 2:1–5).

Overall, Paul's claim about the body is theologically impelled by Paul's own conviction that, through God's apocalyptic in-breaking, in the events of the cross and the resurrection, something fundamental has happened in human history that speaks to the crisis of the human condition in general. Consequently, these events radically call into question

---

22. Conzelmann, *1 Corinthians*, 112.

23. All bodies belong to God. It is countercultural in a context where the general thought is that women's bodies belong to men. In contrast, men's bodies belonged to themselves, and they were free to do with them whatever they deemed fit, hence the problem of sexual immorality threatening the church's health.

24. See Deming, "The Unity of 1 Corinthians 5–6," 289–312, for examples of such cultural perceptions of the body. Referencing Conzelmann (*1 Corinthians*, 112 n. 36), Deming presents an example of such views as a belief that sexual intercourse in some ways injures one's personality (cf. Deming, "The Unity of 1 Corinthians 5–6," 306). His argument in this article is grounded on the premise that 1 Cor 6:12–20 is a continuation of discourse in 1 Cor 5:1–13 and 6:1–11. In his contention, Paul's discourse in 1 Cor 6:12–20 is focused on prostitution because the stepmother in 1 Cor 5:1–13 was selling her services for prostitution (cf. Deming, "The Unity of 1 Corinthians 5–6," 304).

25. Hays, *First Corinthians*, 104.

previous value systems and lifestyles. At all times and in all places, the body of the Christian believer, male or female, is subjected to the lordship of Christ. The difference with human lordship is that human ownership is inherently oppressive, while Christ subverts the conventional understanding of buying and owning the body. Christ buys to liberate! Following Paul's claims, all bodies, not only a particular type of body, possess the inherent dignity and agency to live in the freedom Christ offers.[26] These Christocentric claims give the ethical imperatives of Paul's theology of the body their normative value and legitimacy.

Who are the Addressees of Paul's Discourse in 1 Corinthians 6:12–20?

We have to distinguish between the addressees of the discourse in 1 Cor 6:12–20 and the audience of the discourse. By addressees, I mean the specific target group Paul had in mind. That is, those for whom Paul had the most immediate and obvious goal in couching the various arguments. On the other hand, the audience of the discourse is all who hear and read the discourse.[27] And a third category, through analyzing Paul's rhetorical strategy in chapters 5–6, I argue that the "implied addressees," i.e., those whom Paul wants to persuade with the various arguments, are male believers.

The moral and ethical imperatives in 1 Cor 6: 12–20 specifically address the male target audience. The male focus of the discourse might be explained by the fact that Greco-Roman Christian men are more accountable since

> the sexual latitude allowed to men by Greek public opinion was virtually unrestricted. Sexual relations of males with both boys and harlots were generally tolerated. Thus, the Corinthian men who frequented prostitutes were not asserting some unheard-of new freedom; they merely insisted on their right to continue participating in a pleasurable activity that was entirely normal within their own culture.[28]

26. The Greco-Roman society's cultural commonplace assumed that the "lower hierarchical position of women cannot be challenged until the resurrection of the body, because the bodies of women before the resurrection are constituted differently from men's bodies and are weaker" (Martin, *The Corinthian Body*, 233).

27. See Yafeh, *Paul's Sexual and Marital Ethics*, 48–49.

28. Hays, *First Corinthians*, 102.

Consequently, in 1 Cor 6:12–20, the subject of *porneia* is addressed from the unique perspective of the Christian male *vis-à-vis* the *porne* (i.e., sexual intercourse between the Christian male and the female prostitute, 1 Cor 6:15–16). We do not find a parallel address from the perspective of a Christian female concerning *pornos* (i.e., sexual intercourse between the Christian female and male prostitute). However, I maintain that, although the arguments are designed with Christian males in mind, it does not imply that the *presumed* audience for the discourse was exclusively male. It is couched with a broader audience in mind than simply the Christian male. Though not targeted, it can be inferred that Paul also expects an active response from the female believers. "The various arguments are designed to effect change in the perception and lifestyle of the entire community. Thus, female believers of the community are present in the wider field of vision even if they are not in focus; a responsive action is equally expected from them."[29]

Reading Paul's Discourse in 1 Corinthians 6:12–20 within a Cameroonian Social Location

Patriarchal Marriage Arrangement and Female Agency

The underlying premise of this section is that 1 Cor 6:12–20 offers biblical scholars, ethicists, and theologians a much-needed opportunity to address pressing controversial issues surrounding the sexualization and objectification of the female body in diverse social locations. In the pericope, Paul emphasizes the inherent value of the human body, both male and female. If Paul assumes the intrinsic value of the female body, it implies women's bodies are not the property of men, nor do men have power or control over the female body (cf. 1 Cor 7, on Paul's views of single women and widows). If women, like men, are summoned by Paul to glorify God with their bodies, he must assume female independent agency over their bodies.

  This section offers a series of critical interrogations of Pauline ethics of the body as it relates to actual gender practices among impoverished rural Christian communities in Cameroon. The crux of the interrogation is whether women and girls, in patriarchal social structures with dynamics of relationships structured by gender inequities,

---

29. Yafeh, *Paul's Sexual and Marital Ethics*, 48.

have unconstrained agency over their bodies. Can Paul's claims about the body function as a tool for liberation that empowers women who are multiply oppressed to reclaim independent agency over their bodies and take control of their sexuality?

As a teenager growing up in a steeply patriarchal context, where girls are taught that their primary obligation is to get married and have babies eventually, I found 1 Cor 6:12–20 an essential text of liberation for myself. It energized, empowered, and filled me with extraordinary excitement and conviction that my body was sacred and inhabited by the Holy Spirit. Most importantly, it served as a consciousness-raising tool to help me realize that I could choose to glorify God with my body, in or outside of marriage. Indeed, it affirmed and legitimated my decision to flee to a convent at the age of fifteen, where I lived for the next fifteen years. But now, with my heightened interest in, and commitment to, reading biblical texts for liberation and empowerment within the lived experiences of women in Cameroon, I feel a sense of disquiet rather than empowerment from Paul's discourse. I question whether patriarchal marriages offer women agency and choice over their bodies. Making practical choices and exercising control over one's life is a crucial dimension of one's well-being. Yet, the unfortunate reality for many women and girls in Cameroon is that their bodies are policed and controlled within normalized patrilineal or patriarchal social structures which exert so much power over women's bodies.

Christian women in Cameroon have firm religious commitments and values and hold the Bible as a sacred and authoritative text for their lives. They abide by core biblicist principles and hermeneutics of trust, even when those principles harm their well-being. Their Christian beliefs inextricably shape their social identities. Nevertheless, the patriarchal culture of Cameroon is a critical lens that informs Christian women's reading of the Bible and recontextualizes Paul's injunctions. As such, power relations permeate discussions about female agency in Cameroon because the female body is the site upon which this power is exercised.

Moreover, Christian marriage in Cameroon does not change the core position of patriarchal standards governing marital relations (given the patriarchal underpinnings in the biblical text itself). Culturally, Cameroonian women belong to their husbands because the bride price, or dowry, that a man pays to the woman's family is viewed as "a purchase"—in other words, a property transfer. As the secondary marital partner, the woman is expected to be a docile object in the hands of the male spouse. The fact that families plan to "sell" their daughters legitimates, from an early age, that to be female is to be subject to the regulation and control of men. Women's overall subservience is assumed and normalized, resulting in internalized misogyny. Similarly, the pervasiveness of sexual exploitation, and widespread domestic violence in Cameroon has also become normalized. Indeed, such abuse is often neither prohibited nor punished by law, even when women's rights are extant constitutionally.[30]

Though Paul asserts that believers' bodies are sacred, that both male and female hold value in God's sight and, into both, God pours out God's Holy Spirit, a question yet lingers before us—How do Cameroonian women live out Paul's imperatives within a culture that continuously, and violently, reminds them that their bodies are not their own? To be sure, Cameroonian women of social and economic privilege can flourish and avoid some of the ramifications to an extent. These women's positions of privilege (economic, social, political, religious, etc.) allow them to exercise some agency over their bodies, empowering some even to flee arranged marriages and actively work to destabilize, disrupt, and deconstruct Cameroon's patriarchal cultural narrative.

Unfortunately, most women in Cameroon are not women of means or privilege. Most Cameroonian women have no avenue to escape or challenge the patriarchal culture. While, in comparison, most Western women are empowering one another to stand up, speak out, and fearlessly fight against sexual violence, assaults, and abuses of power, this is not an option for the economically disadvantaged women of Cameroon.[31] Without agency and legal or moral protection, how can such women stand up and demand the right to autonomy over their own bodies—the right to call their bodies sacred and their own? Socially engaged liberationist hermeneutical approaches can invoke 1 Cor 6:12–20 as inspiration for dismantling barriers to women's agency over their bodies and fighting gender inequities. Precisely, the pericope can empower disenfranchised women and girls with tools that would help them seize agency over their bodies.

---

30. Cf. Takwa, "Violence against the women and girl children in Cameroon;" "Advocates for Human Rights, Cameroon;" OCHA, "Gender-based violence; "Sexual violence pervasive in Cameroon's Anglophone regions."

31. While there are no systemic movements like the "Me-Too" movements in the West, Christian women have had sporadic locale initiatives to help address the socio-economic situations of marginalized women and girls. A case in point, some Christian Women Fellowship groups sponsor poor and orphan girls to school.

University Girls and "Sugar-Daddy" Relationships

A "sugar-daddy" (cross-generational) relationship is "characterized by large age and economic asymmetries between [unmarried] partners."[32] In these non-marital, illicit relationships, a wealthy (usually middle-aged) man enters a "sponsored" arrangement (financial and material assistance, for instance) with a much younger (often adolescent) girl in exchange for regular sexual benefits. In Cameroon, the "sugar daddy" phenomenon is prominent among university students. The varied reasons leading young college girls to get into these partnerships can be explained by the deep interlocking of patriarchy, gender, class, religion, socioeconomic status, and other salient social identities. Some girls do so because of the significant amounts of money and gifts they can receive from the "sugar daddy"; others to "boost their status in the eyes of their peers,"[33] through fashionable lifestyles and the latest technological gadgets; while for others, it's means of a financial assistance to afford a university education.[34] This last group will be the focus of this section.

West and Beverly Haddad, in their study of "sugar daddies" and HIV in South Africa, have a point that, sometimes, "young women are not necessarily victims, but active agents in these relationships," indicating that these relationships are more complex and multifaceted.[35] Girls also experience "sugar daddy" relationships differently, based on overlapping identity markers or social locations. The unique experiences of girls from impoverished rural communities, who use "sugar daddy" arrangements as the only available option to acquire a university education, for example,

---

32. Luke, "Confronting the 'Sugar Daddy' Stereotype," 6. Admittedly, there is no consensus on the definition of the "sugar-daddy" relationship due to the complexity and multifaceted reality of the relationship. Some agreed-upon tenets are that it "entails large age and economic asymmetries between partners" (Luke, "Confronting the 'Sugar Daddy' Stereotype," 8, cited in West and Haddad, "Boaz as 'Sugar Daddy,'" 143). (An inverse, "sugar mummy," though less prevalent, increasingly has emerged due to socio-economic changes that have made some older unmarried independent women to seek similar sexual arragements with younger men).

33. Leclerc-Madlala, "Age-disparate Relationship," cited in West and Haddad, "Boaz as 'Sugar Daddy,'" 145.

34. Most university students from poor rural communities engage in sugar daddy relationships for survival. As Leclerc-Madlala cogently states, "the lack of access to education, health services, employment and a weak economy, associated with poverty, often pushed women and girls into age disparate sexual partnerships with potential economic benefits" "Age-Disparate Relationship," cited in West and Haddad, "Boaz as 'Sugar Daddy,'" 144.

35. West and Haddad, "Boaz as 'Sugar Daddy,'" 145.

are obscured by a failure to take seriously the role of family status and socioeconomic status in these relationships.

The relationship between the "sugar daddy" and the girl, on the surface, might seem mutually beneficial. However, a blatant power differential constrains the girl's agential ability to ". . .negotiate safer sexual behaviors."[36] The age and economic asymmetries between the "sugar daddy" and the girl significantly undermine her agency over her body.

Education Inequities among Impoverished Girls and Women, as Major Determinants of "Sugar Daddy" Relationships!

The primary determinant of "sugar daddy" relationships hinges on some girls' abject poverty, especially those from impoverished rural communities, establishing their vulnerability to the promise of a stable economic benefit. In other words, had such girls possessed other means of accessing their university education, they would probably not engage in such risky arrangements. Education is one of the most accessible primary and often singular vehicles for women to move away from traditionally defined gender roles and acquire a voice in society and politics that provides some agency. However, educational inequities remain a glaring problem in impoverished rural communities, putting pressure on girls who earn the opportunity to make it.

Additionally, gender inequities in education in Cameroon are at a statistically significant crisis level among the most marginalized social groups. Poverty and economic vulnerability are so widespread and extreme that increasing numbers of girls, and young women, from a vast range of rural low-income communities cannot afford a university education. Besides, few scholarships or other forms of financial aid help are available to them. Given that education is a prerequisite for women's and girls' attainment of some agency and freedom, a practical means for these girls and young women to acquire a university education is engaging in the risky practice of "sugar daddy" relationships. For a young woman (the "sugar baby"), this relationship usually entails dating an older wealthy man (the sugar daddy or "Mboma" as it is locally called).[37]

36. Luke, "Confronting the 'Sugar Daddy' Stereotype, "6.

37. "Sugar daddy" relationships are locally called "Mboma" in analogy with the ability of the python to swallow its victim. Metaphorically speaking, the "Mbomas," like the pythons, have swallowed their "sugar babies." Consequently, the "sugar daddy" owns and controls the "sugar babies" during the relationship.

Girls and young women who engage in such relationships are labeled prostitutes (exchange of sex for money) because of the assumption that they deliberately enter the "sugar daddy" relationship of their own free will. The stereotypical label "prostitute" that is often assigned to these young women and girls is based on the assumption that self-motivated and age-appropriate sexual activity should not be considered sexual objectification or exploitation. Education is often the only way for a woman from a poor community to escape poverty and patriarchal oppression. This situation leads to acts of desperation to alleviate their economic situations, a vulnerability that older, affluent, upper-class men exploit. These men then retain exclusive access to these university students' bodies, not as equals in a contract of fair exchange, but as sex objects without volition, much less personal agency. This is a variation of servitude and sexual exploitation that most girls and young women engaged in "sugar daddy" relationships suffer. Often, they a subjected to severe physical, emotional, and psychological violence at the hands of their "sugar daddies." Notwithstanding such dire situations of "sugar daddy" relationships, Cameroonian university girls and young women continue to enter into these relationships because they hope that education will empower them with agency, freedom, independence, and a means of generating income.

An "Afro-Womanist-Intersectional" Reading for Liberation

An "Afro-womanist-intersectional" reading for liberation must confront the "sugar daddy" relationship as a form of gender-based violence. Any discussion of the topic must focus on the degree of the agency and autonomy of the girls and young women involved and take the abuse of those in vulnerable situations seriously. The following arguments thus investigate the constraints that shape women's hard choices in these situations and the desperate life circumstances that shape their choices.

Paul's arguments highlight that prostitution has theological significance, but it must be observed that Paul does not call into question the violation of the prostitute's body. He noticeably writes and addresses his arguments for and against the men engaging in prostitution but not the women. Within the social location of the Corinthian church, it was not acceptable, nor possible, for women to have sexual freedom or engage in prostitution for themselves. Indeed, the stigmatized space to which Paul relegates the prostitute blatantly reveals her body as the defiled and polluted object that threatens the health and well-being of the men of the community. The unfair marginalization of the prostitute strikes a reader with sensitivity to Paul's conceptualization of gender as misogynistic.[38]

Even the women in the Corinthian community would understand a hidden truth within Paul's discourse. Shock, having been socialized in Greco-Roman culture with the notion that their husbands bought them at a price and, consequently, owned them, the Corinthians women would have taken Paul's claim that God is the authentic owner of their bodies with shock. From the perspective of African-American women, Paul's assertion, "you are not your own," and "you were bought at a price," conjures up images of enslavement and the literal lack of ownership and agency over their physical bodies. Also, read through the lens of women struggling with forms of bodily self-determination; the metaphor could seem to reinforce and legitimize sociocultural systems that limit women's voices and agency, suggesting that Paul supported the system of gender slavery that commoditized and limited women's bodies for solely male use. Kwok Pui-Lan correctly notes, "Such a metaphor would sound very different to the freeborn than the enslaved. What would it mean to a slave woman who would have experienced double slavery?"[39] Thus, Dale B. Martin makes a salient point by asserting that "any interpretation of Scripture that hurts people, oppresses people, or destroys people cannot be the right interpretation, no matter how traditional, historical, or exegetically respectable."[40]

Unfortunately, in traditional patriarchal societies where men occupy a dominant social position and their power over women is institutionalized, it is commonplace for women to hear their husbands say things like, "I paid your bride price, your body belongs to me, you are my property." Paul's discourse, by contrast, resists, challenges, dismantles, and transcends the core of patriarchal ideologies about female bodies. He strips Christian men and women of full autonomy and control over their

---

38. Keener points out that not only was prostitution a disreputable occupation for women, but "the ranks of prostitutes were especially stocked with slave girls raised from the vast number of abandoned babies" (*The IVP Bible Background Commentary*, 472). It was disgraceful, of course, for men to relieve their sexual appetite with prostitutes.

39. Pui-lan, *Postcolonial Imagination*, 93.

40. Martin, *Sex and the Single Savior*, 49–50. See Tolbert, "When Resistance Becomes Repression," 333. She states, "any interpretation of a text, especially a text as traditionally powerful as the Bible, must be assessed not only on whatever its literary or historical merits maybe but also on its theological and ethical impact on the integrity and dignity of God's creation."

bodies and lives. Both male and female bodies are bought at *a price*. Here, Paul mimics or coopts the language of "buying" and "owning" to subvert their meanings immediately. Rather than coopting such language to reinforce or legitimatize patriarchal policing and control over the body, particularly the female body, it strips the language of its negative power. God is not a new kind of enslaver but a new kind of owner.[41]

The language of buying and owning is Christologically redefined and recontextualized. God's liberationist buying and owning resulted in every believer, without exception, becoming a freed person.[42] Although freed, believers are still responsible for how they use their bodies since they have now become part of the extended family of God. So believers are not independent to do with their bodies as they please but must use their bodies in ways that honor God. Thus, all Christ-followers are on a level playing field within the household of God.[43]

That God owns believers' bodies would have thus directed some Corinthian women to realize their earlier status as earthly objects to men, and must now yield to being God's "object," which entailed their no longer being bound to the patriarchal strictures of their culture, but to God. Therefore, the Corinthian women could construe Paul's arguments as a pushback against the marginalization of the prostitute's body and men's

41. God's redemptive or liberationist action of "buying" from slavery and "owning" ensures believers do not become enslaved again. Hence, Paul's exhortation: "For freedom, Christ has set us free. Stand firm, therefore, and do not submit again to a yoke of slavery" (Gal 5:1). Those within the household of God follow a different logic of freedom. It is a kind of freedom that rejects the pursuit of selfish devaluing and stigmatization of certain types of bodies in the family of God. It is Christ-like freedom that loves all bodies as God's property destined for the resurrection.

42. There is a significant difference between "freed" and "free." Though the language "free" does not occur in the pericope, the language of God's redemptive buying and owning portrays those who self-identify as disciples of Christ as enslaved persons who have been freed. The change in status establishes believers as members of the extended family of God. Since they are members of God's family, they are heirs to God's promises and children of Abraham and Sarah (Gal 3:29). Also, as members of God's family, believers are not entirely independent because they are under the authority of God. However, the yoke or thorn of slavery has been broken and removed. Members of God's household adopt the redefined redemptive yoking that Jesus presents: "Take my yoke upon you, and learn from me, for I am gentle and humble in heart, and you will find rest for your souls. For my yoke is easy, and my burden is light" Matt 11:29–30). Those who take Paul's injunction to use their bodies in ways that glorify God will find rest for their souls that is holistic rest and peace.

43. The categorical class-based differences between freeborn and freedman or freedwoman were erased in Christ. In Christ, every believer is a freedman or woman. They have all been set free.

claim of property rights over their female bodies. Such a reading subverts the conventional practice of males exclusively claiming control over the female body, while also stripping men of their historical power to do with their bodies as they pleased. Now both male and female bodies belonged not to any person but to the purpose of glorifying God.

The argument that God is the rightful owner of all Christian bodies can be easily recontextualized and used to contest how the Church and Cameroonian culture should view the female body, given the deeply entrenched patriarchal power relationships and attitudes. In this way, 1 Cor 6:12–20 can potentially act as a powerful tool, or vehicle, for liberation and social transformation. As we advance, Christian gender justice activists must continue to build on Paul's claims about the body so that those claims' meaning potential are appropriated within Cameroonian Christian readers' localized realities.[44]

A Way Forward

Within Cameroon, education is a crucial antidote to redressing women and girls' social, economic, and political marginalization. The Church is vital in ensuring that vulnerable and impoverished girls, systemically excluded from affordable education, have equal access to quality education. Economic inequality and female agency over the body have an inextricable, complex connection. This makes gender and economic dimensions of bodies central to assessing the effectiveness of Paul's theological and ethical arguments in 1 Cor 6:12–20. Multiple marginalities characterize women in Cameroon. Hence, a socially engaged Afro-womanist-intersectional reading can help provide contextual tools to unpack Paul's arguments in 1 Cor 6:12–20 for the social location of Cameroon. The *telos* of an Afro-womanist gender-centric reading is to underscore how patriarchal power and religious systems intersect to influence and shape the way Cameroonian culture understands and perceives the female body. To effectively address issues about the female body in Cameroon, it is crucial to clearly understand how to reconfigure and recontextualize 1 Cor 6:12–20 in that specific context.

It is the moral and ethical responsibility of Christian institutions to address intersecting systems of oppression that affect women, including(but not limited to) patriarchy, economics, gender, wealth inequity or poor wealth distribution, property, and inheritance. While Paul's theological arguments might not socially directly address "sugar daddy"

44. See West and Haddad, "Boaz as 'Sugar Daddy.'"

relationships in Cameroon because "sugar daddies" operate from a different worldview and value system than that assumed by Paul, he does provide a theological solution for dealing with the structural, cultural, and economic dimensions of how bodies function within the household of God. Concretely, the Cameroonian Church can help create educational systems where the female bodies within God's family are not compelled to seek assistance from "sugar daddies." The current socioeconomic system is creating a market for "sugar daddies;" only a paradigm shift in how the Cameroonian Church educational system operates will change things for economically vulnerable and marginalized female bodies within the Church. A case in point, church institutions can begin by providing educational programs that are affordable and accessible for socially and economically marginalized groups rather than simply maximizing their financial returns as they currently do in Cameroon. Many private educational institutions in Cameroon are under the control of church institutions. However, because tuition in these institutions is costly and unaffordable for poor, marginalized families, the children, especially girls, leave home and engage in "sugar daddy" relationships as a survival strategy, themselves at risk of sexually transmitted infections and mental health problems. The prioritization of education justice for vulnerable and impoverished women and girls will have crucial positive spillover effects on marginalized communities' social and economic fabric, not to mention social ostracism if what they do is deemed socially unacceptable.

The household of God is called to build allyship and solidarity across all liberated or freed bodies. This allyship and solidarity cohere with West's theological vision of a socially engaged scholarship by scholars who have intentionally stepped out of their academic ivory towers to connect with the lived realities of everyday readers of the Bible, with an aim for social transformation.[45] Martin Luther King's superb quote aptly characterizes such a vision of the household of God:

> We are tied together in the single garment of destiny, caught in an inescapable network of mutuality. And whatever affects one directly affects all indirectly. For some strange reason, I can never be what I ought to be until you are what you ought to be. This is the way God's universe is made; this is the way it is structured.[46]

45. West argues correctly that "ordinary Africans have their own resources for appropriating the Bible for their own purposes, including survival, resistance, liberation, and life" ("Reading Other-Wise," 57).

46. King, Jr., "Remaining Awake through a Great Revolution," 1968.

As mentioned earlier, for Paul, mutuality is the power structure of the family of God. Therefore, 1 Cor 6:12–20 can be used as a weapon "of survival, resistance, liberation, and life"[47] against systems of institutionalized oppression that have created economic inequities that often restrict girls' and women's autonomy.

Conclusion

Paul's theological reconceptualization of what Christian bodies are significantly impacts gender justice as it relates to women's bodies. Gender-justice activists and scholars should hold up 1 Cor 6:12–20 as an indictment of the brutal policing and objectification of women's bodies under Cameroonian patriarchal social norms and structures. Paul disrupts social conventions by forcing "eschatological hopes onto a pre-resurrection body."[48] An implication of Paul's moral reasoning in 1 Cor 6:12–20 is that the male and the female body have inherent value, and all bodies belong to God and will be resurrected. So, we are not done with the body at death. To single out the female body for policing and objectification "is to hold the creator in contempt."[49]

Education-justice activists can, in turn, invoke Paul's moral reasoning in their critique of socio-economic and cultural systems that push young girls into sexual relationships with older men who exploit their vulnerability and control their sexuality in inequitable "sugar daddy" arrangements. This line of reasoning collides with and disrupts the ideological underpinnings of sociocultural systems that create and perpetuate the sexual objectification and commodification of female bodies. The repudiation of patriarchal, masculinist convictions about the hierarchy of the body could function as a liberationist and countercultural force for raising critical gender justice awareness, particularly among women in Cameroonian rural communities who have internalized a broader societal objectification of the female body.

Paul's moral reasoning should also serve as an ethical framework for critiquing some of the many ways the female body has been constructed culturally and has continually been controlled and objectified through the male gaze. Women's bodies are equally significant and not

47. West, "Reading Other-Wise, "57

48. Martin, *The Corinthian Body*, 229.

49. Hays, *First Corinthians*, 108.

inconsequential. Belonging to God, women, like men, have choice and agency conferred to them by God. This view of the body and female agency directly opposes our culture's imagination of female bodies and traditional normative gender roles.

Bibliography

Bailey, Kenneth E. *Paul through Mediterranean Eyes*. Downers Grove, IL: IVP Academic, 2011.

Barrett, C. K. *A Commentary on the First Epistle to the Corinthians*. 2nd ed. Black's New Testament Commentaries. New York: Continuum, 1994.

Bartchy, S. Scott. "Power, Submission, and Sexual Identity among the Early Christians." In *Essays on New Testament Christianity*, edited by C. Robert Wetzel, 50–80. Cincinnati: Standard, 1978.

Blount, Brian K. *Cultural Interpretation: Reorienting New Testament Criticism*. Minneapolis: Fortress, 1995.

Braun, Willi. "Body, Character and the Problem of Femaleness in Early Christian Discourse." *RT* 9 (2002) 108–17.

Cameroon. "Advocates for Human Rights, Cameroon: Committee on the Elimination of Discrimination against Women 57th Session," 2014. http://www.theadvocatesforhumanrights.org/uploads/cameroon_cedaw_vaw_february_2014.pdf/.

Cameroon. "Sexual Violence Pervasive in Cameroon's Anglophone Regions." Aljazeera. https://www.aljazeera.com/news/2021/4/29/gender-based-violence-pervasive-in-Cameroons-anglophone-regions/.

Caragounis, Chrys C. "'Fornication' and 'Concession'?: Interpreting 1 Cor 7:1-7." In *The Corinthian Correspondence*, edited by Reimund Bieringer, 543–59. Bibliotheca Ephemeridum Theologicarum Lovaniensium 125. Leuven: Leuven University Press, 1996.

Cohick, Lynn H. "Women, Children, and Families in the Greco-Roman World." In *The World of the New Testament: Cultural, Social, and Historical Contexts*, edited by Joel B. Green and Lee Martin McDonald, 179–87. Grand Rapids: Baker Academic, 2013.

Conzelmann, Hans. *First Corinthians: A Commentary on the First Epistle to the Corinthians*. Translated by James W. Leitch. Hermeneia. Minneapolis: Fortress, 1988.

Craig, Jess. "Sexual Violence Pervasive in Cameroon's Anglophone Regions." *Aljazeera*. https://www.aljazeera.com/news/2021/4/29/gender-based-violence-pervasive-in-Cameroons-anglophone-regions/.

Deming, Will. *Paul on Marriage and Celibacy: The Hellenistic Background of 1 Corinthians 7*. Grand Rapids: Eerdmans, 2004.

———. "The Unity of 1 Corinthians 5–6." *JBL* 115 (1996) 289–312.

Farley, Margaret A. "Sexual Ethics." In *The Encyclopedia of Bioethics*, edited by Warren Thomas Reich, 5:2363–75. New York: Macmillan, 1995.

Fee, Gordon D. *The First Epistle to the Corinthians*. Rev. ed. New International Commentary on the New Testament. Grand Rapids: Eerdmans, 2014.

Fisk, Bruce N. "Πορνεύειν as Body Violation: The Unique Nature of Sexual Sin in 1 Corinthians 6:18." *New Testament Studies* 42(1996) 540-558.

Furnish, Victor P. *The Theology of the First Letter to the Corinthians*. New Testament Theology. New York: Cambridge Press, 1999.

Grindheim, Sigurd. "Wisdom for the Perfect: Paul's Challenge to the Corinthian Church (1 Corinthians 2:6–16)." *JBL* 121 (2002) 689–709.

Hays, Richard B. *First Corinthians*. Interpretation. Louisville: John Knox, 1997.

———. *The Moral Vision of the New Testament: A Contemporary Introduction to New Testament Ethics*. San Francisco: Harper San Francisco, 1996.

Hollinger, Dennis. *The Meaning of Sex: Christians Ethics and the Moral Life*. Grand Rapids, MI: Baker Academic, 2009.

hooks, bell. *Yearning: Race, Gender, and Cultural Politics*. Boston: South End, 1990.

Horsley, Richard A. "1 Corinthians: A Case Study of Paul's Assembly As an Alternative Society." In *Paul and Empire*, edited by Richard A. Horsley. 242–52. Harrisburg, PA: Trinity, 1997.

———. *Paul and Empire: Religion and Power in Roman Imperial Society*. Harrisburg, PA: Trinity, 1997.

———. "Rhetoric and Empire—and 1 Corinthians." In *Paul and Politics*, edited by Richard A. Horsley, 72–102. Harrisburg, PA: Trinity, 2000.

Isherwood, Lisa, and Elizabeth Stuart. *Introducing Body Theology*. London: Continuum, 1998.

Kanyoro, Musimbi R. A. *Introducing Feminist Cultural Hermeneutics: An African Perspective*. London: Continuum, 2002.

Keener, Craig S. *1–2 Corinthians*. New Cambridge Bible Commentary. New York: Cambridge University Press, 2005.

———. *The IVP Bible Background Commentary: New Testament*. Downers Grove, IL: InterVarsity, 2014.

Kwok, Pui-lan. *Postcolonial Imagination & Feminist Theology*. Louisville: Westminster John Knox, 2005.

Leclerc-Madlala, Suzanne. "Age-Disparate and Intergenerational Sex in Southern Africa: The Dynamics of Hypervulnerability." *AIDS* 22 Suppl 4 (2008).

Levine, Amy-Jill, and Marianne Blickenstaff, eds. *A Feminist Companion to Paul*. Feminist Companion to the New Testament and Early Christian Writings 6. London: T. & T. Clark, 2004.

Lightfoot, J. B. *Notes on the Epistles of Paul*. Peabody, MA: Hendrickson, 1995.

Luke, Nancy. "Confronting the 'Sugar Daddy' Stereotype: Age and Economic Asymmetries and Risky Sexual Behavior in Urban Kenya." *International Family Planning Perspectives* 31/1(2005) 6–14.

MacDonald, Margaret Y. "Virgins, Widows and Wives: The Women of 1 Corinthians 7." In *A Feminist Companion to Paul*, edited by Amy-Jill Levine with Marianne Blickenstaff, 148–68. Feminist Companion to the New Testament and Early Christian Writings 6. London: T. &T. Clark, 2004.

Martin, Dale B. *The Corinthian Body*. New Haven: Yale University Press, 1995.

———. "Paul without Passion: On Paul's Rejection of Desire in Sex and Marriage." In *Constructing Early Christian Families: Family as Social Reality and Metaphor*, edited by Halvor Moxnes, 201–15. New York: Routledge, 1997.

———. *Sex and the Single Savior: Gender and Sexuality in Biblical Interpretation*. Louisville: Westminster John Knox, 2006.

May, Alistair Scott. *The Body for the Lord: Sex and Identity in 1 Corinthians 5–7*. JSNTSup 278. New York: T. & T. Clark, 2004.

Økland, Jorunn. *Women in Their Place: Paul and the Corinthian Discourse of Gender and Sanctuary Space*. JSNTSup 269. London: T. & T. Clark, 2004.

Punt, J. "Postcolonial Biblical Criticism in South Africa: Some Mind and Road Mapping." *Neot* 37 (2003) 59–85.

Rosner, Brian S. *Paul, Scripture and Ethics: A Study of 1 Corinthians 5–7*. Arbeiten zur Geschichte des antiken Judentums und des Urchristentums 22. Leiden: Brill, 1994.

———. "Temple Prostitution in 1 Corinthians 6:12–20." *Novum Testamentum* 40 (1998) 336–51.

Segovia, Fernando F. *Decolonizing Biblical Studies: A View from the Margins*. Maryknoll, NY: Orbis, 2000.

Segovia, Fernando F., and Mary Ann Tolbert. *Reading from this Place*. Vol. 1: *Social Location and Biblical Interpretation in the United States*. Minneapolis: Fortress, 1995.

———. *Reading from this Place*: Vol. 2: *Social Location and Biblical Interpretation in Global Perspective*. Minneapolis: Fortress, 1995.

Takwa, Teke Johnson. "Violence Against the Women and Girl Children in Cameroon." *Central Bureau for the Census and Population Studies*, 2009. http://iussp2009. princeton.edu/papers/90344.

Thielman, Frank. *Paul and the Law: A Contextual Approach*. Downers Grove, IL: Inter-Varsity Press, 1994.

Tolbert, M. A. "When Resistance Becomes Repression: Mark 13:9–27 and the Poetics of Location." In *Reading from this Place: Social Location and Biblical Interpretation in Global Perspective*, edited by Fernando F. Segovia, and Mary Ann Tolbert, 2:331–46. Minneapolis: Fortress, 1995.

UNOCHA, "Gender-based Violence: Financial Independence and Economic Empowerment Key to Survivors' Recovery." 2019, https://www.unocha.org/story/ gender-based-violence-financial-independence-and-economic-empowerment-key-survivors-recovery/.

West, Angela. "Sex and Salvation: A Christian Feminist Study of 1 Corinthians 6:12—7:39." *MC* 29 (1987) 17–24.

West, Gerald O. *Biblical Hermeneutics of Liberation: Modes of Reading the Bible in the South African Context*. Pietermaritzburg: Cluster, 1991.

———. "Contextuality." In *The Blackwell Companion to the Bible and Culture*, edited by John F. A. Sawyer, 399–413. Blackwell Companions to Religion. Oxford: Blackwell, 2006.

———. "Mapping African Biblical Interpretation: A Tentative Sketch." In *The Bible in Africa: Transactions, Trajectories, and Trends*, edited by Gerald O. West and Musa W. Dube, 29–59. Leiden: Brill, 2000.

———, ed. *Reading Other-Wise: Socially Engaged Biblical Scholars Reading with Their Local Communities*. Semeia Studies 62. Atlanta: Society of Biblical Literature, 2007.

———. "Some Parameters of the Hermeneutical Debate in the South African Context." *JTSA* 80 (1992b) 3–13.

West, Gerald O., and Beverly G. Haddad. "Boaz as 'Sugar Daddy': Re-reading Ruth in the Context of HIV." *JTSA* 155 (2016) 137–56.

Wire, Antoinette Clark. "Response: The Politics of the Assembly in Corinth." In *Paul and Politics*, edited by Richard A. Horsley, 124–29. Harrisburg, PA: Trinity, 2000.

Yafeh-Deigh, Alice. *Paul's Sexual and Marital Ethics in 1 Corinthians 7: An African-Cameroonian Perspective*. Bible and Theology in Africa 22. New York: Lang, 2015.

13

From Tool of Imperialism to Tool of Patriarchy

The Early African Appropriation of the Bible in Southern Africa

Dora Rudo Mbuwayesango

Introduction

Gerald O. West has masterfully depicted the story of the reception and appropriation of the Bible by Africans in ways that were contrary to Western missionaries' intentions and expectations. He does this with a close reading of the writings of some key European explorers and missionaries who participated in the early stages of the process that resulted in the colonization of Southern Africa—the stages that led to the European claim and possession of African land. The Bible started as a hidden object to the Africans, to a "gaze," and finally to its appropriation by the Africans. As patriarchy is one among many of the interlocking systems of oppression in Africa, it is important to consider how the Bible is appropriated in the context of patriarchal oppression in Southern Africa, by looking at the example of early appropriation that West presents. Although West does not present an appropriation of the Bible by women, he still places them in the early stages of the initial African and Bible encounter.

African Women and the Bible

African women's first encounter with the Bible is situated in the early stages of the Bible's journey from the Colony into the Southern African interior in which there is a shift from the "embargoed Bible of the Dutch East Africa Company" to the Bible as "common property among the Europeans who travel into the interior."[1] West analyzes the period in which the Bible was first introduced to the BaTlhaping people in the 1700s, and aptly identified the stages in the changing status of the Bible in the precolonial period—"[b]efore European greed gazed upon the mineral wealth of the interior" when "the interior was firmly and fully in the control of the indigenous African peoples."[2] The status of the Bible shifts chronologically from "the bartered Bible" to "the covered Bible" to "the uncovered Bible" to "the probed Bible."[3] An African woman's first encounter is situated in the stage of the uncovered Bible. Prior to that, the encounter has been reflected in the interactions of male European trader-missionary travelers and African males (chiefs).

Since the Africans were fully and firmly in control of the interior in the precolonial period, the European visitors did not have the freedom to work among the African peoples without the permission of African chiefs. To demonstrate this fact, West uses the interaction between Chief Mateebe Mothibi and John Campbell when Campbell sought permission to instruct the people. When Campbell is impatient and wants to move on, Mmahutu, Mothibi's senior wife, is sent to relay a message from the chief, a message to persuade him to stay in the city and not venture into a nearby village to preach. West identifies significant revelations that can be gleaned from this African woman's early encounter with the Bible and its contents as presented by the missionaries:

> emerging evidence from this very encounter of a recognition that the Bible represents forms of power and knowledge, and that this power and knowledge can be manipulated by those that control it . . . signs that Africans are already bringing their own questions to the Bible, the beginning of a long process in which the Bible is prised from the hands of missionaries by indigenous

---

1. West, *The Stolen Bible*, 85.

2. West, *The Stolen Bible*, 3.

3. West, *The Stolen Bible*, 85–119.

alliances."[11] Given that many women and girls were followers of Shembe against the wishes of their husbands and fathers, it is doubtful that the prevalence of polygamy/polygyny was not a colonial missionary exaggeration, especially given the many accounts of conflict between women who wanted to follow Shembe and their men who tried to stop them. Joel Cabrita gives the examples: "Chief Msebenzie of the Lower Umzimkhulu complained in 1915 to the Magistrate that since 1913 Shembe has drawn 'women and children, (who) have gone away with these preachers to Ixopo and Durban for two and sometimes three months at a time, without the permission of their husbands and fathers'." Also, Chief Mthengeni of Eshowe District appeared in court for assaulting a Nazaretha preacher and in his defense, he claimed that the Nazaretha "induce our womenfolk to their kraal and they co-habit with them . . . we object to our women going to them but they persist." Despite these objections from men and chiefs, women continued to follow Shembe.[12] However, the fact remains that women comprised the majority of the members of Ibandla lamaNazaretha, as it was estimated that in the 1920s "women and children made as much as 95% in 1921 of the religious community."[13] Polygamy/polygyny started to increase in colonial times, especially in African Independent/Initiated churches (AIC). According to Adam Kuper, polygamy actually increased among the Nguni in the early colonial period.[14]

In pre-colonial Southern Africa, the practice was mostly a privilege of royalty and wealthy members of the society. In colonial and post-colonial Southern Africa the practice became widespread in AIC and ordinary people relatively. Even in the case of wife inheritance, there were rituals in which a widow or targeted inheritor would refuse the offer. In fact, with colonialism and the migration of Africans (young men) to towns or even other countries, the occurrence of a man having more than one family increased.

Following West's analysis that shows how Shembe appropriated the Bible for liberation, I would like to also show that he appropriated it in ways that emboldened African patriarchy. While his interpretive hermeneutic may be different from that of the missionary-Kolwa Christianity,

---

11. Muller, *Rituals of Fertility and the Sacrifice of Desire*, 27. The characterization of the prevalence of polygamy/polygyny in Southern Africa was an exaggeration for the colonial missionary agenda.

12. Cabrita, "A Theological Biography of Isaiah Shembe," 114–15.

13. Jarvis, "A Chief Is a Chief by the Women?," 57–75.

14. Kruper, "Traditions of Kinship, and Bridewealth in Southern Africa."

the outcome for women as it relates to patriarchy is the same. Isaiah Shembe's patriarchal appropriation of the Bible is reflected in his laws on marriage and adultery and virgin girls.

Laws on Marriage and Adultery

Marriage was one of the African institutions that both colonial governments and missionaries saw as needing civilizing. West demonstrates how Shembe, in his instructions concerning marriage and adultery for the Ibandla lamaNazaretha, uses the Bible in ways that depart from their biblical contexts to the advantage of women. He analyzes how Shembe reconstitutes (re-members) the Bible in his pronouncement about marriage and adultery. The end product is a view of marriage that is neither Nguni nor biblical. In this way, West seems to be arguing that the Bible is also a tool for dismantling patriarchy. But these pronouncements and laws need more scrutiny.

West notes that the pronouncement on marriage starts by focusing on the responsibility of the man in which Shembe uses a biblical text (Romans 7) that highlights how "the law of marriage is binding until, but not beyond, the death of her husband." In Shembe's recasting of the law, the man is prohibited from ever deserting his wife.[15] Shembe uses the same biblical allusion to address the responsibility of the wife but now it is conditional. A woman may leave her husband if it becomes unbearable. A process is then laid out for how such a woman can leave her husband. Her ability to leave an unbearable marriage situation rests on the decision of the elders. If she succeeds in convincing the elders and is allowed to leave her husband, then both should not remarry while the other is alive. However, there is another specific condition for the wife after she leaves her husband—the focus on the woman is the exercise of her sexuality after leaving her husband—not only is she not to remarry but she is forbidden from ever having sex. She is required to join "widows, and those who have foregone marriage and chosen celibacy in the name of the Lord."[16] While West notes that Shembe has a particular site in mind for the woman but not for the man, he does not explore the implications for the sexuality of men and women. Here Shembe is clearly endorsing the biblical and Nguni view of sexuality that gives

15. West, *Stolen Bible*, 276–77.
16. West, *Stolen Bible*, 272.

sexual autonomy to the males while female sexuality belongs to the Lord or to a husband. But if we are to take Shembe's use of the Bible in his reconstruction of the Ibandla lamaNazaretha community, should we not interrogate it so as to avoid reconstructing communities that recreate the oppressive systems rather than dismantle them?

West shows that Shembe's "remembering" of the Deuteronomy texts on adultery retains from the text "the rhetorical mode of instruction, general topic (marriage, divorce, adultery) and the communal context in which the matters are to be decided. What Shembe re-members is a focus on the man as the person primarily responsible for adultery." West concludes that, "throughout these teachings there seems to be a concern for providing protection and provision for the women."[17] But as it becomes much clearer in the laws, this comes at the expense of giving sexual autonomy and agency to the woman which seems to maintain the patriarchal hold on women and their bodies.

The same is the case with Shembe's instructions on polygamy. Shembe stipulates the requirement for a wife's permission for a man to take a second wife. If the wife gives permission, the responsibility of asking for permission from the elders is laid on the woman, which West interprets as according to "the woman substantial agency in the process. She should be asked, she should be given the opportunity to agree, and if she does so, it is she who should go to the elders, saying that it is her wish that husband take a second wife. If such is the case, Shembe continues, 'The church is not in a position to refuse if happens in this way'"[18] But this is an endorsement of the way patriarchy works—it is women who are put in the role making certain that male interests are met, especially in the institution of marriage. But even more, the insignificance of the woman's agency is evident in that the woman's refusal does not stop a man from marrying a second wife. That the interests of the wife are superseded by the man's wish for a second wife is underscored by the fact that the man is not required to give a reason for wanting a second wife.

A provision is designed to sidestep a woman's refusal to allow her husband to marry another wife—he must ask the elders three times within a protracted time and a range of congregational consultation. West sees the instructions as positive for a woman as the provision for the man not to use the cattle already at the homestead as economic protection for

17. West, *Stolen Bible*, 275.

18. West, *Stolen Bible*, 276.

the woman, and the location of the second wife elsewhere as spatial protection for the first wife. The requirement for cattle from elsewhere may simply reflect that polygamy was limited by a man's wealth.[19] The spatial location may not be for the protection of the first wife, but is influenced more by the concern for communal harmony (stories of strife between co-wives). West is closer to the truth in his analysis of how Shembe uses Genesis 16 and 21 in the instructions here: "Shembe instructs the man who marries a second wife to ensure that the kind of tension that develops between Ishmael and Isaac does not happen in their Nazarite community. Shembe proves wiser than Abraham, learning from him and instructing the man who takes a second wife to establish separate economic and familial space for each wife's household."[20] It seems that in a patriarchal society, women's interests are limited for the sake of communal interests while a man's interests are accommodated in the communal interest.

West analyzes Shembe's detailed discussion of adultery in "Histories and Laws" and highlights Shembe's use of the Bible in designing laws and regulations for the Ibandla lamaNazaretha.[21] He begins by noting how the introductory statement places the full weight for adultery on the man and not the woman and the reason for it—"as it is he who ought to use the most control in that matter because woman is but a child in bodily strength compared to a man's strength."[22] This declaration is validated by demonstrating why primary blame for adultery is placed on man and not woman by the use of overt and explicit citation of biblical text which West analyzes. The placement of blame primarily on the man is based on Shembe's re-constituting of the biblical text by mixing elements from Genesis 2, and 1 Timothy 2 to argue for the passivity of the woman in adulterous act because "(s)he is acted upon, and 'lacks the strength to hold herself back' but only 'if' [or 'when,' *uma*] the man succumbs to his (and, in Shembe's opinion, the principal) weakness."[23] West observes that Shembe's re-constituting of the text maintains the man-woman hierarchy but elevates the male's nurturing role. In this reconstitution, the male becomes both the mother and father of the woman. In sexuality, the woman is perpetually infantilized. Although, as West notes, Shembe does not

19. See above on the prevalence of polygamy in Southern Africa and exaggerations by missionaries.

20. West, The *Stolen* Bible, 278–89.

21. West, *The Stolen Bible*, 279–88.

22. West, *The Stolen Bible*, 279.

23. West, *The Stolen Bible*, 280.

cast the women as the temptresses but as the tempted who are incapable of resisting, this interpretation does not give women sexual autonomy and agency. In the use of a woman being "rib" to a specific man, Shembe argues that women do not have independent knowledge to which specific man they belong. Although West seems to interpret Shembe's statement, "Adam's stock rib upon rib" in a monogamous context,[24] thus limiting one rib to each man, it seems the phrase needs to be interpreted in the context of polygamy. As this is a case of adultery, the reference is in relation to a man luring another man's wife into adultery. Shembe posits that married women can respond to another man's advances because women do not have the capability to identify the man determined for them since they depend on men to tell them. That the context is about a woman already belonging to another man is underscored by Shembe's conclusion to this instruction on adultery, which makes explicit reference to the rib as already given to another man:

> Keep hold of yourself so that if [God] *has already given the rib to another of your spiritual brethren*, don't trouble it by saying, "Come my flesh," don't cause that rib to sin before God (1 Corinthians 7 v39). The law should be obeyed (Romans 7 v 4).[25]

Although the woman is not the cause of the congregational/social strife or sin, the supremacy of the man is endorsed and validated. Shembe's *re*-construction and use of the Bible do not seem to be designed to build up the esteem of the woman and promote female agency in the Nazarite community. It seems that women are sacrificed for the communal good which is also underscored in Shembe's appropriation of the story of Jephthah's daughter. As West concludes from his analysis of Shembe's use of 2 Tim 3:6, "For Paul women are inherently weak, for Shembe they are passive, they tend to remain the objects of men's volitions."[26] In both cases, however, the outcome is the same—the emboldening of patriarchy as men and women are not equal. Shembe's argument that women are passive is buttressed by the infantilization of women.

24. West, *The Stolen Bible,* 284.
25. West, *The Stolen Bible,* 286; italics are mine.
26. West, *The Stolen Bible,* 294.

Conclusion

Although Shembe is reconstituting the Bible in a way that is different from that of missionary Christianity, in the case of patriarchy, the outcome is the same—patriarchy is emboldened and not dismantled. In the relationship of men and women in the community, missionary Christianity characterizes women as weak and Shembe characterizes them as passive. In both characterizations, women are not granted autonomy and agency in liberating. As the Bible is inherently imperial and patriarchal ideologically, it seems there is a need to interrogate how the Bible continues to be a tool of imperialism and patriarchy, especially in its iconic appropriation in contemporary societies in Southern Africa.

Bibliography

Cabrita, Joel M. "A Theological Biography of Isaiah Shembe, c. 1870–1935." Phd Diss., University of Cambridge, 2008.

Jarvis, Lauren V. "A Chief Is a Chief by the Women?: The Nazaretha Church, Gender, and Traditional Authority." *Journal of African History* 56 (2015) 57–75.

Kuper, Adam. "Traditions of Kinship, and Bridewealth in Southern Africa." *Anthropology in Southern Africa* 39 (2016) 267–80. http://eprints.lse.ac.uk/68966/1/Kuper_Traditions%20of%20kinship_2017.pdf/.

Muller, Carol Ann. *Rituals of Fertility and the Sacrifice of Desire: Nazarite's Performance in South Africa.* Chicago: University of Chicago Press, 1999.

West, Gerald O. *The Stolen Bible: From Tool of Imperialism to African Icon.* BIS 144. Leiden: Brill, 2016.

(No) Laughing Matter and (No) Looking Back!?

Remembering Lot's Wife and Genesis 19:12–29

Kenneth N. Ngwa

Introduction

For Gerald West, biblical interpretation is a work of contestation that is developed in relation to theory, methodology, and exegetical outcomes. West has devoted his scholarship to theorizing African biblical hermeneutics, developing a methodology, and interpreting biblical texts for the sake of liberation. This work is embodied particularly in Contextual Bible Study (CBS). As defined in its manual, CBS is a cyclical process with three intersecting steps:

> The Bible study process begins with analysis of the local context (See), and then re-reads the Bible to allow the biblical text to speak to the context (Judge), and then moves to action as we respond to what God is saying (Act). Social analysis enables us to understand our reality; re-reading the Bible enables us to judge whether our reality is as God intends it to be; and our plan of action enables us to work with God to change our reality. This process is an ongoing process, it is repeated, as each action leads to further reflection (See), etc. This is the cycle of praxis.[1]

---

1. The Ujamaa Center for Community Development & Research, *Doing Contextual*

What interests me in this definition is the double role of "See": First, it focuses on the lived experiences of the interpreter. Second, it evokes an interpretive flow of meaning ("further reflection"). This double formulation and role of "See" implies that context is more than an interpretive receptacle for meaning, more than a form of indigenization; instead, context is a form of intersectional genre analysis that deploys sociological, literary, and ethical theories for the purpose of understanding and engaging in the work of biblical interpretation as a struggle for liberation.

Contextual questions, much like genre-related questions, address the final (written) form of a text, or associated form-critical issues in oral settings. But genre, like context, also addresses the social currency of communication: for whom is a particular genre intelligible and why? How do power, gender, and authority function in classifications of texts into specific genres? That is, the genre is interested in more than the literary features of a (con)text, the relation between form and content, or the classification of (con)texts. To pursue this line of inquiry is to move beyond understanding context as a mode of historical (diachronic) or contemporaneous (synchronic) distribution of meaning; it is to move beyond the noun (context) to the adjective (contextual), and understand that move as a trope of interpretation (the second "See" of CBS).

This understanding of context is informed by Carolyn Miller's argument that genre is how societies develop conventions for acting together. For Miller, this understanding of genre "does not lend itself to taxonomy, for genres change, evolve, and decay; the number of genres current in any society is indeterminate and depends upon the complexity and diversity of the society."[2] Miller provides five features of this understanding of genre: (1) genre as a conventional category of discourse and action that acquires meaning from a situation and the social context in which the situation arose; (2) genre as meaningful action that is interpreted by rules situated at high levels of symbolic meaning; (3) genre as distinct from form, and constituted by a fusion of "lower-level" forms of action within a hierarchy; (4) as recurrent patterns of discourse and enablers in the constitution of the substance of cultural life; and (5) genre as a rhetorical means of mediating private intention and social exigence, "connecting the private with the public, the singular with the recurrent."[3]

Bible Study, 4.

2. Miller, "Genre," 163.

3. Miller, "Genre," 163.

A few years after the founding of the Ujamaa Center that houses CBS research and work in 1989, West—trained in historical-critical approaches to biblical interpretation—published an article on relationships between different modes of reading the Bible. West started his article with a striking statement: "Something is missing in contextual biblical hermeneutics in South Africa." West then named what he saw as missing: ". . .the voice(s) of 'the people' or what I have called 'the ordinary reader' is missing." West's aim in the article was to bring together the "trained reader" and the "ordinary reader."[4] The discussion unfolded around the relationship between these two categories of readers, and West emphasized that the distinctive element that separates the two is that ordinary readers read the Bible pre-critically, while trained readers do critical or post-critical readings. In doing work with communities of ordinary readers, West included the See–Judge–Act process and the layers of reading that accompany it: reading the world behind the text, reading the text, and reading the world in front of the text.[5] For West, the work of CBS requires a particular kind of biblical scholar: a socially engaged biblical scholar. But the work begins with, and ultimately belongs to, the interpreting community's quadruple gathering (1) around their experiences, (2) around the details of the biblical text (in its literary form), (3) around the social world behind the biblical text, and finally (4) back again to the world of the interpreting community.[6]

The transformative work that West envisioned coming out of this approach recognized the tension between "colonized consciousness" and "critical consciousness," the power dynamics and differentials between trained readers and ordinary readers, and a willingness for trained readers to learn from below.[7] This invitation for an epistemological turn to the subaltern, and the methodology associated with such a turn, is part of West's own decolonial turn in postcolonial hermeneutics. West speaks of "re-membering" as "an attempt to capture the creative agency of indigenous Africans."[8] Using Isaiah Shembe, whose engagement with the Bible is located outside of the official structures and ideologies of colonial and missionary Christianity, West examines how African "re-membering" engagement with the Bible is simultaneously contested

4. West, "The Relationship," 87.

5. West, "The Relationship," 95–98.

6. West, "Reading the Bible," 244–45.

7. West, "The Relationship."

8. West, "Reading Shembe," 160.

and creative—a process that draws on African cultural, linguistic, and patriarchal systems, oral practices, and storytelling. As part of a decolonial turn, West calls for engagement with notions of class within African cultural systems. Using the works of Gunther Wittenberg, Makhosazana Nzimande, and Hulisani Ramantswana, West argues that in addition to analyses of culture, race, and religion (ATRs and African Independent Churches), there is a need for a fourth stage: class analyses in both the ancient biblical and African cultural contexts.[9] A full development of West's work is found in *The Stolen Bible*. Thus, although the CBS process revolves around three categories (See–Judge–Act), West's scholarship has in fact included a fourth: "re-membering."

Lot's Wife as a Communal Monument (Body): A CBS Analysis

The narrative about the destruction of Sodom and Gomorrah in Genesis 19 begins with the divine messengers announcing impending violence, which appears to the indigenous characters (Lot's sons-in-law) as a laughing matter (ויהי כמצחק בעיני חתניו), Gen 19:14. When the story concludes, one of the indigenous characters (Lot's wife) becomes a pillar of salt (ותהי נציב מלח: Gen 19:26). How does a story of laughter become a story of violence, of anxious movement, incestuous genealogy, and the memorialization of one of its indigenous characters as a pillar of salt? From a decolonial perspective, the laughter is the embodied indigenous response to the ideology of destruction; the turning of Lot's wife embodies resistance to marginalization; and the salt signifies the embodied indigenous response to the actual destruction. Haunting these three realities—laughter, turning, and salt—is the reality of (forced) migration/displacement, as Lot and part of his family are physically removed from the city and set on their way to another city. In contrast to that colonially-induced migration/movement, Lot's wife stands—literally and figuratively—as a monument. That is, her turning around and becoming a pillar/monument of salt are not simply iconic scenes at the end of the violent assault on the community; her actions and positionality also function as persistent, semantic tropes of resilience and ultimate liberation.

The story of Sodom and Gomorrah has received deserved and significant attention in African biblical hermeneutics, especially since the 1990s. Some of that attention has been shaped and guided through

---

9. West, "A Decolonial (Re)turn," 530–33.

the work of West and the Ujaama Center and its series of Contextual Bible Studies (CBS).[10] The story's depiction of devastating violence—on humans and city alike—leaves many interpretive gaps, discrepancies, and traumas that require transgressive and transformative readings. The ethical, hermeneutical, and exegetical impetus is to name and engage the structural and ideological traumas of the text, especially on marginalized characters. Thus, Robert Wafula has argued that the divine judgment on the city also strikes at the family of Lot, repeatedly portrayed as unequal to Abraham. The devastating effects of such narrative and ideological marginalization are especially borne by Lot's wife and daughters. L. Juliana Claassens has further examined the impact of that story on Lot's daughters.[11]

Paul Zeleza has argued that some forms of diaspora studies represent a rejection of old notions of settled identity around nation, race, class, and gender, and an embrace of cosmopolitanism and a celebration of the "energies of multiple subjectivities."[12] These multiple subjectivities of historic diasporas are organized around four sections: (a) a process, (b) a condition, (c) a space, and (d) a discourse: "the continuous processes by which a diaspora is made, unmade, and remade, the changing conditions in which it lives and expresses itself, the places where it is molded and imagined, and the contentious ways in which it is studied and discussed."[13] The act of turning around and being immortalized as a pillar of salt, therefore, invites consideration of Lot's wife as embodying these layers of identity formation and resistance against colonial and imperial systems of erasure, marginalization, and the privileging of single narratives.

These issues of process, conditions, spaces, and discourses are integral to the story of Sodom and Gomorrah. In one of the most nauseating acts of attempted appeasement in the Bible, Lot promised to "bring out" (יָצָא) and give his daughters to a violent mob that was threatening to abuse his guests (Gen 19:8). The offer, as gruesome as it is, does not satisfy the marauding band, who threatens to break the door of the house. To save Lot, the angels bring (בּוֹא) him into the house (Gen 19:10)—a house

---

10. West, Zwane, and Van der Walt, "From Homosexuality," 5–23; West and Van der Walt, "A Queer," 113–15.

11. Wafula, "Violence and Lessons," 201–6; Claassens, "Excavating Trauma Narratives," 115–27.

12. Zeleza, "Rewriting African Diaspora," 35.

13. Zeleza, Rewriting African Diaspora," 41.

occupied by indigenes and migrant residents. As violence threatens to consume the entire community, Lot and his family are brought out (Gen 19:16, 17), left outside the city (Gen 19:16), and told not to look back or stand anywhere (Gen 19:17). Somewhere just outside the city stands a narrative and embodied monument (female body/pillar of salt) that is missing in plain sight. Lot's wife's body is written into apparent non-existence, or written into visible erasure, by being portrayed as an artifact of disobedience (she disobeyed the command not to look back)—the body that fell victim to the ideology of violence and erasure. Ironically, her embodied erasure—supposedly an example of what not to do—is visible only to those who, like her, look back. Therein lies the paradox of her presence within the story and its interpretive history, and the power of her presence to be seen otherwise—to be seen in spite of its being portrayed by the violent colonial ideology as an emblem of disobedience, an emblem of the unseeable. By turning around and looking back, she not only exits the incestuous logics of colonialism, which continues to attach themselves to Lot and his daughters, even after they left the city (Gen 19: 30–38), but she also counters the blinding act of boundary enforcement that animates "indigenous" and "alien" relations (Gen 19:9–11).

Elements of the See–Judge–Act theory of CBS are discernable in the details of the narrative. For example,

a. The cities of Sodom and Gomorrah are already subjected to "seeing" by visiting men/angels (Gen 18:16) and by the Lord (Gen 18:21). When the men arrive and speak seriously about impending destruction, Lot's sons-in-law think that such discourse is a laughing matter (Gen 19:14). In portraying the indigenous characters (the sons-in-law) as unaware of the impending doom, does the story seek to ridicule them as naïve, or does it rather portray them as representative of the unthinkable nature and act of the disaster? Indigenous laughter unfolds as a form of resistance to colonial and imperial erasure.

b. Between sunrise and sunrise (Gen 19:15, 23)—that is, in one day's time, a colonial restructuring of sound and genealogy—Lot and his family (without his sons-in-law) are urged, commanded, and physically removed from the city about to be destroyed, to a small city that apparently stands a chance of surviving the devastation. Does the small city represent a temporary safety space, the custodian of memory based on imperial patronage (compassion), or does the small city stand as a signifier of decolonial resistance against imperial marginalization?

    c. In decolonial work, devastation itself becomes an artifact of memory: Lot's wife looks back and becomes a pillar of salt, and Abraham witnesses the smoke rising as though from a furnace. Does Lot's wife represent the disobedient wife or does the pillar of salt represent a monument in honor of the woman who would not leave without her people? Perhaps, she is both: she disobeys the imperial command not to look back, and she becomes a hero for the inside group (for indigenous epistemology and methodology). Her looking back becomes a signifier of resistance against imperial singularizing constructions of liberation narratives—narratives in which only a few survive.

In Gen 19:12, Lot is instructed to bring out all his relatives. This command echoes the demand from the men who had arrived at Lot's house (Gen 19:5). Lot performs the first act of "going out"—he informs his relatives of the impending violence/destruction, but his sons-in-law think it is a laughing matter (Gen 19:14). That this town of laughter was about to be turned into a place of destruction narratively anticipates the golden calf story in Exod 32. But more immediately, this laughter anticipates Abraham's journey to Moriah where he will bring laughter (Isaac) into direct confrontation with violence/death at the altar. And as with Lot's wife, so with Sarah: they are both left behind; they are not a part of that journey towards the sacrifice of laughter. Given the "failures" of these "departure/diasporic" stories to create one-directional movements, might the stories also be beckoning the need to envision "return" as a restoration of indigenous laughter where colonial and patriarchal death has occurred? Here, the more useful antecedent kin to Lot's wife might not be Sarah, but Hagar: the one who moved from seeing God to hearing God, through her son, Ishmael. Lot and Hagar are introduced in the story at unique moments: when the migrant/diasporic Sarah is barren (Gen 11:30–31 and Gen 16:1); that is, when laughter is impossible. To remember Lot's wife is to remember indigenous laughter—theoretical, methodological, and exegetical laughter—at the absurdity of colonial and patriarchal machinations and processes that extract (a select few) from larger ecologies of their existence, and then subject those ecologies to devastation. To laugh against (in the face of) such ideologies of erasure is to infuse revitalization where destruction has taken over.

To remember Lot's wife is to hermeneutically and epistemological-ly encounter and challenge colonial and indigenous violence, through contextual analyses in which context functions as a literary and cultural genre. Ron Eyerman argues that "as opposed to psychological or physical trauma, which involves a wound and the experience of great emotional anguish by the individual, cultural trauma refers to a dramatic loss of identity and meaning, a tear in the social fabric, affecting a group of people that has achieved some measure of cohesion."[14] Thus, personal experience of the traumatic event is not necessary for participation in cultural trauma, which is transmitted through mediation—artistic representations and interpretations, through ritual practices and symbols, stories, tales, fables, and even riddles, and through monuments, etc.—that is, genre as a mechanism of social interaction, cohesion, and survival. Cultural trauma develops and sustains its presence and power through ongoing narration, not just through the initial act or wound. Thus, although Lot's wife does not succumb to the violence visited on her community, she nevertheless bears the communal trauma unleashed by the violence, trauma to which she responds by turning and becoming a monument of salt.

Lot's Wife as a Communal Monument/Body:
A Specter of Post/Colonial Trauma

In his fictional autobiographical narrative, *Pillar of Salt*, Albert Memmi wrote:

> I am amazed at not being afraid; but habit gives one courage, and I have actually watched for my self-discovery for a long time: I am dying through having turned back to look at my own self. It is forbidden to see oneself, and I have reached the end of discovering myself. God turned Lot's wife into a pillar of salt—is it possible for me to survive my contemplation of myself?[15]

Similarly, in *Forgetting Lot's Wife*, Martin Harries writes that "the story of Lot's wife evokes things we may feel we cannot not know about—sex, remembrance, the spectacle of mass death—and yet it estranges them."[16] Harries works within the field of psychoanalyses and trauma studies, with

14. Eyerman, *Cultural Trauma*, 2.
15. Memmi, *Pillar of Salt*, 335.
16. Harries, *Forgetting Lot's Wife*, 6.

a focus on the relation between trauma and image. Lot's wife, then, as a visual representation, symbolizes an allegory of "universal trauma only partly hidden in the every day of sight; Lot's wife's refusal to recognize a blind spot, a place where she cannot look, marks the trauma of vision's limits."[17] Might Lot's wife then represent something of the "necessity of forgetting"? Harries ultimately reads Lot's wife as a reflection of modernity's encounter with three things: watching disaster, retrospection, and masochism. Harries asks: "What happens when retrospection begins to look like, to feel like, masochism, a choice to damage the self?"[18]

Self-damaging retrospection is possible within the story only if the prohibition not to look is considered valid and credible. But if that prohibition is colonial, then the choice to look back, the choice of retrospection can only be liberative. In that sense, the image of Lot's wife embodies both the risk of colonial defiance and the hope for restorative work.

Writing about the role of the body (human and social) in understanding the effects of the Chinese Cultural Revolution (1966–1976), Arthur Kleinman and Joan Kleinman identify three "paradigmatic symbols"— dizziness, exhaustion, and pain—that "created an interpersonal space of suffering in which bodily complaint indirectly expressed (remembered, directly experienced) social distress and shared criticism."[19] Dizziness represented a medical condition of dis-ease (or lack) related to health and well-being, but also a cultural signal of imbalance. Exhaustion represented vital signs of having reached the end of a tough process of political revolution; the life force (qi) had been drained. And pain, for its part, represented in muscle aches, backaches, headaches, and cramps, signaled the turmoil of revolution, linking personal anatomy to the social body. Accordingly, "the exhausted, painful, and vertiginous body—the body that had lost its social force and moral face—became the grounds for negotiations over jobs, time, responsibilities, and resources."[20]

17. Harries, *Forgetting Lot's Wife*, 18.

18. Harries, *Forgetting Lot's Wife*, 20–21. Harries goes on to argue that Lot's wife might represent a "willingness . . . to look back when you know that looking will destroy you." I am unwilling to follow Harries' assumption that looking back will destroy; it might not. And I will in fact argue that Lot's wife—memory of her—represents something more than the trauma of the limits of sight; she forges an image that survives erasure and the trauma of the end. She does not refuse to die; she refuses not to live, she refuses erasure.

19. Kleinman and Kleinman, *How Bodies Remember*, 174–75.

20. Kleinman and Kleinman, *How Bodies Remember*, 176.

Beyond individual or personal memory, there is "collective memory,"[21] understood as a social bonding phenomenon, just like language, culture, cuisine, sports, war, and education. Collective memory contemplates the credibility of "other" memories and the inevitable interaction that learning to remember produces between memory partners. In *How Societies Remember*, Paul Connerton explores how two forms of social memory—commemorative ceremonies and bodily practices—inform the constructions and structuring of social identity and behavior. Drawing on ritual studies and psychoanalysis to interpret major political events in Europe—the French Revolution and Nazism—Connerton argues that, as part of commemorative ceremonies, ritual behavior is best understood in three ways. First, from a psychoanalytical standpoint, rites are a form of "symbolic representation" of struggle—personal or collective—which the rite indirectly references and then denies. Second, from a sociological standpoint, ritual behavior is best understood as "a form of quasi-textual representation" intended to communicate shared values and reduce in-group dissensions (irrespective of variations, evident in carnivals). Third, from a historical standpoint, rites cannot be adequately understood in terms of "internal structure" alone. Rather, they are a creative process of invention in response to external realities.[22] With respect to bodily practices, Connerton speaks of "habitual memory"—the way in which "the past is sedimented in the body" and then called upon for use without any need for representational activity.[23] The body learns to perform certain social etiquettes—handshakes, bowing down or kneeling, table manners, dress codes, sitting or standing positions, etc.—all of which become habitual, that is, "normative" in specific occasions. Yet, these habits of the body are more than technical skills, more than mental predispositions, and more than a sign of language: "Habit is knowledge and a remembering in the hands and in the body; and in the cultivation of habit it is our body which 'understands.'"[24]

What is it that Lot's wife understands when she defiantly looks back? And what is it that we understand when we look back when we remember her? Sigmund Freud's work on trauma was attuned to biblical historical-critical scholarship and its focus on narrative fragments in the biblical text, and forging those fragments into traditions about possible

21. Halbwachs, *The Collective Memory*.

22. Connerton, *How Societies Remember*, 48–52.

23. Connerton, *How Societies Remember*, 72.

24. Connerton, *How Societies Remember*, 95.

distinct communities. In light of that methodology, Freud made his her-meneutical move: narrative gaps and discrepancies in the biblical text are covert evidence of historical processes of violence and fragmentation. He then postulated an analogy between narrative violence and real violence: ". . .the distortion of a text is not unlike a murder. The difficulty lies not in the execution of the deed but in doing away with the traces."[25] In *Unclaimed Experience*, Cathy Caruth sets parameters for exploring Freud's theories in relation to violent experiences that are at once intimate and yet unclaimed (and unclaimable, e.g., the holocaust, genocide, slavery) by the traumatized subject. For Caruth, trauma experience constitutes "the un-witting reenactment of an event that one cannot simply leave behind"[26]—a process that compels traumatized persons and communities to negotiate the relation between knowing and unknowing in a compulsory man-ner. Caruth rereads Freud's take on Tasso's romantic epic, *Gerusalemme Liberata*, in which Tancred unwittingly wounds his disguised beloved, Clorinda, whose soul is imprisoned in a tree. In this exploration of trau-ma, it is not just that Tancred (repeatedly) wounds his lover, but also that the voice of the wounded Clorinda speaks back to Tancred as "the moving and sorrowful *voice* that cries out, a voice that is paradoxically released *through the wound*."[27] Here, Caruth implies a profound, simultaneously re-petitive but also creative, process of identity formation and consciousness that binds Tancred and Clorinda together, and that opens up the space for exploring the relation between traumatic experience and narrative, the wound and the voice. It is a psychosomatic framing of trauma applied to literary theory and epistemology.

This story of the wound and the voice, as well as the truth or reality to which it points, describes a traumatic encounter and the experience of ongoing survival, akin to the story, embodiment, and signification of Lot's wife. "At the core of these stories," Caruth writes, "is thus a kind of double telling, the oscillation between a *crisis of death* and the correla-tive *crisis of life*: between the story of the unbearable nature of an event and the story of the unbearable nature of its survival."[28] It is not just that Tancred ought not to have inflicted violence on his beloved; it is also that, having been so wounded and killed, Clorinda ought not to have survived, independent of the expectations and machinations of her killer.

---

25. Freud, *Moses*, 52.

26. Caruth, *Unclaimed Experience*, 2.

27. Caruth, *Unclaimed Experience*, 2; italics original.

28. Caruth, *Unclaimed Experience*, 7; italics original.

And yet, both unexpected realities become realities; a different kind of history is set in motion, in which both unexpected realities constitute the very fabric of the story: Clorinda is unexpectedly (and unacceptably) killed, but she also unexpectedly survives in the voice and speaks back to Tancred from the quintessential landscape and site of erasure (war). Such analyses open up the possibility for postcolonial and decolonial repositioning. It is possible for "*history* to arise where *immediate understanding* may not."[29] Lot's wife may represent the possibility that history may yet emerge where understanding may not.

Lot's Wife Turned Around

Devastation is visited upon the cities. The catastrophe is so immense that its origins, causes, rationale, and possibilities of survival include reflection on the presence, attention, and voice of the divine sovereign. The crisis accelerates quickly. Lot's Wife and daughters have just survived an assault on their home and the grotesque willingness by Lot to offer *his* daughters (his language is specific: "I have . . .") to be assaulted. The city is already in uproar and the crimes of war and violence are everywhere. Then there is an emergency plan!? Get out?! How is that possible? The visiting angels provide a pathway: a literal pathway and a narrative (perhaps imperial orthodox) pathway to safety in a neighboring village (assuming that hospitality is available where Lot and his family are ordered to go). Somehow, the narrative suggests—or expects—that the survivors simply move on without looking back. Most do. But not Lot's wife. In Gen 19:26, we read: "But Lot's wife, behind him, looked back, and she became a pillar of salt" (NRSV). For unstated reasons, she looks back (Gen 19:26) in direct contradiction to the command given in Gen 19:17. She disobeyed the orders governing this devastating scene. Does she have a future? Does her local community have a future? She becomes a monument of salt. Is that her liberation? Is that her legacy? Is that ultimately the legacy and the liberation work of the community? As Lowell Gallagher argues, ". . .between the two scenes of imminent expectation, between hope and dread, stands Lot's wife, fully accomplished, it appears, as the figure of a precipitous eschaton."[30] That eschaton—what she became—is connected to her initial act of looking back.

29. Caruth, *Unclaimed Experience*, 11; italics original.

30. Gallagher, *Sodomscapes*, 21.

Specifically, I am informed by the literary, socio-rhetorical, and political context of Gen 19 in the depictions of identity, exile, and violence within the patriarchal and matriarchal narratives; and I am compelled by the struggle for identity, resilience, survival, and imagined flourishing that has animated a way of being among Anglophones in Cameroon since the outbreak of violence with state power in 2016. Gareth Browne's description of the crisis in *Foreign Policy* is apt:

> When Anglophones initially took to the streets in 2016, talk of independence for Cameroon's Anglophone regions was limited. Protesters were driven by a range of everyday grievances. They were frustrated with the inflexible school curriculum that privileged Cameroon's French-speaking majority and kept English speakers at a disadvantage, and they were tired of a legal system that made justice harder to get for English speakers because it was dominated by Francophones.
>
> That changed in late 2017, when President Paul Biya's government responded to nonviolent protests with force. Cameroonian security forces fired live ammunition from low-flying helicopters into crowds, and videos circulated of them beating demonstrators on the ground. The signal was clear: the government in Yaounde had no intention of entertaining Anglophone demands.[35]

As the violence has spiraled on, kidnappings have become a regular occurrence. In 2017, both of my parents were kidnapped from their home and threatened with death unless we (the children) paid a ransom. When we secured the release of our parents and moved them to a more secure location away from their home, they managed to bear that displacement for a couple of weeks. Then they decided to return to their home, in defiance of the obvious threat to their lives. For me, they embodied a refusal to leave their fellow community members behind; they literally and metaphorically turned around. Although not a recommendation for all who find themselves in similar circumstances, their decision to return and be present has been a source of material and epistemological boost for those who could not afford to pick up and leave. Instead, turning around signifies the daily strategies of resilience and hope-filled work that defy the forces of marginalization, erasure, and singularization. That is how I understand Lot's wife: her subjectivity (what she became), her strategy ("from behind"), and her epistemology (she looked).

35. Browne, "Cameroon's Separatist Movement."

Remembering Lot's Wife

Remembering Lot's wife therefore is akin to CBS work: it involves turning away from the histories and trajectories of colonial patronage, looking at indigenous epistemologies that support and enhance communal flourishing, and committing oneself to the task of revitalization. As the story unfolds, Lot and his family are hesitant about leaving the city but are physically removed from the home (homeland) they know, placed outside the city, and asked to go to the hills. The physical act of "bringing out" (יצא) Lot, and part of his family, from the city recalls the demands of the violent mob to "bring out" the visiting men (Gen 19:6) and Lot's offer to "bring out" his daughters for abuse (Gen 19:8). In this convoluted and layered episode/story of violence and marginalization, the human/divine emotion evoked is no longer laughter but compassion (Gen 19:16). It is an emotion that mitigates against "othering," against alienation and marginalization.

After being brought out of the city, Lot refuses to go to the mountains and negotiates access to a small city. The human/divine emotion evoked here is no longer laughter or compassion, but human grace/favor, and steadfast love (Gen 19:19). The prohibition is against looking back (Gen 19:17). For reasons that are unstated, but might be conjectured, the men on a mission to destroy the city command the fleeing survivors not to look (back); not to see. This is anti-CBS; it is hermeneutics that does not take seriously the reality of life being altered as a result of the ongoing violence. And that is precisely what Lot's wife dares to challenge; she, in fact, looks back.

Remembering Laughter: A CBS Decolonial Approach

In his commentary on this text, Gordon Wenham argues that "by looking back, Lot's wife contravened the instruction not to look back in Gen 19:17. By disobeying a God-given instruction, she forfeited her God-given salvation. In looking back, she identified herself with the damned town." And then, in a staggering form of interpretive misogyny, Wenham speaks empathetically for Lot but condemns Lot's wife and their daughters:

> It is not so much his bereavement that evokes sympathy but the fact that he was a husband who did not enjoy whole-hearted support from his wife. While the narrator does not condone Lot's lapses, he helps the reader appreciate a contributory cause

and suggests why his daughters had few scruples about their behavior. Like their mother, they too had imbibed a love of Sodom and its attitudes.[36]

Danna Fewell and David Gunn, by contrast, argue that in this patriarchal story—("the narrator . . . is recounting a man's story")—Lot is able to offer hospitality even though in actuality, his wife, much like Sarah and servants, likely prepared the food; that is, Lot's wife and servants are the architects of hospitality. So, "Lot's wife is visible only by inference."[37] The inference is a function of her subsumed status, agency, and presence in the story, as exemplified in the fact that the command of the angels is framed in male-gendered language—directed to Lot. Furthermore, how exactly she became a pillar of salt is unclear. Fewell and Gunn wonder—given the role of the divine in destroying the city— whether the narrator is "just a little nervous about signaling divine responsibility."[38] What then does she represent? Might Lot's wife have turned towards the indigenous epistemology of laughter that defined the city before the invasion of violence?

Within the larger narrative arc of Genesis, laughter is already established as a trope of incredulity about imperial messages. When God's visiting messengers (en route to Sodom) promise that Sarai would become pregnant at an advanced age, Abraham falls down in laughter (Gen 17:17); in response to Abraham's laughter, God insists that Sarah's son shall be called laughter/Isaac (Gen 17:19, 21). Later, when Sarah hears the same divine promise of a child, she laughs (Gen 18:12), followed by the divine dialogue with Sarah about laughter (Gen 18:13–14). God's concluding words to Sarah affirm her laughter ("Oh yes, you did laugh") and transition the reader from the household of Abraham and Sarah to the household of Lot and his wife in Sodom. The theme/character of laughter will return in the birth of Isaac and the expulsion of Ishmael (Gen 21:1–20), and in the Akedah, the binding of Isaac/laughter (Gen 22).

Given this narrative history, it is unsurprising that when the messengers send Lot to inform his sons-in-law of impending disaster, we are told that the sons-in-law (indigenous characters) perceive Lot to be joking; the idea is laughable but laughter is also the body's reaction to the enormity of the toll that such imperial messages (of patronage) my

---

36. Wenham, *Genesis*, 59.

37. Fewell and Gunn, *Gender, Power*, 64.

38. Fewell and Gunn, *Gender, Power*, 64.

take on the subject addressed. Dan Rickett wonders why: "Why would they believe Lot to be joking?" and proceeds to argue that perhaps the sons-in-law do not necessarily view Lot to be a jester; perhaps they "are the real foils in the story. Perhaps their negative response is in contrast to Lot's positive response to the messenger's warning."[39] A decolonial approach would move differently: the sons-in-law are not the foils for a story about the ruin; they are set up to be the foils in this imperial story. They function as an ancient version of victim blaming. In this light, Rickett's compassionate reading of Lot's hesitation to leave (effective resistance to the angel's commands) in Gen 19:16 should be equally applied to the sons-in-law: "Lot's hesitance is actually an act of compassion and forbearance which would be quite commendable."[40]

What about Lot's wife? What about her decision to turn around, from behind Lot, and look? Wenham points out that Gen 18:16—19:28 is "arranged palistrophically so that the second half of the story is a mirror image of the first."[41] In this arrangement, the turning point of the story takes place inside Lot's house. That turning point is driven by the angels' monologue, which effectively seals the fate of the city and commands Lot and his family to leave.[42] The story, however, moves beyond Lot's household and includes the entire city; that was the initial intention of the divine—to investigate the city, not a single household. In fact, the preceding narratives repeatedly portray Lot settling in the city—at the gate (Gen 19:1), where legal and cultural matters would be handled. Progressively from Gen 13 onward, Lot has gradually settled in Sodom; that is, he has become a resident and an important leader.

Remembering Salt

A UK-based company, Hoxton Street Monster Supplies, produces and sells salt made from tears of laughter. "This exquisite salt has a fiendishly spicy flavour, and is by far the safest way to experience the peculiar pleasure of human laughter. Collected only from sincerely amused humans, it is one of our rarest salts." The production process boasts a combination

39. Rickett, *Separating*, 51, 52.

40. Rickett, *Separating*, 53.

41. Wenham, *Genesis*, 41.

42. Wenham, *Genesis*, 42. Wenham notes other concentric themes/cycles that govern preceding and succeeding narratives, including the narratives around the garden of Eden, Noah, and the Abraham and Sarah cycles. Wenham, *Genesis*, 42–44.

of "centuries-old craft with the freshest human tears which are gently boiled, released into shallow crystallisation tanks, then harvested by hand and finally rinsed in brine."[43] This capitalist commodification of tears and laughter is nothing like the kind of laughter and salty tears that emerge from the work of marginalized subjects and communities.

Salt was used for birth ritual (Ezek 16:4), in sacrifice ("salt of covenant," Lev 2:13; Num 18:19; Ezek 43:24), as an ingredient expression of loyalty and friendship; to eradicate death and miscarriage in water (2 Kgs 2:19–22); and as a preservative (Mark 9:50; Col 4:6; Luke 14:34). If Lot's wife prepared the food for the hosts, then it is an irony—a brutal one at that—to turn her into a pillar of salt at the end. Might she have returned to the production of hospitality at the moment when salvation seemed to be a man's story about departure? "Salt preserves Lot's wife as a monument which cries out in distress to heaven. For salt is tears, anguish for the women and children of Sodom."[44] Furthermore, the sea of salt is: (1) a place where oppressed peoples gathered and strategized resistance (Gen 14:3) and (2) a geographical boundary-marker (Num 34:3, 12; Deut 3:17; Josh 3:16; 12:3; 15:2, 5; 18:18). That is, in the narrative and material world of exilic/postexilic violence and existence, the sea of salt was an important subject of identity formation and belonging.

The Nigerian historian, Foyin Talola, has documented the value of salt in Nigeria (and across Africa) during the Second World War. Because salt was a commodity of high value to the culinary, medical, cultural, religious, and economic system of precolonial kingdoms, the British colonial government needed to manage the scarcity of salt during the war. Because salt was not a luxury item, the ruling government could not persuade people to wait until after the war when, presumably, prices would fall. Colonial administrators feared that the lack of salt could lead to uprisings from the masses in resistance to colonial rule.[45]

Might remembering Lot's wife signify the presence of enduring resistance against patriarchy and imperialism? As Fewell and Gunn put it: "in the middle of YHWH's concern to silence the outcry and Abraham's concern for justice stands a pillar of salt. A disturbance? A distraction? A seasoning? For salt makes a difference."[46] That difference is about outcomes but also about strategy and process. Consider, for example, this

43. Salt Made from Tears of Laughter.

44. Fewell and Gunn, *Gender, Power*, 67.

45. Falola, "Salt," 415–17.

46. Fewell and Gunn, *Gender, Power*, 64–65.

story from John Jusu and Matthew Elliott about the role of salt among villagers in a southern region of Africa:

> Consider the text on the Sermon on the Mount, where Jesus is preaching, 'You are the light of the world, and the salt of the earth.' Well, I (John Jusu) spoke to a theologian from the southern region of Africa, and he explained that the Western commentaries on this topic did not make sense to him. These commentaries explain that salt preserves and adds flavor. But he told me that to him, light gives direction and reveals our path, and therefore salt should follow the metaphor and also give direction. I asked him to explain, and so he told me a story: 'In my village, when there is drought, the monkeys know where there is water. But, they will not lead humans to that water. So, the people will trap a monkey and tie it up. Then, they will feed it salt. After a day or two, the monkey will become very thirsty. At this point, the humans will release the monkey. Then, the monkey will not care if the human beings are following it or not; it will make straight for the source of water in order to satisfy its thirst.'"[47]

As Rickett points out, what happens next to Lot's wife is "quite unexpected in the story." The fact that she looked back while also being positioned behind Lot may suggest that "she became a pillar of salt while standing, or traveling, behind Lot."[48] For Rickett, the key point of the story is that she disobeyed the commands, while Lot fully obeyed. By contrast, Blake Leyerle's exposition on Lot's wife as a border figure illustrates the complexities of interpretation at the intersections of identity formation, religious conversion, geography, monuments, and temporality.[49] Her turning and looking corresponds to the second "See" of CBS; it is an invitation to engage in theoretical, methodological, and interpretive work that resists and seeks to overcome the manifestations and attempted legitimizations of erasure, marginalization, and singularity in the narrative. By turning back, she removes herself from the ideology of violence, the marginalization of "othered" characters, and the productions of single heroes (which in the story unfold in the horrors of incestuous genealogy). To remember Lot's wife is to turn toward laughter and revitalization.

47. Jusu and Elliott, "The Africa Study Bible," 4.
48. Rickett, *Separating*, 57.
49. Leyerle, "Lot's Wife on the Border," 59–80, especially 61–62.

Bibliography

Browne, Gareth. "Cameroon's Separatist Movement is Going International: Armed Groups are Slipping into Nigeria and Appealing to the Cameroonian Diaspora to Fuel their Fight for a Breakaway State." *FP*, Mar. 13, 2019.

Caruth, Cathy. *Unclaimed Experience: Trauma, Narrative and History.* Baltimore: Johns Hopkins University Press, 1996.

Claassens, L. Juliana. "Excavating Trauma Narratives: Haunting Memories in the Story of Lot's Daughters." In *Transgression and Transformation: Feminist, Postcolonial and Queer Biblical Interpretation as Creative Interventions*, edited by L. Juliana Claassens *et al.*, 99–114. New York: Bloomsbury, 2021.

Connerton, Paul. *How Societies Remember.* Themes in the Social Sciences. Cambridge: Cambridge University Press, 1989.

Fewell, Danna, and David Gunn. *Gender, Power and Promise: The Subject of the Bible's First Story.* Nashville: Abingdon, 1992.

Eyerman, Ron. *Cultural Trauma: Slavery and the Formation of African American Identity.* New York: Cambridge University Press, 2001.

Falola, Toyin. "'Salt is Old': The Management of Salt Scarcity in Nigeria during World War II." *Canadian Journal of African Studies / Revue Canadienne des Études Africaines* 26 (1992) 412-436.

Freud, Sigmund. *Moses and Monotheism.* Translated by Katherine Jones. London: Hogarth, 1951.

Gallagher, Lowell. *Sodomscapes: Hospitality in the Flesh.* New York: Fordham University Press, 2017.

Halbwachs, Maurice. *The Collective Memory.* Translated from the French by Francis J. Ditter, Jr., and Vida Yazdi Ditter. Introduction by Mary Douglas. New York: Harper & Row, 1980.

Harries, Martin. *Forgetting Lot's Wife: On Destructive Spectatorship.* New York: Fordham University Press, 2007.

Jusu, John, and Matthew Elliott. "The Africa Study Bible; God's Word through African Eyes." *Reading the Bible in Context* 2 (2016) 4–7.

Kleinman, Arthur and Joan Kleinman, "How Bodies Remember: Social Memory and Bodily Experience of Criticism, Resistance, and Deligitimation Following China's Cultural Revolution." *NLH* 25 (1994) 707–23.

Leyerle, Blake. "Lot's Wife on the Border." *HTR* 107 (2014) 59–80.

Masenya, Madipoane (Ngwan'a Mphahlele). "Normative Masculinities Turned Upside Down? Reading Gen 19:30–38 Side by Side with Selected African Proverbs." In *Transgression and Transformation: Feminist, Postcolonial and Queer Biblical Interpretation as Creative Interventions*, edited by L. Juliana Claassens et al., 115–27. LHBOTS 707. London: Bloomsbury, 2021.

Mbuvi, Andrew M. *African Biblical Studies: Unmasking Embedded Racism and Colonialism in Biblical Studies.* London: T. & T. Clark, 2023.

Memmi, Albert. *Pillar of Salt.* Translated by Edouard Roditi. Boston: Beacon, 1992.

Miller, Carolyn R. "Genre as Social Action." *Quarterly Journal of Speech* 70 (1984) 151–67.

Niang, Aliou Cissé. *A Poetics of Postcolonial Biblical Criticism: God, Human-Nature Relationship, and Negritude.* Eugene, OR: Cascade Books, 2019.

Rickett, Dan. *Separating Abram and Lot: The Narrative Role and Early Reception of Genesis 13*. Themes in Biblical Narrative 26. Leiden: Brill, 2020.

Wafula, Robert S. "Violence and Lessons that we Never Learn: A Postcolonial Reading of Genesis 18–19." In *Navigating African Biblical Hermeneutics: Trends and Themes from Our Pots and Calabashes*, edited by Madipoane Masenya (Ngwan'a Mphahlele) and Kenneth Ngwa, 199–215. Cambridge: Cambridge Scholars, 2018.

Wenham, Gordon J. *Genesis 16–50*. Word Biblical Commentary 2. Grand Rapids: Zondervan, 2000.

West, Gerald O. "A Decolonial (Re)turn to Class in South African Biblical Scholarship." *OTE* 34 (2021) 530–53.

———. "Reading Shembe Re-membering the Bible: Isaiah Shembe's Instructions on Adultery." *Neot* 40.1 (2006) 157–83.

———. "Reading the Bible with the Marginalised: The Value/s of Contextual Bible Reading." *SJT* 1.2 (2015) 235–26.

———. "The Relationship between Different Modes of Reading (the Bible) and the Ordinary Reader." *Scriptura* 9 (1991) 87–110.

West, Gerald O., and Charlene Van der Walt. "A Queer (Beginning to the) Bible." *Concilium* 5 (2019) 109–18.

West, Gerald O., Sithembiso S. Zwane, and Charlene Van der Walt. "From Homosexuality to Hospitality: from Exclusion to Inclusion: From Genesis 19 to Genesis 18." *JTSA* 168 (2021) 5–23.

Zeleza, Paul Tiyambe. "Rewriting African Diaspora: Beyond the Black Atlantic." *AA* 104/414 (2005) 35–68.

Salt Made from Tears of Laughter. Hoxton Street Monster Supplies. https://www.monstersupplies.org/products/salt-made-from-tears-of-laughter.

The Ujamaa Center for Community Development & Research. *Doing Contextual Bible Study: A Resource Manual*. Rev. ed., May 2015.

15

Pope Francis' Art of Wielding Soft Power

The Transformation Strategies of Pope John XXIII

KJETIL HAFSTAD

Introduction

WHEN I WAS YOUNG, some Dominican friars who had their monastery close to our Norwegian home visited us frequently. They were invited by my father, a Lutheran pastor and journalist, and my mother, a sculptor who subscribed to Catholic piety. I remember how these monks, highly educated, some French, some Norwegians, spoke fondly and respectfully of Pope John XXIII. They looked forward with great expectations to proceedings of the Second Vatican Council. So, in my immaturity, inspired by the conversations with them, I even wrote about these changing events in a church paper. I, too, was moved by the soft power of the good pope.

Now I want to look at similar events in the contemporary Catholic Church. Can the Gospel be sent into battle? In *Domination and Arts of Resistance: Hidden Transcripts,* the American political scientist and anthropologist, James C. Scott, made a seminal analysis of how power works in the real world. His study was primarily based on fieldwork in a Malay village. He supplemented his fieldwork with illuminating examples from the world of literature. Programmatically, Scott suggests that "the analytical strategy pursued here . . . begins with the premise that is structurally similar forms of domination will bear a family resemblance to one another."[1] He goes on to say, ". . .what I do wish to assert . . . is that to the degree structures of domination can be demonstrated to operate in comparable ways, they will, other things being equal, elicit reactions and patterns of resistance that are also broadly comparable."[2] On the one hand, dominating power can be regarded as overpowering yet will often fail because seemingly weak resistance undermines it. Power is always in play, and it is fascinating, but also important to understand and value the impact of different types of power and different forms of resistance.

The Election of Cardinal Jorge Bergoglio as Pope

A very special situation unfolded in the Catholic Church at the Vatican conclave of 2013 which chose Pope Francis to replace the retiring Pope Benedict. In theory, few people on earth possess the kind of unimpeded power of the Pope who is, essentially, the sovereign monarch of the Vatican State and always has the last word. The Pope is the last *monarch* on the planet with infallible sovereignty, as it was declared at the first Vatican Council in 1870. For this reason, the pope can make decisions by himself, without consensus from the Church "*ex sese, non autem ex consensu Ecclesiae.*"[3]

In a practical sense, however, the Pope is of course dependent on his collaborators including the Curia (administration), the Cardinals, and the worldwide community of bishops, priests and the people of God, and all members of the Catholic Church. Also important to note is the fact that his power is more moral than it is political. According to legend, British Prime Minister, Winston Churchill, called for the involvement of the pope in the deliberations of the Yalta Conference. In response to Churchill's request, Russian leader Josef V. D. Stalin is said to have commented wryly: "How many divisions has the Pope?"—indicating that the

1. Scott, *Domination*, ix. This is an important theoretical observation that in a similar way also came to Alexander von Humboldt's mind when he observed similarities in vegetation, in different heights in mountain areas in so different surroundings as Tenerife and Venezuela. Such similarities encouraged Humboldt to form theories of general patterns in nature, and he observed how life of all forms are in interaction, and then founded ecology. Wulf, *The Invention of Nature*.

2. Scott, *Domination*, xi.

3. "Pastor aeternus," approved in the Council's IV Session, July 18, 1870, including condemning everyone teaching otherwise (*anatema sit*). Cf. Denzinger-Schönmetzer, *Enchiridion Symbolorum Definitionum*, 3074.

Pope was militarily powerless in the real world. And yet, the Pope can play a decisive role in many arenas, both within the Church and beyond, and can talk eye to eye with the political leaders of the world.

Pope Francis has demonstrated this, in his old age, with an amazing impact. He has an agenda to change the Catholic Church and align it with the vision of, the beloved Pope John XXIII's "aggiornamento," to bring the Church and the Gospel adequately in communication with contemporary society. He clearly intends to re-introduce the enthusiasm from the Vatican II Council to revise old patterns and come closer to the people of God—and "all people of goodwill."[4] This task of bringing the Catholic Church closer to the people now seems harder than at any other time in history. Currently, the Church is blemished by accusations of corruption, and by clerical sexual abuses of children and women. There are several cases of corruption and the misuse of money collected for the Church, and after centuries of secularization, people everywhere are more critical of the Church and its institutions. People of the Global South and East are critical of churches that originated in the West. In the Vatican, and among conservative Cardinals and bishops, many fear losing their accustomed privileges. For this reason, they are opposed to the candid efforts of Pope Francis to support the weak and marginalized in the Church.

The Inspiration, and Strategies, of Pope Francis

Pope Francis uses all the available tools to bring forth his message, including the "arts of resistance," which I will discuss below. He is a complex pastor, inspired by Liberation Theology, but also the spiritual impulses of Church Fathers like Francis of Assisi—and, in modern times, from among others, Romano Guardini.[5]

Liberation Theology has now come to a new stage with Pope Francis. During his time as principal for the Jesuits in Argentina, then Cardinal Bergoglio, he was removed from this office, and experienced years of isolation, with limited freedom and left only to pray and think by himself. Afterward, when he was reinstated and became a church leader in Buenos Aires, he began quietly working, mostly undercover, during

---

4. The way John XXIII spoke respectfully about people outside the Church, was captured both in the preparations and conclusion of the Second Vatican Council. See *Pacem in Terris*, Encyclical of Pope John XXIII, April 11, 1963.

5. Cf. Borghesi, *The Mind of Pope Francis*.

the military dictatorship. Later, he began openly taking a stance for the poor and underprivileged, in line with the Latin American Liberation Theology views.[6] As Pope, he has shown how deep the influence of the Liberation Theology movement is, even while publicly not making any claims to be part of it.[7]

His actions as Pope have confused and angered the traditionalists in the Vatican and elsewhere.[8] I will, with simple lines, try to pinpoint some of the novelties that have inspired so many, from within the Catholic Church, and within Christianity, in general,—and far beyond Christianity. One observation at the start is that Liberation theologians from Latin America were eagerly trying to grasp the local structural reality in society. They analyzed how the poor were subjugated and marginalized, and they tried to resist the brutality of belligerent governments, often bravely amidst dangerous opposition. Such opposition could be powerful in its model of simplicity.

In Northeast Brazil, for example, Dom Helder Camara invited poor land workers to attend Bible study meetings.[9] After long and hard days of work, they came together to read the Bible and talked about what they found. The effect was revolutionary. The workers discovered their own faculties, they were able to learn to read, understand, and present their own ideas of the stories from the Bible. They then became *subjects* in their own life and could speak up. These "ordinary" readers who encountered the stories from the Bible, were empowered in surprising ways. This is a cornerstone of Gerald West's significant theological contribution. Reading with "ordinary" African readers, West likens this to putting vital members of the community together: a "*re*-membering." In his studies, West shows how "ordinary" readers can bring completely new insights to Biblical studies.[10]

---

6. Borghesi, *Mind of Pope Francis*.

7. Borghesi, *Mind of Pope Francis*.

8. West, *The Academy of the Poor*, 10–13.

9. West, *The Academy of the Poor*, 107–8.

10. A good example from West: "In reading with ordinary African 'readers' we have found . . . as they transgress the boundaries of our methodologies and use our analytical tools together with their own 'well-crafted weapons' against us and our alienated and dominating interpretations . . . .' Re-membering', they . . . make syncopated and subversive methodological moves to recover subjugated, forgotten and neglected meanings, as they applaud a Jesus who is tricky and debate with a God who is undemocratic." West, *The Academy of the Poor*, 107–8.

Camara was focused on how the common reading made the readers subjects and gave them the power to resist oppression. *Reading* in-community set them free. This, however, worried the landowners, who tried to silence Camara, without success.[11] Like Camara, liberation theologians and their supporters in Latin America were often persecuted, both by dominating governments and, more surprisingly, for a long time by conservatives from within their own local churches. In 1984, Camara was forced into retirement, just as Leonardo Boff, the prominent, outspoken Brazilian liberation theologian, and author of over fifty books was ordered into silence.[12] Soon afterward, in 1989, perhaps the most prominent Liberation theologian in Brazil, Cardinal Evaristo Arns,[13] Archbishop of São Paulo, who fervently opposed the military dictatorship in Brazil, had his wings clipped by his own Church. He, however, remained with a fifth of his diocese, isolated from his treasured people from the poor favelas. He, nevertheless, remained an outspoken Liberation Cardinal, in clear opposition to Pope John Paul II.

Pope Francis learned from these Liberation Theologians, but he had a long and hard route to travel to do so.[14] After many years of study,

11. West, *The Academy of the Poor*, 107–8.

12. West, *The Academy of the Poor*, 107–8.

13. Created Cardinal by Pope Paul VI, March 05, 1973.

14. His commission as Provincial Superior of the Jesuits in Argentine (1973–79) stains him, as he indirectly caused the arrest of two Jesuits and failed to help two nuns and his mentor. Nancy Scheper-Hughes and Jennifer Scheper-Hughes, in their article, "The Final Conversion of Pope Francis," write that he was removed from leading the Argentinean Jesuits in 1979, and set to teach theology at a seminary, then sent to Germany for further studies, and on return, exiled to Córdoba for two solitary years, praying, reading, barely talking with anybody. They suggest that his exile and solitude marked the beginning of his "conversion," where he began to remake himself into the resolute, powerful, and charismatic leader he is today (67). As they state: "During his period of enforced solitude, Father Bergoglio barely spoke to anyone. He was even cut off from the other Jesuits with whom he was living. Bergoglio was coming to terms with his (self-defined) rigid, even authoritarian, personality that had contributed to his decision to dismiss and 'let go' of the two 'disobedient' liberation theology Jesuits, Father Franz (Francis) Jalics, his former theology teacher, and Orlando Yorio, who had refused to give up their ecclesiastical base community in a poor parish of Buenos Aires. Bergoglio's decision put the men in mortal danger" (17). They were afterward kidnapped and tortured for six long months by the military police—and rescued by Father Bergoglio's intervention in person, who appealed to General Videla and Admiral Massera. They were afterward brutally dropped by a plane near Buenos Aires and were found in a confused, drugged, and poor physical state. Unfortunately, Bergoglio failed in helping the two nuns and his former boss and mentor, Esther Ballestrino de Careaga. All three were drugged and pushed out of a police aircraft while over the Atlantic Ocean. The bodies of two of the women were later retrieved from the ocean and buried in pauper graves

and two full years in isolation, praying and thinking, he returned to normal duty of the Church in Buenos Aires, as auxiliary bishop in 1992, and archbishop in 1998. He lived simply in an ordinary downtown flat, used public transport or his own two feet, advocated for the poor in society, and promoted the social ethics of the Church in vivid exchanges with politicians. He openly spoke out against both President Néstor Kirchner, and his successor, Cristina Fernández de Kirchner, for their misuse of power, and failure to help the least well-off in society. "Power is born of confidence, not with manipulation, intimidation, or arrogance," Bergoglio said in 2006.[15] Because of this, he lived with the consequences of his outspokenness which included negative rumors about his actions and failures.[16]

Pope Francis' Strategies and Tactics for Changing the Church

When Bergoglio was surprisingly elected Pope, he immediately began to try and change the Catholic Church, understanding sharply what was going on, analyzing on his own, and acting surprisingly freely, like no former Pope before him. His actions, this time, began to have their impact, not only in the Church but on global politics and world leaders. How does he do it? Simplicity! In public, he is relaxed and open to what may happen. When he, for the first time after his election, met the people who had gathered in their tens of thousands at Saint Peter's Square, he looked at the crowd, and instead of using Latin as is the papal custom, simply spoke like a regular local citizen of Rome at that time of the day,

---

(58). Under a deadly dictatorship, the possibilities to oppose, are limited, and fosters "arts of resistance." It is easy to judge when we are in peace. Wolf Krötke, a prominent opponent of the Stasi-regime in the former German Democratic Republic, told me that humor was helpful, when called into interrogation. "We lied, all of us," he told me. "In one or another way, we all were part of the system there; no-one was innocent." Few come out of confrontations with persecuting regimes as clear heroes. Such experiences may offer valuable life lessons to learn. Krötke, *Kirke og Kultur,* 510; Hafstad, *Forsonet med Fortiden,* 193–215.

15. Lamb, *The Outsider,* 11. President Néstor Kirchner (2003–2007) and his wife and successor, Cristina Fernández de Kirchner (2007–2015) "wanted to put Bergoglio in jail," one senior Argentine official told Lamb. "They made his life difficult." Lamb, *The Outsider,* 11.

16. Lamb, *The Outsider,* 9. Lamb further describes how people from finance and politics, keep up the rumour mill from Bergoglio's service in Argentina, and critique Pope Francis' initiatives in that light (50ff.). One ardent critic among them was the former advisor to President Donald J. Trump, Steve Bannon (69–70.).

"Buona sera!"—"Good evening!" And the crowd broke out in laughter and applauded. So simple, just connecting, no elevated phrases. This has remained his papal trademark and reflects Vatican II's shift from Latin as the primary language of mass. And, after every short homily, at noon, following the *Angelus* from the window of his apartment, looking out on the square, he, like his predecessors, greets and addresses the different groups who are present. However, after giving his blessings, it is back to complete normality for everyone in Italy, when he says, *'Buon pranzo!'*—"Have a nice lunch!" Again, small, yet rich tokens of nearness and intimacy.

As Francis was being elected pope, Cardinal Re, presiding over the conclave asked him whether he accepted the election. Pope Francis did not immediately say "Yes!" Knowing well that he was now entering the highest office in the Catholic Church, and would personally be associated with the turbulent discussions going back to the first Vatican Council, in 1870, where papal infallibility was proclaimed, he stood by his turf and, in simplicity, contradicted this tradition (in English, instead of Latin) and stated: "I am a great sinner, trusting in the mercy and patience of God, in suffering, I accept."[17] In some sense, this is a commonplace way of referring to the *Ave Maria* prayer ("Sancta Maria, Mater Dei, ora pro nobis peccatoribus"). But, in the context where the holy responsibility is being transferred, it added a sharp image and critical note to the high office he was entering, with hints of second thoughts!

When he was dressed up in a pure white cassock, befitting his new dignity, he gave signs of impending new rules, by refusing to change his well-worn black shoes, marred by his years of walking about in the city streets and favelas of Buenos Aires, and always using public transport. He rejected the new red shoes prepared for the Pope, and a favorite of his predecessor, Pope Benedict XVI. Furthermore, Pope Francis declined to wear the golden cross and string offered and, instead, retained his old silver one.[18] And, finally, when it came to the choice of transportation, he chose to go together with his colleagues in a coach bus to dinner after the ceremony, rather than in the limousine which had been prepared for him.

Other signs of the new winds of change continued in the first days of Pope Francis' papacy, in the way he greeted people with humility and warmth. As the new bishop of Rome, Pope Francis wasted no time in immediately reaching out to his colleague, the Rabbi of Rome.[19] He refused to

17. O'Connell, *The Election of Pope Francis*, 227.

18. O'Connell, *The Election of Pope Francis*, 229.

19. O'Connell, *The Election of Pope Francis*, 239.

move into the papal luxury apartment, instead, preferring to stay together with younger priests in Domus Sanctae Marthae, a hostel also used for clergy visiting the Vatican. Pope Francis, to this day, continues to occupy a small bedroom and a simple study and is often seen eating in the common cantina. The view from his room overlooks a gas station outside the Vatican, in contrast to the luxuriously appointed roof-top papal apartment he refused, which was renovated by a former secretary of state as a retirement home for himself, and paid for by funds originally raised to benefit sick children at the Vatican-owned Bambino Gesù pediatric hospital.[20]

Pope Francis is at home in this "ordinary" dwelling, where coworkers and visitors come and go, live, and meet. Only for official meetings with leaders of state and other dignitaries, will he use his official apartment. In Domus Sanctae Marthae, he is often found walking around in civilian garb. Once, a more traditional cleric who met the pope dressed down like this, exclaimed loudly when seeing his ordinary clothing, "Holy Father, this is not permitted!" As he passed by, Pope Francis was heard to mutter, "says who?," and kept on walking.[21]

These are but small tokens of his efforts to change the attitude at the Curia, and the leaders of the Catholic Church to live humbly and modestly. Indeed, he regularly declines being transported in luxury cars, preferring to be driven in a modest Ford Focus, or even as he did, driving himself from 1984, in a Renault 5 belonging to a friend. Pope Francis is a complex person; warm, affectionate, and direct. However, he is also firm and resolute. He evidently wants to change the Catholic Church, with all the means and insights he can muster, and by so doing, also contribute towards making the larger human society warmer and more affectionate. His primary tools are the central thoughts of the Bible, interpreted with a contextual emphasis and contemporary edge. He seems to say very simple things, always referring to the Gospel. But what he presents in his

20. BBC report from Vatileaks, November 05, 2015. "In the country he rules with absolute power, Pope Francis has chosen for himself one of the worst views. The pontiff's small suite of rooms in the Vatican's Santa Marta guest house looks out beyond the enclave's walls on to a small street and the rear of a petrol station. By contrast, a retired Italian cardinal living nearby enjoys a top-floor apartment in an old building with a view out over the Vatican itself. Documents leaked to reporters allege that a charitable foundation paid €200 000 to renovate the apartment that Cardinal Tarcisio Bertone is using as his retirement home. The leaks reveal that the Pope has been unable to persuade many of his Vatican officials to follow his own frugal example." See also: Martel, *In the Closet of the Vatican*, 464.

21. Lamb, *The Outsider*, 13.

sermons is often new, illuminative, often with provocative angles, with the power of resistance seeping through.

Select Prayers, Reflections, and Homilies of Pope Francis

For several years now, Pope Francis has published the daily prayers he leads in his papal home, at Domus Sanctae Marthae. These take the form of simple reflections and prayers to start the day, but often also include admonitions for change of scope. One such homily was given on Sunday, May 17, 2020, as the COVID-19 Pandemic had brought the whole world to a standstill.[22] He began that day with a prayer for those with humble, yet important jobs: "Today our prayer is for the many persons who clean hospitals, streets, empty trash from the dumpsters, who go to each house to remove trash: work that no one sees, but it is a job that is necessary to survive. May the Lord bless them and help them." Together with the few close coworkers in Domus Sanctae Marthae, he focused on the many who work tirelessly and thanklessly at their jobs, which, when done perfectly, almost nobody notices. This is, however, the kind of work that can be very meaningful and rewarding.

An example was the case that the German newspaper *Die Zeit* had recently reported about. The paper's reporter spoke with Andrée Ellsel who, every day, even during the time of the COVID-19 pandemic, would descend the steps to the city toilet under Alexanderplatz, in Berlin, where he would greet every guest and clean the interior of all the toilet stalls.[23] Throughout his 7½ hour daily job as a janitor, he would work without the benefit of daylight. But, together with his guests, of both high and low status, he liked to shared a friendly word during the few spare moments of the day. He was content with his job and cared for everyone without preference, even the homeless who lived at the Alexanderplatz.

With such people in mind, the Pope then changes the scope of his homily and recalls Jesus' soothing farewell speech to his disciples in John 14:18. "Jesus gives them tranquility, He gives peace, with a promise: 'I will not leave you orphans,'" the Pope remarks and continues: "Today we can say that we live in a society where the Father is missing, a sense of being orphaned that specifically affects belonging and fraternity." Jesus promises

22. See Pope Francis, "Homily of the Holy Father Francis: Celebrazione Mattutina Trasmessa.

23. See Holl, "Reinigungskraft am Alexanderplatz."

to remain present even as he goes to his Father. "The Holy Spirit does not come to 'make us His clients'; He comes to point out how to access the Father, to remind us how to access the Father . . . Only with this awareness of being children, that *we are not orphans*, can we live in peace among ourselves. Wars, either small ones or large ones, always have a dimension of being orphans: the Father who makes peace is missing."[24]

So, this short homily points to gentleness and tenderness reminding listeners to do the same:

> The Holy Spirit does not teach us to insult. And one of the consequences of this feeling like orphans is insulting, wars, because if there is no Father, there are no brothers, fraternity is lost. They are—this tenderness, reverence, gentleness—they are attitudes of belonging, of belonging to a family that is certain of having a Father.

And then, turning from a society bombarded by lies and insults from the then US president Trump, the Pope opens the eyes of his audience to another reality, and prays: "And to this civilization, with this great feeling of being orphaned, may He grant the grace of rediscovering the Father, the Father who gives meaning to all of life, and that He might unite humanity into one family." Quiet words of assurance at the start of a new day. To keep in mind those who do modest, necessary work, and all who do those important tasks. To do what you do with tenderness, to unite humans in peace. Simple words with possible great, life-changing impact.

The Pope's last homily, at the time of writing this essay, also begins in a humble way. On the first day of 2022, Saturday, January 01, 2022, the Pope addressed the World Day of Peace,[25] At the outset, the Pope reflected on the baby Jesus being laid in a simple crib: "Jesus touches our hearts by being born in littleness and poverty; he fills us with love, not fear. The manger foretells the One who makes himself food for us. His poverty is good news for everyone, especially the marginalized, the rejected and those who do not count in the eyes of the world. For that is how God comes: not on a fast track, and lacking even a cradle! That is what is beautiful about seeing him there, laid in a manger." As so many

---

24. Pope Francis, "Homily of the Holy Father Francis: Celebrazione Mattutina Trasmessa."

25. See Pope Francis, "Homily of the Holy Father Francis: Holy Mass on the Solemnity of Mary, Mother of God."

times before, in his encyclicals, homilies, and discourses, Pope Francis underlines the closeness of the Gospel to poverty.

His homily continues by way of providing a traditional contemplation on the mystery of salvation, reflecting on "the scandal of the manger"—Jesus was born to an unmarried young woman, and an ignorant, but faithful husband, whose stress-filled and painful birth in a menial feeding trough being completely disharmonious with the expectations of a birth of the the Messiah.

> What can be more painful for a mother than to see her child suffering poverty? It is troubling indeed. We would not blame Mary, were she to complain of those unexpected troubles. Yet she does not lose heart. She does not complain, but keeps silent. Rather than complain, she chooses a different part: *For her part*, the Gospel tells us, Mary 'kept all these things, pondering them in her heart' (cf. *Lk* 2:19).

This is the inspiration of Christmas—the unexpected beginning of course, but eventually pointing to the meditative mature faith. As the Popes explained:

> Mary, instead, is pensive; she keeps all these things, pondering them in her heart. We ourselves can have the same two different responses. The story told by the shepherds, and their own amazement, remind us of the beginnings of faith, when everything seems easy and straightforward. We rejoice in the newness of God who enters into our lives and fills us with wonder. Mary's pensiveness, on the other hand, is the expression of a mature, adult faith, not a faith of beginners. Not a newborn faith, it is rather a faith that now *gives birth*. For spiritual fruitfulness is born of trials and testing.

Here is the constant tenor in Pope Francis' homily, bringing together the difficult, and often incomprehensible experiences of life, with a contemplation on the importance of faith.

Pope Francis and the Liberation of Women

The next step is to comment on women's role in the Church via this contemplation on Mary. "That is what mothers do: they know how to overcome obstacles and disagreements, and to instill peace. In this way, they transform problems into opportunities for rebirth and growth. They can do this because they know how to 'keep', to hold together the various threads of life. We need such people, capable of weaving the threads of communion in place of the barbed wire of conflict and division. Mothers know how to do this."It is highly significant, that the outcome on this day is praying for world peace, where the Pope confronts every known transgression made against women.

> And since mothers bestow life, and women 'keep' the world, let us all make greater efforts to promote mothers and to pro-tect women. How much violence is directed against women? Enough! To hurt a woman is to insult God, who from a woman took on our humanity.

Looking to the Mother of the Church (*Mater Ecclesiae*), the Pope gives hope and confidence to a world in conflict: "let us place ourselves un-der the protection of this woman, the Mother of God, who is also our mother. May she help us to keep and ponder all things, unafraid of trials and with the joyful certainty that the Lord is faithful and can transform every cross into a resurrection."

Along such traditional deliberations, the Pope finds inspiration for the Catholic Church to change and put women at the center. He has started on this track, giving high positions to women in the Catholic Church that were earlier reserved for male clerics. He does not, how-ever, seem to desire to start a "revolution" by endorsing women's ordina-tion to the priesthood, although this remains a possible next step for him.[26] The steps he has taken so far are small, but give signs of coming incremental change. Of course, women do have an immense impact on the Catholic Church, not the least through the tens of thousands of women's Orders, which are doing vigorous work throughout the world. Often, the Orders have important women generals representing

26. Pope Francis has made cautious steps to promote women. Reuters reported (January 1, 2020) that: "He named the first woman to hold a high-ranking post in the Secretariat of State, the male-dominated Vatican's diplomatic and administrative nerve center. Italian laywoman Francesca Di Giovanni, 66, will assume the newly-created post in a division known as the Section for Relations with States where she takes the rank of under-secretary, effectively one of two deputy foreign ministers." Again, Reuters report-ed (February 07, 2021) that: "Pope Francis has appointed two women to Vatican posts previously held only by men, in back-to-back moves giving women more empowerment in the male-dominated Holy See. He appointed Nathalie Becquart, a French member of the Xaviere Missionary Sisters, on Saturday as co-undersecretary of the Synod of Bish-ops, a department that prepares major meetings of world bishops held every few years on a different topic. The previous day, Francis named Italian magistrate Catia Summaria as the first woman Promoter of Justice in the Vatican's Court of Appeals."

them in Rome, like the well-known Mother M. Tekla Famiglietti, OSsS (1936–2020), and Abbess General of the Bridgettine Sisters, who served from 1979–2016. However, the question of women's ordination is still an *open* question in the Catholic Church, and the Pope is well aware of the Catholic Church being out of date, not only on questions of equal rights for women but also in a range of burning questions on gender and celibacy, which also may have had an impact on the catastrophic stories of sexual abuse committed by the clergy.[27]

Pope Francis on Homosexuality, Family, and Marriage

On homosexuality, Pope Francis has been especially careful. Recently, Frédéric Martel published his report on homosexuality at the center of the Vatican, *In the Closet of the Vatican: Power, Homosexuality, Hypocrisy*. Martel maintains that many Catholic Church leaders in the Vatican, and overseas, hold double standards on this issue. Those who are officially and theologically against practicing homosexuals are often themselves practicing homosexuals, Martel maintains. This is such a large problem for the Catholic Church. The Pope is mostly silent on this issue, but everyone remembers his open and spontaneous response to journalists who asked for his opinion on homosexuality during an air flight back from Brazil in July 2013: "Who am I to judge gay people?"[28] For many, this was a sign of hope for a change of attitude in the Church.[29] Mercy comes first, doctrine follows, is the simple argument Francis here intimates. It marks a deep difference in the way of thinking that has been self-evident in former papacies.

Head on, the Pope took two very important initiatives, both released in 2015. First, on marriage, remarriage, and the traditional exclusion of the remarried to the Eucharist; and, second, the encyclical,

---

27. A comment I gratefully heard from the great French theologian Hervé Legrand, now Professeur émérite à l'Institut Catholique de Paris, in a conversation in Oslo, Norway, 1993.

28. See BBC News, "Pope Francis: Who Am I to Judge Gay People?"

29. Martel, *In the Closet of the Vatican*, 56. In an interview with the journalist Andre Tornielli, the Pope explains this further referring to this statement "Who am I to judge gay people?" See Pope Francis, *The Name of God Is Mercy*. Asked whether there is an opposition between truth and mercy, or doctrine and mercy, the pontiff responds: 'I will say this: mercy is real; it is the first attribute of God. . . Theological reflections on doctrine or mercy may then follow, but let us not forget that mercy is doctrine.' See also McElwee, "Francis Explains 'Who Am I to Judge?'"

Laudato Sí, ("Praise Be to You") on the environment, the relationship existing between nature and the society which lives in it, and the future. Both caused much discussion and will still affect the Catholic Church in a positive way, I think, in the years to come, presumably far longer than Francis' papacy.

Impact of Pope Francis on the Bishops' Synod of October 2015

The preparation of the Bishop's Synod in October 2015, was far-reaching and delved deeply into issues affecting the family. "On October 08, 2013, Pope Francis announced that in October 2014, there would be an Extraordinary General Assembly of the Synod of Bishops on topics related to the family and evangelization. Subsequent communications made clear that "the Extraordinary General Assembly would be followed by an Ordinary General Assembly of the Synod of Bishops in October 2015, on the same topics," as reported by The United States Conference of Bishops.[30] The 2014 preparatory Synod on the Family, collected material from all parts of the Catholic Church worldwide, and paved the way ahead for the 2015 Synod on the Family which profited from the work of numerous conferences, calling for points of view from everyone interested.

Many participants in the different preparatory meetings were optimistic about a change of climate in the Catholic Church. For example, Werner Jeanrond reported on a very promising meeting called in May 2015, in Rome, by the leaders of Bishops' conferences of France, Germany, and Switzerland. This conference gathered bishops, theologians, biblical scholars, people from the press, and representatives from the Vatican, for open discussion on the different themes included in the discourse on family, marriage, divorce, homosexual cohabitation, and abortion. A central point of departure was the discussions on hermeneutics, on how to understand the complexities involved—and understanding of tradition today. They identified also the possibilities for "courageous pastoral choices," in continuation of Vatican II's *Dei verbum* on growth in faith and understanding, guided by the Holy Spirit.[31]

Pope Francis followed the preparatory process very closely. Knowing very well the opposition against any change in traditional views on

---

30. United States Conference of Catholic Bishops, "2014–2015 Synods of Bishops on the Family." Marriage and Family Life Ministries."

31. Jeanrond, "Å omfavne den andre," 224–28.

the related subjects, Pope Francis limited his opening address to the Synod, on October 05, 2015, calling the bishops to apostolic courage and evangelical humility. "Assume *apostolic courage* which refuses to be intimidated in the face of the temptations of the world that tend to extinguish the light of truth in the hearts of men, replacing it with small and temporary lights; nor even before the petrification of some hearts, which, despite good intentions, drive people away from God."[32] Pope Francis went on to cite his *Domus Sanctae Marthae* morning homily of May 28, 2015, where he asks for "apostolic courage to live life and not to make a museum of memories of our Christian life."[33] He thus addressed the Synod further: "Assume *evangelical humility* that is able to overcome its own conventions and prejudices in order to listen to Brother Bishops and be filled with God. Humility that leads neither to pointing a finger at, nor to judging others, but to hands outstretched helping people to rise again without ever feeling superior." Finally, Pope Francis pointed to the possible failure of the Synod, not willing to listen. "Without allowing ourselves to be guided by the Spirit, all our decisions will be but *'decorations'* that, instead of exalting the Gospel, cover and hide it."

During the Synod, the Pope also celebrated the fiftieth anniversary of the institution of the Synod of Bishops at Rome in October, 1962.[34] He used the opportunity to renew his encouragement to listen to all voices heard in preparation for the Synod. "Such was the conviction underlying my desire that the people of God should be consulted in the preparation of the two phases of the Synod on the family, as is ordinarily done with each *Lineamenta*. Certainly, a consultation of this sort would never be sufficient to perceive the *sensus fidei*. But how could we speak about the family without engaging families themselves, listening to their joys and their hopes, their sorrows, and their anguish?[35] Through the answers given to the two questionnaires sent to the particular Churches, we had the opportunity at least to hear some of those families speak to issues which closely affect them and about which they have much to say."

32. See: https://www.vatican.va/content/francesco/en/speeches/2015/october/documents/papa-francesco_20151005_padri-sinodali.html

33. See: https://www.vatican.va/content/rancesco/en/cotidie/2015/documents/papa-francesco-cotidie_20150428_open-to-surprises.html [Accessed: January 29, 2022].

34. The Second Vatican Council was held in Rome, October 11, 1962 to December 08, 1965.

35. Cf. Second Vatican Ecumenical Council, Pastoral Constitution *Gaudium et Spes* (December 07, 1965), 1.

Pope Francis further deliberated upon "listening as work," in order to comprehend what the Holy Spirit is saying: "A synodal Church is a Church which listens, which realizes that listening 'is more than simply hearing,"[36] It is a mutual listening in which everyone has something to learn. The faithful people, the college of bishops, the Bishop of Rome: all listening to each other, and all listening to the Holy Spirit, the "Spirit of truth" (John 14:17)." He reminded the Synod that the very word "synod" means "journeying together." Not just keeping on standing in the same spot, but going forward and not regarding oneself as elevated above others. Citing John Chrysostom, Pope Francis stated that the

> Church and Synod are synonymous, inasmuch as the Church is nothing other than the 'journeying together' of God's flock along the paths of history towards the encounter with Christ the Lord, then we understand too that, within the Church, no one can be 'raised up' higher than others. On the contrary, in the Church, it is necessary that each person 'lower' himself or herself, so as to serve our brothers and sisters along the way."[37]

In this regard, Pope Francis seemed to be shocked by some of the proceedings and his remarks at the end of the Synod were particularly sharp:

> As I followed the labors of the Synod, I asked myself: *What will it mean for the Church to conclude this Synod devoted to the family?* Certainly, the Synod was not about settling all the issues having to do with the family, but rather attempting to see them in the light of the Gospel and the Church's tradition and two-thousand-year history, bringing the joy of hope without falling into a facile repetition of what is obvious or has already been said."

The task for the Synod, he continued:

> . . .was about listening to and making heard the voices of the families and the Church's pastors, who came to Rome bearing on their shoulders the burdens and the hopes, the riches and the challenges of families throughout the world . . . It was about

36. Apostolic Exhortation Evangelii Gaudium Of the Holy Father Francis to the Bishops, Clergy, Consecrated Persons and the Lay Faithful on the Proclamation of the Gospel in Today's World November 24, 2013, 171.

37. Ceremony Commemorating the 50th Anniversary of the Institution of the Synod of Bishops, Address of His Holiness Pope Francis, Paul VI Audience Hall, Saturday, October 17, 2015. See: https://www.vatican.va /content/francesco/en/speeches/2015/october/documents/papa-francesco_20151017_50-anniversario-sinodo.html   [Accessed: 29.01.2022].

showing the vitality of the Catholic Church, which is not afraid to stir dulled consciences or to soil her hands with lively and frank discussions about the family.

The Pope did not indicate to what extent this took place in the Synod, but instead pointed out that the Synod, ". . .was also about laying closed hearts bare, which frequently hide even behind the Church's teachings or good intentions, in order to sit in the chair of Moses and judge, sometimes with superiority and superficiality, difficult cases and wounded families." Free speech has its costs, he said, and "In the course of this Synod, the different opinions which were freely expressed—and at times, unfortunately, not in entirely well-meaning ways—certainly led to a rich and lively dialogue; they offered a vivid image of a Church which does not simply 'rubberstamp,' but draws from the sources of her faith living waters to refresh parched hearts."[38]

What seemed like deep disagreements in the Sythat came to the fore and gave the Pope a possibility to address the reality that the Catholic Church is always contextualized in different regions. This requires enculturation, adaptation, and understanding so the teaching of the Church can be adapted without changing, and so gradually transform different cultures. This remains a hopeful view in the midst of deep conflicts. This goes back to a Pontifical Biblical Commission report that pointed out the following:

> And—apart from dogmatic questions clearly defined by the Church's Magisterium—we have also seen that what seems normal for a bishop on one continent is considered strange and almost scandalous—almost!—for a bishop from another; what is considered a violation of a right in one society is an evident and inviolable rule in another; what for some is freedom of conscience, is for others simply confusion. Cultures are in fact quite diverse, and every general principle—as I said, dogmatic questions clearly defined by the Church's magisterium—every general principle needs to be inculturated, if it is to be respected and applied.[39]

38. Cf. Letter of His Holiness Pope Francis to the Grand Chancellor of the Pontifical Catholic University of Argentina on the Centenary of its Faculty of Theology, March 03, 2015.

39. Cf. Pontifical Biblical Commission, *Fede e cultura alla luce della Bibbia. Atti della Sessione plenaria 1979 della Pontificia Commissione Biblica*, LDC, Leumann, 1981; Second Vatican Ecumenical Council, *Gaudium et Spes*, 44.

The 1985 Synod, which celebrated the twentieth anniversary of the conclusion of the Second Vatican Council, had spoken of *inculturation* as "the intimate transformation of authentic cultural values through their integration in Christianity, and the taking root of Christianity in the various human cultures."[40] Further, "*Inculturation* does not weaken true values, but demonstrates their true strength and authenticity, since they adapt without changing; indeed they quietly and gradually transform the different cultures."[41]

In the end, Pope Francis looked forward, hopeful for the true defenders of doctrine about whom he said, "The Synod experience also made us better to realize that the true defenders of doctrine are not those who uphold its letter, but its spirit; not ideas but people; not formulae but the gratuitousness of God's love and forgiveness."[42] Through this process, he was also trying to move a small stone of established, traditional thinking of marriage and sexuality. The Pope propelled both hope and new energy among the members of the Catholic Church worldwide, and among ordinary people hearing new tones from the Vatican and among professional journalists, bishops, and theologians, etc. Yet, while at "home" in the Synod, Pope Francis seemed rather pessimistic, understanding that the mountain ahead is and remains steep. This conflict is a paragon for his Papacy.

Pope Francis and His Management of Controversy and Disagreements

Pope Francis summed up the result of this Synod in the Apostolic Exhortation, *Amoris Lætetia*, published on March 19, 2016.[43] Among the traditionalists who will not even consider any changes in the Catholic Church's teachings on marriage, and other questions on cohabitation, were four

40. *Final Relatio* (7 December 1985), *L'Osservatore Romano*, December 10, 1985, 7.

41. "In virtue of her pastoral mission, the Church must remain ever attentive to historical changes and to the development of new ways of thinking. Not, of course, to submit to them, but rather to surmount obstacles standing in the way of accepting her counsels and directives." (Interview with Cardinal Georges Cottier, in *La Civiltà Cattolica* 3963–3964, August 08, 2015, 272).

42. The passages are taken from Conclusion of the Synod of Bishops. Address of His Holiness Pope Francis, Synod Hall, Saturday, October 24, 2015.

43. Post-Synodal Apostolic Exhortation *Amoris Laetitia* of the Holy Father Francis to Bishops, Priests and Deacons, Consecrated Persons, Christian Married People and all the Lay Faithful on Love in the Family, March 19, 2016.

Cardinals. They published worried questions to the Pope, the so-called *dubia* ("doubts") to the way *Amoris Lætetia* posed questions about the situation. Pope Francis, however, remained silent in response to their inquiring questions. The most active among them, American Cardinal Leo Burke, upset by this silence, repeated the main points again in the National Catholic Register, a year later: "One year after the publication of the *dubia* on *Amoris Laetitia*, which have not received any response from the Holy Father, we observe an increasing confusion about the ways of interpreting the apostolic exhortation."[44] According to Cardinal Burke, for example, whether remarried divorcees could receive the sacraments, the reception of which was strictly prohibited under Canon Law, remained unclear: "*Dubia* sought to ascertain, among other matters, whether previous Church teaching forbidding civilly 'remarried' divorcees engaging in sexual relations to receive the sacraments remained in force."[45]

Cardinal Burke maintained that a Pope cannot but talk clearly on these matters, evidently meaning that Pope Francis, even with his open questions, lacked such clarity: Cardinal Burke went on:

> Thus, the questions arise from the recognition of the Petrine office that Pope Francis had received from the Lord for the purpose of confirming his brothers in the faith. The magisterium is God's gift to the Church to provide clarity on issues that regard the deposit of the faith. By their very nature, affirmations that lack this clarity cannot be qualified expressions of the magisterium.[46]

As a traditionalist, Cardinal Burke could be expected to honor Vatican I's decree on papal infallibility. However, by his insinuating that Pope Francis was not promoting *sana dottrina* ("sound doctrine"), Cardinal Burke's allegiance to the teaching of papal infallibility was in question.[47] For his part, Pope Francis has not responded to these claims, evidently understanding that these are hostile questions aimed at counteracting his approach to questioning church teachings. Instead, as Lamb reports,

---

44. Pentin, National Catholic Register, November 15, 2017.

45. Pentin, National Catholic Register, November 15, 2017.

46. See: https://www.ncregister.com/blog/cardinal-burke-addresses-the-dubia-one-year-after-their-publication [Accessed: January 13, 2021].

47. Burke et al., "La Plenitudo Potestatis del Romano Pontifice nel Servizio dell' Unità della Chiesa, in Burke," in *Dove Vai?*, 37.

> Francis has responded with a mixture of silence and lightheart-
> edness to the doctrinal charges brought against him," using the
> arts? of resistance, taking the accusations "with a sense of hu-
> mor" e.g., noting "It does not hurt me at all. Hypocrisy and lies
> hurt me, these hurt me . . . I also pray for them because they are
> wrong and poor people, some are manipulated. And who are
> those who signed . . . ?[48]

So in subtle ways, Pope Francis undermines the opposition from clerical-ists. He annoys them by not responding and, also, not receiving them when they ask for private audiences. It is a silence that *speaks volumes.*

The significance of the silence becomes even clearer when we look at Pope Francis' public speeches and interviews. He has given more in-terviews to the media than any Pope before him in recent memory. Not only does he answer questions at press conferences without requiring to see them beforehand, but to general audiences, he can be stopped and asked questions and he responds off the cuff. This directly contrasts with the silence he has shown toward his opponents. And as Lamb observes, the Pope Francis' opponents, if they give interviews, only do so with those reporters they know will not ask difficult questions: "So many of Francis's opponents demand he answer their questions, yet are unwilling to face any scrutiny of their own from reporters. They want to put this Pope to the test but will not submit their own theology or ideas to detailed examination."[49] So, in the end, Pope Francis says what he has in his heart when speaking with everyone else, and exposes his opponents through his short homi-lies on poverty, grace, and generosity. This is his "art of resistance," which causes much anger from the hard-hearted opponents.

Nevertheless, Pope Francis has experienced much more of a tailwind with his other processes, which began soon after his election on March 13, 2013, and again in 2015, with the release of his encyclical, *Laudato Sí.* Pope Francis was elected at close to eighty years of age and felt he had limited time. Therefore, he started several parallel processes, trying to face openly the uncountable cases of child and women abuses, ordering a full revision of the management of the Vatican's economy, while also in-troducing a new openness with regard to the closed and secret archives in the Vatican. And, he has shown undisguised disgust when subordinates have counteracted these initiatives.[50]

48. Lamb, *The Outsider,* 44.

49. Lamb, *The Outsider,* 37.

50. Pope Francis has sacked close employees when he understood their hidden

Pope Francis on the Climate and Environmental Crisis

The papal encyclical, *Laudato Sí*, signed by the Pope on May 24, 2015, as the Synod on marriage was under preparation, is an unusual papal encyclical. In form, it is a traditional discourse gathering points of view from Church history, from the Bible, from former pope's encyclicals, and motions. However, the theme is thoroughly up-to-date on the climate crisis, and on possible ways to avoid an environmental catastrophe. This encyclical may be the most important Pope Francis has delivered, choosing Church Conferences to discuss it broadly. I will restrict the presentation to short comments on the process of making this remarkable document, which illustrates how Pope Francis gets things done.

First, speaking only to the profile of *Laudato Sí*, Pope Francis tells us that he found inspiration for this work in the legends of St Francis of Assisi. "I believe that Saint Francis is the example par excellence of care for the vulnerable and of an integral ecology lived out joyfully and authentically. He is the patron saint of all who study and work in the area of ecology, and he is also much loved by non-Christians . . . He shows us just how inseparable the bond is between concern for nature, justice, for the poor, commitment to society, and interior peace."[51] At a Conference in Gregoriana, Rome titled, "Radical Ecological Conversion After *Laudato Sí*: Discovering the Intrinsic Value of all Creatures," in March 2018, I learned about how the *Laudato Sí* encyclical had been prepared. This Conference was arranged by the European Forum for the Study of Religion and the Environment. The Ghanaian curia, Cardinal Peter Turkson, who also oversaw The Pontifical Council for Justice and Peace, told us that the Pope had put him in charge of a small task force. Turkson further disclosed that Pope Francis personally followed the work on the encyclical, almost on a weekly basis.

In order to present the actual environmental problems the world faced in an updated scientific fashion, the task force worked in close contact with researchers on climate change at The Potsdam Institute for Climate Impact Research. According to his spokesperson, Rev. Dr. John

---

resistance. For instance, Cardinal Giovanni Angelo Becciu, was degraded from being a powerful second in charge for the Secretary of State in the Vatican to an ordinary priest, in a twenty minutes session with a furious Francis, in September 2020, when Francis detected that this man in his confidence was corrupt. See *La Repubblica*, October 05, 2020, *Cosa nasconde il nuovo terremoto che ha investito le finanze del Vaticano e illuminato la corruzione della Curia.*

51. *Laudato Sí*, 10.

Chryssavgis, these perspectives were further deepened through close contact with the Ecumenical leader of the World Council of Churches, Patriarch Bartholomew. The draft for *Laudato Sí* was conveyed to the Pope for changes and signing one whole year before he signed it. Every encyclical is presented in the name of the Pope, written in the first person. Therefore, Turkson could not tell anything about who wrote what, or where the Pope himself wrote, but Turkson indicated a tight bond. Most often, the Pope signed such encyclicals after a couple of months. Pope Francis used a full year on *Laudato Sí*. The rich result of this process is now studied in churches, universities, and engaged groups all over the world. Further work offers many rich rewards. The process is open, bringing material not only from theology but also contemporary science, inviting the responses of ecumenical representatives and other diverse voices, to be heard.

The Pope's response, thus is to use free language, talk directly to people, to journalists, to powerful people, using the well-known stories from the Bible, mostly with an original twist. At the same time, he exercises his full power, to restrict those who he counteracts with, thereby stripping some oppositional Cardinals of their dignity. After 35 years of a very conservative regime in the Vatican (the eras of John Paul II and Benedict XVI), which not only appointed likeminded Bishops and Cardinals, but also suppressed Liberation Theology (e.g., in 1984, Leonardo Boff silenced), Pope Francis now *not* only turns the tables upside down, but openly presents the vision, inspired by the Gospel, as the only durable means for the Catholic Church to win back the hearts of the faithful. Pope Francis is well experienced in the intricate power structures within the Church, and after having acted questionably in stressful situations during a "career" with many bumps, as Principal for the Jesuits, he has now moved to rethink the foundations of being the Catholic Church,.

So, facing a Catholic Church beset with many faults in leading positions, and which has overwhelmed so many of the faithful and well-meaning people of God, Pope Francis chose to start with the evident, and pure Gospel. And then, he moved to what he believes needs to be done. Yet, he also seems to know pretty well the limits of what he can accomplish. Therefore, he can be silent in the face of accusations from not well-meaning conservatives, even as he chooses to speak freely to journalists, whenever and wherever he chooses, and frequently in frank, open, and surprising tones. That is his soft strategy to effecting deep changes, and his use of the "art of resistance," which seems very effective, even *ex-cathedra* ("from the throne") of St. Peter's Basilica.

Bibliography

Borghesi, Massimo. *The Mind of Pope Francis: Jorge Mario Bergoglio's Intellectual Journey.* Translated by Barry Hudock. Collegeville, MN: Liturgical, 2018.

Burke, Raymond Leo, et al. *Chiesa cattolica, dove vai?: Una dichiarazione di fedeltà.* Verona: Fede & Cultura, 2018.

Denzinger, H., and A. Schönmetzer. *Enchiridion Symbolorum Definitionum et Declarationum de Rebus Fidei et Morum.* Freiburg: Herder, 1976.

Hafstad, Kjetil. *Forsonet med fortiden: Teologer om oppgjør med DDR-tiden.* Oslo: Norsk Teologisk Tidsskrift, 2010.

Jeanrond, Werner. *Å Omfavne den Andre.* Oslo: Kirke og Kultur, 2015.

Lamb, Christopher. *The Outsider: Pope Francis and His Battle to Reform the Church.* Maryknoll, NY: Orbis, 2020.

Martel, Frédéric. *In the Closet of the Vatican: Power, Homosexuality, Hypocrisy.* London: Bloomsbury Continuum, 2019.

O'Connell, Gerard. *The Election of Pope Francis: An Inside Account of the Conclave that Changed History.* Maryknoll, NY: Orbis, 2019.

Pontifical Biblical Commission. *Fede e cultura alla luce della Bibbia: Atti della Sessione plenaria 1979 della Pontificia Commissione Biblica.* Rome: Elle di Ci, 1981.

Pope Francis. *The Name of God Is Mercy: A Conversation with Andrea Tornielli.* London: Bluebird, 2016.

Scheper-Hughes, Nancy, and Jennifer Scheper-Hughes. "The Final Conversion of Pope Francis." *Berkeley Review of Latin American Studies* (Spring, 2015) 13–17, 58–59, 64–67.

Scott, James C. *Domination and the Arts of Resistance: Hidden Transcripts.* New Haven: Yale University Press, 1990.

West, Gerald O. *The Academy of the Poor: Towards A Dialogical Reading of the Bible.* Interventions 2. Sheffield: Sheffield Academic, 1999.

Wulf, Andrea. *The Invention of Nature. The Adventures of Alexander von Humboldt: The Lost Hero of Science.* London: Murray, 2015.

Internet Sources

BBC News. "Pope Francis: Who Am I to Judge Gay People?" July 29, 2013. https://www.bbc.com/ news/world-europe-23489702.

Francis, Pope. "Apostolic Exhortation *Evangelii Gaudium* of the Holy Father Francis to the Bishops, Clergy, Consecrated Persons, and the Lay Faithful on the Proclamation of the Gospel in Today's World." The Vatican, November 24, 2013. https://www.vatican.va/content/francesco/en/apost_exhortations/documents/papa-francesco_esortazione-ap_20131124_evangelii-gaudium.html.

———. "Homily of the Holy Father Francis: Holy Mass on the Solemnity of Mary, Mother of God, 54th World Day of Peace." St Peter's Basilica, Jan. 1,

2022.   https://www.vatican.va/content/francesco/en/homilies/2022/documents/
20220101_omelia-madredidio-pace.html.

———. "Homily of the Holy Father Francis: Celebrazione Mattutina Trasmessa in
Diretta Dalla Cappella Di Casa Santa Marta. Lo Spirito Santo ci ricorda l'accesso al
Padre." May 17, 2020. https://www.vatican.va/content/francesco/it/cotidie/2020/
documents/papa-francesco-cotidie_20200517_spiritosanto-accesso-al-padre.
html.

———. "Letter of His Holiness Pope Francis to the Grand Chancellor of the Pontifical
Catholic University of Argentina on the Centenary of its Faculty of Theology." The
Vatican, Mar. 3, 2015. https://www.vatican.va/content/francesco/en/ letters/2015/
documents/papa-francesco_20150303_lettera-universita-cattolica-argentina.
html.

———. "Post-Synodal Apostolic Exhortation *Amoris Laetitia* of the Holy Father
Francis to Bishops, Priests and Deacons, Consecrated Persons, Christian Married
People and All the Lay Faithful on Love in the Family." The Vatican, March 19,
2016.   https://www.vatican.va/content/dam/francesco/pdf/apost_exhortations/
documents/ papa-francesco_esortazione-ap_20160319_amoris-laetitia_en.pdf.

John XXIII, Pope. "*Pacem in Terris*: Encyclical of on Establishing Universal Peace in
Truth, Justice, Charity, and Liberty." Vatican. April 11, 1963. https://www.vatican.
va/content/john-xxiii/en/encyclicals/documents/hf_j-xxiii_enc_11041963_
pacem.html.

Holl, Nikolas. "Reinigungskraft am Alexanderplatz: Die Geschäfte der anderen."
Zeit Online, Jan. 6, 2022. https://www.zeit.de/arbeit/2021–12/reinigungskraft-
alexanderplatz-toiletten-gaeste.

Mauro, Ezio. "Cosa nasconde il nuovo terremoto che ha investito le finanze del Vaticano
e illuminato la corruzione della Curia." *La Repubblica*, October 5, 2020. https://
www.facebook.com/ Repubblica/posts/cosa-nasconde-il-nuovo-terremoto-che-
ha-investito-la-gestione-delle-finanze-del-/10160659054321151/.

McElwee, Joshua J. "Francis Explains 'Who Am I to Judge?'" *NCR*, January 10, 2016.
https://www.ncronline.org/news/vatican/francis-explains-who-am-i-judge.

Pentin, Edward. "Cardinal Burke Addresses the 'Dubia' One Year after Their Publication." *NCR*, November 15, 2017. https://www.ncregister.com/blog/cardinal-burke-
addresses-the-dubia-one-year-after-their-publication.

Second Vatican Ecumenical Council. 1965. Pastoral Constitution on the Church in the
Modern World *Gaudium Et Spes*. Promulgated by His Holiness, Pope Paul VI on
December 07, 1965. https://www.vatican.va/archive/hist_councils/ii_ vatican_
council/documents/vat-ii_const_19651207_gaudium-et-spes_en.html.

United States Conference of Catholic Bishops. "2014–2015 Synods of Bishops on the
Family." Marriage and Family Life Ministries. https://www.usccb.org/topics/
marriage-and-family-life-ministries/2014-2015-synods-bishops-family.

16

The Leader Who Became a Silent Leper

*African Postcolonial Reflections on Miriam (Numbers 12:1–16) with Reference to Women in Politics in Uganda and Rwanda**

Robert W. Kuloba

Introduction

ALTHOUGH ACKNOWLEDGED AS A leader and prophet, Miriam's role and memoirs in the Hebrew Bible are *nihil*. Miriam is accused and judged before the ideological jury of the Hebrew Bible for being slanderous against Moses, on accounts of his Cushite wife and claiming prophetic monopoly. She is afflicted with leprosy and silenced until pronounced dead. Miriam evokes ambiguous imaginations when read in African postcolonial contexts, in relation to female leadership. Reading Miriam in the context of historical and contemporary political space for women, in which ways does Miriam inspire and inform female political participation in Africa? The essay critiques the ideological spaces that sanction women to lower leadership levels and challenges the dominant ideological perception of male leadership as superior. It draws illustrations from the diversity of African female politicians who have suffered

*In honor of Professor Gerald Oakley West's indelible contribution to African Biblical Studies and Hermeneutics—researching, teaching, and reading scripture/the Bible with humans.

similar fates as Miriam. The chapter takes a postcolonial African trajectory that seeks to read the Bible as an African story.

Who Is Miriam?

Miriam is mentioned as the daughter of Amram and Jochebed in Numbers 26:59 (cf. Exod 6:20). She is a sister to Aaron and Moses although very little is known about her from the Bible. The book of Exodus vaguely mentions a young girl who played the heroic role of saving a Hebrew boy named Moses in the Sea of Reeds. Her naïve courage yielded positive results after the dramatic discovery of the baby by Pharaoh's daughter. She got a chance to participate in the historical making of the man who would not only become the political and religious leader of the people of Israel, but also whose name is iconic in all liberation polemics. She tactfully arranged for Moses' motherly care and nourishment, which groomed Moses into the man who would identify with his people; a leader and servant of God whose authority no woman would challenge and go scot-free, thanks to the daring character of the little girl. The young girl is not named in the texts, but from the rabbinic literature and unfolding events of the exodus episodes, she was apparently Miriam. She is not named in Exodus 6:20 among the children of Amram and Jochebed, but named in Exodus 15:20 and Numbers 26:59 as a Levite, sister to Aaron the brother of Moses (Exod 4:14, c.f 2:1 and Num 26:59).

If Miriam was the girl at the shores of River Nile, who reunited Moses with her family, then that defines her character as a keen woman, right from her childhood. In Midrashim, Miriam is even identified with one of the two midwives in Exod 1:15. She is Puah, while her mother, Jochebed, is Shiphrah (their Hebrew names suggest their roles in saving babies).[1] Miriam had a unique personality of ambition, aggression, and bravery that were required of a leader of her time. Once again, in Midrashim, Miriam was brave enough to tell the Egyptian Pharaoh that he would be punished by God for his cruelty to the Hebrews.[2] She challenged her father Amram to return her mother after divorcing her, as a result of the cruel edict referring to the exposure of the children, and she sang and danced on the day of the remarriage of her parents. She predicted to her father the birth of Moses who would liberate the

---

1. Dame, "Paradoxical Prophet," 5.
2. Singer and Lauterbach, "Miriam."

Hebrews from the Egyptian slavery, and when Moses was born, her father kissed her and said, "Your prophecy, my daughter, is fulfilled."[3] Thus, in Israelite lore, she was a woman of prophetic calibre and significantly influenced family decisions.

In Exodus 15:20–21, she is described as מִרְיָם הַנְּבִיאָה ("Miriam the prophetess"), though her prophecies and teachings are not recorded in the biblical book. She is a priestess and leads women in the celebration dance at the Sea of Reeds, with a timbrel (Exod 15:20), one of the traditional ritual implements of Near Eastern priestesses, leading the people (וַתַּעַן לָהֶם מִרְיָם) in choral song; another priestess role. Prophet Micah regards her as one of the leaders who brought the Israelites from Egypt (Mic 6:4). As Enid Dame has put it, Miriam is a powerful but silenced woman. She is doubly silenced: in the text (by God) and in the arrangement of the texts, by writers and editors who reduce her story to a few brief mentions.[4]

Numbers 12:1–16: An Analysis

Our study of Numbers 12 presents a sad and enigmatic situation that involved Miriam, Aaron, and Moses. Accordingly, Miriam and Aaron spoke ill of Moses on two accounts: Moses' marriage to a Cushite woman, and Moses' claim of prophetic monopoly. God reprimanded them both in defence of Moses but punished Miriam alone severely. Due to difficulties associated with studying this text from its historical context (as also the rest of the Pentateuch), this paper will therefore focus on the ideological overtones of the story of Miriam's plight following the theophany.

Verse 1 וַתְּדַבֵּר מִרְיָם וְאַהֲרֹן בְּמֹשֶׁה עַל־אֹדוֹת הָאִשָּׁה הַכֻּשִׁית אֲשֶׁר לָקָח כִּי־אִשָּׁה כֻשִׁית לָקָח

["And (they) Miriam and Aaron, criticized Moses on the account of the Cushite woman whom he had married. For Moses had married a Cushite wife"].

There is a grammatical problem in relation to the verb וַתְּדַבֵּר, which is 3rd person feminine singular but supposedly Miriam and Aaron as subjects. From its root (דבר), this word is often used as a synonym to אָמַר, and both are translated in simple terms as "speak" or "say"

---

3. Singer and Lauterbach, "Miriam."

4. Dame, "Paradoxical Prophet," 9.

(Gen 8:15; 23:8, Exod 4:14). However, the context of its usage in this verse carries the sense of criticism or slander. It is apparently meant that both Miriam and Aaron are culpable for criticizing Moses' marriage to a Cushite wife. Cush designates the Sudan (Nubia), land south of Egypt, though it is sometimes identified with Ethiopia (Gen 10:6, 8; Isa 11:11; 20:3, 5; and 43:3). However, there is no evidence in the Bible to suggest that this area included Moses' sphere of activity. Martin Noth, however, opines that the area could be identified with Cushan of Habakkuk 3:7, where the reference is to a tribe or confederacy of tribes mentioned as a parallel to Midian.[5]

Verse 2: וַיֹּאמְרוּ הֲרַק אַךְ־בְּמֹשֶׁה דִּבֶּר יְהוָה הֲלֹא גַּם־בָּנוּ דִבֵּר וַיִּשְׁמַע יְהוָה ("And they said: Has the Lord spoken only to Moses? Hasn't he spoken and listened to us also?").

This verse introduces a new reason for Miriam and Aaron's slander against Moses. It is now not the case of Moses' Cushite wife but, rather, about prophetic revelation and authority. Once again, the verb וַיֹּאמְרוּ in its grammatical form implicates both Miriam and Aaron. Both Miriam and Aaron are heard by God questioning Moses' prophetic monopoly.

In Numb 12:4–5, God intervenes. God spoke to all the three: Moses, Aaron, and Miriam. In this verse, there is a reversal of name order between Miriam and Aaron in contrast to the previous verse, with Aaron mentioned first. And while God summoned three of them to come out into the tent of meeting, it would seem to be common in the Hebrew Bible that before the deity, man precedes a woman.

In Numb 12:6–9, God speaks to Aaron and Miriam in the presence of Moses. The scene is outside the "tent of meeting" under the cover of the clouds. Yahweh addressed Aaron and Miriam in defense of Moses. In this section, God affirms that, to other prophets, God speaks in dreams and visions, but to Moses, God speaks directly פֶּה אֶל־פֶּה because Moses is trusted in God's house. Moses is set apart as a special prophet and leader from the other two, Aaron and Miriam (to whom God can only appear in visions and dreams). God rhetorically questions Aaron and Miriam's fearless talk against God's servant Moses. Verse 9 describes God as angry against the accused slanderers—Miriam and Aaron.

In Numb 12:10–12, God's presence departs and the cloud is rolled away. What is left behind is a spectacle of Miriam who is stricken by צָרַעַת

---

5. Noth, *Numbers*, 94.

("skin disease"). Aaron pleads with Moses to heal Miriam, addressing Moses as a superior even though he is the youngest of the three, with an entreaty בִּי followed by אֲדֹנִי (see Gen 44:18, Josh 6:13; 1 Sam 1:26). But, even though Moses in Numb 12:13–15, intercedes for Miriam, the unforgiving narrative subjects her to suffer for seven days with a skin disease.

Discussion: Unfair Divine Punishment and Silencing of Miriam

Though the text presents a lot of inconsistencies associated with a general lack of cohesion, we are intrigued by the situation of bias in dispensing divine justice between two culpable siblings. The scene in the narrative is situated at a key point when leadership was crucial, and about to change hands. The text presents two accusations against Miriam and Aaron: Criticising Moses' marriage and challenging Moses' prophetic "monopoly." The use of תְּדַבֵּר, in Numb 12:1, may not be accidental but an outright emphasis and victimization of Miriam. As earlier stated, the verb is in feminine, singular form but prefixed to two characters' names, Miriam and Aaron.

The discussion on who the Cushite woman in question is has been made by Bernard Robinson,[6] David T. Adamo,[7] Eryl W. Davies,[8] and Gershon Hepner[9] among others. On the usage of a feminine singular verb, Robinson contends that Miriam was punished because she was the one who took the initiative of criticizing Moses. Robinson's argument comes as a negation of the view that Aaron was equally guilty but was spared because of his priestly rank, or because he was a male.[10] To Robinson, Miriam was a Prophetess and was therefore in a position to question any ideas that Moses had a monopoly on divine guidance, but Aaron could not, with credibility, make such a claim on his own account, since he was not a prophet of God, but a prophet of Moses.[11] In verse two, the accusation against Miriam and Aaron changes from Moses' marriage to that of Moses' prophetic authority. Accordingly, Miriam and Aaron spoke against Moses' prophetic authority, claiming

6. Robinson, "Jealousy of Miriam," 429–30; Levine, *Numbers 1–20*, 328.

7. Adamo, "A Silent Unheard Voice in the Old Testament."

8. Davies, *Numbers*, 119.

9. Hepner, "Moses' Cushite Wife."

10. Robinson, "Jealousy of Miriam," 429–30.

11. Robinson, "Jealousy of Miriam," 431.

that they equally had divine revelation from Yahweh. This is the very reason Yahweh comes down to intervene and clarify Moses' relationship with Him.

As already noted, the challenge to Moses' prophetic authority was made by both Miriam and Aaron. But the theophany left only Miriam afflicted with צָרַעַת—a form of skin disease. צָרַעַת in ancient Israel was not an accurate term for leprosy (KJV). But it was believed to be a punishment from God, like all other diseases. Miriam's afflictions became a basis for the postbiblical Jewish interpretations that regarded צָרַעַת as a punishment for malicious talk.[12] Yair Zakovitch, in his study of 1 Kings 5, has demonstrated that in all the biblical narratives in which a person is punished with צָרַעַת, the punishment is due to his or her failure to submit to the proper authority; the authority which the narrator approves.[13] Failure to serve the right party with full loyalty would result in affliction. In Babylon, the Akkadian equivalent of צָרַעַת was *saharsubbû*. In the treaty between Ashurnirari V and Mati'ilu, the latter was threatened with *saharsubbû* as punishment for not serving the former in full loyalty.[14] In 2 Kings 5, Gehazi is punished with צָרַעַת for undermining prophetic authority of Elisha. In Numb 12, Miriam is punished with צָרַעַת for challenging Moses' authority; and when Aaron appeals to Moses to heal Miriam in Numb 12:11–12, he is acknowledging Moses' prophetic authority over that of Miriam, which he and Miriam had challenged.[15] It demonstrated that neither Miriam nor Aaron can speak directly to God to get healed, but only Moses could do so on her behalf.

Lev 13 elaborately outlines the impact of leprosy and other related skin illnesses. Accordingly, צָרַעַת has an effect of uncleanliness and isolation from the general public to avoid contamination. A leper was confined to private space, and was inadmissible to the public. In our text צָרַעַת also had a silencing effect on Miriam. She became unclean and could not talk, lead, or be part of the community she associated with right from Egypt. In the text, this begins a period where she is isolated from the people, alienated, and perpetually silenced till her death.

The thematic (dis)continuity between verses 1 and 2 has been a subject of analysis in the midrashic tradition, which in some circles identifies

---

12. Levine, *Numbers 1–20*, 332.

13. Sperling, "Miriam, Aaron and Moses," 48 and n. 64.

14. Sperling, "Miriam, Aaron and Moses," 48 and n. 66.

15. Sperling, "Miriam, Aaron and Moses," 48–49.

the Cushite woman as Zipporah—Moses' wife.[16] The verb לקח is taken as a pluperfect, that is, Moses had previously married Zipporah, a beautiful woman, referred to by the dysphemism "Cushite," as a precaution against the evil eye.[17] Subsequently, however, he had divorced her or, in another account, had stopped having sexual relations with her. The divorce tradition is based on Exod 18:2–6. In either case, Miriam and Aaron had attributed Moses' dismissal of Zipporah to his haughty belief that prophetic office precluded sexual intimacy. The complaint by Miriam and Aaron was that, inasmuch as they too were prophets and had not abandoned their spouses through either divorce or marital celibacy, there was no need for Moses to abandon Zipporah his Cushite wife.[18] Miriam and Aaron were therefore not against Moses' marriage to a Cushite woman, but are siding with her to challenge Moses' status of marital celibacy.[19] This view is consonant with other midrashic views of Miriam as a family builder.[20] In our texts, the midrashic tradition would suggest that Miriam's effort to restore the marital life of Zipporah and Moses was followed by a rude divine rebuke that left her sick and completely silenced.[21]

Worth emphasizing is the fact that Aaron, in Exod 18:11, is presented interceding for Miriam, while at the same time repenting for his own part. Aaron in his plea clearly admits that he played an active part in the crimes committed against Moses. What remains startling in this text is that Miriam alone was harshly punished for the crime(s), and Aaron was left unpunished for the crime he admits to have committed. There are varying opinions about this issue. The popular view held is based on the order of names that place Miriam first in verse 1. It is thought that because she is named first, she must have been at the forefront of the accusation and Aaron followed her opinion. Aaron's sin is that he compromised with Miriam, in a similar way Adam compromised with Eve.[22] The arrangement of names in verse 1, where Miriam comes first is different from verse 4, where her name is last. This may not be accidental but by design to echo the hierarchical order of superiority and ideological preference for male authority.

16. Sperling, "Miriam, Aaron and Moses," 42.

17. Sperling, "Miriam, Aaron and Moses," 42.

18. Sperling, "Miriam, Aaron and Moses," 46, also n. 46, 47 and 48.

19. See Fischer, "Authority of Miriam," 167.

20. Dame, "Paradoxical Prophet," 5–6.

21. Dame, "Paradoxical Prophet," 5–6.

22. Graetz, "Did Miriam Talk Too Much?," n. 9.

Generally, information about Miriam in the Bible is very scanty. However, there are a few allusions that present the significance of Miriam: In Exod 15:20–21, she is described as מִרְיָם הַנְּבִיאָה ("Miriam the prophetess") though her prophecies are not recorded. Although Prophet Micah regards Miriam as one of the leaders who brought the Israelites from Egypt (Mic 6:4), Miriam is not only differentiated but also disconnected from Moses in Exodus 15: She is the sister of Aaron, and a leader of women in the celebration dance at the Sea of Reeds with a timbrel (Exod 15:20), while Moses is the leader of Israel (v. 22).

Though Miriam seems to have had well-grounded prophetic, priestly and leadership roles, working in trinity with Moses and Aaron (Mic 6:4), her roles, portrait and character in the Hebrew Bible are ideologically mutilated, disfigured and distorted—presenting an ambiguous and disarticulated whole, which preserves Miriam's afterlife as a denigrated and loathed figure. Miriam is silenced forever with the pronouncement of her death as the final nail on her coffin into silence in Numbers 20:1, in the wilderness of Zin. Her roles in Moses' childhood and leadership of Israel, disappear from history and only get remembered as by-the-ways. No mourning or burial rights either are accorded to her, unlike her brothers (Num 20:28–29 and Deut 34:5–8). Naming of her successor after her death to carry on her roles became unnecessary (cf. Num 20:27 and Deut 34:9). Her punishment with leprosy rendered her unclean, distanced and silent from the leadership chart. Moses was set aside as God's chosen leader, while Miriam was ornamented as an iconoclast in the leadership ideology.

Ideologically, Miriam became a byword for illicit behaviours in biblical tradition. There is a warning in Deut 24:9, which recalls Miriam's plight: "Remember what the Lord your God did to Miriam on the way as you came forth out of Egypt." But what did Miriam actually do, that she became a warning for the future generations? The answer is that she gave her opinion on Moses' conduct whatever it was. And she is punished with leprosy for that. Deut 24:9 serves to warn future generations against Miriam. Miriam shouldn't be a character to emulate or else risk leprosy. As Naomi Graetz has argued, "women in the biblical world were not supposed to be leaders of men, and that women with initiative were reproved when they asserted themselves with the only weapon they had, that is: their power of language . . ."[23] The story of Numbers 12 portrays Miriam

23. Graetz, "Did Miriam Talk Too Much?," 233.

as an antithetical to authority. To In agreement with Graetz, Miriam's punishment was a discriminatory decision against her, and has the effect of ending her legitimate public aspirations.[24]

Beyond Num 12:1–16, Miriam is eliminated from the leadership scene, confined in silence and killed off. The narrative is silent about Miriam's activities and life after her punishment. From the texts, it remains a figment in the readers' minds about what became of Miriam after the theophany: Did she ever lead fellow women again, sing songs and probably influence issues as she had been doing? Was she still grateful for the Lord's salvation? Or did she join those who wished they had remained in Egypt? What became of her relationship with Moses' wife or wives? What is clear is that Miriam's leadership and prophetic career ended there. The theophany had an alienating effect on Miriam, who is apparently ridiculed, confined, silenced, stereotyped and isolated. Her attempt to equal herself to Moses not only earned her divine rejection, but made her unclean with leprosy, which forced her into private isolation, leaving the public space for men.

David Sperling has argued instructively that Pentateuchal narratives are all set temporally in the period before the rise of the Israelite states. They refer to events and institutions of the Israelite states and then of the Jewish communities in the years between ca. 1200–300 BCE. He maintains that these same narratives are not primarily antiquarian, but rather ideological, in that they advocate positions intended to influence the contemporaries of the authors in matters which to them were of contemporary concern.[25] He therefore reads the story of Miriam in relation to Aaron and Moses as an ideological investment on the subject of authority. Deborah and Huldah are exceptional cases. The story of Deborah who operates as Judge and Prophetess is apparently meant to highlight the feebleness of Israel's enemies (Judg 4:9) before Yahweh. Yahweh can use an army not strong enough and led by a woman to defeat a strong army led by Sisera. She is leading men in war against the enemies of Israel. Prophetess Huldah (2 Kgs 22:14; 2 Chr 34:22), as with Deborah, has her name and prophetic office mentioned alongside her husband's name. This is probably meant to stress that though they were prophetesses and leaders, they were under the authority of their male partners, unlike Miriam whose sexual life is not mentioned.

24. Graetz, "Did Miriam Talk Too Much?," 235.

25. Sperling, *The Original Torah*; also, Sperling, "Miriam, Aaron and Moses," 39.

It should be emphasised that Bible narratives don't deny Miriam's authority as a prophetess and leader. What is clear is that Miriam's story is halved and incomprehensible, and her position not clearly defined. Whereas the Hebrew Bible lays the antecedents that clarify Mosaic and Aaronic leadership, there is no similar parallel for Miriam, which places her as an imposter. Moreover, it is not clear whether Miriam was deputising Moses or a co-leadership entity that took control and leadership of a section like the women's wing. Miriam instead is painted as a rival that is bent to illegitimately usurp authority and dim Moses' visibility. It is not premature to state that the punishment and humiliation of Miriam constituted a rejection and silencing of female leadership in the Hebrew Bible, largely giving credence to male leadership. Similar characters like Athalia of Judah, who usurp political power, are diabolised and vilified as ideological misfits on political thrones.[26] Unlike the case for Aaron and Moses, Miriam's successor remains unnamed date.

The Story of Miriam and
African Postcolonial Bible Interpretation

Numb 12 presents a creative story of a female leader who is discriminately punished, humiliated, isolated, and eliminated from leadership. The text overtly tells Miriam that "yes, you are also a leader, but you are not like Moses the man . . . You are a woman and should not challenge or equate yourself to men! If men challenge each other like Aaron has done, you should be modest and decent in your conduct. . .! So because you have played a man and challenged male authority, you are more guilty than Aaron and you should suffer leprosy! With this leprosy you are made unclean and you have a right to remain silent or whatever you say shall be used against you with much more severe consequences. You shall be expelled from leadership and your name shall never be heard of again as a leader from this moment till you die!"

It is not wrong to imagine that, to Miriam, Moses was a brother and a co-leader with Aaron in this noble cause of liberating the Israelites from suffering—leading them to the promised land. Miriam understood "leadership to embrace diverse voices, female and male."[27] In identifying with Moses and Aaron, Miriam probably viewed herself in royal terms

26. Kuloba, "Athalia of Judah."
27. Trible, "Miriam: Bible."

as the princess. She probably had learned how Egyptian women played significant roles in the political leadership of Egypt.[28] The presence of her mother and brother in Pharaoh's courts probably availed Miriam opportunities to observe Egyptian princesses and queens and other women of royal origin act freely and exchange opinions. But in the theophany, which was partly a tutorial scene about Moses' unique relationship with God, Miriam is taught a new lesson about the dynamics of power and gender hierarchies. She is situated at the bottom of the pyramid. She is criminalised, invalidated, silenced and eliminated.

In this section of the paper, I read Miriam as the African woman in the political leadership struggle. Right from colonial times, it can be said without fear of criticism, African women have suffered more heinous humiliations and denigrations than their male counterparts. For instance, the colonial government in Kenya heavily punished female sympathisers and fighters of Mau Mau, especially in Kamiti and Athi River prisons where women suffered several beatings, congestion, sanitary problems, inadequate food and clothing and excessive manual work.[29] Women were eventually relegated to political silence as members of the "Maemdeleo Ya Wanawake Organization" (Women's Progress movement) and hostages in colonial villagisation schemes.[30] Women were reminded that they were women who should not challenge colonial men. Theirs werejust basic skills in home economics, as wives and mothers.

Even after independence, women suffered more in the hands of post colonial governments, as prominence was given to male leadership. It is not surprising that African female nationalists and politicians like Mary Nyanjiru (1922) are hardly remembered in the political history of East Africa. Prominence has been given to male politicians like Jomo Kenyatta (Kenya's first president after independence) and his colleagues, who are celebrated to date as freedom fighting heroes. Political authority in Kenya was left in the hands of men like Kenyatta whose government did not have a single woman in it, as if the war against colonialism was fought by only men. Priscilla Abwao, the sole female Kenyan delegate in Lancaster House Conference (1962) that negotiated Kenya's independence, had argued for equal treatment and representation by men and women in the New Kenya, but none of her appeals were taken seriously by her Kenyan brothers who became the political

28. Trible, "Miriam: Bible."

29. Kuloba, "Athalia of Judah."

30. Kuloba, "Athalia of Judah."

leaders of the nation.[31] The horrendous experiences suffered by personalities like Noble Laureate, Wangari Maathai, under Kenyan authorities are well documented in her book.[32]

In contemporary East Africa, my attention will be focused on the two sister countries of Uganda and Rwanda. The irony is that these two countries score highly on women's representation at various levels of government. Uganda, for example, currently boasts of 188 female members of Parliament, representing almost 34% of total members of parliament.[33] In 2021, President Museveni allocated 45% of the Cabinet ministerial posts to women—with key portfolios like Vice President, Prime Minister, and Deputy Prime Minister to women among many others. The situation in Rwanda is even more glamorous. Known as the number one country for women in politics globally, Rwanda has over 60% of its parliament made up of women,[34] while the cabinet is composed of 52% women.[35] The gender achievements in Rwanda are well discussed in scholarly works such as Claire Wallace, Christian Haerpfer, and Pamela Abbott,[36] and Swanee Hunt,[37] among many others. The figures in both these countries exclude female representations in local councils and other non-political appointments on affirmative action tickets.

The high presence of women in politics, however, has not provided a blank cheque. It has checks and balances, and players have had to navigate certain rules, which are predominantly patriarchal. Women's presence, it can be said, is just a silver lining in the thick clouds of patriarchy, which still undermine women's political freedoms of thought, expression, participation, and activism. Recent developments in both Uganda and Rwanda point to gross harassment, humiliation, and criminalization of women politicians whose views contradict the dominant ideology of their male counterparts.

For purposes of illustration, there are a number of cases of women politicians who have suffered sexual abuse and humiliation in Uganda. A case in point is Zainabu Fatuma Naigaga—who belonged to the Forum for Democratic Change (FDC) rival party to the ruling National

31. Kuloba, "Athalia of Judah."

32. Maathai, *The Challenge for Africa.*

33. https://data.ipu.org/node/180/data-on-women?chamber_id=13479

34. https://data.ipu.org/content/rwanda?chamber_id=13513

35. Iribagiza, "Women Now Constitute 52% of Rwanda Cabinet."

36. Wallace, et al., "Women in Rwandan Politics," 111–25.

37. Hunt, "The Rise of Rwanda's Women," 150–56.

Resistance Movement (NRM), who was stripped naked in public by the police in 2015.[38] Her story resonates with Nabila Nagayi Ssempala and Ingrid Turinawe, the female Members of Parliament who have either publicly undressed themselves or had their breasts fondled by policemen.[39] Other forms of intimidation and harassment against women in Ugandan politics take forms of patronage by the dominant political figure, including verbal ridicule and insults.

In 2021, when Rebecca Alitwala Kadaga attempted to contest, again, for the position of Speaker of the 11th Parliament, it is alleged(with some evidence) that the head of state undermined her candidacy and patronized the election process. Through the Central Executive Committee of the ruling party, the president swayed the members of Parliament loyal to the ruling party, NRM, to vote for Jacob. L Oulanyah.[40] Undeterred, Kadaga defied the party's position and contested as an independent candidate, in an election where the president was, in person, at the polling station. Though she lost the race to her rival, Kadaga had cultivated popularity across the political divide, both in parliament and nationally. Unsurprisingly, her political rise has been noted, with anxiety, by the State House, and her elimination from the race became a means to contain her growing internal political star turn. Kadaga was then appointed Minister for the East African Community—to coordinate Uganda's interests externally—within the East African region, removing her, for now, from the local political scene.

The situation in Rwanda is similarly as bad as it is glamorous. Women who have attempted to contest for the presidency have been criminalized and imprisoned. For instance, Victoire Ingabire was arrested and imprisoned in 2012, with charges of inciting violence and having contrary opinions on the genocide ideology.[41] Diane Rwigare equally suffered similar treatment when, in 2018, she made her intentions known to run for the nation's presidency. Rwigare was eventually sentenced on similar charges to Ingabire's (inciting violence and harbouring contrary opinions on the genocide ideology) scuttling any hopes of political office. Other Rwandan politicians, like Yvonne Idamanga, remain languishing in prisons for their political ambitions. Idamanga's charges include accusing the president of being a dictator,

38. Kaaya, "How FDC Woman was Undressed."

39. Mwesigye, "Breasts in Protests."

40. https://www.independent.co.ug/may-24–date-set-for-oulanyah-versus-kadaga/

41. Human Rights Watch, "Rwanda: Eight-Year Sentence for Opposition Leader."

and that the president has instrumentalized the 1994 genocide for his political interests instead of helping the genocide survivors. She was derogatorily accused of being mad and of inciting violence.[42]

As Dan Ottemoeller has noted, the increased emphasis on having women in national and local politics is just instrumentalized by the power-seeking regimes to build electoral support from the block vote of women. As such, women's presence in politics is seen as just a symbolic gesture, without concrete political power.[43] Power still belongs to the patriarchy—the culturally approved ideology. In the wake of women's liberation movements, patriarchy then has been modernized. It has changed the relevant clauses to welcome women into leadership—with certain terms and conditions to be adhered to. Female politicians in this ideological space are expected to uphold the set patriarchal rules and serve the dominant male ideology. Their survival in Parliaments, Cabinets, and other political appointments, is primarily based on their loyalty to the male-dominated power centre. This had been earlier intimated on, parabolically, by Ugandan president, H. E. Y. K. Museveni, *Sowing the Mustard Seed*:

> A subject . . . did a distinguished service for the king. And the king asked his subject how he could reward him. He said to the king: 'My Lord the King, your servant does not want any gift from you. All I want is that when we are in a public place, may my Lord the King call his subject by name . . . it will help me very much because if the king calls his servant by name in front of so many people, everybody will wonder who I am and they will all come to your subject and help him.' . . . this is what we did for the women.[44]

Museveni's parable reveals some important questions: What distinguished service did women provide for Museveni's political career? In which way has the government paid off this service and to what effect? What is this public place? Patriarchy keeps power in the hands of men as Kings.

Museveni's proverb also reveals tensions between democratic ideals of equality and ideals of sovereignty where men, as kings, award and revoke positions of power and recognition to their subjects. It projects a

---

42. Rugemintwaza, "Rwanda: Idamange Yvonne Sentenced." See also Rwandan Govt Critic on YouTube Sentenced to 15 years."

43. Ottemoeller, "The Politics of Gender in Uganda," 87–104.

44. Museveni et al., *Sowing the Mustard Seed*, 191–192.

wishful image of a docile subject, a woman, happy to be a servant so long as she is called by name and title. She is one with modest aims, and she would face a harsh response were she to attempt asserting influence in her own right or make claims that make the king anxious. However, in the political space, some women made "the king" anxious. Actions that would annoy "the king" are responded to in accordance with the ancient laws of the male ego that incriminate and silence culprits, punitively.

Miriam and East African Women Politicians

Turning back to the biblical story of Miriam, I will now seek to establish a conversation between Miriam and her East African female counterparts, in their experience in their respective political spaces. Women in both biblical and East African environments are victims of political marginalization. Miriam was criminalized when she criticized Moses on moral and leadership grounds. Yet, Miriam simply stood on the platform of equality—to assert that she too was a leader in equal measure with Moses. Her claims have been observed ideologically within the text, as a challenge to Mosaic authority, for which she is punished and invalidated. As a result, her voice, and that of her supporters, was silenced perpetually in the Hebrew Bible. Though Miriam is pronounced dead and buried soon after the challenge to Moses, she still lives and finds vitality and fidelity embodied in women around the world—Rwanda and Uganda included.

Both Miriam's and Rwanda's political opponents feared they would incite violence against the dominant leader. For example, accusations against Victoire Ingabire, Diane Rwigare, and Yvonne Idamanga in Rwanda bear commonalities: They all criticized the leader, President Kagame, with at least two of them, Ingabire and Rwigare, having shown political ambition in running for the presidency. They also have accused the president of dictatorship, resulting in a counteraccusation of holding contrary opinions on genocide ideology and of making statements with intent to incite violence. Ingabire's and Rwigare's attempts to run for president posed a threat to the President. It meant that they, as women, were portrayed as being ungrateful for what the regime had offered to women, and they had crossed the gender lines and broken the patriarchal rules, which ideologically protected the position of the presidency for men only.

Like Miriam, the political women of Rwanda may have misread the direction of the wind—to think that high numbers of women meant a levelled playing ground toward the presidency. They may have assumed they had certain rights and freedoms of expression, and that their opinion with the hopes to galvanize support for the higher office were acceptable. Miriam, with her right-hand man Aaron, assumed similar rights and freedoms, while standing on the unnoticeably patriarchal ideological ground. Miriam, like Ingabire and Rwigare, criticized Moses on moral issues and his claims for prophetic and leadership monopoly. Uganda and Rwanda share the motif of political power monopoly, where both presidents have stayed longer in power than most African leaders.

Using an analogy of market theory, power monopoly simply put means "intolerance to competition." There is no close substitute in a monopoly setting. Monopoly power, also known as "market power," denotes that a firm or an individual sets the price of goods and services.[45] If the goods and services are essentials, "the consumer faces a pay-to-live or die choice"[46] as there are no alternative means for survival. Monopolies derive their market power from the ability to erect barriers for competition to enter their domain. These are circumstances deliberately created legally or ideologically to prevent potential competitors' abilities to compete in a market.[47] One of the salient features of monopolistic firms is price discrimination—charging different prices to different customers. Using the concept of reservation price denotes the maximum price—as reserved by the monopolist and expected of a customer to pay.[48] The inception of alternative or close substitutes definitely makes the monopolist anxious, and there can be both overt and covert efforts to deal with the potential competitor in order to continue enjoying the economies of scale associated with monopoly.

In the Hebrew Bible, criticisms of Miriam and her claims for equal leadership authority signified a challenge against Mosaic rule. In the texts, Miriam is ideologically dealt with decisively—invalidated, silenced, and killed off—as Moses, the ideologically approved leader, reigns. In this ideological landscape, Miriam was deemed so dangerous a character, that efforts to put her out of the public eye were sought. Miriam was capable of causing or inciting the already rebellious people in the exodus to support

45. Barkley, *The Economics of Food and Agricultural Markets*, 93.

46. Beckman et al., "Dictator Monopolies," 6461.

47. Goodwin et al., *Microeconomics in Context*, 307–8.

48. Goodwin et al., *Microeconomics in Context*. 130

her course or at best reject Mosaic rule. In contemporary terms, she had the potential to captivate the support of the masses which was tantamount to inciting violence against Moses and the possibility of leadership change. The women in the East African context—like Miriam—are feared they would incite violence against what they call dictatorial regimes. In the case of Rwanda for illustration, accusations of inciting violence carry deeper ideological symbolism. Violence against who, what, and to what effects?

I opine that a numerical increase of women in politics, either by decree or action plans like Affirmative Action (AA), is not the solution to women's marginalization. The problem lies in androcentrism which affects the entire social-political structural landscape, that calls for a transformation agenda. For full emancipation and perfect equality to be realized, there should be a fundamental change in the entire psycho-social and political structure. Sylvia Tamale thinks that there should be an establishment of a theoretical framework that will integrate gender dynamics into the analysis of female and male legislators.[49] She argues that cultural socialization experiences transmitted through parents, education, peers, and the media, among others, create stereotyped expectations of the sexes by Ugandan (and, by extension, many an African) society. Girls are oriented towards feminine roles that include mothering and wifely roles, which limit their perception of life to domestic domains, while boys are aligned with roles that nurture aggressive and ambitious traits to venture into the world beyond the domestic and local arena.[50]

Girls are trained for stable marriages and homes through lessons aimed at imparting humility, obedience, and endurance to men's needs. In churches and Christian fellowships, for example, they are reminded that they are the "weaker sex" (1 Pet 3:7), and as Christians, they should be like the women of the Old Testament, such as Sarah "who addressed her husband Abraham as Master." (1 Pet 3:5) Inevitably, this is not like Miriam, who on the assumptions of equality challenged traditional assumptions when she not only perceived Moses as an equal but also claimed credence for the prophetic and leadership office. In many African political contexts, power and legitimacy are controlled by the patriarchy, and women simply appear as either intruders or guests into political spaces—away from their "rightful place," the domestic domain.

---

49. Tamale, *When Hens Begin to Crow*, 27.

50. Tamale, *When Hens Begin to Crow*, 27; Nzomo, "Women in Politics," 204–5.

Patriarchy creates and defines political spheres and domains for women, as a way of shielding its interests. In some policy documents, like the 1995 Uganda constitution, affirmative action created a gendered enclave for women's political participation in Uganda. Some of the electorate assume that these reserved seats are the only legitimate spaces for women candidates to seek political roles. As such, women who compete for electoral positions with men, outside of these reserved political positions, are viewed as greedy transgressors, assuming a masculine position, and are derogatorily labelled "mad," "un-husbandable" and "prostitutes."[51]

Under similar imaginations, women are presumed to be no more than simple deputies to their male counterparts, as either Vice Presidents, deputy ministers, vice-chairpersons, etc. This deputizing of men ends up reflecting a tendency to assume transference of the husband-and-wife relationship in an African homestead, into the public sphere. Supposedly, the husband is the "head" of the homestead, and the wife is a "second in command"—whose influence is only interim, as in the husband's absence, but not absolute. As such deputies, women are reminded of their subordinate roles and powers, and the dangers of criticizing or undermining the authority of the dominant leader, their boss. Like wives, they should therefore cover the weaknesses of their male bosses instead of undermining them in public.

In this way, women who have voiced views against dominant male leaders in the African patriarchal settings are criminalized. That the political activities of characters like Ingabire and Rwigare as tantamount to inciting violence is simply the fear patriarchy has for the female politician. Reflecting on the idea of incitement brings a realization that the regime in power fears that should the population come to know about certain facts and perspectives, it would discredit the regime and seek for change. The truth is ideological. For example, in the context of Rwanda, there is an official ideology that the regime wants to maintain about the 1994 genocide. Any other challenging views on the 1994 ideology that contradict the official ideology are characterized as dangerous, by the regime. Like Miriam, the female politicians of Rwanda, it can be argued, are criminalized on the basis of variation of opinions, which they hold; opinions that make the establishment anxious.

Maintaining a narrative that is aimed at controlling masses takes forms of overt and covert suppression, including the killing off of other

---

51. Kuloba, "Athalia of Judah."

narratives—creating a monopoly of opinion, in effect dictatorship. Like in Numb 12, the victims are presented before the jury, punished, invalidated, and isolated in prison cells with the hope that they remain perennially silenced.

Bibliography

Adamo, David T. "A Silent Unheard Voice in the Old Testament: The Cushite Woman Whom Moses Married in Numbers 12:1–10." *IdK* 52.1 (2018).

Barkley, Andrew. *The Economics of Food and Agricultural Markets.* Manhattan, KS: New Prairies, 2019.

Beckman, Steven R., *et al.* "Dictator Monopolies and Essential Goods: Experimental Evidence." *AE* 47/59 (2015) 6461–6478.

Dame, Enid. "A Paradoxical Prophet: Jewish Women Poets Re-Imagine Miriam." *Bridges* 12.1 (2007) 4–11.

Davies, Eryl W. *Numbers.* New Century Bible Commentary. Grand Rapids: Eerdmans, 1995.

Fischer, Irmtraud. "The Authority of Miriam: A Feminist Rereading of Numbers 12 Prompted by Jewish Interpretation." In *The Feminist Companion to the Bible: Exodus to Deuteronomy*, edited by Athalya Brenner, 159–73. Sheffield: Sheffield Academic, 2000.

Goodwin, Neva et al. *Microeconomics in Context.* London: Routledge, 2018.

Graetz, Naomi. "Did Miriam Talk Too Much?" In *The Feminist Companion to the Bible: Exodus to Deuteronomy*, edited by Athalya Brenner, 6: 231–242. Sheffield: Sheffield Academic,1994.

Hepner, Gershon. "Moses' Cushite Wife Echoes Hosea's Woman of Harlotries: Exposure of Unfaithfulness in the Wilderness." *SJOT* 23 (2009) 233–42.

Human Rights Watch. "Rwanda: Eight-Year Sentence for Opposition Leader: Victoire Ingabire Found Guilty of Two Charges in Flawed Trial." https://www.hrw.org/news/2012/10/30/rwanda-eight-year-sentence-opposition-leader.

Hunt, Swanee. "The Rise of Rwanda's Women: Rebuilding and Reuniting the Nation." *FA* 19.3 (2014) 150–56.

IPU Global Data on National Parliaments: Rwanda. https://data.ipu.org/content/rwanda?chamber_id=13513.

IPU Global Data on National Parliaments: Uganda. https://data.ipu.org/node/180/data-on-women?chamber_id=13479.

The Independent Newspaper—Uganda. https://www.independent.co.ug/may-24-date-set-for-oulanyah-versus-kadaga/.

Iribagiza, Glory. "Women Now Constitute 52% of Rwanda Cabinet." *New York Times*, Nov. 5, 2019. https://www.newtimes.co.rw/news/women-now-constitute-52-rwanda-cabinet.

Kaaya, Sadab K. "Uganda: How FDC Woman Was Undressed." *The Observer*, Oct. 14, 2015. https://www.observer.ug/news-headlines/40441-how-fdc-woman-was-undressed.

Kuloba, W. Robert. "Athalia of Judah (2 Kings 11) A Political Anomaly or an Ideological Victim?" In *Looking through a Glass Bible: Postdisciplinary Biblical Interpretations from the Glasgow School*, edited by A. K. M. Adam and Samuel Tongue, 139–52. BIS 125. Leiden: Brill, 2014.

Levine, Baruch A. *Numbers 1–20: A New Translation with Introduction and Commentary*. Anchor Bible 4. New York: Doubleday, 1993.

Maathai, Wangari. *The Challenge for Africa*. New York: Pantheon, 2010.

Museveni, Yoweri, et al. *Sowing the Mustard Seed: The Struggle for Freedom and Democracy in Uganda*. London: Macmillan, 1997.

Mwesigye, Shifa. "Breasts in Protest." *The Observer*, Apr. 26, 2012. https://www.observer.ug/component/content/article?id=18409:breasts-in-protest.

Noth, Martin. *Numbers: A Commentary*. Translated by James D. Martin. OTL. London: SCM, 1968.

Nzomo, Maria. "Women in Politics and Public Decision Making." In *African Perspectives on Development*, edited by Ulf Himmelstrand et al., 203–17. London: Currey, 1994.

Ottemoeller, Dan. "The Politics of Gender in Uganda: Symbolism in the Service of Pragmatism." *ASR* 42.2 (1999) 87–104.

Robinson, Bernard P. "The Jealousy of Miriam; a Note on Numbers 12." *ZAW* 101 (1989) 428–32.

Rugemintwaza, Erasme. "Rwanda: Idamange Yvonne Sentenced to 15 Years in Prison." *The Rwandan*, Oct. 2, 2021. https://www.therwandan.com/rwanda-idamange-yvonne-sentenced-to-15–years-in-prison/.

Singer, Isidore, and Jacob Z. Lauterbach. "Miriam." In *Jewish Encyclopedia*. http://www.jewishencyclopedia.com/view.jsp?artid=655&letter=M&search=Miriam#1.

Sperling, S. David. "Miriam, Aaron and Moses; Sibling Rivalry." *HUCA* 70/71 (1999–2000) 39–55.

———. *The Original Torah: The Political Intent of the Bible's Writers, Reappraisals in Jewish Social and Intellectual History*. New York: New York University Press, 1998.

Tamale, Sylvia. *When Hens Begin to Crow: Gender and Parliamentary Politics in Uganda*. Boulder, CO: Westview, 1999.

Trible, Phyllis. "Miriam: Bible." http://jwa.org/encyclopedia/article/miriam-bible.

Wallace, Claire, Christian Haerpfer, and Pamela Abbott. "Women in Rwandan Politics and Society." International Journal of Sociology 38/4(2008/2009) 111-125.

17

Deuteronomic Law and Africa's Quest for Democracy

Gilbert Okuro Ojwang[1]

Introduction

THE BOOK OF DEUTERONOMY (hereafter, D), and especially Deut 12–26, has been rightly recognized as a political document. Already, in the first century CE, Josephus (see below) saw Deuteronomy as the "polity" for ancient Israel, in the sense of a national constitution.[2] Scholars have recognized the level of constitutional sophistication in Deuteronomy as one that is unmatched in the ancient world. Granted, we cannot expect

1. Author's Note: I am pleased to offer this essay in honor of Gerald O. West. I have met Professor West at several annual meetings of the Society of Biblical Literature (SBL), especially in the context of the African Biblical Hermeneutics program section, where I am currently serving as a member of the steering committee. At these meetings, I have admired Professor West's deep command of the discipline of biblical scholarship. A cursory look at his more-than-thirty-page curriculum vitae will quickly reveal that Professor West's scholarship spans numerous themes and interests, including contextual readings of Scripture, and his emphasis on giving voice to ordinary readers. His interest in reading the Bible in the context of the readers' socio-cultural, economic, and political location runs throughout his works. It is in this vein that I offer brief reflections on how Deuteronomic laws can and should be read against the backdrop of postcolonial Africa's democratic project. This version contains minor revisions to the paper originally read at the annual meeting of the Society of Biblical Literature, in Denver, Colorado, USA, November 17–20, 2018.

2. Cf. McBride, "Polity," 223–44.

congruence in all aspects. Nevertheless, Deuteronomy's constitutional ideals can be shown to compare well with the tenets of the constitutions of many modern democratic states. Against this backdrop, this paper seeks to read Deut 16:18—18:22 (with a specific emphasis on the law of the king, in Deut 17:14-20), using sociopolitical lenses in the context of Africa's fledgling democracies. The study is divided into three sections. In the first section, I briefly discuss questions of provenance of Deuteronomic law. In the second section, I seek to justify the socio-political methodology as a fruitful approach to the study of Deuteronomic law. In the third section, I demonstrate how an African biblical scholar might receive this biblical text and use it to provide the vocabulary with which to critique and contribute to Africa's elusive quest for democratic ideals. It is my submission that Deuteronomy offers a model that biblical scholars can use in conversations around advocacy for proper constitutionalism, the rule of law, and good governance in Africa.

Provenance of Deuteronomy 16:18—18:22

Deut 16:18—18:22 is part of the larger Deuteronomic law code of Deut 12–26. It deals with the establishment of various offices in ancient Israel. Duane L. Christensen extends this section to include Deut 19:1–21:9 (dealing with laws on judicial and military matters).[3] The inclusion of this extended material yields a structure that places leadership at the center, flanked by the themes of justice[4] in an ABA' pattern as follows:

A—justice Deut 16:18—17:13

    B—leadership in Deut 17:14—18:22 (King [Deut 17:14-20]— Priest [Deut 18:1-8]—Prophet [Deut 18:9-22])

A'—justice Deut 19:1—21:9

Apart from noting the inclusion of Deut 19:11-13, which recognizes the institution of elders (see also Deut 21:1–9, 19–20; 22:15–19; 25:7–9), I will

---

3. Christensen, *Deuteronomy*, lxxv, 381

4. Further, Christensen's seven-part menorah structure also places Deut 16:18—21:9 (laws on leadership and authority), at the center of the book. See his *Deuteronomy*, lxxv, 381. He concludes that "This fact suggests that a primary concern of the book of Deuteronomy, and perhaps the Pentateuch as a whole, is the matter of leadership of the people of God," 381.

limit my examination to the establishment of leadership offices in Deut 16:18—18:22, especially the offices of judge and of the king.

Provenance of Deuteronomic Laws

The provenance of the Deuteronomic law code in general is heavily debated. Opinions range from those who see the covenant renewal at Shechem (Josh 24), which the narrative places at the period shortly after Israel settles in the land of Canaan, as the occasion for the composition of most of the Deuteronomic legislation. For example, Peter Craigie argued that the essential elements of D, "substantially in its present form," would have been composed soon after the covenant renewal ceremony at Shechem.[5] This view is supported by the similarities between Deuteronomy and Hittite vassal treaties. This early dating of Deuteronomic law makes it almost contemporaneous with the Book of the Covenant (Exod 21:12—22:16), also dated to the settlement period.[6]

Another major scholarly assumption is to see D's legal material as a reform document.[7] This assumption has led scholars to look to periods in which there were reform movements in Israel and Judah. Consequently, some trace the earlier form of D, or at least some parts of it, to the time of Ahab/Elijah in Israel in the ninth-century and in the eighth-century, during Hosea.[8] This is strengthened by the presence of Northern Israelite themes, such as the use of "Horeb" (for Sinai), the Shechem traditions (Deut 11:29–30; 27:1–26), and the similarities between D and Hosea. Closely connected to this reform movement assumption, a number of scholars place D during the time of Hezekiah and his reforms, with another edition placing it during the time of Josiah (640–609 BCE).[9] Most scholars, accepting the theory that D, and especially the Deuteronomic law code of Deut 12–26, is the book of the covenant discovered in Jerusalem during Josiah's reign and which is believed to have informed Josiah's

---

5. Craigie, *Book of Deuteronomy*, 28, 32, 50–51.

6. Cf. Mann, *Deuteronomy*, 4–5.

7. Mann, *Deuteronomy*, 5.

8. Mann, *Deuteronomy*, 5.

9. According to Mann, *Deuteronomy*, Deut 4–28 could have been composed during Hezekiah's reforms, Deut 1–3, 29–34 added during Josiah, and D placed at the introduction of the Deuteronomistic History; Deut 4:25–31; 28:64–68; 30:1–10 added during the Babylonian exile, and D (Deuteronomy) separated from DtrH and included among the Tetrateuch to make Pentateuch, 6.

reforms, see the provenance of D in the Josianic period (2 Kgs 22–23). This view is supported by the evident influence of the Assyrian loyalty oaths.[10] According to this view, the reform movement was triggered by the excesses of Manasseh. This accounts for the presence of scribal activity, priestly[11] interests, legal concerns, and wisdom tradition.[12] Based on the extent to which the powers of the king has been reduced, Norbert Lohfink sees the socio-historical background of D's laws to be the effort to reduce the earlier powers of the king and the priesthood, and to redistribute the powers among the four offices: the judiciary, the king, the temple priests, and the freestanding charismatic prophets.[13]

In spite of the late dating of D's final redaction, scholars generally acknowledge that the laws themselves predate the seventh and sixth centuries BCE. For example, Georg Braulik notes that while the laws concerning offices can be dated to the period of the exile, this "says nothing about the age of the laws that were included" in the final redaction.[14] Similarly, Moshe Weinfeld argues that the "kernel of the law is ancient (cf. v. 14b with 1 Sam 8:5–6, 16 with Hosea 8:13b, 9:3b)."[15] My examination of the various positions, so far, leads me to the conclusion that a northern Israelite provenance (prior to 722 BCE), for the core of D, is the best explanation for its many northern Israelite features.

A Socio-Political Approach

If reform constitutes the socio-historical background of D, as argued by many scholars, this fact lends support for a reading of the final form of D's laws against the backdrop of Africa's struggle for democracy, championed by political reform movements across the continent. For

10. Nelson, *Deuteronomy*, 6.

11. Gary N. Knoppers has questioned the relationship between D and DtrH, see his "Rethinking the Relationship," 393–415.

12. Nelson, *Deuteronomy*, 7; he states that D is the work of a "a covert undertaking by dissident Jerusalem scribal circles during the reign of Manasseh and the minority of Josiah, with collaboration from aristocratic families, elements of the priesthood, and those schooled in wisdom. Traditional legal materials formed the basis for a document fashioned through a series of scribal micro-redactions. Older laws were formed into a program of religious, social, and political reform fashioned in part on the model of Assyrian loyalty treaties," 8.

13. Lohfink, "Distribution," 336–52 (345, 349).

14. Braulik, "Sequence of the Laws," 313–35 (334).

15. Weinfeld, "Deuteronomy," 21–35 (28), see n.40, see also 28, 35.

example, one may cite the agitation for multiparty politics and the push for constitutional reforms in Kenya beginning around 1990, culminating in the promulgation of the 2010 constitutional reform, in what has been dubbed, the "second liberation."[16] Certainly, most postcolonial African countries are in need of political reforms, each in its unique ways, in social, political, and economic regimes. This is more urgent as Africa is finding itself increasingly in the middle of a new "cold" war between the west and China. Therefore, reading D as a reform document, which addresses nearly the same kinds of issues, is apropos for African biblical scholarship.

This is best done through the lenses of what I call the "socio-political approach." By socio-political approach, I mean simply the interaction between the biblical text and a reflection on Africa as a set of political systems. *The Encyclopedia Britannica* defines a political system as "the set of formal legal institutions that constitute a 'government' or a 'state,'" or more broadly "actual as well as prescribed forms of political behavior, not only the legal organization of the state but also the reality of how the state functions."[17] A socio-political approach acknowledges that D shares, at least thematically, similar concerns of modern social scientists, civil societies, religious organizations involved with their states, as well as those involved in governance generally.

Deuteronomy 16:18—18:22 as Polity of Ancient Israel and a Model Constitution

That D is thoroughly a political document is now widely acknowledged. For example, it is recognized by modern western scholars as a "social charter of extraordinary literary coherence and political sophistication, thereby also recognizing the work to be the archetype of modern western constitutionalism."[18] The laws of Deuteronomy can easily "form a draft of a constitution that is based upon the distribution of functions of power."[19] As I mentioned earlier, Josephus referred to it [D] as the "polity" of

16. Katola, "Church-State Relationship," 44–59.

17. Heslop, "Political System." The third way to define a "political system," but which does not form a part of my present interest: "a set of 'processes of interaction' or as a subsystem of the social system interacting with other nonpolitical subsystems, such as the economic system," which relates to my earlier work: *The House of Omri.*

18. McBride, "Polity," 77; cf. Christensen, *Deuteronomy,* lvii.

19. Lohfink, "Distribution," 339; Weinfeld, "Deuteronomy," 28.

ancient Israel. This assertion was made in the context of debate as to who had attained an advanced form of statecraft in the ancient world and for Josephus, Israelite polity antedated Greek and Roman laws.[20]

S. Dean McBride cites the following from Polybius, "Now the chief cause of success or the reverse in all matters is the form of a state's constitution; for springing from this, as from a fountainhead, all designs and plans of action not only originate, but reach their consummation."[21] Put simply, a constitution can make or break a nation. As a national constitution, D's legal regime is markedly different from those of Israel's ancient Near Eastern neighbors (cf. the laws of Eshnunna, Hammurabi, Lipit-Ishtar, Middle Assyria, Hittite laws, etc.).[22] The most outstanding differences have to do with how biblical law, for example, valued human life and the individual worth of a person (based upon Gen 9:5ff) over property.[23] The second major difference between biblical law and the ancient Near Eastern laws has to do with the law-giver. In biblical law, God is the author, the law-giver, whereas the king is the law-giver in ancient Near Eastern laws.[24] Third, the Deuteronomic law of the king of Deut 17:14–20 is almost anachronistic as far as the ancient Near Eastern conception of kingship is concerned,[25] when one considers how much kingly power is constrained.

On the other hand, biblical law shares some of the fundamental purposes of law in the Ancient Near East (ANE), namely, concern for national well-being and material prosperity (Exod 23:20 ff; Lev 26; Deut 11:13ff, etc.).[26] The purpose of ANE laws, and indeed the purpose of law today is "'to establish justice,' 'that the strong might not oppress the weak,' to give good governance,' 'stable government,' 'to prosper the people,' 'abolish enmity and rebellion.'"[27] Here, I should hasten to admit

20. Josephus' assertion was a polemic against Roman Polybius and Cicero's claim that Rome was the first in the "cultivation of virtue, the exercise of rational governance, and the practical implementation of social justice." McBride, "Polity," 62–77 (63) and the references there.

21. McBride, "Polity," 63.

22. Greenberg, "Postulates," 283–300. For these laws, see Hallo and Younger, Jr., eds., *Context*.

23. Greenberg, "Postulates," 291. McBride, *Polity*, 75. For the argument that the laws of D are an elaboration of the Decalogue, see Braulik, "Sequence of the Laws," 313–335.

24. Greenberg, "Postulates," 288ff.

25. Cf. Christensen, *Deuteronomy*, 387.

26. Greenberg, "Postulates," 288.

27. See the laws of Lipit-Ishtar, and Hammurabi, cited in Greenberg, "Postulates,"

that post-modern readers will have qualms about any entity claiming to wield the power to "abolish enmity and rebellion," as such power is sure to be misused. Be that as it may, D's laws on governance are comparable to the constitutions of many modern democracies. For example, according to McBride, D is "arguably, the [US] Constitution's most ancient antecedent."[28] Without providing evidence, Christensen also says that "together with the law of the prophets (Deut 18:9–22), this law [of the king] played a formative role in the separation of powers as drafted in the U.S. Constitution."[29] For these and other reasons, reading Deuteronomic law from the socio-political perspective is warranted for scholars who recognize that all reading occurs from a reader's given social location is "reading from this place."[30]

Leadership and a Just Society

In Deuteronomic law, the highest social value is justice (צְדָקָה וּמִשְׁפָּט *mishpat-zedek* "righteous judgment," Deut 17:18).[31] The structure of the Deuteronomic law on leadership suggests that justice in all its aspects (social, or juridical) is the responsibility of leaders, as well as the people as a whole. As an African biblical scholar, it is almost inescapable to find resonance with Deut 16:18–18:22, and especially Deut 17:14–20 (law of the king), in the wake of perennial misrule of many an African country. Needless to mention, misrule is not the preserve of African nations, but rather a global phenomenon. It has not spared even the most advanced democracies (including western democracies). The killing of Jamal Khashoggi,[32] for example, and the caravan of 4000 to 5000 men, women, and children which moved north on its way to the US, fleeing poverty and gang violence in their (misruled) countries,[33] provide ample illustrations.

287; Cf. The Constitution of the United States: "to establish justice, ensure domestic tranquility, promote the general welfare."

28. McBride, "Polity," 64.

29. Christensen, *Deuteronomy*, 387; Mann, *Deuteronomy*, 9, avers, D is the "polity of Israel, similar to the way that the Declaration of Independence and the Constitution represent the polity of the United States of America."

30. See Segovia and Tolbert, *Reading from This Place*.

31. See McConville, *God and Earthly Power*, 78ff.

32. See BBC News, "Jamal Khashoggi."

33. See Agren, "Migrant Caravan to Leave Mexico City on Foot for U.S–Mexico border."

The Deuteronomic passage elicits the following question: How does this ancient text speak to the issues of governance in the 21st century?[34] The fact that it does, as I have maintained, in itself suggests that the need and desire for just rule is fundamental and indeed universal human, as captured by the US declaration of independence:

> We hold these truths to be self-evident, that all men [and women] are created equal, that they are endowed by their Creator with certain unalienable Rights, that among these are Life, Liberty and the pursuit of Happiness.—That to secure these rights, Governments are instituted among Men, deriving their just powers from the consent of the governed.[35]

If democracy is defined as that system of government that best delivers the above promises, then democracy is not only a western notion, it is also biblical.[36] Democracy has the following four components: 1. A political system for choosing and replacing the government through free and fair elections. 2. The active participation of the people, as citizens, in politics and civic life. 3. Protection of the human rights of all citizens. 4. A rule of law, in which the laws and procedures apply equally to all citizens.[37]

Democracy is as native to Africa as justice is a universal human need. Therefore, it comes as no surprise that in Deuteronomic law, these very themes dominate (except the element dealing with elections in the modern sense; in D, YHWH appoints leaders). Deuteronomic law highlights the central role of the people, the separation of powers and checks and balances through the establishment of various offices, limitations on executive authority of the president/king, emphasis on the rule of law and equal treatment of all citizens, men and women, and moral and ethical rectitude in governance.

---

34. Cf. For those who "struggle for social justice and human rights, the Deuteronomic model of theocentric humanism remains an eminently practicable legacy," McBride, "Polity," 77.

35. National Archives, "America's Founding Documents."

36. For the relationship between biblical law and democracy, see Ska, "Biblical Law," 146–58 (148–49).

37. See Diamond, "What Is Democracy?"

The Role of the People

D's legislation emphasizes the role of the people. The audience is addressed as a single united people by the use of the second person singular pronoun (you). It is the people who have responsibility to hold their leaders accountable. Unfortunately, in Africa, the people are either not informed sufficiently to hold leaders accountable, or merely support unqualified, non-performing or corrupt leaders primarily on the basis of their ethnic backgrounds ("our man/woman"). Ultimately, the people are responsible for the governments they elect, even if some governments are in office against the wish of the people, the consequence of manipulated electoral processes. I am aware that when elections are "stolen," resulting governments tend to be so repressive against their own citizens, that the citizens find it difficult (but not impossible) to remove such dictatorial regimes.

The Role of Leaders: Establishment of Constitutional Offices

As we have seen, the laws on leadership, namely king, priest and prophet, in Deut 17:14–18:22, are sandwiched between Deut 16:18–17:13 (which establishes the courts and the office of judges) and Deut 19:1–21:9 (which spells out other judicial procedures). This suggests that next to the people, leadership is central in the realization of a just and prosperous society.

The first principle of D's constitution is the separation of powers. Power is not concentrated in any one office or individual. It would seem as though Deuteronomic drafters were well aware of the now famous statement by Lord Acton: "power tends to corrupt, and absolute power corrupts absolutely."[38] Lohfink traces the modern idea of the separation of powers of state to Charles Baron de Montesquieu (1748). Most modern democracies tend to have the powers separated into legislature, executive and the judiciary. Lohfink states that while Montesquieu cited classical sources to support his theory, he might have cited the Bible as well.[39] As McBride notes, "the affirmation that egalitarian justice is

38. Quoted in Christensen, *Deuteronomy*, 387.

39. Lohfink, "Distribution," 336–37. For Lohfink, the Bible offers principles for the distribution of power that can be adapted to ecclesial leadership, instead of most ecclesial bodies copying/mimicking secular government systems. According to Lohfink, the Bible does not advocate the centralization of power in a human leader, as is done in the Roman Catholic Church, which bases its monarchical papacy on the supposed theology of Jesus entrusting leadership of his church to Peter and the apostles, a theology

the crux of theocratic government (Deut 10:17–19); [is] the single most important contribution of Deuteronomic constitutionalism to our political heritage . . ."[40] The immediate custodians of this constitutionalism are the judges—the courts.

The Judge: The Judicial Branch of Government

The legislation at Deut 16:18–20 provides for the appointment of judges and officials in local towns. The other office established is that of "officials" שׁוֹטְרִים/*shoterim*, Deut 16:18) who may have been secretaries, or scribes, or bureaucrats of some sort. As we have seen, the addressee is the second person singular (you). This placement among the established offices shows that justice is the highest social value which must be upheld by the people and, by extension, the judges, and indeed all the leaders. Possible impediments to justice are "partiality"[41] and bribery (שָׁחַת *shachat* Deut 16:19, cf. YHWH is identified as "one who does not take bribes," 10:17). Social wellbeing depends on justice and justice only (צדק צדק תרדף/*zedek zedek tirdoph* "you shall pursue justice or 'rightness' or 'justness' only," Deut 16:20). Deut 16:18–17:7 deals with worship as well as social wellbeing. Here too, the theme of justice is infused.

Deut 17:2–7 provides for due process in the administration of justice. A person who is accused of capital offense (in this case, false worship) has a right to fair hearing. The alleged crime must be investigated "thoroughly" הֵיטֵב (/*hitab* Deut 17:4). A minimum of two (Deut 17:6) credible (Deut 17:7) witnesses is required. Men and women are treated equally (Deut 17:2, 5, see also Deut 7:3; 13:6; 15:12–17; 17:2–5; 22:22; 12:12, 18; 16:11, 14; 29:11, 18).[42] The section from Deut 17:8–13 provides for a higher court to which more difficult cases must be referred. Here the bench is made up of the Levitical priest and the judge. The decision of this court is final (Deut 17:11). Contempt of the court is a

---

of "unified authority" which he says can no longer be supported (Lohfink, "Distribution," 337), because it is "exegetically untenable" (338). The Catholic church bases its theology on the notion that Jesus, who is one, held in himself all the offices of prophet, priest and king of the Old Testament and those of teacher, priest, and pastor in the New Testament.

40. McBride, "Polity," 72.

41. Brown, Driver, and Briggs, s.v. Rkn, 648.

42. Phillips, "The Decalogue," 225–46 (231).

capital offense (Deut 17:12).[43] Even the king is within the purview of this and all other laws. According to the Deuteronomist, a society that permits itself to look the other way in the face of injustice is sacrificing its own well-being (encapsulated in the phrase "in order that you may live and possess the land which the LORD your God is giving to you," Deut 16:20b). The well-being of the nation is predicated on adherence to the rule of law, and society as a whole is held responsible for the injustices perpetrated in its midst.

These concepts of constitutionalism, the rule of law, and justice were epitomized recently in the Supreme Court of Kenya, in the case of Raila Odinga vs the Independent Electoral and Boundaries Commission and Uhuru Kenyatta (as third respondent). Since then, the chief justice has become famous for his opening statement before he read the ruling which nullified the August 8, 2017, election of the president of Kenya. He stated: "The greatness of any nation lies in its fidelity to the constitution and adherence to the rule of law and above all respect to God."[44] And he went on to read the ruling to a nation waiting with bated breath. There was rejoicing and a sigh of relief as the court nullified the election which was adjudged to have been characterized by "irregularities" and "illegalities." Kenya became only the fourth nation in the world in which an election of a president was nullified by its courts.

Unfortunately, the repeat polls saw the same strategies that had been used to compromise the first election, the same individuals who had committed the "irregularities" and the "illegalities," (as declared by the Supreme Court), and the same structures still in place. This led the true winner of that election, believed to be Raila Odinga, who had challenged the fraudulent results in court, to boycott the repeat polls. In spite of this boycott, and in spite of the overwhelming evidence that the repeat polls too could not be credible,[45] but buoyed by the support of western embassies, led by the US Ambassador Robert F. Godec, the repeat polls took place with less than 30% voter turn-out. The US, and

43. Cf. Hittite law: "If anyone rejects a judgment of the king, his house will become a heap of ruins. If anyone rejects a judgement of a magistrate, they shall cut off his head," §173a (*Context of Scripture*, 2:117).

44. See Kimuyu, "Maraga's Quote," for full judgment.

45. Already, a week prior to the August 8, 2017 election, a key electoral official in charge of the electronic infrastructure, Chris Musando, who had promised to ensure that the technology was not interfered with, had been brutally murdered, by forces that were intent to compromise the electronic voting equipment; just to mention one among many killings of opposition supporters, simply because Uhuru had to "win" at all costs!

other western envoys, had supported a fraudulent election in shocking betrayal of the democratic ideals that they claim to stand for. Many parts of the country boycotted these polls. Not surprisingly, the incumbent supposedly "won," against himself, by 98%. In spite of this drawback, Kenyans had tasted what is possible when the courts are truly independent and the judges truly committed to upholding justice (צדק צדק תרדף/*zedek zedek tirdoph* "you shall pursue justice or 'rightness' or 'justness' only," Deut 16:20). And Kenyans had its acclaimed and progressive 2010 Constitution to thank for this historic verdict.

The King: The Executive Branch of Government

The Deuteronomic constitution, having laid down the law on the judiciary, moves to the other arm of government, kingship. This is the executive arm of government in modern democracies, whether the president, or prime minister. Deut 17:14–20 establishes kingship as an institution, but one whose powers are greatly reduced in contrast to the practice in the ancient Near East. However, scholars tend to exaggerate the extent to which D reduces kingly powers.[46] These scholars make too much, in my view, of the silence of the passage as to what the king's actual duties were. However, this assumption ignores the preposition (לְךָ/*alay* Deut 17:14) which in this context is used metaphorically to express "rank,"[47] correctly translated "over me" (with the suffix). YHWH then affirms it by using the same preposition in Deut 17:15 (yes, you shall certainly place a king "over you"). The king was to "rule" the people with all that "ruling" implies. That is the reason YHWH is quick to limit the possible excesses of kingly power. YHWH anticipates the people's need for a king (Deut 17:14). However, it is YHWH's prerogative to "choose" (בָּחַר/*bachar* Deut 17:15) the king, the same way YHWH chose the children of Israel.

The king must be a native-born citizen (Deut 17:15); it can be assumed that non-Israelite who had become an Israelite (per Lev 19:34) is included among the brother-citizen. The "foreigner" (נָכְרִי/*nokri*, one who does not share the same kinship ties) is barred from being king (see below). Further, the king is also not allowed to own too many horses (Deut 17:16). He is not allowed to marry too many wives (Deut 17:17a), nor to accumulate too much money (Deut 17:17b). Rather the king

---

46. See for example, Knoppers, "Deuteronomist," 329–346.

47. Waltke and O'Connor, *Introduction to Biblical Hebrew Syntax*, 217.

must thoroughly study and adhere to both the letter and spirit of the constitution.[48]

Most scholars assume that the institution of kingship was not divinely mandated, but rather that YHWH merely acquiesced to the people's demand. This line of thinking suggests that YHWH did not really wish for Israel to have a king. Representing this view, Christensen argues, "Kingship originated in the desire of the people, not as a divine ordinance." According to this reading, what we have Deut 17:15 is a "concession not a command."[49] So, was kingship only a divine concession? I find the evidence to be insufficient. It seems clear to me that the institution of kingship was divinely mandated, even if this mandate coincided with human desire. Indeed, this reading may seem to be supported by the syntax of שׂוֹם תָּשִׂים/*som tasum* ("you shall certainly place" a king over you, Deut 17:15). When understood with the modal "may"/ "can," this yields the reading, "you may freely put a king over you," which is how Joüon and Muraoka understand it. This sense derives more from the use of the *yiqṭōl* form. The added infinitive absolute, שׂוֹם/*som* (to put), serves to strengthen this sense of permission[50] beyond mere concession, to a divine mandate.

Permission itself does not require the infinitive absolute. Otherwise, what is the purpose of strengthening the 'concession' if not to express divine legislation? A similar construction can be found, for example, in Gen 2:16 "you may freely eat." Here, YHWH is not just permitting humans to eat, but is also legislating what humans should eat. It is not as though YHWH did not want Adam and Eve to eat from the trees of the garden, and only conceded at Adam's insistence. For this reason, this infinitive absolute (in Deut 17:15) is best understood as "[a]ffirmation."[51] It is even more plausible to see it as "emphatic imperative" (similar to what we find in Deut 6:17; 7:18).[52]

---

48. Cf. Mwalimu Julius Nyerere of Tanzania, who in a speech stated that he carries around with him two documents wherever he goes: the New Testament and the Arusha Declaration—which spells out Nyerere's ideology of *Ujamaa*—"familyhood."

49. Christensen, *Deuteronomy*, 384, Craigie, *Book of Deuteronomy*, 253; Christensen goes on to group together the laws on kingship, slavery, polygamy, or divorce as only being acknowledged in the Bible, but this acknowledgement does not amount to endorsement, 387–88.

50. Joüon and Muraoka, *Grammar of Biblical Hebrew, Part III*, 370 §113*l.*, 423 §123h.

51. See Waltke and O'Connor, *Introduction*, 585 §35.3.1 d–f.

52. See Cowley and Kautzsch, *Gesenius' Hebrew Grammar*, 346 §113bb(a).

What we seem to have here is permission and legislation at the same time. YHWH was waiting for the people to feel the need for a king so that the king in turn should recognize his accountability to the people. If kingship had been designated by divine fiat, there would be very little difference from ancient NE royal ideologies which held that kingship had descended from the gods. In the effort to dissociate Israelite conception of kingship from her neighbors, the Deuteronomic law has kingship initiated by humans.[53] This is in line with the limitations which D wishes to place on the institution of kingship. The elaborate requirement that YHWH must choose, and that the king must be a native Israelite, and the elaborate restriction on what he must not do, and the injunction to read and obey the law, do not make much sense when the legislation is only permissive.[54]

What we have, then, is a not very successful attempt on the part of the Deuteronomic lawyers to deemphasize the divine aspect of kingship, namely, its divine origin. In the end, Deuteronomic lawyers finally capitulate to the fact that indeed kingship is a divinely mandated institution, as it is patterned after YHWH's kingship. We may conclude that D's approach to kingship is intended to subject the king to the law. The overarching theme is that the king is not above the law. Even the idea of forbidding the appointment of a non-Israelite is intended to secure this one thing, allegiance and fidelity to the constitution, in ways that a non-Israelite might not feel obligated to do. The other reason it seems to me that the king must be a native Israelite is that kingship is going to be a representative and embodiment of the nation as a whole. He or she is going to be a model citizen, to represent what a citizen ought to be and do. While in our democracies the legislators are the representatives of the people, the president who is elected through universal suffrage also represents the people and the nation in a unique way.

The Limitations on Presidential Powers

Beside the Deuteronomic law's implicit limitations on the king's power (by virtue of kingship being instituted only when the people request for one, the king is not the giver of the law, other responsibilities such

53. Cf. Goswell, "The Shape of Kingship in Deut 17," 169–81.

54. A slightly similar view as mine is held by Goswell, "The Shape of Kingship in Deut 17," 172.

as administration of justice are assigned to other offices), there are explicit restrictions without which kingly power is almost always sure to be abused. First, the king is instructed not to multiply horses (Deut 17:16). This restriction points to the exercise of the powers of state, the use of force. The prohibition against multiplying women[/men], in Deut 17:17, points to unrestrained licentiousness.[55] The third restriction on kingship is the prohibition against multiplying "silver and gold" (Deut 17:17, "money"). This points to the restriction against political leaders committing economic crimes against the people.

Niccolò Machiavelli, while advising princes that it is better to be feared than to be loved, if the prince cannot have both, argues that being feared is certainly better than being hated. And a prince can avoid being hated "if he abstains from the property of his subjects and citizens and from their women."[56] Power and prestige are the motivation for wanting to accumulate many horses and money. As noted above, horses functioned the same way today's security apparatus functions. The king may desire to raise a standing army (or personal mercenaries, or an elite force), to serve at least two functions: personal protection from would-be assassins, and to ensure the king's monopoly of the means of violence, and with it the consolidation of kingly power. The freedom to exercise royal (or presidential) authority unmitigated and unrestrained is a tendency that is difficult to resist. And once a ruler has started on this path, there is no stopping until the ruling elite have captured all the institutions of the state.

Once power has been thus consolidated, the king moves to diminish the independence of other state institutions and branches of government. In most African 'demo[n]cracies' [pun intended], this begins by emasculating the independent electoral bodies so that elections are conducted merely to endorse pre-determined outcomes. Other arms of government, such as parliament, once compromised, merely rubber stamp the whims of the ruling elite. And once its independence and process of appointment are compromised, the judiciary decides cases, sometimes even on technicalities, or undue delays, so as to favor the ruler. With power arising from the control of security agencies, and money, the other institution to be brought under the president's control is the flow of information, the media. The compromised media helps cover-up

55. Criado, "King of Swaziland to Marry His 15th Wife."
56. Machiavelli, *The Prince*, 97.

abuses, and suppresses the truth, twist stories, or divert attention from the real issues. The recent attempt of the Saudi Government to cover up the murder of journalist Khashoggi is a good example. In many cases, murders are committed and the perpetrators, being connected to those who wield state power, are never apprehended or charged and convicted. The ruling elite embark on the effort to silence state critics. There is widespread extra-judicial killings and assassinations. Seen against this backdrop, Deuteronomic laws are truly prescient.

Economic crime, too, in all its forms begin to be perpetrated in a system where the checks and balances have broken down; among them, corruption. Public funds are plundered but no one in a significant position of power is charged and convicted. At most, those lower in the power structure fall victim as scape-goats, and end up losing their jobs or going to jail. Another form of economic crime, nepotism, is perpetrated. Only those perceived to be friendly to the regime, which in Africa often takes a tribal angle, are appointed to government jobs. Further, nepotism takes the form of skewed allocation of resources, and in the awarding of government tenders (in Kenya, coined as 'tenderpreneurship'), which follow the same tribal pattern. This state of affairs raises ethnic tensions and hatred to the point of pushing the nation to the precipice of violence. All this can be forestalled by paying attention to Deuteronomy's principle of "the king shall not accumulate too much money."

Meanwhile, whole regions or tribes, perceived to be anti-establishment, are subjected to well-calculated economic and political marginalization, yea, even cultural marginalization as such regions are portrayed as inferior or backward. Media, having been captured by government forces, craft narratives that portray those "enemy" regions as poor and underdeveloped, when it is the government that has marginalized these regions in the first place. Once the "opposition" has been cast in such unfavorable light, the media campaign targets the gullible young people from those communities. As a result of the distorted portrayal of their communities, the youth grow up hating their own cultural heritage. Having been defined, caricatured and maligned by the powers that control the media, the young people from marginalized groups now seek or attempt to emulate the manners and adopt the values of the domineering groups. The domineering groups, in turn, portray themselves as civilized, mannered, and indeed propertied. The dominated groups are left to blame themselves for their woes. Some communities are resilient, while others barely withstand adverse effects of political, social, and economic marginalization.

One might protest that in a scholarly paper, like this one, I should not raise issues that have not been verified (actually some will never be, by design) by investigating agencies, or issues to which the courts have not pronounced their official findings. One might accuse me of engaging in hear-say. How do we know that elections have been stolen? How do we know that some of the gruesome murders were carried out by government agents? How do we know that public funds have been plundered? How do we know that not all the culprits have been arrested? These questions play directly into the hands of the rulers, for it is precisely because of their belief that the truth will not be known that they are able to carry out all the atrocities.

In the case of Kenya, some of these questions have been borne out by courts, and by official institutions. But even if official institutions like courts, or electoral bodies did not declare themselves on some of these claims, there is the important element of public perception and knowledge. So much for executive power that is not curtailed by strong checking-and-balancing institutions. Deuteronomic law knows better to distribute power between the offices of king, priest, prophet, and judge, and so should model for African democracies to invest in strong institutions which can withstand undue influences of those who have access to instruments of state power.

V. Conclusion

This study has shown that, indeed, to borrow the words of McBride, for those who "struggle for social justice and human rights [and I should add, good governance], the Deuteronomic model of theocentric humanism remains an eminently practicable legacy."[57] The success of Africa's democracy is more assured if Deuteronomic constitutional principles are brought to bear in that quest. And African biblical studies has the unique opportunity to lead in that political conversation. A conversation that extends beyond the social, economic, and gender issues that have largely characterized African biblical scholarship thus far.[58] After all, African Biblical Hermeneutics has as its true context

---

57. McBride, "Polity," 77.

58. I have discussed African Biblical Hermeneutics in Ojwang, "Juridical

and audience, average African men and women who are likely to be middle-class, church-going, and Bible-believing (as well as men and women of other religious persuasions) whose daily lives are profoundly affected by the political realities in Africa.

Bibliography

Agren, David. "Migrant Caravan to Leave Mexico City on Foot for U.S-Mexico Border after Failed Request for Buses," *USA Today*, Nov. 9, 2018. https://www.usatoday.com/story/news/world/2018/11/09/migrant-caravan-mexico-president-trump-us-southern-border-immigration-asylum-central-americans/1939241002/

BBC News, "Jamal Khashoggi: All You Need to Know about Saudi Journalist's Death." Oct. 31, 2018. https://www.bbc.com/news/world-europe-45812399.

Braulik, Georg. "The Sequence of the Laws in Deuteronomy 12–26 and in the Decalogue." In *A Song of Power and the Power of Song: Essays on the Book of Deuteronomy*. SBTS 3; edited by Duane L. Christensen, 313–35. Winona Lake, IN: Eisenbrauns, 1993.

Brown, F., S. Driver, and C. Briggs, *s.v.* rkn. *The Brown-Driver-Briggs Hebrew English Lexicon*. Peabody, MA: Hendrickson, 1906 [1999].

Christensen, Duane L. *Deuteronomy 1:1—21:9*. Word Biblical Commentary 6A. Rev. ed. Nashville: Nelson, 2001.

Cowley, A.E., and E. Kautzsch. *Gesenius' Hebrew Grammar*. Oxford: Clarendon, 1910.

Craigie, Peter C. *The Book of Deuteronomy*. New International Commentary on the Old Testament. Grand Rapids: Eerdmans, 1976.

Criado, Elisa. "King of Swaziland to Marry His 15th Wife." *Independent*. Tuesday 17 September 2013. https://www.independent.co.uk/news/world/africa/king-of-swaziland-to-marry-his-15th-wife-8820432.html/.

Diamond, Larry. "What Is Democracy?" https://web.stanford.edu/~ldiamond/iraq/WhaIsDemocracy012004.htm

Goswell, Gregory. "The Shape of Kingship in Deut 17: A Messianic Pentateuch?" *TJ* 38 (2017) 169–81.

Greenberg, Moshe. "Some Postulates of Biblical Criminal Law." In *A Song of Power and the Power of Song: Essays on the Book of Deuteronomy*, edited by Duane L. Christensen, 283–300. SBTS 3. Winona Lake, IN: Eisenbrauns, 1993.

Hallo, William W., and K. Lawson Younger, Jr., eds. *The Context of Scripture*. Vol. 2: *Monumental Inscriptions from the Biblical World*. Leiden: Brill, 2000.

Heslop, D. Alan. "Political System." *Britannica*. https://www.britannica.com/topic/political-system.

Katola, Michale. "The Church–State Relationship in Kenya after the Second Liberation Struggle." *JEPER* 3 (2016) 44–59.

Kenya Law Review. http://kenyalaw.org/caselaw/cases/view/140716/.

Kimuyu, Hilary. "Maraga's Quote Left Kenyans Mesmerized." *Nairobi News*, Sept. 2, 2017. https://nairobinews.nation.co.ke/news/maragas-quote-left-kenyans-mesmerized/.

Impotence," 65–94.

Knoppers, Gary N. "Rethinking the Relationship between Deuteronomy and the Deuteronomistic History: The Case of Kings." *CBQ* 63 (2001) 393–415.

———. "The Deuteronomist and the Deuteronomic Law of the King: A Reexamination of a Relationship." *ZAW* 108 (1996) 329–46.

Lohfink, Norbert. "Distribution of the Functions of Power: The Laws Concerning Public Offices in Deuteronomy 16:18—18:22." In *A Song of Power and the Power of Song: Essays on the Book of Deuteronomy*, edited by Duane L. Christensen, 336–52. SBTS 3. Winona Lake, IN: Eisenbrauns, 1993.

Machiavelli, Niccolò. *The Prince*. Translated by George Bull. Penguin Classics Middlesex, UK: Penguin, 1975.

Mann, Thomas W. *Deuteronomy*. Westminster Bible Companion. Louisville: Westminster John Knox, 1995.

McBride, S. Dean, Jr. "Polity of the Covenant People: The Book of Deuteronomy." In *A Song of Power and the Power of Song: Essays on the Book of Deuteronomy*, edited by Duane L. Christensen, 62–77. SBTS 3. Winona Lake, IN: Eisenbrauns, 1993.

McConville, J. G. *God and Earthly Power: An Old Testament Political Theology*. LHBOTS 454. London: T. & T. Clark, 2008.

Muraoka, T., and Paul Joüon, S.J. *A Grammar of Biblical Hebrew, Part III: Syntax*. Subsidia Biblica—14/II. Rome: Pontifical Biblical Institute Press, 2005.

National Archives. "America's Founding Documents." https://www.archives.gov/founding-docs/declaration-transcript.

Nelson, Richard D. *Deuteronomy: A Commentary*. OTL. Louisville: Westminster John Knox, 2002.

Nyerere, Julius. Speech on New Testament and the Arusha Declaration, nd.

Ojwang, Gilbert Okuro. *The House of Omri: A Sociohistorical Study of Israelite Political and Economic Systems (885–841 BCE)*. Saarbrücken: Scholars, 2013.

———. "Juridical Impotence in the Naboth Story in the Context of Kenya's New Land Laws." In *Samuel, Kings, and Chronicles*, edited by Athalya Brenner-Idan and Archie C. C. Lee, 65–94. Texts@Contexts 5. London: Bloomsbury T. & T. Clark, 2017.

Phillips, Anthony. "The Decalogue: Ancient Israel's Criminal Law." In *A Song of Power and the Power of Song: Essays on the Book of Deuteronomy*, edited by Duane L. Christensen, 225–46. SBTS 3. Winona Lake, IN: Eisenbrauns, 1993.

Segovia, Fernando, and Mary Ann Tolbert, eds. *Reading from This Place: Social Location and Biblical Interpretation in the United States*. Vol. I), and *In Global Perspective*, vol. II. Minneapolis: Fortress, 1995.

Ska, Jean Louis. "Biblical Law and the Origins of Democracy." In *The Ten Commandments: The Reciprocity of Faithfulness*, edited by William P. Brown, 146–58. Library of Theological Ethics. Louisville: Westminster John Knox, 2004.

Waltke, Bruce K., and M. O'Connor. *Introduction to Biblical Hebrew Syntax*. Winona Lake, IN: Eisenbrauns, 1990.

Weinfeld, Moshe. "Deuteronomy: The Present State of Inquiry." In *A Song of Power and the Power of Song: Essays on the Book of Deuteronomy*, edited by Duane L. Christensen, 21–35. SBTS 3. Winona Lake, IN: Eisenbrauns, 1993.

18

Liberating, Spatial Theology

Some Reflections on How Theology Can Transform,
in Dialogue with Gerald West

Trygve Wyller

Introduction

"People's theology"[1]—reading the Bible with the people—is an
inspiring concept from Gerald West. Whatever the approach has been,
whether in the "Kairos Movement" or in the permanently developing
Ujamaa movement[2] theologies of the people have been fundamental
even if he uses different concepts to explain what he is after. . Reading
with the people leads to a transforming theology of the people. In my
view, the best tribute to West is to (critically) continue to dig into this
concept to discuss and interpret what a theology of the people really
means and implies. For many decades, this renowned professor has
provided inspiring contributions to how churches, organizations, theologies, and individuals can provide liberation, justice, and change for
the precarious. The following essay presents some reflections from my
side on the political/ecclesial implications of people assuming the role
of subjects in theology. It addresses how to theologically interpret how

---

1. West, "People's Theology.
2. West, "The Biblical Story," 1ff.

the theology of the people changes not only the world but the presence of God in it as well.

One point of departure for responding to this ambitious question is to join West in underlining the significance of space in the Contextual Bible Study (CBS) praxis. Specific safe spaces are specific conditions for a trustworthy Bible reading with the people. West writes:

> Here the Ujamaa Centre's praxis is informed by the work of James Scott. The organized, marginalized have "a shared interest in jointly creating a discourse of dignity, of negation, and of justice." "They have, in addition," Scott continues, "a shared interest in concealing a social site apart from domination where such a hidden transcript can be elaborated in comparative safety." As Scott indicates, a safe social site enables articulation. Put differently, the question posed by Gayatri Spivak, of whether or not the subaltern can speak, should be recast as a question that takes space seriously. A more appropriate question would be: "Where can the subaltern speak?" For, as Scott so eloquently argues, subordinate classes are less constrained at the level of thought and ideology than they are at the level of political action and struggle "since they can in secluded settings speak with comparative safety." Human dignity, even in the most damaged and denigrated subaltern, demands some form of "speaking." How the subaltern speaks depends almost entirely on local "sectoral" control of space."[3]

One such space is presented in a recent critical reading of Gerald West's theological profile. In 2021, Meshack Njinga, a theologian from Mbeya, Tanzania, defended his PhD thesis "The Kingdom of God and the Poor: The Bible Reading of the Economically Underprivileged Christians in Tanzania"[4] at the University of Oslo. The thesis presents a detailed reading of many of West's texts to discuss whether the CBS in Tanzania differs from that initiated by the West-based Ujamaa CBS in South Africa. The difference is precisely connected to the role of people in the CBS process. This has, in my view, significant theological implications.

A second space comes from a place far away from Norway. The social and cultural distance to South Africa and Tanzania is obviously more than significant. Nevertheless, efforts to establish spaces to open hidden transcripts take place also in the North. Despite the evident differences

---

3. West, "The Biblical Story of Tamar," 2–3.

4. Njinga, "The Kingdom of God."

between the two cases, there are, in my view, also important things to be learned from the Norwegian case as well.

In 2021, I co-organized a new BA/MA course at the Faculty of Theology, University of Oslo. This specific course invites local people living in areas of the nonwhite majority in Oslo to join in a class together with regular students. The course topic is how to facilitate spaces where locals and students encounter and discuss if there are some basic values they both share and the kind of conflicts that hinder them or contexts that enhance them. The course is supported also by the local dean of the Lutheran Church. Nationally, this church is the majority church; in this local, suburban area, however, it represents a small minority. Nevertheless, the course is explicitly connected to ethical and theological reflections, even if many participants belonged to Islam or other non-Christian confessions. One of the central considerations inspiring the course is the concept of space: The local space is theologically significant, even if the specific faith is a space-minority practice. God is more than faith practice.

At first sight, there seem to be no connections between CBS groups in Southwest Tanzania, on the one hand, and an unconventional university course in far-away Norway, on the other hand. Nevertheless, both activities are spatial: They both facilitate spaces where encounters, discussions, and transforming practices take place. A closer look might lead to further reflections relevant to a future people's theology. In this way, according to Njinga, the Tanzanian CBS had its first premise that social realities should be discussed independently of any theological preferences. In the Oslo course, participants reported that it was the encounter between people from different social/ethnic groups that had impacted them most. The interesting parallel between the Mbeya groups and the Oslo course is that both spaces are spaces of independent voices and practices, even if the respective organizer is part of a theological/ecclesial context and/or institution. This is an interesting position for discussing what people's theology implies today. I would like to reflect on some of these aspects in the concluding section of this article. First, we need to have some more details from the two spaces.

Starting from Below: Tanzania

According to Meshack Njinga, the CBS groups developed in the South African Ujamaa context and the parallel groups in Mbeya, Tanzania, differ in one sense. In the technical terminology of the early liberation theology, it regards the interpretation of the so-called "first" and "second" act.[5] Njinga claims that Gustavo Gutierrez underlined that theologians first had to analyze—the "first act"—the social reality they lived in. Only as a second step should the faith-based "second act" be initiated. This is, again according to Njinga, different in the Ujamaa groups: They move more directly to the faith-based second act.

Njinga writes:

> according to liberation theologians, the poor are the source of liberation theology . . . They do 'see–judge–act' accordingly in facing their socioeconomic reality, which is full of injustice, and then when they meet, they reflect according to the word of God where theology takes its part. For Gerald West, see, judge, and act moments take place within the Bible study 'venue.'[6]

Njinga's interpretation of West is that, on this point, West does not follow the model initiated by Gustavo Gutierrez and his Latin American followers. Against this background, Njinga finds that there are significant differences between the Ujamaa CBS groups in South Africa and the CBS in Southwest Tanzania, as researched by Njinga around 2017–2019. The difference is important and, in my view, influences how spaces of people's theology can be reflected today.

The CBS groups studied by Njinga in Tanzania originated from the so-called Village Community Banks (VICOBA) groups, which are active in many areas of Tanzania and beyond. The Vicoba groups work by distributing microcredit loans for people living in areas of precarity. They have a certain amount of money at their disposal, and in weekly group meetings, the money is distributed as microcredit loans to individual group members. The loan makes it possible to buy a cow, a pig, a chicken, or any other item relevant to their small farming businesses.

Over the last decades, some of these Vicoba groups have expanded. They still meet, as usual, for the microcredit planning. However, after a break, they then meet a second time for CBS. These groups are called IR ("Inter-Religious") VICOBA and are chaired by a person with some theological competence. The group members are laypersons, poor farmers from the village, usually people who have known each other for a long time. This area in Tanzania belongs to districts once colonized by

5. Gutiérrez, *A Theology of Liberation*, 11.

6. Njinga, "The Kingdom of God," 161–62.

Germans and therefore have German (and sometimes Scandinavian) Lutheran church traditions and dogmatics, which survived even after the colonizers left.

Njinga focuses on how this mixed space of microcredit and bible groups approach the social reality around them. This is a context dominated by people with only a minimum of cash, farmers who grow vegetables and fruits and later sell them for the local and global market. Njinga's taped material from the group discussions is unique by giving insight into how uneducated farmers and ordinary (poor) people in Western Tanzania read the Bible. The outcome is important and significant.

One member comments: "We should continue to empower each other regardless of our being poor, and we should learn to work hard so that we become capable economically." For helping others, you hear them saying, "To be Christ-like, we need to continue to assist the needy people who are poor, assist the church when it starts the orphanage centers." And others claim, "We are supposed to unite together and make our market system work so that we can avoid other middlemen exploiting us. So, we can ask our local government to interfere on this issue."[7]

For Njinga, such comments indicate that the IR-VICOBA people, during their Bible study groups, first relate directly to the immediate social context without explicitly referring to the Bible. In my interpretation, this makes the specificity of the Vicoba space. In this regard, the Ujamaa space is different. Njinga's presentation of West focuses on the difference between the Ujamaa and the Vicoba on this critical point. It is important to see that this interpretation is referred to when the Bible is applied as an analytical tool. Here, according to Njinga, lies the main difference with Gutierrez and his distinction between the "first and second" act. The interpretation starting with the reality is not the difference; the difference is how one interprets and acts in this given reality, and from which sources one finds the interpretation. Gutierrez finds it from the social praxis of the poor, while West (according to Njinga) finds it in the Bible (no "first act") giving a way forward to act directly from the Bible.

In this way, there are two spaces of liberative praxis discovered within a single CBS tradition. Both aim distinctively at transformation, and both contribute to spaces where the hidden transcript is explicitly present. The difference is connected to a certain "autonomy" in the interpretation and transformative acts in the social contexts. In my reading,

7. Njinga, "The Kingdom of God," 172.

the Vicoba version allows for social acts and interpretations that are not expressly Christian, despite their presence in a space that is constructed also for Christian discourses and practices.

It is not my main interest in this article to judge whether Njinga gives an absolute accurate presentation of West's position compared with the one established by Gutierrez and—according to Njinga—followed implicitly by the poor farmers in Southwestern Tanzania. What is significant is that the West/IR-Vicoba difference reveals that also liberation within a theological space is not the same thing. The (unjust) social context can be independently read and then, in a second step, interpreted from a Biblical perspective. Or, as in the Ujamaa context, it can be interpreted immediately from a biblical perspective.

What we do have to recognize, however, is that both alternatives work within an ecclesial/theological context. The IR-Vicoba groups define themselves as CBS groups, and the chairpersons are always educated theologians or other people with theological competence. The Ujamaa groups are, of course, also part of a theological/ecclesial project. They are, however, not "more" part of theology/ecclesia than the IR-Vicoba. This spatial difference points to differences regarding the role of the people in the people's theology concept.

Starting from Below: Norway

In 2021, together with a group of strong colleagues,[8] I was responsible for a BA/MA course called "Beliefs in Places" (Norwegian: *Tro på stedetā*). at the Faculty of Theology, University of Oslo.[9] The idea is to invite both local people and a group of established students to the same course. The course venue, for those classes where both locals and regular students meet, is a building in the suburban area of Oslo where the local people lived. One main ambition is to establish discussions on concrete social/cultural/political challenges people are experiencing here. A second objective is that all participants elaborate whether the presented challenges might be rooted in common ethical positions, beyond the obvious

---

8. Kaja Rønsdal and Dr. Carsten Schuerhoff, Oslo.

9. The data material is collected by Dr. Schuerhoff. SIKT Norwegian Agency for Shared Services in Education and Research has approved the procedures for the interviews, and all participants have given their informed consent to collect data from the course. All interviewees are anonymized.

cultural/social/ethnic/religious differences.[10] The number of white ethnic Norwegians living here is about 35%. Originally, the area was built to house the expanding new, white "working-class" population of Oslo in the 1960s. Some decades later, as in most big and middle-sized European cities, the area today is dominated by first- and second-generation immigrant families, most of them non-Christian, often Muslim.

This is, obviously, a context where Christian theology and ecclesiology need to reformulate and reconstruct many traditional positions. Norway (and the other Nordic countries) has been, and is still, strongly dominated by Lutheran traditions. The Lutheran churches were majority churches for centuries. In suburban areas like the one where the BA/MA course was located, however, that is no longer the case. Nevertheless, the Lutheran Church, built when the area was still "white," is located in the middle of the local center. One important question is whether the church today is able to contribute to significant social transformation, despite its new minority role.

The BA/MA course was developed by a mixed group, chaired by the local Lutheran dean of the area, other local Lutheran ministers, some representatives from one of the local mosques, leaders of the local sports club, some people from local politics, interreligious and voluntary organizations, and colleagues from the University of Oslo. Together, the group worked out the model for course content and recruiting policy. The result was that a group of 20 locals turned up to join the first course day. During four 3–hour seminars, the locals and the regulars developed discussions on explicitly local issues, among them the local community garden, young women's anxiety about walking around after darkness, racist tendencies, initiatives to create community-relevant activities, etc.

The classes took place every Wednesday. In the time slots between the classes, the students were asked to elaborate further on group issues on Messenger in closed chat rooms. Here are some sentences from these discussions:

- I was thinking . . . about how the community is in our area and the pride you feel to belong here. I never saw something like it on the Westend. Where we live, everyone strives to stretch out a hand, create common spaces, cooperate, meet, etc. And then, among others, racism, the low average income, language challenge, which

10. A first, Norwegian publication from this project is: Schuehoff and Wyller, "Hverdagsreligion Eller Hverdagens trosbetydning?."

again lead to school dropouts, criminality, and exclusion—these all threaten these good values.

- Local people have asked for more visible police. I think many like to see the police around . . . A youngster was knifed just outside the youth club last year. In August, two boys were shot approximately 100 meters from the same club. This is scary, and the police visibility is good. However, they must behave.[11]

One short passage from a taped interview with one of the participants tells us something about how she has assessed the significance of the course:

- TW: We think it was you, in one of the first-class meetings, who claimed this was the first time you really spoke with white people in this area?

Interviewee:

- What I said was, this is the first time I really saw white people living in this area. One of them was a doctor, but there were others also. One very often thinks that there are only foreigners living here. The school has only foreign-born teachers, all the kids are from other countries, it is the same at the other school here as well.[12]

One finds similar passages in other parts of the course material. Meeting other groups more substantially seems to be an important topic for many participants. In the course evaluation, more local, nonethnic Norwegian students also underlined the significance of the encounters with white ethnic Norwegians in the class and during the group discussion. This intercultural/social space seems to be a kind of space acknowledged by many participants.

This is about spatial encounterings and sharings of kinds of often not formulated vulnerabilities that lead to transforming practices. They do not mean that racism is not a topic anymore. They might indicate, however, that spaces which allow for a freer sharing (of tabooed "hidden transcripts") of the kind are important to fight racism.

11. "Messenger" App discussions, Oct 2021.
12. Interview 01/22/22.

Contributing to "People's Theology"

There is, in my view, much to learn from the two cases from Tanzania and Norway. They both pursue transformative spaces where people's view on politics and justice is given autonomy and independence, even if the context remains Christian/religious. These autonomous voices within specific spaces might be important contributions to a future people's theology. Theology is only convincing when it recognizes spaces not occupied only by itself. And such spaces contribute to social change because people recognize the strength in spaces that do not try to colonize their participants.

There are, of course, obvious differences between the Tanzanian and the Norwegian case. The Tanzanian case is a context where there are explicit religious aims connected to the Bible study group. There is no doubt that the first part of the group discussions is connected to the microcredit situation and the clear tendency to avoid a Biblical overinterpretation of the surrounding social world, both of which take part within a broader Christian-religious context. The participants in the IR-Vicoba groups are active Christians from the local context.

The Norwegian case is different. Formally, the religious context for the BA/MA course is also evident. The course is a cooperation between the local diocese and a Faculty of Theology. There are, however, two other perspectives that make this course different from the Tanzanian case.

The first perspective is the heterogeneous group in the committee that planned the course. Some were ministers and theologians, some came from the mosque. There were, however, also members recruited from grassroots initiatives, sports organizations, and local politics. The second perspective is that the group participants are not like that in Tanzania. The students in the course belong to a study program, which does not serve the education of ministers. Most of the students were recruited from another study program, which educates people who plan to serve as leaders in different religious organizations or to increase their competence in counseling people in multireligious contexts. The local participants are even more heterogeneous: Some are recruited from a local mosque, some from the local (Lutheran) church, and some have a background in classic neighborhood organizations.

In sum, there are differences between the two cases, and furthermore: The most obvious one is, of course, the cultural/political context. To compare a case from Southeast Tanzania and one from Norway is, in most cases, impossible because the social and cultural differences are just too many. Nevertheless, from the viewpoint of theology, one perspective remains the same in both cases: Everyday issues are being discussed in both contexts in a non-Biblical language, even if the context is wholly Christian (Tanzania) or nonbinary religious/secular (Norwegian).

Both cases show a different space than the Ujamaa. The hidden transcript has other aspects in these spaces. In the context of (Christian) religion, the participants put forward everyday issues as urgent matters. Njinga, inspired by first-generation Latin American liberation theology, calls this the "first act," which is an analysis of social and cultural context. In the Tanzanian case, there is both an (autonomous) first and a Biblical second act. In the Norwegian case, the second act was not on the program in the BA/MA course. In the course evaluation, however, many students said they had wished for a stronger religious interpretation of the everyday discussions in the study groups. So, if not literally, at least in principle one could see a tendency, where there is accepted space for non-Biblical discussions in the context of Christian/religious(secular) organizations within both spaces.

The important question is: Why is this a tendency relevant to further development of people's theology? In my view, there are two different answers. The first connects to what took place in the meetings where non-Biblical analysis was dominant. The other aspect relates to the institutional setting where all this happened. Together, both the internal aspect and the institutional aspect are highly relevant to what people's theology is about.

Starting with the internal aspect, what seems to be explicit among many course participants—and among those interviewed afterward—is the significance of the encounters. People with immigrant backgrounds said it was the first time they had really sat down with ethnic white Norwegians; ethnic white Norwegians talked about the significance of having been able to elaborate on both everyday issues concerning normativity, racism and justice together with nonethnic Norwegians in the neighborhood.

Accordingly, the encounters themselves seem to have enabled new experiences and insights. Participants also reported a desire for ongoing discussion and encounters, which portends well for a future theology of the people. In the Tanzanian case presented by Njinga, the significance of sharing in the Vicoba groups facilitating and distributing microcredit to local farmers is evident. Different from the Norwegian BA/MA course, the participants do not explicitly discuss what the significance of this sharing means. However, the whole microcredit is built on sharing and the solidarity of those participating. And we also see from the discussions in the CBS sessions that the same kind of sharing priority is highlighted. Again and again, participants underline how people in the villages and in the local context should join to resist poverty so that all people are lifted to better living conditions. This means that, here too, the sharing and connecting aspect of the encounter are important elements of these practices.

Against this background, the significance of these encounters and sharing encounters for interpreting what people's theology is about becomes clearer. "People's theology," in the literal sense of the word, happens when the people's own sharing and encounters lead to new common power within a social context. Decisive is that the sharing takes place in spaces not dominated by Biblical discourse, even if the context of these places is ecclesial/theological. One could call this the power of an inclusive people's theology. The power comes from encounters and a sharing of what West (using a concept from James Scott) calls "hidden transcripts." In the social space of the BA/MA course some kind of "safety" seems to have been developed in such a way that sometimes taboo-like interpretations could be shared, even if they belong to transcripts not covered by a Biblical language. The unity and sharing of the many are what contribute to the power of this theology of the people.

Presenting, Not Representing Spatial Presences

The two cases above enable discussions on why the spaces of hidden transcripts benefit from independent voices of people, even when located within an ecclesial/religious context. One might say that these spatial "hidden transcripts" are theological/ecclesial because it is part of an ecclesial/theological responsibility to build and enhance them. One significant aspect of this kind of theological significant spaces is that they are primarily developed and established by the people themselves. In the Vicoba groups, the social spaces are the spaces where people live and work. In the BA/MA course in Oslo, the encountering space is constructed by the course leadership. Nevertheless, the specific encounters that many locals define as the most significant happened when local people encountered and started to share.

This means that these theological spaces come close to Bruno Latour's distinction between representation and presentation[13] In a discussion on philosophies of ecology, his ambition was to show why it is so important that people, especially indigenous people who are affected by climate changes themselves, talk. Then they *present*, different from the *representation* (on behalf of) done by all Non-Governmental Organizations (NGOs).

In my view, this means that presentation is also a theological significant value of both the IR-Vicoba people and the participants in the BA/MA course. The independent and authentic voices of those most inflicted must have priority. This is one basic aspect of people's theology.

In the area of theology, this means to trust that presenting is a language more inherent to theology than representing. In the case of the Tanzanian CBS groups, the consequence is discussing social reality with their own voices. People articulate decisive theology even if they do not use explicit Biblical language. The reason is that theology recognizes and trusts that integrity and authenticity are decisive aspects of God's creation. Further, it is also decisive that the independent discussions on microcredit and social reality within the Vicoba groups seem to empirically enhance their concrete life situation. This again means that this theology is about transformation. The decisive thing, however, is that this is a transformation initiated by the independent voices of the people themselves, within an ecclesial/theological context, which *presents* the articulations of people.

A parallel situation occurs in the Norwegian BA/MA course. The case itself is, of course, nothing more than a microcosmos in the big world of tensions. Nevertheless, when participants present voices of lived experiences from the local area—and some describe the lasting impact of encountering ethnic white people from the neighborhood substantially for the first time—then they symbolize small traces of transforming

13. Latour et al., "Down to Earth Social Movements," 1–9.

So I have never tried to extend politics to science or to ecology, but exactly the opposite: I have shown how, by following those who make non-humans speak, we could rely upon what politics has always been. So the Parliament of Things has nothing especially 'republican' about it. Or rather, res publica understood as public 'things' or public 'issues' has been the interest of all collectives from the beginning of politics, and the Western notion of representative democracy has been nothing but a small excerpt of the vast experience of humanity in what may be considered. Milstein *et al.* dispute resolution around common and composed issues. We, the Westerners, are immersed in a process of learning or relearning all those other solutions we have tried to eradicate or simplify. That's my starting point." Latour, et al, "Down to Earth Social Movements," 9.

theology. The important aspect is that presenting includes both authentic voices and encounters that have transforming potentialities.

What needs to be discussed further is whether this (*decentering*) ecclesio-theological context contributes to this transforming strength of both the Tanzanian and Norwegian case. In my view, ecclesial bodies that endorse independent voices to present within their own bodies give strong signals. The main signal is that Christian love implies that others, not yourself present.

Bibliography

Gutiérrez, Gustavo. *A Theology of Liberation: History, Politics, and Salvation.* Rev.Ed. London: SCM, 1988.

Latour, Bruno, Denise Milstein, Isaac Marrero-Guillamón, and Israel Rodríguez-Giralt. "Down to Earth Social Movements: An Interview." *Social Movement Studies* (2018) 1–9.

Njinga, Meshack Edward. "The Kingdom of God and the Poor: The Bible Reading of the Economically Underprivileged Christians in Tanzania." PhD diss., University of Oslo, 2021.

———. *The Kingdom of God and the Poor: The Bible Reading of The Economically Underprivileged Christians in Tanzania.* Research in Contemporary Religion 36. Göttingen: Vandenhoeck & Ruprecht, 2024.

Schuerhoff, Carsten, and Trygve Wyller. "Hverdagsreligion Eller Hverdagens Trosbetydning?" *NNK* 4 (2023) 16–26.

Scott, James C. *Domination and the Arts of Resistance: Hidden Transcripts.* New Haven: Yale University Press, 1990.

West, Gerald O. "The Biblical Story of Tamar: Training for Transformation, Doing Development." In *For Better for Worse: The Role of Religion in Development Cooperation*, edited by Robert Oden, 135–47. Uppsala: Swedish Mission Council, 2016.

———. "Locating Contextual Bible Study within Praxis." *Diakonia* 4 (2013) 43–48.

———. "People's Theology, Prophetic Theology, and Public Theology in Post-Liberation South Africa." University of Oslo Podcast, Oct 15, 2013. https://www.tf.uio.no/tjenester/kunnskap/podkast/gjesteforelesninger/gerald-west-041013.html.

———. "Reading the Bible with the Marginalized: The Value/s of Contextual Bible Reading." *STJ* 1 (2015) 235–61.

PART FIVE

Bible, Decolonization, and Liberation

19

"So These Stones Shall Be to the Israelites a Memorial"

(Joshua 4:1–8) The Memorial Stone/s

Dorothy Bea Akoto

Introduction

This very important Festschrift in honor of Professor Gerald O. West springs from an appreciation for West's focus on contextual Bible study, particularly among ordinary readers of the Bible. The importance of this Festschrift is intensified by the dramatic shift of the epicenter of Christianity and biblical studies with their accompanying theology/ies, from the Global North to the Global South (i.e., from the West to Sub-Saharan Africa, South America, Asia, and elsewhere).

This shift has included the methods of interpretation, from those dominantly used in the works/studies of western Euro-American biblical scholars and theologians that appeared to have been the yardstick for most studies in these fields. These methods appeared to have overshadowed every other interpretive approach that did not emanate from the West. The metaphor of "memorial stones" proposed in this article, could be used to highlight the one-sidedness of the Euro-American scholarship in the field of biblical studies by showing the shift to the other side, evident in the works of African biblical scholars and theologians. Though the latter works did not emanate in the West, they should not, and must not be considered as less important. This is because the works of African scholars like West, among those of several other African biblical scholars and theologians, are soundly grounded in the biblical context but do not woodenly toe the line of Western scholarship. Rather, they are focused on addressing the contemporary needs of not only sophisticated academicians but also of "ordinary readers" of the Bible. This article, therefore, celebrates West as a seasoned African biblical scholar and theologian, who has become one of the "memorial stones" of African biblical scholarship.

The shift referred to above could be captured in the following assertion by another stalwart of African biblical scholarship, Justin S. Ukpong, that,

> In recent times, African biblical scholars have also expressed concern about the relevance of the classical mode of biblical interpretation for the socio-cultural context of Africa and have pointed to the need for developing a framework of academic biblical interpretation that would be responsive to the social, cultural and religious contexts of Africa and that would involve the perspectives and concerns of the ordinary African reader.[1]

Ukpong's words could probably be interpreted as reflecting a shift from received [Western Euro-American] modes of interpretation to contextual [African socio-cultural] interpretations. West's contextual Bible studies, with their focus on "ordinary readers," are described by Andrew D. Mayes as "The interpretation of the text [that] takes place in the interaction between the text and the interpretative community, a community, which may or may not have religious commitments, or may be characterized by different political or ethical concerns."[2] This definition represents a significant shift in biblical interpretation and theology as exemplified in West's interpretive approaches that insist on focusing on non-academic readers of the Bible.

As African biblical scholars, like the Israelites of old, we need to begin to "remember" the biblical scholars and theologians that have abounded in our African socio-cultural contexts by identifying them as "memorial stones" and uphold their legacies as the Israelites upheld those of their legendary figures and their legacies by celebrating them along with the

---

1. Ukpong, "Popular Readings of the Bible in Africa," 582. See also West, "Some Parameters of the Hermeneutic Debate."

2. Mayes, ed. *Text in Context*, xv.

important landmarks (like the crossing of the Jordan River) in their history "*until* forever" (Josh 4:7). In summary, the works of our African brothers (like West) and sisters, which focus on contemporary contextualized interpretations of the Bible, clearly indicate that there has been a major "paradigm shift"[3] from how biblical interpretation and theological studies have been done in Western (Euro-North American) contexts. It is on this basis that this paper seeks to identify West as one of the "memorial stones" of biblical interpretation and theology in Africa.

As a springboard to firmly ground the metaphor of "memorial stones" proposed in this article, Josh 4:1–8 will first be read using the traditional critical methodology. This methodology addresses textual, form, historical, redaction, narrative and other criticisms and is used to both "get back there" (*then*) as well as get at "what it means"[4] (*today*). Krister Stendahl, in describing contemporary biblical theology, used these two expressions to refer to the historical context of the text, which is what the text meant "back then" and for what the text means "now" (i.e., the application of the text to the contemporary interpretative context). But Stendahl's "now" context is not West's "now" context. Though the text from Josh 4:1–8 may have come from a particular religious and political context, with different ethical concerns, its message to the contemporary interpretative context is re-read with the present context in mind. In other words, after attempting to discover the probable historical context of the text, the theological findings embedded in the text are then applied to today's African Christian religious setting, and/or other socio-cultural contexts. In this way, I metaphorically identify West with the concept of "memorial stone" within contemporary African biblical and theological scholarship.

The chapter then concludes its re-reading of Josh 4:1–8 by offering a suggested way forward in contextual biblical study, in general. While this latter application is intended to highlight West's idea of "contextual Bible study," it also reiterates an idea I coined in 2004, called a "hermeneutic of grafting."[5] This "hermeneutic of grafting" involves taking "cuttings" from the western/Euro-American Bible tree and splicing these "cuttings" into an already existing full-blown African "tree," which is

3. Bosch, *Transforming Mission*, 1992. The sub-title of Bosch's book captures the shift that had occurred in mission and theology that had moved the epicenter of Christianity from the Global North to the Global South.

4. Stendahl, "Biblical Theology, Contemporary," 418–32.

5. Akoto, "Hearing Scripture in African Contexts, 283–306.

firmly rooted in the African contextual soil. The grafting of these two (i.e., the Euro-American and African contextual) "trees" produces hybridized "fruit," which has the unique taste combining both the Western and African "trees." Gayraud S. Wilmore's assertion that "The religious beliefs and rituals of a people are inevitable and inseparably bound up with the material and psychological realities of their daily existence" reflects such a reading which accounts for West's, postcolonial Africa's, African, and European heritages.[6]

The Context of Joshua 4:1–8

The immediate context of Josh 4:1–8 could be traced to the crossing of the River Jordan. This narrative appears to be a duplication or reenactment of the crossing of the Red [Reed] Sea earlier in Exodus 14. After the people had crossed the River Jordan, God commanded Joshua to choose twelve men to pick up stones from the riverbed, where the priests had stood. Joshua, in obedience, instructed the twelve men who had been chosen, from among the Israelites, to wade into the middle of the Jordan River and lift twelve stones on their shoulders. After they had crossed before the ark of the YHWH,[7] they picked up twelve stones, with each stone representing one of the tribes of Israel. The reason for picking up these stones is given in Josh 4:7, "then you shall tell them that the waters of the Jordan were cut off in front of the ark of the covenant of the LORD . . . So, these stones shall be to the Israelites a *memorial forever*." Even though this statement is used to keep an ecological occurrence in mind, it could be likened to an etiology. The event of crossing the River Jordan, initiated by YHWH, had occurred among the Israelites (i.e., in their socio-cultural context), and they were commanded to carry this memory with them "*until forever*" by passing it down to their succeeding generations.

Textual Criticism

Trent C. Butler's textual critical work compared the Hebrew text of Joshua with the earliest Greek translations that date back to the second century BCE. These texts had been preserved only in manuscripts that date from

---

6. Wilmore, *Black Religion and Black Radicalism*, 1.

7. YHWH is used primarily for the Hebrew sacred name for God (יְהוָה), translated as LORD in most versions of English Bibles.

the fourth century C. E. In his comparison, Butler noticed "numerous divergences of the Greek from the Hebrew text in every chapter and at times in every verse of a chapter."[8] For Butler, these divergences either came from simple mechanical errors made while hand-copying the text or were probably due to the translators' lack of understanding of the precise nuances of the Hebrew words encountered in the text (e.g., in Josh 4:3). In this light, the Greek translators must have attempted to improve the literary style of the book of Joshua for the continuity of the narrative (e.g., Josh 4:1–3, 5 and 7). As such, the Greek appeared to sometimes be a better preservation of the original Hebrew text. The theological changes were probably attempts to make the Greek text relevant to the needs of the translator's particular community. Joshua 4:7–8 could, therefore, be the result of homiletic interpretation and exegesis.

Alberto Soggin also did text-critical work on Joshua and discovered that the LXX probably had several different recensions. This made the critical work on Joshua complex. However, in spite of a number of traditional errors, the Masoretic Text (MT) was retained in such a way that whenever the "Masoretic Text lacked a passage or two, these passages were usually restored in the LXX."[9] For instance, the ark is mentioned in the MT of Josh 4:5 but is omitted in the LXX. Soggin attributed this omission, and/or restoration of texts, to Deuteronomic redaction with the conclusion that the LXX seems to be harmonizing two recensions.[10] The probability of two different versions of the same incident could be implicit in Josh 4:8 and 9 as well. In the former (Josh 4:8), the twelve men had taken up the twelve stones from the riverbed after the Ark had passed, but in the latter (v. 9) the men had probably replaced the earlier stones with other stones.

Adrian H. W. Curtis, in his Old Testament Guides, *Joshua*, asserted that the "whole of the MT tradition of Joshua is good."[11] Curtis suggested that the Dead Sea Scrolls (DSS) of Qumran cave 4 (4Q) produced two manuscripts of Joshua (i.e., "a" and "b"). He claimed that the shorter Greek version was complicated because it had several recensions in the Codex Vaticanus, which reflected a different Hebrew text than the MT. From the work of Butler and Curtis, it could be suggested that the MT

8. Butler, *Word Biblical Commentary*, xviii.

9. Soggin, "Joshua," 187–95.

10. Soggin, *Joshua*, 49.

11. Curtis, *Joshua*, 12.

was used by the LXX and was abbreviated according to the shorter Hebrew original in the Vorlage.[12]

In my reading of the Septuagint (LXX) and Masoretic Text (MT), slight differences could be noticed, none of which were of any great significance to suggest that there was a major textual problem. I concluded, in agreement with Curtis, that the Masoretic Text (MT) of my pericope (Josh 4:1–8) was preferable. The omission of certain elements like references to the Ark and "where the feet of the priests stood" in Josh 4:3–5 in the LXX, appear to be either attempts to tone down the prophetic element in the story or, perhaps, were mere simplifications of the story.

From the information gained from these textual critics, the translation of Josh 4:1–8 could be based on the BHS. To be noted, however, are the several duplications in the Biblical Hebraica Stuttgartensia translation. These duplications include the choosing of the twelve men, taking up the twelve stones, and the cutting off of the waters of the Jordan. These duplications seem to suggest that there probably must have been more than one manuscript of the incident narrated in Josh 4:1–8. In light of the foregoing, I think, in the attempt to produce this text, the final editor [i.e., the Deuteronomistic Historian (DtrH)], strove to harmonize the sources at their disposal.

Form Criticism

John H. Hayes was one of the earliest scholars to study the form of this story, which he described as a "religious processional"[13] on the journey of the entry into the land. Robert G. Boling and G. Ernest Wright, later than Hayes, studied the form of this story and concluded that it was an "etiological narrative."[14] This kind of narrative involved a sign (e.g., Josh 4:6), which was a "physical reminder, a long-standing visual aid to historical memory."[15] This narrative also involved an event connected with prophecy, which was accompanied by a miraculous deed performed by YHWH alone. Additionally, Boling and Wright considered the events of such narratives as characteristic of theophanies (i.e., stories of encounters with the divine, e.g., Judg 6:11–21).

12. Curtis, *Joshua*, 13.

13. Hayes, *An Introduction to Old Testament Study*, 220.

14. Boling and Wright, *Joshua*, 65.

15. Boling and Wright, *Joshua*, 173.

Similarly, Norman K. Gottwald had asserted that "Stories containing an explanatory motif of this sort were often called "etiological" [origin] sagas."[16] Soggin suggested that Joshua did not play any part in some of the stories attributed to him but that he probably only was the "protagonist of the book."[17] Curtis also described this occurrence as an "aetiological story, used to refer to a story, which explains the origin of some existing phenomenon or custom or practice."[18] The story originally probably belonged to a realm of myths, which is marked by the expression "to this day" and Curtis suggested that the writer attempted to confirm a tradition that was being passed on, and concluded that just as it was in the case of prophetic sagas, perhaps, the stories of historical figures were told and elaborated upon by the addition of other tales that made the historical figures heroes.

I agree with Gottwald and Curtis that this story is etiological. My agreement with the previous scholars is based on the formulaic expressions, like "to this day," and "these shall be a memorial . . . until forever" used in relation to the story. The importance of memory, which was to be indelibly imprinted on the minds of the succeeding generations and which was to last "until forever," for me, is endorsed by these expressions. Additionally, since these stones were physically visible signs (Josh 4:6), they served and could still serve as historical memories, which could stand the test of time. Furthermore, this miracle proved the omnipotence of YHWH, who alone could have parted the Jordan, just as the Red [Reed] Sea was parted (Exod 14).

My further agreement with these scholars that this narrative is etiological lies in the predictive prophetic undertone, which though not immediately obvious, could be gleaned from YHWH's instruction that the stones will be a memorial from the day of the miracle and into the future. My agreement with them is further based on the fact that etiological stories abound in African socio-cultural contexts. In these contexts, any phenomenon that could not be explained physically or logically became shrouded in some form of mystery, and the story was passed down from one generation to another, from parents to children, or from adults to younger generations. This passing on from one to another generation was mostly done through oral tradition in the form of stories and proverbs or other didactic means. The stories usually became accepted as explanations

16. Gottwald, *The Hebrew Bible*, 234.

17. Soggin, *Introduction to the Old Testament*, 187.

18. Curtis, *Joshua*, 66.

for inexplicable mythical and superstitious occurrences, which were neither doubted nor were their veracity questioned by anyone.

The stones in Josh 4:1–8 were to be set up as a memorial so that when in later generations, the children of the Israelites should pester their parents to know what the stones stood for, the miracle of the parting of the Jordan River would be recounted to them. In this article, I attempt to metaphorically liken the work of biblical interpretation and theology from the purely western Euro-American and the African contextual perspectives to "memorial stones." I consider the change in methodological perspectives from the former to the later (i.e., from the two different contexts) as a pragmatic "paradigm shift." This shift is from the purely western Euro-American historical interpretation of the Bible and doing theology, to reading and interpreting the Bible and doing theology with African contextual interpretative lenses. These two contexts and their interpretative perspectives have often been considered in terms of the global North and global South, respectively. In my proposed metaphor, the scholars of both contexts and their works could be identified as "memorial stones." This is because both sets of scholars and their works appear to be legacies that have become landmarks to which biblical scholars and theologians have turned for research throughout many generations.

Whereas Euro-American scholarship had tended to stand very tall for several generations, the works of African scholars had not been much celebrated in the past. The contextualized biblical/theological works of African patriarchs and matriarchs (i.e., biblical scholars and theologians), like West, could be identified as "memorial stones." At the same time, these patriarchs and matriarchs, whose works stand tall as legacies for future generations could themselves be identified as "memorial stones." In relation to the story of Josh 4:1–8, the "memorial stones" of Africa could be identified as those chosen from among the people of their own contexts and instructed by the LORD to carry the stones that were to be buried in the Jordan and which were to be remembered "until forever." Their dint of hard work, through study and research, could be identified with obedience to the LORD. They have, thus, become identifiable visual signs (i.e., "memorial stones") of biblical/theological studies, throughout the generation.

Narrative Criticism

As suggested earlier in this article, the story found in Josh 4:1–8 is in the form of a narrative. One of its major ingredients is characterization. Nothing elaborate was mentioned about YHWH but the divine initiative and miraculous act are clear in the story. Joshua, the supposed protagonist, was poorly developed. Though his unquestioning obedience and military character could be felt in the story, he remained more or less passive throughout. The names of the twelve men, who were chosen and charged to carry the twelve stones, were not mentioned and whether they obeyed the instruction or not was not recounted in the story because Josh 4:8 states that "So the Israelites did as Joshua commanded them." Initially, twelve men were chosen to carry the stones but here Joshua instructs all the Israelites to do it and they obeyed Joshua's command. There appears to be a gap here.

Another ingredient of narrative in this story is dialogue. The story follows the sequence of divine command and human execution. This speech form is new because hitherto YHWH had addressed the whole nation or the elders. In this narrative, the address is directed to an individual, named Joshua. Even though it appeared as though YHWH was speaking to Joshua, from the beginning of Josh 4:2 to the end of Josh 4:3, in which it appeared as if Joshua was speaking. Structurally, it appears difficult to determine where the speech of Joshua ends because it appeared as though YHWH had begun to speak again in Josh 4:6–7. Joshua did not speak much throughout the narrative but it appeared as though the final editor/redactor was interested in projecting Joshua's qualities as an obedient and perhaps, docile leader. He was portrayed as a second Moses, perhaps because he had succeeded Moses and was shown as listening to the voice of YHWH in order to obey it without question. YHWH spoke to Joshua as to Moses to whom YHWH spoke face to face. The narrative could also be considered as the response to a question posed to a father (parent) by a son (child), which is similar to the stories in Exod 12:26–27; 13:14–15; Deut 6:20–21; Josh 4:6–7; 21–23.

The narrative set out to explain a certain phenomenon (i.e., the stones standing among the Israelites). The narrative presupposed that the Israelites were already constituted into a league of twelve tribes hence the choice of twelve men from among them to represent each tribe and each tribe was to have a stone monument to endorse this presupposition. This presupposition could also be founded on the reference to "the full corpus of possibly authentic pre-monarchic references to the twelve tribes operating as a normative."[19] These passages appeared to be connected with cultic material, which was not accessible to young children. As such, adults needed to be taught specific formulas, which they in turn would teach their children with the intention that the children would follow the meaning of the history of YHWH in relation to the people of Israel. With the foregone findings, Boling and Wright were probably right in describing this narrative as a "cultic teaching or proclamation (. . . a developed piece of tradition within Israel's cultic history)."[20]

Historical Criticism

This pericope and the entire book of Joshua belong to "part of a larger historical work, from Deuteronomy 1 to 2 Kings 25."[21] Martin Noth had put forth a proposal, which designated this historical corpus as "Deuteronomistic History" (*hereafter* DtrH).[22] These books had also been designated as the Former Prophets.[23] Noth had argued that the language of these books, except for Ruth, appeared similar and as such there must be a single hand responsible for the authorship of this collection. The main distinguishing characteristic of the books belonging to this historical corpus, which included Joshua, was that they specified that blessings resulted from obedience to YHWH's commandments whereas curses were the result of disobedience to same. Thus to the Deuteronomistic Historian (DtrH), who authored these books, divine initiative and human response were of primary importance. Apart from Noth, several other scholars had worked on the Deuteronomistic history. One of their proposals was that three stages in the writing of the DtrH were found in Jerusalem after 580 BCE (i.e., during the exile). This proposal was endorsed by Andrew Mayes, who also had claimed that the editing of Deuteronomy was "a process rather than an event or events."[24]

19. Gottwald, *The Tribes of Yahweh*, 359.

20. Boling and Wright, *Joshua*, 43.

21. Butler, *Joshua*, xx.

22. Noth, *The Deuteoronomistic History*.

23. Cottrill, "Joshua," 103. Cottrill, here, describes Deuteronomy as "the first book of the Hebrew (former) prophets."

24. Mayes, *Deuteronomy*, 29. Mayes had also suggested that the work of the Deuteronimist was a "process or a movement," which was not completed in a single editing context, 43.

The story in this pericope probably had historical links with the Exodus story (i.e., Exod 14 and 15) and some scholars had considered it to be another Exodus miracle. In this story, as in the exodus story, YHWH was represented by the ark, which was instrumental in the parting of the Red [Reed] Sea, as well as in cutting off the waters of the Jordan (Josh 4:6–7). YHWH appeared to be central to the narrative due to the event of the cutting off of the waters of the Jordan before the ark, which had been evident in Josh 3:2–4, 6, 9, 11–14, 16b and 4:4–7 and 11). These references should probably be considered as pointers to pre-existing stories, which were used by the final editor of the chosen pericope (Josh 4:1–8) as well as for the entire book of Joshua. In this story, YHWH is portrayed as both the God of the Exodus and the God of the Land that the people would possess after they had crossed over the Jordan. As in the Exodus story, the miraculous act of YHWH in parting the Red [Reed] Sea was not automatic. It was the result of Moses' obedience at that time and now in this story, obedience was required from Joshua, the twelve chosen men, and the people as a whole.

The references made to cultic practices in the chosen pericope were similar to those in the earlier exodus story. Additionally, the later mention of Gilgal in Josh 4:19–20, as the place where the people lodged for the night (Josh 4:8), appeared to point to some influences of writings from monarchic times. References to the "waters" (Josh 4:7) seemed to point to the influence of Canaanite cultic practices on this writing. The cultic use of water for cleansing, purification, and sacrifice among the Canaanites must have had a strong influence on the cultic practices of the Israelites. It is in this light that Frank Moore Cross suggests that this episode involves a divine warrior, who fights a holy war as evident in the Canaanite cosmogonic myth or the myth of *Enuma Elish*, where YHWH is portrayed as victorious over the waters of chaos.[25]

Redaction Criticism

From the various divergences found in the text of the LXX by scholars and personal reading of the text, it might be safe to conclude that the final editor of my pericope had more than one manuscript from which they copied. Boling and Wright had claimed that the transmission of

25. Cross, *Canaanite Myth and Hebrew Epic*, 58–59. Cross's idea of the cutting off of the waters of the Jordan appears to be reminiscent with the waters of chaos in Mesopotamian/Babylonian/Canaanite creation stories.

texts, (not only that of my pericope but texts in general) underwent active interpretation. This claim appeared to be very much at work in my chosen pericope, especially in the theological element added to the stones to make them a sign, a memorial to Israel forever. This is also evident in the numerous repetitions/duplications of structural elements in the text. For instance, twelve men were chosen to carry the stones. The waters of the Jordan River were cut off and the parents were instructed to teach their children the importance of the miracle connected with the stones in the text. These duplications seemed to point to not only duplicate motifs and traditions used by the final redactor but also to the use of probable duplicate sources. The question could be asked. "If the final editor had had a single authentic manuscript on hand, why did they have to repeat the names of places or events that had already been referred to in previous or even later narratives?" The prominence of the ark is perhaps, a case in point. According to Boling and Wright, this prominence of the ark, "might indicate that [*the cult of* italics mine] Shiloh or even Jerusalem had influenced the material" here.[26] The foregone assertion seemed to indicate that though the events of my pericope appeared to be pre-monarchical, the DtrH must have used material from monarchical times. These materials probably were from traditions of the Gilgal shrine and from the tribe of Benjamin and they were probably used to fill in the gaps that might be evident in the narrative of the editor.

I tend to agree with Curtis that "It is probable to think that the Deuteronomistic editor/s used an existing collection of traditions, which comprised something similar to the present book (Joshua), in telling the story of the conquests."[27] Leslie Hoppe is also of the opinion that stories connected with the crossing of the Jordan were preserved stories of memorial stones set up at Gilgal (Josh 4:1–3, 6,7, 8b and 20). Traditions about the ark and the concern that future generations would learn about God's fidelity when they heard this story, were of major concern for the final editor.[28]

The number "twelve" is of very great importance to the editor of my pericope. This number is used five times in the first eight verses of Joshua 4. This number appeared to be prominent also as the twelve tribes of Israel, which constituted the whole nation, were represented under the leadership of Joshua. This event also appeared to be a commemoration

26. Boling and Wright, *Joshua*, 43.

27. Curtis, *Joshua*, 33.

28. Hoppe, *Joshua and Judges*.

of the covenant made at Sinai (Exod 24:4), which Gottwald explained as "expressing the pleroma of Israel as a totality of tribes."[29]

"So These Shall Serve the People of Israel as a Memorial until Forever" (Josh 4:7)

Why is so much importance attached to this statement? The chain of events that surrounded this story made it very important. It was at the initiative and order of YHWH that the story took place. Joshua is given the instruction to choose twelve men. These men were not just ordinary men but choice men appointed by Joshua. The Masoretic Text (MT) referred to them literally as "men who were hkm "fixed" [i.e., established]. They were to be chosen from among the entire nation. No partiality was to be shown in choosing them. There was equality and indispensability of all the twelve tribes before YHWH. The men were instructed to pick up twelve stones according to the number of the tribes of Israel. They were to carry the stones with them to the other side of the Jordan and deposit them at the place where they would lodge for the night. The question may be asked, "Why all this trouble? The answer could be simple but the reason behind it all is very loaded. It was to commemorate another mighty act of YHWH, at the particular time the act was accomplished as well as commemorating it "until forever" at all times in the future.

Yes, YHWH was familiar with the sudden bouts of change in the behavior of the Israelites, their constant apostasy in returning to the sin they had repented of, and how they easily forgot the mighty acts YHWH performed among them. As such these memorial stones were to be visible signs to remind the Israelites about how YHWH had parted the waters of the Jordan for them to cross over so that the possession of the Land at the other side would be accomplished. This was not the only reason. It was also intended for the future generations of the Israelites to be taught about the mighty acts performed by YHWH in their history. These stones were also to serve as a source of legitimatizing, not only the story about YHWH's mighty acts but also of that of the sanctuary that sprang up from the stone monument that was set up. The story also hinted at how children constantly pestered their parents to tell them about the things they saw their parents do and which they (i.e., the children) were required to do. In this light, these stones were to help parents address the insatiable

29. Gottwald, *Tribes*, 244.

inquiring nature of the children, who would ask about the stone monument in the future. A great responsibility was thus placed on parents to give instructions to their children about the history of Israel and their relationship with YHWH. This story was specifically for the sons of Levi however, it became a universal charge to the entire nation.

With the foregone reasons behind the "memorial stones," I think the Deuteronomistic writer made a conscious attempt to interpret the tradition of Israel with regard to these "memorial stones" but at the same time, they were careful to interpret the law in particular to the children of Israel. It appears as though African tradition strictly followed this Israelite tradition. The elderly members of the community, ranging from the heads of households, through family heads, to clan heads, and on to the bigger community, had the responsibility of teaching the younger generations the norms of the society. Appropriate activities and/or ceremonies that maintained peace and harmony among neighbors, between the Supreme Being, living-dead, and the living were carefully and conscientiously passed down from generation to generation. This was and still is to ensure that when succeeding generations heard the stories that were passed down, heard proverbs, saw the trees, stones, mountains, or particular pieces of farmland, houses, rivers, and some animals, they would remember the miracles connected with them and reverence these things or places.

Just as the "memorial stones" in Josh 4:1–7 were to be a sign for the children of Israel "until forever," certain celebrations and natural phenomena in the African socio-cultural context have remained memorials and signs to the African peoples, from generation to generation [until forever]. It is no wonder that a wise saying among the Ewe peoples of South-eastern Ghana has it that "The beard may grow longer than the eyebrow but the beard can never pass down tradition to the eyebrow." By this saying, children are admonished to be humble and to respect the more experienced in the community. Adults were also admonished by this saying to rise up to the task of teaching and training the younger generations by transmitting the good traditional norms of the community, clan, families, households, etc., to their children. This ensures peace and tranquility in the lives of all and sundry in their existential socio-cultural contexts.

Conclusion/Way Forward:

In conclusion, the aim of the final redactor of Josh 4:1–8 was to first and foremost, narrate a story that explicated an Israelite tradition and secondly, to carefully interpret a particular cultic demand of the law of YHWH. Jerome F. D. Creach, commenting on this story, suggested that the purpose of this story was to create "a proper memory of the Jordan crossing and instructing each generation as to its importance in Israelite history"[30]

The MT text of this pericope could be said to be "good" because it does not raise any serious textual critical issues. The matters of harmonization, dittography, explication, or glosses, etc., could be attempts to make the story suit the tastes and demands of the particular community (i.e., the Israelites). That the story is etiological appears indisputable. The narrator had set out to explain the origin of a particular cultic practice among the Israelites and succeeded in doing so. The historical link of this story to the first exodus story appears evident in that there probably might have been stories of the first exodus tradition in circulation and the redactor made use of them. The divine initiative and miraculous act of YHWH, and the human response to them, are crucial to the success of the story.

The importance of parental responsibility for the instruction of children appears to be a universal charge here. Parents or leader figures are obliged to pass on their traditions and cultural practices to succeeding generations so that those customs and traditional practices would become "signs" and "memorial stones" to all members of their nations, communities, and societies "until forever." The younger/succeeding generations also have the responsibility of giving due respect to the leader figures in order to learn from the latter. As much as these obligations and responsibilities pertain in various socio-cultural contexts, the role of the priests [church leaders, who listen for the voice of God and communicate the same to members and the responsibility of members to take leadership seriously, also constitute major lessons for the Christian community.

In terms of this Festschrift, our African "memorial stones" (like West) must be considered as leaders/priests, who listened and obeyed the word of God to bring the message to us in understandable contextual ways so we can in turn act on them. We like the children of Israel, are the enquiring ones, who continue to probe to understand the way forward in theology and Bible studies in our cultural contexts.

30. Creach, *Joshua*, 45.

The journey of West, whom we celebrate in this Festschrift, as far as Bible study and theology are concerned, could be identified with the events of the story in Josh 4:1–8. West stands in the tradition of Joshua as the leader, who listened to God's command and obeyed. West went for "chosen [fixed] people" through South African Black Theology and contextual Bible study. West empowered the הֵכִין—*hkn* ("chosen") to carry on the message. Like the priests, West had stood on sacred ground in "the Jordan River of theology and contextual Bible study" and instructed many "chosen" to pick up "memorial stones" from where his feet had stood. The original "twelve stones" were for all the twelve tribes of Israel. By implication, the South African Black Theology and contextual Bible study, pioneered by West, are universal and inclusive of all without discrimination.

Perhaps, the celebration of West in this Festschrift could be summed up in the *bola*[31] "divining beads" of his [pre-Christian missionary] South African ancestors. West had proposed this idea very early in his biblical/ theological journey. The *bola* had been with our ancestors long before the inception of Euro-American Bible studies. When the missionaries introduced the Bible to West's ancestors, it dawned on them that what their *bola* was to them, in divining the will of the traditional gods, was similar to the Bible that was used by the Christian missionaries to divine the will of God and they (i.e., West's ancestors) came to contextualize the Bible as *bola*. The foregone could be explained in West's words, in reference to South African Black Theology that "the literary dimensions of the biblical text together with a focus on the central *symbols* and *thematic* semantics axis [or trajectory] of the final canonical form are fraught with a hermeneutics of suspicion, trust and resistance."[32] I would like to submit here that our "memorial stones" received and took the message of the Bible and contextualized it in line *bola* or it could be said that they employed the African *bola* to bring hybridized interpretations of the Bible to future generations, in spite of their suspicions, trust and resistance. As such, the enquiring "children" (i.e., "ordinary readers" and all who engage in theology, contextual Bible studies/interpretation), would understand the Bible (the word of God) and act on it.

31. The "ditola" beads that his ancestors used to decipher the will of the traditional gods and which they later equated to the Bible which the missionaries to his native South Africa, used to determine the will of God.

32. West, "The Bible in South African Black Theology."

Bravo Professor West for "birthing" South African Black Theology just as Gustavo Gutierrez[33] had "birthed" Liberation Theology in Latin America. We celebrate you for leaving a legacy of [emphasis mine, *Black liberation*] contextual theology, Bible study, and interpretation by providing us with modes of reading the Bible contextually and doing sound biblical interpretation in our own African context. Above all, you have through the foregone means, empowered us by providing us with the resources to be able to reclaim and regain our lands, our dignity, and identities. We celebrate you as one of Africa's "memorial stones." Your legacy has become a place of lodging for us, just as Gilgal was for the Israelites after they had crossed the Jordan. Your legacy has been established and firmly fixed like the memorial sacrificial stone altar in Gilgal "until forever." Many "enquiring children" (emphasis mine, *rising scholars*) will be taught by them. You have brought awareness to both females and males, non-literate and literate, poor and wealthy, the "ordinary" as well as the seasoned. Mercy Amba Oduyoye, while addressing the evils of patriarchy used these words, which I would like to use to describe how you have equipped and liberated us too.

> We seek to discard the fetters of oppression of culture [addition mine, western *Euro-American carbon copying*]. We seek full humanity and some principles to guide our lives in community. The meaning of full humanity cannot be defined by only one sector of humanity without listening to the voices, the hurts, and the delights of all the Fatimas. Even more important, what constitutes the fetters of oppression should be defined by those who experience it and not those who simply observe it.[34]

Many are following in your footsteps toward unique contextualization of the received word of God now, and many more future generations will follow in them *"until forever."* Just as the Israelites had to move tents again and again, your legacy will not remain stagnant but will continue to move on.

Bibliography

Ackroyd, P.R. Leaney and J.W. Packer. *Joshua*. Cambridge: Cambridge University Press, 1974.

33. Gutierez, *A Theology of Liberation*.
34. Oduyoye, *Daughters of Anowa*, 82.

Akoto, Dorothy Bea. "Hearing Scripture in African Contexts: A Hermeneutic of Grafting." *OTE* 20 (2007) 283–306.

Benton, Lancelot C. L. *The Septuagint with Apocrypha: Greek and English.* 1851. Reprint, Peabody, MA: Hendricksen, 1995.

Boling, Robert G., and G. Ernest Wright. *Joshua: A New Translation with Notes and Commentary.* Anchor Bible 6. Garden City, NY: Doubleday, 1982.

———. "Joshua" & "Joshua, Book of." In *The Anchor Bible Dictionary*, 3:999–1005. New York: Doubleday, 1992.

Bosch, David J. *Transforming Mission: Paradigm Shifts in Theology and Mission.* American Society of Missiology Series 16. Maryknoll, NY: Orbis, 1992.

Butler, Trent C. *Joshua.* Word Biblical Commentary 7. Waco, TX: Word, 1983.

Cottrill, Amy E. "Joshua." In *Women's Bible Commentary.* Edited by Carol Newsom, Sharon H. Ringe and Jacqueline E. Lapsley. Louisville: Westminster John Knox, 2012.

Creach, Jerome F. D. *Joshua.* Interpretation. Louisville: Westminster John Knox, 2003.

Cross, Frank Moore. *Canaanite Myth and Hebrew Epic: Essays in the History of the Religion of Israel.* Cambridge: Harvard University Press, 1973.

Curtis, Adrian H. W. *Joshua.* Old Testament Guides. Sheffield: Sheffield Academic, 1994.

Elliger, Karl, ed. *Biblia Hebraica Stuttgartensia.* Stuttgart: Deutsche Bibelgesellschaft, 1990.

Ellison, John W. *Nelson's Complete Concordance of the Revised Standard Version of the Bible.* New York: Nelson, 1957.

Gottwald, Norman K. *The Hebrew Bible: A Socio-Literary Introduction.* Philadelphia: Fortress, 1985.

———. *The Tribes of Yahweh: A Sociology of Religion of Liberated Israel 12500–1050 B.C.E.* Maryknoll, NY: Orbis, 1993.

Gray, John. *Joshua, Judges and Ruth.* New Century Bible. Greenwood, SC: Attic, 1946.

Gutierrez, Gustavo. *A Theology of Liberation: History, Politics, and Salvation.* Translated by Sister Caridad Inda and John Eagleson. New York: Orbis, 1988.

Harrison, R. K., gen. ed. *The New International Commentary on the Old Testament.* Grand Rapids: Eerdmans, 1981.

Hayes, John H. *An Introduction to Old Testament Study.* Nashville: Abingdon, 1979.

Hayes, John H., and Carl R. Holladay. *Biblical Exegesis: A Beginner's Handbook.* Atlanta: John Knox, 1987.

Hoppe, Leslie J., OFM. *Joshua and Judges with an Excursus on Charismatic Leadership in Israel.* Old Testament Message 5. Wilmington, DE: Glazier, 1982.

The Jewish Bible: Tanakh A New Translation of the Holy Scriptures according to the Traditional Hebrew Text. Jerusalem: Jewish Publication Society, 1985.

Mayes, Andrew D. H. *Text in Context: Essays of the Members of the Society of Old Testament Studies.* Oxford: Oxford University Press, 2000.

———. *Deuteronomy.* New Century Bible Commentary. Grand Rapids: Eerdmans, 1981.

Noth, Martin. *The Deuteoronomistic History.* JSOTSup 15. Sheffield: Sheffield Academic, 1981.

Oduyoye, Mercy Amba. *Daughters of Anowa: African Women and Patriarchy.* Maryknoll, NY: Orbis, 1995.

Smith, Robert H. "The Book of Joshua." In *The Interpreter's One Volume Commentary on the Bible*. Nashville: Abingdon, 1991.

Soggin, Alberto J. "Joshua." In *Introduction to the Old Testament*, 187–95. 3rd ed. Louisville: Westminster John Knox, 1989.

———. *Joshua: A Commentary*. Translated by R. A. Wilson. OTL. Philadelphia: Westminster, 1972.

Stendahl, Krister. "Biblical Theology, Contemporary." In *The Interpreter's Dictionary of the Bible*, edited by George A. Buttrick, 1:418–32. Nashville: Abingdon, 1962.

Strong, James. *Abingdon's Strong's Exhaustive Concordance of the Bible*. Nashville: Abingdon, 1990.

Ukpong, Justin S. "Popular Readings of the Bible in Africa and Implications for Academic Reading." In *The Bible in Africa: Transactions, Trajectories and Trends*, edited by Gerald O. West and Musa W. Dube, 582–84. Leiden: Brill, 2000.

West, Gerald O. "The Bible in South African Black Theology." In *Biblical Interpretation in African Perspective*, edited by David Tuesday Adamo, 31–59. Lanham, MD: University Press of America, 2006.

———. *Biblical Hermeneutics of Liberation: Modes of Reading the Bible in the South African Context*. Maryknoll, NY: Orbis, 1991.

———. "Contextual Bible Study in South Africa: A Resource for Reclaiming and Regaining Land, Dignity and Identity." In *The Bible in Africa: Transactions, Trajectories and Trends*, edited by Gerald O. West and Musa W. Dube, 595–610. Leiden: Brill, 2000.

———. "Some Parameters of the Hermeneutic Debate in the South African Context." *JTSA* 80 (1992) 3–13.

Wilmore, Gayraud S. *Black Religion and Black Radicalism: An Interpretation of the Religious History of Afro-American People*. 2nd ed. Maryknoll, NY: Orbis 1992.

20

"But a Promise is a Promise"

Trauma and Recognition in the Sarah and Hagar Narrative (Genesis 16; 21) and Damon Galgut's The Promise

L. JULIANA CLAASSENS AND ROBERT R. VOSLOO

Introduction

(Do you promise me, Manie?

Holding on to him, skeleton hands grabbing, like in a horror film.

Ja, I'll do it.

Because I really want her to have something. After everything she's done.

I understand, he says.

Promise me you'll do it. Say the words.

I promise," Pa says, choked-sounding.)[1]

DAMON GALGUT'S CRITICALLY ACCLAIMED novel, *The Promise*, follows the lives of a white Afrikaner family over the four decades that saw the end of the apartheid regime and the birth of a democratic South Africa. Being awarded the Booker Prize in November 2021, this haunting novel offers a candid, though also a rather grim look at what has become of the so-called rainbow nation of God. Central to this novel is the theme of a promise made by Manie, the father of the ironically named Swart family

---

1. Galgut, *The Promise*, 24.

(the Afrikaans word for "Black") to his dying wife, Rachel, to give their servant, Salome, ownership of the house in which she and her son Lucas reside. Structured around four funerals, *The Promise* demonstrates how this promise is *not* kept by the father, nor in effect by the next generation represented by the three children Anton, Astrid, and Amor.

The Promise is reminiscent of yet another promise made to a biblical character which to some extent is just as silent, or rather silenced, by its author than the servant Salome, who, for four decades, patiently has been waiting for the promise to be fulfilled. In Gen 16, it is significant that Hagar, the runaway slave girl of Sarah, receives a similar promise also made to Abraham that involves progeny and divine protection.[2] However, it is a question of what had happened to this promise to Hagar, who in ages since, has been read as representing the outcast, the disenfranchised—in terms of race and class, exposing the injustice of slavery, segregation, #BlackLivesMatter,[3] and in our context the ongoing struggle with Apartheid as institutionalized racism.

In this essay, we will explore how a creative conversation between Galmut's *The Promise* and the Sarah and Hagar narrative may help us consider the role of stories, both ancient and modern, to not only offer a candid look at ourselves and our world, but also to imagine a more just world. A central theme in both of these stories is the way in which trauma is linked to the experience of not being seen, of not being recognized and respected. This intersection of trauma and recognition is of particular importance in a context in which the blatant failure to recognize the needs, hopes, and desires of individuals and the communities they represent does great harm, not only to others, but also to the self.

In this regard, it is the youngest daughter in *The Promise*, Amor, whose name aptly means "love," and whose words, "But a promise is a promise!" are echoed in the title of this essay that serves not only as the family's conscience but also of the readers'. With this exploration of the way in which the characters in Galmut's *The Promise*, as well as in the Sarah and Hagar narrative, come to represent a nation's struggle to make sense of their traumatic past, we would like to honor Prof. Gerald West's

---

2. Cf. Okoye, "Sarah and Hagar," 170–73; and Trible, "Ominous Beginnings for a Promise of Blessing," 42. Okoye highlights the fact that Hagar is the only woman to be the recipient of an epiphany as well as to receive a promise regarding descendants. However, he notes that having been circumcised, Ishmael ought to have been included in the covenant with God that also includes a portion in the Promised Land.

3. Williams, "Hagar in African American Biblical Appropriation," 172–75. Cf. also Reaves, "Sarah as Victim and Perpetrator," 486.

legacy. Over many years, Prof. West has distinguished himself as an exegete and reader of biblical texts in such a way that seeks to bring about transformation in society. As a socially engaged biblical scholar, West's work through the Ujamaa Center and Contextual Bible Reading, dealing with topics such as gender-based violence and the violence done to the LGBTIQ+ community, involves holding up the biblical text as a mirror to expose injustice in our context of South Africa.[4] But at the same time, Prof. West's contextual Bible readings always offer creative suggestions that make it possible for individuals and communities to act in such a way as to bring about much-needed change.

What Happened to the Promise to Hagar?

Many readers, particularly readers who have found themselves in disenfranchised positions, have identified with Hagar precisely because her plight (and her flight) resonated with their concrete experiences of suffering and misrecognition. For instance, in a sermon at the closing event of the German Kirchentag in Wittenberg in May 2017, the Anglican archbishop of Cape Town, Thabo Makgoba notes that "[f]or any African, Hagar's story is deeply etched into both our historical DNA and our contemporary experience."[5] Drawing on Dolores Williams' description of Hagar's predicament, which involved slavery, poverty, sexual and economic exploitation, surrogacy, rape, domestic violence, and homelessness,[6] Makgoba laments: "Black people generally but particularly black women in

---

4. Cf., e.g., West and Zondi-Mabizela, "The Bible Story That Became a Campaign," 4–12; West, "Deploying Indecent Literary," 57–78; West, van der Walt, and Kaoma, "When Faith Does Violence," 1–8; West, "The Contribution of Tamar's;" West and Haddad, "Boaz as 'Sugar Daddy.'"

5. Conger, "Archbishop Makgoba's Sermon."

6. Williams, *Sisters in the Wilderness*, 3, writes as follows about her realization of the striking similarities between Hagar's story and the stories of African-American women: "Hagar's heritage was African as was black women's. Hagar was a slave. Black women had emerged from a slave heritage and still live in light of it. Hagar was brutalized by her slave owner, the Hebrew woman Sarah. The slave narratives of African-American women and the narratives of contemporary day-workers tell of the brutal or cruel treatment black women have received from the wives of slave masters and from contemporary white female employers. Hagar had no control over her body . . . The bodies of African-American slave women were owned by their masters . . . Like Hagar and her child Ishmael, African-American female slaves and their children, after slavery, were expelled from the homes of many slave holders and given no resources for survival."

South Africa know exactly the same realities. They know that in so many contexts, 'black lives do not matter.'"[7]

In a fascinating article that interrogates how "whiteness has assumed ownership to Sarah's story,"[8] Jayme Reaves contends that white people, like herself (and we authors as well), have not always recognized how our whiteness and privilege blind us to our complicity in unjust systems of oppression.[9] With her specific United States context of White Evangelical women in mind (who incidentally, in 2016, overwhelmingly voted for Trump),[10] Reaves demonstrates how white privilege is responsible for (white) readers' sympathies to be primarily focused on Sarah.[11] Our whiteness, moreover, makes us oblivious to the pain of the unseen characters, such as that of the slave woman Hagar and her son Ishmael, who, in a profound act of anti-hospitality on the part of Sarah, is banished into the wilderness.[12] In this regard, Reaves highlights Sarah's indifference towards Hagar, how despite sharing a household and a life with Hagar and her son, with Abraham, she can speak of "this slave-girl and her son" in Gen 21:10.[13] Moreover, this lack of recognition is evident in the fact that Sarah never directly addresses Hagar, not once using her name.[14]

Despite having a profound encounter with the God who "truly sees" (רֳאִי אֵל—*El Roi*) the runaway slave woman and her unborn son in the wilderness, and bestows a similar promise to her and her descendants as the one offered to Abraham and his son (Gen 16:13), it seems that the dominant narrative is, and almost always has been, the story of Israel.[15] Reaves, drawing on the work of Okoye, argues that Hagar's vision of

7. Conger, "Archbishop Makgoba's Sermon." Makgoba continues: "But as we read the Hagar story further, we find that alongside this litany of suffering and exclusion, there is also the story of a God who acts in a powerful way. When Hagar finds herself vulnerable on the periphery, God gives her the resources to survive. Just like the Syrian refugee you have welcomed into Germany, Hagar stands as a beacon of hope to all who suffer, to the oppressed around the world."

8. Reaves, "Sarah as Victim and Perpetrator," 491.

9. Reaves, "Sarah as Victim and Perpetrator," 490.

10. Reaves, "Sarah as Victim and Perpetrator," 487.

11. Reaves, "Sarah as Victim and Perpetrator," 489.

12. Reaves, "Sarah as Victim and Perpetrator," 490. Sarah's inhospitality towards Hagar is juxtaposed with the hospitality bestowed upon the (divine) visitors in Genesis 18 by Abraham and Sarah.

13. Reaves, "Sarah as Victim and Perpetrator," 497.

14. Reaves, "Sarah as Victim and Perpetrator," 497; Okoye, "Sarah and Hagar," 167.

15. Reaves, "Sarah as Victim and Perpetrator," 490, 492; Okoye, "Sarah and Hagar," 164–65.

a God who sees and hears and makes promises is "displaced and subsumed" by the narrator's construction of God who in Genesis 21 all but "write[s] Ishmael out of direct inheritance."[16] As Reaves remarks:

> We must remember as readers, however, that it is not in Sarah's, or Israel's, interest to recognize the legitimacy of Ishmael's inheritance claim . . . This story feels rigged against Hagar and Ishmael, supplying Israel (and us as readers) with convenient justifications for setting one's self, tribe, nation, or even our theological understanding over and above the interests of another.[17]

In terms of the central theme of this essay, one could thus ask, "What happened to the promise to Hagar?" Even though Ishmael is the legitimate firstborn son, who also is circumcised and, hence, included in the covenant made between God and Abraham in Gen 17, Ishmael and his descendants are excluded by the descendants of Israel from any claim to the Promised Land. The story ends with Hagar and her descendants in the wilderness—Ishmael becoming the ancestor of twelve tribes, who is said to be in constant strife with the neighbouring nations (Gen 35:9. Cf. also Gen 16:12).[18] According to Okoye, "as far as the narrator is concerned, Ishmael was content with his inheritance in the desert!" However, as Okoye reminds us, such a notion of the "contented and happy black slave" quite often is a construction that helped "assuage [the] consciences" of the slaveowners.[19]

Reaves uses her honest engagement with the story of Sarah to challenge her own whiteness, her position of power and privilege, and her complicity in structures that continue to perpetuate injustice. She admits that, personally, it was quite a shock for her to realize that she, as also many other white feminist scholars who have been drawn to Hagar trying to highlight "her exploitation and abuse because we want to be on her side and show our 'wokeness,'" has instead failed to face up to the fact that "we"

---

16. Reaves, "Sarah as Victim and Perpetrator," 490; Okoye, "Sarah and Hagar," 170.

17. Reaves, "Sarah as Victim and Perpetrator," 490; Okoye, "Sarah and Hagar," 172.

18. One should note that the promise is fulfilled in terms of abundant progeny, in addition to a long life and a good death as evident in the genealogy in Gen 25:7–8, Trible, "Ominous Beginnings," 56. However, it is telling that there is no mention of land. In this regard, Okoye observes that the Hebrew term used in Gen 21:10, "to drive out" (גָּרֵשׁ—gršֿ) also is used for driving out the indigenous nations suggesting that in effect Ishmael is banished from the Promised Land," "Sarah and Hagar," 171.

19. Okoye, "Sarah and Hagar," 172.

may well be Sarah in this narrative.[20] In this regard, this study proposes that *The Promise* may have a similar effect, helping readers everywhere to see what white privilege may prevent white readers from seeing.

What Happened to the Promise to Salome?

A central theme in *The Promise*, which follows the lives of one particular Afrikaner family that paradigmatically represents the white population as a whole, is whether the next generation will keep the promise to give Salome the house that she had been living in. None of the three siblings of the family, whose names all start with an "A"—Anton, Astrid, and Amor, seem to be doing terribly well. Their lives over the course of four decades, in different ways, reflect the painful legacy of the apartheid regime into which they were born.

For the oldest daughter Astrid, her failure to keep this promise is rooted in a self-indulgent lifestyle that manifested early on in the novel in terms of her self-destructive eating disorder, coupled with her shopping obsession. Her life, ironically, ends in violence as she, upon returning from one of her many shopping trips, is highjacked and killed.

As for the first-born son, Anton, he struggles throughout the novel, representing the crisis in masculinity experienced by many white males in South Africa, who have grown up with an exaggerated sense of their sense of self rooted in white-male privilege. Traumatized by his having shot an elderly woman while doing compulsory military service in the 1980s, during the State of Emergency, Anton goes AWOL, turning into a conscientious objector to forced conscription. However, unable to come to terms with the demons of the past, as well as failing at life (as exemplified by being a failed novelist), Anton ends his life by means of a self-inflicted gunshot.

Despite having, at least, the will to keep the promise her father made to her mother, the youngest daughter, Amor, also is unable to do much. For 40 years, paralyzed by her inability to convince her family to do what is right, Amor exiles herself as far away as possible from the family farm where she grew up to go work as a nurse in an HIV-AIDS hospital in Durban—her choice of a career dedicated to healing people, perhaps

20. Reaves, "Sarah as Victim and Perpetrator," 484, 491. Cf. also Trible and Russell, *Hagar, Sarah and Their Children*, 195–96, where Russell reflects on her own "patterns of privilege" as a "white, North American, Christian woman" that are mirrored in "Sarah's actions in casting Hagar out."

serving as penitence to somehow absolve herself and her family. Amor's character development is traced through an emphasis on her looks as she is first shown as a shy teenager, then as a beautiful young woman returning from London, and by the end of the novel, a middle-aged woman looking much older than her age; tired and worn-out.

Employing the divergent roads followed by these three siblings, *The Promise* showcases the blindness that comes with whiteness, the inability to recognize one's innate power and privilege associated with being born white. Reaves reflects on how her social location as a white woman has implicitly taught [her] to identify with Sarah . . . the matriarch of [her] inherited faith tradition," who is seen as "the heroine or protagonist in the story."[21] This position of whiteness, moreover, makes it difficult to sympathize with the plight of Hagar and her descendants. As Reaves writes:

> In the same way, whiteness can blind us to the oppression and injustice in the text, reinforcing a privileged worldview and assumptions of others' experiences and readings, whereas an informed reading seeks to account for these and see beyond them.[22]

A similar argument can be made in terms of the various positions presented by the three children in *The Promise*: that all relate to the failure to keep the promise to Salome and her children.

However, despite spending most of its time on the rather tragic lives of the Swart children, it is clear that this story really should have been about Salome (the family's Black servant), the unexpected beneficiary of this unfulfilled promise made all those years ago by Rachel (the mother of the family). Not only was Salome intimately involved with raising Rachel's three children, but she also faithfully cared for Rachel herself during her long struggle with cancer. Nevertheless, Salome remains just as invisible as Hagar had been in the Genesis story. As the narrator muses: "She was with Ma when she died, right there next to the bed, though nobody seems to see her, she is apparently invisible. And whatever Salome feels is invisible too."[23]

Salome is also not seen at Rachel's funeral, and this time, not because nobody noticed her but because Tannie Marina "told her in no uncertain

---

21. Reaves, "Sarah as Victim and Perpetrator," 489–490.

22. Reaves, "Sarah as Victim and Perpetrator," 490.

23. Galgut, *The Promise,* 24; Wood, "A Family at Odds."

terms that she would not be allowed to attend" the funeral.[24] And, even when Anton's wife, Desirée, does notice her after Astrid's death, all she can do is make the following snide comment about Salome: "She's incredibly lazy, that old one . . . Really you should get rid of her."[25]

The reader is also somehow implicated. The narrator accuses the reader of a similar indifference to Salome that is evident in members of the Swart family: "If Salome's home hasn't been mentioned before, it's because *you* have not asked, *you* didn't care to know."[26] Thus, even if Salome is not literally chased into the wilderness like Hagar, the continuous non-recognition and misrecognition of Salome's identity and dignity throughout the novel must have left its marks on her body and soul.

The narrator of *The Promise* challenges this invisibility of Salome by, for instance, imagining Salome's inner world in which she offers up her prayer after Rachel's death: "Oh God. I hope You can hear me. It is me, Salome. Please welcome the madam where You are and look after her carefully because I wish to see her again one day in heaven."[27] It is evident from Salome's prayer that she sees her own life as inextricably intertwined with that of Rachel. As we read: "I have known her a long time, from before she was a madam even, from when she and I were both young women, and in these past days we were sometimes one person."[28]

It is significant that Salome, in her prayer, also thanks God that Rachel promised her the house.[29] On the one hand, one could say that Salome does receive some affirmation and recognition through Rachel's desire and persistence, which compelled Manie's promise to give Salome the house. On the other hand, the narrator, immediately after imagining Salome's prayer, contemplates the impossibility of truly knowing what Salome thought:

> Perhaps she doesn't pray in these words, or in any words at all,
> many prayers are uttered without language and they rise like all

24. Galgut, *The Promise*, 72.

25. Galgut, *The Promise*, 164.

26. Galgut, *The Promise*, 237; Anderson, "The Promise by Damon Galgut."

27. Galgut, *The Promise*, 72.

28. Galgut, *The Promise*, 72. Amor also indicates the family's longstanding connection with Salome early on in the novel when she says, regarding Salome, that "she has been here on the farm forever, or that's how it feels," and adds that her grandfather used to say, "Oh, Salome, I got her along with the land" (23). These references demonstrate the complexity of this connection, which at least in the grandfather's mind is equated to possession.

29. Galgut, *The Promise*, 72.

the rest. Or perhaps she prays for other things, because prayers are secret in the end, and not all to the same God.[30]

The reviewer in *The Guardian*, Jon Day, writes that this is a central moment in the novel that on the one hand "wants to be able to speak on Salome's behalf while simultaneously disavowing any hope of doing so." As he writes: "Perhaps this is just one more example of Salome's disenfranchisement—no home, no voice, no narrated inner life."[31]

So, what happened to the promise to Salome? In the following section, we will further consider the role that misrecognition plays in the failure of keeping the promises made to Salome (and Hagar) but, conversely, how it is also a renewed appreciation of the importance of recognition that may help future readers to take responsibility for doing what is right.

The Struggle for Recognition in a Context of Mis-Recognition

In recent decades much has been written on the need for recognition as a vital force connected to the identity of persons and groups.[32] Recognition is most often understood in a positive sense as identity-affirming, while misrecognition and disrespect are seen as functioning as a harmful strategy of Othering, especially given how human identity is so closely aligned with the need for recognition. As the Canadian moral philosopher Charles Taylor claims at the beginning of his influential essay, "The Politics of Recognition":

> (O)ur identity is partly shaped by recognition or its absence, often by the misrecognition of others, and so a person or group of people can suffer real damage, real distortion, if the people or society around them mirror back to them a confining or demeaning or contemptible picture of themselves. Nonrecognition or misrecognition can inflict harm, can be a form

---

30. Galgut, *The Promise*, 72.

31. Day, "*The Promise* by Damon Galgut."

32. In the early 1990s, Taylor spoke within the context of discussions on multiculturalism about "the politics of recognition," whereas Axel Honneth engaged the Hegelian idea of "the struggle for recognition" within the discourses on critical theory, to put forward a normative theory for understanding social conflicts and struggles. See Taylor, "The Politics of Recognition," 5–73 and Honneth, *The Struggle for Recognition*. Since then, the notion of recognition has become a key concept in social and political theory. For an overview discussion, see, for instance, Cillian McBride, *Recognition*.

of oppression, imprisoning someone in a false, distorted, and reduced mode of being.[33]

The notion of recognition can also be brought to bear on social and political conflicts and struggles within the South African context. At the heart of colonialism and apartheid, one can argue, lies an inherent logic of nonrecognition, misrecognition, and disrespect. And the protest movements against these ideologies can indeed be described in a positive and affirming way as struggles for recognition and dignity.

Yet, one must also take note of the more critical discourses that rightly point to the ambivalence of the notion of recognition.[34] Kelly Oliver, for instance, has argued that there is a type of recognition bestowed by the dominant group that actually serves merely as a repetition of power dynamics, privilege, and domination, leaving the oppressed with the sense that they lack something only their dominators can bestow on them.[35] In this way, stereotypes of inferiority and superiority are kept in place, making recognition a symptom of the pathology of oppression. Drawing on Franz Fanon's reference to the Hegelian master-slave dialectic, Oliver points out that within colonial contexts, accounts of recognition often presuppose, rather than challenge, the inherent pathologies of recognition within oppressive cultures.[36]

One should, therefore, expose what McBride has described as "the recognition-deficit" model that presents people as passive receptors and does not sufficiently take cognizance of destructive power relations, wider inequalities in society, and concrete socio-historical realities of systemic and structural injustice.[37] The ambivalence of this idea of recognition rightly challenges us to be cognisant of how positive interpersonal regard is often undermined, and even negated, by deeply entrenched structural deficiencies.

In Galgut's *The Promise*, we find that the trace of recognition that Salome received in being the recipient of a promise made to Rachel by her husband, Manie, is negated or seriously hampered by systemic and

33. Taylor, "The Politics of Recognition," 25.

34. See in this regard, Ikäheimo, Lepold, McNay, and Stahl, eds., *Recognition and Ambivalence.*

35. Oliver, *Witnessing,* 9.

36. Oliver, *Witnessing,* 28.

37. McBride, *Recognition,* 6–7.

structural barriers of racism and patriarchy, that made it impossible for the promise to be enacted or concretized.

Initially, we see how the promise cannot be fulfilled because of the law apparatus of the apartheid society. When the young Amor told Anton that she heard her father promise the house to Salome, Anton responded by saying "Even if Pa wanted to, he can't give it to her . . . It is against the law."[38] But, we also see how over time, even when it is not against the law any longer, the promise is not kept, reminding us that the heart of the problem lies deeper than the legal excuse proffered.

Although the promise is not enacted, it remains a haunting presence. Anton, for instance, mentions how it returned to his thoughts at an arbitrary moment: "The question about the house has travelled from his mother to his sister to Lukas to Salome and has now been planted in him, a tiny dark seed just starting to sprout."[39] Nonetheless, notwithstanding the persistent presence of the promise in the minds and conversations of the family, their dominant response remains that of denial, contestation, and repression. Most crudely, this is expressed by Manie's retort when Amor tells him that he should do what he promised, and give Salome the house: "I never did . . . I never promised anything."[40] Ironically, Manie, who has difficulty honouring his promise to his wife, gives a piece of land to the charismatic pastor, Alwyn Simmers, for a spiritual/capitalist project—a decision that, in effect, makes possible the events that lead to his death.

Amor's own relationship to the promise—of a house being given to Salome—is ambivalent. For many years, she does not act upon the promise that she had overheard as a young girl (ironically, while she also experiences not being seen), even if she shows the intention to do so. Yet it keeps bothering her; this promise is described as "this buried question from long ago" and as that particular stone that "never seems to find a resting place, no matter how often it is turned."[41] But, at the end of the novel, after Anton's death, we read of Amor's plans to make good on the promise. In the conversation with a lawyer—who reminds her "I'm a lawyer. Promises don't mean a thing"[42]—she learns of a land claim against the farm, and that the "gift" of the house, the one promised, may

38. Galgut, *The Promise*, 74.

39. Galgut, *The Promise*, 51.

40. Galgut, *The Promise*, 58.

41. Galgut, *The Promise*, 178.

42. Galgut, *The Promise*, 234.

turn out to be a poisoned chalice. When Amor goes to the house, Salome is there with her son Lukas. The accusation addressed to Amor by Lukas is clear: "My mother was supposed to get this house a long time back. Instead, she got lies and promises. And you did nothing."[43]

For Lukas, the deferral of the promise nullifies any belated gift of the house. It is a form of recognition that is highjacked by the pathologies of oppression within apartheid society. In strong language, Lukas states: "And still you don't understand, it's not yours to give. It already belongs to us, and the land it's standing on. Ours! Not yours to give as a favour when you're finished with it. Everything you have, white lady, is already mine. I don't have to ask."[44] In this context, Amor feels that she is not recognized, hence her response to the description of her as a "white lady": "I have a name. You used to know it. I told you about the house that day I met you at the koppie. Do you remember?"[45] In this situation one senses that there is still the memory of a shared, albeit a divided and traumatic, past. But the mutual experience of the deepening gulf between them is real.

So where is the hope in this rather tragic story? Rand Cooper of the *New York Times* warns not to expect "much hope in this novel. Its 'negative and destructive power,' as one character says about the Swarts' bad karma, is relentless."[46] Galgut himself is said to be rather cynical about South Africa, which held so much promise, particularly after the euphoria associated with the first democratic elections. In an interview with the *Financial Times,* he writes "There has always been a feeling that South Africa was a country on the edge, but that it somehow always managed to veer away from that edge . . . But now, the feeling is maybe we won't."[47]

Nevertheless, despite the fact that neither *The Promise* nor the story of Sarah and Hagar can be said to have happy endings, the act of storytelling always implies a measure of hope that the reader will read and "go do differently." In this regard, we would like, in the final part of this essay, to offer some thoughts on the imperative of reclaiming mutual recognition, which may offer our best hope for a more just future.

43. Galgut, *The Promise*, 237.

44. Galgut, *The Promise*, 238.

45. Galgut, *The Promise*, 238.

46. Cooper, "A Family."

47. Studeman, "Damon Galgut on His Booker Winner *The Promise.*"

Becoming Promise-Keepers

One of the interesting narrative devices in *The Promise* is the way in which the four sections of the novel are structured around four funerals, each reflecting a different religious tradition. Shortly before dying, Rachel returns to her Jewish roots; the father, Manie, "converts" to a charismatic church with a former Dutch Reformed Church dominee, proclaiming a type of prosperity theology that, quite literally, results in Manie's death following the failed attempt to demonstrate God's protection of/from a poisonous snake bite; daughter, Astrid's funeral, being conducted by a Catholic priest who had refused to absolve her before her highjack; and Anton's funeral reflecting a "new age" spirituality propagated by his wife's yoga instructor. These divergent religious expressions associated with the funerals attest to the fact that, even though South Africa indeed is a deeply religious country, none of these religious traditions are able to help the children of this family (and one could say country) to do justice; to become promise-keepers.

The exception is Amor who, even though not overtly religious, ends up being the one having a transcendental encounter of her own when struck by lightning as a young girl. This event becomes conceivably responsible for her enlightenment and decision to choose a different path. Coincidentally, at the end of *The Promise*, one finds a stripped-down Amor on the roof during a raging storm, in the presence of the divine, whose power has scarred her once before. The fact that Amor is the sole survivor of the Swart family suggests that love, service, and promise-keeping may be the only option that does not end in death.

Read through the lens of "recognition theory," one could indeed say that the ending (and the novel as a whole) amplifies the critique of an account of a form of recognition that is abstracted from the entrenched realities of systemic, structural, and insidious forms of injustice and exploitation. Alternatively, one can also read the ending in the light of the philosopher Paul Ricoeur's question, in his discussion of mutual recognition, in *The Course of Recognition*, where he asks: "Can we build a bridge between the poetics of *agape* and the prose of justice?"[48] For Ricoeur, "the prose of justice" refers to just laws, policies, and institutions. Without this attention to the form and language of the juridical plane, the talk of recognition can stay trapped within pathologies of oppression because it does not address structural and systemic injustices.

48. Ricoeur, *The Course of Recognition*, 224.

Ricoeur, moreover, also makes a plea for what he calls "the poetics of *agape*." Here the emphasis is not so much on the logic of equivalence, with all receiving their due. Instead, the focus is on the logic of super-abundance marked by gift-giving and excess. We give to and receive from others more than what we owe them legally.

For Ricoeur, the language of such a "poetics of agape" is similar to the hymn we find in 1 Cor 13. The "poetics of agape" is therefore "based on symbolic meditations as exempt from the juridical as from the commercial order of exchange."[49] In this context, Ricoeur also affirms the power of gestures to witness to such "a poetics of agape." These gestures—such as a handshake or an embrace—can unleash "an irradiating and irrigating wave that, secretly and indirectly, contribute to the advance of history towards states of peace."[50] In reading *The Promise,* we are mindful of Ricoeur's emphasis on "the poetics of agape" and the way it finds expression through gestures, which may help us to reconfigure recognition as it pertains to our divided and traumatic past. The truth of the matter is that we continue to find ourselves between structure and gesture, between the rule and the gift, between justice and love.

In *The Promise,* we have become acutely and painfully aware of the structural barriers that prevent the fulfillment of the promise, and how this failure to be promise-keepers at a deeper level may be the result of a lack of love, of *agape,* of *amor.* Nevertheless, at the very end of the novel, one finds a hint, a gesture, that could serve as a reminder to commit ourselves to "the prose of justice" as well as to an ongoing embodiment of "the poetics of agape." When, in one of the final scenes of the novel, Amor says goodbye to Salome one hears the voice of the narrator that goes to the heart of the ambivalent and fragile bond that characterizes the relationship between these two women: "Both women know that they won't see each other again. They're close, but not close. Joined but not joined. One of the strange, simple fusions that hold this country together. Sometimes only barely."[51] As the narrator describes their encounter: "They embrace a last time. Frail basket of bones, containing fire. Pulse beating dimly under your hand."[52] This encounter is marked by a touching act of recognition, of naming, of gratitude:

49. Ricoeur, *The Course of Recognition,* 219.

50. Ricoeur, *The Course of Recognition,* 245.

51. Galgut, *The Promise,* 239.

52. Galgut, *The Promise,* 242.

> Goodbye, Salome. Thank you.
>
> Goodbye, Amor. And thank you.[53]

This gesture of mutual recognition points to how these individual stories were and continue to be an interwoven narrative that collectively is linked to past trauma, even if it means the ambivalent reality of being "joined and not being joined." Amor, who throughout the novel is portrayed as the one who is most conscious of being "joined" to Salome and her family is, by means of this final gesture, able to help realize something of the mutuality that she has experienced all along with Salome and her son, Lukas.[54]

This shared past, furthermore, makes it clear why truthful memory, in addition to remorse, forgiveness, and reconciliation, are such crucial categories. In *The Promise,* it is Desirée (who would become Anton's wife) who has no desire to be joined in any way to Salome and her family, as evident in her harsh and racist words about Salome and Black people. Her father, we read, appeared before the Truth and Reconciliation Commission, and in the novel, her stance represents something of the attitude still prevalent in South Africa, that any engagement with the past that involves proximity, commitment, and restoration is disavowed.

The power of *The Promise* is rooted in a moral appeal to its readers which challenges a type of engagement that dislocates a truthful grappling with the past from a future-orientated memory, as symbolized in the idea of a covenant or a promise. In her book, *The Human Condition,* Hannah Arendt (in the section on "Action") argues that human capacity to act is linked to forgiveness. As she states: "Without forgiveness, release from the consequences of what we have done, our capacity to act would, as it were, be confined to one single deed from which we could never recover; we would remain the victims of our consequences forever."[55] But Arendt also writes how the remedy for the unpredictability and uncertainty of the future is encapsulated in the ability to make and keep promises. Therefore, if we were not committed to promise-keeping, we would lose our sense of self: "We would be condemned to wander helplessly and

---

53. Galgut, *The Promise,* 242.

54. Cf., e.g., how Amor in the beginning of the novel shares with Lukas, who also had lost a parent (his father died in a gold mine) the news of the promise about the house that she had overheard. The thirteen-year-old Amor's experience is that something "joins them together," Galgut, *The Promise,* 25.

55. Arendt, *The Human Condition,* 237.

without direction in the darkness of each [hu]man's lonely heart, caught in its contradictions and equivocalities."[56]

Arendt also makes it clear that both the capacity to forgive and to promise, depend on the presence and actions of others. As she argues: ". . .forgiving and promising enacted in solitude or isolation remain without reality and can signify no more than a role played before one's self."[57] Thus, the ethical force of Galgut's *The Promise* may well reside in the way it exhibits the fragile reality of "being joined," and how the engagement with the trauma of the past cannot be dislocated from embodied acts of mutual recognition and promise-keeping.

Conclusion: A Different Future for Sarah and Hagar?

In this essay, we asked what had happened to the promise to Hagar and Salome in Galgut's *The Promise*. We considered how these two stories, from two very different contexts, helped us to analyze the importance of reclaiming recognition in a context in which the Hagar's and Salome's of the world are not seen and not respected. This essay also helped us to acknowledge that white privilege and power are responsible for the fact that we, despite our best efforts, have allowed Hagar (and one could also say Salome) to recede into the background, to render invisible her suffering.

However, Letty Russell argues that beyond a story which helps readers to recognize our culpability, the narrative of Sarah and Hagar, (also that of Salome, Amor, and the other members of the Swart family) can also be viewed as a "story of blessing that comes to us as children of struggle seeking the courage and faith we need to share God's peace and justice together as one human family."[58] Thus, in light of our engagement with *The Promise* and in terms of a renewed appreciation for the important role of recognition in moving towards a more just future, we want to believe that we can imagine the story of Sarah and Hagar ending differently. As Reaves says it well:

> The text implies that, if we are concerned about liberation, the responsibility lies with those who have power and privilege to bear witness in their lives and communities to a different story: a story recognizing Sarah and valuing Hagar, acknowledging

56. Arendt, *The Human Condition*, 237.
57. Arendt, *The Human Condition*, 237.
58. Russel, "Children of Struggle," 196.

the wrongs committed, enabling Hagar's agency, giving space for Hagar to speak for herself, and using her privilege to support Hagar's worth and need through reparative measures.[59]

With this goal in mind, we want to conclude our exploration of trauma and recognition in Galgut's *The Promise* and the story of Sarah and Hagar in Gen 16; 21 with a poem by the Syrian-American poet Mohja Kahf that imagines such an alternative ending for the two women titled "Hagar Writes a Cathartic Letter to Sarah as an Exercise Suggested by her Therapist."[60] By means of this creative engagement with the story of Sarah and Hagar, we are inspired to see the way in which we are indeed "joined," and how we are all called to deal with the wounds of the past and to find life-giving ways to live together in the future.

In her letter, Kahf's Hagar writes Sarah, saying that although they have been rivals, it can be so different. She suggests that they both "ditch the old man," and perhaps "set up house" together. They could "raise [their] kids" together, and perhaps even "start a catering business" or travel beyond this godforsaken place of Ur "with its tribes of hooligans."[61]

Kahf's Hagar does not shy away from the traumatic memory of being abandoned and almost watching her child die in the wilderness. And returning, once more, to her experience of constant disapproval, of feeling unseen, and of—perhaps—being seen as a threat, Hagar also narrates her trauma of how it felt to live in a context of non-recognition and misrecognition. But then, Kahf's poem concludes with Hagar directly addressing Sarah with an appeal to recognize the pain she had experienced, to "admit . . . for just one second" that what Abraham did to Hagar was cruel: just "[L]ong enough to pity him, yourself, me."[62]

Hagar ends this cathartic letter to Sarah with the invitation to Sarah to become the Sarah who laughs (Gen 18:12; 21:6), who has seen the God for whom nothing is impossible (Gen 18:14). As she signs off:

Love,
Hagar[63]

59. Reaves, "Sarah as Victim and Perpetrator," 16. As Reaves argues: "If I, as a white woman, am Sarah in this story, then I am called to recognize my power and do differently—to interrogate the ways in which I perpetuate injustice through personal behaviors and complicity in systemic abuse, and to work for positive, liberating change."

60. Kahf, *The Waters of Hajar*, 31–32.

61. Kahf, *The Waters of Hajar*, 31–32.

62. Kahf, *The Waters of Hajar*, 32.

63. Kahf, *The Waters of Hajar*.

Bibliography

Anderson, Eric Karl. "The Promise by Damon Galgut: A Review." (June 18, 2021). Available at https://lonesomereader.com/blog/2021/6/18/the-promise-by-damon- galgut <Acc'd: Jan16, 2022>.

Arendt, Hannah. *The Human Condition*. Chicago: University of Chicago Press, 1958.

Conger, George. "Archbishop Makgoba's Sermon at 500th Anniversary Celebration of the Reformation." Anglican.ink—May 28, 2017. Available at https://anglican.ink/2017/05/28/archbishop-makgobas-sermon-at-500th-anniversary-celebration-of-the-reformation/ <Acc'd: Jan 16, 2022>

Cooper, Rand Richards. "A Family, and a Nation under Apartheid, Tears at the Seam." *New York Times*, Apr 15, 2021. https://www.nytimes.com/2021/04/15/books/review/damon-galgut-promise.html <Acc'd: Jan 16, 2022>.

Day, Jon. "*The Promise* by Damon Galgut review—Legacies of Apartheid." *The Guardian*, June 18, 2021. Available at https://www.theguardian.com/books/2021/jun/18/the-promise-by-damon-galgut-review-legacies-of-apartheid <Acc'd: Jan 16, 2022>.

Galgut, Damon. *The Promise*. Cape Town: Umuzi, 2021.

Honneth, Axel. *The Struggle for Recognition: The Moral Grammar of Social Conflicts*. Cambridge: Polity, 1995.

Ikäheimo, Heikki, Kristina Lepold, Lois McNay, and Titus Stahl, eds. *Recognition and Ambivalence*. New Directions in Critical Theory. New York: Columbia University Press, 2021.

Kahf, Mohja. "The Waters of Hajar and Other Poems." *TMW* 91 (2001) 31–44. Available at https://www.academia.edu/24440889/The_Water_of_Hajar_and_Other_Poems/.

Makgoba, Thabo. "Archbishop Makgoba's Sermon at 500th Anniversary Celebration of the Reformation." *Anglican Ink*, May 28, 2017. https://anglican.ink/2017/05/28/archbishop-makgobas-sermon-at-500th-anniversary-celebration-of-the-reformation

McBride, Cillian. *Recognition*. Cambridge: Polity, 2013.

Okoye, James C. "Sarah and Hagar: Genesis 16 and 21." *JSOT* 32.2 (2007) 163–76.

Oliver, Kelly. *Witnessing: Beyond Recognition*. Minneapolis: University of Minneapolis Press, 2001.

Reaves, Jayme R. "Sarah as Victim and Perpetrator: Whiteness, Power, and Memory in the Matriarchal Narrative." *Review & Expositor* 115 (2018) 483–99.

Ricoeur, Paul. *The Course of Recognition*. Cambridge: Harvard University Press, 2005.

Russell, Letty. "Children of Struggle." In *Hagar, Sarah, and Their Children: Jewish, Christian, and Muslim Perspectives,* edited by Phyllis Trible and Letty M. Russell, 185–98. Louisville: Westminster John Knox, 2006.

Studeman, Frederick. "Damon Galgut on His Booker Winner *The Promise*: 'Death Sets Things Off.'" *Financial Times*, Nov. 4, 2021. https://www.ft.com/content/2ff91d34-93eb-42d8-bf36-62d5fef69cd2.

Taylor, Charles. "The Politics of Recognition." In *Multiculturalism*, edited by Amy Gutmann et al., 25–73. Princeton: Princeton University Press, 1994.

Trible, Phyllis. "Ominous Beginnings for a Promise of Blessing." In *Hagar, Sarah, and Their Children: Jewish, Christian, and Muslim Perspectives,* edited by Phyllis Trible and Letty M. Russell, 30–77. Louisville: Westminster John Knox, 2006.

West, Gerald O. "The Contribution of Tamar's Story to the Construction of Alternative African Masculinities." In *Bodies, Embodiment, and Theology of the Hebrew Bible,* S. Tamar Kamionkowski and Wonil Kim, 184–200. LHBOTS 465. New York: T. & T. Clark, 2010.

———. "Deploying Indecent Literary and Socio-Historical Detail For Change: Genesis 2:18–24 as a Resource for Choice of Sexual Partner." In *Teaching for Change: Essays on Pedagogy, Gender, Health and Theology in Africa,* edited by Charlene van der Walt and Funlola Olojede, 57–78. Stellenbosch: Sun Media, 2019.

West, Gerald O., and Beverly Haddad. "Boaz as 'Sugar Daddy'; Re-reading Ruth in a Context of HIV." *JTSA* 155 (2016) 137–56.

West, Gerald O., and Phumzile Zondi-Mabizela. "The Bible Story That Became a Campaign: The Tamar Campaign in South Africa (and Beyond)." *MF* 103 (2004) 4–12.

West, Gerald O., Charlene van der Walt, and Kapya John Kaoma. "When Faith Does Violence: Reimagining Engagement between Churches and LGBTI Groups on Homophobia in Africa." *HTS* 72/1 (2016) 1–8.

Williams, Delores. "Hagar in African American Biblical Appropriation." In *Hagar, Sarah, and Their Children: Jewish, Christian, and Muslim Perspectives,* edited by Phyllis Trible and Letty M. Russell, 171–84. Louisville: Westminster John Knox, 2006.

———. *Sisters in the Wilderness: The Challenge of Womanist God.* New York: Orbis Books, 2013.

Wood, James. "A Family at Odds Reveals a Nation in the Throes." *New Yorker,* April 19, 2021. https://www.newyorker.com/magazine/2021/04/19/a-family-at-odds-reveals-a-nation-in-the-throes/.

21

An American Axe and the Power of the God's Word

Concepts of Technological and Religious Superiority in the Encounter between Norwegian Missionaries and Zulu Royalty in the 1860s

KNUT HOLTER

Introduction

OUR DESTINATION IS ZULULAND but let me first take you on a detour to Kuruman in the Northern Cape. Actually, I made this detour on the ground some years ago. During a research visit to Stellenbosch, I decided to use a weekend to drive up north along the Atlantic coast, then turn eastwards at Springbok all the way to Kuruman, and finally turn southwards via Britstown and go back to Stellenbosch. It was a long journey, three thousand kilometers in three days, and it included a kudu collision that resulted in a headache, some bruises, a heavily damaged car, and a dead kudu. Afterwards, some colleagues asked me why I had "risked my life" setting out on this journey. My answer was that I did it because of Gerald O. West. I wanted to see the mission station that he and his scholarly ancestors, Jean and John Comaroff, have discussed in their respective studies of the nineteenth-century missionary enterprise of Robert and Mary Moffat

establish missionary work within the Zulu Kingdom; first at Empangeni (1851) and Entumeni (1852), and then followed Eshowe (1861) and several more stations throughout the 1860s.[7]

From the late 1840s, more Norwegians arrived to take up missionary work from these stations, and due to the growth of the work, Schreuder was in 1866 consecrated bishop of the Church of Norway mission fields in Zululand and Madagascar. In the church history of South Africa, the Lutheran bishop Schreuder is for various reasons overshadowed by the much more famous Anglican bishop John W. Colenso. Nevertheless, for some years there were actually two missionaries in the field who saw themselves as bishop of the Zulus, and the reports from Norwegian and British missionaries accordingly have many parallels, such when they describe their interaction with the Zulu royalty. Colenso's interaction with king Mpande and prince Cetshwayo is well documented,[8] and so is also that of Bishop Schreuder and some of his co-workers.[9] Kielland's report about an encounter with prince Cetshwayo is accordingly part of an ongoing interaction between Zulu royalty and Western missionaries.

The first actor in Kielland's report about his visit to Cetshwayo is the missionary himself. Pastor Kielland—or *uKjelane*, as he was called by the Zulus—was born in Norway in 1833, did a theology degree at the Royal Frederick University in Kristiania (now University of Oslo) in 1858, was ordained in 1862, and served as a missionary at Empangeni in Zululand from 1863 to 1874, when he returned to Norway where he served as a pastor until his death in 1898.[10] Being in charge of the oldest, permanent missionary residence within the borders of the Zulu Kingdom, Kielland felt a special duty to preach God's Word to Cetshwayo, whose residence Ulundi—later capital of the Zulu Kingdom under Cetshwayo's reign—was located in the area where the Norwegian missionaries concentrated their work.

The second actor in the report is then prince Cetshwayo, who eventually became the last reigning king of the Zulu Kingdom, from 1873, after the death of his father Mpande, and till the Zulu defeat to the British in the Anglo-Zulu War, in 1879. Before the coronation (organized by the British) in 1873, Cetshwayo had experienced decades of struggle

---

7. Myklebust, *Historie*, 29–52.

8. Colenso, *Bringing Forth, passim*.

9. Simensen et al, "Christian Mission," 190–94; Jørgensen, *Contact and Conflict*, 195–211.

10. Danbolt, *Misjonærer*, 24–25.

with other throne pretenders, and after the defeat to the British, he experienced both imprisonment at the Castle in Cape Town and a visit to Queen Victoria in London.[11] In the midst of all this, he had quite a regular contact with the Norwegians. One example is pastor Ommund C. Oftebro, who served at Empangeni (1854–1861) and Eshowe (1861–1893) and who refers to several points of contact.[12] In the tension between Zululand and Natal in 1861, Oftebro actually acted as Cetshwayo's secretary *vis-à-vis* the British colonial authorities.[13] Another example is Robert C.A. Samuelson—son of a Norwegian missionary (who eventually joined Colenso)—who served as Cetshwayo's secretary during the latter's imprisonment at the Castle in Cape Town in 1880.[14]

Let me now turn to Kielland's report about his encounter with Cetshwayo and his giving of an American axe to him. The report is dated 2 January 1868, and it is formally addressed to the Home Board of the Norwegian Missionary Society.[15] However, during the 1850s and 60s such reports were also published more or less *in extenso* in *Norsk Missions-Tidende*, the magazine of the mission society,[16] and so is also the case with this report, being published later the same year.[17] Accordingly, one must assume that Kielland had this quite broad readership in mind when he wrote the report.

Norwegian missionary reports from Zululand in the 1860s and 1870s—like the one by Kielland—take the colonial context for granted. Admittedly, there are examples of criticism of the increasing colonization, but the missionaries only to a limited extent realized that they themselves were part of the same.[18] In the Norwegian scholarly interpretation of the missionary enterprise in Zululand, it took more than a century before its colonial aspects were acknowledged. In the 1970s, the Norwegian historian Jarle Simensen initiated a broad research project on Norwegian mission work in Zululand (from 1844) and Madagascar (from

---

11. As for his visit to London, cf. Theron, "King Cetshwayo in Victorian England." The time spent at the Castle in Cape Town is crucial in Webb and Wright, *Zulu King*.

12. Holter, "Did Prince Cetshwayo."

13. Jørgensen, *Contact and Conflict*, 202.

14. Webb and Wright, *Zulu King*, 73.

15. Kielland, "Til den ærede Hovedbest."

16. Skeie, "Misjonsmateriale som historisk kilde."

17. Kielland, "Empangeni."

18. Hovland, *Mission Station Christianity*, 193–97, 209–13.

1867).[19] In a later work, discussing the historiographical development of Norwegian mission history related to Zululand, Simensen distinguishes between a "theological paradigm" in studies from around the centenary of the Zululand project (1940s) and a "historical-sociological paradigm" of the project that he directed, with dissertation titles like "Vanguards of European Imperialism" and "Collaborators of Imperialism."[20]

In the following, I will quote from my translation of Kielland's handwritten original report, but there are only minor differences (mainly orthographic ones) between the original report and the version published in the magazine of the mission society. The report is, if not unique, then at least one of quite a few examples where we have a substantial sermon part, although of course in a reconstructed form, from mid-eighteenth-century missionary work in Zululand, together with explanatory notes from the missionary's side. In my first and longest excerpt from the report (two other excerpts will be given later), Kielland jumps back and forth between words of the sermon to his Zulu audience, and explanatory notes for his Norwegian audience, and the first excerpt has the following structure:

> Explanatory note: Cetshwayo has asked Kielland for an American axe, Kielland brings it as a gift.
>
> - Sermon part: Kielland contextualizes his service; it is parallel to Zulu *inkonzo*, the service for the king, but it has a different content: to preach God's Word.
>
> - Explanatory note: Cetshwayo praises the beautiful axe, Kielland decides "taking the occasion thereof."
>
> - Sermon part: Kielland contextualizes his message, using the axe as a case, arguing that the technological skills of the whites result from their having God's Word. Cetshwayo and the Zulus are therefore invited to receive the power of the same God's Word.

In my translation from the Norwegian original, the report goes like this:

[Explanatory note:]

> With prayers to God that he would give me opportunity and boldness as well as skill to speak that which could be beneficial for the sake of truth, I went there (to the prince's kraal). Having

19. Simensen et al., *Norwegian Mission in African History.*
20. Simensen, "Norsk misjonsforskning," 228–36.

waited 1½ hours before it pleased the servants to announce my arrival, and only after repeated reminders to them, I was allowed to enter. I brought the Prince an American axe, which he had previously requested through a messenger, and with which he seemed well pleased. I spoke—with various interruptions, during which he partly addressed the many chiefs and servants sitting around either one thing or the other I had uttered on or other matters, and partly answered me with a "yes" or a question—approximately, the following words:

[Sermon part:]

I have heard that you will soon return to Undi again. I have therefore come to see you before you go, so that I bear no guilt. I do not mean guilt just before you, but before God too, if you had been staying here so close to my residence and I had failed to speak the Lord's Word to you, my Government. For we teachers, too, have, as you know, our *inkonzo* (service), with which we serve both you and your people, which is to preach God's Word. You know this is our work, which we cannot fail to do, and therefore it is my intention to speak God's Word to you even today, if you permit me.

[Explanatory note:]

When he had kindly consented, after he had admired the axe, I had brought and addressed his people praising the beautiful work, I continued, taking the occasion thereof, approximately as follows:

[Sermon part:]

You often admire the work of white people and their skills and abilities, that they can make such things, but you, too, could obtain similar skills. Therefore, also, we teachers have come to you, that you black people may become like us whites in all things, also in the skills of doing useful and good works. For you, too, can obtain the wisdom and power that is needed thereto. From where have white people got it, and why do they now surpass the blacks in so many things? Is it not chiefly God's Word which they have received that has done such great things among them that has taught them and thereby enlightened them so that they now stand high in all knowledge and insight? God's Word has such power also for you. I do not say that this will happen in one day, but it will happen gradually.

Reading Kielland's text today, its colonial language is striking. But it is also striking that he expects his concepts of the Zulus to be well received by the intended readers, the subscribers to the mission magazine. Norway had at the time not yet obtained national freedom from its Scandinavian neighbors (Denmark: 1380/36–1814, Sweden: 1814–1905), but a similar kind of freedom for the Zulus seems to have been outside the imagination of Kielland's readers.

The American Axe—As Part of a Broader Societal Web

Pastor Kielland's gift to prince Cetshwayo—an American axe—is but one of a large number of examples of exchange of gifts referred to in nineteenth-century reports from Western explorers, colonialists, and missionaries visiting Africa, and for that matter other parts of the world, too. As far as Zululand is concerned, both Norwegian and British missionary reports have examples of how the exchange of gifts—being concrete objects or mutual services—played important roles in their interaction with the Zulus. Such as in the words of Bishop Colenso, in a report dated 3. October 1859, from his traveling through Zululand:

> While I write, the front of my wagon is stopped up with ten or twelve of the King's daughters; the eldest of whom, Nokwenda and Tandile, have been made very happy by the present each of a tin teacup. I am reduced to extremity for presents for the people; having exhausted my blankets, coloured neckerchiefs, knives and scissors, I am obliged to make presents of *matches* and *pills!* which last have been begged, *in case* there should arise at any future time a pain of some kind. The young prince gets a fork, and the King himself sends to ask if I can spare my gridiron. Then come the four chief indunas, next to Masipula, and they want blankets too but are told all are gone.[21]

On the Zulu side, the key favor the king could give the missionaries was of course access to the Zulu Kingdom and permission to do missionary work there. On the missionary side, both Kielland and Bishop Colenso use typical expressions from the colonial narrative to describe the supposed fascination of the Zulus for European small gifts like mirrors, knives, forks, etc.

21. Colenso, *Bringing Forth*, 121.

The first ones to be granted access to Zululand to do missionary work by king Mpande, in the early 1850s, were the Norwegians, Schreuder and his men. An initial reason seems to have been Schreuder's medical competence. His medicine box, his ability to cure both people and cattle, but also his practical abilities—such as making a wheelchair for the king (the wheelchair that can still be seen at Fort Nongqayi Museum Village in Eshowe)—convinced king Mpande to allow the Norwegians to operate within the borders of the kingdom.

However, king Mpande could also provide more touchable favours to the Norwegians. In connection with the opening of the borders of the Zulu kingdom for Norwegian missionaries in 1850, he gave Schreuder ten cattle and four ivory tusks (two of the tusks can actually still be seen in the Mission Museum in Stavanger). Accidentally, Colenso received the same number of ivory tusks from Mpande in 1858.[22] However, such a gift consisting of four ivory tusks was not restricted to missionary leaders, it seems to have been a rather fixed amount for diplomatic encounters. In 1830, King Dingane—King Mpande's half-brother—sent four ivory tusks to the British representative in Grahamstown, expressing the hope of living together in peace, and welcoming a missionary that could instruct his people.[23] Likewise, in 1881, the now imprisoned King Cetshwayo—Mpande's son—wrote to the Governor of the Cape, emphasizing his loyalty to the British, though indirectly referring to the hopeless situation he had been placed in by the British colonizers. King Cetshwayo notices that he at an earlier stage had given the British representative:

> . . . three hundred head of cattle, in order to thank him and the government for coming to settle the country under my rule; I gave him also four elephant's tusks.[24]

The exchange of colored neckerchiefs and blankets, or symbolically and strategically heavier ivory tusks and access to the kingdom, is the immediate context of Kielland's giving an American axe to prince Cetshwayo. The axe was part of a long chain of exchange of gifts and favors, and the question is then what functions this exchange may have had.

First, as one can deduce even from a surface reading of reports from Norwegian and British missionaries operating in Zululand, it is clear that a gift is never only a gift. The missionaries saw the endless requests for

22. Colenso, *Bringing Forth*, 124.
23. Kirby, *Andrew Smith*, 5–6.
24. Webb and Wright, *Zulu King*, 47.

gifts as part of a pattern of mutually giving and receiving favors. An interpretive perspective on the phenomenon could be found in the insights of early twentieth-century anthropologists working with economic practices in traditional societies. The classic study as far as the exchange of gifts is concerned, is Marcel Mauss' essay on "the gift" as a societal practice.[25] Building on Bronislaw Malinowski's studies of exchange practices among the Melanesian Trobrianders,[26] Mauss acknowledged the complexity and at the same time cohesiveness of exchange practices, and he especially emphasized the perspective of reciprocity.

Using Mauss as a lens for interpreting Kielland's American axe—and its function as a "gift" to Cetshwayo—could help us understand some of its overall function. It was an *American* axe, which is a steel axe, different from the traditional iron axes produced by Zulu smiths. It had little economic or strategic value when compared with Mpande's oxen, ivory tusks, and missionary access to the kingdom. Still, the American axe—or for that matter Colenso's fork to a prince and tin teacup to a princess—represent what Jean and John Comaroff refer to as "goods of strange power" (1991:182).[27] They were seen as part of the technological skills—but also of the political and economic power—of the whites. And, when they are received as "gifts" by members of the royal family, and when the receivers are "pleased" (such as prince Cetshwayo, according to Kielland) and "very happy" (such as princesses Nokwenda and Tandile, according to Colenso), the function of the gifts is, in the terminology of Mauss, a reciprocal building of broad relationships between missionaries and Zulu leadership.

Second, and not that easily deductible from a surface reading of the missionary reports, is that an axe is never only an axe. Narratives about missionaries—and others from the North—who introduce steel axes into a pre-modern society is a well-known topic in anthropology discourses, such as in the American anthropologist Lauriston Sharp's famous analysis of the aboriginal Yir Yoront society in Australia in the 1930s.[28] Well-intending missionaries aiming to raise the living standards of the Yir Yoront aboriginal community introduced steel axes—in considerable numbers—as payment for services and as gifts for special occasions. However, they did not realize that the steel axe interfered with a broad

25. Mauss, *The Gift.*

26. Malinowski, *Argonauts.*

27. Comaroff and Comaroff, *Of Revelation and Revolution*, 182.

28. Sharp, "Steel Axes."

range of societal webs related to the traditional stone axe, until then the only sort of axe. Partly on a symbolic or religious level, as the stone axe was an important totem of the clan, referring back to its mythical ancestor. And partly also on the level of production; the stone for the stone axe came from quarries hundreds of kilometers away, and played a key role in regional trading chains, which now were disturbed. Partly also as far as gender roles were concerned; the production of stone axes required knowledge and skills that traditionally were the proprium of adult men, and the stone axe itself was an important symbol of masculinity. The steel axes, on the other hand, were given out indiscriminately, regardless of the gender and age of the receiver, with the result that the role of adult men lost some of its distinct identity.

What we learn from Sharp is then that an axe is never only an axe. The "indigenous axe" of a traditional society is part of its social, cultural, and religious webs, and when a "new axe," such as that of the missionary is introduced, it creates interfaces with the whole spectrum of existing webs. So might have been the case also in the encounter between prince Cetshwayo and missionary Kielland, although it should be admitted that the sources are quite silent. The axe brought by the missionary would relate to a wide spectrum of social and cultural webs of the traditional Zulu society. One example is that it would interfere with the economy of the smiths, the producers of the indigenous axes. The traditional Zulu society had few skilled professions; an exception, though, was the guild of smiths.[29] According to Eileen J. Krige, who did fieldwork in Zululand in the 1920s and 30s, but with strong attention to older traditions, the smiths have traditionally played a crucial role in the economy of the Zulu society:

> The true commercial man among the Zulus was the smith, the products of whose labour were essential to every man and woman. It was he who forged the hoes, without which no woman could till the fields and grow food for her household; it was he who made the assegais that every man must have as the warrior of his chief. The smith was thus the most indispensable man in any neighbourhood. He did not work for nothing, however, but received payment in cattle or goats for his goods.[30]

29. Krige, *Social System*, 209–11.

30. Krige, *Social System*, 212.

Axes were not the only product of the guild of smiths; more important were hoes for women working in the fields and assegais for men serving as warriors. The smiths also produced various kinds of ornaments; Cetshwayo himself is said to have kept two smiths constantly at work, making bracelets of copper and iron. The introduction of an axe from the outside world would therefore have the potential of disturbing the social structure. It would—at least if it were, as in our case, an axe "with which he [the prince] seemed well pleased," as missionary Kielland writes in his report—be able to threaten the economic position of the existing guild of smiths.

Another example is that the introduction of new sort of axes would interfere with the symbolic role of the smiths and their work with iron. The smiths were not only what the missionaries would consider, more or less, skilled manufacturers; as ironworkers, they were in the possession of a kind of traditional wisdom and knowledge. In their production of—amongst other things—axes, they were, according to Axel-Ivar Berglund, exercising *amandla*, a divine power entrusted them "from above":

> In Zulu thinking power, *amandla*, is related to wisdom and knowledge. To these there are two approaches. Firstly, they are related to a particular ability given to a specific clan, i.e., those who are the ironworkers as are *ama-Shezi*, the *Nzuza* clan having the particular ability of preparing men for warfare, while rainmakers were of the *Ntlangwini* clan. Secondly, there is the concept of *ukuhlakanipha*, cleverness or profound wisdom, which is regarded as a special gift to a particular person of any clan and not necessarily limited to specific tasks. Informants agree that both kinds of knowledge and wisdom "come from above."[31]

In other words, the prince's liking for the missionary's alternative axe would have the potential of being interpreted as an expression of a corresponding liking for the missionary's alternative religious concepts.

In sum, Kielland's giving of an American axe to Cetshwayo is part of a regular, if not an institutionalized, exchange of gifts and favors. However, a gift is never only a gift, and an axe is never only an axe. A gift may create a relationship, but in this case, where the gift is an American axe, it also has the potential of disturbing or challenging existing societal and religious patterns.

31. Berglund, *Zulu Thought-Patterns*, 36–37.

The American Axe—As a Pretext for Preaching

Let me now turn more directly to Kielland, and his rhetorical use of the gift to Cetshwayo. As I pointed out above, Kielland argues that the wisdom and power that lie behind the technological superiority of the whites comes from the Bible, God's Word, and he invites Cetshwayo to take part in this:

> God's Word has such power also for you. I do not say that this will happen in one day, but it will happen gradually. Nor did it happen with us in one day. 800 years have passed since God's truths were first brought to our country on the other side of the sea. Our ancestors were immersed like you in sin and darkness, in the deepest ignorance of God and his kingdom. They, too, worshipped their idols, ensnared like you in error and deceptive doctrines. But God's Word came and was preached among them, and it gradually triumphed over the darkness. And they went forth in the enlightenment of the heart until this day.

The power of God's Word, accordingly, is not conceptualized in charismatic terms, as a kind of power exercised by the help of the Holy Spirit and experienced here and now. Kielland expresses only contempt for the charismatic practice of the traditional healers in the Zulu society, the *isangoma*, such as their practice of "smelling out" the supposedly responsible for certain deeds. Neither is the power of God's Word found in natural phenomena or in examples of manipulating nature.

There is a secularizing drive in much of the Western mission practices in the nineteenth century, rejecting what is seen as magical concepts of traditional religion and instead explaining nature according to the contemporary modern worldview. An illustrative example, also from the 1860s, is provided by the German missionary Gottlieb F. Bühler, who served amongst the Yoruba in Nigeria for the British Church Missionary Society, building up a structure of primary schools. The pupils were taught reading, writing, and arithmetic, of course, but also subjects like playing the harmonium. In a report to the CMS directors in London, Bühler even asked for a machine that could demonstrate the principles of electricity, and the reason he gives is interesting. The pupils, he says, come from "this country where the god of thunder & lightning is worshipped."[32] This is clearly not an accurate description of traditional Yoruba religion, yet, it is a good illustration of how Bühler conceptualizes the difference between

32. Olabimtan, *Samuel Johnson*, 67.

his own religious tradition and that of traditional Yoruba religion with regard to their respective understandings of technology.

Rather, in Kielland's report, the power of God's Word is conceptualized in historical terms. Using the history of the church in Norway as an illustration, and reflecting a typically Lutheran theology, Kielland links the power of God's Word to that of convincing the individual about sin, but then also liberating this sinner, so that he—or she—can contribute to the building of a better society. This experience of the Norwegians, Kielland argues, can also be experienced by the Zulus, and in the following paragraph he elaborates on the similarities between Norwegians and Zulus:

> So it should also go with you, and what could hinder you? Have you, as many would assert, a different origin than we? Far from it! We have all come from one human couple, so says the Book of God and it is true. What is it then that separates us? Nothing except the color of our skin. We come from a cold country, whereas you live here under the burning sun, and your naked bodies are burned by the sun, which makes them dark. But in your veins runs the same red blood as in ours, and your bodies are formed in the same way as ours. And inside you there is, as inside us, a heart that feels, a soul that understands, that knows what it wants. There is only one thing that makes a very great difference, and that is God's Word! We have it and you do not. It makes the main difference between us. Skin and color and everything else is nothing, it makes no real difference between people, but to have God's Word and obey it, or to be without God's Word is what makes a difference. For God's Word has extraordinary power, it enlightens people and transforms people. It transforms whole peoples and countries, and there is nothing on which it does not exert its effect when people receive it.

The key perspective in this paragraph is a theology of creation that binds all human beings together. Kielland rejects polygenism, the idea that the human races are so different that they must reflect different origins, that is different acts of the Creator. This was an idea that had a number of followers throughout the eighteenth and nineteenth centuries, such as for example in Kielland's neighbourhood, in the teaching of Bishop Colenso.[33] "Have you, as many would assert, a different origin than we?," Kielland asks rhetorically, and perhaps the "many" refers to the competing missionary enterprise headed by Colenso. However,

33. Kidd, *Forging of Races*, 153–56.

Kielland immediately rejects the possibility: "Far from it!" And, in detail he emphasizes the similarities between the Norwegians and the Zulus: the same red blood, the same form of the body, both with a heart, and both with a soul. Then there is skin colour, but that difference does not matter, it simply reflects different climatic conditions.[34]

The only real difference between the two, Kielland argues, is that the former has God's Word, whereas the latter has not. This is, however, a problem that can be solved here and now. Hence the missionary's invitation to the Zulu prince to receive God's Word, which has extraordinary power, being able to enlighten people, to transform people, eventually with the result that they reach the same technological level as those whites who have made this American axe.

Conclusion

Let me conclude. I started by asking how missionary Kielland conceptualizes his gift—an American axe—to prince Cetshwayo as an example of a typically colonial concept of technological and religious superiority of the whites, a concept which then is used as a basis for inviting the prince and other members of the Zulu royalty to acknowledge and experience the power of God's Word.

The overall function of the gift is to strengthen the relationship to the prince and his court, as part of a reciprocal exchange pattern. At the same time, it is not an innocent gift; in this particular context, there is more to the American axe than being just another—though somewhat improved—cutting tool. From the Zulu side, the traditional iron axe is part of economic as well as symbolic webs, and from the missionary side, the American axe is an example of the technological superiority of the whites.

In Kielland's reconstruction of his encounter with prince Cetshwayo, he lets the American axe play a crucial role. He explicitly argues that after Cetshwayo "[. . .] had admired the axe I had brought and addressed his people praising the beautiful work, I continued, *taking the occasion thereof*" (my emphasis). Kielland uses the axe as proof of the power of the Bible, or as he puts it, God's Word. And then by explaining the technological superiority of the whites as being due to an external factor, a religious

34. Cf. a recent study of whiteness and racism; by Maluleke and Mathebula, "From Being Black."

22

Bible Abuse, Silence and Denial

Exploring Successful Community Responses

Philippe Denis

Introduction

Sadly, the Bible, which is meant to be life-giving, can also be abused and produce death. It can be used by abusers to subjugate, to confuse, and to silence their victims. Such abusers instrumentalize the biblical text, and the figures or symbols associated with it, to destabilise their prey and destroy their body and soul. The Bible is used as a cover-up. In religious circles, the Bible then becomes an essential component of the system of denial and silence that protects abusers and allows them to perpetuate their evil deeds.

The Bible itself, in fact, not infrequently refers to this type of abuse. It documents how well-to-do people and members of the political elite used the name of God, and biblical precedents, to oppress the poor. Prophets in the Hebrew Bible, such as Samuel and the authors of the Psalms, raised their voices to restore the truth. In the New Testament, Jesus denounced and then fell victim to religiously motivated abuse. He did not keep silent but his disciples, when it came to the crux, did. The religious establishment of the time actively contributed to, or made possible through its silence, Jesus' passion and death.

Gerald West, a long-time colleague, and fellow "traveller" in the study of the Bible, to whom this essay is dedicated, knows all of this very well. The 1985 *Kairos Document* and its various successors, a chain of texts to which he often refers,[1] show how the Bible can be twisted to proclaim the opposite of what it is meant to say. The Contextual Bible Studies (CBS) he co-initiated, and groomed other people into as part of the work of the Ujamaa Centre, aims precisely at helping vulnerable people to resist Bible abuse and regain the proper initiative. Women's organisations, Young Christian Workers, HIV/AIDS support groups, dispossessed people, LGBTQI activists, etc, are part of the long list of the victims of abuse who, who through Ujamaa Center, learned novel ways of reading and interpreting the Bible to resist such abuse. Initiatives such as the "Tamar Campaign," the "Worker Sunday Campaign" and the "Redemptive Masculinities Campaign" are based on the same principles of fighting for justice.

In this chapter, I shall examine three extreme cases of Bible abuse: they relate to apartheid in South Africa, to the genocide against the Tutsi in Rwanda and to sexual violence among priests and religious men and women in the Catholic Church. For each, I shall look at strategies used by the victims—or, better said, the survivors—to combat denial and silence, share their experience and, sometimes but not often, obtain justice. In most cases that was a long, painful, and uncertain process, relying on third parties who listened to their painful stories and gave credence to them.

Other manifestations of Bible abuse could be found, for example, in Christian antisemitism, which justified a long list of anti-Jewish pogroms and ultimately the Holocaust; in biblically-motivated aggressions against LGBTQI people; or the evangelical right in the United States which supports, on religious grounds, a party and a programme that is openly anti-poor, racist and xenophobic, presenting, in an odd way, its champion, Donald Trump, as a reincarnation of Cyrus, the Persian leader who authorized the Jewish exiles in Babylon to return to the Promised Land.[2]

---

1. See for example West, "Tracing the 'Kairos' Trajectory," 4–22.
2. Block, "Is Trump Our Cyrus?"

The Biblical Justification of Apartheid

The *Kairos Document*, a document published by a group of priests, pastors, and laypeople mostly from Johannesburg and Soweto in the aftermath of the first state of emergency in July 1985 to promote a faith-based response to state violence, proposed a critique of "State Theology" premised on the idea that the discourse of the proponents of apartheid "misus[ed] theological concepts and biblical texts for its own political purposes."[3] By then, various forms of racial discrimination had been imposed on all people of colour in South Africa for more than a century and, since 1948, a humiliating and violent regime of strict territorial, institutional, and cultural separation based on pseudo-scientific concepts of race had been put in place in the country. Apartheid, as this regime was generally known, was also euphemistically presented as separate religious development to disguise its real nature which was to subordinate, by force if needed, groups of people deemed to be inferior.

As Hermann Giliomee, a historian of Afrikaner politics and culture, pointed out, this ideology found its roots—in the interwar period—not in political circles, as one would have expected, but in the Church. One of its main artisans was Gustav Bernhard August Gerdener, the founder of the Dutch Reformed Church (DRC) mission in the Transvaal, in the early 1930s. He later took a post at the University of Stellenbosch and exercised a wide influence through his teaching and writings.[4] Key to the biblical argumentation developed in those years was the idea that, if God ultimately wanted all "peoples" to be reunited on the day of judgment, God never wanted them to mix on earth. God wanted people from different racial backgrounds to be physically separated. In 1947, a conference of DRC ministers in Pretoria, led by Daniel Johannes Keet, argued that mixing people of different races is against God's will:

> In its broad features, the Holy Scriptures maintain the existence of separate peoples and condemns mixing between different peoples and races which can impair the Christian religion and civilization . . . The church's policy of race-Apartheid is in agreement with the Bible.[5]

3. Leonard, ed., *The Kairos Documents*, 9.

4. Giliomee, "The Making of the Apartheid Plan, 1929–1948," 375.

5. Pienaar, "An Evangelical Afrikaner Patriot?," 127.

For someone not familiar with South African history, this interpretation of the Bible seems bizarre, especially when one considers the New Testament, where Jesus challenged the cultural, political and territorial divisions of his time and never prescribed that ethnic groups or 'races' should be separated. Instead, he created a space for these divisions to be contested. This is why it is legitimate to speak about DRC ministers' statements to reflect Bible abuse.

The following address, delivered at the National People's Congress (NPC) on "Race Policy," held in 1944 in Bloemfontein, shows how pregnant, despite the quasi-absence of scriptural evidence, the notion was among leading Afrikaners, that God had wanted, from all eternity, that the different ethnic groups should be separated and the white "race," in effect, should dominate. For them, the "equality of all races" was a dangerous myth. The author of the address, Jacob Daniel du Toit, also known as Totius, was a prominent theologian and publicist of the *Gereformeerde Kerk*, a dissident Dutch Reformed church. His speech was titled "The Foundation of Our Race Policy, in which he stated the following.

> 'Give me a Bible text,' says the opponent of our colour policy, 'a text that proves that segregation is in agreement with the utterances of Holy Scripture.' 'I have no text,' is my answer. 'Then I have won the case, says the advocate for equality' . . . I answer: . . . 'I don't have a text, but I have the Bible, the whole Bible. My argumentation would proceed from Genesis to Revelation.[6]

While Totius may have overstated his case the proponents of apartheid did have at their disposal a few scriptural texts, though not many, to justify apartheid. An important one was the story of the Babel Tower in Genesis. At the beginning of all things, so the argument went, God, the "Divider" (*Skeidingmaker*), separated day and night, light and darkness, water and earth, animals and humans. God's children were meant to live in harmony, but they sinned: first Adam and Eve, then Cain who killed his brother, lastly, the sons of Noah who attempted to build a tower reaching toward heaven that 'would make a name for [them]selves' (Gen 11:4). According to Totius, God punished them for wanting to live all in one place without respecting the necessary boundaries. God created the confusion of languages and dispersed them.[7]

---

6. Du Toit and Du Toit, *Die Afrikaanse Rassebeleid en die Skrif*, 5.

7. Vosloo, "Bible and Justification of Apartheid," 197.

This dubious exegesis, in the service of an oppressive system, points to a manipulation of the Bible. Being together for different peoples, in fact, was not the problem in the biblical story. At issue was Aaron's sons' desire to "make a name for themselves." (Gen 11:4) So, other parts of the Old Testament were mobilised to justify apartheid. All were interpreted in the same manner. The commentator transformed a factual observation—there *is* a diversity of peoples—into a command—there *should be* a diversity of people, that is wanted by God. This hermeneutical shift comforted the proponents of the theory of "God the Divider."

From the New Testament, the most often quoted text to defend apartheid ideology was Acts 17:26: "From one man he made every nation of men, that they should inhabit the whole earth; and he determined the times set for them and the exact places where they should live." Totius and Evert Philippus Groenewald, a biblical scholar from the University of Pretoria, also skewed the meaning of the text by seeing in it, as noted in the previous paragraph, a divine command and not simply a factual observation.[8] Who could deny the existence of territorial boundaries in human society? Yet, saying that God, not only accepted the existence of boundaries but refused for people to cross them and live together in peace, if so they wished, was an extrapolation that, knowing the human cost of apartheid, one can rightfully qualify as abusive.

This type of biblical exegesis appeared in the mid-1940s, a few years before the victory of the South African National Party at the general elections of May 1948, and the implementation of a strict programme of racial segregation in South Africa. It, therefore, contributed to making acceptable to the white population that would vote for the National Party, the idea that separating racial groups geographically was a command from God. The use of euphemisms like "separate development," which gave good conscience to the apartheid planners and their church backers, did the rest. Calling apartheid "separate development" is tantamount to denial. It hides the reality of race-based abuse, violence, and oppression associated with apartheid.

The scriptural justification of apartheid continued to be taught in the DRC until the 1980s.[9] Only a minority of Afrikaner theologians such as Ben Marais and Bennie Keet, objected to it.[10] Two DRC synodical documents, from 1966 and 1974, respectively, explicitly endorse

8. Vosloo, "Bible and Justification of Apartheid," 201.

9. Vosloo, "Bible and Justification of Apartheid," 201.

10. Vosloo, "Bible and Justification of Apartheid," 204–9.

the "separate development" ideology of apartheid, noting that, "In specific circumstances and under specific conditions," the New Testament makes provision for the regulation of separate development of the co-existence of various people in one country."[11]

There was little resistance from the English-speaking South African churches, apart from a few statements condemning apartheid in general terms, until the 1970s.[12] The Christian Institute, founded by Beyers Naudé, a DRC minister, in 1963 and banned in 1977, though effective, was isolated and considered with great suspicion among the South African white population.[13] The DRC, which instrumentalised the Bible to support apartheid, did not face much of a challenge. Things started to change in the DRC only when Allan Boesak, a bi-racial theologian from the Dutch Reformed Mission Church, linked to the Christian Institute and who worked as chaplain at the University of the Western Cape [a university reserved, according to the apartheid laws, for the Coloured population—("Coloured" is the South African term for bi-racial people], was elected as president of the World Alliance of Reformed Churches (WARC), in August 1982, in Ottawa. At the same meeting the white members of the Alliance that supported the South African regime, were suspended and apartheid was declared a heresy.[14] That was an important step, coming from an international Reformed Church body. It assisted the members of the Black and Coloured Reformed churches in opposing the absurd claim that apartheid was biblical, and in using their own theological and spiritual resources to resist the associated apartheid abuse.

Let us now return to the *Kairos Document* and to "Evangelical Witness in South Africa," a similar document issued in 1986 by a group of evangelical ministers and theologians, who were members of Pentecostal and Mainline churches, under the auspices of a still informal movement called "Concerned Evangelicals."[15] Both documents condemned the manipulation of the Bible but, instead of targeting the texts commonly used by DRC theologians to justify apartheid, they focused on Romans 13, the text used by the South African government, and its church backers, to condemn any attack against the regime. Good Christians, the Black members of the churches were told by their (white) pastors and elders, should stay

11. De Gruchy, *The Church Struggle in South Africa*, 68–70.

12. De Gruchy, *The Church Struggle in South Africa*, 68–70.

13. De Gruchy and Villa-Vicencio, *Apartheid Is a Heresy*.

14. De Gruchy and Villa-Vicencio, *Apartheid Is a Heresy*.

15. Denis, "The Splintering of South African Evangelicalism."

away from politics and abstain from criticising the government because Paul, in the Epistle to the Romans, had enjoined his disciples to submit to the governing authorities. That was the Word of God!

This form of instrumentalization of the Bible dominated the last years of apartheid. It provoked bitter resistance in the Black churches, especially in Soweto, and contributed to the development of new forms of faith-based political mobilisation. As Luke Ngoetjana, a Pentecostal minister who was sacked from the Bible School in Soweto, where he was teaching (by the white leadership of his church) and whose house was subsequently petrol-bombed, the *Kairos Document* aimed less at the South African government—its oppressive character was a foregone conclusion—than at the white churches which supported the status quo, through their actions or their silence:

> The message [of the *Kairos Document*] was not about challenging the apartheid regime, I must say, but about challenging ourselves as churches. How can a born again live in a segregated society and not feel it? We are divided. We need to do something about segregation in the church. We need to challenge the church to do something prophetic and to address segregation. We reacted as ministers. Some of us were a bit educated. When we came to meetings, those from Black Consciousness told us: You sold us to the whites. It is not the government. It is the church which is separating the participation. The morning is for white people and in the afternoon the blacks preach to the blacks. When the whites have gone home, it is the domestic servant's turn to come. For me, I had to take a taxi from Soweto to minister to the domestic servants. It was dividing us. I was picking up the pain. We spoke about ourselves. But, of course, when you ask questions the government feels challenged.[16]

Ngoetjana was not alone. In the 1970s and 1980s, the instrumentalization of the Bible by the defenders of the apartheid status quo provoked among Christian activists, a yearning for new ways of reading the Bible and among those, men and women, who wanted to challenge the churches' conservatism at the theological level. This began a search for a new biblical hermeneutics which anticipated the work of Gunther Wittenberg, West, and others in the subsequent period.

16. Luke Ngoetjana, interviewed by Philippe Denis, on 3 September 2020, in Pietermaritzburg, SA.

Bible and Biblical Symbols during the Genocide against the Tutsi[17]

Between April and July of 1994, Rwanda was the scene of one of the most devastating genocides in recent human history. Three-quarters of the Tutsi population, then residing in the country—an estimated 800,000 people, including children and elderly people—were hunted to death and massacred. Tens of thousands of Tutsi women were raped. This episode of mass violence is called a genocide because of the intention, on the part of the perpetrators, to exterminate a group of people for ideological reasons—just like the Jews were targeted for extermination during the Holocaust's in the Nazi's "final solution." The immediate reason for the Genocide was the invasion of Rwanda by the Rwandan Patriotic Front (RPF) in October 1990, an army of Tutsi refugees who had been based in Uganda for many years, and the ensuing war which caused massive displacement of civilians and many deaths on both sides. The Tutsi—a minority group which shares the language, culture, and religion of the Hutu, the other people group in Rwanda, and often had family links with them—were accused of being "accomplices" of the RPF, and were killed for that reason. The trigger was the shooting down of the plane transporting Juvénal Habyarimana, the Rwandan president, a Hutu, on 6 April 1994. The authors were almost certainly Hutu extremists who wanted to destabilise the country and take over the government.[18]

The genocide ended when the RPF defeated the Rwandan army in mid-July 1994. Nearly two million people, including many genocide perpetrators, fled to Tanzania and Zaire (today's DR Congo) where they remained until late 1996. Low-intensity warfare continued until the early 2000s. The RPF also committed crimes, but on a smaller scale and out of revenge, not with the intention of exterminating the Hutu as Hutu. The authorities who had planned and actively supported or condoned the genocide never apologised. Instead, they denied all responsibility, accusing, against all evidence, the RPF of having also perpetrated genocide.

---

17. This section borrows from research carried out in Rwanda, Burundi, the DRC, and several European countries between 2014 and 2020, which led to the publication of a book titled *The Genocide against the Tutsi and the Christian Churches*. On the use of religious symbols during the genocide against the Tutsi, see also Loumakis, "Genocide and Religion," 47–83.

18. Even though certain aspects of the history of the genocide against the Tutsi still deserve exploration, there is no shortage of studies on this topic. For a start, see Forges, *Leave None to Tell the Story*.

That is what is called the "double genocide theory." Quite a few church people, including missionaries, still support this theory today.

Churches in Rwanda, and the Catholic Church, the oldest and the biggest confession, in particular, were deeply affected by the genocide. They lost hundreds of priests, pastors, and religious men or women. Many massacres took place in churches. A non-negligible number of Hutu people, and among them many Christians, took risks to save Tutsi lives. Yet, the Catholic Church bears a responsibility in the genocide for having failed to denounce it. Closely linked to the Rwandan government since the time of independence (1962), the Church leaders merely called the warring parties to a ceasefire without saying a word on the systematic extermination of Tutsi people which was taking place before their eyes. A fair amount of Hutu priests and pastors—a few dozen, if not more— were reported to have directly and personally assisted the killers. Some of these were eventually convicted of genocide at the International Criminal Tribunal for Rwanda (ICTR), in Arusha.[19]

Testimonies from eyewitnesses, and transcripts of messages broadcast on radio, show that the use of religious symbols during the genocide, far from being anecdotal, was common. The organisers and the executants claimed, again and again, that God was on their side and that God had abandoned the Tutsi. Also mobilised, were Jesus, the Virgin Mary, and the Bible. As noted by Malachie Munyaneza, the interim government called itself *Leta y'Abatabazi* (Government of the Saviours) in reference to Jesus *Umutabazi* (the Saviour).[20]

In May 1994, Valérie Bemeriki, a particularly violent radio presenter on notorious Radio Télévision Libre des Mille Collines (RTLM), put across the religious message of the *génocidaires* in the following terms:

> If somebody takes arms and shoots you, you will not say: I shall pray, that's it. Well, God helps the one who helps himself. It means that each time we shall ask for it, each time we shall stand up, God will always be with us, Jesus will be behind us and, as a result, we shall lead and win the war.[21]

According to her, the Virgin Mary also took part in the fight against the Tutsi:

19. Munyaneza, "Violence as Institution," 57.

20. Munyaneza, "Violence as Institution," 57.

21. Chrétien, ed., *Rwanda Les Médias du génocide*, 330.

> In fact, the Virgin Mary is with us and we are with her. She
> knows that we are innocent victims. Because she knows that we
> are innocent victims, she shall encourage us.[22]

In the diary he kept during the genocide, Gabriel Maindron, a French priest in Congo-Nil, near Kibuye, told the story of a killer who was sporting a rosary around his neck. A religious sister asked him: "Why do you carry this rosary'" He responded: "The Virgin Mary helps me to find the hidden enemies."[23] According to Bemeriki, Valentine Nyiramukiza, one of the girls who saw the Virgin Mary appearing in Kibeho in the 1980s, had asked Our Lady whether God's children would continue the fight. "The Virgin in person," Bemeriki declared, "did not hesitate to respond: Only the vanquished will stop fighting."[24]

The Bible was also instrumentalized. In 1990, the Hutu extremist newspaper *Kangura* published "ten commandments," modelled on the ten commandments entrusted by God to Moses on Mount Sinai (Exod 20:1–17), which reproduced the stereotypes of the Tutsi as power-hungry and deceitful, and incited the Hutu to distrust them at all times.[25] According to a witness at the Arusha ICTR, in May 1994, Jean-Baptiste Ruzindaza, the president of the Court of First Instance, in the town of Butare, held the Bible and said that the people who would fight the enemy with success would be rewarded by God. On another occasion, he urged the Hutu people to leave behind no traces, quoting Jesus' words that all things secret would be brought into the open (Luke 8:17).[26] Justin Mugenzi, the minister of trade and industry in the Rwandan interim government, reminded those who did not fight the RPF of Isaiah's warning that the people who neglected their duties would face misfortune.[27] Donat, a convicted *génocidaire*, interviewed by Amélie Faucheux, believed that killing was a normal thing. Even Longinus, the Roman soldier who had pierced Jesus' heart, he argued, had been allowed to do so.[28]

Of all the manipulations of the Bible to incite or defend violence, the most shocking is the one Emmanuel Mwezi, a genocide survivor from

---

22. Faucheux, "Massacrer dans L'intimité," 417.

23. Maindron, "Rwanda: L'horreur," 54.

24. Chrétien, ed., *Les Médias du Génocide*, 330.

25. *Kangura* 6 (1990), 6–8: quoted in Chrétien, ed., *Les Médias du Génocide*, 141–42.

26. Loumakis, "Genocide and Religion," 60.

27. Loumakis, "Genocide and Religion," 61.

28. Faucheux, "Massacrer dans L'intimité," 990.

Muhazi in north-east Rwanda, attributed in an interview, to a Presbyterian pastor of the area:

> There was a pastor that one could see on the shore [of Muhazi Lake], a churchman. I heard him saying when we were hiding, that he had read the Old Testament and the New Testament and that he had not found in the holy pages that killing a Tutsi was a sin. He explained that only the Book counted and that in it one only heard of 'humans'. Who had written in the Bible that Tutsi were humans? The term Tutsi did not appear in it. Therefore, no wrong had been committed. The Bible did not mention the word Hutu either but the absence of the word Tutsi was enough since the Hutu were humans.[29]

An important theme in the religious discourse of the *génocidaires* was that God had abandoned the Tutsi. In Ndera, an *Interahamwe* (member of a Hutu extremist militia) told Cesar Murangira: "You, the Tutsi, you claim to know the Lord? He abandoned you, the Lord!"[30] In Mugonero, one of the survivors testified that Elizaphan Ntakirutimana, the chief pastor, had responded to his Tutsi colleagues before they were killed: "You must be eliminated. God no longer wants you."[31] In an interview, Damas Gisimba, the director of an orphanage in Kigali, described an extraordinary scene of sacrilege and murder in the church of St. André College, in Nyamirambo. The killers, he explained, wanted to convince themselves that God was on their side and that the Tutsi had nobody to turn to:

> At St André College, they killed more than 40,000 people who had taken refuge there. Even in the church because the killers came to kill in the sanctuary. I saw it. Some dressed as priests and used the chalices of the parish to put beer in them and drink it. Even in the stoups. That was to say, they claimed, that God himself accepted what they were doing by killing the Tutsi. When killing them, they would say: 'Even God, abandoned you.' I also heard them say: 'You look like Jesus, with your nose . . . But Jesus saw that you are traitors, and then he gave us the right to kill you.[32]

In the same manner, Emmanuel Murangira, a genocide survivor from Nyarusiza, near Gikongoro, recounted that the town's burgomaster and

---

29. Faucheux, "Massacrer dans L'intimité," 679.

30. Murangira, *Un Sachet D'hosties Pour Cinq*, 49.

31. Gourevitch, *We Wish to Inform You*, 28.

32. Faucheux, "Massacrer dans L'intimité," 1186.

the councilors of Nyamagabe, came to tell the crowd: "Go and destroy the houses of the Tutsi! Kill them! God has abandoned them." During the first attacks, on 11 April 1994, the Hutu killers blew their whistles and chanted: "The God of Tutsi is no longer around," and "The God of the Hutu is the only one that remains."[33] Jean-Marie Twambazemungu, a lay leader of the Emmanuel Community in Kigali, wrote that, on the first day of the genocide, an *Interahamwe* leader, finding a crucifix in his house, remained silent for a moment and then said: "You say that you are not an accomplice and you pray to Jesus who is a Tutsi!"[34]

This explains why, throughout Rwanda, the *Interahamwe,* and the mobs following them, engaged in so many acts of iconoclasm. Numerous cases of attacks against statues have been reported. A beautiful Christ was seen as a "Tutsi Christ" and had, therefore, to disappear just like his human followers. In the Centre Saint-Paul, in Kigali, the *Interahamwe* tried to break the neck of a wooden Christ with their machetes. He was, they said, "the God of the Tutsi."[35] The same happened in Nyamasheke near Cyangugu, where they broke the leg of Christ in one of the statues.[36] The Virgin Mary was also accused of being Tutsi, in Kibeho, where the *Interahamwe* cut off her hands.[37] In Nyange, they smashed her hands and nose, saying: "See how ugly you will become now, and even your God will no longer be your God!"[38] The Centre Christus, in Kigali, has on display a wooden Christ with the arms and the nose cut off that was found in the town of Gisenyi, after the genocide.

What we have here is a phenomenon of ethnicization of the faith. The Hutu extremists claimed that God had chosen them and abandoned the Tutsi. The Bible was hijacked in the process. They did not explain why God would have chosen one group against the other and accepted, or even encouraged, mass murder. That warring armies tried to enlist the support of God should not surprise us. During the First World War, prayers were addressed to God on both sides. All armies have chaplains who, of course, pray for the success of their own country on the battle-field. But in Rwanda, the weaponization of religion went further. It justi-fied and exacerbated a genocide.

33. Totten and Rifiki, eds., *We Cannot Forget,* 85.

34. Kagoyire, Ngarambe, and Twambamezungu, *Rescapés de Kigali. Témoignage,* 75.

35. Mukagasana, *La Mort ne Veut Pas de Moi,* 239.

36. Ndorimana, *Rwanda,* 41.

37. Audoin-Rouzeau, *Une Initiation,* 114.

38. Faucheux, "Massacrer dans L'intimité," 1003.

The response came later. After July 1994, in a landscape of desolation, the survivors gathered their forces and tried to mobilise support. They formed survivor organisations such as *Ibuka* (Remember) or *Avega* ("Association of the Genocide Widows") which, in association with the current Rwandan government, churches, and NGOs commemorate the genocide every year, and provide material and emotional support to the families of survivors. Their main concern is that the truth should be told. They find any form of denial—which, unfortunately, remains common in some sectors of the churches—distressing. They want to be heard.

Misuse of the Bible by Catholic Priests and Members of Religious Congregations Implicated in Sexual Violence

Until the 2000s, clerical pedocriminality, sexual abuse of religious women by priests or members of religious congregations and confusion of spirituality and eroticism in counselling or penitential sessions were largely underreported. They have always existed but are only attested in the period following the Second World War.[39] Most affairs are prescribed and cannot lead to prosecution, but some were taken to court and the perpetrators are in jail. Depending on the countries, between 2 % and 5% of all priests and religious men seem to have been implicated in cases of sexual abuse, with or without sexual penetration.

For so long, bishops and religious superiors only paid attention to the needs of the perpetrators and failed to hear the victims, especially the children. The parents themselves, in many cases, minimised the problem. Often the bishops, or religious superiors, would move a priest to another parish or ministry, where he would repeat the offense. The main cause of silence and denial is "clericalism"—a culture exalting the dignity of priests and bishops in the church, creating unequal relationships of power between clergy and laity, women especially.

Another factor was the emotional and sexual immaturity of the priests involved in sexual abuse. More often than not, the formators (guides) in seminaries and novitiates (trainees) are not equipped to assist young men in discovering their sexuality and handling it appropriately.

39. Claude Langlois, one of the few historians who studied the history of "pedocriminality" found several references to sexual abuse of minors by priests in 19th-century France, but they were usually not recognised as such. See Langlois, *On Savait, Mais Quoi?*

Some candidates that should have been turned down are ordained. Once in ministry, they do not receive adequate support. The fact that the Catholic Church only ordains celibate men to the priesthood, and excludes women from the ministry, complicates the equation. It is reckoned that about 80 percent of Catholic priests or members of religious congregations accused of having sexually abused young boys, with or without sexual penetration, are homosexual.[40] Many were unable or unwilling to come to terms with their sexual orientation in a church which, officially, considers homosexuality as an "intrinsic disorder."[41]

All those who have dealt with cases of sexual abuse of children, myself included, know well that when children are molested—through words with explicitly sexual content or physical contact—most of the time they are unable to respond. They freeze. They experience total confusion. They do not have words to describe what happened to them. It sometimes takes decades for them to name the aggression. Support groups are of great help in this journey.

This is where religion—and, for what concerns us here, the Bible—comes in. In an extraordinarily perverse way, some priests or members of religious congregations (though not all, of course) employ religious language to confuse their victims and disarm them or victim-blame them. If the priest invokes God or the Virgin Mary, and quotes the Bible, how can he be wrong? The abusers use their sacred status to maintain s strangle-hold on their prey. They blur the boundaries between the licit and illicit. When the crime is completed, they impose silence on their victims, not in their capacity as perpetrators, but in their authoritative capacity as priests or members of a religious congregation. They invoke the name of God to silence the child or the adult that they have abused. They trap them, and it takes a long time for the victims to recover from this ordeal.

Our main source here will be the report of the Independent Commission on Sexual Abuse in the Church (CIASE),[42] mandated by the Conference of French Bishops (CEF) and the Conference of French Men and Women Religious (CORREF), in February 2019, and chaired by Jean-Marc Sauvé, a respected civil servant. The 2500-page-long CIASE report was released in October 2021. It is complemented by a detailed historical and sociological study of sexual abuse in the Catholic Church,

40. *Catechism of the Catholic Church* (1992), art. 2357.

41. *Catechism of the Catholic Church* (1992), art. 2357.

42. Report of the Independent Commission: *Les Violences Sexuelles dans l'Église.*

based on the archives of a certain number of French dioceses and religious congregations, on a psychological study, and on a 200–page long compilation of testimonies of survivors entitled *De Victimes à Témoins* ("From Victims to Witnesses"). The CIASE report received wide coverage in the media. It has been endorsed by the Bishops' Conference and by the Conference of Religious Men and Women during their respective assemblies in November 2021.

The CIASE report is not the only one of this nature. Similar reports have been released in the United States (2004, 2018), Ireland (2009), Belgium (2010), the Netherlands (2011), Australia (2017) and Germany (2018).[43] Some were entrusted to independent commissions, like in France. Others were appointed by the local bishops' conference. Their time frame varied. For many, the *terminus a quo* was in the 1950s or 1960s. Some commissions only focused on the sexual abuse of minors by priests. The CIASE report, by contrast, also investigated sexual abuse of adults, mostly women but also, occasionally men, by priests and religious men or women. For our purpose, it is particularly valuable for the richness of the information it provides on sexual abuse by priests and religious leaders, for its attention to the historical, sociological and psychosocial context of sexual abuse in the Catholic Church in France, and for the conscious and deliberate decision to hear the voices of the victims.

The CIASE report devotes an entire section to the manipulation of the Christian doctrine which includes a paragraph on the misuse of the Bible:

> The misuse of the Bible (*detournement de la Bible*) to the benefit of perverse justifications is present everywhere. The list is long of biblical expressions diverted from their original meaning. For example, the notion of 'election', essential for the comprehension of the biblical revelation, is diverted by the predator to mean: 'You are my favourite; it is our secret.' The 'seed' to which the parables in the Gospel refer becomes something else than a grain. The *Canticles of Canticles* is taken literally. The mystical union between Christ and the Church gives rise to very prosaic interpretations, etc. In this regard one observes that biblical expressions used for manipulation purposes are so to say cut from the context which gives them life and deploys their real

---

43. But not in Italy, Spain and Poland nor in any African country. In the United Kingdom there is a commission called Independent Inquiry into Child Sexual Abuse (IICSA), created in 2014, which works on an ongoing basis. It investigates, among others, sexual abuse in the churches.

and profound meaning. Thus the use of the figure of the Virgin
Mary 'who said yes to everything', figure of unconditional obedience. This corruption (*dévoiement*) relies both on a denial
and a misuse of the evangelical meaning. For this reason, the
commission considers positively the move of Catholic culture
towards a better understanding of the Bible, as recommended
by Vatican II and the rules of interpretation.[44]

Gilles Berceville, a Dominican theologian who gave testimony at the
Commission, used similar language in a book on sexual abuse in the
Catholic Church: "It is not only in spite of their faith that Catholic communities become places of abuse," he wrote, "it is because of their faith
that these communities produce very specific and particularly harmful
forms of abuse."[45] He elaborated on this argument in an interview with
a French Catholic newspaper:

> The abuser priest deviates the fundamentals of trust to his own
> profit. It is the worst form of ascendency (*emprise*), the spiri-
> tual ascendency: taking the place of God in the mind of the
> other, to take possession of his faith. When the person realises
> it, it is a terrible shock because they do not know anymore
> whom to trust. Yet this is the biggest question to which reli-
> gions claim to have a response: telling us what is worthy of our
> faith. The suffering caused by spiritual abuse is one of the most
> important causes of atheism.[46]

Three examples, drawn from the appendices of the CIASE report will
illustrate the phenomenon of Bible abuse among predator priests and
religious persons.

One of the survivors, a married man who had spent time in a psy-
chiatric hospital after flashbacks of the abuse he had suffered as a child,
recounted how, at the age of thirteen, he used to visit a chapel in his
neighbourhood. Years later, he was still seeing himself on a particular day,
barefoot, with a yellow tee-shirt and shorts of the same colour. He found
the key in the interstice of the door, came in, grabbed the chalice, and swallowed consecrated hosts as naughty children do. At that point, the priest
arrived, shouted at him, and told him that it was a grave sin to eat the Body
of Christ. He came closer to him, made him sit, and forced him to do a

---

44. CIASE Report, *Les Violences Sexuelles dans L'Église Catholique*, 264 (my trans.).

45. Berceville, "La Foi Manipulée," 29 (my trans.).

46. Berceville, interviewed by Cécile Hoyaux, *La Croix*, 20 February 2019 (my trans.).

fellation (oral sex). "God gives life," the priest warned afterward in a clear reference to the biblical message, "but he can also take it. If you speak of this to your parents, that is what will happen to them."[47]

Second example, in a testimony analysed by a team of historians and sociologists of the École Pratique des Hautes Études, in Paris, a survivor by the name of Yves, abused at the age of thirteen in the 1980s, pointed out that the first response that his Christian upbringing had given him was: "Yes I am sacrificed. It is my cross. I must learn to forgive eventually. All the time my biblical references reminded me that I should not talk. Woe to the one by whom the scandal comes."[48]

Third example: a priest was accused of aggression on vulnerable people in the 2010s. In a letter to his bishop, he tried to justify his actions by explaining how difficult it was for a celibate man, living alone, to cope with the stress of parish life. "Does not the Bible say," he commented, twisting the meaning of the passage, "that it is not good for the man to be alone?"[49]

Victims of clerical abuse keep emotional scars for the rest of their lives. Those who manage to overcome the trauma, at least to a certain degree, are those who find the courage to speak and, for this, they need a lot of support. For some, the CIASE process provided such an opportunity. Others created pressure groups to alert public opinion, like the victims of a priest from Lyon called Bernard Preynat in the 1970s, who created the highly mediatic group La Parole Libérée (The Liberated Word).

When support comes from inside the church structure, that is even better. Philippe Lefèvre, another Dominican priest, and a lecturer in Old Testament at the University of Fribourg (Switzerland), is a case in point. In 2006 still in France, he published a theological critique of certain points developed by Tony Anatrella, a priest and psychoanalyst, aggressively homophobic, who enjoyed a high reputation in the French Bishops' Conference and in the Roman Curia. This brought him a flow of criticism and veiled threats from conservative Catholics. More unexpectedly, though, he received the visit of several sexual abuse survivors who told him that Anatrella had abused them during sessions of 'corporal therapy' meant to 'cure' them of their homosexuality. Philippe Lefèvre reported the matter to the president of the bishop's conference, and six other bishops, who did not respond. A few years later, however,

47. Appendix to the CIASE Report, *De Victimes à Témoins,* 37.

48. Pottier, ed., *Les Violences Sexuelles,* 406. Cf. Matt 18:7.

49. Pottier, ed., *Les Violences Sexuelles,* 244–45. Cf. Gen 2:18.

more complaints were made against Anatrella and, in July 2018, Michel Aupetit, the newly-appointed archbishop of Paris, barred Anatrella from administering sacraments and running spiritual or therapeutic sessions. Lefèvre was vindicated, but the matter has still not been referred to a court.[50]

Out of this came a remarkable book entitled *Comment Ruer Jesus? Abus, Violences et Emprises dans la Bible* (Trans: *How to Kill Jesus? Abuse, Violence and Ascendency in the Bible* by Lefèvre.[51] With his own experience as a whistle-blower and counsellor in the background, Lefèvre reinterprets biblical stories of abuse. And there are many. We see for example how Cain who had refused all true connectedness with God, and offered God a vain sacrifice, killed his brother, a true believer, out of jealousy, in what can be termed a scene of domestic violence (Gen 4:1–14). The Psalms often speak of abuse, most notably Psalm 73, which describes victims of abuse confronted by perpetrators claiming close proximity to God: "They scoff, and speak with malice; with arrogance, they threaten oppression. Their mouths lay claim to heaven, and their tongues take possession of the earth (Ps 73:7–8)."

Lefèvre takes us through the various episodes of sexual abuse that are narrated in the Bible. He shows that, if Levi the high priest welcomed Samuel, he tacitly accepted the evil conduct of his two sons who slept with women at the entrance of his tent (1 Sam 2:22). He mentions the story of Tamar, raped by her half-brother Ammon and enjoined to silence by her brother Absalom (2 Sam 13:20), which became the focus of one of the Ujamaa Centre's campaigns. Lefèvre reminds us that, on two occasions, old men handed over their daughters to rapists to obtain security: Lot in Sodom (Gen 19:8) and an elder in Gibeah (Judg 19:23–24). The book ends with a description of Jesus' passion portrayed as a scene of abuse.

For clerical perpetrators of sexual abuse on children, the Bible is a redoubtable weapon. They use it to affirm their position of authority and to give sacred sanction to their criminal actions. The Bible, and religious language in general, becomes an instrument of abusive power. Victims, if they ever recover, take years to come to terms with this particular form of abuse.

50. Cordelier, "Abus Sexuels dans l'Église."
51. Lefèvre, *Commet Ruer Jesus?*.

Conclusion

We have evoked here three types of abuse: the ongoing oppression, humiliation, and marginalisation of one part of a population by another, on basis of superiority; the systematic extermination, with acts of extreme cruelty, of an almost entire population group under the false pretext that they supported the "enemy"; lastly, the sexual abuse of adults and children by priests and religious men and women. In all three cases, the perpetrators used religious language to justify their actions, and reduce their victims to silence. And, not infrequently, they quoted the Bible or, if they did not, they implicitly referred to it.

Viewed with a bit of distance, these forms of biblical interpretations, if they were not so frightening and harmful, would appear quit ridiculous. How can the God of the Bible be described as a "Divider," as the apologists of apartheid claimed he was? Some parts of the Old Testament/Hebrew Bible may justify this view, but certainly not the New Testament, or at least its key passages. It is as if the apologists of apartheid voluntarily turned their back to the evangelical message. And what about the Hutu extremists who pretended that God—and the Virgin Mary—had "abandoned" the Tutsi, as if they took sides in this nasty civil war? Then there is the weaponization of the Bible, and of the symbols associated with it, by Catholic priests, and religious men and women, who should have known that "one does not invoke God in vain." (Exod 20:7).

This points to the "contested nature of the Bible," to borrow a theme familiar to West. Like the tongue of Aesop (Babrius and Phaedrus, Fables), it can be used for good or evil. Yes, the Bible can be abused or used to abuse. We should know it. One can only support the recommendation of the CIASE report: "Working out the biblical expressions that are diverted for manipulation purposes and promoting a reading of the Bible that is at the same time critical and spiritual at all levels of formation."[52]

The only way of resisting abuse, and defeating denial and silencing, is to give a voice to the victims. Bible-based abuse consists primarily of silencing the abused. Denial is the epitome of the crime. It takes a long time, sometimes a lifetime, for a victim to name the abuse and abuser. Apartheid was defeated when people everywhere started to talk about it, and organise resistance. The survivors of the genocide against the Tutsi found relief and solace in support groups. The victims of clerical abuse, often rebuked by

---

52. Pottier, *Les Violences Sexuelles dans L'Église Catholique*, 54 (my trans.).

church leaders who wanted to protect the reputation of the institution, also started to breathe only when they found somebody prepared to listen to, and believe their stories. Denouncing the instrumentalization of the Bible and using the sacred text, on the contrary, to discredit abusive practices, is a key moment in survivors' journeys of liberation.

Bibliography

Appendix to the CIASE Report. *De Victimes à Témoins*, 37.

Audoin-Rouzeau, Stephane. *Une Initiation: Rwanda (1994–2016)*. Paris: Seuil, 2017.

Babrius and Phaedrus. *Fables*. Loeb Classical Library. Editor and Translated by Ben Edwin Perry. Cambridge: Harvard University Press, 1965.

Berceville, Gilles. Interviewed by Cécile Hoyaux. *La Croix* (20 February 2019).

Berceville, Gilles. "La Foi Manipulee." In C. Fino, G. Berceville, G. Drouin, L. Forestier, and E. Vincon. In *Scandales dans L'Église, des Théologiens S'engagent*, 25–51. Paris: Cerf, 2020.

Block, Daniel. "Is Trump Our Cyrus? The Old Testament Case for Yes and No." *CT* (29 Oct 2018).

Catechism of the Catholic Church, 1992.

Chrétien, Jean-Pierre, ed. *Rwanda Les Médias du Génocide*. Paris: Karthala, 2002.

Cordelier, Jérôme. "Abus Sexuels dans l'Église: Tony Anatrella a Eté Couvert par Une Omerta Organisée." *Le Point* 5 (July 2018).

de Gruchy, John. *The Church Struggle in South Africa*. Minneapolis: Fortress, 2005.

de Gruchy, John, and Charles Villa-Vicencio. *Apartheid Is a Heresy*. Grand Rapids: Eerdmans, 1983.

Denis, Philippe. *The Genocide against the Tutsi and the Christian Churches: Between Grief and Denial*. Melton, Suffolk: James Currey, 2022.

———. "The Splintering of South African Evangelicalism During the Last Decade of Apartheid." *SAHJ* 73/3 (2001), 706–726.

Des Forges, Alison. *Leave None to Tell the Story: Genocide in Rwanda*. New York: Human Rights Watch, 1999.

Du Toit, J. D., and S. Du Toit. *Die Afrikaanse Rassebeleid en die Skrif: Artikels van Prof. D. J. D du Toit en Prof. Dr. du Toit* (Tweede Druk). Potchefstroom: Pro Rege Bpk, 1955.

Faucheux, Amélie. "Massacrer dans L'intimité. La Question de la Rupture des Liens Sciaux et Familiaux dans le Cas du Génocide des Tutsi du Rwanda de 1994." PhD thesis, Paris, École Pratique des Hautes Etudes, 2019.

Giliomee, Hermann. "The Making of the Apartheid Plan, 1929–1948." *JTSAS* 29 (2003) 375–92.

Gourevitch, Philip. *We Wish to Inform You that Tomorrow We Will Be Killed with Our Families: Stories from Rwanda*. New York: Farrar, Straus & Giroux, 1998.

Kagoyire, Y-S., F-X. Ngarambe, and J.-M. Twambamezungu. *Rescapés de Kigali: Témoignage*. Paris: Emmanuel, 2014.

Langlois, Claude. *On Savait, Mais Quoi? La Pédophilie dans l'Église de la Révolution à Nos Jours* [People Knew, but What?: Pedophilia in the Church from the Revolution to Our Days]. Paris: Seuil, 2020.

Lefèvre, Philippe. *Commet Ruer Jesus? Abus, Violences et Emprise dans La Bible.* Paris: Cerf, 2021.

Leonard, Gary, ed. *The Kairos Document.* Pietermaritzburg, SA: Ujamaa Centre, 2010.

Loumakis, Spyridon. "Genocide and Religion in the 1990s." In *The Global Impact of Religious Violence*, edited by André Gagné, Spyridon Loumakis, and Calogero Miceli, 47–83. Eugene, OR: Wipf & Stock, 2016.

Maindron, Gabriel. "Rwanda: L'horreur." *Dialogue* 177 (1994) 54.

Mukagasana, Yolande. *La Mort ne Veut Pas de Moi.* Paris: Fixot, 1997.

Munyaneza, Malachie. "Violence as Institution, an African Religious Experience: The Case of Rwanda." *Contagion* 8 (2001) 39–68.

Murangira, César. *Un Sachet D'hosties Pour Cinq. Récit d'un Rescapé du Génocide des Tutsi Gommis en 1994 au Rwanda.* Nantes: Amalthée, 2016.

Ndorimana, Jean. *Rwanda: Idéologie, Méthodes et Négationnisme du Nénocide des Tutsi à La Lumière de la Chronique de la Région de Cyangugu.* Rome: Vivere In, 2003.

Ngoetjana, Luke. Interviewed by Philippe Denis, on 3 September 2020, in Pietermaritzburg, SA.

Pienaar, Jacques. "An Evangelical Afrikaner Patriot? The Life and Work of GBA Gerdener With Special Reference to His Contributions to Afrikaner Identity Formation and the Racial Discourse in South Africa from 1925 to 1950." Unpublished PhD Thesis, University of Stellenbosch, 2020.

Pottier, Philippe, ed. *Les Violences Sexuelles dans L'Église Catholqique 1950–2020: Une Analyse Sociohistorique: Rapport du Groupe de Recherche de L'École Pratique des Hautes Études pour La Commission Indépendance Sur Les Abus Sexuels dans l'Église.* Paris: École Pratique des Hautes Études, 2021.

Report of the Independent Commission on Sexual Abuse in the Church. *Les Violences Sexuelles Dans L'Église Catholique France 1950–2020. Rapport de La Commission Independente Sur Les Abus Sexuels dans L'Église* [Trans: *Sexual Violence in the Catholic Church France 1950–1920*]. October, 2021.

Totten, Samuel, and Ubaldo Rifiki, eds. *We Cannot Forget: Interviews with Survivors of the 1994 Genocide in Rwanda.* New Brunswick, NJ: Rutgers University Press, 2011.

Vosloo, Robert. "The Bible and The Justification of Apartheid in Reformed Circles in the 1940's in South Africa: Some Historical, Hermeneutical and Theological Remarks," *STJ* 1 (2015) 195–215.

West, Gerald O. "Tracing the 'Kairos' Trajectory from South Africa (1985) to Palestine (2009) Discerning Continuities and Difference." *JTSA* 143 (2012) 4–22.

23

The Bible as an Instrument for Social Change in Contextual Reading with the Poor and Marginalized Communities in South Africa

Repression, Resilience and Resistance

SITHEMBISO S. ZWANE
UNIVERSITY OF KWAZULU-NATAL,
PIETERMARITZBURG, S.A.

Introduction

THE CONTEXTUAL READING OF the Bible with the marginalized communities has the potential for social change. This potential finds expression in the process of reading "with" rather than "for." First, the paper will argue that elements of State *Repression* through socio-economic marginalization of the communities undermines social change and transformation of the conditions of the marginalized communities. This is expressed through a critical reflection on labour and social movements.

Second, the paper will postulate that theological *Resilience* takes place through a contextual reading of the Bible with the materially poor and marginalized communities which has the potential to empower and nurture people's agency in the context of marginalization. This section prioritizes the contextualization of the Bible in reading with the poor and marginalized in black working-class communities in the South African context.

Third, the paper will argue that theological *Resilience* facilitates community *Resistance* through People's campaigns and pragmatic actions. These campaigns and actions are organized by communities in a public act of defiance against elements of repression by the State. In their act of defiance, the communities are supported by the Ujamaa Centre using the See–Judge–Act method for critical reflection. This method begins with social analysis (See) of repression, which moves to biblical analysis and discernment (Judge) which builds resilience and ultimately pragmatic action (Act) through resistance by the communities affected by repression and marginalization.

Repression: Labour and Social Movements

During the dark days of apartheid under white minority rule, the state repression was not unprecedented. The state used its military force to control and dominate law abiding citizens contributing to anarchy. The policies adopted were designed to oppress and marginalize the black working-class majority.

The ushering of the new dawn post-1994 brought hope and optimism for the majority of black South Africans. The theme of 'a better life for all' resonated with the black working class who had been oppressed for decades without recourse. The socio-economic and political oppression of black people in South Africa was institutionalized by the apartheid system. When the black majority rejected this illegitimate government, the state unleashed its military machinery to silence the "voices" of the oppressed.

Christopher McMichael states, "More radical voices have suggested the police are a brutal mechanism of state violence, targeted primarily against the black poor."[1] This statement is a synopsis of the past atrocities against the black poor communities who were at the receiving end of a brutal force at the hands of police. The post-1994 period came with its own challenges against black people in South Africa. The project of liberation is not complete with a growing socio-economic inequality that

---

1. McMichael, "Police Wars," 1.

exists in the community. The high levels of chronic unemployment, abject poverty and huge income inequalities characterize the South African reality post political liberation.

Sbu Zikode argues "Many things have been said. Many things have been seen. Many policies have been passed. Many people have voted. But what has been done has not been done for the poor. It has been done for the rich. The poor are outside. We have no country."[2] Both McMichael and Zikode are raising critical contextual challenges about the state before and after 1994 respectively. The apartheid government's response to the plight of the black working class people was repression in a desperate attempt to legitimize their rule as a government without dealing with the socio-economic exclusion of black communities.

But has the current state corrected the socio-economic ills of the past apartheid government? Zikode's statement suggests that a lot still needs to be done by the current government to mitigate against the socio-economic exclusion of black communities. Issues of chronic unemployment have severely compromised our labour system and the economy. Zikode reflects on the frustration social movements like Abahlali base-Mjondolo[3] have been subjected to under the democratic government. The formation of Abahlali Basemjondolo was a result of the failures of the democratic government to adequately address the socio-economic challenges of the black majority.

According to Richard Pithouse, social movements in South Africa have collapsed and those that remain are not strong enough to effectively challenge the government.[4] Part of the problem is the "othering" of the "poor who are fragmented."[5] The shift from standard to non-standard employment has reduced employment opportunities for social movements and the working class. The mining sector, for example, is among those sectors that have shifted to non-standard employment and have failed to provide living wages for workers resulting in a Marikana massacre. According to Patrick Bond and Shaun Mottiar, "34 workers were killed and 78 others suffered bullet-wound injuries, all at the hands of police weapons, leaving some crippled for life."

Bond and Mottiar are apprehensive about the state repression against the Marikana workers killed for raising labour issues

2. Zikode, "The GreatestThreat," 113.

3. Gibson, "Fanonian Practices."

4. Pithouse, "NGOs and Urban Movements," 256.

5. Gibson, "Fanonian Practices," 5–6.

challenging an exploitative neoliberal capitalist economy. The state re-action towards the workers was unprecedented in post-apartheid South Africa. Furthermore, they argue that the "formalized migrancy system and evolution of labour relations on these mines did not improve the socio-economic conditions of workers, given the rising debt burden."[6] The Marikana workers were asking for an increase of SA Rands 12.500 from the LONMIN directors. They had been negotiating for this in-crease with their company for a prolonged period without success. The state repression did not end with the apartheid government against the black poor, it has continued post liberation.

The state repressions have been characterized by evictions of the poor social movements from their homes especially in the area of eThe-kwini (Durban) displacing thousands of shack dwellers and moving them away from their places of work. These socio-economic challenges confronting workers and social movements undermine social change and transformation of communities in South Africa. The Ujamaa Cen-tre has been invited by these social movements and workers to "read the Bible with" them in search of a socio-economic alternative from a theological perspective. As an organization working with the Bible, the focus has been the creation of invigorated spaces of theological resil-ience through contextual Bible reading.[7]

Resilience: A Contextual Reading of the Bible with the Marginalized

Liberation theologies in South Africa have laid a firm foundation for biblical and theological reflection on an array of contemporary issues af-fecting the poor and marginalized communities. Over the past 30 years, contextual biblical and theological analysis has featured prominently in the work of the Ujamaa Centre for Community Development. A body of literature published in the field of biblical and theological studies by scholars from 1990 engages with the notion of contextual Bible reading with the marginalized communities.[8]

---

6. Bond and Mottiar, "Movements," 294.

7. Zwane, "Invited," 1–24.

8. Cochrane, "Theology;" Cochrane, "Circles of Dignity;" Sibeko and Haddad, "Reading the Bible," 83–92; Mandew, "War and Memory Salvation:" Mandew, "Power and Empowerment;" Philpott, "Jesus is Tricky;" Walker, "Tradition;" Walker, "Engaging Popular Religion;" West, "Biblical Hermeneutics;" West, "Contextual Bible Study and/

The Ujamaa Centre's strategic location within the University of KwaZulu-Natal provides access to a wide range of academic resources. But it has also meant navigating a bureaucratic red tape with the propensity to undermine the contribution of marginalized communities that we read the Bible with.

The Ujamaa Centre's "Theory of Change" (ToC) underscores the critical role of enabling the poor and marginalized communities. The ToC is therefore an attempt at creating an enabling environment for a redemptive and inclusive religious narrative. This redemptive and inclusive narrative should offer an alternative religious system to a dominant religious system that is premised on what the *Kairos Document* (1985) defines as "Church Theology." "Church Theology" offers contributions that are devoid of ideo-theological praxis.

The ToC's ultimate goal is to facilitate the creation of spaces of resilience among the marginalized communities. The concept of resilience is diverse; attempts to define it have been made by scholars in different contexts.[9] Ujamaa Centre's understanding of resilience finds expression in Contextual Bible Study (CBS) praxis and interpretive resources.[10] These biblical and theological interpretive resources have contributed immensely to building theological resilience among the poor and marginalized communities in South Africa.[11] The use of the tools of analysis in the process of building and nurturing theological resilience among the marginalized communities have challenged the dominant socio-economic and political narratives.

The CBS resources have been used to deconstruct the oppressive biblical narratives against the marginalized communities. Readers of the Bible come from different theological and denominational backgrounds which shape their theological posture. Conceptual biblical and theological methods have been developed to read the Bible prophetically to effect social change in the communities.

---

or as Interpretive Resilience," West, "Difference and Dialogue;" West, "Academy of the Poor;" West, "Contextual Bible Study in Africa;" West, "Reading the Bible;" West, "Lord's Prayer" West, *Contextual Bible Study*, 1–9.

9. Lynch, "Who Is Resilient?;" Cretney, "Resilience for Whom?," 627–40. Bene et al, "Resilience."

10. West, "Reading the Bible," 235–61.

11. West and Haddad, "Boaz as Sugar Daddy," 137–56. West, "Senzeni Na?," 260–77. West, "Facilitating Interpretive Resilience," 17–37. West and Zondi-Mabizela, "The Bible Story," 5–17. West and Zengele, "The Medicine of God's Word," 51–63. West and Zwane, "Why Are You Sitting There?,"175–88.

The theological methods include thematic-semiotic, socio-historical and the literal-narrative. Each of these conceptual methods makes a significant contribution to the reading of biblical texts. In the community, we have often used the literal-narrative approach because it considers the "historical and sociological" aspects of the biblical text which attempts to "slow down" the process of reading.[12]

This section often deals with the "details" of the text in the form of characters and their historical relations. The focus is on the narrative "setting" engaging with the characters in the biblical text.[13] The socio-historical methods interrogate the world of the text in terms of culture, race, class, and gender struggles that form part of the biblical text. This process of reading the text can include the socially engaged biblical scholars who bring their resources of biblical scholarship to the interpretive reading process when called upon by the members of a group in the CBS workshop.

According to West, "the socially engaged Biblical scholar is called to read the Bible with them ('ordinary readers'), but not because they need to be conscientized and given interpretations relevant to their context. No, socially engaged biblical scholars are called to collaborate with them because they bring with them additional interpretative resources which may be of use to the community group."[14]

As articulated by West, the role of the socially engaged Biblical scholar in the interpretive process of reading the Bible is a collaboration with "ordinary readers" (organic intellectuals and activists as defined by their community). However, this does not mean that the socially engaged scholar manipulates the text and ignores the hermeneutical foundational principles of biblical scholarship in the analysis of the text in a collaborative process.

Socially engaged scholars use their tools of biblical scholarship to engage the text from its socio-historical context. Each participant in this process brings their own contextual interpretive experience. Each "voice" in the reflection and analysis is important whether it be the "voice" of an unemployed individual, an HIV-positive person, an LGBTQA+ member, a church bishop or a university professor. What becomes crucial is the liberating interpretive narrative that is transformative and brings social change.

12. West, "Do Two Walk Together?," 431–49.

13. West, "Do Two Walk Together?"

14. West, "Contextual Bible Study," 601.

Therefore, the Ujamaa Centre holds the view that ordinary readers of the Bible are not "voiceless" but are often "silenced" by those who control the "invited spaces" of control and marginalization.[15] These so-called leaders masquerading as the vanguard of the working class are the elites that maintain and sustain the oppression of the poor and marginalized. For West, the idea of interpretive theological resilience has been a defining characteristic for the poor and marginalized communities.[16]

The communities of the poor and marginalized that we have read the Bible with have agency and the capacity to speak prophetically and theologically when their resilience is activated through the interpretive praxis. The reading of the Bible "with" the marginalized engages critically with contexts of marginalization. These contexts include the marginalization of women primarily because of systemic structures of patriarchy and heteronormativity that dominates in the communities. The role of organic intellectuals and socially engaged biblical scholars is to use the Bible redemptively to disrupt these oppressive systems and structures in our contexts.

According to Beverley Haddad, "it is these contexts of oppression and marginalization where 'the poor and marginalized women articulate their faith practices that activist intellectuals need to relocate, practically and theoretically.'"[17] The practical and theoretical commitments of the Ujamaa Centre activist-intellectuals have been to relocate oppressed and marginalized communities from social exclusion to social inclusion through the CBS methodology.

The CBS method is the contextualization of biblical studies to effect social change and transformation. The tools of analysis in the CBS methods accept that the Bible speaks with different "voices," which includes the rich and poor, men and women, etc. Itumeleng Mosala conceded that the Bible was a "site of struggle" suggesting that it offered diverse hermeneutical approaches to the readers.[18] The notion of "struggle" is not a peculiar concept when it comes to the "black masses" in the South African context.[19] Part of the struggle was the post lib-

---

15. West and Zwane, "Re-reading 1 Kings 21:1–16," 179–207; Zwane, "Invited," 1–24.

16. West, "Facilitating Interpretive Resilience," 20.

17. Haddad, "The Manyano Movement," 12.

18. Mosala, "The Use of the Bible," 175–99.

19. Mofokeng, "Black Christians," 34–42.

eration dislodging of black theology from the centre raising questions about its relevance post 1994.[20]

Black theology along with other liberation theologies was crucial in the struggle for political emancipation in South Africa. These liberation theologies in South Africa contributed to challenging socio-economic and political oppression of black people. These liberation theologies rediscovered the agency of the oppressed African people in the South African context.[21]

The CBS adopted similar ideo-theological liberation methods and critical approaches to the reading of biblical texts. Elelwani Farisani argues that "any uncritical reading of the biblical text tends to further oppress and sideline the poor and marginalized."[22] Farisani is apprehensive about the impact of uncritical analysis of the biblical text for the poor and marginalized. The lack of criticality has the potential to undermine attempts to use the bible as a tool for liberation rather than oppression.

The poor and marginalized are the interlocutors in the reading process. As dialogue partners with socially engaged scholars, their liberation from oppression depends primarily on their ability to engage critically with their lived experiences and reality. Furthermore, uncritical reading of the Bible as 'revealed Word of God' assumes that the Bible is non-ideological.[23]

The notion of the Bible as a revealed Word of God is contested from an ideological perspective. The Bible is ambiguous because it offers both life and death hence the importance of criticality in the interpretive reading process. Paulo Freire states that "true dialogue cannot exist unless the dialoguers engage in critical thinking which perceives reality as a process, a transformation, rather than as a static entity—thinking which does not separate itself from action, but constantly immerses itself in temporality without fear of risks involved."[24]

Freire underscores the importance of criticality in praxis which challenges dominant discourses perpetuated by the oppressors of the poor and marginalized. Criticality is a prerequisite for theological resilience among marginalized communities. The core values of the CBS identify criticality

20. Vellem, "Hermeneutical Embers," 35–48; Zwane, "Transition," 1–8.

21. Maluleke, "Rediscovery," 19–37.

22. Farisani, "Ideologically Biased," 628–40.

23. Mosala, "Biblical Hermeneutics," 6.

24. Freire, "Pedagogy," 69.

as one of the key liberation instruments.[25] The emphasis on criticality elucidates the argument that the CBS is not "just a liberation discourse, but a form of liberation pedagogy."[26] Sarojini Nadar asks an important critical question, "has the CBS as a method been able to help us towards our goal of overcoming injustice—of getting us out of the mud?"[27] This is an ideo-theological question that seeks to move the process of CBS from a liberation *discourse* to a liberation *pedagogy*.

The liberation discourse is both a conceptual and methodological contribution of the CBS process to the struggle for social justice in the South African context. Liberation discourse, both as conceptual and methodological praxis, has created a culture of critical analysis in the public realm. However, it is not obvious how liberation pedagogy facilitates progress from liberation discourse in transforming the conditions of the marginalized.

Nadar seems to be persuaded by Alissa Jones Nelson's "contrapuntal hermeneutics" as the appropriate progression framework, against what she terms as "glossing over" the "intellectual" and the "community."[28] But how do all these terms, concepts and methods escape the academic rhetoric that has no substance or impact at the community level? What then is appropriate theological hermeneutics for the liberation of the poor and marginalized African people?

Olehile Buffel writes, "As the poor reflect theologically on the Bible in their various contexts characterised by poverty and the associated socio-economic and political ills, they do so from a liberative hermeneutics, even though they may not refer to their contextual reading as such."[29]

Buffel is suggesting that the poor are not ignorant, they might not have the theological discourse to articulate their own comprehension and appropriation of the text; however, they still engage in liberative hermeneutics as praxis using their context of poverty to speak theologically about their socio-economic and political ills. It is in the context of "appropriate" biblical hermeneutics premised on the notion of social justice that the Bible becomes an important contextual tool for liberation. Contextual reading of the Bible is therefore an attempt to

25. Nadar, "Beyond the 'Ordinary Reader,'" 384–403; West, "Reading the Bible," 235–61.

26. Nadar, "Beyond the 'Ordinary Reader,'" 390.

27. Nadar, "Beyond the 'Ordinary Reader,'" 387.

28. Nadar, "Beyond the 'Ordinary Reader,'" 400.

29. Buffel, "Bible of the Poor," 2.

privilege marginalized "voices" through the biblical text. It is a process of participation that enables social transformation and change. The approach to social transformation finds expression in the invented spaces of resilience and resistance.[30]

There are three important projects focusing on contextual readings of the Bible with the marginalized communities that the Ujamaa Centre facilitated in the past decade. The Ujamaa Centre was invited by the Siyaphila HIV and AIDS network to facilitate CBS workshops aimed at building theological resilience and resistance among their members.

Reading with People Living with HIV and AIDS

The facilitation of contextual reading of the Bible "with" people living with HIV and AIDS through the Siyaphila (meaning "We Are Alive") network strengthened activist solidarity in the Natal-Midlands region. This was a period where Antiretroviral treatment (ARVs) was limited to a few who could afford it. This was also a period of debate about the HIV and AIDS pandemic. The last thing on the minds of those affected by the virus was a discussion about the Bible especially because it was being used to condemn and judge those who were HIV-positive.[31] Ujamaa Centre partnered with Siyaphila for more than a decade facilitating CBS processes with their members.

The Bible was a bone of contention as they struggled with HIV as a chronic illness. In the initial stages of the collaboration, it became evident that the members of the Siyaphila group believed that the Bible belonged to the church leaders or professional theologians.[32] This view was justified at the time because it was the church and religious leaders who were using the Bible against the members of the Siyaphila and other HIV-positive people condemning and judging them about their HIV-positive status. For the members of the Siyaphila, the Bible was a "holy" book and belonged to a church.[33]

In the early stages of the CBS process the consensus among the members of Siyaphila was that the Bible did not engage with real-life

---

30. West and Zwane, "Re-reading 1 Kings 21: 1–16," 179–207; Zwane, "Invited," 1–24.

31. West and Zengele, "Medicine of God's Word," 57.

32. West and Zengele, "Medicine of God's Word," 57.

33. West and Zengele, "Medicine of God's Word," 57.

struggles of people living with HIV, and HIV-positive people, in particular.[34] This was a troubling conclusion but not unexpected because of a toxic theological context at the time which was influenced by what the *Kairos Document* (1985) refers to as "Church Theology."

This dominant theological narrative asserted that HIV infection was a punishment for promiscuous behaviour. After a series of structured CBS sessions on "positive" living, using CBS as a tool for reflection and analysis of their lived reality, the negative attitude towards the Bible began to gradually dissipate. The Bible was no longer perceived as just a "holy" book for the select few.[35] The collaborative interpretive process involved a re-reading of the book of Job in the context of suffering. In this biblical narrative, Job lost everything materially including his own family and friends. Eventually, Job was vindicated, and God restored his life. This narrative was read in conjunction with the book of John 9: 1–12 which engages with issues of sin and suffering.

The contextual redemptive reading of these texts engaged the issue of sin and suffering from the perspective of the people living with HIV. This contextual and redemptive reading changed their perception of the Bible. The CBS process brought hope among Siyaphila members and engaged HIV-positive members and their Bibles during the most difficult time in South Africa.[36]

The Bible became a source of life rather than death, happiness rather than hopelessness. The Bible for the members of the group was no longer distant, "what had brought judgement, stigma and discrimination brought happiness, hope and life."[37] The fundamental change in this project was that the members of Siyaphila had discovered that the CBS had brought life to their situations. Furthermore, "Another member told the group that she had actually felt secure enough in her new-found sense of ownership of the Bible that she had confronted her own pastor about the way he was using the Bible against people like her."[38] This is how the members of Siyaphila were able to reclaim their space within the church. They used the CBS praxis to build and activate their theological

---

34. West and Zengele, "Medicine of God's Word," 58.

35. West and Zengele, "Medicine of God's Word," 58.

36. West, *The Stolen Bible*, 377–92.

37. West and Zengele, "Medicine of God's Word," 58.

38. West and Zengele, "Medicine of God's Word," 59.

resilience through a contextual reading of their Bibles challenging the dominant oppressive church narrative.[39]

This is what theological resilience looks and feels like for many who have used the CBS process in their own contexts. This includes the marginalized LGBTQIA+ community who have been experiencing hate crime and homophobic attacks because of their sexual orientation.

Reading with the LGBTQIA+ Community

The reading of the Bible "with" members of the Pietermaritzburg Gay and Lesbian Network (GLN) now operating as "Uthingo Network" in Pietermaritzburg created spaces of critical engagement with the "toxic" texts.[40] The Ujamaa Centre started working with Uthingo Network in 2013 facilitating CBS workshops on the subject of the Bible and homosexuality. These were paired workshops using the See–Judge–Act method to facilitate contextual re-reading of the biblical texts that had been used to discriminate and marginalize members of the LGBTQIA+ community within Uthingo Network.[41]

The paired workshop engaged with Gen 18–19 as a CBS process. The first workshop provided the basis for a contextual re-reading of Gen 18–19 as a unit rather than two separate and unrelated texts. The second workshop began with a report back on the work done with the CBS on Gen 18–19 by the participants. Part of the workshop was a young (self-identified) gay man who initially did not want to be part of the first workshop the reason being that his role was primarily to film the process on behalf of GLN.[42] In the second workshop, he requested to be part of the report back which surprised many because he did not participate in the first workshop. In his report back, he narrated why he was apprehensive about the Bible detailing how it was used against him "since he had been open about his sexuality, was one of stigmatisation and condemnation."[43] This young man shared with the group that he

39. West, "Reconfiguring a Biblical Story."

40. See the website: "About us." Uthingo Network (gaylesbian.org.za) formerly known as the Pietermaritzburg Gay and Lesbian Network (GLN).

41. De Gruchy, "See–Judge–Act," 1–10.

42. West, "Facilitating Interpretive Resilience," 18.

43. West, "Facilitating Interpretive Resilience," 18.

had paid careful attention to the CBS process while filming the plenary sessions and small group discussions.[44]

Furthermore, he stated categorically that his apprehension with "religion" and the Bible changed after observing the process, "listening and watching" the process of re-reading Gen 18–19 from the perspective of homosexuality to hospitality was fundamental in challenging the dominant narrative on these biblical texts.[45] The participant observation of CBS on Gen 18–19 had given him reasons to reconsider his position on the Bible because he had found the CBS "empowering."[46] For this young gay man, the CBS process activated theological resilience. The young man had used the CBS to liberate his family and his LGBTQA+ community. The CBS had created invigorated spaces of interpretive theological resilience for the LGBTQA+ members.

This approach to reading the Bible takes into consideration the important role of restorative theology for those marginalized and discriminated against.[47] The young gay man used the CBS experience to reclaim his agency against a homophobic church and community that used his sexuality to discriminate and marginalize him and others in the LGBTQA+ community.

The CBS methods restored his faith and trust in the Bible and "religion" in general. His restored faith in the Bible was a sign of change in the attitude and perception. The oppressive heterosexual patriarchal system is not different from a capitalist oppressive system that exploits the labour of vulnerable casual workers.

Reading with the Casual Workers

The reading of the Bible with casual workers in Pietermaritzburg attempted to critically discuss the shift from standard (permanent) employment to non-standard (casual) employment. Initially we read Matt 20:1–16 to deal with issues of chronic unemployment. Subsequently, the focus shifted to casual work which became dominant in the area. The literal reading of Matt 20:1–16 with casual workers in Pietermaritzburg "aroused our hermeneutic of suspicion, and we wondered if this parable *should* be

44. West, "Facilitating Interpretive Resilience," 18.

45. West, "Facilitating Interpretive Resilience," 18.

46. West, "Facilitating Interpretive Resilience," 18.

47. West, "Senzeni Na?," 260–77.

read in a liberative manner."[48] It is unequivocally evident that it *could* be read as supporting aspects of socialism, "but only if we ignored some of its detail."[49] The socialist re-reading of this parable with casual workers presented two important elements.

First, the reading of the text laid the basis for theological resilience against a capitalist system that undermines the rights of workers. The casual workers argued vehemently that the text reflected their own lived reality of work under capitalism. The creation of precarious non-standard casual work makes working class workers susceptible to exploitation by the owners of the means of production.

Second, the reading of the text challenged the dominant narrative that parables are mythological and have no contextual relevance. The casual workers could easily identify their own economic struggles with the parable of Jesus. Prior to doing a CBS on this parable, we struggled to find biblical scholars who were engaging critically with the economic dimensions of the parable. We kept on hoping that progressive readings on the parable would emerge and finally it did with an array of socially engaged biblical scholars like Gunther Wittenberg, Norman Gottwald, Herman Waetjen, and Richard Horsley, among others.

Their progressive and insightful work enabled Ujamaa Centre to reconstruct a socio-economic reading of the biblical story, beginning with the God of liberation who is invoked by the cry of the slaves (Exod 3:7–10), and "who try to construct an alternative socio-economic society."[50] An egalitarian socialist reading of the parable was used to highlight the plight of the casual workers in a capitalist economic context shedding standard employment. This type of employment makes workers vulnerable to exploitation by their employers.

The Ujamaa Centre observed from the families and communities of the poor and marginalized that when they are "unable to discern the systemic dimensions of unemployment, families and communities often blame the individual for their failure to find work. So, to some extent, those sitting on the sides of the downtown street waiting for work have been driven there by shame as much as by economic necessity. Intervening in this situation, the Ujamaa Centre, through its Theology and Economic Justice Programme has used formations like the Young Christian

48. West and Zwane, "Why Are You Sitting There?," 175–88.

49. West and Zwane, "Why Are You Sitting There?," 175–88

50. West and Zwane, "Why Are You Sitting There?," 175–88.

Workers (YCW) and any other forum offered to us to reflect together on the systemic dimensions of unemployment."[51]

In an attempt to mitigate against desperation caused by chronic and systemic unemployment affecting families and communities, the Ujamaa Centre invoked its CBS method as a tool for building and nurturing resilience among the poor and marginalized families and communities. Furthermore, the

> Contextual Bible Study is our primary resource for collaborative work like this. We activate the Bible as a weapon of struggle for economic liberation, wrestling it from the hands of those who use it to stigmatise and blame those who are unemployed for what is a systemic predicament. A text that Ujamaa Centre has wrestled with through the years has been Matthew 20:1–16. Initially, this text was used to explore a socialist vision of society.[52]

Prior to this, we were apprehensive about the capitalist elements demonstrated by the landowner in the parable. Most of all we were disturbed by the landowner's capitalist-sounding rhetorical question, "Am I not allowed to do what I choose with what belongs to me?"[53] This rhetoric from the landowner is typical of some of the capitalist's tendencies. It is in this context that the working-class participants develop their resilience against a system of oppression and marginalization. The theological resilience is not an event, but a process of praxis that uses the See–Judge–Act moment to effect social transformation and change in the community.[54] This change is not intended to be paternalistic nor tokenism. It is a radical and progressive movement challenging the structural and systemic oppression and marginalization.

A similar approach was used in the reading of the Lord's Prayer in Matt 6:9–13 with a focus on "Debt" and "Bread" as symbols of the "Kingdom of God" on earth. The marginalized working-class communities appreciated a dialogical process allowing space for critical engagement. The unemployed in the workshop observed that the CBS transformational methods advocating for an alternative radical

---

51. West and Zwane, "Why Are You Sitting There?," 8.

52. West and Zwane, "Why Are You Sitting There?," 8.

53. West and Zwane, "Why Are You Sitting There?," 175–88.

54. West, "Recovering the Biblical Story of Tamar," 135–47.

economic system and change contributed to their increased knowledge and positive change in their analysis.[55]

Reading biblical texts "with" the unemployed poor and marginalized communities became a redemptive and liberating process. This text was also read with the unemployed groups during the lockdown due to Covid-19 highlighting issues of debts and food shortage because of retrenchments, as a result of the pandemic.[56] Theological resilience developed through contextual reading of the Bible with the poor and marginalized facilitated People's Campaign and pragmatic actions of resistance.

Resistance: People's Campaigns and Action

The theology of resilience is intended to facilitate pragmatic action using a theology of prophetic resistance. The theology of prophetic resistance emerged from the struggle for political emancipation in the South African context. Allan Boesak writes,

> I am speaking of the tradition represented by the theology of prophetic resistance, which early on in history had broken with the theology of accommodation to existing situations of oppression. I mean that a theology of protest would never be enough, understating that protest is always a form of begging, and that only a theology of resistance could respond adequately to the call of costly discipleship."[57]

Boesak's proposed prophetic theology of resistance is not an event but a process of praxis. Liberation from racism orchestrated by a white minority government required the oppressed to engage in critical praxis. As correctly articulated by Boesak, protest alone was inadequate for the struggle for liberation. The consideration of the historical injustices of the past in the praxis process justified a comprehensive pragmatic theological response to the apartheid regime.

Sharon Welch writes, "The important consideration for liberation theologians is not the universal or a priori conditions of resistance, but the historical conditions of struggles against domination."[58] Welch's challenge to liberation theologians postulates the importance of

55. West, "Recovering the Biblical Story of Tamar."

56. Zwane, "Solidarity Assurance," 159–73.

57. Boesak, "Kairos, Crisis and Global Apartheid," 26.

58. Welch, "Community of Resistance," 41.

historical struggles against domination and how the communities engaged in struggles to overcome domination should approach their struggle. The Ujamaa Centre's liberation praxis process has used the historical struggles of domination of the working class to advocate for a theology of resilience that facilitates resistance. The CBS methods offered a base from which to develop campaigns designed to conscientize and mobilize communities to adopt a theology of resilience and resistance against domination and oppression. There are two important campaigns that have been used as the foundation for a theology of resilience and resistance in the communities of KwaZulu-Natal.

First, it is the "Tamar Campaign" which began in 1996 as a response to the call by women who attended the Bible and violence workshop.[59] The primary focus and emphasis of the Tamar Campaign is the prioritizing of the "voices" of the marginalized women affected by Gender-Based Violence (GBV). These "voices" of marginalized women participated in the CBS workshop building and nurturing resilience.

From the established praxis of CBS, both resilience and resistance forged a path towards a theology of resistance. The Tamar campaign is no longer just a South Africa Campaign but has received international recognition as an important tool for the deconstruction of patriarchal and systemic oppression of women. Oppressive systems have one common element, domination and oppression. The Campaign has empowered women because they are no longer silenced.[60] Furthermore, the campaign has incorporated elements of HIV and AIDS that have affected the majority of women.

Second, it is the "Worker Sunday Campaign" started in 2003 as a response to neo-liberal capitalist economic system oppressing and marginalizing the working-class communities. The Campaign was established by the Industrial Mission of South Africa (IMSA) Network which included the Institute for the Study of the Bible and Worker Ministry (ISB-WM), Pietermaritzburg Agency for Community for Social Action (PACSA), Ecumenical Service for Socio-Economic Transformation (ESSET) and a Catholic Church and Work programme. The primary objective of the campaign is to develop critical reflection on socio-economic justice. This

59. West and Zondi-Mabizela, "Bible Story," 5–13; West et al., "Rape in the House of David," 36–41.

60. West and Zondi-Mabizela, "Bible Story," 5–13; West et al., "Rape in the House of David," 36–41.

reflection included the call for a Basic Income Grant (BIG) challenging the government through lobbying and advocacy.[61]

These campaigns have contributed immensely to the building of the theology of liberation that facilitates a movement from resilience to resistance among marginalized groups in the communities. The Ujamaa Centre continues to nurture prophetic theological resilience and resistance through its Body Theology and Bread Theology programmes respectively. The theology of resilience and resistance contributes significantly to social change and transformation.

Conclusion

First, I attempted to argue that elements of state repression characterized by socio-economic marginalization of communities still exist in the post-apartheid dispensation which undermines social change.

Second, I sought to show that theological resilience takes place through a contextual reading of the Bible with the marginalized communities and has the potential to effect social change, empower, and nurture people's agency in the context of marginalization.

Third, I also argued that theological resilience facilitates community resistance through People's campaigns and pragmatic actions.

Bibliography

Bene, Christopher, Rachel G. Wood, Andrew Newsham, and Mark Davies. "Resilience: New Utopia or Tyranny? Reflection About the Potentials and Limits of the Concepts of Resilience in Relations to Vulnerability Reduction Programme." *IDS Working Papers* (2012) 1–61.

Boesak, Allan A. *Kairos, Crisis, and Global Apartheid: The Challenge to Prophetic Resistance.* Black Religion/Womanist Thought/Social Justice. New York: Palgrave, 2015.

Bond, Patrick, and Shaun Mottiar. "Movements, Protests and a Massacre in South Africa." *JCAS* 31 (2013) 238–302.

Buffel, A. Olehile. "The Bible of the Poor in the Context of Poverty, COVID-19 and Vaccine Nationalism: Hermeneutics of Liberation from the Perspective of the Poor." *HTS* 77 (2021) 6920.

Cochrane, James R. *Circles of Dignity: Community Wisdom and Theological Reflection.* Minneapolis: Fortress, 1999.

———. "Conversation or Collaboration? Base Christian Communities and the Dialogue of Faith." *Scriptura* 57 (1996) 103–24.

61. ISB-WM, "Annual Report," 3, 8.

———. "Theology and Faith Tradition, Criticism and Popular Religion." In *Doing Theology in Context: South African Perspectives*. edited by J. De Gruchy and C. Villa Vicencio, 26–42. Theology and Praxis 1. Maryknoll, NY: Orbis, 1994.

Cretney, Raven. "Resilience for Whom? Emerging Critical Geographies of Socio-Ecological Resilience." *GC* 8 (2014) 627–40.

De Gruchy, Steve. "See–Judge–Act: Putting Faith into Action." *A Handbook for Christian Groups Engaged in Social Transformation*. Unpublished Training Manual. University of KwaZulu-Natal, n.d.

Farisani, Elelwani. "The Ideologically Biased Use of Ezra–Nehemiah in a Quest for an African Theology of Reconstruction." *OTE* 15 (2002) 628–46.

Freire, Paulo. *Pedagogy of the Oppressed.* Rev. Ed. Translated by Myra B. Ramos. New York: Herder & Herder, 1970.

Gibson, Nigel C. "Fanonian Practices and the Politics of Space in Post-Apartheid South Africa: The Challenge of the Shack Dwellers' Movement (Abahlali baseMjondolo)." Presentation at the Frantz Fanon Colloque, Algiers, Algeria on July 7, 2009. https://abahlali.org/node/5540/.

Haddad, Beverley. "The Manyano Movement in South Africa: Site of Struggle, Survival and Resistance." *RS* 61 (2004) 4–13.

Institute for the Study of the Bible and Worker Ministry (ISB-WM). *Annual Report*: Pietermaritzburg, SA, 2003, 2004.

The Kairos Document: A Theological Comment on the Political Crisis in South Africa. Braamfontein, SA: The Kairos Theologians, 1985.

Lynch, Cecelia. "Who Is Resilient? Problematizing the Appropriation of 'Resilience In Humanitarian Action." *CIHA Blog* (2017). https://www.cihablog.com/resilient-problematizing-appropriation-resilience-humanitarian-action/.

Maluleke, Tinyiko S. "The Rediscovery of the Agency of Africans. An Emerging Paradigm of Post-Cold War and Post-Apartheid Black and African Theology." *JTSA* 108 (2000) 19–37.

Mandew, Martin. "Power and Empowerment: Religion, Imagination and the Life of the Local Base Ecclesial Community." Master's thesis, University of Natal, 1993.

———. "War, Memory Salvation, the Bulhoek Massacre and the Construction of a Contextual Soteriology." PhD diss., University of Natal, 1997.

McMichael, Christopher. "Police Wars and State Repression in South Africa." *JAAS* 51/1 (2004) 3–16.

Mofokeng, Takatso. "Black Christians, the Bible and Liberation." *JBT* 2 (1988) 34–42.

Mosala, Itumeleng J. "The Use of the Bible in Black Theology." In *The Unquestionable Right to Be Free: Essays in Black Theology*, edited by I. J. Mosala and B. Tlhagale, 175–99. Johannesburg, SA: Skotaville, 1986.

———. *Biblical Hermeneutics and Black Theology in South Africa*. Grand Rapids: Eerdmans, 1989.

Nadar, Sarojini. "Beyond the 'Ordinary Reader' and the 'Invisible Intellectual': Shifting Contextual Bible Study from Liberation Discourse to Liberation Pedagogy." *OTE* 22 (2009) 384–403.

Philpott, Graham. *Jesus Is Tricky and God Is Undemocratic: The Kin-dom of God in Amawoti*. Pietermaritzburg: Cluster, 1993.

Pithouse, Richard. "NGOs and Urban Movements: Notes from South Africa." *City* 17 (2013) 253–57.

Sibeko, Madika, and Beverley Haddad. "Reading the Bible 'with' Women in Poor and Marginalized Communities in South Africa." *Semeia* 78 (1997) 83–92.

Ujamaa Centre for Biblical and Theological Community Development and Research (formerly Institute for the Study of the Bible and Worker Ministry). Ujamaa School of Religion, Philosophy and Classics. ukzn.ac.za.

UThingo Network (formerly Gay and Lesbian Network). Pietermaritzburg. About us | Uthingo Network (gaylesbian.org.za)

Vellem, Vuyani S. "Hermeneutical Embers from the 'Zone of Non-Being.'" In *Mission and Context*, edited by Jione Havea, 35–48. Lanham, MD: Lexington, 2020.

Walker, Megan. "Engaging Popular Religion: A Hermeneutical Investigation of Marian Devotion in the Township of Mpophomeni." *Semeia* 73 (1996) 131–60.

———. "Tradition, Criticism and Popular Religion: A Hermeneutical Investigation of Marian Theology with Special Reference to the South Africa Context." Master's thesis. University of Natal, 1992.

Welch, Sharon D. *Communities of Resistance and Solidarity: A Feminist Theology of Liberation.* 1985. Reprint, Eugene, OR: Wipf & Stock, 2017.

West, Gerald O. *The Academy of the Poor: Towards A Dialogical Reading of the Bible.* Interventions 2. Sheffield: Sheffield Academic, 1999.

———. *Biblical Hermeneutics of Liberation: Modes of Reading the Bible in the South African Context.* Pietermaritzburg, SA: Cluster. 1991.

———. *Contextual Bible Study.* Pietermaritzburg: Cluster, 1993.

———. "Contextual Bible Study and/or as Interpretive Resilience." In *That All May Live! Essays in Honour of Nyambura J. Njoroge*, edited by Ezra Chitando, Esther Mombo, and Masiiwa Ragies Gunda, 143–59. Bamberg: University of Bamberg Press, 2021.

———. "Contextual Bible Study in South Africa: A Resource for Reclaiming and Regaining Land Dignity and Identity." In *The Bible in Africa: Transactions, Trends and Trajectories*, edited by Gerald O. West and Musa Dube, 595–610. Leiden: Brill, 2000.

———. "Difference and Dialogue: Reading the Joseph Story with Poor and Marginalized Communities in South Africa." *BI* 2 (1994) 152–70.

———. "Do Two Walk Together? Walking with the Other through Contextual Bible Study." *ATR* 93 (2011) 431–49.

———. "Facilitating Interpretive Resilience: The Joseph Story (Genesis 37–50) as a Site of Struggle." *AT* 38 (2018a) 17–37.

———. "The Lord's Prayer as Economic Renewal." In *Global Perspectives on the Reformation: Interactions Between Theology, Politics and Economics*, edited by Anne Burkhardt and Simone Sinn, 85–94. Leipzig: Evangelische Verlagsanstalt, 2017.

———. "Reading the Bible in the Light of HIV/AIDS in South Africa." *TEC* 55 (2003) 335–44.

———. "Reading the Bible with the Marginalized: The Value/s of Contextual Bible Reading." *STJ* 1 (2015) 235–61.

———. "Reconfiguring a Biblical Story (Genesis 19) in the Context of South African Discussions about Homosexuality." In *Christianity and Controversies over Homosexuality in Africa*, edited by Ezra Chitando and Adriaan van Klinken, 135–47. Religion in Modern Africa. London: Routledge, 2016.

————. "Recovering the Biblical Story of Tamar: Training for Transformation, Doing Development." In *For Better or Worse: The Role of Religion in Development Cooperation*, edited by Robert Oden, 135–47. Halmstad: Swedish Mission Council. 2016.

————. "*Senzeni Na*? Speaking of God 'What is Right' and the 'Return' of the Stigmatising Community in the Context of HIV." *Scriptura* 116 (2017) 260–77.

————. *The Stolen Bible: From Tool of Imperialism to African Icon.* BIS 144. Leiden: Brill, 2016.

West, Gerald O., and Beverley Haddad. "Boaz as 'Sugar Daddy': Re-Reading Ruth in the Context of HIV." *JTSA* 155 (2016) 137–56.

West, Gerald O., and Bongi Zengele . "The Medicine of God's Word: What People Living with HIV and AIDS Want (and Get) from the Bible." *JTSA* 125 (2006) 51–63.

West, Gerald O., and Phumzile Zondi-Mabizela. "The Bible Story that Became a Campaign: The Tamar Campaign in South Africa (and Beyond)." *WCC Ministerial Formation* 103 (2004) 4 -12.

West, Gerald O., Phumzile Zondi-Mabizela, Martin Maluleke, Happiness Khumalo, Phidian Smadz Matsepe, Mirolyn Naidoo. "Rape in the House of David: The Biblical Story of Tamar as a Resource for Transformation." *RS* 61 (2004) 36–41.

West, Gerald O., and Sithembiso S. Zwane. "Re-Reading 1 Kings 21:1–16: Between Community-Based Activism and University-Based Pedagogy." *JIBS* 2 (2020) 179–207.

————. "Why Are You Sitting There? Reading Matthew 20:1–16 in the Context of Casual Workers in Pietermaritzburg, South Africa." *Matthew: Texts@Contexts* (2013) 175–88.

West, Gerald O., Sithembiso Zwane, and Charlene van der Walt. "From Homosexuality to Hospitality: From Exclusion to Inclusion: From Genesis 19 to Genesis 18." *JTSA* 168 (2021) 5–23.

Zikode, Sibusiso. "The Greatest Threat to Future Stability in our Country is the Greatest Threat of the Abahlali Base Mjondolo Movement (SA) (Shack Dwellers)." *JAAS* 43 (2008) 113–17.

Zwane, Sithembiso S. "Invited, Invigorated and Invented Spaces: Trans-Development Approach." In *Faith, Class and Labor: Intersectional Approaches in a Global Context*, edited by Jin Young Choi and Joerg Rieger, 1–24. Intersectionality and Theology Series. Eugene, OR: Pickwick Publications, 2020.

————. "Solidarity Assurance: Reality, Faith and Action." In *Doing Theology in the New Normal: Global Perspectives*, edited by Jione Havea, 159–73. London: SCM, 2021.

————. "Transition, Reflection, Rethinking and Re-Imagining: The Relevance of Black Liberation Theology (BLT) in South Africa Post 1994—A Tribute to Vuyani Vellem." *HTS* 76 (2020) 99–106.

Post-Script

Gerald Oakley West: A Great African Biblical Scholar

Tinyiko Maluleke

Although I do not remember where, when, or how I first met Gerald Oakley West, I do know that I have known him for three decades, at least. I could not have met him in the late eighties when he was briefly a part-time lecturer at the historic Federal Theological Seminary (FED-SEM), for I had already left FEDSEM in the mid-eighties.[1] Nor could we have met earlier. While West was at Kimberly Boy's High School, I was a thousand kilometers away, at the Swiss missionary founded, Valdezia Higher Primary School, outside Louis Trichardt.[2] Nor was I lucky enough to hear one of West's—presumably—thunder and brimstone sermons, during his time as a pastor of the Assemblies of God denomination in the early eighties.

But for a moment, that was as brief as it was profound, between 1998 and 2000 West and I were colleagues, at the School of Theology, University of Natal (UN), Pietermaritzburg. There was no real push for me to leave my previous post at the University of South Africa (UNISA) to join the School of Theology (UN) at that time, except for the collegiality and encouragement of West.

1. Denis and Duncan, *The Native School.*
2. Maluleke, "The Valdezia Mission Station."

Among the many great scholars who formed part of the School of Theology (UN) team during my time there, were the likes of Jonathan Draper, Beverly Haddad, Tony Balcomb, Andrea Fröchtling, Philippe Denis, Kwame Bediako, Edwina Ward, Lucas Ngoetjana, Sue Racoszy, and Klaus Nurnberger. Added to this was an exciting group of postgraduate students from all over the African continent and, indeed, all over the world. The postgraduate seminars were energetic, robust, and very loud. These seminars became a platform for laying bare and the examination of the ecclesio-political problems of a continent and a world that was only coming to grips with the post-cold-war democratic era. Amongst the most robust "agent provocateurs" in these seminars were none other than the likes of Bediako and West himself.

While the precise details and circumstances of my first meeting with West may elude me for now, I knew within an hour of my first encounter with him, that I had found a great theological interlocutor, a great dialogue partner, and wonderful colleague. During my stay in Pietermaritzburg, West was the one colleague with whom I spent the most amount of social time. The recurring theme of our dozens of conversations was none other than that of the troubled place of the Bible in African Christianity,[3] especially in Apartheid South Africa.[4] West and I also spoke about the fortunes of our beloved Mamelodi Sundowns Football Club, the trailblazing music of Juluka (Johnny Clegg and Sipho Mchunu) illustrated by such songs, "Scatterlings of Africa" and "Impi" (war) as well as the unconventional spoken-word poetry of the "voice of reason," by one Mzwakhe Mbuli.

Three, out of at least a dozen conferences I attended with West, stand out for me. One took place within South Africa and two elsewhere on the continent. Sometime in 1998, West and I joined a few other colleagues—including Tony Balcomb, Lucas Ngoetjana and Patrick Pillay—during a week-long seminar that took place at Bediako's Akrofi-Kristaller Institute, in Akropong, fifty kilometers North-East of Accra, in Ghana. During our brief sojourn in Ghana, West and I took it upon ourselves to use every opportunity for vigorous theological engagement with Andrew Walls (the great mentor and friend of Bediako, who was also in attendance) and Bediako, who was our host.

3. West, *The Stolen Bible.*
4. Maluleke, "Black and African Theologies."

We were particularly concerned with the underlying historiography and implicit biblical hermeneutics on which were based Kwame Bedaiko's two seminal books, *Theology and Identity*[5] on the one hand and *Christianity in Africa*,[6] on the other. Also interesting for us was Kwame Bediako's attempt—especially in his Theology and Identity book—to make linkages between modern African Theology and second-century African Theology. While in Akropong, we also took the time to visit the social and community spaces of the town, savoring the local cuisine, and tasting the waters of the local wells—all the while interrogating and mulling over Bediako's bold and powerful propositions. It was a special moment for us to meet and engage with one of Africa's best 20th-century theologians—Bediako—in his home context.

The second conference at which both West and I were present was the Multi-Event, multi-disciplinary academic workshop in Cape Town, organized in September 1999, by colleagues at the University of Cape Town. Typical of West's established trajectory of a relentless focus on the poor and the marginalized, the Multi-Event program had West speaking to the topic of the citizenship of marginal and subjugated voices. For my part, I was asked to speak about "Black Theology, Yesterday, Today and Tomorrow," or something to that effect. Unbeknown to me at that time, the obituary of South African Black Theology had already been written. The section of the program in which I was featured, was meant to be a "reading" of the final rites for Black Theology. But I stood up and caused a stir. My Multi-Event presentation can be summarized in the slogan: "Long live Black Theology, Long Live!" Immediately after my presentation, West came over to request a copy of my presentation. At the Multi-Event, I also met Sarojini Nadar,[7] who was to later become one of no less than 25 PhD students that West has supervised.

The third memorable conference that I attended in which Gerald West was also present, took place in March 1998, in Sagana, Kenya, a hundred kilometers North of Nairobi. It was the Ecumenical Symposium of the Eastern Africa Theologians. As well as a few other colleagues from South Africa, the symposium was also attended by such leading African theologians as Jesse Mugambi (Kenya), John Mary Waliggo (Uganda), Laurenti Magesa (Tanzania), Anne Nasimiyu-Wasike (Uganda) and

---

5. Bediako, *Theology and Identity*.

6. Bediako, *Christianity in Africa*.

7. Nadar, "Womanist and Literary Perspectives on Esther."

Hannah Kinoti (Kenya), amongst others.[8] At its prime, the Ecumenical Symposium of the Eastern Africa Theologians published and inspired the publication of a dozen books on various topics in African Theology.

Perhaps, Mugambi's *From Liberation to Reconstruction* is among the most influential of the books to come directly and indirectly out of the Ecumenical Symposium of the Eastern Africa Theologians.[9] While Mugambi's book was clearly prophetic, it is a book we received with caution in South Africa. For one thing, we did not think *liberation* and *reconstruction* were mutually exclusive. But, I remember how animated the room was after West presented at the 1998 Sagana symposium. West delivered a paper on what he termed "neglected dimensions of Biblical interpretation in African contexts and how churches should be equipped to respond to the cries of the poor."

Whereas one may not have agreed with every dimension of West's interpretative trajectory,[10] he has been consistent in his insistence on the critical role of biblical hermeneutics in foregrounding the voices and needs of the poor—to whom he often refers as "ordinary readers" of the Bible. This theme of "ordinary readers" cuts through the dozens of publications—books, book chapters, peer-reviewed journal articles, workshops, and conference presentations, as well as Bible studies, which West has published over the span of his career.

To navigate the distances from "reading *at*" and "reading *for*" towards "reading *with*" ordinary readers, West steeped himself deeply into the liberationist hermeneutical methodologies of such scholars as Itumeleng Mosala,[11] and those who worked with the Hebrew Bible scholar Norman Gottwald.[12] But for West, the ultimate fountain of hermeneutical wisdom was to be found among the poor and the marginalized readers of the Bible located in the townships and the squatter camps of South Africa, Kenya, and Uganda.

The collection of essays contained in this Festschrift is made up of contributions by peers of West from across the world, each one of them an expert in their respective field. It is a fitting tribute to a scholar who must be counted among the best African biblical hermeneuticians of the last forty years period, beginning roughly in 1981 and ending in

8. Mugambi and Magesa, eds., *Jesus in African Christianity.*

9. Mugambi, *From Liberation to Reconstruction.*

10. Maluleke and Nadar, "Alien Fraudsters."

11. Mosala, *Biblical Hermeneutics and Black Theology.*

12. Gottwald, *The Bible and Liberation.*

2021 with his retirement from academia. West is definitely one of the most beautiful theological minds that (South) Africa has shared with the world in recent times.

For me, it has been a special privilege to be part of a group of scholars who have orchestrated this special Festschrift in honour of such an esteemed colleague. I consider it a blessing for me to have worked and interacted with West, and his partner Haddad, during my time at the University of Natal (1998 to 2000). It is indeed an invaluable privilege to count West among my friends, theological interlocutors, and dialogue partners.

Bibliography

Bediako, Kwame. *Christianity in Africa: The Renewal of a Non-Western Religion.* Maryknoll, NY: Orbis, 1995.

———. *Theology & Identity: The Impact of Culture upon Christian Thought in the Second Century and Modern Africa.* Oxford: Regnum, 1992.

Denis, Philippe, and Graham Duncan. *The Native School That Caused All The Trouble: A History of the Federal Theological Seminary of Southern Africa.* Pietermaritzburg: Cluster, 2011.

Gottwald, Norman K., and Richard A. Horsley, eds. *The Bible and Liberation: Politics and Social Hermeneutics.* Bible & Liberation. Maryknoll, NY: Orbis, 1984.

Maluleke, Tinyiko. "The Valdezia Mission Station, Then and Now: A Missiological Appraisal." *Missionalia* 31 (2003) 156–76.

———. "Black and African Theologies in Search of a Comprehensive En-vironmental Justice." *Journal for Theology in Southern Africa* 167 (2020) 5–19.

———. *Biblical Hermeneutics and Black Theology in South Africa.* Grand Rapids: Eerdmans, 1987.

——— and Sarojini Nadar. "Alien Fraudsters in the White Academy: Agency in Gendered Colour." *JTSA* 120 (2004) 5–17.

Mugambi, J. N. K. *From Liberation to Reconstruction. African Christian Theology After the Cold War.* Nairobi: East African Educational Publishers, 1995.

Mugambi, J. N. K., and Laurenti Magesa, eds. *Jesus in African Christianity. Experimentation and Diversity in African Christology.* Nairobi: Initiatives, 1989.

Nadar, Sarojini. "Womanist and Literary Perspectives on Esther: Resources for Social Transformation." PhD diss., University of Kwazulu Natal, 2003.

West, Gerald O. *The Stolen Bible: From Tool of Imperialism to African Icon.* BIS 144. Leiden: Brill, 2016.

Author Index

Scripture Index

Genesis (*continued*)

19:14	287, 289–90
19:15	289
19:16–17	289
19:16	289, 299, 301
19:17	13, 289, 295, 299
19:19	299
19:23	289
19:26	287, 295–96
19:30–38	289, 304
21	viii, 281, 406, 410, 422–23
21:1–20	300
21:6	422
21:10	409, 410n18
21:33	77n65
22	300
23:8	336
25:7–8	410n18
35:9	410
37–50	31, 33, 482
44:18	337

Exodus

	xiv, 66, 70, 86, 96, 173, 191, 296, 334, 397
1–18	86
1–3	65
1:15	334
2	86
2:1	334
3:4	83
3:7–10	63, 476
3:7–8	62
3:7	64
3:9–11	64
4:14	334, 336
5:1	63
6:20	334
12—Num 16	66
12–16	64
12:1–26	63
12:25–26	66

12:25	66
12:26–27	395
12:29–51	63
13:14–15	63, 395
14	390, 393, 397
15	182, 194n31, 340, 397
15:20–21	335, 340
15:20	334–35, 340
15:22–25	63, 76
15:22	340
16	65
16:4–5	63, 76
16:13	65
16:31	65
17:1–6	76
18:2–6	339
18:11	339
20:1–17	451
20:7	460
20:22—23:33	96
21–23	194, 198n40
21:12—22:16	355
22:24	67
22:25–27	98
22:25	99
22:26–27	98
23:10–11	96n32
23:20ff	358
24:4	399
32	290
33:8b	296

Leviticus

	64, 96, 191, 194
2:13	302
13	338
17–26	96
19:34	364
25	62, 65
25:1–7	96
25:2	64
25:23a	64
25:23b	64
25:23c	64

Apocryphal/ Deutercanonical Books

Rabbinic Literature